I0094433

Germans Against Nazism

Germans Against Nazism

Nonconformity, Opposition and Resistance in the Third Reich

Essays in Honour of Peter Hoffmann

Edited by
Francis R. Nicosia
and Lawrence D. Stokes

berghahn
NEW YORK • OXFORD
www.berghahnbooks.com

First published in 1990 by
Berg Publishers Ltd

Revised edition published in
2015 by Berghahn Books
© 2015 Francis R. Nicosia and Lawrence D. Stokes

All rights reserved. Except for the quotation of short passages
for the purposes of criticism and review, no part of this book
may be reproduced in any form or by any means, electronic or
mechanical, including photocopying, recording, or any information
storage and retrieval system now known or to be invented,
without written permission of the publisher.

Library of Congress Cataloging-in-Publication Data
A C.I.P. cataloging record is available from the Library of Congress.

British Library Cataloguing in Publication Data
A catalogue record for this book is available from the British Library

Printed on acid-free paper

ISBN 978-1-78238-815-9 (paperback)
ISBN 978-1-78238-816-6 (ebook)

Feiger Gedanken
Bängliches Schwanken,
Weibisches Zagen,
Ängstliches Klagen
Wendet kein Elend,
Macht dich nicht frei.

Allen Gewalten
Zum Trutz sich erhalten,
Nimmer sich beugen,
Kräftig sich zeigen,
Rufet die Arme
Der Götter herbei.

Goethe, *Beherzigung*

(Craven thoughts and
of timid vacillation,
unmanly dread, and
fearful lamentation
can avert no affliction,
nor render you free.

Stand firm against
all the powers that be,
never yield,
be strong,
summon the arms
of the gods to your aid.)*

* This translation is taken from Inge Jens (ed.), *At the Heart of the White Rose: Letters and Diaries of Hans and Sophie Scholl*, trans. J. M. Brownjohn, NY, 1987, p. 292, n. 72. Hans Scholl is said to have scribbled this poem on the wall of his cell before being led into the so-called People's Court, presided over by Roland Freisler, for his trial. Hans and his sister Sophie Scholl were sentenced to death on 22 February 1943 and, with their friend Christoph Probst, were executed that same day by the guillotine at Stadelheim prison in Munich.

Contents

List of Tables

Preface

This collection of essays deals with individual and organised nonconformity, opposition and resistance to Hitler and National Socialism in Germany. It is intended as a *Festschrift* in honour of Professor Peter Hoffmann of McGill University, who has been one of the leading scholars in the field of anti-Nazi resistance for a generation, on the occasion of his sixtieth birthday.

The contributors reflect a diversity which is unusual in volumes such as this. They represent a cross-section of historians in their fields of research, their generations and their relationship with Professor Hoffmann. Some are known for their work in the area of resistance, while others have established their reputations in other areas of the history of the Third Reich. Some are well-established scholars, while others, having more recently gained recognition for their scholarship, stand at the mid-point of their careers. Some are personal as well as professional acquaintances of Professor Hoffmann, while others know him only by name and reputation. A few have been his students, and have had the good fortune of also becoming his colleagues.

The editors have endeavoured to solicit essays that are in some degree original contributions to an understanding of resistance to National Socialism. Recognising that this took many forms, from organised assassination attempts to symbolic individual acts of dissent and disobedience, we have sought articles that consider the activities of institutions, organisations and individuals across a wide spectrum, prompted by a variety of motives.

We wish to express our appreciation to Dr Ronald Provost, Vice-President for Academic Affairs of Saint Michael's College in Vermont, and the Faculty Council of Saint Michael's College for their financial and logistical support. Most of all we extend our special thanks to Kelly McDonald of Saint Michael's College. She applied her extraordinary skills and untiring effort to putting most of the manuscripts on the computer, while her meticulous editorial assistance proved invaluable. Our appreciation is also extended to Professor Dr Peter Wulf of the University of Kiel, Siegbert Thiedemann of Flensburg and Erika Stokes of Halifax, Nova Scotia, as well as to the Durick Library of Saint Michael's College, the Killam Library of Dalhousie University in Halifax and the McLennan Library of McGill University in Montreal, for their bibliographic assistance.

We would like to thank the following for their kind permission to reproduce the illustrations in this book: W. Kohlhammer Verlag GmbH and the Hauptstaatsarchiv, Stuttgart; Firma F. Urbahns and the Stadtarchiv, Eutin; Dr med. Clarita von Trott zu Solz, Berlin; the Hon. F. D. L. Astor, London; the Bundesarchiv, Koblenz; Kapitänleutnant a.D. Robert Hering, Gärtringer.

F. R. N., L. D. S.
September 1989

Preface to the Paperback Edition

In a conversation with Marion Berghahn several years ago, we discussed the fact that Berg Publishers of Oxford had never published an affordable paperback edition of *Germans Against Nazism: Nonconformity, Opposition and Resistance in the Third Reich. Essays in Honour of Peter Hoffmann*. Coincidently, that conversation occurred at around the time of the publication in 2010 of *Das Amt und die Vergangenheit. Deutsche Diplomaten im Dritten Reich und in der Bundesrepublik*, by Eckart Conze, Norbert Frei, Peter Hayes and Moshe Zimmermann. The appearance of this unique and controversial volume was also a factor in my decision to move forward with a paperback edition of *Germans Against Nazism*. Not surprisingly, *Das Amt* generated fierce debate among scholars on the general question of resistance to Hitler and National Socialism in Germany, and specifically on the issue of German Foreign Office bureaucrats and civil servants and their relationship to the questions of resistance and complicity in the crimes of the Third Reich. The authors questioned what they argued was the blindly accepted and largely unchallenged postwar narrative that the German Foreign Office had been a bastion of opposition and resistance against Hitler and his regime. Moreover, they rejected many of the claims of Foreign Office officials from the Nazi period who went on to serve in the postwar Foreign Ministry of the German Federal Republic, namely that they had in fact opposed Hitler and National Socialism and had engaged in anti-Nazi resistance from within the system.

The appearance of *Das Amt* was followed by a conference in Tutzing am Starnberger See in Germany in September 2011. This conference, in which I had the privilege of participating, focused on the question of the German Foreign Office and its relationship to anti-Nazi resistance efforts in Germany after 1933. The conference was followed by the publication in 2013 of the conference proceedings in the volume *Widerstand und Auswärtiges Amt. Diplomaten gegen Hitler*, edited by Jan Erik Schulte and Michael Wala. The conference and the resulting book offered readers nuanced conclusions that while most of the bureaucrats in the German

Foreign Office went along with the regime and its policies, there were some among them who in fact did oppose the Nazi state, and that there existed different levels of opposition or resistance among Hitler's Foreign Office bureaucrats and diplomats that reflected their individual circumstances, personalities and decisions. This conference and its published proceedings provided a further impetus for moving forward with the publication of an affordable paperback edition of this book.

Published in 1990, the original Berg edition of *Germans Against Nazism* was meant to honour Peter Hoffmann on the occasion of his sixtieth birthday. Marion Berghahn was at Berg Publishers in 1990 when Lawrence Stokes and I worked with her on the project. Not long after that, Marion founded Berghahn Books. She was familiar with this volume and its contents from her time at Berg, and generally with the renewed and continuing debates surrounding the question of resistance in Nazi Germany, as reflected in the publication of many significant works on the topic since 1990. Therefore, she agreed in 2013 that Berghahn Books would republish the volume in a paperback edition in 2015, twenty-five years after the publication of the original hardback edition. Its publication in 2015 also marks the seventieth anniversary of the end of the Second World War. This anniversary will undoubtedly see the appearance of additional works, scholarly and otherwise, that will focus on the many issues associated with the war's end. Among those issues, the topic of anti-Nazi resistance, its place in the larger society of wartime Germany, its failed attempts to realize the overthrow of Hitler and his regime, and the possible reasons for those failures, will be at the forefront of this new literature. In that context, the essays in this volume will continue to shine a necessary and timely light on the resistance efforts of individual Germans and specific groups of Germans between 1933 and 1945. This edition will find a wider audience of general readers, scholars and students with a specific interest in the history of the resistance to National Socialism in Germany, as well as in the larger history of the Third Reich.

When *Germans Against Nazism* first appeared in 1990, there were relatively few significant and comprehensive collections of scholarly essays in English on the subject of resistance to Hitler and National Socialism in Germany. Indeed, besides Peter Hoffmann's pathbreaking *Widerstand Staatsstreich Attentat. Der Kampf der Opposition gegen Hitler*, first published in 1969, there were relatively few that covered the subject of resistance in Nazi Germany in its larger sense, beyond discussion of the 20 July 1944 assassination attempt against Hitler. On one level, *Germans Against Nazism* considers "resistance" in the broader context of its relationship to acts of what some have identified as "nonconformity" or "opposition" to Hitler and his Nazi state in Germany, largely individual actions that might have carried less risk than those that are labelled as "resistance." It was also an early opportunity to examine different examples of nonconformity, opposition and resistance within the broader spectrum of German political, social and institutional life between 1933 and 1945. These sectors included, among others, the state bureaucracy, the national conservative right, the socialist and communist left, the Christian churches, the Jewish community and Jewish organizations and the German military establishment, as well as the contacts of some of these sectors with foreign governments, particularly toward the end of the war.

Much new scholarship on resistance to Hitler and National Socialism in Germany, among them significant works by Peter Hoffmann, has appeared in the twenty-five years since the publication of this collection of essays in 1990. These works include, but are certainly not limited to, general histories of the resistance in Nazi Germany that appeared in the 1990s and the turn of the new century, such as those by Theodore Hamerow, Klemens von Klemperer, Hans Mommsen and Peter Steinbach. They also include works by scholars such as Arnold Paucker and Avraham Barkai on Jewish resistance in Germany, as part of the greater acceptance by scholars of the reality of Jewish opposition and resistance to Nazi persecution in Germany and throughout Europe before and during the war. Recent works by scholars such as Nathan Stoltzfus, Barbara Beuys, Kurt Schilde and Harald Steffahn consider acts of opposition and resistance among ordinary Germans, including some in mixed marriages, as well as acts of opposition and resistance among German youths and in movements such as the White Rose.

Other studies have appeared that deal with issues of gender and women in the German resistance, such as the books by Martha Schad, Frauke Geyken and Dorothee von Meding. Additionally, significant new scholarship on resistance within the socialist and communist left has appeared, including works by Shareen Blair Brysac, Hans Mommsen, Anne Nelson, Hans-Rainer Sandvoß, Francis Carsten and Johannes Tuchel. The always sensitive and controversial question of the Christian churches and resistance to National Socialism in Germany has also generated much new scholarly literature, including works by Suzanne Brown-Fleming, Beth Griech-Polelle, Michael Phayer, Robert Ericksen and Gerhard Ringshausen. There has been a wealth of new scholarship on prominent individuals in the resistance such as Adam von Trott zu Solz, Dietrich Bonhoeffer, Helmuth James von Moltke, Carl Goerdeler and Claus von Stauffenberg. These include works by Günter Brakelmann, Sabine Dramm, Olaf Jessen, Ines Reich, Benigna von Krusenstjern, Jochen Thies, Marikje Smid, Gerd Ueberschär, Henric Wuermeling, Elizabeth Stifton and Fritz Stern, and of course Peter Hoffmann. Resistance to National Socialism in Austria has also become a topic of interest, for example, in books by Wolfgang Neugebauer and Gisela Hormayr. Moreover, the role of resistance to Hitler and National Socialism, as part of postwar German society's somewhat belated efforts in the 1980s to confront its recent past, is evident in the works of Jürgen Danyel, Michael Geyer and John Boyer, Peter Steinbach and others.

The past twenty-five years have also seen considerable interest in, and scholarship on, the extent to which the professions in general – including, for example, the medical and legal professions – were complicit in, rather than in opposition to, Nazi crimes. Mention has already been made of the professional diplomats and civil servants in the German Foreign Office, and the extent to which they actually resisted, were complicit in or generally indifferent to Nazi policy and crimes. Finally, much greater attention has recently been paid to the role of Nazi anti-Semitism, Nazi Jewish policy and the persecution and mass murder of the Jews in Europe as a motivating factor for some in the German resistance. Examples of this can be found in works by Jörg Wollenberg, Susanna Keval, Michael Kißener and, most recently, Peter Hoffmann's two volumes (in English and German) on Carl Goerdeler and the impact of Nazi persecution and mass murder of the Jews in Germany and beyond on him.

This edition of *Germans Against Nazism* is meant to honour Professor Peter Hoffmann once again, this time on the occasion of his eighty-fifth birthday. When Lawrence Stokes and I wrote the original preface to this volume in 1989, one might naturally have assumed that Professor Hoffmann would retire some five, six or seven years later. As I write this new preface, however, some twenty-five years later, Peter Hoffmann is still teaching full-time at McGill University in Montreal, and still producing new and original scholarship on the topic of resistance to Hitler and National Socialism in Germany. Indeed, over the past half-century, both before and since 1990, many noted and outstanding scholars have written about this always difficult and contentious subject. Among them, none has contributed more to the literature, and to the discussions and debates that always accompany this particular topic, than Peter Hoffmann.

This new edition is also meant to pay tribute to eight of the contributors to the original edition, colleagues who have passed away over the course of the last twenty-five years. They include William Sheridan Allen, Michael Balfour, Harold C. Deutsch, Donald Dietrich, Leonidas E. Hill, Karol Jonca, Henry O. Malone and Lawrence D. Stokes (or Larry), who, with his essential expertise in the subject of resistance in Nazi Germany, was the co-editor of the original volume in 1990. With the expertise and collaboration of these eight scholars, and that of the other eleven, this volume is able to cover much of the broad political, economic, social and cultural spectrum of "nonconformity," "opposition" and "resistance" to Hitler and National Socialism in Germany between 1933 and 1945.

The twenty essays in this edition are reprints of the original essays in the volume published by Berg Publishers in 1990, including the brief introduction on the work of Peter Hoffmann to that date. I have updated the original bibliography of Peter Hoffmann's scholarship on the German resistance, which appears at the end of the original introduction, with a selected list of his major works on the subject since 1990, which appears at the end of this new preface. I have also attached to the original bibliography at the end of the book an additional list of selected works on resistance in Germany that have appeared since 1990. The very brief biographies of the contributors that appear in the contributors section have also been updated. It was a somewhat more complicated task to update the brief biographical descriptions of the work of our deceased colleagues. However, with the help of some of their spouses and the internet, I have been able to piece together what I hope are reasonably up-to-date short biographies that will do justice to their many contributions and achievements after 1990.

We have learned a great deal about the overall history of the Third Reich from Peter Hoffmann's scholarship on the resistance in Germany during the Nazi years. Perhaps most of all, we have come to understand why it has taken us so long to learn the full extent of the resistance of the relative few during those years. Because of feelings of shame and guilt on the part of the many, who either looked away out of fear or indifference or who actually participated in some way in the crimes of the Nazi state, that history is still being revealed. As a young graduate student in the 1970s, it was my good fortune to have Peter Hoffmann as my *Doktorvater* at McGill University. Although I did not pursue the specific topic of resistance in Germany for my Ph.D dissertation research or in my subsequent scholarly projects, Professor Hoffmann was the ideal mentor, and for that I will always be grateful. Most importantly, his scholarship on the resistance has provided me and countless others with a lens into so many other aspects of modern German history and the history of the Third Reich.

I would like to thank Marion Berghahn, scholar and publisher, for her support and cooperation in the publication of both the original edition of this book twenty-five years ago at Berg Publishers, and for this long-overdue paperback edition a quarter-century later. My gratitude is also extended to Adam Capitanio and the rest of the staff of Berghahn Books for their assistance.

FRN
Middlebury, Vermont
June 2014

Peter Hoffman's Bibliography since 1990

The following contains a selected list of Peter Hoffmann's books and articles and chapters on the subject of the German resistance to Hitler and National Socialism published since 1990.

Books

Claus Schenk Graf von Stauffenberg und seine Brüder. Stuttgart, 1992.
Stauffenberg: A Family History, 1905–1944. New York, 1995.
Stauffenbergs Freund. Die tragische Geschichte des Widerstandskämpfers Joachim Kuhn. Munich, 2007.
Behind Valkyrie: German Resistance to Hitler. Documents. Montreal and Kingston, 2011.
Carl Goerdler and the Jewish Question, 1933–1942. New York, 2011.
Carl Goerdler gegen die Verfolgung der Juden. Cologne, 2013.

Selected Articles and Chapters

'Roncalli in the Second World War: Peace Initiatives, the Greek Famine and the Persecution of the Jews.' *The Journal of Ecclesiastical History,* vol. 40, 1989, pp. 74–99.
'The German Resistance and the Allies in the Second World War.' In George O. Kent (ed.), *Historians and Archivists: Essays in Modern German History and Archival Policy.* Fairfax, VA, 1991, pp. 201–227.
'The Question of Western Allied Co-operation with the German Anti-Nazi Conspiracy, 1938–1944.' *The Historical Journal,* vol. 34, 1991, pp. 437–464.
'The Second World War, German Society, and Internal Resistance to Hitler.' In David Clay Large (ed.), *Contending with Hitler: Varieties of German Resistance in the Third Reich.* Cambridge, 1992, pp. 119–128.

'Persecution of the Jews as a Motive for Resistance against National Socialism.' *Proceedings of the Biennial Conference on Christianity and the Holocaust. "The Holocaust: Progress and Prognosis 1934–1994."* Lawrenceville, NJ, 1994, pp. 267–291.

'Ludwig Beck - Oberhaupt der Verschwörer.' In Klemens von Klemperer, Enrico Syring and Rainer Zitelmann (eds.), *'Für Deutschland.' Die Männer des 20. Juli.* Frankfurt and Berlin, 1994, pp. 26–43.

'Claus Schenk Graf von Stauffenberg - Der Attentäter.' In Klemens von Klemperer, Enrico Syring and Rainer Zitelmann (eds.), *'Für Deutschland.' Die Männer des 20. Juli.* Frankfurt and Berlin, 1994, pp. 233–246.

'Stauffenberg und die Kontakte der Umsturzverschwörung mit England, 1943–1944.' In Klaus-Jürgen Müller and David N. Dilks (eds.), *Grossbritannien und der deutsche Widerstand 1933–1944.* Paderborn, 1994, pp. 95–104.

'Die britische Regierung, die deutsche Opposition gegen Hitler und die Kriegszielpolitik der Westmächte im Zweiten Weltkrieg.' In Ernst Willi Hansen, Gerhard Schreiber and Bernd Wegner (eds.), *Politischer Wandel, organisierte Gewalt und nationale Sicherheit. Beiträge zur neueren Geschichte Deutschlands und Frankreichs. Festschrift für Klaus-Jürgen Müller.* Munich, 1995, pp. 315–329.

'Der deutsche Widerstand gegen den Nationalsozialismus.' In Hans-Erich Volkmann (ed.), *Ende des Dritten Reiches - Ende des Zweiten Weltkriegs. Eine perspektivische Rückschau.* Munich, 1995, pp. 293–315.

'The German Resistance, the Jews, and Daniel Goldhagen.' In Franklin H. Littell (ed.), *Hyping the Holocaust: Scholars Answer Goldhagen.* East Rockaway, NY, 1997, pp. 73–88.

'July 20, 1944.' In Harold C. Deutsch and Dennis E. Showalter (eds.), *What If? Strategic Alternatives of WWII.* Chicago, IL, 1997, pp. 162–167.

'The Persecution of the Jews as a Motive for Resistance Against National Socialism.' In Andrew Chandler (ed.), *The Moral Imperative: New Essays on the Ethics of Resistance in National Socialist Germany, 1933–1945.* Boulder, CO, 1998, pp. 73–104.

'Die britische Regierung, die deutsche Opposition gegen Hitler und die britische Kriegszielpolitik im Zweiten Weltkrieg.' In Wolfgang J. Mommsen (ed.), *Die ungleichen Partner. Deutsch-britische Beziehungen im 19. und 20. Jahrhundert.* Stuttgart, 1999, pp. 170–183.

'The German Resistance to Hitler and the Jews.' In David Bankier (ed.), *Probing the Depths of German Antisemitism: German Society and the Persecution of the Jews, 1933–1941.* Jerusalem and New York, 2000, pp. 463–477.

'The Development of the German Resistance to Hitler.' In Julie M. Winter (trans. and ed.), *Marion Yorck von Wartenburg, The Power of Solitude: My Life in the German Resistance.* Lincoln, NE, 2000, pp. xi–xxxi.

'Claus von Stauffenberg and the Military Ethos.' In Brian P. Farrell (ed.), *Leadership and Responsibility in the Second World War*. Montreal and Kingston, 2004, pp. 167–181.

'The German Resistance and the Holocaust.' In John J. Michalczyk (ed.), *Confront! Resistance in Nazi Germany*. New York, Washington, DC, Baltimore, MD, Bern, Frankfurt, Berlin, Brussels, Vienna and Oxford, 2004, pp. 105–126.

'Major Joachim Kuhn: Explosives Purveyor to Stauffenberg and Stalin's Prisoner.' *German Studies Review*, vol. 28, 2005, pp. 519–546.

'Stauffenberg und Tresckow.' In Günter Brakelmann and Manfred Keller (eds.), *Der 20. Juli 1944 und das Erbe des deutschen Widerstands*. Münster, 2005, pp. 159–172.

'The German Resistance to Hitler and the Jews: The Case of Carl Goerdeler.' In Dennis B. Klein et al. (eds.), *The Genocidal Mind: Selected Papers from the 32nd Annual Scholars' Conference on the Holocaust and the Churches*. St. Paul, MN, 2005, pp. 277–290.

'Ludwig Beck: Soldatentum und Verantwortung. Ein Widerstandskämpfer aus Hessen.' *Polis*, vol. 42, 2005, pp. 19–36.

'Stauffenberg –Tat und Denkmal.' In Peter I. Trummer and Konrad Pflug (eds.), *Die Brüder Stauffenberg und der deutsche Widerstand*. Stuttgart, 2006, pp. 31–41.

'Oberst i.G. Henning von Tresckow und die Staatsstreichpläne im Jahr 1943.' *Vierteljahrshefte für Zeitgeschichte*, vol. 55, 2007, pp. 331–364.

Introduction:
Resistance to National Socialism
in the Work of
Peter Hoffmann

Francis R. Nicosia

There has long been a debate among interested scholars over what constituted 'resistance' against Hitler and National Socialism during the Third Reich. Should individual acts of nonconformity with the wishes or policies of the state be permitted to bear the same label of 'resistance' as acts of those who participated in the conspiracy to assassinate Hitler on 20 July 1944? Was the refusal to accept certain aspects of National Socialism by isolated individuals on a daily basis as much 'resistance' as were the organised attempts to overthrow the Nazi state entirely?

The *Concise Oxford Dictionary* defines the verb 'to resist' in several ways: actively to oppose or seek to stop the course of; to prevent penetration; to repel, to remain unaffected by; to abstain from. 'Resistance' is defined as refusal to comply; hindrance; impeding or stopping the effect exercised upon another. Of course, formal definitions found in dictionaries do not always take into account meanings that are specifically dependent on a particular context. Moreover, definitions of resistance in a political context have come to reflect primarily the existence of an organised conspiracy, assassination, para-military activity, a *coup d'état*.

Definitions of resistance are also relative to time and place; criticism of the state, dissent from or nonconformity with its policies in a democratic environment are not thought of as constituting resistance in a traditional political or historical sense, but they may all be considered forms of resistance on different levels in a totalitarian society such as Hitler's Third Reich. So central was *Gleichschaltung* (co-ordination) in the theory of National Socialism, and so brutally explicit was its application, that even the most individual and private forms of dissent or non-compliance with the policies of the government carried with them varying degrees of risk and the potential for grave consequences. For example, some paid with their lives for refusing to utter the greeting 'Heil Hitler', or for remarks that the war might be lost for Germany.[1]

The essays in this volume address the question of resistance in its broadest sense to Hitler and National Socialism in the Third Reich. This should not be construed as an attempt to dilute the nature and substance of the kind of resistance undertaken by the relatively powerful and well-placed few in the armed forces and the bureaucracy who were at least remotely in a position in some significant way to alter or to actually destroy the Nazi regime.[2] Rather the intention is to suggest that there were very different levels of resistance to National Socialism during the Third Reich,[3] reflecting in some measure the wide range of position, power and influence among the population as a whole. In that sense, individual acts of non-compliance among ordinary citizens usually reflected the extent to which many of them were realistically capable of resisting certain policies of the Nazi state – for that matter the state in general. For example, one might consider the votes of the majority of Germans in the Reichstag elections of 5 March 1933 for parties other than the National Socialist German Workers' Party (NSDAP), a week after the suspension of civil liberties and a month and a half after the beginning of the Nazi reign of terror, as a form of resistance.[4] The inclination of most to resist in some way could not be expected to include active conspiracy against the Nazi government and the assassination of its leaders. Even if the will to kill them had been present, the average citizen had virtually no access to the important figures of the regime, least of all to Hitler. Peter Hoffmann has alluded to the resistance in Germany as a 'phenomenon of a determined but largely ineffective reistance . . . made up of a variety of forms of behavior, from semi-public gestures to direct anti-government activity at the highest level'.[5] That he does not believe that only involvement in a conspiracy to do away with Hitler constituted opposition to the regime is evident in his assertion: 'It makes no sense today to demand that every opponent of the regime and of National Socialism had to have been a fanatical potential assassin in order that his opposition be believed.'[6]

The following contributions, and indeed almost anything written about resistance in Germany during the Third Reich, also reflect the complex nature of the response of individuals, groups, and organisations to the emerging danger and evil which they perceived. Probably for most critics and opponents of Hitler and the Third Reich, National Socialism contained positive elements as well; certainly the majority of Germans were disinclined to return to the liberal democracy of the Weimar Republic. Nevertheless, for virtually all Germans who might fit into this broad categorisation of resistance, nationalism and patriotism inevitably intruded in a more or less complicating manner, impeding or confusing their opposition to all or part of the status quo, particularly during the Second World War. For many, moreover, especially in the Churches, their fear of communism conflicted with their apprehensions about or opposition to the Nazi 'New Order' in Germany and Europe. Thus, the essays presented here also reflect the broad scope of resistance to Hitler, as well as the complexity of its nature.

There can be little doubt that between 1933 and 1945 the great majority of Germans did succumb to a greater or lesser extent to the propaganda of the Nazi regime, and acquiesced in the state's exercise of total control over every aspect of their individual lives. Peter Hoffmann has argued: 'On the whole, at all times from 1933 to 1945 the majority of German voters, indeed of the entire population, supported the government, albeit with varying degrees of willingness.'[7] Although many no doubt felt apprehensive about aspects of National Socialism and its policies, relatively few were able to muster the courage or the will to resist the state on any level, particularly after the first two years of Nazi rule. Popular opposition 'remained scattered, isolated and easily controlled' by the police, while the conspirators who planned the overthrow of the regime and the arrest or assassination of Hitler and other leaders lacked unity, favourable access, popular backing at home, and diplomatic support abroad. Hoffmann has concluded: 'This resistance was therefore not effective, since it was incapable of changing the regime.'[8]

Of course, success has not been the only, or even the primary, standard according to which the German resistance has been debated, interpreted and judged by scholars. Peter Hoffmann asserts: 'To declare these individual or collective acts of heroism in the struggle against Nazism to have been ineffective is not a judgement on their moral value. Isolated individuals and groups, without hope of being effective, did not make success the criterion for their commitment, any more than did other resistors with better access to the centres of power.'[9] The actions of those who resisted were motivated even more by a sense of moral responsibility to demonstrate to themselves, to their communities and to the world that some Germans stood in fundamental opposition to the policies and actions of the Nazi state. In so doing, they took upon themselves the obligation to save Germany from self-inflicted spiritual collapse as well as from physical destruction at the hands of the Allies.[10] That such considerations counted for much more than the prospect of success in the resistance to Hitler is evident in the words of Major-General Henning von Tresckow, one of the conspirators in the 20 July 1944 assassination attempt against Hitler: 'The assassination must be attempted, at any cost. . . . We must prove to the world and to future generations that the men of the German resistance movement dared to take the decisive step and to hazard their lives upon it. Compared with this object, nothing else matters.'[11] Without a strong idealistic component in the motivation of individuals and groups, it is questionable whether their actions can or should be labelled 'resistance'.[12] Moreover, this moral imperative has also been a primary motivating factor for many scholars who address the subject in their work.

In one of the earliest studies of indigenous opposition to Hitler and National Socialism, the German historian Hans Rothfels acknowledged the existence of a substantial amount of resistance and the complexity of its composition, motives and history. In this book, first published in the United States in 1948,[13] Rothfels aimed his conclusions primarily at an American audience at a time immediately after the war when the very notion of Germans in appreciable numbers actively resisting the Nazi regime was not at all palatable to public opinion in any of the victorious Allied countries. During those years and among the generation that followed, there was little distinction in the West between Nazis and Germans; most people simply assumed that all Germans supported everything that Hitler had done and for which he had stood. It is not surprising, therefore, that Allied censorship in occupied Germany from 1945 to 1949 would not permit the publication of works which addressed specifically and directly the question of resistance to National Socialism between 1933 and 1945, and that the first studies did not appear in Germany until after 1949. Thus, Rothfels's book had relatively little impact on the Western audiences that he was trying to influence. While he stressed that he did not wish to deny the responsibility of the German people as a whole for the horrors unleashed in their name by the Nazis, he did try nevertheless to demonstrate that there had been that 'other Germany', which, in a complex variety of ways, had stood in opposition to Hitler and National Socialism.

A generation later, in the 'Foreword' to his *magnum opus Widerstand Staatsstreich Attentat.* *Der Kampf der Opposition gegen Hitler*, Peter Hoffmann alluded to 'a calmer atmosphere' then prevailing than that which followed the Second World War, one in which a more sensible and productive discussion of the German resistance could take place.[14] In addition to the far greater availability of primary source materials, including perhaps an increased willingness of some persons who were key witnesses to the events between 1938 and 1945 to talk, Professor Hoffmann was clearly looking to Germany and to what by the end of the 1960s was an audience somewhat more receptive to an airing of the issue of resistance by Germans to Hitler. Prior to that time, Germans were preoccupied by the psychology of defeat, economic distress, occupation and denazification; the fact that many had resisted the Nazis must have been a particular embarrassment to the millions who had enthusiastically supported them, and probably discouraged public interest in the resistance.[15] In the 1950s and 1960s, surviving resisters were regarded by many in Germany as traitors, and accordingly resistance was not a popular topic among academics, publishers, educators and the public at large. However, public opinion polls taken from 1951 to 1970 in the Federal Republic were also revealing a somewhat more positive attitude toward those who had been involved in resistance, set against a declining negative attitude.[16] Peter Hoffmann's work represents, therefore, the first comprehensive examination of the theory and practice of resistance in Germany on the level of conspiracy, assassination and *coup d'état*, which, in conjunction with other seminal scholarly works on the history of the Third Reich, began to confront Germans with their recent past on a large scale during the late 1960s, a generation after the end of the Second World War and the immediate post-war period.[17]

That Peter Hoffmann has devoted much of his scholarly energy to the question of the resistance to Hitler and National Socialism in Germany is not surprising. It is too facile simply to conclude that he is a German driven by the need to demonstrate to the world that not all Germans were Nazis, that some opposed Hitler's crimes and that Germans in general are capable of human decency. That many German authors might want to do this is both understandable and desirable, as long as the crimes of the Third Reich and responsibility for them are not denied. In his work, Peter Hoffmann clearly portrays the criminal nature of the Nazi regime, while the tragedies of the relatively few who did resist, particularly although not exclusively on the level of conspiracy and assassination, are contrasted sharply with the indifference or acquiescence of the many in all ranks of German society: 'Whereas the Resistance was representative of all German society in sociological, economic and political terms, it was not representative in quantitative terms. . . . Broad support, actual or potential, among the population was lacking for the actions of the Resistance as well as for its ideas.'[18]

There are personal, family ties to the German resistance which in part explain Peter Hoffmann's ongoing interest and scholarship in this area of research. His father, the late Dr Wilhelm Hoffmann, was a *Bibliotheksrat* (academic librarian) at the *Landesbibliothek* (State Library) in Württemberg from 1931, and its director after 1945. The Hoffmann family had long been acquaintances of the Weizsäckers, the Stauffenbergs and the Bonhoeffers among others in Württemberg – that is, with some of the leading families who were representative of the German conservatives to whom Peter Hoffmann has devoted much of his attention in his work on resistance. Wilhelm Hoffmann met Adam von Trott zu Solz several times during the war. Trott secured for the elder Hoffmann the necessary visas for travel to Switzerland on library business; at the same time, Hoffman acted as a courier for the conspirators to make contact with the British there. Dr Eugen Gerstenmaier, apparently with the knowledge and consent of Trott, confided to Wilhelm Hoffmann that an assassination attempt against Hitler would take place in July 1944. In that month Trott gave Hoffmann a pistol and asked him to see that it reached his (Trott's) wife in Berlin. Presumably intended for Frau von Trott's suicide in the event that the impending assassination attempt against Hitler failed, Wilhelm Hoffmann entrusted the weapon to his brother-in-law, who was travelling to Berlin and who turned it over to Hans Schönfeld, a member of the conspiracy who was employed by the World Council of Churches. Thus Peter Hoffmann's father was intimately connected with the resistance against Hitler during the Second World War. Despite the obvious risks, he assisted the conspirators in their efforts and generally enjoyed their confidence.

Wilhelm Hoffmann was also among the first publicly to raise the question of German resistance in print during the immediate postwar period in Germany, albeit rather briefly. In his book *Nach der Katastrophe*,[19] published in 1946, he made observations about Germany during the Third Reich that to some extent must have helped to prepare the ground for Peter Hoffmann's research efforts a generation later. Wilhelm Hoffmann stressed the ability of the Nazis to use German nationalism as a cover for their criminal intentions, making it difficult for the majority of Germans to distinguish between their patriotism and National Socialism, or overtly and actively to object to the policies of the Nazi state. If in the occupied countries of Europe during the war there was no conflict between the desire for freedom and nationalist feelings, in Germany there clearly was. Hoffman senior also pointed to a major weakness of the resistance, namely its inability to formulate a clear and unified idea of what would follow the overthrow of the Nazi regime. Thus, there was no concept developed of a future order which, even given the visible brutality, and the preparations for war and the hardships these caused, might have offered an alternative to the status quo around which substantial numbers of Germans might have rallied. Peter Hoffmann has built on all these themes in his own work on the resistance.[20]

As a young student pursuing his doctorate at the University of Munich, Peter Hoffmann was inclined to pursue his research in the history of Germany in the nineteenth century; his *Doktorvater*, the renowned Professor Franz Schnabel, was at the time perhaps the leading authority on that period. His dissertation dealt with the diplomatic relations between the Kingdoms of Bavaria and Württemberg during and immediately after the Crimean War.[21] As he was finishing his graduate studies, Peter Hoffmann was approached by the '*Stiftung Hilfswerk 20. Juli 1944*'[22] and invited to undertake a definitive history of the resistance. He already possessed an interest in the topic in any case, and might also in some small way have been attracted to it as a result of his knowledge of his father's activities during the war. Moreover, the assurance of the '*Stiftung*' that it possessed large quantities of hitherto unused documents, papers, etc., was also an inducement to move into this field of scholarly activity. The result, of course, was his definitive volume, referred to above, first published in 1969.

Certainly a hallmark of Peter Hoffmann's scholarship on the resistance in Germany has been its comprehensive nature. He has written to a varying extent on most of the themes, individuals and groups upon which the essays in this volume focus. He has studied the ubiquitous nature of the police and security authorities in the Nazi state. The question of morality versus narrow class self-interest as a motivating factor among the conservative élite has been another question receiving his intense scrutiny. He has looked at the complexity surrounding the disappointing failure of the *Wehrmacht* as an instrument in the resistance against Hitler between 1938 and 1944. The attitude of the Allies toward resistance inside Germany, particularly in conjunction with their war aims, as well as their role in its ultimate failure, have been topics that he has addressed in several important publications. Peter Hoffmann has also considered the uneven and at times selective nature of the resistance, within a general context of compliance with the regime, on the part of the Protestant and Catholic Churches. He has examined the generally heroic but futile efforts of socialist and communist resistance against the Nazi state, especially during the early years of the Third Reich, and has subsequently taken up the question of popular disaffection and nonconformity with aspects of National Socialism. Finally, few scholars have treated the theme of Jewish resistance within Germany, an immensely sensitive and difficult one because the natural weakness of such activity was the result of the uniquely vulnerable position of the German-Jewish community before and after 1933. However, Peter Hoffmann has placed particular emphasis on Nazi atrocities against the Jews as a factor provoking the resistance by German conspirators during the Second World War.

Clearly, the emphasis in Peter Hoffmann's work over the years has been on the history of the organised conspiracy to assassinate Hitler and to topple the Nazi regime; however, he has placed this within the context of the wider history of resistance in the Third Reich by also undertaking a detailed examination and assessment of other forms of opposition. He has recognised that resistance in the 'broad sense' began even before 1933, has argued that in the 'true sense' it commenced after 1933 and has focused on 'the real hallmark of resistance' that began in 1938, namely the active conspiracy to destroy Hitler's regime outright.[23] In some respects, therefore, the essays in this volume stand in a dialogue with him on the nature and course of resistance to Hitler and National Socialism in Germany. Some papers supplement topics on which his scholarship has led the way, while others complement his work by expanding upon matters which he has already considered in greater detail in his writing.

Thus, Robert Gellately's contribution on the political policing of the Nazi state demonstrates the ability of its authorities to create an effective 'surveillance society' which eliminated the 'relatively safe enclaves in which disobedience might have developed structurally'. Lawrence Stokes and Leonidas Hill consider the moral and ethical component of resistance in conservative circles during the Third Reich, notwithstanding some of the more dubious political inclinations these groups manifested and their general rejection of the liberal democracy of the Weimar Republic. Arnold Paucker and Karol Jonca address the difficult question of the manner in which the Jewish community sought to resist the Nazi assault on its rights and position in Germany both before and after the Nazi *Machtüber-nahme* in 1933.

The essays by John Conway, Robert Ericksen and Donald Dietrich present a picture of a resistance to National Socialism in the Protestant and Catholic Churches which was sporadic, selective, and very mixed, one that includes examples of the great personal courage of a few believers on an individual level against a backdrop of institutional reticence, fear, confusion and overall compliance. Ian Kershaw, Ernst Hanisch and Jill Stephenson consider the question of popular non-compliance with and opposition to certain policies of Hitler's regime, specifically levels of resistance against the *Gleichschaltung* of German society by the Nazi state. Whether it was popular opposition to the 'guns versus butter' priorities of the regime between 1934 and 1936, disobedience to Nazi policies which stood in conflict with religious and social customs in the Austrian Alps, or the refusal of German citizens in Württemberg to comply with the 'no surrender' dictates of the authorities during the waning months of the war, these three authors provide examples of the extent, however limited, to which ordinary individuals would go to resist total subordination to the will of Hitler's state. William Sheridan Allen and Eve Rosenhaft provide a broader context for treating the subject of resistance on the Left. Allen looks at Social Democratic responses to National Socialism within the context of a developed tradition of underground movements in Europe, while Rosenhaft considers the legacy of communist resistance in the early years of the German Democratic Republic.

The important topic of the contacts of the German resistance with the outside world, and its dependence on them, is the focus of the contributions by Ger van Roon, Henry Malone and Rainer Blasius. Malone and Blasius discuss the German and British sides respectively of those connections, while van Roon considers parallel ties with resistance groups in Holland. Harold Deutsch and Heinrich Walle address the question of resistance in the German armed forces; Deutsch considers the perennial question of the inclination or disinclination of top military commanders to act to remove Hitler from power in 1938, and Walle presents the story of one naval officer's questioning of and final non-compliance with the overall aims of the Nazi state. Finally, in his concluding piece Michael Balfour raises one of the more important 'what ifs' in the history of the Third Reich, namely what might have happened had the resistance to Hitler and National Socialism been successful in eliminating him from power. In so doing, Balfour proposes reasons why the resistance in Germany in general, and the conspiracy to assassinate Hitler in particular, ultimately had to fail.

Peter Hoffmann has suggested that it is not possible fully to comprehend the evil of the Third Reich without an understanding of the resistance which it produced. He has written:

> The Nazi crimes, and the battle waged against them by a few within Nazi Germany, challenge all human beings to comprehend the nature of tyranny. Hitler's rule cannot be understood without a grasp of the resistance to Nazi crimes, for the very nature of the Third Reich evoked the most uncompromising opposition as well as the enthusiasm of the masses. The relation between National Socialism and the Resistance is a key to comprehending the Nazi system.[24]

That there is a direct correlation between the essence of a tyranny and the nature and degree of opposition to it, has been a constant thread throughout Peter Hoffmann's work on the German resistance for a generation. Therefore his writing on the subject has been and will remain for years to come a standard for all scholars, because its ultimate contribution has been a fuller understanding of Hitler, National Socialism and the history of the Third Reich.

NOTES

1. For much more on this, see: W. Wagner, *Der Volksgerichtshof im nationalsozialistischen Staat*, Stuttgart, 1974, pp. 277–415.
2. See, for example, H. Mommsen, 'Die Geschichte des deutschen Widerstands im Lichte der neueren Forschung', *Aus Politik und Zeitgeschichte*, vol. 50, 1986, pp. 3–38.
3. See, for example, the discussions of resistance on a variety of levels, beyond the confines of organised attempts at *coup d'état*, in: L. E. Hill, 'Toward a New History of the German Resistance to Hitler', *Central European History*, vol. 14, 1981, pp. 369–99; and G. van Roon, *Widerstand im Dritten Reich. Ein Überblick*, 4th edn, Munich, 1987, pp. 11–28.
4. See, for example, van Roon, *Widerstand im Dritten Reich*, pp. 11 ff.
5. P. Hoffmann, *German Resistance to Hitler*, Cambridge, Mass., 1988, p. 55.
6. P. Hoffmann, *Widerstand Staatsstreich Attentat. Der Kampf der Opposition gegen Hitler*, 4th rev. edn, Munich, 1985, p. 54.
7. Hoffmann, *German Resistance*, p. 51.
8. Ibid., pp. 60, 71–2.

9. Ibid., p. 60.
10. See: H.-A. Jacobsen (ed.), *July 20, 1944: The German Opposition to Hitler as Viewed by Foreign Historians – An Anthology*, Bonn, 1969, pp. 6–7.
11. F. von Schlabrendorff, *Revolt Against Hitler: The Personal Account of Fabian von Schlabrendorff*, G. von S. Gaevernitz (ed.), London, 1948, p. 131.
12. See, for example, R. Pommerin, 'Demokraten und Pazifisten oder Rowdies und Rebellen? Die Einschätzung der "Edelweißpiraten" im britischen Außenministerium 1944/45', *Geschichte im Westen*, vol. 2, 1987, pp. 135–44.
13. See H. Rothfels, *The German Opposition to Hitler*, Hinsdale, Illinois, 1948. The German edition was published one year later as *Die deutsche Opposition gegen Hitler; eine Würdigung*, Krefeld, 1949. (New and enlarged edn, ed. H. Graml, Frankfurt am Main, 1977.)
14. Hoffmann, *Widerstand*, p. 12. In 1968 Hans Rothfels strongly recommended the publication of this volume to the Piper-Verlag in Munich. Although he was still the leading German authority on the resistance in Germany at the time, Rothfels insisted that there was still much to be said on the subject. The book first appeared in English under the title *The History of the German Resistance 1933–1945*, published simultaneously in the United States and Great Britain by the MIT Press and Macdonald and Jane's Publishers, respectively, in 1977. It was first published in French as *La résistance allemande contre Hitler* by Éditions André Balland in Paris in 1984.
15. See Hoffmann, *German Resistance*, p. 1.
16. See Institut für Demoskopie Allensbach, *Der Widerstand im Dritten Reich. Wissen und Urteil der Bevölkerung vor und nach dem 40. Jahrestag des 20. Juli 1944*, Allensbach, 1984.
17. There were two important studies on the resistance published in Germany during the 1950s between the work of Rothfels and Hoffmann. However they consider only special aspects of the overall topic. They are G. Ritter, *Carl Goerdeler und die deutsche Widerstandsbewegung*, Stuttgart, 1954; and E. Zeller, *Geist der Freiheit. Der Zwanzigste Juli*, Munich, 1952. Like Hans Rothfels, they emphasise the moral basis of the opposition to Hitler.
18. Hoffmann, *German Resistance*. p. 71.
19. See W. Hoffmann, *Nach der Katastrophe*, Tübingen–Stuttgart, 1946, pp. 60 ff., 111 ff.
20. For Hoffmann's views on the inability of most Germans to avoid confusing their nationalism with National Socialism see, for example, his *German Resistance*, pp. 52 ff. The problem of the failure of the resistance to formulate a unified program of what was to follow the Nazi regime was naturally linked to the question of its foreign contacts and the inherent problems associated with them. See, for example, his 'Peace Through Coup d'État: The Foreign Contacts of the German Resistance 1933–1944', *Central European History*, vol. 19, 1986, pp. 3–44.

21. It was published as *Die diplomatische Beziehungen zwischen Württemberg und Bayern im Krimkrieg und bis zum Beginn der italienischen Krise (1853–1858)*, Stuttgart, 1963.
22. There was very little official, institutional support for the survivors, widows and children of the German resistance during the first years after the war. The *'Stiftung'*, partly funded by the West German government, undertook this kind of assistance.
23. Hoffmann, *Widerstand*, p. 10.
24. Hoffmann, *German Resistance*, p. 3.

BIBLIOGRAPHY

The following bibliography contains only those published works by Peter Hoffmann that deal specifically with the question of the resistance to Hitler and National Socialism during the Third Reich.

Books

Widerstand Staatsstreich Attentat. Der Kampf der Opposition gegen Hitler, Munich, 1969; 2nd rev. edn, 1970; 3rd rev. edn, 1979; 4th rev. edn, 1985.
Die Sicherheit des Diktators. Hitlers Leibwachen, Schutzmaßnahmen, Residenzen, Hauptquartiere, Munich–Zürich, 1975.
The History of the German Resistance 1933–1945, London–Cambridge, Mass., 1977; rev. edn, Cambridge, Mass., 1979.
Hitler's Personal Security, Basingstoke–London–Cambridge, Mass., 1979.
Widerstand gegen Hitler und das Attentat vom 20. Juli 1944. Probleme des Umsturzes, Munich, 1979; 2nd rev. edn, 1984.
La résistance allemande contre Hitler, Paris, 1984.
German Resistance to Hitler, Cambridge, Mass.–London, 1988.

Articles

'Zu dem Attentat im Führerhauptquartier "Wolfsschanze" am 20. Juli 1944', *Vierteljahrshefte für Zeitgeschichte*, vol. 12, 1964, pp. 254–84.
'Zum Ablauf des Staatsstreichversuches des 20. Juli 1944 in den Wehrkreisen', *Wehrwissenschaftliche Rundschau*, vol. 14, 1964, pp. 377–97.
'Der 20. Juli im Wehrkreis II (Stettin): Ein Beispiel für den Ablauf des Staatsstreichversuches im Reich', *Aus Politik und Zeitgeschichte*, No. 28, 14 July 1965, pp. 25–37.
'The Attempt to Assassinate Hitler on March 21, 1943', *Canadian Journal of History/Annales Canadiennes d'Histoire*, vol. 2, 1967, pp. 67–83.
'Claus Graf Stauffenberg und Stefan George: Der Weg zur Tat', *Jahrbuch*

der Deutschen Schillergesellschaft, vol. 12, 1968, pp. 520–42.

'Hitler's Personal Security', *Journal of Contemporary History*, vol. 8, 1973, pp. 25–46.

'Problems of Resistance in National Socialist Germany', in F. H. Littell and H. G. Locke (eds), *The German Church Struggle and the Holocaust*, Detroit, 1974, pp. 97–113.

'Handeln aus dem Zwang des Gewissens: Der tragische Befreiungsversuch am 20. Juli 1944', in K. Piper (ed.), *Piper-Almanach zum 70. Jahr. 1964–1974*, Munich–Zürich, 1974, pp. 711–18.

'Der Hergang des Attentats', in H. J. Schultz (ed.), *Der zwanzigste Juli. Alternative zu Hitler?*, Stuttgart–Berlin, 1974, pp. 36–49.

'Maurice Bavaud's Attempt to Assassinate Hitler in 1938', in G. L. Mosse (ed.), *Police Forces in History*, London, 1975, pp. 173–204.

'War Stauffenberg "ostorientiert"?', *Die Zeit*, No. 53, 29 December 1978, p. 10.

'Beck, Rommel and the Nazis: The Dilemma of the German Army', in E. Denton III (ed.), *Limits of Loyalty*, Waterloo, Ontario, 1980, pp. 101–25.

'Ludwig Beck: Loyalty and Resistance', *Central European History*, vol. 14, 1981, pp. 332–50.

'Generaloberst Ludwig Becks militärpolitisches Denken', *Historische Zeitschrift*, vol. 234, 1982, pp. 101–21.

'Srodowisko Ludzi Nauki a Faszyzm', in C. Madajczyk (ed.), *Inter arma non silent Musae. Wojna i kultura 1939–1945*, Warsaw, 1982, pp. 99–101.

'La resistenza militare antinazista in Germania', *Il Ponte*, vol. 39, 1983, pp. 956–69.

'Der militärische Widerstand in der zweiten Kriegshälfte 1942/45', in Militärgeschichtliches Forschungsamt (ed.), *Vorträge zur Militärgeschichte 5. Der militärische Widerstand gegen Hitler und das NS-Regime 1933–1945*, Herford–Bonn, 1984, pp. 110–34.

'Warum mißlang das Attentat vom 20. Juli 1944?', *Vierteljahrshefte für Zeitgeschichte*, vol. 32, 1984, pp. 441–62.

'Alexander, Berthold, and Claus Graf Stauffenberg, the Stefan George Circle, and Greece: Background to the Plot Against Hitler', *Journal of the Hellenic Diaspora*, vol. 11, 1984, pp. 89–97.

'Stauffenberg und die Veränderungen der außen- und innenpolitischen Handlungsbedingungen für die Durchführung des "Walküre"-Plans', in J. Schmädeke and P. Steinbach (eds), *Der Widerstand gegen den Nationalsozialismus. Die deutsche Gesellschaft und der Widerstand gegen Hitler*, Munich–Zürich, 1985, pp. 1003–20.

'Motive', in J. Schmädeke and P. Steinbach (eds), *Der Widerstand gegen den Nationalsozialismus. Die deutsche Gesellschaft und der Widerstand gegen Hitler*, Munich–Zürich, 1985, pp. 1089–96.

'Claus Graf Stauffenberg und der Widerstand gegen Hitler', *Meyers Großes Universallexikon*, vol. 15, Bibliographisches Institut, Mannheim–Vienna–Zürich, 1986, pp. 406–9.

'Peace through Coup d'État: The Foreign Contacts of the German Resistance 1933–1944', *Central European History*, vol. 19, 1986, pp. 3–44.

'Claus Graf Schenk von Stauffenberg: 1907–1944', in H. Schumann (ed.), *Baden-Württembergische Portraits. Gestalten aus dem 19. und 20. Jahrhundert,* Stuttgart, 1988, pp. 379–87.

'The War, German Society and Internal Resistance', in M. Laffan (ed.), *The Burden of German History, 1919–1945: Essays for the Goethe Institute,* London, 1988, pp. 185–209.

'Colonel Claus von Stauffenberg in the German Resistance to Hitler: Between East and West', *The Historical Journal,* vol. 31, 1988, pp. 629–50.

2

Surveillance and Disobedience:
Aspects of
the Political Policing of
Nazi Germany

Robert Gellately

Studies of resistance, opposition or dissent in Nazi Germany have had little to say about the process by which the country was brought under surveillance and control by the Gestapo (Secret State Police). This neglect is surprising since the Gestapo, which stood at the head of an extensive police and Party network, represented the most important formal–institutional obstacle faced by conspiracies against Hitler. This body did not only attempt to search out and destroy serious threats to the regime; it also endeavoured to suppress all non-compliance by the population at large. Within a remarkably short time, this concerted effort severely reduced the possibilities for even the most innocuous forms of disobedience, all of which were politicised, characterised as 'opposition' and, therefore, criminalised. Historians are beginning to see that the Gestapo's activities played a vital role in establishing and enforcing the strictest possible parameters on behaviour, so that there emerged in Germany an extreme example of what Michel Foucault calls a 'surveillance' or 'panoptic' society.[1] However, though historians might agree that these terms represent a more or less apt description of post-1933 Germany, they have not explored the nature of this development and its implications for everyday life. As a consequence, they have failed to understand the structural limitations placed upon possible expressions of disobedience in Nazi Germany.

15

Review of the literature

The Institute for Contemporary History in Munich has contributed greatly to our understanding of 'resistance and persecution' in Bavaria. Although its six-volume study completed several years ago touches on some aspects of the Gestapo and the court system, it never addresses the persecutors in any depth.[2] One might have expected that oral histories, such as the recent three-volume study yielded by the research project on the Ruhr workers,[3] would highlight the role of controlling organisations of the Party and state, since terroristic elements of Nazism ought to have stamped indelible impressions on the memories of non-Nazis, especially in such a working-class milieu. Yet that series, too, is practically silent when it comes to the Gestapo and how it operated.

At the opposite end of the spectrum, some accounts of working-class resistance exaggerate the role of the Gestapo as an explanation for the failure of workers' resistance; they tend to overestimate the numbers formally and informally part of the Gestapo and attribute comprehensive abilities to it.[4] In fact, given the conception of Nazism held by the Left, which saw it primarily as a kind of conspiracy of the capitalists and the Nazis against the workers instead of a social movement with broad (if by no means universal) support *also* in the working-class milieu, it is not so surprising that the Left pictured the Gestapo and Nazism in general as a kind of foreign apparatus imposed on German society.[5] The repeated suggestion that the working class was reluctant to volunteer information to the authorities does not stand up under closer inspection, although such contentions echo the perceptions of the Left at the time, both inside Germany and abroad.[6] Without diminishing the role of the Gestapo, there is a need here for some demythologising.

For the most part, the police and other control organisations are either not mentioned at all or taken for granted in studies of resistance. At an international conference on the fortieth anniversary of the July 1944 plot to assassinate Hitler, for example, there were some sixty-five papers presented which dealt with virtually every conceivable kind of resistance, but not a single contribution was devoted to *any* control organisations.[7] Why is it that works on resistance do not see fit to examine how the persecutors went about their daily tasks? Certainly, such neglect cannot be attributed simply to an oversight on the part of any particular historian, but is rather a result issuing in large measure from the ways in which these studies have been conceptualised. The Gestapo – to the limited extent that it receives attention at all – is mostly a synonym for ruthless, arbitrary and inescapable terror, the quintessence of the 'police state'. Peter Hoffmann's observation in his latest account of the resistance is representative. He states that 'the Gestapo terrorised dissidents with the mere possibility of a knock on the door at five o'clock in the morning and two leather-coated figures standing outside saying, "Come with us".'[8] Although such widely-held perceptions of the 'ubiquitous Gestapo' certainly contain some truth, it is high time to examine, more systematically and in depth, the many issues surrounding the policing of Nazi Germany. As Tim Mason points out, it is insufficient merely to attribute the absence of resistance 'to the unique power of the totalitarian state'; that is to use 'a sort of shorthand rather than to offer an explanation'.[9] It is certainly true that the emergence of the Gestapo and the obliteration of most opposition were directly related.

Barrington Moore has pointed out that in the final analysis the 'one prerequisite' for expressions of disobedience to take place anywhere is the existence of 'social and cultural space' which 'provides more or less protected enclaves within which dissatisfied or oppressed groups have some room', so that a minimum of mobilisation can occur.[10] The Gestapo, and the other negative inducements to obey, the awareness of the widespread incidence of tip-offs to the authorities, in conjunction with the so-called positive accomplishments of the regime (such as curing unemployment or tearing up the Treaty of Versailles) and 'self-coordination', worked to reduce to a minimum the space for any kind of disobedience to blossom.[11]

The effectiveness of any enforcement body is to a greater or lesser extent dependent upon the co-operation or collaboration it receives from the society of which it is a part. This was certainly true in Nazi Germany, in which general surveillance was felt to be inescapable, so that it became increasingly difficult for any disobedience to be expressed, let alone for resistance and opposition to crystallise.[12] Clearly, accounts of resistance cannot afford to overlook the extent and nature of organisations of surveillance and suppression.

Local Organisation of the Gestapo and its Spy Network

According to the recollections of many who once lived in Nazi Germany, the effectiveness of the Gestapo and the surveillance system rested on a numerically large police force and an 'army' of spies and paid informers.[13] It is true that no one felt far from the scrutiny of the Nazi state whether in public, at work, or even at home. However, this sense of being watched could not have been due to the sheer physical presence of Gestapo officials, because membership in the Gestapo was remarkably small. By the end of 1944 there were approximately 32,000 persons in the force, of whom 3,000 were administrative officials, 15,500 or so executive officials, and 13,500 employees and workmen, 9,000 of them draftees. 'Administrators' had the same training as other civil servants, and dealt with personnel records, budgets, supplies and legal problems such as those stemming from passport law. Especially trained 'executive officials' were assigned tasks according to the various desks (*Referate*) into which the State Police was sub-divided, and they 'executed the real tasks of the Gestapo', although 'a number of these officials also were engaged in pure office work'.[14] The Gestapo also took over other organisations and some of their personnel, such as the customs frontier guards, but these had little to do with day-to-day policing inside Germany and can be left out of account here. Otto Ohlendorf, head of the *Sicherheitsdienst* (Security Service, SD), estimated that there was 'one specialist' or executive official 'to three or four persons' in the Gestapo.[15]

Given the small number of officials in the Gestapo, their distribution had to be thin on the ground. A March 1937 survey of personnel in the Düsseldorf Gestapo region, for example, showed a total of 291 persons, of whom 49 were concerned with administrative matters and 242 involved more directly with police work (in the *Außendienst*). At that time 126 officials were stationed in Düsseldorf, a city with a population of approximately 500,000. Other cities within the overall jurisdiction of the Düsseldorf headquarters were assigned additional personnel: Essen had 43 officials to cover a population of about 650,000, while Wuppertal had 43 and Duisburg 28 each for populations in excess of 400,000. Oberhausen had 14 officials and Mönchen-Gladbach 11, while Kleve and Kaldenkirchen, with 8 each, were the smallest two of the eight cities in the jurisdiction to have their own Gestapo posts. In comparison with the rest of the country, numbers for Düsseldorf were relatively large, partly because of the 165 kilometres of national border for which it was responsible.[16] Still, given the demands made by the regime, this was a small force to police the roughly four million inhabitants of a jurisdiction known for its support of opposition parties such as the Social Democratic (SPD) and Communist (KPD) parties, for being a haven of 'political Catholicism', and for its relatively large Polish and Jewish populations.

Information from other localities indicates that the personnel in each post were divided into officials, teletypists, assistants, clerks, typists, drivers, and so on. These were normally subdivided into departments and separate subsections (*Referate*) more or less on the ever-changing patterns of Berlin headquarters.[17] Moreover, the range of political behaviour that came within the sphere of the Gestapo was varied and constantly growing. For example, the desk in the Düsseldorf Gestapo concerned with Polish and Eastern European workers in July 1943 had twelve separate subsections dealing with everything from 'refusal to work' and 'leaving the workplace without permission', to 'forbidden sexual relations'. The section on the 'Economy' was divided into eight subsections. While the regular police were in charge of enforcing economic regulations enacted for the duration of the war, the Gestapo was to be called in when, for example, the deed caused unrest in the population or when the perpetrator was a public figure.[18]

Outside the largest cities such as Berlin, Hamburg or Munich, the various desks (*Referate*) in any given local Gestapo post could consist of a single official, and in many cases this person had to look after more than one desk.[19] The numbers of the officials in the Gestapo survey of 1937 may even be inflated, if the example of the town of Eutin in Schleswig-Holstein is any guide. The 1937 survey counted three Gestapo men there, but Lawrence Stokes maintains that three local civic administrators in succession looked after political police matters along with their other tasks. They had to take care of between 15 and 25 areas of administration (*Referate*), a number of which had nothing whatsoever to do with police work. Thus, the 1937 survey may exaggerate the numbers in the Gestapo and convey a false impression of the extent of its professionalism.[20]

A number of additional organisational and personnel questions that are especially important to studies of resistance might also be discussed if space permitted. For example, mention might be made of the police network beyond the Gestapo, such as the Criminal and Order Police, and also the part played by the Nazi Party and the Security Service of the SS in the surveillance of the country. It would also be useful to consider the limited purge of the Weimar Republic's state political police forces, because the 'cleansing' was not nearly as complete as is often claimed in the literature.[21] One topic which must be addressed, however, is the Gestapo spy network, so often the subject of speculation in resistance circles at the time.

Little information has survived on Gestapo spies, thought to be so numerous that it was all but impossible to escape from their 'silent, mysterious, unperceived vigilance'.[22] In fact, there seem to have been far fewer than believed then and since. The most important of the agents were 'V-persons' (contacts), often, but not always, paid and recruited by the various 'desks' or specialists in the local Gestapo branches; there were also 'G-persons' (informants), occasional tellers of tales; and, finally, 'I-persons' (informants), who were not part of the spy network proper, but kept track of the public mood and reported to the police. Not much is known about such people, their number, turnover, occupations and contributions. One Bavarian locality where some information has come to light is Nuremberg. As of 1 September 1941, a total of 150 Gestapo officials were centred there, responsible for a population which totalled 2,771,720 distributed over 14,115 square kilometres.[23] Elke Fröhlich discovered that in the years 1943–44 six of these officials were in charge of the informers' department – section IVn – and that there were some 80–100 people regularly informing the Gestapo.[24] The ratio of informers to full-time officials in Nuremberg was therefore at the very most one paid informer for every official. Normally these people conveyed information on a specific area of concern to the police while continuing their regular jobs and professions. Thus the Gestapo was far from being at the head of an 'army' of agents.[25]

The Gestapo's confidential informants have been the subject of a study by Walter Weyrauch.[26] In 1945, under the auspices of the United States military government, Weyrauch analysed a collection of the Frankfurt Gestapo card files on informers. His up-dated summary deals only with the 1,200 or so cards of people who at one time or another were paid to inform. He deliberately excludes other kinds of collaborators such as those he calls 'spite informers', even though, as indicated below, they were of far greater significance in generating police investigations than those who were paid and/or who worked regularly for the Gestapo on a voluntary basis. Weyrauch sees the 'typical Nazi informant' in the Frankfurt data as 'unconnected with the Nazi party or the official German government structure', and known 'as unsympathetic' to Nazism: the sort of person who 'sometimes seemed suited for a leadership position after the war'.[27] Informants were also drawn from among foreigners in the country, from known opponents to the regime, and from those considered 'tainted' for 'ethnic or religious reasons'.[28] Weyrauch notes that some priests even turned over to the police confidential information gained via the confessional.[29]

Presented with these facts, Weyrauch's account loses its plausibility when he continues to insist that the primary motive for collaboration was what he terms 'circumstantial coercion'. He himself maintains that 'the index cards were silent about specific threats', that the extent to which these putative threats 'amounted to duress as a legal defence is a matter of speculation', and that 'significantly the vast majority of suspect persons seem to have been able to avoid becoming confidential informants after having been interrogated and detained by Gestapo officials'.[30] It is strange that such evidence, provided by Weyrauch himself, did not lead him to suspect that many collaborators might also have had their own reasons for co-operating with the Gestapo.[31]

Such an impression is confirmed by material on several Gestapo agents that survives from Aachen. It is clear that the Gestapo and its regular informers were always on the lookout for recruits. An Aachen report to the Cologne Gestapo on 24 August 1942 stated that an agent on holiday chanced to meet a priest whom he had known for some time. The priest was characterised as 'suitable' for the job of informant because of his favourable disposition toward the regime. Other agents' files in the Düsseldorf archive give the distinct impression that many responded positively to working for the Gestapo, and those who wished to discontinue doing so, or who failed to show the requisite enthusiasm, were dropped or quit of their own accord.[32]

Detlev Peukert also believes that the information passed on to the Gestapo from planted spies was not as useful as the tips received from the population at large or the reports of 'the smaller agents on the periphery of the Communist milieu'.[33] Still, there is evidence that planted agents at times played an important role. The Aachen Gestapo, for example, wrote in October 1944, that one of them was working undercover on the Communist Party; he is described as 'very gifted' in making contacts with 'enemy circles', 'intelligent, cautious, but nevertheless unerring'. He could be regarded as 'reliable. . .his reports were flawless and led to the greatest success'. 'His active and gifted collaboration' is mentioned in a letter to Cologne headquarters. On the basis of one of his reports, it was possible to destroy a very large 'terror organisation of mixed character'.[34]

Gertrud Meyer's account of Gestapo methods of tracking the workers' movement in Hamburg shows that, in a number of instances, undercover agents were crucial in the arrest of Communist functionaries.[35] A Gestapo spy in Würzburg, acting as an *agent provocateur* in the autumn of 1934 went so far as to initiate and organise an underground KPD group, even getting the needed illegal literature from the police, only then to turn in those who could be recruited.[36] A number of other works also show that the Gestapo had to make greater efforts in planting spies in the working-class movement than was usually the case when it came to dealing with other 'opponents'. However, while some collaborators may have had to be intimidated to work with the police, this was not invariably the case.[37] And it may well be that a few spectacular 'successes' led to an overestimation of the strength of the Gestapo and its agents, especially within the underground opposition movements.[38]

The Everyday Operation of the Gestapo

Many studies of resistance tend to focus on isolated and fragmentary arrest statistics, which necessarily convey an inaccurate picture both of the resistance and the energy the Gestapo had to devote to combating it.[39] Firmer generalisations about the resistance can be made by exploiting the resources of the Gestapo files which have survived for Düsseldorf and Würzburg. Some interesting findings emerge from Reinhard Mann's work, even though he was not particularly concerned with the question of resistance. Mann studied a random sample of 825 cases drawn from the 70,000 surviving Düsseldorf Gestapo files. His results have the advantage of taking reflections about the general preoccupations of the Gestapo out of the realm of pure speculation and uninformed impressions.

Table 2.1, which is based on Mann's investigations,[40] shows the preoccupations of the Düsseldorf Gestapo over the course of the Nazi dictatorship. Thirty per cent of his sample (245 cases) pertained to tracking prohibited, mostly left-wing organisations. Of the 204 cases of people involved in illegal political parties or organisations, 61 were suspected of having links with the KPD and 44 with the SPD. In 49 cases, it was not possible to establish specific political affiliation. When it came to organised political parties, the main opponents were clearly the Marxists, while the pursuit of religiously oriented or youth organisations took up a much smaller share of all Gestapo activities.

Efforts to destroy illegal organisations increased after 1933, when only 14 of the 245 cases came to light, while the highest number of such proceedings began in 1935 with 57 cases, up from 30 the year before. Thereafter a more or less steady decline set in. In 1937, 42 cases were opened, but the number fell the next year to 18, and the following year to only 13; after a brief flurry in 1940, the drop

Table 2.1 Proceedings of the Düsseldorf Gestapo between 1933 and 1945

	Number	Total	%
Continuation of forbidden organisation:			
Political parties and associations	204		
Forbidden religious associations and sects	15		
Dissolved associations and activity for forbidden youth groups	26		
		245	30
Non-conforming behaviour in everyday life:			
Verbal utterances	203		
At work or in leisure activities	38		
		241	29
Other forms of nonconformity:			
Acquiring or spreading of forbidden printed matter	37		
Listening to foreign radio	20		
Political passivity	7		
Assorted others	75		
		139	17
Conventional criminality		96	12
Administrative control measures		104	13
Totals		825	100

Source: R. Mann, *Protest und Kontrolle im Dritten Reich*, Frankfurt, 1987, p. 180.

continued with only 2 in 1941. There were 7 cases in 1942, 4 in 1943, and 1 in 1944. The declining number of cases in the sample after 1935 in part reflects the success of the Gestapo in eliminating organised opposition.[41]

The Düsseldorf Gestapo pursued nearly as many persons suspected of 'non-conforming everyday behaviour' – 29 per cent of all its cases – as it did those involved in outlawed organisations. Much energy was expended to control the spoken word, and the majority of cases of this kind of nonconformity brought to the Gestapo's attention (203 cases out of 241) pertained to airing opinions in public. Many of these kinds of investigations must have depended on the observations of people beyond the ranks of the Gestapo, since it simply had too few members to keep watch or to listen in on its own.

The Gestapo was also keen to enforce policies with regard to obtaining and/or spreading information disallowed by the regime: 7 per cent of the sample (57 instances) concerned such matters. Other forms of nonconformity – 'political passivity' and a wide variety of deviations lumped together as 'other kinds' of nonconformity – constituted nearly 10 per cent of the Gestapo case-load. The last named category, with 75 investigations, is a catch-all which contains everything from the anti-Hitler caricaturist, to the reluctant military recruit of 'mixed race', to the Catholic school rector denounced for insufficient Nazi zeal.[42] It is evident that the Gestapo was operating with a concept of opposition and security which went well beyond conventional definitions. A further 13 per cent of all proceedings (104 cases) were commenced by the Gestapo upon suspicion that someone had broken 'administrative control measures', such as bending or breaking rules on residency requirements. Because crime in the Third Reich was to a great extent politicised, the Gestapo spent much time (12 per cent of all the cases in the sample) dealing with what in Table 2.1 was called 'conventional criminality'. It investigated accusations involving 'morals charges' such as homosexual activity[43] and supplying false information to the authorities; but the largest single category of 'conventional crime' was 'economic' charges of various kinds.[44]

A brief comparison of the Gestapo offices in Düsseldorf and Würzburg reveals a remarkable similarity in organisation and *modus operandi*.[45] This finding is to be expected, given the efforts that were made to achieve central control. But the preoccupations of each Gestapo post varied according to local circumstances. One obvious and persistent concern of the Düsseldorf Gestapo, which emerges with special clarity in contrast to Würzburg, is that the former had to police both the Rhine river and the border with respect to the flow of people, goods and money. The border was located far from Würzburg, and is hardly mentioned in the files. Nor were the illegal Communist and Socialist movements as important in the largely agricultural and rural Würzburg area as in the Rhineland, and the Gestapo divided its time accordingly. Other variations undoubtedly existed, for example, in places which had neither Jews nor much of an illegal workers' movement. In both Düsseldorf and Würzburg Catholicism and policing the pulpit were also of great importance.

It would appear that the activity, even the effectiveness of the Gestapo, if measured in terms of the quantity of new cases undertaken, began to fall off after 1941. Mann's statistics can be read to show that, with important exceptions (namely concerning foreign workers, on which more is said below), virtually every form of disobedience it tracked began to decline from 1942 onwards. This reading is troubling in that, for example, it indicates a decrease in the frequency of 'non-conforming expressions of opinion' handled after 1941 by the Düsseldorf Gestapo, while data from other (non-quantifiable) sources and secondary accounts suggest that across the country grumbling, rumour-mongering, and even 'malicious' gossip probably began to grow at precisely that time.[46] Moreover, although Mann's figures show that 'conventional criminality' handled by the Gestapo declined after 1940, there are indications from other writers that certain kinds of crime, especially in the broad area of the economy, almost certainly increased.[47] It is clear that the Gestapo's vigilance continued right to the bitter end; yet it was becoming less successful in picking up disobedience at the very moment it is likely to have been increasing. While the number of Gestapo cases dropped after 1941, those which were initiated on the basis of information received from the population declined even more precipitously, and virtually ceased by 1944.[48]

No reliable statistics on Gestapo arrests from 1933 to 1945 appear to have survived. There are indications in the admittedly fragmentary statistics of arrests during the war years which suggest that a major transformation took place in its activities. It may well be, as Mann's figures for Düsseldorf establish, that after 1941 the *absolute* number of new Gestapo cases declined. However, national figures for several wartime years show that the Gestapo then began to devote increasing energy to controlling a new 'race enemy' within the country, namely the army of foreign workers, whose *relative* importance to the Gestapo increased dramatically. In order to supervise these persons and segregate them from the German population, especially when they were employed outside work-camps or the camps attached to factories proper, the police was to a large extent dependent upon the provision of information from attentive citizens, and in the first years of the war apparently had no difficulty in obtaining it. Thus by the summer of 1942 (between May and August) the Gestapo made a total of 107,960 arrests, 79,821 of them foreigners; in addition, there were 4,962 cases in which Germans were caught in forbidden contact with such individuals. While not all those arrested were informed upon by a civilian – a supervisor or Labour Front official in a camp could readily call in the Gestapo – local studies suggest that a substantial proportion of arrests probably resulted from tip-offs from the public. To, be sure, it is also clear that the Gestapo continued its drive to recruit informers inside even the smallest clusters of foreign workers scattered around the country.

In short order, the bulk of the Gestapo's effort went into dealing with the new 'racially foreign' threat inside the country. The police continued to uncover various kinds of German 'opposition', but in relative terms such arrests represented a declining percentage of the Gestapo's workload. Given that in all likelihood non-compliance (broadly defined) was growing, it is plausible to suggest that a large part of the reason for the failure to turn up more of it was that citizens were becoming less inclined to inform on others. By comparison, therefore, the arrests of opponents such as communists and socialists began to assume a relatively smaller place in the Gestapo workload. Thus some 5,161 people had been arrested in those same summer months of 1942 on suspicion of communist or socialist activity; a handful of people (416) were thought guilty of listening to foreign radio stations; and 286 were taken into custody for protesting at official church policies. There were other forms of miscellaneous opposition; but these and others just mentioned paled in comparison to the police problem posed by the foreign workers.[49] The figures for January to June 1943, indicate that of 241,968 arrests, 155,145 pertained to foreign workers and an additional 10,773 to Germans suspected of outlawed contact with them. In the same period, 8,850 people were arrested on suspicion of communist or socialist activities; and there were other opponents caught, such as the 1,314 who were suspected of listening to a foreign radio station, and 638 who protested against Nazi church policy. It is clear, however, that numerically the emphasis of the Gestapo's work was shifting to the workplace – 12,249 Germans were also arrested for shirking on the job – and that the greatest effort was reserved for policing foreigners inside the country.[50]

Between July and September 1943 the figures show a continuation of the trend: of the total of 146,217 arrests, 105,262 were foreigners charged with refusal to work or shirking; 6,549 Germans were also accused of this 'crime'. There were, in addition, 4,637 arrests of Germans for breaking regulations by socialising with these foreigners. Some 5,757 people were arrested for suspected communist or socialist activity, and another 404 for protesting against church policy.[51]

It would be useful to have more information on these statistics, which are known to be flawed, because (among other things) when it came to the despised foreigners, especially those from Eastern Europe, the Gestapo grew inclined to adopt Draconian methods and, before very long, to apply lynch justice.[52] Even so, the figures suggest a reorientation in Gestapo activity, the vast bulk of which pertained to the economy, mostly focused on the foreigners and on keeping them at work and racially segregated. The figures probably underestimate the involvement of the Gestapo with these workers; in 1944 and 1945, as the war was carried into Germany, not all dealings with them were registered, and reports of executions, quite aside from arrests, went astray. As Germans became increasingly reluctant to inform the authorities about the 'criminality' of foreign workers, the Gestapo grew more ruthless in dealing with them, and meted out punishment on its own authority. An examination of cases brought to the attention of the Gestapo in Würzburg shows a gradual decline, beginning with the diffusion of knowledge about the German losses suffered at Stalingrad; and by 1944 and 1945 the flow of information from the population simply evaporated. Isolated evidence from elsewhere in Germany suggests that in the last months of the war the Gestapo dispensed even with the appearance of following procedures and, for example, liquidated foreign workers in their area to eliminate witnesses who might offer testimony on Gestapo misdeeds.[53]

Before concluding, it is useful to provide several specific remarks on denunciations, such a prominent feature of the Nazi era and, until recently, not investigated by historians. Political denunciations, or the provision of information on suspected criminality by the population at large, were the single most important factor behind the initiation of all Gestapo cases.[54] As indicated in Table 2.2, which is also taken from Reinhard Mann's study, 26 per cent of the random sample of 825 cases he examined began with an *identifiable* denunciation from the population, and another 3 per cent came from businesses.

Mann believed that the incidence of information coming from the population was actually much greater, and suggested that the German people had been won over to Nazism. He could not have meant that denouncers as a whole acted out of loyalty to the Nazi system, because his own figures (on which more presently) reveal that they co-operated for all kinds of reasons.[55] Still, the extent of the reliance on denunciations from the population is a dramatic revelation, since it suggests a substantial degree of accommodation, adjustment or even collaboration – a term that denotes active rather than passive participation – by Germans in the workings of the Nazi terror system. This behaviour has hitherto not been fully appreciated. The figures would suggest that the regime's most dreaded enforcer would have been seriously hampered without

Table 2.2 Causes for the Initiation of a Proceeding with the Gestapo –
Düsseldorf, 1933–1944

1. Reports from the population	213 (= 26%)
2. Information from other control organisations	139 (= 17%)
3. Own observations of Stapo–Düsseldorf, V–persons	127 (= 15%)
4. Information via communal or state authorities	57 (= 7%)
5. Statements of interrogations	110 (= 13%)
6. Information from businesses	24 (= 3%)
7. Information via NS organisations	52 (= 6%)
8. No information	103 (= 13%)
Total	825 (= 100%)

Source: R. Mann, *Protest und Kontrolle im Dritten Reich*, Frankfurt, 1987, p. 292.

public co-operation. To be sure, the files themselves have gaps and
are far from exhaustive in providing background information. The
files on 13 per cent of the cases are silent about what moved the
Gestapo into action. The observations of the Gestapo and its net of
regular informers launched a surprisingly small proportion of cases
on their own, namely 15 per cent; but once the authorities proceeded with their own interrogations, they uncovered further
incriminating evidence which led to almost as many new investigations. On its own, however, the Gestapo was clearly not in a
position to deal with the political policing of the country. It
received help both from other 'control organisations', such as the
Criminal, Order, and Military Police, which together provided
information in 17 per cent of the cases the Gestapo pursued, and
from the Nazi Party (6 per cent). Other evidence shows that these
organisations, in turn, had often been informed by someone from
the population at large, so that even greater participation from the
public took place than might be deduced from Mann's statistics.[56]
It is also clear that local Nazi Party officials received many more
denunciations from the population, but sometimes handled these
on their own, and did not pass on all the information they acquired
to the Gestapo.

  Although the Gestapo's power became nearly unchecked, Tim
Mason suggests that this does not explain how it was implemented.[57] When one looks in greater detail at its efforts to police
the more private spheres of social and sexual life, such as for
example to create barriers between Jews and non-Jews and, after
1939, between foreign workers and the German people, it can be
shown that in doing so the reliance on tips from the population was
even greater than the general picture painted by Mann. To give but

one example based on a study of the Gestapo files in Würzburg, over half of all the suspected transgressions of the September 1935 Nuremberg laws forbidding marriage and extra-marital sexual relations between Jews and non-Jews began with a denunciation from the population. Given that Würzburg and the surrounding district of Lower Franconia were among the most reluctant to vote Nazi before 1933, had little or no tradition of anti-Semitism, and remained staunchly Catholic, it is reasonable to suppose that the situation was worse elsewhere. Without the flow of information from the population the regime's attempts to enforce such racial policies would have been severely hampered. According to one recent account, Gestapo surveillance and control was extended down to the shop-floor in factories such as the Volkswagen Works because employees were willing to pass along information about non-compliance. Thus, for example, a foreman turned in a German worker in 1943 for listening to foreign radio broadcasts and expressing doubts about the war's outcome. His reasons for doing so had little to do with the 'political' content of the remarks. Instead, he seems to have informed because he feared that, having overheard the 'treasonous' words, he might himself be denounced by those who worked under him, men whom he knew resented his often demanding approach to daily tasks.[58]

On the question of assessing the motives of those who denounced others to the police, Mann was not able to determine any reason whatever in 39 per cent of all the cases which began with a tip from someone in the population. He claims that of the rest, 37 per cent had identifiable 'private' or instrumental motives, but only 24 per cent what he terms 'system-loyal' ones.[59] Even if one were to allow the latter figure to stand – and it is problematical – such statistics suggest that the Gestapo was repeatedly utilised for purposes completely unintended by the regime. The country's leaders might have preferred to receive tip-offs from loyal Nazis; but all denunciations were structurally useful, even when they were based on the most self-serving motives, were utterly without foundation, and were even consciously false. Nazi leaders from Hitler on down were troubled about how to cope with the denouncers, especially those who laid careless and/or knowingly erroneous charges. After much vacillation and many second thoughts, the attitude prevailed that it was advisable to have too much information rather than too little, so that even at times when the flood of tips threatened to become dysfunctional, the snoopers were not overmuch discouraged nor the false denouncers punished too severely.[60]

Fritz Stern rightly points out that too much should not be made

of the negative factors which led to compliance and accommodation.[61] The same kind of desire to get on-side is mentioned in
William S. Allen's study of Northeim where, for example, a local
non-Nazi school principal 'prompted solely by his awareness of the
new atmosphere' suspended a student for spreading a rumour that
the Nazis were responsible for burning the Reichstag.[62] These
informal reinforcements of the terror system brought the Gestapo
to life, because suddenly towns were flooded by 'amateur "Gestapo" operatives', who thereby helped to undermine the resolve of
anyone wishing to swim against the tide.[63] Even a brief look at
specific instances of resistance, such as that offered by the 'White
Rose' group in Munich, reveals the many ways in which the
population at large internalised the norms of the regime to the point
where they acted as unofficial extensions of the terror by keeping
their eyes and ears open, and by informing the authorities of what
they saw and heard.

Conclusion

This essay has explored several aspects of the surveillance society in
Nazi Germany by focusing on how the Gestapo operated outside
the gaols and concentration camps. It is clear that the elimination of
relatively safe enclaves in which disobedience might have developed structurally required information from the population at
large. While the majority might, as some writers would have it,
remain silent, apathetic or passive – on the 'Jewish Question',[64] for
example – the Gestapo could continue to enforce anti-Semitic
policies as long as it could count on a substantial number of people
to come forward. Germans – both those who co-operated and
those who thought it best to keep their distance – were actively
engaged in the policing process, and such 'auto-policing' or 'auto-
surveillance' needs to be kept firmly in mind in any study of
opposition, resistance, dissent or any other kind of disobedience.

   The emergence of an extreme example of a surveillance society in
Nazi Germany simultaneously eliminated several of the most important preconditions for the existence of disobedience, let alone
opposition or resistance. Other and related factors frequently mentioned in the literature also continued to play a role. The 'atomis-
ation' of society persisted, so that solidarities were difficult to
maintain or to form anew. Political 'criminality' could be tracked
down in short order, and the demoralising perception was that
there was little chance of success. Not only did all these factors

reduce the possibility for some sort of underground to emerge; but also a cardinal fact of life for the citizens in Nazi Germany after 1939 was that the fatherland was at war. The terror bombings of the Reich, and the decision to insist upon unconditional surrender, robbed the Allied cause of much of the moral edge it might otherwise have enjoyed over the Nazi regime.[65]

Given the lack of encouragement from outside Germany and the fortress mentality within, as well as the likelihood of failure, those who would disobey – let alone press on to offer opposition or to organise resistance – were bound to be few in number. Even in the occupied countries, where there were less severe limitations on the space for disobedience, most opposition and resistance did not get under way until after the Nazi grip began to slacken. It should come as no surprise that inside Germany, where secure enclaves remained smaller and more fragile, disobedience was slower to take shape, more restricted in scope and carried the troubling consequence, unique to Germany, of being difficult to dissociate from treason.

Even though there were few enclaves in Nazi Germany, moments of disobedience, of non-compliance, even of opposition and resistance materialised at one point or another. Accounts testify to the courage of many individuals and groups who swam against the tide, who were not swept away by the powerful momentum to comply. Any evaluation of the courage and commitment of such people must reflect on the nature of the situation they faced and the strength of the odds against them. One should also not forget that, in Peter Hoffmann's words, 'on the whole, at all times from 1933 to 1945 the majority of German voters, indeed of the entire population, supported the government, albeit with varying degrees of willingness.'[66]

NOTES

1. M. Foucault, *Discipline and Punish: The Birth of the Prison*, trans. A. Sheridan, NY, 1979, pp. 217, 301. See also his 'The Subject and Power' in H. L. Dreyfus and P. Rabinow (eds), *Michel Foucault: Beyond Structuralism and Hermeneutics*, Chicago, 1982, pp. 208 ff. Foucault disagrees with the 'materialist' interpretation of G. Rusche and O. Kirchheimer, *Punishment and Social Structure*, NY, 1939, reissued 1967, but this neglected work offers valuable insights into the treat-

ment of crime under fascism. They note (p. 179) that the Gestapo operated 'by the general doctrine that politically relevant acts are not subject to judicial review'. I discussed some of the comparative literature at a conference at the University of Pennsylvania in April 1988; see 'Enforcing Racial Policy in Nazi Germany', in T. Childers and J. Caplan (eds), *Re-evaluating the 'Third Reich': New Controversies, New Interpretations*, NY, forthcoming.

2. M. Broszat *et al.* (eds), *Bayern in der NS-Zeit*, 6 vols, Munich, 1977–83 (hereafter cited as *Bayern*, with the appropriate volume number).

3. See L. Niethammer (ed.), *'Die Jahre weiß man nicht, wo man die heute hinsetzen soll.' Faschismus-Erfahrungen im Ruhrgebiet*, Berlin, 1983, especially the contribution by U. Herbert, ' "Die guten und die schlechten Zeiten." ' Überlegungen zur diachronen Analyse lebensgeschichtlicher Interviews', pp. 67 ff. See also L. Niethammer (ed.), *'Hinterher merkt man, daß es richtig war, daß es schiefgegangen ist.' Nachkriegs-Erfahrung im Ruhrgebiet*, Berlin, 1983; also L. Niethammer and A. von Plato (eds), *'Wir kriegen jetzt andere Zeiten.' Auf der Suche nach der Erfahrung des Volkes in Nachfaschistischen Ländern*, Berlin, 1985, particularly Niethammer's remarks on the causes of the silences in his 'Fragen – Antworten – Fragen. Methodische Erfahrungen und Erwägungen zur Oral History', pp. 392 ff. Some of the remarks by a participant in the Ruhr project are available now in U. Herbert, 'Good Times, Bad Times: Memories of the Third Reich', in R. Bessel (ed.), *Life in the Third Reich*, Oxford, 1987, pp. 97 ff. Denunciations and the Gestapo are mentioned at several points in B. Wenke, *Interviews mit Überlebenden. Verfolgung und Widerstand in Südwestdeutschland*, Stuttgart, 1980, pp. 20 ff.

4. See the document from 1936 from a Bochum area trade unionist reprinted in full in D. J. K. Peukert and F. Bajohr, *Spuren des Widerstands. Die Bergarbeiterbewegung im Dritten Reich und im Exil*, Munich, 1987, pp. 133 ff.

5. See D. J. K. Peukert, *Die KPD im Widerstand. Verfolgung und Untergrundarbeit an Rhein und Ruhr 1933 bis 1945*, Wuppertal, 1980, pp. 116 ff. See also his *Volksgenoßen und Gemeinschaftsfremde. Anpaßung, Ausmerze und Aufbegehren unter dem Nationalsozialismus*, Cologne, 1982, pp. 233 ff. Contemporary socialists' interpretations of Nazism can be found in the *Deutschland-Berichte der Sozialdemokratischen Partei Deutschlands (SOPADE) 1934–1940*, Salzhausen, 1980 on. However, that there was *more* than merely a misperception behind the Left's impotence after 1933 is made clear by T. W. Mason, 'The Third Reich and the German Left: Persecution and Resistance', in H. Bull (ed.), *The Challenge of the Third Reich*, Oxford, 1986, pp. 95 ff.

6. See Peukert, *Die KPD im Widerstand*, pp. 121 ff.

7. J. Schmädeke and P. Steinbach (eds), *Der Widerstand gegen den Nationalsozialismus. Die deutsche Gesellschaft und der Widerstand gegen Hitler*, Munich–Zürich, 1985. For other examples of the same neglect, see R. Löwenthal and P. von zur Mühlen (eds), *Widerstand und Verweigerung*

in *Deutschland 1933 bis 1945*, Berlin, 1982, and H. Graml (ed.), *Wider-stand im Dritten Reich. Probleme, Ereignisse, Gestalten*, Frankfurt am Main, 1984.

8. P. Hoffmann, *German Resistance to Hitler*, Cambridge, Mass., 1988, p. 30; cf. his 'The War, German Society and Internal Resistance', in M. Laffan (ed.), *The Burden of German History 1919–45*, London, 1988, p. 197.

9. T. W. Mason, 'Injustice and Resistance: Barrington Moore and the Reaction of German Workers to Fascism', in R. J. Bullen *et al.* (eds), *Ideas into Politics: Aspects of European History 1880–1950*, London–Totowa, NJ, 1984, p. 115.

10. B. Moore, Jr, *Injustice: The Social Bases of Obedience and Revolt*, White Plains, NY, 1978, p. 482.

11. Ibid., p. 483.

12. See, for example, H. Zeisel, *The Limits of Law Enforcement*, Chicago, 1982, pp. 83 ff.; also G. Aly and K. H. Roth, *Die restlose Erfaßung. Volkszählen, Identifizieren, Aussondern im Nationalsozialismus*, Berlin, 1984, pp. 36 ff.

13. The classic example of the emphasis on numbers is E. Kogon, *Der SS-Staat. Das System der deutschen Konzentrationslager*, Munich, 1974, p. 28. Cf. F. Dröge, *Der zerredete Widerstand. Zur Soziologie und Publizistik des Gerüchts im 2. Weltkrieg*, Düsseldorf, 1970, pp. 54 ff. See also n. 38, below.

14. See International Military Tribunal, *Trial of the Major War Criminals before the International Military Tribunal, Nuremberg, 14 November 1945 to 1 October 1946* (hereafter IMT), vol. 21, Nuremberg, 1947–9, pp. 294 ff. See also the testimony of Werner Best in IMT, vol. 20, pp. 123 ff.

15. See IMT, vol. 4, p. 345.

16. Bundesarchiv/Koblenz (hereafter BAK): R58/610, Personalstatistik der Staatspolizei, 31 March 1937.

17. See P. R. Black, *Ernst Kaltenbrunner: Ideological Soldier of the Third Reich*, Princeton, 1984, pp. 297 ff.

18. Hauptstaatsarchiv/Düsseldorf (hereafter HStA-D): RW 36/3, 6 ff. Plan of Gestapo – Düsseldorf.

19. On the Gestapo organisation see BAK: R58/1112, 145–6 and R58/242, 101. Cf. the testimony of Karl Heinz Hoffmann in IMT, vol. 20, p. 160; also Ibid., vol. 21, pp. 293–4; and K. Moritz and E. Noam, *NS-Verbrechen vor Gericht 1945–1955. Dokumente aus hessischen Justiz-akten*, Wiesbaden, 1978, pp. 272–3.

20. See Landesarchiv/Schleswig-Holstein: Regierung Eutin, A II 2 (260/17 462), and L. D. Stokes, *Kleinstadt und Nationalsozialismus. Ausgewählte Dokumente zur Geschichte von Eutin, 1918–1945*, Neumünster, 1984, p. 504.

21. For a discussion of these and other issues, see Gellately, 'Enforcing Racial Policy', and the volume cited in n. 40 below.

22. The quotation (from 1847 but equally apt for the Third Reich) is in

Foucault, *Discipline and Punish*, p. 280. Cf. IMT, vol. 20, p. 128.
23. BAK: R58/856, 1 September 1941.
24. E. Fröhlich, 'Die Herausforderung des Einzelnen. Geschichten über Widerstand und Verfolgung', in Broszat *et al.* (eds), *Bayern*, vol. 6, 1983, p. 212. Cf. G. Meyer, *Nacht über Hamburg. Berichte und Dokumente*, Frankfúrt am Main, 1971, p. 81.
25. Cf. I. Marßolek and R. Ott, *Bremen im Dritten Reich. Anpaßung, Widerstand, Verfolgung*, Bremen, 1986, p. 183; and H. Schwarzwälder, *Geschichte der Freien Hansestadt Bremen*, vol. 4, *Bremen in der NS-Zeit (1933–1945)*, Hamburg, 1985, pp. 407–8.
26. W. O. Weyrauch, 'Gestapo Informants: Facts and Theory of Undercover Operations', *Columbia Journal of Transnational Law*, vol. 24, 1986, pp. 554 ff.
27. Ibid., p. 560.
28. Ibid., pp. 577 ff. Cf. BAK: R58/610.
29. Weyrauch, 'Gestapo Informants', p. 579.
30. Ibid., pp. 565, 567, 568.
31. Cf. M. Maschmann, *Fazit. Mein Weg in der Hitler-Jugend*, Munich, 1981, pp. 43 ff; C. Klessmann and F. Pingel, *Gegner des Nationalsozialismus*, Frankfurt am Main, 1980, pp. 195 ff; and R. Giordano, *Die zweite Schuld oder von der Last Deutscher zu sein*, Hamburg, 1987, pp. 30 ff.
32. See HStA-D: RW 34 Nr. 33, Staatspolizeistelle Köln
33. Peukert, *Die KPD im Widerstand*, p. 123.
34. HStA-D: RW 34 Nr. 33.
35. Meyer, *Nacht über Hamburg*, pp. 77 ff.
36. H. Mehringer, 'Die KPD in Bayern 1919–1945', in Broszat *et al.* (eds), *Bayern*, vol. 5, 1983, pp. 228–9.
37. Cf. Marßolek and Ott, *Bremen im Dritten Reich*, p. 183; also Peukert, *Die KPD im Widerstand*, pp. 125 ff.
38. A. Merson (*Communist Resistance in Nazi Germany*, London, 1985, p. 51) believes the numbers of spies 'must have totalled a high number'; while only a few infiltrated the KPD successfully, they were 'of great individual significance'.
39. Isolated figures on 'protective custody' and related matters are summarised in Hoffmann, 'The War', pp. 192–3.
40. See R. Mann, *Protest und Kontrolle im Dritten Reich. Nationalsozialistische Herrschaft im Alltag einer rheinischen Großstadt*, Frankfurt am Main, 1987, p. 180. Mann rounded off his percentage figures; their total exceeds 100 per cent. For further comments on this work, and on the strengths and weaknesses of Gestapo files as historical sources, see R. Gellately, *The Gestapo and German Society: Enforcing Racial Policy, 1933–1945*, Oxford, 1990. This work is based primarily on a study of the Gestapo case files in the Staatsarchiv/Würzburg.
41. Mann, *Protest und Kontrolle*, p. 182 (chart 1).
42. Ibid., pp. 266 ff.
43. Note the case of one of the Gestapo heads in Würzburg, Josef Gerum,

and his pursuit of such matters; besides the file on him in the Berlin Document Centre, see Fröhlich, pp. 76 ff.

44. See Mann, *Protest und Kontrolle*, p. 252 (table 3).

45. For details, see Gellately, *The Gestapo*, Chs. 1 and 2.

46. Mann, *Protest und Kontrolle*, p. 241. For the growth of all types of dissent, see I. Kershaw, *Popular Opinion and Political Dissent in the Third Reich: Bavaria 1933–1945*, Oxford, 1983, pp. 281 ff; and M. G. Steinert, *Hitler's War and the Germans: Public Mood and Attitude during the Second World War*, trans. T. E. J. de Witt, Athens, Ohio, 1977, pp. 117 ff. Negative rumours about the impending war with the USSR began to circulate widely across Germany in the spring of 1941; see H. Boberach (ed.), *Meldungen aus dem Reich 1938–1945*, vol. 6, Herrsching, 1984, pp. 2273–5. See also the overview of M. Broszat, 'Vom Widerstand: Bedeutungswandel in der Zeitgeschichte', in his *Nach Hitler. Der schwierige Umgang mit unserer Geschichte*, Munich, 1987, pp. 320 ff.

47. Mann, *Protest und Kontrolle*, p. 252. For a local example, see J. Stephenson, 'War and Society in Württemberg, 1939–1945: Beating the System', *German Studies Review*, vol. 8, 1985, pp. 89 ff.

48. See R. Gellately, 'The Gestapo and German Society: Political Denunciation in the Gestapo Case Files', *Journal of Modern History*, vol. 60, 1988, pp. 654–94. Cf. Mann, *Protest und Kontrolle*, p. 294.

49. W. Schumann *et al.*, *Deutschland im Zweiten Weltkrieg*, vol. 2, Berlin (East), 1975, p. 412. The figures are for Germany and its incorporated areas.

50. Schumann *et al.*, *Deutschland im Zweiten Weltkrieg*, vol. 3, Berlin (East), 1982, p. 241.

51. Schumann *et al.*, *Deutschland im Zweiten Weltkrieg*, vol. 4, Berlin (East), 1984, p. 407.

52. As early as August, 1942, the Gestapo executed without trial foreigners (Poles) considered 'guilty' of having sexual relations with German women. See, for example, the detailed local SD report in the Staatsarchiv/Bamberg: M30/1048. Cf. U. Herbert, *Fremdarbeiter. Politik und Praxis des 'Ausländer-Einsatzes' in der Kriegswirtschaft des Dritten Reiches*, Berlin, 1986, pp. 327 ff. For case studies of the Special Courts see K. Bästlein, 'Die Akten des ehemaligen Sondergerichts Kiel als zeitgeschichtliche Quelle', *Zeitschrift der Gesellschaft für Schleswig-Holsteinische Geschichte*, vol. 113, 1988, pp. 157 ff.; and B. Schimmler, *Recht ohne Gerechtigkeit. Zur Tätigkeit der Berliner Sondergerichte im Nationalsozialismus*, Berlin, 1984. For an important local study, and a review of the East German literature, see especially W. Bramke, 'Der unbekannte Widerstand in Westsachsen 1933–1945', *Jahrbuch für Regionalgeschichte*, vol. 13, 1986, pp. 220 ff., and his 'Der antifaschistische Widerstand in der Geschichtsschreibung der DDR in den achtziger Jahren. Forschungsstand und Probleme', *Aus Politik und Zeitgeschichte. Beilage zur Wochenzeitung Das Parlament*, 8 July 1988, pp. 23 ff.

53. This issue is discussed in Gellately, *The Gestapo*, Ch. 8. On the gaps in

the statistics, even those on executions, see M. Messerschmidt and F. Wüllner, *Die Wehrmachtjustiz im Dienste des Nationalsozialismus. Zerstörung einer Legende*, Baden-Baden, 1987, pp. 63 ff. See also H. Obenaus, ' "Sei stille, sonst kommst Du nach Ahlem!" Zur Funktion der Gestapostelle in der ehemaligen Israelitischen Gartenbauschule von Ahlem (1943–1945)', *Sonderdruck* from *Hannoversche Geschichtsblätter*, Neue Folge, vol. 41, 1987, pp. 1–32.

54. See the literature cited in Gellately, 'Political Denunciation'; note especially M. Broszat, 'Politische Denunziationen in der NS-Zeit: Aus Forschungserfahrungen im Staatsarchiv München', *Archivalische Zeitschrift*, vol. 73, 1977, pp. 221 ff.
55. Ibid., pp. 287 ff.
56. Cf. Gellately, 'Political Denunciation', pp. 661 ff.
57. Mason, 'Injustice', p. 115.
58. On Lower Franconia, see the detailed examination in Gellately, *The Gestapo*, Chs. 3–6. On the VW Works see K.-J. Siegfried, *Das Leben der Zwangsarbeiter im Volkswagenwerk 1939–1945*, Frankfurt am Main, 1988, pp. 72–3; see also his *Rüstungsproduktion und Zwangsarbeit im Volkswagenwerk 1939–1945. Eine Dokumentation*, Frankfurt am Main, 1986, pp. 92 ff.
59. Mann, *Protest und Kontrolle*, p. 295.
60. The response of Nazi leaders to denunciations is discussed in Gellately, *The Gestapo*, Ch. 5. For a telling remark from Hitler in 1933, in which he noted that 'we are presently living in a sea of denunciations and human evil', see L. Gruchmann, *Justiz im Dritten Reich 1933–1940. Anpaßung und Unterwerfung in der Ära Gürtner*, Munich, 1987, p. 835.
61. F. Stern, 'National Socialism as Temptation', in his *Dreams and Delusions: The Drama of German History*, NY, 1987, pp. 147 ff. Cf. H. B. Gisevius, *To the Bitter End*, trans. R. and C. Winston, London, 1948, pp. 101 ff.
62. W. S. Allen, *The Nazi Seizure of Power: The Experience of a Single German Town 1922–1945*, rev. edn, NY, 1984, p. 157.
63. Ibid., p. 189.
64. See I. Kershaw, 'German Popular Opinion and the "Jewish Question", 1939–1943: Some Further Reflections', in A. Paucker (ed.), *Die Juden im Nationalsozialistischen Deutschland/The Jews in Nazi Germany 1933–1945*, Tübingen, 1986, p. 384.
65. See the perspective offered by C. Bielenberg, *Ride Out of the Dark*, London, 1968, pp. 119 ff.
66. Hoffmann, *German Resistance*, p. 51. A similar point is made by G. van Roon, *Widerstand im Dritten Reich*, 4th edn, Munich, 1987, pp. 12 ff.

3

Conservative Opposition to Nazism in Eutin, Schleswig-Holstein, 1932–1933

Lawrence D. Stokes

Peter Hoffmann defines opposition against National Socialism as 'a group of activities endangering the lives of those who engaged in them' which 'began years before, but certainly not later than' Hitler's appointment as Chancellor on 30 January 1933. Although his research has focused on the period commencing in 1938, when resistance in Germany reached the stage of attempting a *coup d'état*, its 'true hallmark', Hoffmann also calls attention to several individuals whose rejection of Nazism preceded and continued unabated into the Third Reich. One such person was the Prussian-Pomeranian Conservative landowner and publicist Ewald von Kleist-Schmenzin, who 'belonged among the most resolute and uncompromising enemies of Hitler', for whose benefit he refused to make even the slightest concession. Unlike much early resistance, which, according to Hoffmann, was politically oriented and motivated, Kleist-Schmenzin was a 'fundamental' opponent of the Nazi movement on ethical grounds of moral conscience. Precisely that attitude constituted 'the core of the entire phenomenon' of resistance and 'the key without which everything would be incomprehensible'.[1]

The following essay deals with a much less well-known, regional representative of German Conservatism, whose political career, at least during 1932–3, to a remarkable degree resembled that of Ewald von Kleist-Schmenzin. Dr Ernst Evers was a lawyer and

37

notary in the town of Eutin, Schleswig-Holstein, where from the spring of 1931 he served as district chairman of the German National People's Party (DNVP), in which Kleist-Schmenzin was a prominent figure. Like him, Ernst Evers was a relentless foe of National Socialism as it assumed concrete form in the government of the state of Oldenburg, to which Eutin and its surrounding territory, notwithstanding their geographical location, adhered constitutionally, and which at the end of May 1932 elected Germany's first purely Nazi cabinet. Neither Kleist-Schmenzin nor Evers was a defender of the system of parliamentary democracy associated with the Weimar Republic. However, they did staunchly advocate the preservation of the traditional German *Rechtsstaat*, whose very existence was threatened by Nazism as Evers saw it demonstrated in the arbitrary, violent and incompetent regime installed in Eutin. To combat its rampant lawlessness he arranged, among other actions, for the distribution of a pamphlet written by Kleist-Schmenzin that unsparingly exposed the totalitarian and destructive aims of the Nazi movement. On account of his unyielding opposition to its rule, Evers was briefly incarcerated in the town's concentration camp in 1933, while Kleist-Schmenzin became part of the conspiracy that culminated in the attempted assassination of Hitler on 20 July 1944, for which he paid with his life.

James J. Sheehan has emphasised the importance of studying the local history of Germany for the different perspective it provides on affairs that were not entirely shaped from the centre of the country. The significance of Eutin's Conservative opposition to Nazism as personified by Ernst Evers, just when the Hitler movement gained its first untrammelled foothold in government at the regional level and was poised to take over power in the Reich as a whole, is that it gave all Germans an opportunity to assess the behaviour of the NSDAP ruling one small area of the nation. The country at large could thereby judge the sort of system the Nazis were likely to install in Berlin if they received the chance. The relatively unusual possibility of events on the periphery decisively influencing political developments at the centre was lost, however, when the upper echelons of the DNVP, especially its chairman Alfred Hugenberg, concluded that Eutin's experience should not impede the establishment of a coalition government with the Nazis in order to achieve goals he and the Nationalists had been pursuing since the creation of the Republic.[2] Disregarding the admonitory lesson that Eutin and its short preview of the Third Reich could have taught politicians and voters elsewhere opened the way to the fateful course

Germany would embark upon for the next twelve years.

What circumstances combined to put Conservatives in Eutin during the last half of 1932 in the position of perhaps helping to avert the catastrophe that Nazism ultimately visited upon Europe? The socio-economic structure of the town, situated approximately midway between Lübeck and Kiel, with a population of 7,230 in 1933, went a long way towards explaining its political preferences. Almost totally lacking large-scale enterprise, Eutin was the administrative, educational, banking and commercial hub supplying goods and services to the mainly rural residents of eastern Holstein. Scarcely one in five of its citizens could be categorised as a worker, even including white-collar and domestic employees; the rest were overwhelmingly middle- and lower-middle-class businessmen and shopkeepers, artisans, civil servants and pensioners. Furthermore, 93 per cent of them professed the Lutheran faith. The absence of both a substantial industrial proletariat and more than a tiny minority of Roman Catholics meant that, until the rise of National Socialism after 1929, two parties dominated Eutin's politics. In the elections that followed the November 1918 revolution, and again a decade later, the SPD won the support of up to 40 per cent of the voters (the Independent Socialists at the beginning and the Communists at the close of the Republic each attracted only a few dozen adherents). Otherwise Social Democracy had to content itself with from a quarter to a third of the electorate. Its chief rival, either alone or as the strongest partner in bourgeois alliances, was the DNVP.[3]

In contrast to the Conservatives at the national level, who in the balloting for the Constituent Assembly in January 1919 captured just 10.3 per cent of the votes cast, the Eutin DNVP already counted over twice that proportion. During subsequent years it regularly reached around 30 per cent, whereas in the country as a whole the party only once exceeded 20 per cent in Reichstag elections. However, the local ascendancy of the Nationalists was most evident when they allied with the German People's (DVP) and Democratic (DDP) parties to gain almost two-thirds of the ballots at some municipal and regional polls. In the 1925 presidential election, 61.77 per cent of Eutin's voters supported the joint candidate of the Right, Paul von Hindenburg; the Reich average was less than one-half. Besides the general appeal of its monarchism, its habitual rejection of the foreign and domestic policies of the republican governments, and its pronounced hostility towards the political Left under Weimar, the strength of the DNVP in Eutin derived from its intimate ties with the town's élite. Thus both the town's longtime mayor and senior administrator (*Stadtoberinspektor*) and also the superintendent of the Provincial Lutheran Church were members; most of the latter's pastors also backed the party electorally. The two aforementioned civic officials also successively headed the cartel of veterans' organisations (*Kriegervereine*) that greatly influenced the social life of the town after the First World War. Not even the fiasco of the Kapp *Putsch*, in which the DNVP's chairman, the principal of an Eutin secondary school, was so deeply involved that he was forced to retire from active politics, could harm its prospects; in voting for the Oldenburg legislature just three months later, the DNVP and the DVP – calling themselves the 'National Block' – topped the poll in the town. The Conservatives reached their peak in the pair of elections to the Reichstag in 1924, winning on their own 38 and 37 per cent respectively of all the ballots cast.[4]

The decline in the DNVP's fortunes almost exactly paralleled the upsurge of the NSDAP, which in Schleswig-Holstein set in as early as 1928. Until then relations between the two had been unremarkable in keeping with the political insignificance of the Nazis. Although Eutin members of the Nationalist paramilitary formation *Stahlhelm* had stood ready to assist Hitler's abortive November 1923 attempt to overthrow the authorities in Munich and Berlin, they afterwards found themselves excluded from simultaneously belonging to the Nazi SA. Despite their shared ideological premises, including hatred of parliamentarism, democracy, the Versailles peace settlement and the Jews, National Socialists were usually at pains to distinguish the populism of their infant movement from the reactionary agrarians and big industry behind the Conservatives. Some recruits to the NSDAP, such as the Eutin surgeon and gynaecologist Dr Wolfgang Saalfeldt, had quit the DNVP because it was 'too tame'. This latent conflict, implicit in Hitler's own disdain for all bourgeois parties, surfaced in the course of the 1929 campaign against the government's adoption of the Young Plan. What started out as a common front of Nazis, Nationalists and their friends to block implementation of legislation regulating Germany's reparation obligations degenerated into a bitter public quarrel and finally a lawsuit for defamation brought by local SA leader Johann Heinrich Böhmcker against his opposite number in the *Stahlhelm*. Nevertheless, fully one-third of the town's eligible voters supported the Right's plebiscite, far more than the fewer than 14 per cent who did so nationwide.[5]

The relative weight of the various groups in the anti-Young Plan coalition became clear with the outcome of the September 1930

Reichstag election. The Nazis, who since the onset of the world economic crisis had directed their propaganda away from the working class cultivated by the party's 'socialist' wing and towards the immediately threatened farmers and small-town *Mittelstand* in Schleswig-Holstein, now emerged as serious competitors for the votes of Eutin's non-Marxist Protestants. The result was devastating for the DNVP. While the NSDAP leapt from 4 to nearly 40 per cent in the balloting compared to 1928, the Nationalists plummeted simultaneously to under 6 per cent; only 244 out of 4,166 electors opted for them.[6] This débâcle, followed by almost equally severe losses in voting for municipal and county councils shortly afterwards, led to a change in the local leadership of the DNVP. Its new chairman was Dr Ernst Evers, who became the town's most outspoken opponent of National Socialism.

He was not an obvious choice for this distinction. Since 1927 his law partner and *Duzfreund* (they were fraternity brothers) was none other than J. H. Böhmcker, who had twice failed his probationary *Assessorexamen* and was therefore disqualified from a career in the civil service. Moreover, Evers had a reputation as an enemy of Social Democracy rather than of Nazism. Biographical information about him is scant.[7] He was born on 24 April 1883 into a family long resident in Eutin, where his father owned a brewery and beverage distribution company. Evers graduated from the local *Gymnasium* in 1902. After studying at Göttingen and other universities, he obtained his doctorate from Rostock and then opened a legal practice in the town. A heart condition limited his military service during the First World War; instead, he was employed by the Eutin government. During the 1920s Evers built up his firm into one of the town's best, and was a member of several Nationalist organisations. He entered civic politics in 1925, serving as a *Ratsherr* until October 1928 – the final eighteen months also as deputy mayor – when he suddenly resigned. In these offices Evers amply showed his dislike of the SPD, whose leader he blocked from occupying the latter post. His resignation stemmed, however, from differences of opinion with the bourgeois caucus (*Fraktion*) on the council. The nature of these is not known, but they may have been exacerbated by his aloof demeanour and ready resort to sarcasm. Nazi *Kreisleiter* Saalfeldt perceptively assessed the appointment for his superiors: though he was in partnership with SA chief Böhmcker, Evers was replacing an individual who 'in many respects had worked well together with the Marxists, which had created dissatisfaction and so driven people' into the NSDAP – all in all, 'an unwelcome constellation for us in terms of party politics'.[8]

The accuracy of this evaluation was soon borne out. To be sure, in several elections held during the last year preceding Nazism's triumph in Eutin its 'national' elements attempted to collaborate in the spirit of the so-called 'Harzburg Front',[9] but with limited success. Already in the May 1931 campaign for the Oldenburg legislature, Conservatives and the *Stahlhelm* pronounced their readiness to co-operate with the NSDAP in ministries at the Reich and regional levels, and the Nationalist list of candidates (according to social democratic newspapers) was 'tailored to the wishes of the Nazis'. But representatives of the DNVP also criticised at length article seventeen of the programme of the NSDAP, which called for the expropriation of property by the state without compensation, and just as bluntly rejected the idea of a Nazi dictatorship: 'No one party should assume that it alone can rule Germany. We Germans are much too wilful for that. Our goal can only be achieved by all of us within a Right-wing coalition.' The upshot was that Hitler's movement fell short of winning the absolute majority it had expected in the town, and the Conservatives increased their share of the vote, albeit only to 8.6 per cent. Nor could the parties together muster enough seats to form a cabinet; their attempt to nominate Böhmcker Minister-President was defeated. Although the entire 'national opposition' thereupon supported a Nazi-initiated referendum to force a new election to the *Landtag*, they were only willing to rally behind Hitler in the run-off vote for the German presidency on 10 April 1932 after the *Stahlhelm* commander Duesterberg had stood against him in the first round. The nearly 55 per cent the *Führer* polled in Eutin set the stage for the final legislative elections of the Republic, in which the town gave the NSDAP an even more ringing endorsement. One in ten voters, however, was now to be found on the Nationalist side. The campaigns unmistakably revealed the totalitarian methods of the Nazis: for example, a member of the Eutin youth branch of the *Stahlhelm* was brutally assaulted by some SA men, while other adherents of Hitler systematically undermined the traditional loyalty to the DNVP of the area's farmers by seizing control of their organisation, the *Landbund*, which provided a foretaste of the future all-encompassing pattern of *Gleichschaltung*. In its concluding report, the district leadership of the NSDAP remarked that though Nationalist speakers had adapted themselves to their opponents' views to such a degree that it was difficult to attack them, they also displayed a 'venom' (*Gehässigkeit*) that had been directed solely towards Nazis. This was the attitude, rather than occasional collaboration in organising the region's 'Voluntary Labour Service',

together raising money through charitable undertakings to aid their
unemployed followers (both with the assistance of the Lutheran
Church) or jointly combating their common 'Marxist' enemy,[10]
that continued to characterise the relationship between the DNVP
and National Socialism in the Third Reich which began prema-
turely in Eutin.

The town's new Nazi government was presided over by J. H.
Böhmcker, who promptly proceeded to transform this portion of
Oldenburg in a fashion that would become all too familiar once
Hitler had been installed as Reich Chancellor. First, by a variety of
means, he tried to suppress the activities of the other political
parties, including the DNVP, to which Ernst Evers strenuously
objected. Trouble started during the Reichstag election campaign
called by the von Papen cabinet for 31 July. Evers, who thought the
NSDAP was in the process of breaking up over internal conflicts
involving its 'revolutionary' and 'pragmatic' wings, and the top
candidate of the Nationalists in Schleswig-Holstein, Reichstag
caucus chairman Dr Ernst Oberfohren, therefore concentrated
their speeches upon the supposedly socialist aspects of the Nazi
platform. Thus, Hitler's plan to increase the taxation rate for
higher-paid wage-earners was denounced as 'bolshevistic', and
unlikely to solve the problem of joblessness. 'The DNVP', declared
Oberfohren, 'will remain free of every kind of socialism, however it
is dressed up, and will serve as the reservoir (*Sammelbecken*) for the
nationally-minded bourgeoisie . . . opposed to National Socialist
excesses'. This rebuke of Nazi economic policy was mild compared
to the comprehensive settling of accounts contained in Kleist-
Schmenzin's brochure 'National Socialism – A Danger', of which
Evers had hundreds of copies distributed throughout the Eutin
district. Its author used citations from the Nazis themselves to
depict their movement as an anti-religious 'revival of a dying
Marxism', implacably hostile to the interests of the German
middle-class: 'In any event, the heritage of a National Socialist
government will be chaos.' Intended to check Hugenberg's goal of
obtaining an alliance with the NSDAP, the pamphlet's attacks
upon Hitler and his duplicity particularly outraged Dr Saalfeldt,
who threatened to have future meetings of the DNVP broken up
by the SA unless this form of agitation ceased. Evers took the
warning seriously, and appealed to Böhmcker to implement suitable measures to 'thwart the terror' of his own party and uphold the
freedom of assembly guaranteed under the Weimar constitution.
To this petition, which the conservatives also circulated as a handbill among the voters, Böhmcker responded that Saalfeldt had been

told the government would employ all the force at its disposal to prevent violence from whatever source it originated. But at the same time he admonished the DNVP for provoking the Nazis with advertisements inviting 'both national and international socialists' (thereby bracketing them with the SPD and KPD) to attend and speak at its rallies. Böhmcker added that unless the Nationalists abandoned their 'hate-filled' verbal and printed propaganda, they could not complain if this 'triggered the resort to improper methods' against them in turn.[11]

This scarcely veiled official intimidation made no impression on Dr Evers. He reminded the Nazis that they had earlier called their Conservative opponents 'traitors' (*Volksverräter*) and similar names; his party would henceforth repel such defamation no matter what the price. Nor would he show up any longer as a discussant at Nazi meetings, or allow Saalfeldt to take part in his, for which he was labelled 'cowardly' and 'unmanly'. Evers persisted in criticising the 'socialist tendencies' of Nazi proposals and blamed the NSDAP alone for the failure of the 'Harzburg Front'. As for flying the swastika flag on government headquarters the day Böhmcker took office, this merely showed that the Nazis put their party ahead of the nation. But the most provocative action by the Nationalists was in refusing categorically to withdraw Kleist–Schmenzin's controversial brochure from circulation; indeed, by means of open letters and notices in the press, they disseminated its message about the true nature and aims of Nazism even more widely. The reaction of Hitler's followers went beyond decrying the tactics of the DNVP as 'dirty' and menacing its speakers, who had to be protected by the police. Less fortunate was a distributor of the pamphlet who was ambushed on an Eutin street by two members of the SA; they made off with 200 copies of it and destroyed them, for which each received a fine or gaol sentence. A large Nationalist election sign erected on the town market-place suffered the same fate: Nazis demolished it and threw the pieces into a lake. For the DNVP, the lesson to be drawn from such misbehaviour seemed obvious:

> Let the NSDAP go on in the same fashion with fisticuffs, kicks, stealing and highway robbery, then it will not be long before our impoverished and once-again deluded people recognize the truth. We demand: freedom of thought, speech and assembly! No one has ever succeeded in eliminating a political opponent by brute force in a struggle of ideas; that, too, has to be said to the National Socialists. . . . Wake up, you real German men and women, before it is too late! The verdict will be handed down on 31 July.[12]

It was, though not exactly in the form desired by the central leadership of the DNVP, which had urged voters to give an absolute majority to the parties of the 'national opposition'. This was easily achieved in Eutin, where half the electorate still supported the NSDAP, while the Nationalists – thanks in part to summer vacationers casting absentee ballots – increased their share to 15 per cent; the figures for the entire country, however, were 'only' 37.5 and 5.9 per cent respectively.[13] Evers and the DNVP had shown that staunch opposition to dictatorial rule by the Nazis would be rewarded at the polls. They were therefore all the more determined to keep up their critique of Böhmcker's regime. As far as the Nationalists were concerned, his principal abuse of power involved the arbitrary dismissal of civil servants belonging to or sympathising with the DNVP who before and after July 1932 discharged their responsibilities in ways deemed detrimental to the NSDAP by the Eutin government. They would be replaced by loyal Nazis, so-called *Parteibuchbeamten*, a type of otherwise unqualified appointee (like the new Oldenburg Minister of Justice, who had not studied law) that Evers had already taken issue with to good effect. A spectacular case of this sort, which made the town notorious across northern Germany, was that of its mayor, Dr Otto Stoffregen. A Nationalist since mid-1932, Stoffregen's quarrels with the Nazis originated in their objections to his generous salary provisions, but rapidly escalated to include, among many other things, his administration of police and welfare matters. These were both politically sensitive subjects, about which the NSDAP as Eutin's strongest party claimed it should have a greater voice. The stubborn resistance the mayor put up against such importunities hardened the resolve of the National Socialists to remove him outright. A chance was offered by the investigation into the bombing of the SPD-affiliated Consumer Co-operative Store in the town on 10 August 1932. The perpetrators of this and similar deeds elsewhere in Schleswig-Holstein were SA men, whose leader Böhmcker – ruling the single Nazi jurisdiction in the province – afforded them sanctuary. When Prussian detectives arrived to carry out arrests, he brazenly denied them authority to do so. One of the town's own policemen nevertheless assisted them, so Böhmcker suspended him from duty. Stoffregen backed up his subordinate, and he, too, was dismissed.[14]

Stoffregen's firing, which even the ministry in Oldenburg admitted was illegal, set off a bitter struggle in public and in the courts, involving the mayor, the DNVP and Nazi governments from Eutin to Berlin, that was not finally settled until the Third

Reich had ceased to exist. The victim saw his as 'the first case in which a National Socialist government had proceeded against a German Nationalist civil servant in an especially crass fashion.'[15] On account of the precedent it represented – if Stoffregen could be dropped from office summarily for upholding the law against its blatant infringement, the tenure of no non-Nazi official was secure – the Nationalists, with Dr Evers in the forefront, took up the cause. A petition, circulated in the town over the names of Stoffregen's widely respected predecessor (also a member of the DNVP) and several other prominent citizens, and calling upon the Oldenburg cabinet to restore the mayor to his post, quickly gathered 1,200 signatures from persons of all political persuasions. But the most comprehensive indictment of Böhmcker's regime was a statement composed by Evers and approved at a mass meeting of his party on 13 November. It summarised the events leading up to and immediately following the mayor's dismissal, and culminated in a demand for Böhmcker's recall as the only means of ensuring 'the return of legal conditions and the maintenance of peace and order' in Eutin. In extremely forthright language the document criticised in detail his serious character weaknesses, his lack of impartiality in administering affairs, and his ignorance or disregard of the very laws he was sworn to maintain.

> Böhmcker is not prepared to protect the constitutional rights of the population and to enforce respect for the law. . . . We [therefore] feel obliged to call the attention of the State Attorney's Office to the illegal and improper behaviour of the head of government [in Eutin]. In view of the many extra-legal acts committed in recent months we [also] have appealed to the Reich Minister of the Interior. . . . We are not willing to tolerate any longer the suffering of the overwhelming majority of our people under the biased, arbitrary and illegal conduct of [Johann Heinrich Böhmcker].

However, in attributing Böhmcker's misdemeanours to his repeated failure of his bar examinations years ago, Evers made his own earlier acceptance of the younger lawyer as a partner seem aberrant. Be that as it may, this courageous submission to the government in Oldenburg did not achieve the results for which the Eutin DNVP had hoped. Not only did the Nazi majority in the legislature refuse to lift Böhmcker's immunity as a deputy, thereby effectively preventing his prosecution by the judicial authorities, but the Nationalist caucus also decided that Stoffregen's just claim to reinstatement had to be sacrificed to the overriding need for preserving good relations with the NSDAP. Doubtless for the same reason, Conservative Interior Minister von Gayl declined to intervene by dispatching a *Reichskommissar*, as he had readily done in July to social democratic Prussia. A formal DNVP request on 18 January 1933 for a parliamentary committee to investigate the whole matter was thus quietly dropped when the *Landtag* met again early in February.[16]

What had transpired in the interval, of course, was the formation of the Hitler–Hugenberg cabinet, which alone preserved Böhmcker's hold on power along with that of the NSDAP in the state of Oldenburg. For the outcome of the Reichstag election on 6 November 1932 reflected the accumulated disenchantment of Eutin with Nazism that Ernst Evers had been voicing. At the outset of the campaign he stated that while Social Democracy and the Catholic Centre Party would still be prime targets of the DNVP, 'the struggle must and will also be waged against the National Socialists for what they have done to damage the national cause'. The Conservatives, adopting some of the dynamic terminology hitherto more typical of their rivals (one of their speakers in Eutin, for example, was billed as representing the 'Fighting Circle of Young German Nationalists'), attacked the NSDAP for pandering to the particular economic interests of its supporters, rather than making the welfare of the entire nation its guiding principle. The Nazis responded by incongruously branding the DNVP the 'party of the Jews' and denying responsibility for excesses by the SA such as street battles with Nationalists. Dr Evers, in speeches and open letters to the press, pointed out that it only served the purposes of their common enemy when, because of lack of discipline on the part of some National Socialists, a 'fratricidal nationalist war' was waged between the two sides. Did the Nazis imagine that their movement, which claimed to stand for Germany's revival, would win support by such methods? The result of the vote confirmed the value of this strategy of presenting the DNVP as a law-abiding alternative to Nazism. Despite its ostentatious backing of the highly unpopular von Papen ministry, and notwithstanding clever Nazi appeals to fellow veterans in the ranks of the *Stahlhelm*, 22 per cent of Eutin's electorate – almost three times the average across the country – returned once more to the Nationalist fold, while Hitler's party lost its absolute majority in the town. Since a further one-third of the voters cast their ballots for the Left, observers predicted that the rule of the NSDAP there would soon come to an end.[17]

This prognostication was not borne out; but for that Ernst Evers was not alone to blame. Although it is true that his pronounced hostility towards the SPD helped make any form of collaboration

among all anti-Nazi forces unlikely, Eutin's Social Democrats had
displayed a noticeable lack of aggression *vis-à-vis* National Socialism since their involvement in the violent death of one of its
adherents at the close of 1931.[18] Evers apparently calculated instead
that the DNVP could continue to regain its former position locally
at the expense of the NSDAP. He was encouraged in this belief by
the steady growth in the size of his party, which by December 1932
counted over 200 members in Eutin; at the same time, however,
card-carrying Nazis were still more than twice as numerous. None
the less, he rightly surmised that the rejuvenation of the Nationalists was in no small part due to his own untiring exposure of the
grave shortcomings of Böhmcker's regime, and so he resolved to
press on with his crusade throughout Schleswig-Holstein. The
climax was reached in mid-January 1933 at gatherings of the
DNVP branch in neighbouring Plön and of the provincial organisation meeting in Kiel, where he reported at length on the sorry
state of Oldenburg's Nazi administration: 'From being a "land of
smiles". . . as people used to enjoy calling Oldenburg, it has
become a "land of tears".' Only a strong and united Conservative
movement, in his view, could change this. His outspoken defence
of mayor Stoffregen, as well as his harmful revelations and charges
about developments within the NSDAP, first and foremost the
alleged Jewish ancestry of district leader Saalfeldt, provoked a
heated exchange of correspondence with various Nazis in the Eutin
newspaper that went on for weeks. It was only terminated on the
day the new government headed by Hitler and Hugenberg took
office.[19] The efforts by Ernst Evers to persuade his fellow Germans
of the dangers a Nazi government posed to the rule of law thus
failed to convince even his own party leader. But one prominent
Nationalist, Dr Ernst Oberfohren, on the basis of both his own
first-hand experience of Nazi brutality and Evers's accounts of the
situation in Eutin, came to the conclusion that a coalition with the
National Socialists at the Reich level could only be entered into, if
at all, with a firm determination to preserve the independence of
the DNVP against the machinations of an utterly unscrupulous
partner. When at Hugenberg's insistence such an arrangement
came about on 30 January 1933, immediately followed by incontrovertible proof of Nazi ruthlessness in seeking to expand their
power by displacing Conservative cabinet members and officials,
Oberfohren initially resisted this course of events, before losing
hope and committing suicide at the beginning of May.[20]

Ernst Evers too, as indicated by his almost total absence from the
campaign for the Reichstag election on 5 March 1933 that Hitler

had demanded, only reluctantly accepted the creation of the so-called 'cabinet of national concentration'. Whereas representatives of the DNVP mostly echoed the Nazis in saying the vote would be the last held for a long while no matter how it turned out, and joined them in celebrating Germany's 'awakening', Evers probably agreed with Ewald von Kleist-Schmenzin, who roundly condemned the opportunism of such Conservatives: 'Soon there will be a proverb – spineless like a German government official, godless like a Protestant clergyman, honourless like a Prussian officer.'[21] Renamed the 'Fighting Front Black, White, and Red' (the colours of the imperial monarchy), the now less combative party slipped to below 20 per cent of the ballots cast in Eutin. According to the newly introduced *Gleichschaltung* legislation, this also constituted its share of seats on the revamped town council, to which Evers again belonged. Although excluded from the 'Auxiliary Police' established to safeguard the revolution, local Nationalists expected to be able freely to solicit support for the 'forces within the national front' that did not belong to the NSDAP: 'the task of the DNVP before history is not yet completed'. However, the limits of unfettered political agitation in the Third Reich were quickly made clear to Evers when his group objected to Dr Saalfeldt's nomination as *Ratsherr* and deputy mayor. A sharply worded letter composed by another Nationalist councilman argued that, under the provisions of the 'Law for the Restoration of a Professional Civil Service' of 7 April, the supposedly 'non-Aryan' Saalfeldt, whom the *Führer* personally had confirmed as a Nazi without clarifying his racial status, was not eligible to be appointed. Copiously citing an anti-Semitic tract by Henry Ford, the complaint elaborated the general attitude of the DNVP towards Jewry:

> With respect to the Jewish question, for years the Nationalist programme has demanded above all a halt to the immigration of Jews from the east as well as the elimination of Jewish domination in government, administration and public life. . . . Until now Jewry has known how to preserve its influence under every form of government. . . . Wherever they have been fought as a race, they have been able to prove either that they were not Jews or, if the evidence for this was not quite sufficient, that they have been 'made suspect' and 'persecuted' on account of the base instincts of anti-Semites. For the Jew realises very clearly that when he is 'attacked' it is not because he is a Jew but instead is due to the influences and opinions he represents, which will lead to the destruction of social mores if they are not checked. The Jew is a problem the world over. . . . Entire nations that were in complete agreement about the need to combat Jewry have so far not been able to defend themselves against this race.

Thus the entire world is now looking towards Germany to see what
form anti-Semitism will take here.

The Nationalists, therefore, could not agree that Saalfeldt should
participate in running Eutin: 'Otherwise, outsiders will take up the
case and use it to prove that in Germany, too, the Jewish question is
moving towards a solution wholly acceptable to the Jews; and for
this reason alone the national revolution will be nothing more than
a miscarriage.' There is no evidence that this statement, signed by
Evers as caucus chairman, which was primarily intended to embar-
rass the NSDAP, did not also accurately reflect his own philos-
ophy; certainly, he led the Nationalist delegation that walked out of
the council when its Nazi majority refused to concur in Saalfeldt's
dismissal. But neither on tactical nor on legal grounds did the Reich
leadership of the DNVP approve this 'ineffective political operation' that needlessly harmed relations with its ally. Encouraged by
this stance, the Eutin government delayed replying to the protest
until it was made superfluous by the dissolution of Evers' party.[22]
A similar fate awaited renewed efforts to reinstate Stoffregen;
without its DNVP members, the remaining Nazis on the council
proceeded to endorse the mayor's permanent removal, which
repeated appeals to his party's Berlin headquarters could not
reverse.[23]

The final demise of the Eutin DNVP was preceded by an attempt
to revive the idea of a Hohenzollern restoration. Although Hitler
had already definitively abandoned this gambit he had once used to
attract Conservative support, the town's Nationalists nevertheless
announced a public meeting on 'The Monarchy and the Future of
Germany', to be addressed by a clergyman. It was twice banned by
the Nazi authorities, on the grounds it would only arouse 'disquiet
and uncertainty' among the population; to this also Evers objected.
It was clearly illegal, he said, to forbid a gathering sponsored by a
governmental party because its theme 'was not acute at present'.
However, this was in vain, as was a complaint to Labour Minister
Seldte that the local youth wing of his own *Stahlhelm* had been
barred from an official Youth Festival on account of 'provocative
behaviour' on another occasion. These issues became irrelevant,
though, when the DNVP dissolved itself nationwide on 27 June
1933. A few days later its delegates formally withdrew from the
town council. The confiscation of its property by the Gestapo, the
absorption of the *Stahlhelm* into the SA, and the *Gleichschaltung* of
various bodies associated with the party abruptly terminated Conservatism as an organised political force in Eutin.[24]

The town's Nationalist leaders were not prepared, however, to cease all contact among themselves, notwithstanding a law of 14 July against the continuance of any other party besides the NSDAP. To deal with every form of real and suspected resistance to untrammelled Nazi rule Böhmcker established a 'provisional' concentration camp in an unused section of the Eutin jail. Between 22 and 26 July 1933 Ernst Evers, Otto Stoffregen and three additional Conservatives (including the author of the DNVP submission denouncing Dr Saalfeldt's Jewishness) were taken into 'protective custody' and confined there. They were accused not only of trying to preserve the organisational structure of their party, but also of publicly criticising and ridiculing Böhmcker's conduct in office, despite warnings that such 'carping and grumbling' directed against the regime would not be tolerated. Specifically, in the wake of a 'secret' meeting of these Nationalists in an Eutin restaurant that was raided by the police, thorough searches of their homes were undertaken, which turned up seriously compromising materials, dealing above all with the Stoffregen case. Thus, in correspondence with Evers and two DNVP Reichstag deputies the deposed mayor had depicted himself as 'an innocent victim of Nazi totalitarian pretensions', even though a so-called 'friendship treaty' between both parties recognised their equal contributions to the 'national revolution'. As for Dr Evers, who months before had already been threatened with *Schutzhaft* for his oppositional behaviour, his 'manner hitherto of engaging in political dispute' strongly suggested, according to Böhmcker, that he was likely to continue his 'harmful activities', and by 'concocting and spreading untrue or grossly distorted allegations' greatly harm the welfare of the Reich and the reputation of the government in Eutin and the NSDAP which stood behind it. For this he ordered his former law partner to be held in the concentration camp until 4 August. Unlike most prisoners Evers was not required to perform manual labour, but instead carried out clerical tasks. He was also more fortunate than Dr Stoffregen, who had to pay a hefty fine of 3,000 marks and sign a statement renouncing his rights as a civil servant before regaining his freedom.[25]

This experience, though mild compared to that of many inmates of early Nazi camps, had the effect of extinguishing any further co-ordinated resistance among Eutin's Nationalists for the duration of the Third Reich. Böhmcker saw to it, as long as he remained in control of the town (he became mayor of Bremen in 1937), that even purely social clubs were closed down if they were patronised principally by former adherents of the DNVP; and the Gestapo

promptly arrested any such individuals who actually engaged in
oppositional activity. Like Hitler, Böhmcker was much more
inclined to regard 'reactionary' Conservatives, rather than 'misguided' Marxists, as constituting the most dangerous potential
enemies of Nazism. He nevertheless sought to reconcile both
groups with the 'new order' – often to the distress of his own more
radical followers. Through the mediation of a mutual lawyer friend
he made peace, of sorts, with Dr Evers; but it is extremely doubtful
whether Böhmcker thereby – as his severest critic within the
NSDAP claimed – 'drew a brown shirt over the blue soul' of his
erstwhile friend. An incident in 1935, indeed, suggests otherwise.
According to a confidential report sent to the Reich Minister of the
Interior by his opposite number in Oldenburg, at a *Herrenabend*
held in the officers' mess of Eutin's army battalion, Evers delivered
a ringing speech in favour of the monarchy to an admittedly silent
audience. He was supposed to have been a bit drunk at the time;
however, as Peter Hüttenberger has observed about such actions in
Hitler's Germany, alcohol 'only lowered the threshold of discre-
tion' in persons usually more careful about displaying their essential
hostility towards the regime. This seems to have been the conclusion of the authorities, who placed Evers under surveillance for at
least a year. Afterwards his dossier was turned over to the political
police in Kiel.[26]

Unfortunately, nothing else is known about Evers' doings until
October 1945, when he was named a trustee and administrator of
sequestered Nazi property in Eutin by the British Military Government. It also appointed him two months later to the first post-war
town council, to which he was later repeatedly elected, as he was
several times to the district *Kreistag*. Ernst Evers was a co-founder
and regional chairman of Eutin's branch of the Christian Democratic Union (CDU), and he headed several cultural organisations
in his home town before his death on 14 March 1954.[27]

In an address to the personnel of the Eutin government in July
1937, before departing for Bremen, J. H. Böhmcker counted
among his major accomplishments the victory of Nazism in eastern
Holstein five years previously, against the opposition not only of
the Marxist parties but also and especially of the German Nationalists. This constellation of enemies, at least as far as the latter were
concerned, was largely the work of Dr Ernst Evers, who, almost
from the moment he took over the leadership of the DNVP in the
town, showed himself a fearless and implacable foe of the NSDAP.
His motive in this regard went beyond his profound antagonism
towards any form of 'socialism', or his apparent conviction that the

anti-Semitism practised by the Nazis was insufficiently consistent, attitudes which scarcely qualified him as an unambiguous democrat.[28] Rather, Evers was appalled by the systematic departure from legal norms that the regime which assumed power in Eutin after July 1932 displayed. The fact that the chief perpetrator of this illegality was his personal friend and business associate seems to have intensified the perception in this arch-conservative lawyer of the deadly danger Nazism posed to the foundation of the *Rechtsstaat*. Consequently he was untiring in his efforts to topple Böhmcker, even if this placed his own liberty and possibly his life in considerable jeopardy once Hitler became Chancellor. His and Hugenberg's appointment by President von Hindenburg was just one instance of the disavowal which Evers and the local DNVP suffered at the hands of their party's chairman, who overrode the intimate knowledge they, along with Ernst Oberfohren, had acquired of the frightful reality of Nazi rule throughout Oldenburg. Evers pursued active opposition to National Socialism until he was briefly placed in Eutin's concentration camp; and afterwards he persisted in his dissent from the dictatorship ruling Germany. This principled stance was acknowledged by the Allied occupation authorities, notwithstanding his other more dubious political beliefs. But these should not disqualify Ernst Evers, nor Ewald von Kleist-Schmenzin, from being counted part of the German resistance, which, Peter Hoffmann asserts, owed its very distinction to the fact that it was 'recruited from all social classes, political groups, and ideological and religious persuasions.'[29]

NOTES

1. P. Hoffmann, 'Problems of Resistance in National Socialist Germany', in F. H. Littell and H. G. Locke (eds), *The German Church Struggle and the Holocaust*, Detroit, 1974, pp. 97, 106–7; Hoffmann, *Widerstand – Staatsstreich – Attentat. Der Kampf der Opposition gegen Hitler*, 4th rev. edn, Munich, 1985, pp. 10, 36–7; Hoffmann, *Widerstand gegen Hitler und das Attentat vom 20. Juli 1944. Probleme des Umsturzes*, 2nd rev. edn, Munich, 1984, pp. 14, 17, 59 ff.; and Hoffmann, 'Motive', in J. Schmädeke and P. Steinbach (eds), *Der Widerstand gegen den Nationalsozialismus. Die deutsche Gesellschaft und der Widerstand gegen Hitler*, Munich, 1986, pp. 1089–96; see also B. Scheurig, *Ewald von Kleist-Schmenzin. Ein Konservativer gegen Hitler*, Oldenburg, 1968, pp. 30, 39, 60 f., 64, 74, 78, 84, 199.

2. J. J. Sheehan, 'What Is German History? Reflections on the Role of the *Nation* in German History and Historiography', *Journal of Modern History*, vol. 53, 1981, pp. 21–2; and J. A. Leopold, *Alfred Hugenberg: The Radical Nationalist Campaign against the Weimar Republic*, New Haven, 1977, pp. 127 ff.

3. L. D. Stokes, *Kleinstadt und Nationalsozialismus. Ausgewählte Dokumente zur Geschichte von Eutin 1918–1945*, Neumünster, 1984, pp. 9, 15 ff., 24–9 (tables of election results from which all subsequent such figures on Eutin are drawn); and Stokes, 'Zur Geschichte der Arbeiterbewegung in Eutin während der Weimarer Republik', in R. Paetau and H. Rüdel (eds), *Arbeiter und Arbeiterbewegung in Schleswig-Holstein im 19. und 20. Jahrhundert*, Neumünster, 1987, pp. 365–85. On the role in civic politics of anti-socialist electoral coalitions comprising parties that represented 'essentially the right-wing *Bürgertum*' see R. Koshar, *Social Life, Local Politics, and Nazism: Marburg, 1880–1935*, Chapel Hill, 1986, pp. 57 f.

4. D. Petzina, W. Abelshauser, and A. Faust, *Sozialgeschichtliches Arbeitsbuch. Band III: Materialien zur Statistik des Deutschen Reiches 1914–1945*, Munich, 1978, p. 174 (table 41a on Reichstag election results); A. Dorpalen, *Hindenburg and the Weimar Republic*, Princeton, 1964, p. 82; L. D. Stokes, 'Die Eutiner Landeskirche zwischen Novemberrevolution und Nationalsozialismus', in K. Reumann (ed.), *Kirche und Nationalsozialismus. Beiträge zur Geschichte des Kirchenkampfes in den evangelischen Landeskirchen Schleswig-Holsteins*, Neumünster, 1988, p. 135; and Stokes, 'Der Kapp-Putsch von 1920 in Eutin', *Die Heimat. Zeitschrift für Natur- und Landeskunde von Schleswig-Holstein und Hamburg*, vol. 86, 1979, pp. 231–40; see also C. J. Elliott, 'The Kriegervereine and the Weimar Republic', *Journal of Contemporary History*, vol. 10, 1975, pp. 109–29.

5. Stokes, *Kleinstadt*, pp. 33 ff., 43 ff., 56 f., 62 f., 81–7, 288, 718, 726; Stokes, 'Professionals and National Socialism: The Case Histories of a Small-Town Lawyer and Physician, 1918–1945', *German Studies Review*, vol. 8, 1985, p. 457; R. Zitelmann, *Hitler. Selbstverständnis eines Revolutionärs*, Stuttgart, 1987, pp. 370, 419 f., 440; and D. P. Walker, 'The German Nationalist People's Party: The Conservative Dilemma in the Weimar Republic', *Journal of Contemporary History*, vol. 14, 1979, pp. 627–47. On anti-Semitism in the DNVP, which was every bit as widespread as among followers of Hitler, see D. L. Niewyk, *The Jews in Weimar Germany*, Baton Rouge, 1980, pp. 49–52; and T. Childers, *The Nazi Voter: The Social Foundations of Fascism in Germany, 1919–1933*, Chapel Hill, 1983, pp. 41, 161, 188.

6. R. Rietzler, *'Kampf in der Nordmark'. Das Aufkommen des Nationalsozialismus in Schleswig-Holstein 1919–1928*, Neumünster, 1982, pp. 366 ff., 399 ff.; and Stokes, *Kleinstadt*, pp. 34 ff., 68, 71 f., 91, 95.

7. I am especially grateful to Dr Hans-Jochen Fischer of Oldenburg, as a fledgling lawyer an acquaintance of Ernst Evers, and to Eutin city archivist, Egon Jacob, for many of the following details (letters to the

author, 1 March and 25 May 1988); also Landesarchiv Schleswig-Holstein (hereafter LASH), records of the government in Eutin (hereafter RE), file no. A III 2b; Stadtarchiv Eutin (hereafter SAE), file no. 2490, letter from Evers to the mayor of Eutin, 1 July 1928; and *Eutiner Kreis-Anzeiger* (hereafter EKA), 15 March 1954. See Stokes, 'Professionals', p. 459; and Stokes, *Kleinstadt*, pp. 129, 140 ff., 164, 290.

8. US National Archives (hereafter USNA), microfilm roll 175, frame no. 317879, report of 15 April 1931 to *Gau* Schleswig-Holstein, Kiel, and *Gau* Weser–Ems, Oldenburg, of the NSDAP, reprinted in Stokes, *Kleinstadt*, p. 159. Married without children, Evers was evidently a convivial host in the privacy of his home.

9. On the massed rally of Nazi, Nationalist, and *Stahlhelm* formations and their leaders at Bad Harzburg on 11 October 1931, vainly intended to demonstrate the unity of the anti-republican Right, see Leopold, *Hugenberg*, pp. 97 ff.

10. Stokes, *Kleinstadt*, pp. 39 ff., 121 ff., 165 f., 170 ff., 183 ff., 242 f., 247 ff., 256 f., 266, 278, 281 ff., 302 f., 315 f.; Stokes, 'Professionals', p. 466; and K. Schaap, *Die Endphase der Weimarer Republik im Freistaat Oldenburg 1928–1933*, Düsseldorf, 1978, Ch. 7.

11. *Anzeiger für das Fürstentum Lübeck* (hereafter AFL), Eutin, 11 June, 10, 13–15 July 1932; *Lübecker Volksbote* (hereafter LVB), 18 July 1932; LASH, RE/A Va 4; USNA, 164/302710; Stokes, *Kleinstadt*, pp. 317 ff., 328–9; and Scheurig, *Kleist-Schmenzin*, Ch. 6 and pp. 255–64 (reprint of 'Der Nationalsozialismus – eine Gefahr').

12. AFL, 16, 17, 19, 23, 28, 29, and 31 July 1932; *Ost-Holsteinisches Tageblatt* (hereafter OT), Plön, 23, 24 and 30 July 1932; *Schleswig-Holsteinische Volkszeitung* (hereafter SHVZ), Kiel, 28 July 1932; SAE, 3238; LASH, record group 355, no. 135; and Stokes, *Kleinstadt*, pp. 337 f.

13. AFL, 28 July 1932; and USNA, 164/302703 (DNVP election handbill 'Don't talk – act') and 164/303059, report from Kreisleiter Saalfeldt to *Gau* Schleswig-Holstein, 4 August 1932. On the importance of absentee voting for both the NSDAP and the DNVP in the July 1932 election, see R. F. Hamilton, *Who Voted for Hitler?*, Princeton, 1982, Ch. 9.

14. L. D. Stokes, 'Der Fall Stoffregen. Die Absetzung des Eutiner Bürgermeisters im Zuge der NS-Machtergreifung, 1928–1937', *Zeitschrift der Gesellschaft für Schleswig-Holsteinische Geschichte*, vol. 104, 1979, pp. 256–64; Stokes, *Kleinstadt*, pp. 117 ff., 145 ff., 190 ff., 222 ff., 303, 319, 338, 351–6; and J. Noakes, *The Nazi Party in Lower Saxony*, London, 1971, pp. 229 f.

15. LASH, RE/A XV c1, Stoffregen to Friedrich von Winterfeld, deputy chairman of the DNVP, Berlin, 29 June 1933.

16. Stokes, *Kleinstadt*, pp. 356–62; Stokes, 'Stoffregen', pp. 255, 264 ff.; and Schaap, *Endphase*, pp. 227, 246 f.; also LASH, record group 399, no. 6 (Böhmcker Papers); Stokes, 'Professionals', pp. 465, 472 f.; and letter from Dr H.-J. Fischer to the author, 1 March 1988.

17. AFL, 4, 25, and 29 September, 7, 11, 19, 25, 29, and 30 October, 3, 5, and 6 November 1932; LVB, 29 October, 2 November 1932; SHVZ, 3 November 1932; SAE, 3238; USNA, 164/302962, report from the Eutin district propaganda leader to *Gau* Schleswig-Holstein of the NSDAP ('the DNVP agitated in the foulest manner only against National Socialists'), 9 November 1932; and Stokes, *Kleinstadt*, pp. 321 f., 329 f.

18. On this incident, which the entire Right successfully exploited to eliminate the SPD as a significant political factor in Eutin, see L. D. Stokes, 'Der Fall Radke. Zum Tode eines nationalsozialistischen "Märtyrers" und die Folgen in Eutin, 1931–1933', in E. Hoffmann and P. Wulf (eds), *'Wir bauen das Reich'. Aufstieg und erste Herrschaftsjahre des Nationalsozialismus in Schleswig-Holstein*, Neumünster, 1983, pp. 41–72; and Stokes, 'Sozialdemokratie contra Nationalsozialismus in Eutin 1925–1933', *Demokratische Geschichte. Jahrbuch zur Arbeiterbewegung und Demokratie in Schleswig-Holstein*, vol. 2, 1987, pp. 196 ff.

19. AFL, 2 and 20 December 1932, 11, 14–31 January, and 1 February 1933; SHVZ, 2 and 9 January 1933 ('The whole world is holding its belly laughing about Eutin'); OT, 15 January 1933; LVB, 25 January, 8 February 1933 ('Nazi Chaos in Eutin'); L. D. Stokes, 'The Social Composition of the Nazi Party in Eutin, 1925–32', *International Review of Social History*, vol. 23, 1978, p. 6; and Stokes, *Kleinstadt*, p. 323. On the widespread criticism and ridicule of the Nazi government in Oldenburg including Eutin, see Schaap, *Endphase*, Ch. 8.

20. P. Wulf, 'Ernst Oberfohren und die DNVP am Ende der Weimarer Republik', in Hoffmann and Wulf (eds), *'Wir bauen das Reich'*, pp. 176–80; see also Leopold, *Hugenberg*, pp. 134, 148 ff.; and F. Freiherr H. von Gaertringen, 'Die Deutschnationalen Volkspartei', in E. Matthias and R. Morsey (eds), *Das Ende der Parteien 1933*, new edn, Düsseldorf, 1984, pp. 541–652.

21. Hoffmann, 'Problems of Resistance', p. 107; also AFL, 21, 26 and 28 February, 1, 3–5 and 7 March 1933; SAE, 3238; and Stokes, *Kleinstadt*, p. 371 (Ernst Oberfohren: 'The national government will remain in place in any event; the question for the electorate is simply whether or not to stand behind it.').

22. AFL, 19 April and 12 May 1933; SAE, 3213, minutes of Eutin town council meetings, 22 and 30 May 1933; LASH, RE/A XV c1; Stokes, 'Professionals', pp. 475 f.; and Stokes, *Kleinstadt*, pp. 344 ff., 373, 388, 392–8, 778 ff.

23. LASH, RE/A XV c1, correspondence among Dr Stoffregen, the National Committee for Communal Politics of the DNVP and its Reichstag deputies Steuer and von Winterfeld, 10, 28, and 29 June 1933; Niedersächsisches Staatsarchiv Oldenburg, record group 136, no. 459; and Stokes, 'Stoffregen' pp. 269 ff.

24. Stokes, *Kleinstadt*, pp. 373 f., 399 f., 412 ff., 450, 454 ff.; see also W. H. Kaufmann, *Monarchism in the Weimar Republic*, NY, 1953, pp. 215 ff., 224 f.

25. AFL, 25 July and 6 August 1933; SAE, 3482, letter from Böhmcker to Evers ('presently in the Eutin jail'), 27 July 1933; Stokes, *Kleinstadt*, pp. 398, 402, 406 f., 513, 515, 540–6, 566 f.; Stokes, 'Stoffregen', pp. 271–6; and Stokes, 'Das Eutiner Schutzhaftlager 1933/34. Zur Geschichte eines "wilden" Konzentrationslagers', *Vierteljahrshefte für Zeitgeschichte*, vol. 27, 1979, pp. 570–625.

26. SAE, 3482, correspondence between the mayor and the Gestapo office of the Eutin government, 3 and 7 October 1936; LASH, record group 320/Eutin, no. 182; Stokes, *Kleinstadt*, pp. 502 f., 764, 771, 814, 839 f. (extract from the political *Lagebericht* of 13 April 1935 for the state of Oldenburg); letter from Dr H.-J. Fischer to the author, 1 March 1988; Zitelmann, *Hitler*, p. 414; W. Lührs *et al.*, *Bremische Biographie 1912–1962*, Bremen, 1969, pp. 56–8 (J. H. Böhmcker); R. Mann, *Protest und Kontrolle im Dritten Reich. Nationalsozialistische Herrschaft im Alltag einer rheinischen Großstadt*, Frankfurt am Main, 1987, pp. 237 ff.; and P. Hüttenberger, 'Heimtückefälle vor dem Sondergericht München 1933–1939', in M. Broszat *et al.* (eds), *Bayern in der NS-Zeit*, vol. 4, Munich, 1981, p. 497. Dr D. J. K. Peukert[†], formerly of the University of Essen, helpfully clarified the latter reference for me.

27. LASH, 320/Eutin, no. 13; EKA, 15 March 1954 (obituary of Ernst Evers); and letter from E. Jacob to the author, 25 May 1988. Efforts to locate any surviving personal papers of Evers have proved fruitless.

28. AFL, 5 October 1932. See the highly critical assessment of the response in particular of Conservative–Nationalist members of the resistance towards the 'Jewish question' in Germany by C. Dipper, 'Der Widerstand und die Juden' in Schmädeke and Steinbach (eds), *Widerstand*, pp. 598–616; but also the contrary interpretation of Hoffmann, 'Motive', in ibid., pp. 1089 f.

29. Hoffmann, 'Problems of Resistance', p. 102; and Hoffmann, 'The War, German Society and Internal Resistance', in M. Laffan (ed.), *The Burden of German History 1919–1945: Essays for the Goethe Institute*, London, 1988, p. 197; also G. Buchstab, B. Kaff and H.-O. Kleinmann (eds), *Verfolgung und Widerstand 1933–1945. Christliche Demokraten gegen Hitler*, Düsseldorf, 1986. On Kleist-Schmenzin's activities and death in the anti-Hitler resistance, see Hoffmann, *Widerstand – Staatsstreich – Attentat*, pp. 82 ff., 195 f., 245, 405, 440, 640, 643, 675, 677 f.; and Scheurig, *Kleist-Schmenzin*, Chs. 7–12.

4

Self-Defence Against Fascism in a Middle-Class Community: The Jews in Weimar Germany and Beyond

Arnold Paucker

Already in the early years of the Weimar Republic, activists in the Social Democratic Party of Germany (SPD) were provided with a pamphlet which took the form of an uncompromising, forthright polemic against anti-Semitism, for there were sections of the German working class which, after the defeat of 1918, had not escaped the infection.[1] This pamphlet, which cannot have been issued later than 1924, was used in many areas of Germany before the NSDAP had become a mass movement; it was reprinted more than once, although there are few copies to be found today.[2] The title-page poses the following question for the rank and file of the SPD: Reactionary fascism's political, economic, and religious Jew-hatred and race-hatred – what should the workers know about it? Published by the Social Democratic Party of Germany, Hanover district association, for speakers and functionaries. This is an admirable anti-anti-Semitic and anti-fascist polemical pamphlet, in essence every bit as valid today as it was sixty years ago.

Ten years ago, the late Ernest Hamburger and I undertook an in-depth analysis of this pamphlet and its origins. Dr Hamburger, a former Social Democratic deputy in the Prussian *Landtag*, is of course well-known as the author of the standard work *Juden im öffentlichen Leben Deutschlands*.[3] At a very early stage, we established beyond doubt that this pamphlet was based on material from the *Centralverein deutscher Staatsbürger jüdischen Glaubens* (Central

Association of German Citizens of the Jewish Faith [CV]); comparison with other *Centralverein* publications left no other conclusion possible. In addition, we were able to adduce evidence that *Centralverein* officials must have supplied the SPD with the text for printing. On this point, we noted one further qualification: the functionaries involved must either have belonged to the SPD or at least have been closely linked with that party (and in fact now, ten years later, it is possible to identify the compiler or purveyor with a degree of certainty).[4] This was clear from passages in the booklet which, in formulation, style and choice of words, unquestionably went beyond what would have been practicable or possible for the *Centralverein* itself to publish under its own signature. It was on behalf of the Jewish religious community that the CV had taken on the task of countering anti-Semitism, and its members were for the most part not to be reckoned as protagonists of or voters for Social Democracy.

The *Centralverein deutscher Staatsbürger jüdischen Glaubens* was founded in 1893 by German Jews in order to defend their civic rights from the existing threat of anti-Semitism in Wilhelmine Germany.[5] The German Jews formed a middle-class community, and it is in Germany itself – and with justice – that, for their apathy or sympathy toward fascism, blame was and still is laid heavily upon middle-class groups. As a consequence, we have all come across the complacent assertion which for so many people eases their lives and placates their consciences: 'Well, if Hitler hadn't been an anti-Semite, lots of you Jews would cheerfully have joined the National Socialists.' There are several replies possible, but it is one from my Berlin youth that always springs to my mind; it used to be – and I hope still is – the answer to all such notions: 'Ja, wenn meine Grossmutter Räder hätte, dann wär sie'n Omnibus' (best rendered as 'Oh yes, and if my grandmother had wheels, she'd be a bus').

The reaction of German Jews to anti-Semitism and national Socialism in the Weimar Republic was first explored by myself[6] and then by some other Jewish historians and (to my gratification) most recently – it must be emphasised, in an exemplary way – by a number of younger German historians as well.[7] Having drawn particular attention to these works, I shall here above all try to combat a certain mythopoeia (which may well be classified under the heading *Mythos Berlin*),[8] since figmentary notions about German Jewry at the time of the Weimar Republic still haunt the scene – images which do not correspond to reality; they do not show much real knowledge of the Jewish community in Germany, nor do they help towards an understanding of its precarious position.

My own contention, after all, is not unknown – that German Jewry, despite much initial hesitation within the group as well as very many grave errors in the last phase of the Weimar Republic, made a notable effort to combat fascism.

At least one post-war German historian has clumsily tried to illustrate a potentiality for fascism within German Jewry by pointing to what seems to him a fascist disposition within Italian Jewry.[9] This, of course, must always be a lame comparison; and moreover the example of Italy is not well chosen. The *Risorgimento*, the Italian national movement of the nineteenth century – in this totally unlike its German counterpart – included no hint of an anti-Semitic tendency; nor, similarly, up to 1938 was there any anti–Semitism in Italian fascism, which often posed as the successor to the *Risorgimento* (quite falsely; the true descendants were the Italian partisans). After 1938, a kind of enforced anti-Semitism existed. Italian Jews, however, were divided. The official Jewish bodies surrendered to the fascist regime: to do this in Italy was often a mere matter of form. However, long before 1943 and even before 1939, Italy's Jews played a considerable part in the anti-fascist resistance and, in the *Giustizia e Liberta* movement, their role was virtually decisive. Research on the subject has established these facts.[10]

If, however, we speak of the anti-fascist attitude of *German* Jews, we cannot ignore the lapses and sins of the past which may be exemplified by the case of Italy. For in a way it was just that *non*-anti-Semitic fascism of Mussolini which seduced some otherwise honourable German-Jewish Liberals. Obviously, then, fascism was possible without anti-Semitism. It was felt that this fact should be assiduously brought home to the representatives of the German brand of fascism. From time to time even the *Centralverein*, for tactical reasons, was not too high-minded to indulge in this kind of sophistry. This is understandable; German Jewry was in the greatest danger and people were snatching at any kind of reasoning. Even Liberal personalities such as Theodor Wolff, the chief editor of the *Berliner Tageblatt*, or the prolific biographer Emil Ludwig momentarily warmed themselves a little in Mussolini's sun.[11] Later on, the right-wing Zionist *Betar Youth* were even to parade themselves before the dictator; and, having regard to the *Betar* marine establishment in Italy before the application of the Nuremberg laws, Mussolini is sometimes thought of as a godfather to the Israeli navy. Nevertheless, this wild exaggeration belongs to another chapter. There is no question here of a cover-up; but, in truth, all this was in no way characteristic of German Jewry.

Now, indeed, it is possible to develop a hypothesis as to what would have happened – and here again comes an 'if' – if the German right-wing or German Conservatism from its inception had proclaimed the establishment of Jewish civil rights as a primary demand; while, on the other hand, we imagine that the German left-wing – Radicals, Democrats, Liberals, Socialists, Communists – had always and almost without exception denounced Jewish emancipation and equal rights and had gone on to condemn the Jewish community lock, stock and barrel as the bearer of Capitalism, the people's bane. In such a situation it might very well be conceivable that the bulk of German Jewry in the Weimar Republic would have sided with the political Right, even indeed that the greater number would have taken up a position to the right of the German People's Party (*Deutsche Volkspartei* [DVP]); and then in 1933 . . .? There are, after all, examples enough to show how Christians of Jewish descent were frustrated in their attempts to jump on the Nazi bandwagon;[12] but when it comes to the Jewish community, no historian can work on this kind of unhistorical hypothesis. Germany's political development led to a totally different path for the Jews.

There is, however, no intention here of putting forward the proposition that, by reason of some God-given attribute or natural propensity, Jews have been chosen as a constant progressive factor in the commonwealth of mankind, and that during the Weimar Republic they were thereby automatically turned into good Democrats, upright Republicans and valiant Socialists. Of course, the unquestionable ethical bases of Judaism cannot be left entirely out of consideration. In a lecture given in Berlin after the Second World War, the great Jewish sociologist Eva Reichmann coined the expression 'Jewish class-anomaly'.[13] She was calling attention to the fact that the German-Jewish middle classes of the late 1870s were obliged to take a different path from that of their non-Jewish class-brethren. While it would be wrong to say that Jewish emancipation had entirely failed, it did remain incomplete. A contented German middle class continued its support for National Liberalism, which was by that time moving ever rightward, or else opted for Conservatism. Meanwhile, after 1878 the second-class Jewish citizenry was becoming a sort of 'loyal opposition': the realities of German experience drove them towards the Progressives (*Fortschritt/Freisinn*) and also, from the turn of the century, to Social Democracy. These findings are incontrovertible since, later in the Weimar Republic, even the real right-wing among German Jews hardly went beyond the People's Party. Kurt Tucholsky, a merciless critic of the Jewish middle class when it threw itself into nationalist postures, once remarked that the DVP would have been the natural watering-hole of German Jews, if only . . . but he, too, clearly felt that in the circumstances this was just not on.

Generally speaking, it can be established that after 1878, in round figures, up to 70 per cent of German Jews were voting for the Progressives and that in the Weimar Republic up to two-thirds of them voted for the German Democratic Party (*Deutsche Demokratische Partei* [DDP]), while the remaining one-third cast their vote mostly for the SPD. Very few votes were left for other political parties. After 1930 and the collapse of the bourgeois centre, German Jewry's large-scale move towards Social Democracy (and to a much lesser extent towards the Communists) was set in motion. Even the Catholic Centre Party (*Zentrumspartei*) profited from the desperate position of the Jews; but there is no sign of a comparable migration of Jewish voters in that direction. Orthodoxy and rural Jewry may possibly have seen in the Centre Party a protective patron; yet the assertion that a new 'protected Jewish citizenry' now began to sail under the colours of the Catholic Church is not supported by most historians. Rather, over 60 per cent now voted for the workers' parties – remarkably enough, if it is recalled that in Germany Jewry we are dealing with a middle-class community. If we wish to speak at all of Jewish right-wing tendencies, a small section made up of the moneyed bourgeoisie had found a niche in the DVP and a deranged few leaned towards the German nationalists, the *Deutschnationale Volkspartei* (DNVP). They were motivated by the wild notion that it might be possible to achieve something against anti-Semitism from within the lesser of the two nationalist and anti-Semitic evils (and indeed it would appear that *one* Jewish industrialist even – briefly – supported the Nazis financially).

To complete the picture, one must differentiate and contrast the great mass of so-called assimilating Jews (most of them even today lumbered with the derogatory epithet 'assimilationists') from the Zionist minority; and, unquestionably, there were certain right-wing Zionists carrying on a mild flirtation with fascism. In German Zionism, with its humanistic tendency, this was a very small group, and remained so even under the stifling Nazi dictatorship. The political allegiances and voting patterns of the German Jews have in fact been most reliably researched, and, in speaking of German Jewry's anti-fascist self-defence, these findings must constantly be borne in mind.[14]

There has certainly been much condemnation of German Jews' chauvinism and jingoism. Undoubtedly, they were ardent patriots with an extravagant love – later to be so ill-rewarded – for their

fatherland. At the outbreak of the First World War they instantly
stormed ţhe recruiting offices, with the Zionists first in the race.
Today, with the benefit of hindsight, it is not difficult to realise
who were the most astute ones: precisely that tiny convinced
anti-war group which mistrusted German war aims and abhorred
the mass slaughter.[15] Within German Jewry, it was the religious
pacifists, the opponents of imperialist war aims and even the simple
draft-dodgers who showed good sense: not the 99.5 per cent who
in 1914 thought they were fulfilling their patriotic duty – for which
they were later thanked by being sent to the gas chambers.[16] On the
whole, sadly, our grandfathers were not prophets; and the Jewish
minority, constricted within an imperialist and initially war-
fevered German populace, could not have acted in any other way,
even if at the outbreak of war the Jews had differed substantially in
their attitudes from their fellow-citizens (which, of course, was not
the case). Yet, when speaking of political acumen, it should also be
remembered that in 1912–13 Jewish newspapers were polemicising
vigorously and consistently against the Pan-German pro-war
agitation. Moreover, I am not here referring to the so-called Jewish
press (the *Judenpresse*, as it was dubbed by the anti-Semites) such as
the *Berliner Tageblatt*, but rather to the official publications of the
religious community: the *Allgemeine Zeitung des Judentums* or the
Centralverein paper, *Im deutschen Reich*.[17] And who now remembers
that in the closing stages of the war German Jews overwhelmingly
– and one is tempted to add splendidly – condemned the idea of a
'Victor's Peace' and advocated instead a 'Negotiated Peace'.

The tag 'nationalist', persistently attached to German Jewry, has
created a great deal of confusion. Nationalist postures, wrapping
oneself in the nationalist toga, were expected of the minorities in
the Reich; and, in response to that requirement, the fact that almost
all German Jews were German nationalists, that they were
staunchly *deutsch-national* as opposed to Jewish nationalist, was
continually emphasised. It would undoubtedly have been better to
have dropped such a prejudicial choice of phrase at an earlier stage,
rather than fostering confusion with extreme right-wing German
organisations, parties and groups which were anti-Jewish and with
which a democratic Jewry had nothing whatsoever in common.
On the whole, it would have been an advantage to have stopped the
whole 'patriotic' twaddle much earlier. It was, unfortunately, no
easy matter for German Jews to change their ways; yet all this
patriotic breast-beating, this glorification of the fatherland, did not
exactly help when it came to an out-and-out battle against fascism.

It is also true that in 1918 the majority of German Jews had run into all kinds of 'political awkwardnesses' concerning first the Republic and then anti-fascism. They were undoubtedly somewhat tainted with monarchism and not exactly subversively inclined. The November Revolution, many felt, gave no immediate assurances.[18] Jews, after all, had not enjoyed the happiest experience when it came to violent and revolutionary political upheavals, and a burnt child dreads the fire. Moreover, Imperial Germany could point to a record of more than a modicum of undeniable civic achievements for Jews. Even Zionist pessimists were bound to admit this fact. On the other hand, at the outset the republican future seemed uncertain, and many people might have felt: 'better the devil you know than the devil you don't'. And who can say today that such fears were entirely unjustified? The disjointed and anarchic conditions in Europe after the First World War were certainly among the factors which were eventually to lead to the annihilation of European Jewry. Thus, there were numbers of Jews who were, initially at any rate, merely *Vernunftsrepublikaner* (republicans on rational grounds): for many Jewish groups it was not altogether easy to accustom themselves immediately to the new German democracy, in which for the first time Jews *were* granted unconditional and complete civic equality. Here one must confess to Jewish weaknesses which were very marked even in Jewish defence activity outside the field of anti-anti-Semitism. Of course, such limitations were alien, indeed often incomprehensible, to those Jews who had long declared their solidarity with the workers' movement. Innumerable Jewish intellectuals, who castigated the short-comings of bourgeois Jewish Defence and whose very names have become household words, were from an early stage uncompromising and sincere anti-fascists. Yet these were in most cases Jews already totally divorced from Judaism, who had often resigned officially from the Jewish congregations; while my reflections concentrate on the middle-class Jewish religious community. And here I come to my contention: that it is exactly when we consider the actual social structure of this Jewish community that we find that a real and important change was achieved, one which it is quite impossible to over-estimate.

The following observations are essential in light of the attacks that have been made against 'smug, satisfied, contented Jewry', whether in Wilhelmine Germany or the Weimar Republic. There was, in truth, a certain intrinsic discrepancy between the conservative life-style characteristic of most of the Jewish community and their (partly enforced) political options and voting patterns. In addition, very considerable distinctions existed among German

Jewry, between active élites marked by greater political awareness, which were not always truly representative, and an often apolitical, grass-roots public. On the other hand, with the Association of Jewish Frontline Servicemen (*Reichsbund jüdischer Frontsoldaten* [R.j.F.]), to which almost all Jews who had seen active service in the First World War belonged, one could almost prove the opposite. Its members were adherents of the DDP and the SPD, and sometimes even Zionists. Politically speaking, the leading group in the R.j.F., often right-of-centre in German politics, was unrepresentative of its following, since among the unattractive features of ex-servicemen's organisations, the most striking is quite often a stubborn leaning towards the right. Generalisations, therefore, cannot apply, especially in regard to different anti-fascist stances.

A political avant-garde was always distinct from the main community – and it had a deeper understanding of the dangers threatening Jews. I am speaking here of those Jewish functionaries of the *Centralverein* (and it is fair to term them its 'young guard'), who early on had recognised the grave threat directed just as much against the fledgling Republic as against the continuance of a Jewish community endowed with equal civil rights. The service performed by these men was to have acted as prophets voicing their warning at a point in German history when the authorities in the Republic were still dismissing Hitler and his henchmen as a set of loud-mouths, a passing phenomenon, not to be taken seriously. Recognition is due to them for their tremendous efforts in attempting to rouse the leaders of the Republic from their deadly lethargy and to awaken them to a mortal peril, which even a blind man must have been able to see.[19] No single voice is raised today to maintain that this small Jewish group could possibly have prevented the downfall of the Republic. Their representatives did their duty as Germans and as Jews; nor could they have imagined the extent of the coming catastrophe.

At the outset, Jewish self-defence was restricted to combating anti-Semitism and to defending civic rights, although the famous words 'that a people which oppresses others cannot itself be free' were not unknown in this quarter either. The link between an attack on the Jews and the undermining of democratic liberties and freedom was constantly stressed. Nevertheless, it is a fact that for decades Jews viewed anti-Semitism too much in isolation. It was just not enough to sing the praises of a heartfelt Jewish desire for the good of the fatherland, and to say that one could be sure of earning its gratitude in the end. Yet one must recognise the limitations of a middle-class Jewish organisation and the bounds imposed

on its activities by its very nature. Officially, indeed, Jewish representatives were supposed to remain neutral, in the party-political
sense, a stance not always maintained even in Wilhelmine Germany, and in any case quite impossible to observe in practice.
Compromise here was one thing, but for the Jewish dignitaries
whose distinguished careers had begun in Imperial Germany and
who had grown grey in legalistic activity, anything else would
have been felt to be a grotesque imposition. They refuted baseless
anti-Semitic accusations: when their rights were impeded, they
turned to the state for help or appealed to the courts. Otherwise,
they called for decency and reason. But which of them was prepared to go out into the street and deal with propaganda aimed at
the masses, or who would go so far as to make common cause with
political agitators from the Socialist working class? Even the mere
thought outraged these Jewish worthies. It was not until a new
generation of *Centralverein* officials arose that it was recognised that
an anti–Semitic fascist mass movement could no longer be countered by traditional apologetics, that it no longer sufficed to attack
only the anti-Semitic component of German fascism, but that the
Jewish minority must battle against the phenomenon of fascism in
its entirety. Today it is easy to say that for Jews there can only be,
always and everywhere, a total defence against fascism. For the
representatives of a middle-class community sixty years ago, that
was a very serious step to take.

From this, there developed novel propaganda methods, and after
1929 a characteristic of the new disguised anti-fascist propaganda
was that, in contradistinction to official Jewish self–defence, it was
stripped of every kind of apologetics. This had not yet been the case
with the equally camouflaged material supplied to the SPD five
years before. In the Social Democratic pamphlet mentioned above,
in which are to be found whole passages borrowed from *Anti-Anti:*
Tatsachen zur Judenfrage ('Anti-Anti: Facts on the Jewish Question'), widely circulated at the time and supplied by the *Centralverein* to its speakers, the calumnies about 'vermin' and 'parasites'
were countered by the long list of Jewish Nobel Prize winners, and
accusations of cowardice with the heroic deaths of Jewish soldiers.
All this was quite unexceptionable and, after all, served an anti-
racist purpose. On the other hand, the really clever concealment of
Jewish provenance, the apparent preservation of neutrality, went
way beyond that. The pamphlet further asserted: 'Jewish capitalism
isn't circumcised, the Christian sort is not baptised', both were
'organised exploitation of the worker by the entrepreneurs';
'Whether Christian or Yid, business cannot be gainsaid'; and other

such pleasantries. This recalls some illegal KPD propaganda in Germany, in which the party dabbled even up to the November pogrom in 1938; some of its underground leaflets constantly harped on similar themes. From this it is apparent how far some Jews had let themselves be carried in their anti-fascist ardour; yet we are dealing here with an effective polemic against anti-Semitism written out of a strong anti-fascist conviction.

From 1929 onward, neutrality took on a completely new form. Propaganda emanating from official Jewish quarters simply could no longer counter the NSDAP programme in its entirety. The Party had become so powerful, had captured such large numbers of the German populace, that the very fact of the display of an official Jewish stamp, an avowal of its Jewish origin, left any such anti-fascist publicity impotent. German Jewry found itself in a tragic situation from which tactically only one conclusion could be drawn. Mass propaganda of Jewish origin had to be kept anonymous, and distribution would have to remain the hands of non-Jewish bodies faithful to the Republic. Incidentally, the disguise was so effective that the Nazis never did succeed in tracing the chain of supply. As a result, on the other hand, the fact of this considerable Jewish achievement remained unknown until the 1960s.[20]

It is not possible to describe this propaganda in detail here. However, there is no question but that, in the last years of the Weimar Republic, a considerable portion of the anti-Nazi propaganda of the SPD, the *Reichsbanner*, and the 'Iron Front' can be ascribed to the Jewish self-defence organisation. Some of the leaflets, stickers and posters have been preserved, and their provenance has been reliably authenticated. It meant a vast expenditure of Jewish effort. The propaganda was often sophisticated and above all most persuasive, as strikingly exemplified by the polemical anti-Nazi publication *Alarm*, supplied by the *Centralverein* to the Socialist working class and occasionally even to the Communists for three years. This author has elsewhere detailed the effect of novel methods, undoubtedly developed by the Jewish self-defence organisation, in the electoral districts where they were employed in collaboration with Socialist militants. In these constituencies a considerable fall in NSDAP votes was noticeable even before the elections of November 1932. Not every attempt, therefore, fizzled out ineffectively, and undoubted successes were registered in certain regions. The only drawback was that the advocates of this new propaganda could not prevail on their own party leaderships to carry it into effect to propel their parties to act at the right time. The 'other Germany' was often too lukewarm, here as elsewhere.

The Jewish Defence in Germany, the *Centralverein*, and the vast majority of German Jews retained their faith in that 'other Germany'.[21] Without that belief, in the last years of the Weimar Republic one could have simply given up. Here, too, hindsight has dominated, chiefly in Jewish quarters, and has furthered the development of a comprehensive condemnatory theoretical infrastructure. This presupposes a 'liberal illusion' to which a short-sighted German Jewry prostituted itself for an entire century, portraying to itself an imaginary other Germany which never existed in reality or which was so insignificant that there was no need for that pointless dialogue which neither existed nor could exist, simply because no interlocutor was present. In this view, emigration from Germany as early as 1930 – and what country would then have accepted the Jews *en masse*? – would have been the rational alternative, rather than futile attempts to stem a tidal wave with leaflets and stickers and making appeals to those who stopped their ears and continued to stop them until it was too late. There always have been two Germanies, and German Jews had faith in the nobler, liberal alternative, the democratic, the Socialist Germany. Up to the last, the outcome remained uncertain; and so long as the battle was undecided, the Jews had to defend their civic rights.

German Jewry has since been blamed for having brought its own fate upon itself because of internal fragmentation. This argument – that the victims are abetters in their own doom – is often put forward by people who might more fittingly keep silent on the theme. Quite apart from that, it is obvious that the abrogation of civil rights and the annihilation of Jews were carried out by forces in the face of which Jewish influence – whether or not Jews had been united – could only be insignificant. Moreover, given a Germany split along political lines, so that there were, of course, Jews of all shades of opinion, it would be unreasonable to demand brotherly unanimity from them alone. Even if German Jewry had consisted of 600,000 Ruhr miners stubbornly cleaving to fraternal concord, it still would not have escaped its fate. It is true, however, that neither in Wilhelmine Germany nor in the Weimar Republic did the German Jews ever succeed in creating a centralised representative body. The *Reichsvertretung der deutschen Juden* was established only when the majority of the German people and the criminal Nazi regime had declared Jews to be outcasts beyond the pale of the law. On the other hand, it should also be emphasised that in the latter stages of the Republic there were successful efforts (at least in the struggle against anti-Semitism and National Socialism) to bring about a limited collaboration, even including the

Zionists, among the otherwise often-warring Jewish forces. Undoubtedly this reinforced the campaign against fascism.

Up to 1933, the Zionists formed a small, though significant, minority in German Jewry. Their prognosis as to the continuing existence of the Jewish community was distinctly pessimistic. In their opinion, apologetic defence against anti-Semitism was a sheer waste of time. Despite this, as the threat of danger grew, even among the German Zionists there developed a tendency towards an anti-fascist defence in the Diaspora.[22]

How militant was Jewish anti-fascism? There have been certain grotesque suggestions about paramilitary undertakings. Here it must be stressed that during the Papen coup of July 1932, Jewish functionaries, acting for the Jewish Defence, pleaded with the Social Democratic Prussian government, with which the *Central-verein* maintained close contacts, for armed resistance. However, the leadership of the SPD was unwilling. Whether at the time any such possibility existed at all is still a matter of controversy. The Jews were never more than a small auxiliary force for the Republic: independent military measures belonged to the realm of fantasy. Had civil war broken out in Germany in 1932, following resistance by the Prussian government or a *Putsch* from the Right, then the Jewish population would have been caught in the cross-fire and the Nazis would have organised pogroms. German Jews in their tens of thousands would have fought shoulder to shoulder with the Republican and Socialist formations defending the Republic. No other choice would have been open to them; and there were enough veterans in the R.j.F. who had gained military training during the World War. For the Jews the silent abandonment of democratic positions in Prussia in 1932 already marked the beginning of their tragedy. It can be argued without difficulty that it was this fact alone which was a true pointer to the end of Jewish emancipation in Germany.

Thus far, these limited observations concern Jewish behaviour patterns in the Weimar Republic. However, to mark a total break with 30 January 1933 is too facile. It is still necessary to cast a glance at the very least at the year during which Jewish civic rights were stripped away.[23] The former types of self-defence, naturally, had to give ground. The enemy of the State had now become the authority of State. Nevertheless, in the transition phase during the first years of the dictatorship, there were further attempts at defending Jewish positions and Jewish answers to anti-Semitism (by this time State-based), and this presented a continuation of some forms of traditional Jewish self-defence. The line between self-defence and self-preservation is not always so easily drawn; a growing literature now deals with the many facets of Jewish self-assertion under the Nazi dictatorship.[24]

It has been suggested, long after the event, that the isolated Jewish community should have engaged in militant and military resistance. One can just imagine Jewish *Sanitäts-* and *Kommerzienräte* clambering up the barricades on the Kurfürstendamm; yet even absurdities like this have been put forward by anti–fascists nurtured decades later in the security of the pluralist societies of the West. The fact is that there had to be bargaining with the Nazi authorities for the temporary means of living, and, eventually, 'official' organising of a fairly orderly retreat of the German-Jewish population to foreign countries offering a haven. This has been made a reproach to German Jews, culminating in the cry of 'Collaboration!' spread abroad by pseudo-historians, political agitators and third-rate dramatists.[25] However, this does not mean that German Jewry, too, did not have its black sheep, nor that under pressure inexcusable mistakes did not occur. A small catalogue of these can be drawn up. However, here we are speaking of the behaviour of the great majority of German Jews: what was the state of things with them? In the case of the *Jüdischer Kulturbund*, a liberal-humanist enclave was created – entry reserved only for the outlaws, forbidden to Germans – a remarkable, perhaps unique, cultural oasis in conditions of total oppression.[26] Step by step, the Jews were forced to yield to the relentless abrogation of their rights; yet there was also a degree of resistance by the Jewish leadership wherever it was possible.[27] And, to single out but one remarkable feature of Jewish life in Nazi Germany, not only did the numerous Jewish youth organisations[28] allow the positive values of the German youth movement (now 'co-ordinated' [*gleichgeschaltet*] by the fascist State) to live on, but they also gave thousands of German Jews a Liberal or a Zionist education – and not seldom a thorough Socialist and anti-fascist education as well, and this under the very noses of the Gestapo.[29] Of course, the official representation of German Jewry could not carry out any active resistance; but up to 2,000 Jewish Germans were involved in undercover anti-fascist activity of every kind and degree over a span of twelve years.[30] Here alone impressive comparisons (in percentages) can be drawn in proportion to the surrounding German world.[31]

In conclusion, Zionist functionaries who after 1939 remained voluntarily to carry out *Hechaluz* (Zionist youth) work in Germany and paid for it with their lives – the Director of the *Reichsvertretung*, the liberal Otto Hirsch, who firmly resisted the early deportations

and then perished in Mauthausen; and the Communist activist
Herbert Baum, who organised Jewish youth groups for sabotage
and propaganda against the Nazis and the war and then, with his
comrades, met a martyr's death in Plötzensee – they all died not
only for the Jewish people; they also fell in the fight against German
fascism.[32] Self-defence in a free society – self-defence under the
dictatorship: for Jews as well, there are connecting threads and
continuities. German Jews were a middle-class community. Adherence to democratic values during the Weimar Republic; active
defence against anti-Semitism; dignity and resistance under the
National Socialist tyranny – these are the authentic attributes of
German Jewry.

NOTES

1. This is an expanded and annotated English version of a paper, 'Zur
   antifaschistischen Selbstwehr einer bürgerlichen Gemeinschaft. Die
   Juden in der Weimarer Republik', delivered in Berlin on 25 August
   1987, in a cycle of lectures on *Judentum, Demokratie und Identität in
   Deutschland*, under the auspices of the *Republikanisches Forum* at the
   exhibition 'Mythos Berlin', held from 13 June to 20 September 1987.
   As the paper is largely based on my work over twenty-five years on
   Jewish self-defence in Germany, source references are kept to a minimum; the reader is referred for further details to the various studies
   mentioned below and to the bibliography listed in note 7.
2. Copies are in the Forschungsstelle für die Geschichte des Nationalsozialismus in Hamburg and the Leo Baeck Institute, London.
3. E. Hamburger, *Juden im öffentlichen Leben Deutschlands. Regierungsmitglieder,
   Beamte und Parlamentarier in der monarchischen Zeit 1848–1918*, Tübingen,
   1968. A second volume was never completed; but see n. 14, below.
4. Some of my informants have pointed to the Socialist *Centralverein*
   functionary Arthur Schweriner as a very likely source of this pamphlet. This would correspond with his career in the Jewish Defence.
   He was the only leading CV official who belonged to the SPD in the
   early years of the Republic. On him and the anti-fascist camouflaged
   CV journal *Alarm*, which he edited, see A. Paucker, *Der jüdische Abwehrkampf gegen Antisemitismus und Nationalsozialismus in den letzten Jahren der
   Weimarer Republik*, 2nd edn, Hamburg, 1969, pp. 120–1 and *passim*.
5. On the *Centralverein* in Wilhelmine Germany see I. Schorsch, *Jewish
   Reactions to German Anti-Semitism, 1870–1914*, NY–Philadelphia–London, 1972; J. Reinharz, *Fatherland or Promised Land: The Dilemma of the
   German Jew, 1893–1914*, Ann Arbor, 1975; A. Paucker, 'Zur Prob-

lematik einer jüdischen Abwehrstrategie in der deutschen Gesellschaft', in W. E. Mosse and A. Paucker (eds), *Juden im Wilhelminischen Deutschland 1890–1914*. Ein Sammelband, Tübingen, 1976, pp. 479–548; M. Lamberti, *Jewish Activism in Imperial Germany: The Struggle for Civil Equality*, New Haven–London, 1978; and E. Friesel, 'The Political and Ideological Development of the *Centralverein* before 1914', *Year Book of the Leo Baeck Institute*, vol. 31, 1986, pp. 121–46.

6. Paucker, *Der jüdische Abwehrkampf*, and previously 'Der jüdische Abwehrkampf', in W. E. Mosse and A. Paucker (eds), *Entscheidungsjahr 1932. Zur Judenfrage in der Endphase der Weimarer Republik. Ein Sammelband*, 2nd edn, Tübingen, 1966, pp. 405–99; and 'Jewish Defence against Nazism in the Weimar Republic', *The Wiener Library Bulletin*, vol. 26, 1972, pp. 21–31.

7. See the critical bibliography in my essay 'Die Abwehr des Antisemitismus in den Jahren 1893–1933, in H. A. Strauss and N. Kampe (eds), *Antisemitismus. Von der Judenfeindschaft zum Holocaust*, Bonn, 1984, pp. 164–71. Also now U. Beer, 'The Protection of Jewish Civil Rights in the Weimar Republic: Jewish Self-Defence through Legal Action', *Year Book of the Leo Baeck Institute*, vol. 33, 1988, pp. 149–76.

8. See the reference in n. 1, above, to the exhibition 'Mythos Berlin'.

9. The contentious findings on Italian-Jewish political behaviour by E. Nolte in *Der Faschismus in seiner Epoche. Action française. Der italienische Faschismus. Der Nationalsozialismus*, Munich, 1963, served as a basis for the premises of other historians in regard to German Jewry.

10. An exemplary portrayal of the part played by Italian Jews in the resistance is the recent book by S. Zuccotti, *The Italians and the Holocaust: Persecution, Rescue and Survival*, London–NY, 1987.

11. E. Feder, *Heute sprach ich mit . . . Tagebücher eines Berliner Publizisten 1926–1932*, C. Lowenthal–Hensel and A. Paucker (eds), Stuttgart, 1971, *passim*.

12. See for instance W. Cohn, 'Bearers of a Common Fate? The "Non-Aryan" Christian "Fate-Comrades" of the Paulus-Bund, 1933–1939', *Year Book of the Leo Baeck Institute*, vol. 32, pp. 327–66.

13. E. G. Reichmann, *Die Flucht in den Hass. Die Ursachen der deutschen Judenkatastrophe*, Frankfurt am Main, 1956, p. 172; English edition: *Hostages of Civilisation: The Social Sources of National Socialist Anti-Semitism*, London, 1950, pp. 144 f. See also Paucker, 'Zur Problematik . . .', p. 494.

14. I single out here: Hamburger, *Juden im öffentlichen Leben Deutschlands*; J. Toury, *Die politischen Orientierungen der Juden in Deutschland. Von Jena bis Weimar*, Tübingen, 1966; Paucker, 'Jewish Defence'; and above all E. Hamburger and P. Pulzer, 'Jews as Voters in the Weimar Republic', *Year Book of the Leo Baeck Institute*, vol. 30, 1985, pp. 3–66, in which a chapter of Hamburger's unfinished book (see n. 3, above) has been updated and enriched by Pulzer, and is really the last word on the subject.

15. See R. Horwitz, 'Voices of Opposition to the First World War among

Jewish Thinkers', *Year Book of the Leo Baeck Institute*, vol. 33, pp. 233–59.

16. There is a fatal symmetry here. The subalterns of the First World War became the generals of the Second. They held the front against the Red Army whilst their former comrades-in-arms, German-Jewish officers, were gassed in Auschwitz.

17. See Paucker, 'Zur Problematik . . .'; and B. Suchy, 'Die Jüdische Presse im Kaiserreich und in der Weimarer Republik', paper delivered at an international congress in Duisburg, *Juden als Träger bürgerlicher Kultur in Deutschland*, organised by the Salomon Ludwig Steinheim-Institut für deutsch-jüdische Geschichte, the Universität Duisburg, the Leo Baeck Institute, London, and the Landeszentrale für politische Bildung beim Ministerpräsidenten des Landes Nordrhein –Westfalen, 24–28 April 1988, Sachsenheim, 1989, pp. 167–192. Suchy's essays on the Verein zur Abwehr des Antisemitismus 'From its Beginning to the First World War', *Year Book of the Leo Baeck Institute*, vol. 28, 1983, pp. 205–39, and 'From the First World War to its Dissolution in 1933', *Year Book of the Leo Baeck Institute*, vol. 30, pp. 67–103, also deserve special mention in the context of this essay.

18. See A. Paucker, 'Jewish Self-Defence', in A. Paucker (ed.), with S. Gilchrist and B. Suchy, *Die Juden im Nationalsozialistischen Deutschland/The Jews in Nazi Germany. 1933–1943*, Tübingen, 1986, pp. 55–65.

19. Paucker, *Der jüdiche Abwehrkampf*, pp. 85–109.

20. Ibid., pp. 110–28.

21. The American historian and former German Jew, Peter Gay, bore impressive witness to this at the 1985 conference of the Leo Baeck Institute in Berlin on the Jews in National Socialist Germany. See P. Gay, 'In Deutschland zu Hause . . . Die Juden der Weimarer Zeit', in Paucker (ed.), *Die Juden im Nationalsozialistischen Deutschland*, pp. 31–43.

22. The best treatment of this topic is by J. Reinharz, 'The Zionist Response to Anti-Semitism in Germany', *Year Book of the Leo Baeck Institute*, vol. 30, pp. 105–40.

23. I have dealt with this also in my essay 'Jewish Self–Defence', and in 'The Jewish Community in Germany – Reflections on Jewish Behaviour and Policies under a Fascist Dictatorship', paper delivered at a symposium, *Jewish Leadership and the Holocaust*, organised by the Institute of Jewish Affairs, London, 22 November 1987, (unpublished).

24. See Paucker (ed.), *Die Juden im Nationalsozialistischen Deutschland*, n. 18, above.

25. The reference is, of course, to the play by Jim Allen, *Perdition*. This concoction, condemned by serious historians, portrays Zionist–Nazi collaboration for a gullible public. As regards German Jewry, events are lifted out of context and presented without understanding of the complicated background. Confronted with this travesty of the truth a

historian may well despair. See F. R. Nicosia, 'Victims as Perpetrators: German Zionism and Collaboration in Recent Historical Controversy' in *Remembering for the Future: The Impact of the Holocaust on the Contemporary World*, Proceedings of the International Scholars Conference at Oxford University, 10–13 July 1988, Oxford, 1988, pp. 2134–48.

26. H. Freeden, *Jüdisches Theater in Nazideutschland*, Tübingen, 1964. See also Paucker (ed.), *Die Juden im Nationalsozialistischen Deutschland*.

27. H. S. Levine in his essay 'The Jewish Leadership in Germany and the Nazi Threat in 1933', in C. Fink *et al.* (eds), *German Nationalism and the European Response 1890–1945*, Oklahoma, 1985, p. 206, argues that the *Reichsvertretung der deutschen Juden*, created out of 'confusion and fear', was 'a new structure of Jewish self-organization . . . that eventually became part of the machinery of destruction'. His study deals almost entirely with 1933, and, while instructive for that year, then makes a sudden jump and reaches a much too facile and simplistic conclusion. The Jewish leadership was neither that naïve nor that inept. They may have been misguided at times, but their achievements under crushing oppression were by no means negligible. Given the shifting and only gradually deteriorating situation, any wholesale dismissal of the *Reichsvertretung* today would seem totally unjust.

28. There is a considerable literature on Jewish youth and Jewish youth movements. Of the more recent studies, note in particular W. T. Angress, *Generation zwischen Furcht und Hoffnung – jüdische Jugend im Dritten Reich*, Hamburg, 1985; idem, 'Jüdische Jugend zwischen nationalsozialistischer Verfolgung und jüdischer Wiedergeburt', in Paucker (ed.), *Die Juden im Nationalsozialistischen Deutschland*, pp. 211–21; J. Reinharz, 'Hashomer Hazair in Germany (I) – 1928–1933', *Year Book of the Leo Baeck Institute*, vol. 31, pp. 173–208; idem, 'Hashomer Hazair in Germany (II) – Under the Shadow of the Swastika, 1933–1938', *Year Book of the Leo Baeck Institute*, vol. 32, 1987, pp. 183–229; C. Schatzker, 'The Jewish Youth Movement in Germany in the Holocaust Period (I) – Youth in Confrontation with a New Reality', ibid., pp. 157–81; idem, 'The Jewish Youth Movement . . . (II) – The Relations between the Youth Movement and Hechaluz', *Year Book of the Leo Baeck Institute*, vol. 33, pp. 301–25.

29. The author may be permitted a digression here. For instance, when it came to the musical repertoire of the Jewish youth movements, this not only included Jewish, Zionist and Socialist songs, *Landsknechts- und Bauernlieder*, but contemporary anti-fascist tunes as well. At the time of the Italian aggression against Abyssinia, an 'Abessiniensong' was widely sung in the *Werkleute*. It was composed early in 1936 by F. Aronstein (co-editor of the anthology *Israel, Volk und Land*, Berlin, 1934, later a headmaster in Israel). A Hebrew version was written in 1937 in Ben-Shemen by Asriel Blumberg (shot down as a navigator when serving with the Royal Air Force in the war against Nazi Germany) and Arnold Paucker. A telling stanza in 'near-Italian' may be quoted here:

Adrigat, Dschiputi, Adua
Ras Nasibu, Graziano
La vittoria in Addis Abeba
Morte peste Badoglio.

30. This estimate, based on various studies and used by me elsewhere, may actually be an underestimate. In the mid-1930s well over a hundred Jewish anti-fascist activists were held in Dachau concentration camp alone. (Interview, 2 June 1988, with Dr Alfred Laurence, himself imprisoned there.)

31. A fair amount of work has now been done about Jewish resistance in Germany, though the subject still requires further research. Consult H. Eschwege, 'Resistance of German Jews against the Nazi Regime', *Year Book of the Leo Baeck Institute*, vol. 15, 1970, pp. 143–80; K. Kwiet and H. Eschwege, *Selbstbehauptung und Widerstand. Deutsche Juden im Kampf um Existenz und Menschenwürde 1933–1945*, Hamburg, 1984; and E. Brothers, 'On the Anti-Fascist Resistance of German Jews', *Year Book of the Leo Baeck Institute*, vol. 32, 1987, pp. 369–82. See also my paper 'Jüdischer Widerstand in Deutschland 1933–1945: Tatsachen und Problematik', delivered at the Gedenkstätte Deutscher Widerstand, Berlin, on 3 November 1988 on the occasion of the opening of the section 'Hilfe für Verfolgte und Widerstand von Juden'. This paper was published as a brochure by the Gedenkstätte, Heft 37, 1989; and an expanded English version will appear in the *Year Book of the Leo Baeck Institute*, vol. 37, 1992.

32. I have dealt with the various forms of Jewish resistance to Nazism after 1933 in much greater length in the two papers mentioned in notes 23 and 31.

5

Jewish Resistance to Nazi Racial Legislation in Silesia, 1933–1937

Karol Jonca

The strategic aims of racial indoctrination, adopted from the beginning of the NSDAP, worked towards the separation of Jews from
the German *Volksgemeinschaft*. The notion of 'national community'
soon became a vehicle for integrating the whole of Nazi ideology.
When Hitler took over power in 1933, the doctrine was gradually
established by means of many legal and illegal political and economic measures.[1] From 1933 to 1941, i.e. until the 'final solution of
the Jewish question', the Nazis tried to keep up the appearance of
legal action against German Jews. In Germany the tide of norma-
tive acts and notorious administrative measures against Jews,
the so-called anti-Jewish *Maßnahmen*, abolished elementary human
rights. Since the time of the French Revolution these had been
identified with natural human rights by bourgeois communities.
  In the spring of 1933 various legislative Acts advancing the birth
of the *Führerstaat*, with its leader and his élite NSDAP in authority,
shaped the political situation in Germany. The *Ermächtigungsgesetz*
of 23 March proclaimed that the Reich government was entitled to
make laws even though they were inconsistent with the Constitution, and granted Hitler full legislative powers.[2] Thus, the Act
approved his assumption of authority and provided him with
unrestricted political and legal powers as the head of government
whom other State organs could not control. This legislation became an instrument of authoritarian rule, annihilating principles of
human equality, equality before the law, and equality of rights and
duties. Racial criteria were the basis for social divisions which led to

discrimination against the 'inferior race', i.e. the Jews.

During the first days of the Nazi regime, Jewish rights were compromised when storm-troopers (the SA) began to boycott Jewish shops and enterprises. Simultaneously, repressive measures were taken against Jewish doctors and lawyers. The day Hitler succeeded to the Chancellor's office (30 January 1933), Jewish lawyers in Kassel were denied admittance to the local court of justice.[3] A few weeks later, Jewish lawyers in Breslau (Wrocław) had to share the lot of the Kassel lawyers. On 11 March, during the conduct of trials, Jewish judges and lawyers were driven away from the Breslau courts by SA units. Some of them were mistreated. The same actions were carried out on 13 March, when SA men once again broke into Breslau's courts and drove away all Jewish lawyers.

This unprecedented intervention by storm-troopers in the functioning of the lawcourts did not provoke the disapproval of the Reich Minister of Justice. On the contrary, the Silesian incident gave rise to an unexpected reaction on the part of the Reich legal commissioner, Dr Hans Kerrl. In a circular letter of 31 March addressed to all the presidents of the *Oberlandesgerichte*, he called it a 'defensive action'. Kerrl ordered the presidents of the courts to induce judges of Jewish origin to go on leave. In case of refusal, these judges were to be forbidden admittance to the buildings. As a matter of fact, Jewish judges, assessors and public prosecutors were all sent on leave and banned from the courtrooms.[4] As early as the following day, 1 April 1933, the measures taken by Commissioner Kerrl received the full approval of the Nazi Minister of the Interior, Wilhelm Frick. The Minister expressed the opinion that Jewish contributions to German industry, trade and the free professions infected the soul of the nation and its social and political relations.[5] Kerrl's order of 1 April also forbade Jewish notaries from performing their duties.

The regulations of Commissioner Kerrl and Minister of the Interior Frick were but a prelude to the process of completely abolishing equality of civil rights and limiting the public rights of German Jews. Among the Acts repealing Article 109 of the Weimar Constitution, the statute on the 'Reorganisation of the Civil Service' (*Gesetz zur Wiederherstellung des Berufsbeamtentums*) of 7 April 1933 was of primary importance. The statute excluded from the Civil Service, in the interest of Aryan citizens, all persons of non-Aryan descent, and those whose political past did not guarantee that they would support the national state unreservedly. The well-known 'Aryan paragraph' of the Act permitted the pensioning off of civil servants of non-Aryan descent. The Act, together with executive ordinances, rendered it possible to remove Jews from the Civil Service as well as from other employment. The legislation for the first time used the expression *arische Abstammung*, but typically did not define it. In compliance with the Act of 30 June 1933, non-civil-servants (that is, municipal officials, journalists and the like) came under the 'Aryan paragraph'. Still in April, a decree concerning the overcrowding of German schools and universities and a statute establishing student communities created extensive opportunities for repressing Jewish professors and students. The first legislative Acts containing the 'Aryan paragraph' of April 1933 had already given those Jews identifying themselves with *Deutschtum* a sharp shock. According to Robert Weltsch, the editor of the Zionist newspaper *Jüdische Rundschau*, the legislation had destroyed 'Jewish spiritual existence', because, owing to their identification with Germany, the Jews did not believe that they would be removed from the German community in such a way.[6] In Weltsch's opinion, Jews glimpsed a 'demonic image of Nazism' at that time.

An attempt at a determined, yet seemingly futile, resistance against such Nazi legislation was made by Georg Weissmann and Arnold Wiener, Jewish leaders in German Upper Silesia. The decree on the 'Reorganisation of the Civil Service' having been promulgated, Weissmann, in a letter of 9 April addressed to Reich Commissioner Kerrl, insisted on its suspension with respect to Jewish lawyers and notaries of the *Landgericht* and *Amtsgericht* of Beuthen. This was not an insignificant matter, since Jews made up 16.6 per cent of all German lawyers. In Silesia, there was an even higher proportion of Jews. In the *Oberlandesgericht* Breslau region, 564 out of 1,056 lawyers were of Jewish descent. Ninety–eight Jewish lawyers came within the Act and were immediately suspended from practice. Another thirteen were suspended owing to their defence of Communists.[7] The German–Polish Convention for the Protection of Minorities (the so-called Geneva Convention), in force in the plebiscite area of Upper Silesia, provided Weissmann with an effective argument.

The Geneva Convention of 15 May 1922 obliged Germany and Poland to assure full protection of individual rights, life and liberty to all inhabitants of the former plebiscite area of Upper Silesia (i.e. the German *Regierungsbezirk* Oppeln and the Polish Silesian Voivodship) without distinction of birth, nationality, language, race or religion. Individual immunity and equality before the law were guaranteed. Furthermore, the Convention provided minorities with the same civil and political rights other citizens enjoyed.

It also protected admission to public employment and the right to exercise a chosen profession. The Convention declared that no Act or official action could be inconsistent with its principles. The statute on the 'Reorganisation of the Civil Service' was undoubtedly incompatible with this Convention. It is true that Jews living in a part of *Regierungsbezirk* Oppeln (i.e. the territory of Upper Silesia) had not exercised their right to minority protection between 1922 and 1933. It was only when excesses and boycotts after Hitler's coming to power grew in intensity that the attention of Jews was drawn to the possibility of minority protection provided by the Geneva Convention.[8]

The initiative to use the Convention to protect the Jewish population inhabiting the German portion of Upper Silesia was taken by Upper Silesian Jewish leaders Weissmann and Wiener. They were given effective support by the Czechoslovakian Jewish leader Dr Emil Margulies and by Zionist groups which began to intervene with the League of Nations. However, some non-Zionist circles and the *Reichsbund Jüdischer Frontsoldaten* declared themselves against the intervention of the League. Wiener, who did not become discouraged with their attitude, still intended to defend the rights of the Jewish minority in the League of Nations, the more so when anti–Semitic incidents grew in number in *Regierungsbezirk* Oppeln. Among the many cases of boycotting local shops and industrial enterprises and the dismissing of Jews from their jobs, Arnold Wiener chose a most suitable case to submit a petition to the League.

The case of Franz Bernheim was made into a pretext. Bernheim had been discharged from the DEFAKA store in Gleiwitz on account of his Jewish descent; he was deprived of his livelihood and emigrated to Czechoslovakia. Several other Acts discriminating against the Jewish population and violating the provisions of the Geneva Convention were mentioned in the petition submitted to the Council of the League of Nations by Wiener on 12 May. Among them were the statutes on the 'Reorganisation of the Civil Service' of 7 April 1933 and on admission to the legal profession of the same date, as well as the decree about exercising notarial duties of 1 April, the statute on the introduction of a *numerus clausus* into the educational system of 15 April, and the like.

A report on the situation of the Jewish population in Silesia was delivered to the League by the Irish delegate, Sean Lester. Bernheim's case, presented against the background of new discriminatory statues applied by the Third Reich, led him to draw the conclusion that the Acts infringed upon the provisions of the third part of the Convention by 'unequal treatment of the Jewish population'. Lester emphasised that the discriminating statutes should not be applied in that part of Silesia that was covered by the Convention of 1922. Arguments put forward during the debates by the German delegate, von Keller, were unconvincing and were rejected. During the debates of 26 May and 6 June, von Keller had to give assurances that the Reich legislation would not break international commitments, and that the Reich government would honour those commitments in the third part of the Geneva Convention. Von Keller declared that offences against the Convention had been taking place until then due to the application of the statutes by the German administrative authorities, and that the damage they had caused would be compensated for. The Council of the League declared von Keller's declaration to be satisfactory, and Bernheim's case was transmitted to the President of the Mixed Commission, Felix Calonder, for final resolution.[9] Bernheim was awarded damages on account of his unfounded dismissal from the store. The consequences of the affirmative decision by the League were of much greater significance to the Jewish population of *Regierungsbezirk* Oppeln. In the part of Silesia coming under the Geneva Convention, the Jewish population was recognised as a minority and protected by the minority statute. Only Jews of non–German citizenship were not granted the status of minority members.

Owing to the debates held in the League of Nations in May and June 1933, the German government resolved against application of its racial legislation in Silesia (*Regierungsbezirk* Oppeln). Statutes including the 'Aryan paragraph' were suspended in Silesia with the decree of 22 July 1933 signed by the Prussian Deputy Minister of Justice, Dr Roland Freisler. The decree stated that statutes and orders regarding special treatment for Jews were not applicable in the post-plebiscite area of Upper Silesia on account of the valid German–Polish Convention of 15 May 1922.[10] A few days later, on 29 July, the Prussian Minister of the Interior issued a similar decree stating that 'statute regulations and administrative ordinances of the National Socialist state, providing for special treatment of non-Aryan persons, are inapplicable to inhabitants of the plebiscite area of Upper Silesia'. As it turned out, however, in the circumstances created by the Nazi government in the part of Silesia coming under the German–Polish Convention of 1922, it was not easy to repeal provisions laid down in anti-Jewish legislation. On 7 August two representatives of the Jewish minority, Artur Kochmann and Georg Weissmann, intervened personally with the Minister of

Justice in Berlin. During their discussion they called his attention to
the announced NSDAP boycott of Jewish lawyers and doctors,
which was inconsistent with the Justice Minister's decree of
22 July.[11] In a letter of 16 August addressed to the Minister, thirteen
Jewish lawyers from Upper Silesia also expressed their anxiety
about application of this decree. The lawyers' intervention met
strong opposition from the president of *Oberlandesgericht* Breslau,
who argued that 43 per cent of all the lawyers from Oppeln,
Beuthen and Gleiwitz were Jews, and that in *Landesgericht* Breslau
they even made up 62 per cent. Hence, in his region he advocated
pensioning off lawyers, judges and notaries in accordance with the
statute of 7 April 1933.

Early in September 1933 representatives of the *Synagogenverband
der Provinz Oberschlesien* informed the *Auswärtiges Amt* in Berlin of
their intention to submit petitions to the Council of the League of
Nations regarding the infringement by Germany of the Convention's provisions for minority protection. Undoubtedly to prevent
the submission of these petitions, the State Secretary in the Prussian
Ministry of the Interior, Dr Ludwig Grauert, met the representatives of the *Synagogenverband*, Weissmann, Kochmann and Lustig,
on 19 September in Gleiwitz. Grauert had to listen to a list of
complaints about the slowness of German officials in reinstating
Jewish judges on forced leave, about unceasing boycotts and about
anti-Jewish propaganda undertaken even by administrative authorities. It was finally decided that the Jews would withdraw the
petitions in Geneva and that Secretary Grauert would intervene
immediately with the German authorities involved.

The protest of the *Synagogenverband* representatives, well-
founded in legal argumentation, brought about a relatively correct
enforcement of the third part of the Geneva Convention provisions
in relation to the Jewish population. The *Oberpräsident* of Oppeln
province, in the columns of the local official gazette (*Amtsblatt der
Regierung Oppeln*), reminded the administrative authorities that 'all
the statutes issued after 1 April 1933 as well as future statutes and
decrees, if comprising special provisions concerning persons of
non-Aryan descent', did not apply in the plebiscite area of Upper
Silesia.[12] The regulation that statutes discriminating against Jews
would also not take effect in future was of great significance. Thus,
the Nuremberg legislation of 15 September 1935 establishing the
Reich Citizenship (*Reichsbürgergesetz*) and Protection of German
Blood Laws (*Blutschutzgesetz*) and their executive regulations were
not enforced in the plebiscite area of *Regierungsbezirk* Oppeln.

It is true that day after day there were cases of violations of the

1922 Convention's provisions for minority protection. The *Syna-gogenverband der Provinz Oberschlesien* reacted to them immediately. In his publication prepared in Tel-Aviv in 1940 the indefatigable Georg Weissmann devoted a lot of attention to the significance of 'collective petitions' guaranteed by the Convention.[13] In the atmosphere of the fierce German anti-Jewish campaign, which included boycotts, arrests and other means of obvious terror, the area of Silesia protected by the Convention was regarded as a relatively peaceful one. Non-application of the *numerus clausus* discrimination rules at the Friedrich-Wilhelm–Universität of Breslau to Jews coming from *Regierungsbezirk* Oppeln seemed to confirm this.[14] In the spring of 1934, however, the question of Jewish lawyers was raised again. Although no cases of repression had been reported, they were given no dock briefs at the *Landesgericht* Ratibor. Artur Kochmann called attention to cases of discrimination against Jewish notaries and judges. Discrimination was also initiated by the Nazi government. In July 1935 the *Regierungspräsident* in a report to the Minister of the Interior complained that 'efforts aimed at the suppression of Jewish influences are hindered. We are doing our best to give no occasion for appealing to the competent agencies provided by the Geneva Convention.'[15]

Jewish resistance against the enforcement of the Nazi anti-Semitic legislation turned out to be very effective. The Geneva Convention unquestionably hampered the Nazis' fight against Jews in *Regierungsbezirk* Oppeln. Georg Weissmann was keenly attuned to the benefits of Jewish resistance in Silesia. Owing to protection provided by the Convention thirty-eight Jewish organisations, four Zionist groups and the Zionist Sport Association *Hakoah* were active in July 1938 in *Regierungsbezirk* Oppeln. Moreover, in towns in that part of Silesia such as Beuthen, Gleiwitz, Ratibor and Hindenburg there were eight Masonic lodges or organisations of a similar kind. Owing to the Convention, a few other associations and organisations were founded in four Upper Silesian towns from October 1933 until mid-March 1934.[16]

Jewish minority organisations claimed a 'fair share' of state allocations for religious, educational and charitable purposes. What was unobtainable in other regions of the German Reich at that time was obtained in *Regierungsbezirk* Oppeln under the Geneva Convention. Jewish organisations referring to the Convention and supported by the Swiss President of the 'Mixed Commission', Calonder, made the German government allot 150,000 marks for their purposes. According to Weissmann, 'it was just incredible that this amounted to much more than the state had assigned to communities in the past, rendering it possible to accomplish many educational aims in bringing up the young'.[17] It was possible with the allocation to cover the cost of agricultural courses organised for Jewish young people emigrating to Palestine (*Hachscharah*). Between five and six hundred young people took such courses organised in 1934 and 1935. State allocations rendered it possible in the Falkenberg district to obtain a lease of a farm that became an agricultural centre for young people, the *Lehrgut Ellguth-Steinau*. Data from the *Staatspolizeistelle* Oppeln of July 1937 show that at that time there were two more instruction camps for Jewish youth: *Beth Hechaluz* for fourteen pupils and *Makkabi-Hahair* for thirty Jewish boy scouts, as well as *Kibbuz Jom. Tow.* for thirty-six persons, founded without police permission. Agricultural and vocational instruction of pupils leaving for Palestine was the aim of these centres. In the period of the Convention's validity, Jewish sports organisations and variously oriented political associations could also develop. Although the Nuremberg laws had also been proclaimed in Upper Silesia, they were not applied to Polish and Jewish minorities by decree of the local authorities. The ban on getting married and on Jewish employment to perform housekeeping, as well as regulations about dishonouring the race, were also not applied to members of minorities. Thus mixed marriages could be contracted in the region. The minority status of the Jewish population was valid until 15 July 1937.

When the Convention for the protection of minorities was terminated on that day, Nazi racial legislation henceforth came into effect in the plebiscite area of Upper Silesia. Jews as well as Poles were not minorities any more and were therefore repressed, just as were Jews in other regions of the German Reich. The Jewish population of Upper Silesia, protected as a minority under the Geneva Convention between 1933 and 1937, was subjected to the pogrom of *Kristallnacht* on 9–10 November 1938. Repressive measures adopted after the termination of the Geneva Convention and since November 1938, particularly an intense economic 'aryanisation', drove Jews away from the area. The increased emigration brought about a sudden drop in the number of Jews inhabiting the German portion of Upper Silesia to 3,020 persons by March 1941. Deportations to extermination camps on 16, 20 and 28 May and on 8, 15, 23 and 29 June 1942, and during 1943 doomed the Jewish population of *Regierungsbezirk* Oppeln to annihilation. Artur Kochmann, who rendered a great service in the Jewish struggle for survival, was deported in the last consignment from Gleiwitz. Out of several hundred Jews deported to Auschwitz

death camp, only one German Jew came back to Gleiwitz in
January 1945 after liberation. The others were swallowed up by the
Holocaust.[18]

NOTES

1. K. Pätzold, *Von der Vertreibung zum Genocid. Zu den Ursachen,
   Triebkräften und Bedingungen der antijüdischen Politik des faschistischen
   deutschen Imperialismus*, Berlin, 1980, p. 184; A. Barkai, *Vom Boykott
   zur Entjudung. Der wirtschaftliche Existenzkampf der Juden im Dritten
   Reich*, Frankfurt am Main, 1987, p. 19.
2. F. Ryszka, *Panstwo stanu wyjatkowego*, 3rd edn, Warszawa–Wrocław,
   1985, pp. 207–8.
3. W. Prinz, *Volksgemeinschaft, Volksfeinde, Kassel 1933–1945*, vol. 2,
   Kassel, 1987, p. 177; R. Bessel, *Political Violence and the Rise of Nazism:
   The Storm Troopers in Eastern Germany 1925–1934*, New Haven–London,
   1984, p. 105.
4. Ryszka, *Panstwo stanu wyjatkowego*, p. 242; F. Polomski, *Ustawodawstwo
   rasistowskie III Rzeszy i jego stosowanie na Górnym Slasku*, Katowice, 1970,
   p. 51.
5. F. Celnikier, 'Pojecie Zyda w doktrynie i hitlerowskim ustawodaws-
   twie', *Studia nad faszyzmem i zbrodniami hitlerowskimi*, vol. 9, 1985, pp.
   218–19.
6. R. Weltsch, *Die deutsche Judenfrage. Ein kritischer Rückblick*, Königstein,
   1981, p. 78.
7. *Schlesische Volkszeitung*, no. 251, 27 June 1933.
8. G. Kaeckenbeeck, *The International Experiment of Upper Silesia: A
   Study in the Working of the Upper Silesian Settlement 1922–1933*, London–NY–Toronto, 1942, p. 261.
9. *Journal Officiele*, Société des Nations, 1933, vol. 14, pp. 844, 933. K.
   Jonca, *Polityka narodowosciowa Trzeciej Rzeszy na Slasku Opolskim w
   latach 1933–1940*, Katowice, 1970, pp. 280–1.
10. Wojewodzkie Archiwum Panstwowe (hereafter WAP), Opole, 'Min-
    derheitsamt Oppeln', sign. 380, fo. 24.
11. Geheimes Staatsarchiv – Preussischer Kulturbesitz Berlin – Dahlem,
    Rep. 84c, sign. 1603, fo. 53, Vermerk of 16 August 1933.
12. 'Amts-Blatt der Regierung zu Oppeln für 1934', p. 198.
13. G. Weissmann, 'Die Durchsetzung des jüdischen Minderheitsrechtes
    in Oberschlesien 1933–1937', *Bulletin des Leo Baeck Instituts*, no. 22,
    1963, pp. 157 ff.
14. A. Konieczny, 'Pozbawienie Zydów stopni doktorskich na Uniwer-
    sytecie Wrocławskim w latach 1940–1941', *Acta Universitatis*, Seria
    Prawo XVIII, Wrocław, 1967, pp. 126–7.

15. Jonca, *Polityka*, p. 297.
16. WAP/Wrocław, 'Regierung Oppeln', sig. RO I 1734, fos. 7–13.
17. Weissmann, *Durchsetzung*, p. 174.
18. Zydowski Instytut Historyczny w Polsce-Warszawa/Jewish Historical
    Institute in Poland-Warszawa, Rep, 'Gmina Zydowska w Gliwicach'
    (Jüdische Gemeinde in Gleiwitz), sign. 146; Erich Schlesinger, 'Ge-
    schichte der Jüdischen Gemeinde von 1933 bis 24. Januar 1945'.

6

Between Pacifism and Patriotism – A Protestant Dilemma: The Case of Friedrich Siegmund-Schultze

John S. Conway

Friedrich Siegmund-Schultze is virtually forgotten in Germany today, despite his more than sixty years of public service during the first half of this century; it is safe to say that outside Germany his name is unknown. The noble army of anti-Nazi martyrs, who lost their lives in resistance to Hitler's tyranny, has been extensively praised; but the lesser figures have yet to receive their due acknowledgement. Siegmund-Schultze's notable contributions as a leader in the field of social work, or as one of the early supporters of the ecumenical movement, are occasionally acknowledged as pioneering efforts which have now been superseded.[1] But the neglect of his anti-Nazi activities undoubtedly stems from his vital association with the German peace movement, which has consistently been treated as a lost cause, with its proponents regarded as irrelevant to the mainstream of German history. Yet Siegmund-Schultze deserves greater recognition than he has so far been accorded, both as the most outspoken advocate in the ranks of the German Evangelical Church for the cause of international peace and reconciliation during the inter-war period, and subsequently as a champion of *das andere Deutschland* against the Nazis and their nefarious policies. At the same time his career illustrates a peculiarly German Protestant dilemma – the case of a man who suffered increasingly painful crises of conscience as he tried to reconcile the clash of loyalties between his patriotism and his pacifism, at a time when the Nazi

87

crimes defiled his nation's reputation and all but obliterated the vision of a peaceful Christendom for which he so ardently campaigned.

Friedrich Siegmund-Schultze was born in 1885, the son of a well-established clergyman in the Prussian Evangelical Church. His upbringing was conservative and nationalist, and he retained a life-long attachment to Germany's national achievements and an admiration for its 'high' culture. From his student days, however, he became committed to three significant causes, which were to affect his whole life: a dedication to the social question, an awareness of the opportunity for ecumenical encounters, and a commitment to peacemaking through international friendship and reconciliation. As a pioneer in all three of these endeavours, he became a focal point for those who sought new directions in Germany's social, ecclesiastical and international policies, and vigorously opposed the predominant climates of opinion, even within their own church. During the brief period of the Weimar Republic, real hopes for success brightened his horizons. But the advent to power of the Nazis in 1933, and the rapid implementation of their anti-internationalist, anti-Semitic and anti-pacifist campaigns led to Siegmund-Schultze's becoming one of the first Protestant pastors to suffer persecution at Nazi hands. As early as June 1933 he was expelled to Switzerland, and was unable to return to his homeland for fourteen years. The tragedy of seeing his life's work cut short was compounded by having to watch his nation dragged down into the moral degradation and physical destruction of the Second World War.

The Making of a Pacifist

Siegmund-Schultze's struggle against militarism, self-centred nationalism, and repressive authoritarianism, which formed the basis of his later rejection of Nazism, began with his early dedication to the cause of *Versöhnung*, or reconciliation, between the classes and the nations. At the age of twenty-six, in 1911, he gave up his post in a well-endowed parish in Potsdam in order to establish the first social settlement in the fetid and unchurched slums of east Berlin, where, over the next twenty years, he developed a remarkable system of welfare institutions, caring for the underprivileged and outcasts of society. He gained from this experience a noteworthy sensitivity to the needs of oppressed groups, which led to his early and vigorous response in the spring of 1933, when the Nazis launched their first campaign of persecution against Germany's Jews.

As a young pastor, Siegmund-Schultze was also drawn into the early church-related international peace movement of the pre-1914 years. From his contacts with leading British and American churchmen he caught the vision of a Christian ecumenical pacifism, which called on the churches to renounce the weapons of hatred and militarism, and to unite in service to the needs of the world. Such utopian views were not popular in Germany. Indeed, as Roger Chickering has shown, the leading churchmen of the day treated such ideas with disdain or open hostility.[2] But as one of the founders in 1914 both of the moderate reformist World Alliance of Churches for Promoting International Friendship, and of the more explicitly pacifist Fellowship of Reconciliation, Siegmund-Schultze became a stalwart champion of the pacifist movement in its various branches, which in the following decades was to retain his unbroken, if sometimes exasperated, loyalty. Here, he believed, was preserved that vision of a 'peaceful civilisation in universal goodwill which Christianity has taught mankind to aspire after'.[3]

After 1918, such a new world order seemed a possibility. By binding up the wounds of war and by building new bridges of international reconciliation, Siegmund-Schultze believed, the message of Christianity could again be made credible. During the 1920s he became a leading figure in all ecumenical meetings of churchmen, and sought to arouse support for the new Germany at countless international gatherings organised by the World Alliance and other bodies. The pages of his influential journal *Die Eiche* were devoted to overcoming the legacy of wartime hatreds, and recording the multiple efforts of those seeking to rid the world of war in order to devote themselves to the wider tasks of Christian service. Despite the continued scepticism of leading German theologians, the abolition of war seemed to be the supreme ethical issue of the times.

By the end of the 1920s, however, the rise of dynamic nationalist and racist forces, such as the Nazi Party, made the prospects for a successful propagation of Christian universalism and peace grow steadily dimmer. Attacks on the peace movement were a frequent feature of the Nazi Party's propaganda. The virulent polemics which denounced pacifists as the agents of 'world Jewry', or condemned their efforts to promote international understanding as a betrayal of Germany's national character and interests, left no doubt that the Nazis regarded pacifism along with Marxism and Judaism as one of their main ideological targets. The optimistic

assumption of the peace movement's supporters that the passage of
time would lead to a diminution of past passions and to an increase
in pacifist sympathies proved to be ill-founded and no more than
wishful thinking.

For Siegmund-Schultze, and for the groups of idealistic students
and young pastors he recruited for his social work activities, the
most significant factor arousing his alarm and antagonism came
from his observations of the Nazi Party's activities in the Berlin
slums. Night after night, gangs of Nazi thugs roamed the streets
and alleys, physically attacking their supposed enemies, especially
Jews and Communists, in deliberately staged campaigns of
intimidation 'to uphold German honour and German blood'. This
open cult of violence and racial hatred directly challenged the vision
of social harmony and support of the less privileged to which
Siegmund-Schultze had dedicated so many years' service.

Expulsion from Germany

The subsequent enthusiasm with which the majority of Germans
welcomed Hitler's rise to power in 1933 was a bitter blow to all
segments of the peace movement. The consequences of the Nazi
victory were soon seen. Within a few weeks, German peace organisations were forcibly closed. Prominent leaders were either taken
into custody in concentration camps or forced into exile. For his
part, Siegmund-Schultze was appalled at the readiness with which
his colleagues in the Evangelical Church accepted at face value Nazi
promises of internal renewal and applauded Hitler's programme for
military rearmament. His fears were rapidly confirmed when in
April 1933 the first anti-Semitic laws were issued and a nation-wide
boycott of Jewish businesses organised. The situation of Jewish
shopkeepers and minor civil servants in east Berlin was particularly
precarious, and led hundreds to appeal to Siegmund-Schultze and
his settlement workers for help. With his customary – if, to some,
reckless – energy Siegmund-Schultze publicly denounced these
Nazi measures, and called on the Evangelical Church leaders to
protest against such blatant and unjust discrimination.[4]

To his credit, Siegmund-Schultze was the first leading member
of the German Evangelical Church to recognise that the Nazi
take-over of power would lead to severe repercussions for all the
Jewish people.[5] Unlike most of his colleagues in the leadership of
both church and state, he did not believe that the Nazi anti-Semitic
campaign was merely a tool for mobilising public support by the

use of demagogic agitation. His observations of the Nazis had already alarmed him about their plans to curb 'anti-social activities'. Nor did he share the delusion that such disciplinary measures would lead to a restoration of a stable if authoritarian society. On the other hand, his foresight about the Nazis' ultimate intentions was limited, since he confidently expected that his settlement's activities would be appreciated and supported even under the new regime.

Siegmund-Schultze was dismayed by the damage done to Germany's reputation abroad by the Nazis' brutal and terroristic acts. He was primarily concerned with 'damage control' to offset the numerous protests from his international colleagues in the World Alliance.[6] At the same time, he was equally dismayed that church leaders took no steps at home to condemn publicly such acts of lawlessness and anarchy.[7]

More significant still was the official church reaction to the far-reaching step ordered by Hitler on 7 April with the enactment of the 'Law for the Restoration of the Professional Civil Service', ordering the immediate dismissal of Jews from their posts, which also provided the opportunity for numerous pro-Nazi adherents in the so-called 'German Christian' wing of the Evangelical Church to demand that the same measures be applied to the Church's own ranks. But the response of Church leaders was almost totally passive. They refused to issue any public protests against the anti-Semitic violence or to organise relief measures for its victims. The reasons given showed that the desire to preserve the autonomy of the church's structures far outweighed any feelings of solidarity with fellow Germans of Jewish origin. It was left up to a minority of pastors, later to be forged into the Confessing Church, to oppose these Nazi plans for *Gleichschaltung* in the Church's ranks.

The events of April 1933 reinforced Siegmund-Schultze's conclusion that anti-Semitic violence was central to the Nazi campaign of hatred. He was pessimistic about the likelihood of any protests successfully changing Nazi policy, and came to the remarkably far-sighted realisation that the only practical way to alleviate the situation would be to facilitate the emigration of those involved. At the same time he recognised that such assistance should be undertaken, not merely on a denominational basis, but upon a fully international and inter-faith foundation. As early as May 1933 he therefore sought to mobilise his wide circle of acquaintances in the peace movement and the World Alliance by proposing the creation of an international relief committee which would include representatives of the Catholic Church and the Jewish religious community.[8] Such inter-faith collaboration, he believed, would be necessary to ensure that these religious bodies would arouse their respective constituencies to help and thereby make the governments of the recipient states more agreeable to the proposed relief measures. At the same time, a clear political message would be sent to the new Nazi regime if the world's religious communities combined to express their repugnance at the way German Jews were being treated.

This plan unfortunately came to nothing. The international Protestant, Catholic and Jewish authorities showed a reluctance to collaborate with one another on such a broad venture, while the majority of foreigners believed that, as the problem was engendered in Germany, the solution lay in remedying conditions in that country.[9] And in the circumstances of the Depression, no government was willing to promote fresh immigration projects, even for the most laudable motives.

The decisive blow to the scheme came, however, from Siegmund-Schultze's own fate. In these weeks of May and June 1933 he was increasingly aware that, because of his explicitly pacifist and pro-Jewish sympathies, he was a marked man in the eyes of the Nazi radicals. He had to take the precaution of being escorted home by groups of the young students and workers he recruited for his settlement. But on 21 June, in the wake of a week-long rampage by SA gangs in the neighbouring suburb of Köpenick which cost the lives of many Communists and others, SA storm-troopers attacked the campus of Siegmund-Schultze's children's hospital, the Ulmenhof, and bodily assaulted and arrested him there. He was only rescued through the personal intervention of the head of the Berlin Gestapo, Rudolf Diels. Summoned to Gestapo headquarters two days later, he was accused of having given assistance to no less than ninety-three Jewish families, and presented with an ultimatum: he was to leave the country immediately, or his entire social-work operations would be closed down. On the following day he was escorted to Basle railway station to begin what proved to be fourteen long years of exile.

Saving the Refugees

At first Siegmund-Schultze hoped that his banishment would be brief; but he was eventually forced to recognise that Nazi hostility toward him and the causes he had adopted was implacable. Nevertheless, from his new home in Zürich, Siegmund-Schultze resolved to do what he could to assist the victims of Nazi repression. Hitler's decree of July 1933 making the Nazi Party the sole political entity in the Reich forced thousands of pacifists, liberals, Socialists and Communists to flee Germany. Many found their way to Switzerland for at least temporary refuge, and Zürich became a centre of refugee life and activities. In addition, because of its convenient location, many thousands more Germans, still unresolved about their future, came to Zürich to enquire about the practical consequences if they were obliged to go into exile. A continuous stream of such visitors, particularly those with church connections, came to seek Siegmund-Schultze's advice.[10]

Some of these, such as younger members of the beleaguered Confessing Church, he was able to refer to more influential figures in Swiss Protestant circles, like Alfons Koechlin, the President of the Swiss Protestant Church Council. But increasingly he came to see that the persons most in need of his help were those 'non-Aryan' and nominally Christian Germans who had nowhere to turn to. The majority of these people were baptised Jews who had no connections with Jewish agencies, but had also never been firmly linked to any Christian denomination. Labelled as Jews solely by Nazi fiat, they were regarded by more orthodox Jews as renegades, while at the same time they were not fully accepted by their Christian co-religionists. It was largely left up to the Quakers to organise relief efforts on their behalf. Through his long-standing connections with the Quakers in the peace movement, Siegmund-Schultze was soon engaged in extensive contacts and correspondence, especially with the American Friends Service Committee in the United States, and also with the British Quaker agencies, trying to obtain the necessary affidavits of support which would allow these threatened Germans to emigrate.[11]

The failure or unwillingness of the German churches to support these refugees, and the ineffectiveness of the League of Nations' efforts on their behalf, left the initiative once again to the non-governmental voluntary agencies. But, as Peter Ludlow has shown for the European Protestant organisations,[12] and Haim Genizi for their American counterparts,[13] major obstacles existed to any successful resolution of the problem in view of the numbers of persons involved. Basic among these was the lack of political will on the part of the western democracies, whose policies and lack of initiative were characterised – at least until 1938 – by 'brutal considerations of expediency and political advantage'.[14] These attitudes were compounded by the knowledge that their publics in general were indifferent to the plight of the refugees, Jewish as well as Christian. In addition, however, the difficulties of the situation were aggravated by the short-comings of the refugee organisations. The multiplicity of agencies, their frequent competition for the insufficient amounts of financial support, their rivalries and internal fights, their concentration on divergent limited objectives, and the absence of any efficient centralised international bureaucracy, were all factors which prevented effective co-operation, often leading to overlapping and time-consuming muddle and confusion. And in the international Protestant community, with whose many branches Siegmund-Schultze was so closely involved, there was, in Ludlow's words, 'a structureless incoherence' which led to constant misunderstandings and inadequate co-ordination.

The resulting frustration of this general situation was aggravated by the Nazis' escalating persecution of Germany's Jews with the enactment of the infamous Nuremberg Laws of September 1935. The resulting protests by leading churchmen abroad, such as the Bishop of Chichester, George Bell, against these anti-Semitic policies, stirred up anti-German feeling in the world's churches, and thus inevitably polarised and 'politicised' the issue of refugee assistance. At the same time the sharply increased surveillance of the Confessing Church's activities in Germany through the newly-created Reich Ministry of Church Affairs and the Gestapo made it increasingly unlikely that those churchmen opposed to Nazi policies would dare to raise their voices in protest, let alone be able to organise effective measures to assist their fellow Germans of 'non-Aryan' origins.

Despite these depressing circumstances, Siegmund-Schultze still continued his unflagging efforts to mobilise help for the refugees. His abortive proposal of 1933 for an International Christian Committee for German Refugees was finally resurrected in 1936. But its efforts were singularly disappointing, with exaggerated expectations as to the amount of financial support it could raise and unrealistic schemes for resettling the refugees in rural Latin American countries. In any case, it could only help a tiny fraction of those persons needing assistance. More effective were the efforts made by the churches in Switzerland, particularly in Zürich, to provide immediate relief on the spot, and their example was copied in Britain and Sweden. But it took the dramatic events of 1938 to force the refugee agencies into meaningful collaboration and to arouse public consciousness of the scale of the problem to be faced.

The Approach of War

The German seizure of Austria in March 1938, the incorporation of the Sudetenland six months later, and above all the dreadful events of the *Kristallnacht* of November 1938, made the deliberate course of Nazi militaristic aggression and the brutal terrorisation of their opponents unmistakably clear. Siegmund-Schultze, like other leaders of the peace movement, was appalled by the prospect of the world being once again engulfed by war and racial hatred. No less disillusioning was the evident fact that many of their sometime supporters in the struggle to secure disarmament, inter-state arbitration and international brotherhood were deserting the cause. Sympathy for the pacifist programme dissipated as more realistic measures to halt the rise of Germany's outright and flagrant aggressions seemed to be required, The fortunes of such groups as the World Alliance dwindled rapidly. As Siegmund-Schultze wrote to his American colleague, Henry Atkinson, at the end of 1938: 'The past year has been a torture for me. . . . After all the mistakes of the last year I have not much hope for the World Alliance. I do my duty as a soldier of an army which is soon to die.'[15] But characteristically it was not the techniques, and still less the objectives, of the peace movement which he felt were at fault. Rather he placed the blame on the timidity of its leaders, who seemed to him to have resigned their calling to be a challenging voice against the prevalent acceptance of nationalism and even of armed conflict. By 1939 only a minority of dedicated pacifists remained to raise their voices against the futility and waste of another war.

These gloomy developments only heightened Siegmund-Schultze's personal predicament. Increasingly burdened by the evidence of the vexatious intimidations imposed on the refugees or would-be refugees who daily consulted him by mail or in person, his feelings of moral outrage were compounded by his awareness that any public denunciation on his part would endanger not only the cause but also his friends in Germany. He was compelled to adopt an unwelcome, and indeed agonising, self-denying ordinance of silence, particularly at such large-scale ecumenical gatherings as those of Oxford and Edinburgh in 1937, where the anti-German tone of the discussions and resolutions was galling to his patriotism.

His own personal safety was also endangered. In 1937 he returned unobtrusively to Germany, hoping to give advice to the proposed delegates to Oxford, but had to cut short his stay when warned that the Gestapo was on his heels. In the following year he was placed under surveillance by Gestapo agents,[16] and almost fell into their hands when he arrived in Vienna from Warsaw on the very morning of the *Anschluß*, in March 1938. Later in the same year, he was denounced for some unguarded remarks to a theological gathering in Athens, which resulted in the institution of proceedings for his *Ausbürgerung* or revocation of his German citizenship. In the end this came to nothing, because of the dilatory handling of his case by more sympathetic members of the German consulate in Zürich.[17] But the constant strain of knowing that his position was so vulnerable was never removed.

The onset of the Second World War was a profoundly depressing event, especially as Siegmund-Schultze could predict from his own experiences the untold sufferings it would involve. The realisation that nationalism was still far more powerful a source of loyalty than the dream of an international Christian community was hurtful enough. Even more painful for Siegmund-Schultze and other Germans forced into exile was the evidence that the majority of their fellow-countrymen apparently endorsed Hitler's aggressions with enthusiasm. The conflict of loyalties these feelings induced, and the increased isolation he experienced as neutral Switzerland was horrified at the news of the Nazi-inflicted bloodshed and misery, could only in part be relieved by redoubled efforts to assist the flow of refugees,[18] or by closer links with the Fellowship of Reconciliation, for whose Christian pacifist idealism Siegmund-Schultze had so much sympathy and for which he became the European 'adviser' for the duration of the war.

Yet, like other notable pacifists in exile such as Ludwig Quidde, the former head of the secular German peace movement, Siegmund-Schultze was too loyal a German to abandon his hopes for a better future for his country, and still believed that, one day, Germany could again play an honourable role in upholding the ideal of a world without war and subsume its nationalist past in a new vision of European federalism. Like Quidde he remained staunchly German at heart, and refused to accept the totally pejorative views of Germany and its history which prevailed abroad during the Second World War. His life-style was thoroughly German, his personality still Prussian. After a lifetime of belonging to the German establishment, he retained his belief in the orderly use of the 'proper' channels, and sought to maintain 'correct' relations with the German authorities in Switzerland throughout his years of exile. He was no rebel, still less a conspirator.[19] And yet, his revulsion against the whole Nazi ideology and practice, and his fear that a Nazi victory would mean the end of the kind of

Christian civilisation for which he had so long striven, forbade him
to abandon the struggle in despair.

In 1939, most churchmen in all countries who had participated in
or sympathised with the peace movement were obliged to undergo
a painful rethinking of their views. Unable to ignore the ties of
nationalism, they nevertheless resolved to avoid the mistakes made
in the First World War, when the mutually exclusive claims that
God was on their side had done so much to discredit Christianity
altogether. Instead, already in April 1939 as the danger of war
loomed the leaders of the newly-established World Council of
Churches (in process of formation) had issued guidelines on 'The
Church as an ecumenical community in time of war', which called
for the maintenance of fraternal relations among the churches of the
belligerents, counter-action against the hatred engendered by
propaganda, and the pursuit of the goal of a lasting and just peace.[20]
Such suggestions represented a notable consensus of Christian
opinion, but were inevitably disappointing to more radical pacifists
like Siegmund-Schultze, who believed that the Churches' influence
should first be mobilised to prevent war taking place at all, or then,
if it did break out, to bring the fighting to a close as quickly as
possible.

Understandably, he supported the initiative taken in October
1939 in the name of the World Alliance by Bishop Berggrav of
Oslo in neutral Norway to try to find a basis for the cessation of
hostilities.[21] But in London, both church and government leaders,
while welcoming the World Alliance's step, refused to countenance
any peace-feelers which could leave Hitler's aggression uncon-
demned or result in the intolerable subjugation of eastern and
central Europe to Nazi and Soviet totalitarian rule. In Germany, the
majority of churchmen openly rejoiced in Hitler's conquest of
Poland and anticipated ultimate victory. The opposition Confessing Church was too intimidated by the Gestapo to dare risk not
giving its support, lest further doubt be cast on its patriotism.[22]
This first attempt to fulfil the Church's mission to seek peace
proved to be a disastrous failure.

The Nazis' stunning victories of 1940 still further reduced the
possibility of successful peace initiatives. Many anti-Nazi exiles
now fled from Switzerland to safer havens. But Siegmund-
Schultze, despite pressing invitations from his American contacts
to cross the Atlantic for the war's duration, refused to follow them.
Writing to Nevin Sayre, the American President of the Fellowship
of Reconciliation, in a deeply pessimistic mood in June 1940, he
saw little hope for the future.[23] But by April 1941 he could strike a

more positive note, and referred to his growing circle of contacts, and particularly to visitors from Germany.[24]

Contacts with the German Resistance

Among the unannounced visitors from Germany were not only refugees or would-be refugees seeking to escape from Nazi clutches. There were also clandestine emissaries of the German resistance movement wanting to make use of Siegmund-Schultze's expertise in furthering their plans for the overthrow of Hitler and his nefarious regime. For obvious security reasons Siegmund-Schultze kept no written records of these encounters, so that it is impossible to describe with accuracy the extent and range of his participation. But from his later recollections the main outlines are clear.[25]

Siegmund-Schultze had long been acquainted with the leaders of the conservative resistance movement, in particular Carl Goerdeler, the former mayor of Leipzig, General Beck, the former Army Chief of Staff, and several leading industrialists. Already before war broke out his home in Zürich, according to the noted historian of this Resistance group, 'was a port of call for many emigrants and a post office for Opposition messages; he was kept regularly informed of the situation in Germany by representatives of the Bosch firm' of Stuttgart.[26] He himself readily agreed to make use of his excellent connections with leading foreign churchmen, including those in Britain, and his reputation as an experienced go-between was held to be of great potential value in the dark and desperate days of 1940 and 1941 when Hitler's military victories seemed to presage the triumph of the Third Reich. Furthermore, it is probable that Goerdeler sought his advice on the formulation of future social policies for a post-war Germany.

As is now well-established, from the outbreak of the war the leaders of the German resistance recognised that a *coup d'état* against Hitler would only succeed if they could promise the German people an immediate end to hostilities. But this would depend on whether their enemies, in particular Britain, would be ready to initiate negotiations for a moderate peace with any new non-Nazi German government. In order to overcome the refusal of the Army leadership to engage in such highly treasonous activity the resistance leaders needed to have these assurances in advance of any planned coup. Hence 'the innumerable attempts by members of the opposition to gain contact with Britain'[27] with a variety of rather imprecise plans, all designed to bring the war to an end. But Winston Churchill's appointment as Prime Minister in May 1940, with his resolute determination to carry on the war until the Nazi regime and German militarism were eradicated, led to his prohibition of all negotiations with the enemy and his refusal to entertain any such peace initiatives.[28]

Nevertheless, the German opposition still hoped for a positive British response. In the spring of 1941 its representatives approached Siegmund-Schultze, asking him to send a new proposal for peace terms to the British Government through his church contacts. He was sceptical of success. Not only was Churchill's opposition known, but also the credibility of any attempt he might make would depend on his knowing that it had support in the highest German military circles. But in May 1941 he was given a statement of peace proposals which carried the initial 'B', allegedly indicating approval by the Commander-in-Chief, Brauchitsch.[29] In the same week, the news broke of the dramatic flight to Scotland of Hitler's deputy, Rudolf Hess, presumably to outline his own peace terms. The moment therefore seemed propitious to forward to Britain Goerdeler's latest proposals for peace, and at the same time to call for a British-led appeal to the German people to overthrow the Nazi regime before it was too late.

Siegmund-Schultze chose first to take up the latter suggestion. On 24 May he wrote to William Temple, the Archbishop of York, whose voice he presumed would be listened to by the British Government, as follows:

Your Grace, dear Brother in Christ,
I have come to the conclusion that this is the right moment for an appeal to the German people which should be sent out at once by air to as many parts of Germany as might be possible. . . . There is today in Germany on one hand a great mystery about the disappearing of Rudolf Hess; there is on the other hand a great excitement about the immense preparations which are being made for a war at the eastern front. After careful consideration with friends I have come to the conclusion that the enclosed text, from the German point of view, would be a means of preparing the way for freedom and peace in Germany. I hope very much that on your advice an action of the British government can be arranged.[30]

Speed was essential. Because of the highly controversial character of his message, and because he was aware that 'every letter and telegram sent from Switzerland to England becomes known to others', he could not use regular open channels. He therefore decided to go directly to the British Legation in Berne, asking for his letter to be transmitted at once by diplomatic cipher.

This whole scheme, however, came to nothing, as the British officials in Berne were under strict orders not to encourage any such 'peace moves'. The following day Siegmund–Schultze sent Temple an open telegram:

COULD ZÜRICH BRITISH CONSULATE RECEIVE ADVICE BY FOREIGN OFFICE TO TRANSMIT URGENT MESSAGE TO YOUR GRACE. SIEGMUND-SCHULTZE.

Archbishop Temple, although completely unaware of what was involved, nevertheless took the matter seriously enough to approach the Foreign Office on 4 June, and was told that 'although this must be considered a rather unusual procedure', permission would be granted. In promising to forward the text of the message to the Archbishop, the Foreign Office nevertheless requested him to ensure 'that it was not made public in any way or any use made of it'.

In Zürich Siegmund–Schultze waited impatiently for an answer. However, none came for several weeks. After the Nazi invasion of Russia on 22 June 1941 the project for appealing directly to the German people seemed overtaken by events. But the escalation of the bloodshed made it all the more imperative to find ways to bring hostilities to a stop. At the end of July, prompted by a further request from the resistance leaders in Germany, Siegmund–Schultze resolved to try again. On 4 August he heard that the Legation was now prepared to co-operate, and on the following day he handed over a memorandum on peace aims, dated 24 July, which was addressed to Archbishop Temple, but clearly intended to be read by the British Government.

Siegmund–Schultze's personal position was made clear in his covering letter:

Some weeks ago I was asked by German friends to send a certain suggestion to the British Government. . . . I am no politician but I feel constrained in conscience to follow the appeal of these men, to be a mediator of their attempt to restore justice and peace as far as Germany is concerned. As I have stood for justice and goodwill through the First World War, and since have had to leave my country because of my protest against the violence of Nazism, I think I may hope to be regarded as a sincere messenger in this matter. And I can witness about the leading men of the group for which I am speaking that they have always stood against Nazism, and hold their opinions unchanged during the two years of the war. They feel the deep concern to save Christian civilisation from the disaster which is menacing it, if no peace of justice and goodwill can be freely negotiated.

He asked, if possible, for a reply by the second half of August, as

> it would be of great importance for the responsible men to have evidence that the British government still feels bound by its former declaration to negotiate about peace terms with a German government which overthrows the National Socialist regime.[31]

When Siegmund-Schultze's proposal reached London by diplomatic courier on 27 August, it received close attention at the highest level. The Foreign Secretary consulted the Prime Minister about this and two simultaneous schemes. Churchill's reply, on 9 September, was bluntly negative:

> Prime Minister's Personal Minute
> Most Secret. In a locked box.
>
> Foreign Secretary:
>
> I am sure we should not depart from our policy of absolute silence. Nothing would be more disturbing to our friends in the United States or more damaging with our new ally, Russia, than the suggestion that we were entertaining such ideas. I am absolutely opposed to the slightest contact. If you do not agree, the matter should be raised before the War Cabinet sitting alone.

Nevertheless, on 20 September – possibly through some misunderstanding – the text of Siegmund-Schultze's letter and the peace proposal were forwarded to the Archbishop of York. On 26 September he sent a reply which he asked the Foreign Office to forward to Switzerland, while at the same time suggesting that, if the British Minister were to see Siegmund-Schultze,

> it would be kind and wise so to arrange the meeting that it had the air of a coincidence. Siegmund-Schultze is very carefully watched; he is . . . constantly under observation by Nazis who might cause trouble if he were seen going to the British Legation. . . . In him personally, as a very sincere friend of Great Britain, I should have great confidence. I am bound to say that I should not have equal confidence in his judgement of the reliability of persons with whom he was dealing. I have previous evidence of his being misled by a perfectly genuine enthusiasm.

In the event, alerted by the Prime Minister's opposition, the Foreign Office refused to transmit any reply. The ensuing silence forced Siegmund-Schultze to realise that his efforts had been in vain. This British refusal to offer any help to the anti-Nazi opposition, he concluded, was yet another instance of the British Government's apparently entrenched anti-German hatred, of which he had so much experience, and which now, once again, dashed his hopes for a moderate and just peace settlement.

Despite this rebuff, German resistance leaders made further attempts to use church contacts as go-betweens in promoting peace initiatives with the British Government. The well-known meeting between Bishop Bell and Dietrich Bonhoeffer in Sweden in May 1942[32] was followed very shortly by a similar approach by the General Secretary of the World Council of Churches, Visser't Hooft, to another member of the British Cabinet, Sir Stafford Cripps.[33] Neither was successful. Their failure showed not only that the British Government refused to consider abating its policy of requiring complete defeat, but equally that the interventions of the churches in pursuit of a moderate peace settlement were increasingly unwanted and even counter-productive.

Characteristically, rather than admit the unrealistic nature of the German resistance's plans, or acknowledge the churches' obvious inability to sway events, Siegmund-Schultze blamed British intransigence for this failure. As he bitterly wrote to Nevin Sayre in April 1942:

> I do not like to write about the peace efforts which I had to try in connection with others last year. They have been in vain because of the unwillingness of the British to do anything as long as the military success is so much on the other side. As they would not like to make peace even with an opposition against National Socialism, it seems to be necessary to fight to the bitter end. The losses and the destruction will become harder during this summer. And a part of the life and culture on the continent will be extinguished, as Great Britain will not have the power to prevent the Soviets from their plans for vengeance and one-sided reconstruction after the war.[34]

The global extension of hostilities in 1942, the tightening grip of Nazi military power over the whole of occupied Europe, and the proclamation by the Allies at the Casablanca Conference of their demand for unconditional Axis surrender, destroyed the chances of achieving any mediated peace. The impotence and frustrations of the pacifist movement were reflected in a letter Siegmund-Schultze wrote to his long-term colleague in Britain, Lord Willoughby Dickinson, in July 1942:

I am without illusions regarding a peace which could be in conformity with our wishes. I have made my attempts at first with my German friends, afterwards on the ground of such plans and promises also with British friends; but I have found that there was no willingness to come to any understanding or agreement even with the opponents of National Socialism before there will be reached a full military victory. So we really cannot do anything which could restrain the catastrophe which is hanging over Europe.[35]

Fighting against Hatred

Like other pacifists, and indeed like other church leaders such as Pope Pius XII, Siegmund-Schultze was appalled by the escalation of hostilities through the unrestricted bombing of German cities and towns, regardless of whether they contained significant military or industrial targets. Already in 1941 he had thought of launching an international appeal calling for the protection of civilian lives, but the moment never seemed opportune to issue it. The churches of the warring nations refused to support it.[36] But his justification was percipient and far-sighted:

In my view the bombing of civilian populations does, in fact, more damage to those who carry it out than to those who suffer it. . . . The moral consequences of such bombing . . . will later, in more peaceful times, whenever these come again, leave deep traces in people's lives. . . . I am completely convinced that we, who are called on to fight against hatred, must protest against the wartime evil which has clearly done so much to inculcate hatred. At the moment only a few recognise the danger of such actions. But after the war we shall again see policies condemned in wordy resolutions which today the churches have accepted as normal or at least unavoidable. The view which we expressed in the inter-war period at ecumenical gatherings, that war itself is incompatible with the spirit and practice of Christ, seems today to be almost forgotten in Christian circles.[37]

As more and more German cities came under attack, Siegmund-Schultze's fears for the future only increased. Allied policy seemed to be determined by a desire for revenge or punishment of the entire German population without discrimination. He was therefore encouraged to hear of Bishop Bell's courageous, if highly unpopular, speeches in the House of Lords in 1943 criticising such wanton destruction and calling for a clear distinction in war aims between the Nazi rulers and the mass of Germans they had misled. In March 1943 Siegmund-Schultze sent the Bishop an open telegram of support, assuring him that anti-Nazi opposition circles were gratified by this evidence that not all Britons had succumbed to wartime anti-German hysteria.[38]

Such signs of peacemaking were few. Siegmund-Schultze had to console himself by concentrating on his work for the refugees within the borders of Switzerland, by listening every evening at 9 p.m. to the BBC news, by compiling large files of clippings from the *Völkischer Beobachter* and the Swiss newspapers, and by noting carefully every change in the balance of military forces.

By the start of 1943, the turn of the tide in the war with Germany's defeats at Stalingrad and Alamein raised new fears. Would the eventual overthrow of Nazi tyranny not expose Europe to an equally dreadful Soviet domination? Would the victorious Allies be tempted to impose a still harsher peace than Versailles on the defeated Germans? What contribution could the churches, and especially the Christian pacifist organisations, hope to make in the reconstruction and the re-Christianisation of Europe? The structure of the World Alliance and its national councils had been destroyed, and its work sabotaged by the inadequacy of the Geneva secretary. The Fellowship of Reconciliation was too small and insignificant to be more than a lonely voice for peace. The initiative in church affairs seemed to have been handed over to the World Council of Churches, whose Dutch General Secretary, Visser't Hooft, showed an increasing reluctance to listen to the memoranda and suggestions which Siegmund-Schultze, as one of the pioneers of the ecumenical movement, showered upon him with German thoroughness. Above all, who would be left in Germany to carry out the ideals of Christian service and pacifism he had so long upheld? The news of the imprisonment and later execution at the hands of the Gestapo of so many of his close associates – Elisabeth von Thadden, Father Max Metzger, Dietrich Bonhoeffer, Carl Goerdeler, General Beck and others associated with the abortive 20 July 1944 plot – left him profoundly saddened. The thought of what Germany had lost was almost unbearable. And the knowledge of what had happened to the other victims of Nazi racism and persecution, especially the Jews, was, he reported to the USA, a 'constant torture for me during the last months'.[39]

By 1944, anguish over the casualties and damage inflicted on Germany combined with uncertainty about the future. Possibly the need to reinforce the survivors led Siegmund-Schultze to make common cause with the more radical left-wing 'Free Germany' movement in Switzerland.[40] This group of pronounced anti-Nazis had been suppressed by the Swiss authorities for its alleged pro-

Communist sympathies, but still operated undercover, and now recognised the need for a broader base of support. After the failure of the July plot, its leaders tried to recruit representatives of both the Evangelical and Catholic churches to join in a common front. At the end of the month a new executive committee was established, with Siegmund-Schultze representing the Evangelical Church. But this arrangement was short-lived. Siegmund-Schultze soon discovered that the 'Free Germany' organisation was too Marxist to be a fitting partner for his hopes of a renewed Christian pacifism, while in turn the 'Free Germany' leaders were suspicious of his links to the German establishment, and were relieved when his place was taken by the less threatening figure of Karl Barth's assistant, Charlotte von Kirschbaum.[41]

But all such plans and proposals for the future of Germany once Nazism was overthrown proved illusory when the Allies made it clear that no successor government would be allowed, but that the whole country would be occupied. Siegmund-Schultze's discussions with 'Free Germany', as well as his extensive contacts with other exiled politicians such as the former Reich Chancellor Joseph Wirth and the Socialist Wilhelm Hoegner, later the Premier of Bavaria, were building castles in the air. None of them could predict their conquerors' future intentions nor gauge what the likely response would be to military occupation. But the prospects were minimal that any settlement imposed by military force would be congruent with the pacifists' hopes. And it was clear that their services in the task of reconstruction would not – or at least not yet – be required.

Siegmund-Schultze's relief in May 1945 that hostilities in Europe had at last ceased was offset by the realisation of the terrifying devastation which had been caused. The flood of reports in the world's press revealing the awful details of Nazi atrocities in the concentration camps showed how deep the German moral degradation had become. The Christian response to this disastrous situation, as expressed in a remarkable pamphlet drawn up by Siegmund-Schultze and others in June 1945, was first and foremost to call for an acknowledgement of German guilt.[42] 'The wrath of God has been brought down upon Germany', the statement declared, because

> the German people has yielded to the spirit of violence to such a degree that incalculable harm has been caused to its own and other nations. [Whatever may have been the mistaken policies of other nations] these cannot exonerate the German people from having given

allegiance to a false leader and having yielded to the deceitful mirage of German world-domination. . . . The church herself raised her voice too late and too timidly against the arbitrary rule of the National Socialists, and many Christians have denied Jesus for the sake of a false leader. . . . We expect from the church . . . a word of penitence. . . . Christianity must, far more than hitherto, be the messenger of peace. We believe that it was one of the causes of our downfall that German Christianity failed just here. We confess our fault, our grievous fault.

The similarity is striking between these sentiments and those taken up by Pastor Martin Niemöller and other surviving leaders of the Confessing Church and incorporated in the famous Stuttgart Declaration of Guilt in October 1945.[43] Together they sought to enable the church to take up the challenges it faced and to render its service in the renewal of the German people.

For his part, Siegmund-Schultze shared the same ambition. If events had proved him right about Nazi evil, he now looked forward to the end of his exile. Writing to Bishop Bell in July 1945, he asked for help in getting the necessary permits to get back to Germany.[44] But it was not to be. Bureaucratic delays by the military occupation placed barriers in the way of the emigrants' return. In east Berlin, the Soviet military administration and later the Communist government of the German Democratic Republic made it clear that Siegmund-Schultze's kind of social-work ministry was unwanted. And when he finally did return to West Germany in 1947 he found, like many other exiles, that he faced suspicion and resentment from those who had stayed behind. The widespread refusal of many Germans to face the facts of their more or less willing participation in the Nazi terror was accompanied by an unwillingness to admit that the exiles had more correctly judged the political and spiritual crisis of the times. Opposition to Nazism, whether at home or abroad, still held the taint of national treachery.

Even more dismaying were the increasing rivalries between East and West, the consequent division of Germany and the eventual alignment of each half of the country into competing military alliances, all of which doomed the pacifists' aspirations for reconciliation and peace among the nations. In the climate of the 1950s, Siegmund-Schultze and his small band of followers were again relegated to being largely-ignored prophets in the wilderness. The peace movement's post-war campaign for a disarmed, neutral and reunited Germany had failed – seemingly irrevocably. In his final years, Siegmund-Schultze was a disillusioned and somewhat embittered man. He died in 1969.

Conclusion

As one who opposed the pernicious impact of militarism, totalitarianism and racism from the beginning, Siegmund-Schultze was forced to pay the penalty of exile in 1933, and thus became a bystander as the tide of Nazism engulfed Germany and then most of Europe. But throughout he maintained his belief – most fervently expressed in his book *Die Überwindung des Hasses*, published in 1946 – that there was an alternative destiny for Germany. The frustration he endured and the failure to see his hopes realised was not just Siegmund-Schultze's personal tragedy; it was rather the tragedy of the whole nation whose fortunes he had so closely monitored and to which he remained so closely committed. His outspoken criticisms of the policies of his country and his church often made him an uncomfortable crusader tirelessly proclaiming the truth as he saw it, which revealed at best a lack of caution and at worst a moralising self-righteousness. To his critics, his ideals seemed unrealistic, his self-importance exaggerated, and his attempts to reconcile his patriotism and his pacifism merely the product of wishful thinking. But in a larger perspective Siegmund-Schultze deserves his place in the ranks of those who valiantly opposed the evils of Nazism, and assisted its victims, both Jews and Gentiles, during the twelve cruel years of totalitarian rule.

APPENDIX 1: TRANSLATION OF PROPOSED TEXT OF A LEAFLET APPEAL TO THE GERMAN PEOPLE, MAY 1941:

Appeal to the German People:

Rudolf Hess has flown to Scotland because he could not stand the present situation any longer. He recognised that not only Germany or England, but all Europe, is going to be ruined if this struggle is continued to a bitter end. He is neither sick nor mad, but – like us all – shocked to the core by the fate which threatens to be fulfilled.

But Hitler, who has seen that he cannot overthrow the British Empire in one blow, is now turning south and east in order to carry out his unlimited plans for world domination at the cost of the blood of the German people. Enormous forces are being thrown at the eastern border of the Reich, and more and more peoples are being drawn into the war. The untold misery of millions will be the result.

At this moment the British Government restates its readiness to effect a peace with the German people based on reconciliation and justice. If the German people rejects the plans for world conquest and the brutal system of National Socialism, and gives itself a government which respects the right of self-determination of all people, and holds the present world as sacred, then tomorrow the building of a new world can begin in which all peoples will have the same rights and possibilities.

Let us all in this last fateful hour seek the salvation of mankind!

APPENDIX 2: TRANSLATION OF THE PEACE PROPOSALS FORWARDED BY SIEGMUND-SCHULTZE TO BRITAIN, AUGUST 1941:

A group of German leaders, from many different walks of life, is prepared to take over the responsibility for forming a government, which, at the appropriate time will seek confirmation through a free expression of the will of the German people. All connected steps will exclusively have an inner-German character. These authoritative persons in this regard wish to obtain clarity whether, as soon as a new government opposed to National Socialism has been established, earlier assurances of the British Government regarding peace negotiations can be taken up.

The following peace aims, as adopted by the German group, are suggested as the basis for negotiations:

1. The restoration of the full sovereignty of the neutral countries occupied during the war by the belligerent nations.

2. The confirmation of the pre-war annexations [*Anschlüße*] of Austria, the Sudetenland, and Memel by Germany.

3. The restoration of the German borders of 1914 in respect to Belgium, France and Poland.

4. The settlement of the European land frontiers on the basis of the right of national self-determination at a Peace Conference of all states.

5. The return of the German colonies or of territories of equal value, and at the same time the creation of an international system of mandates for all colonies.

6. No war reparations, but a united reconstruction.

7. Reduction of customs barriers.

8. The appointment of a comprehensive world economic council.

9. International control of currencies.

10. The re-establishment of the work of the International Labour Office.
11. The restoration of Law, and the punishment of the guilty.
12. The extension of the International Court of Justice's jurisdiction.
13. The establishment of a conference of the European states to meet regularly, and corresponding meetings on a regional basis.
14. Universal limitation and reduction of armaments.
15. International control of arms and the armament industries.

NOTES

1. His voluminous papers, covering all aspects of his public career, were carefully preserved, and were later, during his retirement, arranged as an 'Ecumenical Archive', in alphabetical sections according to theme, along with a printed guide. In 1974 they were transferred to the Evangelical Church's Central Archive (Evangelisches Zentralarchiv, hereafter EZA) in Berlin, and can be found there under the title EZA 51 and 626. His career is commemorated in two laudatory *Festschriften*: *Lebendige Ökumene*, 1965, and H. Delfs (ed.), *Aktiver Friede*, Soest, 1972. No full biography has been written but three doctoral students are now working on aspects of his career. See also J. S. Conway, 'Friedrich Siegmund-Schultze (1885–1969)', *Evangelische Theologie*, 1983, pp. 221–50, and *Gestalten der Kirchengeschichte*, vol. 10, *Die neueste Zeit*, Stuttgart, 1985, pp. 86–101. For the significance of his social work activities, see A. Weyer, *Kirche in Arbeiterviertel*, Gutersloh, 1971.
2. R. Chickering, *Imperial Germany and a World without War*, Princeton, 1975, especially pp. 196–217.
3. *Report of the Conference held at Constance, August 1914*, London–NY, 1914, p. 45.
4. For the details of these efforts, see EZA 51/H II b and c. On 6 April he announced his intention to devote space in the July issue of *Die Eiche* to comment on the political situation and in particular on the measures taken against the Jews. In fact, such plans were overtaken by events, and the *Eiche* was forced to carry a short notice stating that sudden 'ill-health' had obliged its publisher to withdraw from all his activities.
5. In 1933, he estimated that there were some 750,000 Jewish 'non-Aryans' in Germany, but also that there were at least three times as many non-Jewish 'non-Aryans'. Even if the suggested figure was too large, as later computations have indicated, the danger could not be ignored. See W. Cohn, 'Bearers of a Common Fate? The "Non-Aryan" Christian "Fate-Comrades" of the Paulus-Bund, 1933–1939',

Year Book of the Leo Baeck Institute, vol. 33, 1988, pp. 327 ff, especially Appendix 1: 'The Size of the Partially Jewish Population'.

6. See his correspondence with Elisabeth Rotten, a well-known Quaker activist, then living in Switzerland, in EZA 51/H II b I 1; for his enumeration of protests received from abroad and his discussion of the steps needed to rectify the situation, see EZA 51/D III 1 and 2.

7. For a description of the various reactions in the Protestant churches, see K. Scholder, *Die Kirchen und das Dritte Reich*, vol. 1, Berlin, 1977, pp. 328–43, translated by J. Bowden as *The Churches and the Third Reich*, 2 vols, London–Philadelphia, 1987–8.

8. For his contacts with Jewish leaders in Berlin, such as Leo Baeck, and with Catholics, such as Prälat Wienken, to see what could be done in this critical situation, see EZA 51/H II b I 1 and 2. For a full description of the origins and fate of this proposal, see W. Gerlach, 'Zur Entstehung des "internationalen kirchlichen Hilfskomitees für deutsche Flüchtlinge" 1933–1936', in H. Delfs (ed.), *Aktiver Friede*, p. 35 ff. Also P. Ludlow, 'The Refugee Problem in the 1930s: The Failures and Successes of Protestant Relief Programmes', *English Historical Review*, vol. 90, 1975, pp. 564 ff.

9. The British President of the World Alliance, Dickinson, to Siegmund-Schultze, 24 June 1933, EZA 51/D VII e 2. The absence of any further references to Catholic or Jewish organisations which might be involved makes clear their scepticism about the whole scheme. For Catholic efforts to assist 'non-Aryan' Catholics, see L.-E. Reutter, *Katholische Kirche als Fluchthelfer im Dritten Reich*, Hamburg, 1971, which makes no mention of any approach by Siegmund-Schultze. Similarly, there is no mention of this plan in the biography of Prälat Wienken: M. Höllen, *Heinrich Wienken – der 'unpolitische' Kirchenpolitiker*, Mainz, 1981.

10. For the details, see EZA 51/H II d 1.

11. For his efforts in one particular case, which lasted for several years, but in the end failed, see J. S. Conway, 'Last Letters of the Brandt-Meyer Family from Berlin', *Yad Vashem Studies*, vol. 11, Jerusalem, 1976, pp. 91 ff. See also L. Darton, *An Account of the Work of the Friends Committee for Refugees and Aliens, First Known as the German Emergency Committee of the Society of Friends, 1933–1950*, London, 1954; and C. Carr-Gregg, 'The Working of the German Emergency Fellowship Committee, 1938–1941', in W. D. Rubinstein (ed.), *Jews in the Sixth Continent*, Sydney, 1987, pp. 185 ff. The last surviving member of the British Quaker team, Miss Bertha Bracey, died in February 1989 at the age of 95.

12. See Ludlow, n. 8.

13. See H. Genizi, *American Apathy. The Plight of Christian Refugees from Nazism*, Ramat-Gan, Israel, 1983.

14. J. G. McDonald to James Rosenberg, 18 September 1934, quoted in ibid., p. 49.

15. Siegmund-Schultze to Henry Atkinson, 31 December 1938, EZA 626/PA 12/1.

16. According to his later recollection, this led to a semi-comic incident while visiting Italy, when he confronted his 'shadow' and proffered a list of his engagements in order not to be followed.
17. See the files of the German Foreign Ministry (Politisches Archiv des Auswärtigen Amts), Bonn: Inland II A/B.
18. For the details, see EZA 51/H II c and d. In 1938, he reported, more than 1,600 refugees had contacted him or been referred by other agencies. Memorandum on the activity of the International Secretary of the World Alliance, Dr F. Siegmund-Schultze, during the years 1938 and 1939, EZA 51/D VIII c.
19. In a later note left among his papers, he recorded his refusal to become involved with the wartime activities of Allen Dulles, the head of the American intelligence agency in Switzerland. 'I took the view that as staunch opponents of the Nazi government we were not called to make common cause with Germany's enemies. Above all I steadfastly refused to become involved in any way with activities which had anything to do with espionage.' EZA 626/AK II, 10, 9.
20. The text is printed in German in A. Boyens, *Kirchenkampf und Ökumene 1933–1939*, Munich, 1969, pp. 385–7; see also the important statement by Bishop Bell, 'The Church's Function in War-Time', printed in his book *The Church and Humanity (1939–1946)*, London, 1946.
21. See P. Ludlow, 'Bischof Berggrav zum deutschen Kirchenkampf' in H. Brunotte (ed.), *Zur Geschichte des Kirchenkampfes. Gesammelte Aufsätze II*, Göttingen, 1971, pp. 221–58; also B. Martin, *Friedensinitiativen und Machtpolitik im Zweiten Weltkrieg 1939–1942*, Düsseldorf, 1974, pp. 194 ff.
22. See Siegmund-Schultze to Pastor Henriod, 24 October 1939, EZA 51/D VII m.
23. Siegmund-Schultze to Nevin Sayre, 9 June 1940, EZA 51/H II d 3. See also EZA 51/J VIII a 1.
24. EZA 626/14/8.
25. See particularly Siegmund-Schultze to G. Ritter, 28 March 1954, EZA 626/PA 37/4.
26. G. Ritter, *The German Resistance*, NY, 1958, pp. 157–8, where Siegmund-Schultze is described rather curiously as 'the well-known sociologist'. His home was used in October 1938 for a meeting between Carl Goerdeler and an English contact, the businessman A. P. Young. See A. P. Young, *The X Documents*, London, 1974, p. 111.
27. Ritter, p. 212. For a complete overview of the early peace-feelers, see B. Martin; a more critical view and an evaluation of the British Government's attitudes to peace-feelers, including the one discussed below, is taken by L. Kettenacker, *Das 'Andere Deutschland' im zweiten Weltkrieg*, Stuttgart, 1977, especially pp. 59–60.
28. The British Foreign Office, however, kept track of such efforts. See 'Summary of Principal Peace Feelers, September 1939–March 1941',

Public Record Office (hereafter PRO), FO 371/26542, and 'Summary of Principal Peace Feelers, April 1941–June 1942', in PRO, PREM 4/100/8, both of which are printed in Kettenacker, pp. 164–200.

29. In Ritter's view 'it is a mystery' how Brauchitsch was induced to support Goerdeler's peace proposals at this juncture. See Ritter, *The German Resistance*, p. 213. According to Siegmund-Schultze's later recollection, Brauchitsch was persuaded by the dangerous situation caused by Hitler's decision to attack the Soviet Union.

30. EZA 626/PA 37/4; for British responses, see PRO, FO 371/265568 and 26543; for an English translation of the text of the appeal, see Appendix 1.

31. For an English translation of these proposals, see Appendix 2. They are given in the German edition only of Ritter's book, *Carl Goerdeler und die deutsche Widerstandsbewegung*, DTV edition, Stuttgart, 1954, p. 551.

32. G. Bell, 'The Background of the Hitler Plot', *The Contemporary Review*, vol. 168, 1945; R. C. D. Jasper, *George Bell, Bishop of Chichester*, London, 1967, pp. 266 ff.; E. Bethge, *Dietrich Bonhoeffer. Eine Biographie*, Munich, 1967, pp. 850 ff. (translated, by Eric Mosbacher *et al.*, as *Dietrich Bonhoeffer: Man of Vision, Man of Courage*, NY, 1970); P. Hoffmann, *The History of the German Resistance, 1933–1945*, Cambridge, Mass., 1977, pp. 216 ff.; Ritter, *The German Resistance*, p. 217; H. Rothfels, *The German Opposition to Hitler*, London, 1970, pp. 134 ff.; Kettenacker, *Das 'Andere Deutschland'*, pp. 193–4; H. Ben-Israel, 'Im Widerstreit der Ziele: Die britische Reaktion auf den deutschen Widerstand', in J. Schmädeke and P. Steinbach (eds), *Der Widerstand gegen den Nationalsozialismus*, Munich–Zürich, 1985, pp. 740–2. The refusal of the Foreign Secretary, Eden, to give any assurances to Bishop Bell was entirely in line with the policy of the previous year. Less well known is Eden's resentment at the church's interference, and his antagonism towards Bell in particular, which found its expression in 1944 in his comments: 'I see no reason whatever to encourage this pestilent priest'. PRO, FO 371/39087/C 10028.

33. For the details see, PRO, FO 371/30912; Visser't Hooft, *Memoirs*, London, 1973, pp. 156–8; Kettenacker, *Das 'Andere Deutschland'*, p. 192. See also, P. Hoffmann, 'Peace through Coup d'État', *Central European History*, vol. 19, 1986, pp. 3–44.

34. Siegmund-Schultze to Nevin Sayre, 29 April 1942, EZA 51/J VII b.

35. Siegmund-Schultze to Lord Dickinson, 13 July 1942, EZA 51/D VII c.

36. In March 1942 Siegmund-Schultze wrote to the British ecumenical leader, Joe Oldham, criticising the British Churches' support of such methods of conducting the war, and reminding him of the pacifists' opposition, EZA 626/AK 14/21.

37. Siegmund-Schultze to Alfons Koechlin, Basel, 10 March 1943, EZA 51/L V a 5.

38. The text is printed in E. Bethge and R. C. D. Jasper (eds), *An der Schwelle zum gespaltenen Europa. Der Briefwechsel zwischen George Bell*

und Gerhard Leibholz (1939–1951), Stuttgart, 1974, p. 104; for an excellent analysis of this correspondence, see E.-A. Scharffenorth, 'Die Aufgabe der Kirche in Kriegszeiten. Der Einsatz von George Bell und Gerhard Leibholz für eine konstruktive Deutschlandpolitik Großbritanniens 1941–1943', *Kirchliche Zeitgeschichte*, vol. 1, no. 1, 1988, pp. 94 ff.

39. Siegmund-Schultze to Nevin Sayre, 14 March 1943, EZA 51/J VII b.

40. See K. H. Bergmann, *Die Bewegung 'Freies Deutschland' in der Schweiz 1943–1945*, Munich, 1974.

41. See R. Kobler, *Schattenarbeit. Charlotte von Kirschbaum. Die Theologin an der Seite Karl Barths*, Cologne, 1987, especially pp. 81 ff.

42. 'Aufruf der Arbeitsgemeinschaft evangelischer Deutschen in der Schweiz', Zürich, June, 1945, reprinted as *A New Germany. A Call from Protestant Germans in Switzerland*, International Fellowship of Reconciliation, London, July, 1945.

43. See M. Greschat (ed.), *Die Schuld der Kirche*, Munich, 1982; also J. S. Conway, 'How shall the nations repent? The Stuttgart Declaration of Guilt, October 1945', *Journal of Ecclesiastical History*, vol. 38, 1987, pp. 592–622.

44. Siegmund-Schultze to Bishop Bell, 14 July 1945, EZA 51/D VII o.

7

A Radical Minority: Resistance in the German Protestant Church

Robert P. Ericksen

The Protestant Church in Germany enjoyed a good reputation after the Second World War, based upon its resistance to and persecution by the National Socialist regime. Pastor Martin Niemoeller had earned international sympathy and respect for his imprisonment from 1937 to 1945. Dietrich Bonhoeffer, pastor and theologian, gained posthumous fame as his participation in the Canaris conspiracy and his martyrdom became known. Each of these men had worked for the Confessing Church in the so-called 'Church Struggle' (*Kirchenkampf*), and this struggle seemed to express the natural or even inevitable truth: Christianity and National Socialism did not mix. The one represented immoral, the other moral values.

Recent scholarship suggests that Christianity and National Socialism mixed more easily than first thought. Many Christians greeted the rise of Hitler in 1933 and most approved of his leadership for the next few years, using words like renewal and rebirth to describe this turning point in German history. Even Christians in the Confessing Church often shared this judgement. Although Christian resistance to National Socialism developed, it did so only among a tiny, radical minority. This is especially true if resistance is defined as working toward or at least desiring the overthrow of the regime. Within a broader definition, that is, resisting certain policies of the regime, a larger proportion of the Christian population took part. However, many people within this category also professed their loyalty to and enthusiasm for Adolf Hitler. This leaves a very ambiguous picture of what 'resistance' actually means.[1]

The problem of defining resistance among Christians is only one difficulty among many, which include also the complicated search for evidence. First, those who claim to have been active resisters usually would have operated secretly and tried to avoid leaving evidence that could be used against them. Those who claim to have been 'passive' resisters bequeath us the daunting task of trying to decipher their intentions. These people can tell us, of course, what was in their hearts and minds, but their memories, and motives, may well be influenced by the overwhelming post-war condemnation of National Socialism. It is inevitable that the full story of resistance behaviour will never accurately be known.

A final difficulty involves the feasibility of resistance in a supposedly totalitarian state. Historians of this topic sometimes arouse the objection that they expect too much. Should they look for resistance among Germans and imply criticism if they do not find it? Was resistance possible for most people? Would resisters not simply have been shot or sent to a concentration camp? The concept of 'inner emigration' has been developed to deal with this problem, covering those individuals who disliked the regime but were not blessed with the necessary circumstances or courage to leave or oppose it. However, the churches provide several examples to illustrate the effectiveness of open resistance in Hitler's state. Given the right issue and the right circumstances, people protested, petitioned and demonstrated in the streets against government policies – and they won. Ironically, however, these same people often supported Adolf Hitler and his general policies enthusiastically.

The difficulties of resistance scholarship noted above are not unique to Christians or to church history. Uniqueness lies only in the positive reputation the churches later enjoyed, which risks giving the benefit of the doubt where it is not necessarily deserved. If we are tempted to think Dietrich Bonhoeffer represents the Confessing Church, and the Confessing Church represents the Protestant Church, that is simply wrong. Bonhoeffer had many critics and very few peers. Most contemporaries in the churches judged his behaviour harshly. We must grow suspicious if too many now claim the protection of his umbrella.

The Early Interpretation and its Problems

Assessing resistance to Hitler proved difficult in the early years after the war. During the last months of 1945, very few Germans wanted to be associated with National Socialism. They were emphatically not trying to locate, recall and publicise those instances in which they had considered Adolf Hitler wonderful. His reputation was now in shambles, suffering from the political, military and physical catastrophe of the final war years and the moral catastrophe evident in photos and news stories from Auschwitz, Dachau or Bergen-Belsen. Furthermore, the victorious Allies were seeking to cleanse Germany of National Socialism, punishing the most criminal Nazis and removing others from positions of influence or power. Under these circumstances, individual Germans tried to look after their own interests and salvage their futures. They also had to reconcile their personal sense of self with the judgement now widespread in the world that Germans were monsters. Such psychological trauma can create problems in historical memory.

To the sceptical Allies, it seemed that 'members of the resistance' popped up like spring flowers. Opportunism helps explain this, of course. Individuals might claim to have participated in secret resistance activity without having to supply very good evidence. Selective memory also must have been involved. In sorting through questions of personal, national or universal guilt, individuals may have remembered, consciously or through psychological repression, only those occasions when they were upset with Hitler or the Nazis for some particular policy or act, forgetting that this 'opposition' was perhaps passive, even unspoken, or undercut by appreciation and admiration for the 'renewal' of Germany under Hitler.

Institutions also had to face up to the moral and physical collapse of Germany. Among those institutions, the churches enjoyed the advantage of their good post-war reputation. Membership in the Confessing Church in particular, an organisation which had earned the goodwill of the western Allies, helped place one quickly on the 'white list' for post-war purposes.[2] The churches were even given the unique opportunity of 'denazifying' themselves, based on the assumption that little cleansing needed to be done and that church leaders could be trusted to do it. As a result, professors thrown out of universities through denazification proceedings often found their path to a small country pastorate unimpeded.[3]

During the awkward transition from National Socialist to post-war Germany, the churches began recording their immediate past, forgetting the many reputable theologians, pastors and church leaders who had welcomed and praised the Nazi regime, and remembering the few prescient heroes who had opposed it. Projects began, including the creation of an archive under the leadership of Wilhelm Niemoeller at Bielefeld and the creation of an

Arbeitsgemeinschaft für kirchliche Zeitgeschichte ('Study Group for Contemporary Church History') in Munich. The Bonhoeffer story also entered public consciousness with the publication of *Letters and Papers from Prison* and other of his writings, as well as the major biography by his friend, colleague and relative by marriage, Eberhard Bethge.[4]

Each of these developments was natural and worthwhile. The problem is that they seemed to suggest that Bonhoeffer, Niemoeller and their like represented the Christian community of their day. They tended to present a picture of good versus evil in which a few villains in the 'Church Struggle', the heretical *Deutsche Christen* (German Christians), supported the Nazi world-view, whereas the real Christians opposed it. Few writings appeared in those early years to indicate this might be a misperception.[5]

This trend matched the interests and directions of church historians outside Germany as well. Niemoeller and Bonhoeffer received massive attention and admiration in North America.[6] If it was difficult for the post-war world in general to comprehend the inhumanity of the Nazi era, especially the Holocaust (how could human beings have perpetrated such crimes?), it was even more difficult for Christians to imagine that other Christians might have supported or contributed to this criminal regime. The simplest explanation, then, was to assume that Christian support for Hitler had been minimal and, ideally, that it came from people who were Christian in name only.

This simple picture of good versus evil has gradually eroded. My work on Gerhard Kittel, Paul Althaus and Emanuel Hirsch, for example, is an attempt to show that significant theologians of international reputation supported the Nazi regime.[7] They did so neither grudgingly nor under the political pressure of a totalitarian state, but enthusiastically, because they liked what they saw. Paul Althaus, established theologian and president of the Luther Society in Germany for thirty years, greeted the rise of Hitler as 'a gift and miracle from God'.[8] Emanuel Hirsch, Kierkegaard authority and arguably one of the most brilliant theologians of this century, supported Hitler from the election of April 1932 right through to 1945. He worked toward the goal of a 'political university' at Göttingen, pushing the Party line and denouncing colleagues who strayed from it. Gerhard Kittel, founding editor of the internationally recognised *Theological Dictionary of the New Testament*, joined Walter Frank's Institute for the History of the New Germany, an organisation designed to give intellectual credibility to the National Socialist world-view, which published anti-Semitic materials prolifically in its journal, *Forschungen zur Judenfrage*.

The story of these three men is significant in showing that educated, widely admired, intellectual Christians found the regime of Adolf Hitler worthy of their support. Nor did these men think of themselves as Christian in name only. By their own reckoning, they were Christians in their personal lives, Christians who read their Bibles, prayed, preached sermons and raised their children in Christian homes. They were also admired by others for their piety and decency as human beings.[9]

Althaus's choice of words in the above quotation is noteworthy. He did not just accept Hitler as one politician among many, the lesser of several evils, or even as quite a good leader as politicians went. He considered Hitler instead a gift from God and a miracle. This represents a view which was widespread among Christians in 1933, one which also lingered on for many years.

Althaus, Hirsch and Kittel based their support for Hitler on several factors. The First World War was a grievous disappointment to each of them, the Versailles Treaty a crime, and each supported a chauvinistic, militaristic nationalism in response to it. They believed this to be in line with God's will and thought love of country, including willingness to fight and die for one's fatherland, a Christian virtue. Proud of their nationalism, they refused to recognise that it might blind them to other valid points of view or to crimes committed in Germany's name.[10] They also believed that Hitler represented respect for traditional values, the values of family, law and order, and obedience to authority. Each disliked certain social and cultural aspects of the modern world, especially changes in behaviour and values which they judged decadent. Hitler promised to end pluralism by enforcing unity through the power of the state, a unity that would be German, 'Aryan' and Christian.[11]

Finally, each of these men accepted enough of traditional, Christian anti-Semitism that the brutalities of Nazi anti-Jewish policies did not cost the government their support.[12] Kittel, in this context, even argued that God did not want Christians to be 'sentimental and soft', but to face the reality of the Jewish 'problem' and deal with it as harshly as necessary.[13]

If Althaus's, Hirsch's and Kittel's conservative nationalism was typical of Christians in Germany, as it appears to have been, that helps explain why so little resistance to National Socialism developed. From the standpoint which these men espoused, Dietrich Bonhoeffer would be regarded as a traitor, not a hero. God called Christians to obedience, especially to the National Socialist regime, which represented God's will for Germans after the awful years of democracy and the pluralist society under Weimar. As Althaus, the most moderate of these three, wrote in 1935:

> As a Christian church we bestow no political report card. But in knowledge of the mandate of the state, we may express our thanks to God and our joyful preparedness when we see a state which after a time of depletion and paralysis has broken through to a new knowledge of sovereign authority, of service to the life of the *Volk*, of responsibility for the freedom, legitimacy and justice of *völkisch* existence. We may express our thankfulness and joyful readiness for that which manifests a will for the genuine brotherhood of blood brothers in our new order of the *Volk*. . . . We Christians know ourselves bound by God's will to the promotion of National Socialism, so that all members and ranks of the *Volk* will be ready for service and sacrifice to one another.[14]

Two years later he elaborated on the concept of *Volk*, the foundation of Hitler's claim to lead the German people:

> My *Volk* is my outer and my inner destiny. This womb of my being is God's means, his *Ordnung*, by which to create and to endow me. . . . The special style of a *Volk* is his creation, and as such it is for us holy. . . . Our life in our *Volk* is not our eternal life; but we have no eternal life if we do not live for our *Volk*. This is not a question of the absolute value of the *Volk*, but of our absolute obligation to the *Volk*.[15]

The above quotations, in fact the political ideas of all three of these theologians, seem shockingly out of place if Christianity and National Socialism were really antithetical to each other. Is it possible that these men were exceptions, outside the mainstream of political attitudes among Protestant Christians? Did the Confessing Church espouse a different and more representative political stance?

First of all, Althaus actually associated himself with the Confessing Church after the first months of struggle.[16] More importantly, many people in the Confessing Church expressed similar attitudes of loyalty to and appreciation for National Socialism. Some supporters held more critical views, but the Confessing Church as such never defined itself as a political movement or a resistance organisation. Rather, it argued for certain theological positions and campaigned for particular ecclesiastical goals. Its main antagonist was not the National Socialist state, but the *Deutsche Christen*.

The *Deutsche Christen* organisation, formed before 1933, consisted of clergy who wanted to combine their enthusiasm for

National Socialism with their Christian faith.[17] Although a minority among Protestants, they assumed that Hitler's victory would
assure theirs as well. Therefore, during 1933 they pushed for the
creation of a new Reich Church to replace the regional churches
(*Landeskirchen*) of the past, and they hoped to secure the position of
Reich Bishop for one of their own, Ludwig Müller. Then they
would be able to offer Hitler a Protestant Church unified within
Germany's borders and congruent with the Nazi world-view.

By September success seemed certain. A Reich Church had been
created, a new church constitution accepted, and, with the support
of a radio address by Hitler, Müller's election had been assured.
Those outside *Deutsche Christen* ranks, however, had already been
made nervous by the involvement of the state in church matters. In
September, enthusiasts in Prussia further aggravated the situation
by insisting that the church should incorporate the 'Aryan Paragraph', that is, remove from church payrolls personnel of Jewish
descent. Then in November, in the so-called 'Sports Palace Scan-
dal', thousands of *Deutsche Christen* gathered in Berlin to hear
Reinhard Krause call for the eradication of all Jewish influence on
Christianity. Resenting the implications of the orthodox concept of
the Judaeo-Christian tradition, Krause suggested removing the Old
Testament from the Bible and cleansing Christianity of any other
Jewish taint.[18] Later the *Deutsche Christen* established an institute for
the 'de-judaisation' of the churches, and some also claimed that
Jesus, contrary to accepted belief, had not been Jewish but
Aryan.[19].

Martin Niemoeller responded to these issues with outrage. He
rejected dismissal of the Old Testament. He also accepted the
orthodox view that Christians are 'one in Christ', thereby making
Jewish-Christian pastors equal to any others. Therefore, he called
for a 'Pastors' Emergency League' to oppose the heresy of the
Deutsche Christen and the interference of politics and the state in
church affairs. In the following months Bonhoeffer, Karl Barth and
others developed a statement of beliefs on which to build opposition to the *Deutsche Christen*. The result emerged in May 1934, a
document called the Barmen Declaration, and this became the
'confession' to which the Confessing Church adhered.[20]

The Barmen Declaration is a theological statement, reaffirming
orthodox views about revelation and the nature of the Christian
faith. It says nothing about the persecution of the Jews or other
injustices in Nazi Germany, nor does it make an attack on the state.
Though Karl Barth and Dietrich Bonhoeffer (then in England)
would have liked a stronger statement, their colleagues argued that

politicisation would have lost them too much support.[21] It thus remained possible to endorse both the Confessing Church in its attack on the heresy of the *Deutsche Christen* and Adolf Hitler and his leadership of Germany. Individuals may well have been opposed to Hitler and even active in resistance activity of some sort, but the Confessing Church did not preach opposition to the regime.

Seen in the light of Barmen, the 'Church Struggle' appears more like ecclesiastical politics than politics *per se*, with the Confessing Church trying to protect itself, its message, and its right to non-interference from the state. But it was not trying to protect other victims, oppose other policies, or advocate the overthrow of the regime.[22] This critique of the Confessing Church, coupled with our knowledge of theologians such as Althaus, Hirsch, and Kittel, has altered our understanding of Christianity and National Socialism. Some have also criticised even the heroes of the church. Dietrich Bonhoeffer, though he expressed Christian concern for Jews as early as April, 1933, still maintained a theology of Judaism which might not pass muster in post-Holocaust Jewish-Christian dialogue.[23] Karl Barth failed to see the Jewish question as a primary Christian concern in the 1930s, and did not oppose National Socialism aggressively until he was forced out of Germany and free to observe from the safety of Switzerland.[24] Martin Niemoeller, a national conservative who had served as a U-boat captain in the First World War, greeted National Socialism in 1933 warmly, along with so many others. After the outbreak of war in 1939, he offered from his prison cell to rejoin the navy and fight again for Germany. This would have got him out of prison, of course, which could have been reason enough for his offer; but he may also have retained a loyalty to his fatherland or even to some of the National Socialist goals for which he would have been fighting.[25]

These criticisms show that in the 1930s, Barth, Bonhoeffer, and Niemoeller did not immediately achieve our retrospective view of the nature and criminality of National Socialism. Shelley Baranowski goes further, offering a class analysis: the Protestant churches represented a middle- and upper-class perspective which made the entire church and its leadership vulnerable to fascism.[26] This may help explain the dearth of support for Weimar and subsequent nationalist enthusiasm in response to Hitler. We find very few proponents of liberal democracy among these people. But it does not answer all the questions about lack of resistance. Upper-class ties, after all, marked many of the 20 July conspirators, too.

Examples of Resistance

It now seems clear that resistance to Nazism did not characterise the Protestant Churches. None the less, it did occur. Dietrich Bonhoeffer provides the best example. He worked within the radical wing of the Confessing Church; he led an illegal seminary; he suffered Gestapo surveillance, speaking and travel bans; he was recruited into the Canaris conspiracy by his brother-in-law, Hans von Dohnanyi; he worked as a spy, using his ecumenical contacts abroad to try to communicate with the Allies about the conspiracy; he suffered arrest in 1943, followed by two years of interrogation and imprisonment; and he was executed on 9 April 1945, singled out as one of the final victims of Nazi revenge. Furthermore, Bonhoeffer wrote about his activities in terms of their theological basis, so that it is clear his actions were rooted in his Christian faith.[27].

Other forms of resistance occurred among Protestant Germans. Martin Niemoeller's role in the Confessing Church, his opposition to the Reich Church leadership under Müller, and his refusal to be careful in his sermons, led to Gestapo surveillance and arrest in 1937.[28] Other Christians, the so-called 'righteous gentiles', hid Jews, helped them escape from Germany, or otherwise tried to interfere with Nazi brutalities.[29] Here, however, I will focus on two incidents of resistance which have not been widely discussed.

The first example comes from the apogee of the Church Struggle in the fall of 1934. During that year Ludwig Müller and his lieutenant, August Jäger, tried to solidify the Reich Church government along *Deutsche Christen* lines, using the power of the state to break down pockets of resistance. Two such pockets were centred in the Lutheran *Landeskirchen* (regional churches) in Württemberg and Bavaria under the leadership of Bishops Wurm and Meiser respectively. These two regional churches remained 'intact', that is, outside the control of the Reich Church in Berlin. *Deutsche Christen* excesses in 1933 had been criticised in southern Germany, and Lutherans there also valued their distinctive confessions which separated them from the Reformed churches and the Old Prussian Union. Many staunch Lutherans, who liked the political goals of the *Deutsche Christen*, could not accept being blended into a broader, not strictly Lutheran, national Protestant church. Thus, Wurm and Meiser fought to maintain the autonomy of their *Landeskirchen*.[30]

August Jäger therefore acted in September and October 1934 to unseat these two bishops and replace them with *Deutsche Christen* administrations. He and Müller argued that the new church constitution of July 1933 gave Müller the right, as *Führer* of the church, to intervene in this way if necessary for the good of the Reich Church. With support from the state for Jäger's action, Wurm and Meiser each suffered removal from office and house arrest. The response of their clergy and parishioners in their defence proved overwhelming.

On 11 October, a Thursday, Jäger arrived at Bavarian church headquarters, accompanied by the political police, and demanded Meiser's removal. Meiser, who had been travelling, hastily returned to Munich and preached that evening to a packed congregation: 'Now is the time for action. Now, community, the act of loyalty is required of you.'[31] An overflow crowd waited at the doors to shout its support, making it difficult for Meiser's car to depart through the mass of well-wishers. A contemporary report said of the crowd, 'They continued to remain in the square for a long time and sang church chorales and patriotic songs until they were broken up by the riot police.'[32] The next day Meiser was placed under house arrest and forbidden contact with the public. Demonstrations spread across Bavaria. Services, for example, were held with black cloth on the altar and candles extinguished. That Sunday, 14 October, pastors throughout Bavaria read a message from Meiser and his *Landeskirchenrat*:

> We complain before God and the community, we complain before people and state, we complain before the *Führer* of the Reich about the *breach in loyalty and faith*, about the *destruction of character and trust*. . . . We summon our pastors and communities to offer *no obedience to this church government, which is contrary to confession and constitution*. . . . The *Landesbischof and the Landeskirchenrat will continue for the future, too, to be the legitimate church authorities*. . . .[33]

On 15 October 1934 Minister-President Siebert of Bavaria wrote to the Reich Minister of the Interior, Wilhelm Frick, describing a crisis situation. Old Party members were worried. For example, a 'Kreisleiter . . . from Central Franconia' complained that his 'time was taken up dissuading the farmers from leaving the Party'.[34] Five days later Siebert complained to Frick of reports that '95 per cent of the farming population of Franconia supported Meiser'. He had been warned that 'unless the question was settled soon along the lines of their demands the farmers could not be restrained from rebelling and their political allegiance would also go astray'.[35] Klaus Scholder observes about these events:

> All this was without doubt one of the greatest and at the same time

most remarkable protest demonstrations ever experienced in the Third Reich. There could be no question here of resistance against the regime in the strict sense; those who protested had no awareness at all of a fundamental political or moral opposition to the system. . . . On the other hand something was happening here which was not happening anywhere else in the Third Reich in any respect: the *Führer* state was manifestly coming up against the limits of its power.[36]

Tension built up for several more days in Bavaria. Events had also run similarly in Württemberg, with the house arrest of Bishop Wurm, followed by widespread appeals, petitions and public demonstrations in the streets in his support. Suddenly, this tension broke dramatically. Meiser and Wurm were released from house arrest and reinstated in office on 26 October. Jäger was forced to resign three days later, and on 30 October Hitler received Bishops Meiser, Wurm, and Marahrens of Hanover in the Chancellery. Müller, Jäger and the Reich Church government had overplayed their hand, run into popular opposition, and lost the support of the Party and state on which they relied.[37]

A second example of church resistance involves theological students and faculty members at Göttingen University. Here the incidents had a much lower profile; but again they involved active resistance to officials trying to force *Gleichschaltung* (co-ordination) with the National Socialist world-view, and again the resisters were able to thwart the Nazis.

Emanuel Hirsch became Dean of the Göttingen theological faculty in 1933. An active national conservative and opponent of Weimar throughout the 1920s, he publicly threw his support to Hitler in April 1932, and later joined the Party.[38] He served as Dean of his faculty through 1939, working closely with the Ministry of Education in Berlin to carry out *Gleichschaltung* and create the 'political university' desired by Nazi enthusiasts. Most students and faculty supported Hirsch at first, but the controversies of the 'Church Struggle' in 1933 and 1934 coupled with his enthusiastic support for Ludwig Müller led to friction. One professor, Hermann Doerries, and a couple of untenured instructors (*Privatdozenten*), Freiherr von Campenhausen and Georg Hoffmann, supported the Confessing Church, and gradually the majority of students also moved to that side of the controversy.

The first sign of conflict came in the form of a student prank. Anonymous postcards began arriving at the Dean's office with rhymed poems attacking *Deutsche Christen* professors, including especially Hirsch himself. The latter was sufficiently incensed to undertake an extensive police investigation, determining the post-box in Hanover from which most of the cards had been mailed, the time of posting, and the train timetables of students travelling through that city. Hirsch added graphological analysis, but all to no avail. The one or more students involved were never apprehended.[39]

Had Hirsch known what the period 1935 to 1938 would offer him in terms of conflict, he may have been less concerned with these few insulting postcards. A new and more serious level of conflict began with the provisional appointment of Walter Birnbaum to the chair of practical theology in March 1935. Birnbaum, who had none of the appropriate academic credentials (no Ph. D., no *Habilitation*), had worked with Jäger in the Reich Church government, but with its collapse by the end of 1934 an alternative position for him had to be found. Thus, his appointment was perceived all round as a reward for his loyalty to the *Deutsche Christen*.[40]

Confessing Church students, some 75 per cent of the total,[41] protested immediately to their *Landeskirche* in Hanover. One accused Birnbaum of an 'unholy confusion and mixing of concepts, and an incapacity to think theologically'. Birnbaum also allegedly deified Hitler's role with statements such as 'National Socialism is an outbreak of life against death' and 'now National Socialism is entrusted with the job of saving the church'.[42] Even Hirsch, though he supported Birnbaum throughout this conflict, seems not to have been entirely impressed. Alluding to Birnbaum's lack of appeal as a lecturer, Hirsch reportedly said, 'If the Garden of Eden had contained a *Birnbaum* (pear-tree) instead of an *Apfelbaum* (apple-tree), the Fall would never have occurred.'[43]

With support from Doerries and Hoffmann at Göttingen and officials of the *Landeskirche* in Hanover, students began boycotting Birnbaum's lectures and seminars and attending secret, *ersatz* (substitute) courses taught from a Confessing Church perspective.[44] Hirsch reported to the Minister of Education, Bernhard Rust, suggesting that perhaps such behaviour could be countered by regulating the examination process. Accordingly, Rust wrote all theological faculties on 4 July 1935, specifying that substitute lectures and seminars were illegal. Furthermore, theological students must complete three years at a recognised German university and then undergo legal, officially recognised examinations in order to be eligible for future employment as clergy.[45]

Over the next three years Hirsch and the Ministry of Education tried to control these Confessing Church students and their supporters, Doerries, Hoffmann and von Campenhausen. For example, Hirsch wrote threatening letters to both Hoffmann and von Campenhausen, each of them untenured and vulnerable, forbidding them to give any support to boycott or *ersatz* course activities. These men, however, responded courageously, refusing to back down and defending their freedom of conscience on church matters and their right to advise and assist students when requested to do so. Hirsch said it was his job as Dean, not theirs, to determine which activities were healthy and which destructive. He also sent secret reports to Berlin, naming these individuals plus Doerries, as well as giving the names of student ringleaders. But he never felt his evidence strong enough nor the legal issues sufficiently clear to go beyond intimidation.[46]

The Ministry of Education tried another tack in November 1936 with the following decree:

> It is forbidden for any student of Protestant theology to attend any *ersatz* course or similar contrivance in place of university lectures or to participate in a boycott against university instructors. If offences occur, rectors must on the basis of the law for students of 1 April 1935 ban offending students permanently from any further study at any German university.[47]

Hirsch publicised this decree and used it to try to intimidate leaders of the *ersatz* courses. Then, in February, Heinz Rettberg petitioned the Ministry of Education on behalf of forty fellow students. He claimed the need and the right to study under teachers with proper ties to scripture, the confessions and the students' future ordination vow. Rettberg sent this petition through proper channels, that is, through his Dean's office. Hirsch took the opportunity to add a covering letter, describing Rettberg as the leader of the Confessing Church group which had caused all the trouble over Birnbaum in the first place. Hirsch also blamed Martin Niemoeller, who had spoken in Göttingen just the week previously, for stirring up students and prompting them to submit this complaint. He recommended that the protest be ignored, which it was.[48]

Bishop Marahrens and the *Landeskirche* in Hanover observed these events in Göttingen with anxiety. They had opposed Birnbaum's appointment, though to no avail, and questioned the theology of both Birnbaum and Hirsch because of their ties to the *Deutsche Christen*. Furthermore, Confessing Church students were important to the Hanoverian church on account of its future clergy roster and political direction. So the discontent of students, their boycott of lectures, and their potential boycott of examinations pushed the *Landeskirche* into a more radical response than it probably desired.

Theological studies normally concluded with two examinations, the first theological, the second confessional. Examination committees had always been composed of professors from the theological faculty along with representatives of the church. In the spring of 1937, the Hanoverian church altered this pattern, conducting examinations solely on its own, without participation by Hirsch or one of his appointees.[49] This approach, if allowed to proceed, would enable Confessing Church students to become pastors without studying under Birnbaum and without succumbing to the various threats by Hirsch and the Ministry of Education. Hirsch responded in May 1937 with a memorandum to all his faculty, forbidding their co-operation with the church on its examining committees and requesting reports about any contacts initiated by the church.[50] For months, however, Hirsch and the regime were stymied.

This crisis finally came to a head in the spring and summer of 1938, beginning with a decree from the Minister of Church Affairs, Hans Kerrl, who thereby joined the struggle for the first time. He decreed on 16 May that, from the autumn of 1938, students who failed to take an approved examination, that is, one with the official participation of a university faculty, would be ineligible for a state salary or pension. In the German church, with all salaries paid by the state, this decree appeared the kiss of death. Students, however, were not cowed. About sixty students petitioned the *Landeskirche*, proclaiming they would not sit examinations in which either Birnbaum or Hirsch participated. An internal memo in the Church Office noted with concern: 'It can already be seen that the ecclesiastically and confessionally clear and stable youth avoid testing in Hanover and, for the most part, will be lost to the Hanoverian church. And that is the group most valuable to the church. On the other hand, the German Christians . . . who used to avoid Hanover, will now feel very encouraged.'[51]

Bishop Marahrens tried to open negotiations with the Ministry for Church Affairs, but Kerrl simply responded with this blunt decree:

According to the church law on education of clergy of 31 October 1928, every first theological examination must include participation of a full professor from the Protestant theological faculty of the university.

1. This provision has not been followed since spring 1937.

2. All first examinations since then (beginning with March 1937) have been illegal.[52]

Hirsch posted a letter on the bulletin board the next day, addressed
to Göttingen students:

> I warn students of theology against taking part in first theological
> examinations under the auspices of the regional church office in the
> autumn of 1938 without participation of the theological faculty. The
> examination is worthless to you, since it contravenes the decree of the
> church minister of 31 May 1938 [*sic*]. Salaries and pensions for
> candidates who sit these examinations cannot be paid from church
> taxes or state funds. I have been officially told that participants in the
> autumn examinations in Hanover will fall under the full economic
> consequences of this decree. No exceptions will be made.[53]

Directly challenging the church's authority, Hirsch went on to
offer an autumn examination arranged entirely by the faculty and
specially authorised by the Ministry.

In less than two weeks Hirsch and the *Landeskirche* backed away
from the strident positions they had been taking, reaching an
unexpected compromise. Hirsch agreed that he would not examine
in the future, and that Birnbaum would not examine students
'decisively opposed' to him. Marahrens accepted this solution. It
also appears to have satisfied the students, and the entire controversy
over boycotts and examinations disappears from the records.[54]

It is interesting that in the examples of resistance cited here:
response to the attempted removal of Bishops Wurm and Meiser in
1934 and the question of boycotts and examinations at Göttingen
from 1935 to 1938, the resisters won. They drew from the standard
arsenal of resistance techniques: petitions, demonstrations, boycotts. They risked their personal well-being, confronting Nazi
enthusiasts such as Jäger and Hirsch who called upon Party, state
and police power. And in the end, Party and state backed down, so
that the resisters achieved essentially what they desired. Another
example, better known and drawn more from the Roman Catholic
side, involved opposition to the euthanasia programme begun with
the outbreak of war in 1939. As the secrecy of this programme of
'mercy death' for 'unworthy life' in German hospitals unravelled,
Clemens Count von Galen, the Catholic bishop of Münster, led a
courageous public attack which forced the regime to change its
policies.[55] The Protestant Bishop Wurm of Württemberg also
contributed to this protest, writing to both Goebbels and Hitler in
protest in late 1941.[56]

Are these examples of church resistance also resistance to
National Socialism? None involved attempts to overthrow the
regime. In the Göttingen case, for example, Confessing Church

students regularly declared their loyalty to the regime and routinely belonged to the SA.[57] Hermann Doerries, their faculty supporter, had joined the NSDAP in May 1933, and never left the Party.[58] Franconian farmers who supported Bishop Meiser, moreover, were old-time Party members.[59]

The significance of these issues to the regime also varies considerably. Euthanasia, presumably, derived directly from the wishes of Party leaders. The attempt to remove Wurm and Meiser, on the other hand, was the brainchild of Jäger and Müller. Had they managed to take over the Protestant Church, peacefully and/or successfully, in a short space of time, Hitler would have been pleased. But when their incompetence grew increasingly evident, Hitler's interest decreased. By 1935 the *Deutsche Christen* no longer enjoyed significant Party support.[60] The issue of student boycotts and examinations presumably did not even provoke the attention of Party leaders, though Emanuel Hirsch and the Ministries of Education and Church Affairs certainly believed they were pursuing an important aspect of *Gleichschaltung* and the creation of a 'political university'.

Though these issues vary in significance, they share one thing in common. Each concerned the church directly on an issue which many or most Christians took to be significant. Therefore, whether it was a matter of opposing the murder of German citizens, state interference in regional churches, or government influence on the content of theological education, individuals were willing to act boldly and effectively, despite the risk involved in confronting a regime aspiring to totalitarian control.

Conclusion

True resistance designed to overthrow the Nazi regime was undertaken by a tiny minority of Protestants in Germany. Contrary to the early post-war picture, Christian support for Hitler was broad and enthusiastic, with Christians and Nazis mixing more easily than has generally been thought. This helps explain why resistance to those measures now deemed crimes as well as to the regime as a whole occurred so rarely. On the other hand, resistance to specific National Socialist measures was more widespread. In fact, all members of the Confessing Church opposed some policies of the National Socialist state. Furthermore, they often exercised more leverage than we would expect, actually affecting policy in some instances.

This picture breeds confusion. Few resisted the regime. Many opposed certain policies. Should we call this resistance? At least we can argue that German Protestants were an impediment to totalitarian control. That raises a question, however, with regard to the nature of the things they opposed. In the post-war era we have drawn up a list of complaints against National Socialism which is heavily weighted by our knowledge of the Holocaust. Thus, anti-Jewish policies in the thirties, failure to protect the human and civil rights of Jews and others, and finally the creation of death camps are things we condemn. The Nuremberg Trials also condemned the invasion of Poland in 1939 and Germany's desire generally to expand by force at the expense of its neighbours. Some version of this list makes up the basis on which post-war observers look for resistance within Germany. German Protestants failed almost completely to resist Hitler on the basis of these crimes which we now deplore.

We know Christians could resist effectively on issues of great concern. May we ask what issues did not concern them? The creation of concentration camps? Denial of citizenship and basic rights to Jews? The imposition of law and order by harsh, extra-legal measures? Foreign policy conducted by armed force? The burning of synagogues, the disappearance of German Jews, and rumours of mass murder in the East? Measured in terms of resistance, these issues simply did not arouse the concern of Christians to the same extent as did the other questions described here.

Finally, our definition of resistance must question whether it was enough to think bad thoughts about Hitler, or whether some action was necessary to place one among his recognised opponents. This is a point where the possible list of Protestant resisters could expand exponentially. Even Gerhard Kittel, who joined the Party in 1933 and worked actively in Walter Frank's anti-Jewish institute, later claimed he only did so to bring a Christian critique to the racism of Nazi fanatics. Unfortunately, even in 1946 he defended his own version of spiritual as opposed to racial anti-Semitism.[61]

Kittel's self-definition as a resister can be dismissed, perhaps, but there remains a huge grey area in which difficulties of evaluation will constantly recur. This results from problems of definition about resistance and opposition, problems of proof about behaviour which was secret, problems of knowledge about what intentions were in peoples' minds, and problems of memory in which historical and psychological pressures toward selectivity and distortion are enormous. We now know, however, that despite the 'Church Struggle', active Protestant resistance or committed opposition to the regime as such was rare.

132   Robert P. Ericksen

NOTES

1. Peter Hoffmann describes 'the attempt at a coup d'état' as 'the real hallmark of resistance'. See The History of the German Resistance, 1933–1945, rev. edn, Cambridge, Mass., 1979, p. x.
2. Records on British plans for denazification and the creation of 'white lists' for post-war purposes can be found in the Public Record Office (hereafter PRO). The creation of 'black', 'grey' and 'white' lists is described, for example, in PRO, CAB 87/67, 228.
3. See Directive on Education, Youth Activities and German Church Affairs, 36. (b), of 22 November 1945, in PRO, FO 371/20573, for a statement on denazification in the churches: 'You will normally take action through the offender's superior ecclesiastical authority.' See also G. Besier, 'Selbstreinigung' unter britischer Besatzungsherrschaft. Die Evangelisch-lutherische Landeskirche Hannovers und ihr Landesbischof Marahrens 1945–1947, Göttingen, 1986. Eugen Mattiat is one of those professors removed for cause who then accepted a parish near Göttingen. For some discussion of his career, see R. P. Ericksen, 'Kontinuitäten konservativer Geschichtsschreibung am Seminar für Mittlere und Neuere Geschichte: Von der Weimarer Zeit über die nationalsozialistische Ära bis in die Bundesrepublik', in H.-J. Dahms (ed.), Die Universität Göttingen unter dem Nationalsozialismus. Das verdrängte Kapitel ihrer 250jährigen Geschichte, Munich, 1987, pp. 234–5; and R. W. Brednich, 'Volkskunde – die Völkische Wissenschaft von Blut und Boden', in Dahms pp. 313–19.
4. Eberhard Bethge has edited Bonhoeffer's published works and written extensively about him, including the major biography, Dietrich Bonhoeffer: Man of Vision, Man of Courage, NY, 1970.
5. One exception is found in F. Baumgärtel, Wider die Kirchenkampflegenden, Neuendettelsau, 1959.
6. Martin Niemoeller made speaking tours of America after 1945. Bonhoeffer's influence can be noted in his impact on major American theologians (Harvey Cox, the 'God is dead' theologians) and in the fact that there is an active North American Bonhoeffer society. Eberhard Bethge has indicated his view that Bonhoeffer is more appreciated in America than in Germany (interview with the author, May 1984).
7. See R. P. Ericksen, Theologians under Hitler: Gerhard Kittel, Paul Althaus and Emanuel Hirsch, New Haven, 1985.
8. P. Althaus, Die deutsche Stunde der Kirche, 3rd edn, Göttingen, 1934, p. 5.
9. See Ericksen, Theologians under Hitler, passim, for further details. Althaus and Kittel gathered so-called Persilscheine ('soap certificates') to get them through denazification proceedings. Other evidence too, however, supports the impression of Christian piety and human decency. The one exception is Hirsch, but only in so far as he had a biting, sarcastic style which made him appear less warm and friendly.
10. For a recent essay on the significance of nationalism which makes

extensive use of my *Theologians under Hitler*, see C. C. O'Brien, 'A Lost Chance to Save the Jews?', *The New York Review of Books*, 27 April 1989, pp. 27–35.

11. Typical expressions of these attitudes can be found in Althaus, *Die deutsche Stunde der Kirche*; or E. Hirsch, *Die gegenwärtige geistige Lage im Spiegel philosophischer und theologischer Besinnung*, Göttingen, 1934.

12. For reactions to the 'Aryan Paragraph' issue in the church, see E. Hirsch, 'Theologisches Gutachten in der Nichtarierfrage', *Deutsche Theologie*, vol. 5, May 1934, pp. 182–4; or P. Althaus and W. Elert, 'Theologisches Gutachten über die Zulaßung von Christen jüdischer Herkunft zu den Ämtern der deutschen evangelischen Kirche', *Theologische Blätter*, vol. 12, November 1933.

13. G. Kittel, *Die Judenfrage*, Stuttgart, 1933, pp. 61–2.

14. P. Althaus, *Kirche und Staat nach lutherische Lehre*, Leipzig, 1935, p. 29.

15. P. Althaus, *Völker vor und nach Christus*, Leipzig, 1937, pp. 3–5, 8.

16. Klaus Scholder notes that Althaus attended the Dahlem Synod of the Confessing Church in October, 1934, as the Bavarian representative. See *The Churches and the Third Reich*, vol. 2, Philadelphia, 1988, p. 270.

17. On the *Deutsche Christen*, see J. C. Zabel, *Nazism and the Pastors*, Missoula, Montana, 1976.

18. This incident is described in K. Scholder, *The Churches and the Third Reich*, vol. 1, Philadelphia, 1987. For a description of these events see also J. S. Conway, *The Nazi Persecution of the Churches, 1933–1945*, Toronto–London–NY, 1968.

19. Walter Grundmann, a former student of Kittel, founded this institute. See A. Henze, 'Walter Grundmann and the "Institute for the Dejudaization of the Christian Church"', forthcoming in R. P. Ericksen (ed.), *German Professional Groups and the Holocaust*. For an example of the arguments to 'prove' Jesus non-Jewish, see E. Hirsch, *Das Wesen des Christentums*, Weimar, 1939, pp. 158–65.

20. The Barmen Declaration did not purport to be a 'confession'. This word was too heavily freighted, especially for Lutherans, who had never been able to accept a common confession with Reformed Protestants of their basic principles of belief. See R. P. Ericksen, 'The Barmen Synod and its Declaration: A Historical Synopsis', in H. G. Locke (ed.), *The Church Confronts the Nazis: Barmen Then and Now*, NY, 1984.

21. See G. Niemoeller, *Die erste Bekenntnissynode der Deutschen Evangelischen Kirche zu Barmen. I. Geschichte, Kritik und Bedeutung der Synode und ihrer Theologischen Erklärung. II. Text, Dokumente, Berichte*, Göttingen, 1959; and C. Nicolaisen, *Der Weg nach Barmen. Die Entstehungsgeschichte der Theologische Erklärung von 1934*, Neukirchen–Vluyn, 1985.

22. The one exception is a statement from the Confessing Church leadership to Hitler in 1936, protesting at the brutal treatment of Jews as a violation of Christian conscience. See R. T. C. Gutteridge, *Open Thy Mouth for the Dumb: The German Evangelical Church and the Jews,*

1879–1958, London, 1976. By 1943, even Bishop Wurm, though a Christian anti-Semite, became sufficiently upset about anti-Jewish brutalities that he wrote several outspoken letters in protest. See W. Gerlach, *Als die Zeugen schwiegen. Bekennende Kirche und die Juden*, Berlin, 1987, pp. 339–52.

23. For example, see E. Fackenheim, *Quest for Past and Future: Essays in Jewish Theology*, NY, 1983.

24. Barth wrote to Eberhard Bethge in the mid-1950s, admitting that the Jewish question had not concerned him enough early on. Though he certainly opposed National Socialism in 1933 and 1934, his opposition became clearer and more assertive after 1935. See Scholder, *The Churches and the Third Reich*, vols 1 and 2; also E. Busch, *Karl Barth: His Life from Letters and Autobiographical Texts*, Philadelphia, 1976.

25. See J. S. Conway, 'The Political Theology of Martin Niemoeller', *German Studies Review*, vol. 9, October, 1986; also J. Bentley, *Martin Niemoeller: A Biography*, London, 1986.

26. S. Baranowski, *The Confessing Church, Conservative Elites, and the Nazi State*, NY, 1986.

27. See Bethge, *Dietrich Bonhoeffer*.

28. See Bentley, *Martin Niemoeller*.

29. A film, 'The Courage to Care', has been produced by the Anti-Defamation League of B'nai B'rith (1987). Note that the Christians highlighted in this film tend to be Dutch, Polish, etc. It was much more difficult for Christians in *Germany* to oppose their own government than for those living in the occupied countries to resist the Nazis. Nationalism added a significant obstacle for Germans, making opposition seem like treason. In the occupied countries, however, opposition was also patriotic.

30. See Scholder, *The Churches and the Third Reich*, vol. 2.

31. Quoted ibid., p. 261.

32. Quoted ibid., p. 262.

33. Quoted ibid.

34. Quoted ibid.

35. Quoted ibid., p. 263.

36. Ibid.

37. Ibid., *passim*.

38. E. Hirsch, 'Ich werde Hitler wählen!', *Göttinger Tageblatt*, 9/10 April 1932. Hirsch's Party membership number was 5,076,856, dated 1 May 1937.

39. See Göttingen University Archive (hereafter GUA), S 10, I.ld. Nr. 599 (5), 'Disziplinarangelegenheiten 1931–1936'.

40. See his own account of these events in W. Birnbaum, *Zeuge meiner Zeit. Aussagen zu 1912 bis 1972*, Göttingen, 1973.

41. This is Hirsch's estimate. See Emanuel Hirsch to Bernhard Rust, Minister of Education, 17 June 1935, in GUA, Theologische Fakultät (hereafter TF), 140.

42. Wolfgang Schroeder to Pastor Klügel, 25 July 1935, in the

Landeskirchlichesarchiv (hereafter LKA) Hannover, S 1, H II, 133a.
43. This report came from a long-time faculty member and was confirmed by several other of Hirsch's colleagues.
44. See LKA, S 1, H II, 133a.
45. Circular from Rust to the Evangelical Theological Faculties, 4 July 1935, in TF 140.
46. See correspondence in TF 140.
47. Circular from the Minister of Education to Deans, 17 November 1936, in TF 140.
48. Heinz Rettberg to the Minister of Education, 16 February 1937; Hirsch to the Minister of Education, 19 February 1937; and the Minister of Education to Hirsch, 22 March 1937, all in TF 140.
49. See correspondence in LKA, S 1, H II, 133a, especially Minister for Church Affairs to the Landeskirche Hannover, 15 August 1938.
50. Hirsch to members of the theological faculty, 15 May 1937, in TF 140.
51. 'Denkschrift: Die Zukunft der theologischen Prüfungen', June 1938, in LKA, S 1, H II, 133a.
52. Minister of Church Affairs to the Landeskirche Hannover, 15 August 1938, in LKA, S 1, H II, 133a.
53. Hirsch to students of theology, 16 August 1938, in LKA, S 1, H II, 133a.
54. Stalmann to Marahrens, 27 August 1938, and 'Erwägungen zum Schreiben von 27.8' initialled by Marahrens, in LKA, S 1, H II, 133a.
55. See Hoffmann, *History of the German Resistance*, p. 24.
56. Ibid. See Gerlach, *Als die Zeugen Schwiegen*, p. 341, for reference to the protest letters.
57. Testimony to this effect was given at the 250th anniversary of Göttingen University, May 1987, by students from that era.
58. Doerries had Party number 2,872,330, dated 1 May 1933. See my account in 'Widerstand als ambivalenter Gegenstand historischer Forschung: Am Beispiel der evangelisch theologischen Fakultät der Universität Göttingen', *Kirchliche Zeitgeschichte*, vol. 1, 1988, pp. 76–7.
59. See Scholder, *The Churches and the Third Reich*, vol. 2, pp. 260–3.
60. Ibid. The *Deutsche Christen* did receive some support from the Ministries of Education and Church Affairs, but they were no longer a high priority for the Party.
61. G. Kittel, *Meine Verteidigung*, June 1945, December 1946. These two documents are in the Tübingen University Archive.

8

Catholic Resistance
to Biological and Racist
Eugenics in the Third Reich

Donald Dietrich

I

As *Führer*, Hitler assumed the role of eschatological saviour and of calculating political leader. This process required that traditional theological concepts and terminology be metamorphosed into secular and political forms. The dogma of the Nazi creed, at least for Hitler and his intimate followers, included racial purity, the supremacy of the 'Aryan' race, and the resettlement of conquered territories by a 'pure-blooded' stock. Axiomatically, the Jew was seen both as the symbol and the concrete representative of everything evil. In the Nazi view, the new political leadership was to be based on race and blood. Structurally, Nazism was a political movement analogously rooted in the traditional Christian experience in which faith precedes understanding.[1] The *Volksgemeinschaft* was consecrated as a substitute religion, a transcendent community based on race, which provided the individual with his religious and social identity. Equally attractive, Nazism could also offer a scientific dimension by advocating the eugenic and genetic solutions to socio-political issues prominent in the Second Reich as well.

Nazi racism was designed to provide a new social model that would yield a 'natural' internal alignment of Germans. All groups that deviated from the norm were to be eliminated – 'asocial' elements, the disabled, the insane, homosexuals and, of course, the Jews. Eugenics, the classification and selection of people on the basis of genetic value, was not restricted only to sterilisation,

137

euthanasia, and the annihilation of Jewry, but also laid down regulations applicable to the population as a whole. The establishment of this *Volksgemeinschaft* would mean the eradication of those who could not enter this utopia. In the final analysis, social behaviour in the Third Reich helped uncover 'racial character'.[2] From the sterilisation legislation of 1933 onward, those who formulated National Socialist racial policy helped continue the eugenic and demographic tradition originating in the Second Reich, when academics and the middle-class intelligentsia became concerned that the 'good Germans' were producing at a lesser rate than the 'non-respectable' elements of the population. A desire for better genetic stock had long been debated, although there was little public support before 1933 for the 1920 views of Karl Bindung and Adolf Hoche, professors of law and medicine respectively, who called for the elimination of 'ballast existences'. The National Socialists' goal of social selection, based on genetic criteria scientifically observed in individuals, rested on a lengthy tradition of psychological, anthropological and medical research. For the Nazi regime, this ideology would link practice and theory by combining action with a consciousness of historical purpose. Resistance to such a system could cover anything from nonconformist attitudes to civil disobedience to the stimulation of conflicts designed to overthrow the system.[3]

Although Catholics historically had condoned religious and socio-economic anti-Semitism, they had also generally opposed the biological eugenics that served as the dogmatic principle supporting Hitler's agenda. As a minority group in a unified Germany, Catholics were obsessed with institutional survival, and for decades this translated into religious, although not racist or biological, anti-Semitism.[4] Not surprisingly, then, in the Weimar era and the Third Reich, a congruence existed between Catholic attitudes and the dominant political value system that featured national revival, imperial expansion, the abolition of democratic pluralism and anti-Semitism.

Although highlighted in earlier works on resistance,[5] there actually was little public opposition by the institutional Church. Historically, the Catholic Church exhibited a patriotism previously intensified by its *Kulturkampf* experiences. As an institution, it was gravely compromised during the Third Reich by its approval of what Hitler had promised politically before 1933 and subsequently delivered.[6] Most Church leaders saw institutional survival as a value in itself, a policy that superseded the plight of the victims of Nazism. With respect to the Jews, Church leaders spoke of 'justice and charity', but generally practised diplomacy and conciliation.

The Church, however, did confront the biological bases of racism and the Nazi pseudo-religion. Racism challenged the Church's claims in baptism and marriage, elements in the Catholic religious identification. As a result, Catholics openly expressed dissatisfaction with Nazi biomedical ideals in the Catholic press, in meetings and in Church activities, thereby limiting the *Gleichschaltung* based on neo-paganism.[7]

II

During the Weimar period, institutionalised German Catholicism had repeatedly opposed the radical Nazi programme, which placed the welfare of the political community before that of the individual and which rooted morality in the race. But anti-Semitism as such was not the primary issue. Indeed, such Catholic writers as Erhard Schlund, a Franciscan priest, could agree with the Nazis on the importance of fighting the Jews' 'hegemony in finance, the destructive influence of the Jews in religion, morality, literature and art and in political and social life'. The nationalist movement, he continued, had a healthy core, 'the endeavour to maintain the purity of German blood and the German race'. Even as late as 1940 Father Tharsicius Paffrath, a Franciscan scholar specialising in the Old Testament, could write: 'The religion of the Old Testament did not arise from and in accordance with the [Israelite-Jewish] natural, peculiar character. . . . It is altogether unique, fundamentally independent of the peculiar racial character of Israel.' Pleas for moderate anti-Semitism as well were fairly typical and perfectly respectable in the Church. Gustav Gundlach, a Jesuit writing for a reference work edited by Bishop Michael Buchberger of Regensburg, argued that political anti-Semitism could be used to fight the Jews' 'exaggerated and harmful influence', and was permitted as long as it utilised normally admissible means. Buchberger himself insisted in 1931 that it was justified self-defence to ward off the rule of 'overly powerful Jewish capital'. It was unjust and unchristian, however, to blame all Jews for these failings or to convert this economic struggle into one of race or religion. In confronting Hitler before as well as after 1933, the German bishops declared their philosophical appreciation of the natural values of race and racial purity without fully realising until the war the biological ramifications of such support. Generally they limited their dissent to insisting that Aryan goals be achieved without resort to immoral or violent means.[8]

Although Church leaders as well as other Germans responded positively at first to the religious, economic, political and social anti-Semitism characterising the viewpoints of the NSDAP, they simultaneously opposed the biomedical solutions to political problems advanced by the Nazis, who sought eugenically to create and nurture the 'new man', an ideal that Catholics had historically and vigorously opposed.[9] While it would be erroneous to attribute the Final Solution to the eugenicists of pre-Nazi Germany, they did help create a climate of opinion within the professions and society that made such horrors as the euthanasia programme and Auschwitz into realities. Both the eugenics programme to improve racial hygiene and racist anti-Semitism were derived from a biological, Social Darwinist anthropology. Both aimed through racial hygiene to eliminate diseases that undermined a healthy *Gemeinschaft*. Nazi racism was designed to excise, in the words of Gerhard Wagner, the *Reichsärzteführer*, the 'Jew as sick, the Jew as diseased'. Even to be sick was now an infraction against the state, which was deprived of valuable labour resources.[10] This eugenic view found little support even among pre-1933 German theologians, bishops, and priests.

III

To protest against pagan Nazi anthropology and racist eugenics, Christian theologians focused on man's place in God's scheme; the image of Man, stressing the basic unity of the human species, meant to them the denial of the Nazi racial myth at the source of which was the *Judenfrage*. Throughout the 1930s Catholic writers pointed out that the unity of the Jews was neither biological nor political but rather religious. Belief in God was the soul of this *Volk*.[11] Generally, Catholic theologians reminded their readers that a Christian anthropology, diametrically opposed to the *Totalstaat* and biological anti-Semitism, was at the apex of all their reflections. Increasingly, the theologians seemed to realise that they had to critique a Nazi eugenics which still resembled, in broad contours at least, the positions taken by social scientists and physicians, as well as even by some Catholic scholars, during this period.[12]

Otto Schilling, a Catholic professor of theology at Tübingen, for example, reminded his readers that the Church applied natural law, not medical eugenics, to the norms governing procreation, and within this context the focus was to be primarily on the welfare of the individual and only secondarily on that of the race. As an example of applied reason, he noted that Pius XI in *Casti Connubii* had urged care in selecting a marital partner, since the Church opposed artificial birth-control and sterilisation. Eugenicists, Schilling reminded his readers, offered noble motives to recommend birth-control, but actually relied on individual egoism. He also warned that reducing the quantity of children could limit the quality of the species. The state, he insisted, had the strict duty to protect the life of the innocent child, whose helplessness itself should be a touching appeal to justice, the foundation for the political community. Schilling condemned eugenic sterilisation; the sanctity of procreation and the rights of the family were personal and sacred rights. Only with a refined sense of morality, which to him seemed unlikely, could a political eugenics plan operate within the parameters established by God. In essence, man was to use his reason as he conformed to natural and divine law.[13]

In 1935, still cognisant of the quantity–quality eugenics debate, Karl Frank, a Jesuit professor of theology in Düsseldorf, stated that in any *Volk*, descended from a specific race or racial mixture, there were valuable and less valuable offshoots. The current, restricted eugenics discussion, he observed, was concerned with helping the hereditarily superior elements triumph over the inferior. Working from a Mendelian perspective, however, he suggested that an intelligent approach actually should mean crossing races for a healthier stock. But from the Hitlerian national eugenics standpoint, this would be forbidden. Hence, in his opinion a scientifically realistic eugenics policy was not really being sought by the *Reich*. Frank stressed that such recent attacks on the family as the 1933 sterilisation legislation could not ultimately achieve the eugenic goals of improving humanity genetically and morally. Eugenics, he felt, should properly support that procreation which would strengthen the racial stock, while still striving to protect the rights of the chronically ill. Frank pointed out that man's goal was to seek fulfilment in eternal life. This meant leaving to the Creator how this goal could be achieved even by those in chronic pain or who were hereditarily mentally ill, since no one except God had control over the genetic possibilities inherent in procreation. Catholics, of course, could attempt to control marriages between the hereditarily ill as well as between the hereditarily ill and the 'healthy', but the plans had to be shaped by the rational natural law that respected the individual. In a practical vein, Frank insisted that economic activities should be provided so that everyone could be self-supportive.[14] Such a programme would undermine the eugenic fear of escalating social-welfare expenses. He felt that eugenics could be practised, but only within the charitable confines of divine and natural law. Apparently ignorant of the escalating Nazi goals, Frank naïvely maintained that at least euthanasia was not being seriously discussed in responsible governmental circles. Actually, however, as early as 1935 Hitler had decided on a euthanasia programme to improve the quality of the race, but hesitated to implement it for fear of the Church's reaction. In the chaos of a wartime situation, he cleverly reasoned, opposition would be muted.[15]

Theologians discussed the issues of racial differentiation as well. Frank, for example, insisted that all members of mankind from the beginning had been endowed with a rational essence. Cultural levels had historically served only to distinguish among, and not to rank, human groups. Had such a position been developed more explicitly and promoted more vigorously, of course, it would have obviated the entire concept of the *Untermensch* as well as the need for a racial eugenics policy, including sterilisation, euthanasia and extermination. Who could tell, Frank insisted, when a particular quality might become necessary for the next stage in the onward development of mankind? Similarly, Franz Walther, an early Catholic opponent of euthanasia from Munich, argued that euthanasia was rooted in the historical collapse of religion and could never really improve God's creation. Walther located the deepest roots of the pro-euthanasia movement in a culture conditioned by the collapse of natural-law morality, horrified by the experiences of the First World War, and powered by the surrender of religious faith.[16] Theological opposition to Nazi racial eugenics was emerging, even while the institutional Church simultaneously was adapting politically.

The theologians and the bishops as well insisted repeatedly that race as a cultural concept, although important, could not determine morality. They opposed the idea of a biological master race. Even though rejecting classical liberalism, Church leaders were quick to alert the faithful to the extravagant claims of the *Volksgemeinschaft*, which, they contended, could deprive the individual of sacred rights. Divine law was to be superior to all dogmas of nation and race. Such boldness infuriated the Nazis. No matter what the tactics of the Church, declared an SD report, and regardless of whether the bishops used legal or illegal means, 'between the National Socialist state and the Catholic Church there can be no peace. The totalitarian claims of the Church challenge those of the state.'[17]

Naturally, given the attempted Nazi transformation of societal values under the aegis of Social Darwinism, Catholic theologians felt compelled to reassert the traditional precepts of a morality not grounded in racial struggle. The year 1935 marked a transformation from watchful concern to a more incisive critique of the new regime. Negative analyses of the government, of course, were nearly always surrounded by a patriotic camouflage that insisted on connecting Germany and Christianity. Critical of the regime, for example, Bishop Konrad Preysing stated in 1935 that the battle to drive Christianity 'from our Fatherland' was being waged. Max Pribilla, an internationally respected Jesuit theologian in Düsseldorf, urged that Catholic and not racist marriage manuals should be developed for the moral guidance of the German faithful. As war approached, Pribilla focused on the very survival of the Church itself and on the moral decisions made by Catholics. A good Christian society, he insisted, was necessary to form a good man. As an indication that the goal of being a good Christian was becoming more difficult to attain, Pribilla asserted that for many even the mere fulfilment of religious duty had become heroic.[18]

By 1938 such scholars as Anton Artweiler from Cologne were similarly highlighting the tension existing for Catholics as German citizens. If human brotherhood were ignored, he opined, then the fatherhood of God could not be accepted. Following the lead of the moral theologians Michael Schmaus, Professor of Dogmatic Theology at Münster, and Fritz Tillman, Professor of Moral Theology at Münster, Artweiler avoided a narrow apologetical approach. He felt that man should concentrate on the spiritual life nourished by faith in God and in Christ's redemptive acts. The Church was the body of Christ, and the faithful were its members. Focusing on the dangers of Nazi racism, Artweiler insisted that race was not *the* absolute, but was limited by its very essence. All men belong to one human race, since man is Man, although there were such communities as the family and nation. The state was only the politically organised form of the *Volk*, united through blood or culture. Every political community, however, could be equally derived from God and so was beneficial. In fact, the Church, not the racial *Gemeinschaft*, was to be the community (*Gemeinschaft*) most closely approximating God's ideal.[19] Just as eugenics and racism permeated every aspect of Nazism, since the 'New Man' was an anthropological goal, Catholic theologians found themselves drawn to the same battlefield no matter where their theological speculations on National Socialism began.

In 1939, as tensions increased, Schilling clarified the issues that Catholics were facing. To de-emphasise Nazi organicism, which stressed the common good versus private need, Schilling insisted that the foundation of social justice was the community in which individuals could morally develop. The individual in a specific community was the alpha and omega of the social order. Law was to have its basis in natural law, not in the will of the *Führer* seen as the embodiment of the race. He reminded his readers that social justice and the organic *Volk* belonging to the *Gemeinschaft* could be included in traditional Christian patterns of thought, and that only from this *Weltanschauung* was it possible to mediate values seemingly at odds with one another.[20] Intellectually ruminating on the *Volk* or race could have been a harmless academic exercise focusing on theological anthropology had the Nazi theory not been literally applied to the Jews and to others who did not conform to Aryan ideals. The historical religious and cultural hatred of the Jews initially prevented Catholic leaders from seeing that Hitler's anti-Semitism was one facet of his eugenic racism, which was intended to reshape German society.

After 1935 theologians generally stopped stressing the so-called 'Jewish question'. Apparently sensitive to the fact that Nazism was not 'normal' racism, respectable academics even ceased speculating on religious anti-Semitism itself. Wilhelm Moock, a theologian from Munich, for example, noted that German leaders historically could be found with a variety of surnames, indicating that spiritual values, not blood, made a person German. Moock went even further by insisting that the Church might well talk metaphorically about a marriage blossoming in the *Volk*, but that simultaneously the Church had no interest in racial breeding.[21] Respected members of the profession no longer commented on either *Volk* or *Blut* with the unabashed enthusiasm so apparent in the early years of adaptation to the Third Reich. But, unfortunately, they failed to chastise the Nazis for proclaiming their racist ideology and its subsequent implementation. Still, under the circumstances, lack of comment could be construed as a realisation among Catholics that anti-Semitism was giving support to more than merely political or cultural racism. Increasingly, Catholic theologians seemed to perceive that the Nazi leaders were more than conservative, authoritarian and anti-Semitic politicians. This is not to suggest that anti-Semitism had died. Rather, the theologians apparently had only stopped using anti-Semitism in order more clearly to distinguish Catholic from Nazi ideals. Their continued use of such terms as *Volk* and *Vaterland*, however, unfortunately reinforced the persistence of the insider–outsider matrix which in practice sustained anti-Semitism. Nowhere did there appear a condemnation as clear as the 1965 Vatican II statement in *Nostra Aetate* that for the sake of her common patrimony with the Jews, the Church decried hatred, persecutions and displays of anti-Semitism staged against the Jews at any time in history.

Peter Lippert, a Jesuit theologian from Düsseldorf, viewed the community as the highest form of human interaction. Properly conforming to God's will, communities of two or three or the Church of several hundred million overflowed with power and plentitude, since each person as a social creature would contribute to and receive his political and cultural essence from the community in which he existed. Lippert agreed with the Nazi slogan, *Gemeinnutz geht vor Eigennutz* (common need precedes individual need), but only for the specific socio-economic dimensions of community life. Such an approach was invalid when applied to spiritual concerns. Even the 'common good' of the human community could not be decisive in a matter of conscience. Values inherent in Man superseded the political *Gesellschaft*, since human well-being in the community was based on love, not politics, and certainly not on hatred for others. Ultimately, the true community existed when the individual gave to those in need, since all men were brothers.[22]

Ivo Zeiger, also a Jesuit theologian in Düsseldorf, defended the Church by focusing on man himself. Any debate centring on the issues of ethics and moral doctrine ultimately had to be referred back to anthropology, i.e. to man's image of himself as God's creature. The moral law was peculiar to man. Hence, the individual could only become true Man when he totally obeyed God's moral precepts, an ethic not rooted in race. Zeiger did not even mention race, but emphatically insisted that revelation was God speaking to man and so affirming His superiority to man. God continued to speak to mankind through the creation of a universe in which obedience to man's true nature as a creature of God was his natural law. Man was to obey God's natural law, not that proposed by the Social Darwinists. Real natural morality was, ultimately, verified in revelation. In Christ, Man became a new creature, and natural law, combined with revelation, was designed to help man reach the ideals created by God.[23]

IV

Catholics could also attack Nazi racism in the work of Alfred Rosenberg. In 1930, Rosenberg had published his *Myth of the*

Twentieth Century. This hateful book was never given Hitler's *imprimatur* publicly, and so Catholics found they could attack this semi-official bible of the NSDAP without impugning Hitler. Rosenberg offered a religion of blood. Each race evolved its own religion, and each had its own racial soul. Although official racial propaganda was controlled, knowledge of the Nazi élite's hatred of the Jews was apparent, and an array of Catholic institutional protests, supported by theological scholarship, can be documented. Those leaders who actively resisted had a *Weltanschauung* that repudiated Rosenberg's Nazi neo-paganism. On 12 February 1931 the Bavarian bishops condemned Nazism because Hitler's minions insisted that race superseded religion. In his 1933 Advent sermons, Michael Cardinal Faulhaber of Munich reminded the faithful that they were redeemed by Christ's blood, not German blood. Wilhelm Neuss of Cologne, supported by members of the hierarchy, published a formal attack on Rosenberg.[24] Sensing the gravity of the Catholic attack, in 1937 Rosenberg stated: 'National Socialism has always claimed the whole man and his entire personality.'[25] Very few Church leaders, however, publicly addressed the specific pre-war, 'legal' anti-Semitic acts aimed at the Jews, which prepared the way for the Final Solution. No amount of research can basically alter the Church leaders' moral responsibility for these events. Ultimately, they sought the salvation of souls, not lives. Their acquiescence in 'legal' anti-Semitism is unquestioned, and the extent of their culpability seems clear. Church leaders were reluctant to speak out against racial persecution in a consistent fashion after 1933 not only because of their long history of religious anti-Semitism, but also because of such objective factors as their battle with the Nazi regime for institutional autonomy and the difficulty of publicly opposing its racial policies without encountering harsh counter-measures in response to what could be construed as political disloyalty.[26]

Although Catholic leaders did not offer more than a pittance of support for or aid to Jews unless they were also baptised Catholics, they consistently opposed the pseudo-pagan, racial ideology of the regime as an institutional issue. Rosenberg's glorification of biological race rather than religion undermined the foundations and dogmas of the Church itself. The persecution of non-converted Jews, however, never seemed to arouse much sustained interest among Catholic leaders, although Adolf Cardinal Bertram of Breslau did ultimately protest against the death of Jews in concentration camps in private letters to Himmler and the Ministry of the Interior. Only when the Nazi Party infringed upon the Church's ministrations to its Jewish converts or to Jews married to Catholics was it strenuously and publicly opposed as well as privately resisted, at least according to Nazi sources. The overwhelming majority of *Sicherheitsdienst* (SD) reports on religious institutions were on the Roman Catholic Church, since the Nazi leaders considered it to be a formidable opponent, protecting its organisational viability as well as attacking the biological racism which the Nazis insisted was the foundation for all values. In fact, the reader of these SD reports is almost led to assume that the Nazis were in a position of defensive holding, jealously recognising Church successes and impatiently awaiting the moment of attack after a victorious war.[27] The reports were certainly biased, since it was the goal of the SD to establish enemies simply to justify its own institutional survival. But enough materials do exist to suggest fear of the Church, at least during the war.

After 1941 Catholic leaders became more aggressive as the tempo of the Final Solution picked up. A Jesuit priest, Franz von Waldburg-Zeil, noted that the German people seemed only to respond to the phrases of 'people's community' and 'community of blood'. Many, he feared, perceived their god in *Blut, Boden* or *Volk*. The bishops, in 1941, circulated *Hirtenbriefe* (pastoral letters) which criticised racial ideology, referred to Jesus as the King of the Jews, and called for the blood-brotherhood of all men.[28] In 1942 Archbishop Konrad Gröber of Freiburg insisted that all men were equal, sharing the same path and destiny.[29] Dr Alois Weber, Bishop of Leitmeritz, charged that the Nazis had 'declared it to be the basic law of morality that everyone may permit himself to be guided by his own advantage, his own lust . . . that whatever secures a healthy new generation was permissible and good'. Nazism was responsible for the fact that 'adultery and divorce are glorified . . . and thereby the downfall of the people is prepared'.[30] In September 1943 the Fulda Bishops' Conference came closest to taking a position on racial injustice and crimes perpetrated by Nazism when the bishops stated: 'We act on behalf of . . . those innocent people who are not of our people and blood . . . for the prisoners or foreign labourers, for their right to treatment worthy of human beings.'[31] Despite all its short-comings, the Catholic Church did not fail to resist Nazism. Its very existence and activities were effective barriers to the realisation of the Nazis' totalitarian claims. As long as the Church could preach Christian doctrine and morality, *Gleichschaltung* was a dream and not a reality.

Outside the hierarchy, Catholic priests who were not academic theologians were not hesitant about attacking the biological racism they perceived at the base of the Nazi system. One priest, for example, circulated a flyer in which he said, 'What is going on in the Church struggle? . . . Salvation comes not from the Aryans, but, as Christ said, from the Jews.' In 1935 the police seized the Catholic weekly *Ketteler Wacht* because it contained an article entitled 'Christianity and Judaism' which was contradictory to Nazi racial ideology. A Catholic priest from Duisberg gave a lecture in 1935 condemning the views of the Berlin anthropologist and eugenicist, Hermann Muckermann, SJ, who was interested in racial hygiene, but was not a biological anti-Semite. Catholics attacked the Nazi attempt to make the care of German blood the primary duty of the political community.[32]

A 1935 report of the *Regierungspräsident* in the Aachen Government District indicated that racist anti-Semitic propaganda was not well-received there, since a large part of the population disapproved of it, especially as it appeared in *Der Stürmer*. It was suggested that very serious differences with the Catholic Church would result if such propaganda continued.[33] Another report states: 'The treatment of the Jewish Question in my district has in any case elicited the greatest indignation, since in their values the Catholic population appraise the Jews first as men and only secondarily judge the matter from a racial-political standpoint.'[34]

In what was clearly an example of moral outrage, Roman Catholic clergymen during the war spoke out against SS eugenic practices. In 1940 Faulhaber attacked 'Himmler's appeal to the SS to do its biological duty'. Two years later clergymen became more explicit. They denounced the practice of encouraging and even paying girls in the Reich Labour Service to engage in sexual relations with members of the *Waffen-SS*. An SD agent vigorously denied the claim and attacked clergymen who, 'in their allegations that girls in the Labour Service are required to have a child by an SS man, will stop at nothing to defame the regime'. Clerical attacks did not compel the SS to revise its eugenic policy, but they may have encouraged some women not to offer themselves voluntarily to SS men. In any case, Himmler was hardly pleased with the final results. The SS *Lebensborn*, established in 1936 to care for the offspring of selective mating, had recorded only 11,000 births by 1945, an inauspicious beginning for the Thousand Year Reich.[35]

Such policies as euthanasia were also halted in Germany owing to popular opposition, especially when this was also articulated publicly by Church leaders. On 11 August 1940 Bertram, as Chairman of the Fulda Conference, wrote to Hans-Heinrich Lammers, head of the Reich Chancellery, and reviewed the historical and recent controversies in the field of eugenics. He stressed that assurances had been formally given that at least euthanasia was still illegal, even if sterilisations were not. Bertram spoke of the 'unqualified inadmissibility of acts of this kind, which were most strictly forbidden' and 'not only by the moral and religious teaching of the Catholic Church, but by the religious and moral convictions of all Christians'. The slightest exception would lead to grave consequences: 'If this principle is once set aside, even with limited exceptions, on the ground of an occasional need, then, as experience teaches us, other exceptions will be made by individuals for their own purposes.' The letter overflows with references to the sanctity of human life.[36] On 6 November 1940, Faulhaber wrote to the Minister of Justice, Franz Gürtner. He reminded Gürtner that in 1934 the German bishops had affirmed the irreconcilability of euthanasia with the Christian conscience. Concluding, he appealed: 'But even during wartime one may not discard the everlasting foundations of the moral order, nor the fundamental rights of the individual.' Because of the rigorous censorship, the outcry was not as great as it might have been. Often such important public statements were not printed in the *Amtsblatt* of the diocese for fear of confiscation, but were sent secretly by courier to the local pastors, who frequently duplicated them. Some found their way to the foreign press in this fashion, and were never officially printed in Germany itself.[37] Following these episcopal observations on eugenics, and sensitive to the high degree of public support already existing, Bishop Clemens August von Galen of Münster created an international uproar by his three famous sermons of 13 and 20 July and 3 August 1941.[38] Reich officials at the time noted that the Church was still a major 'uncoordinated' force. Galen's protest provided the Church with renewed public credibility, and offered it the possibility of retaining a consistency in its moral theology. Unfortunately, Church officials did not extend and continue their critique once the Nazis moved their racial purification machinery east. In a move indicative of the regime's rage, a *Gaustabsleiter*, Arnold F. (Essen), accused Galen of being a paid English agent. But in all of the furore at home and abroad concerning Galen's sermons, it should be recalled that he attacked the National Socialist Party and ideology, not his German fatherland. Belatedly, the bishops had observed that strictly eugenic reasons justifying racial purification were not limited by the traditional parameters of the eugenics debate. The regime was engaged in mass murder. Until it was too late, the bishops failed to see that the soil had been prepared for this development by cultural anti-Semitism and a stress on the *Volk* as a unique *Gemeinschaft*, a view rarely criticised by Church leaders.

V

There is an intrinsic connection linking the pre-1933 eugenic debates, the sterilisation law of 1933 to which the Church never
mounted meaningful opposition, the euthanasia measures of 1939,
and the Final Solution launched in 1941. These policies did not
originate in a vacuum, but rather had a unique and traceable
genesis. The eugenic roots of these genetic and racial policies can be
found in earlier popular, medical, juridical, and moral-theological
debates which supported the control and, in some cases, the elimination of the medically, socially and, ultimately, the racially unwanted. Sterilisation and euthanasia, at least in their involuntary
eugenic forms, and their associated procedures launched a massive
assault on traditional religious and natural morality, and made the
individual merely an appendage of the State or the race. Compounded with doctrines of racial supremacy, they were the prelude
to and the preparation for the wholesale elimination of *Untermens-
chen* by any definition.[39]

Gordon Zahn, Hans Müller and Guenter Lewy have rightly
asserted that the Catholic Church as an institution failed to exert the
vigorous moral and political leadership which might have mitigated the horrors of Nazi racism.[40] In an introduction to Müller's
work, Kurt Sontheimer states that by failing to protest against the
gross injustices of the regime as vigorously as against those measures
which affected its institutional structure, the Church violated its
own moral teachings.[41] Sontheimer has also correctly contended
that Catholic endorsement during the Weimar years of such specific
programmatic aspects of National Socialism as its authoritarianism,
its intense nationalism and its fervent opposition to liberalism and
communism prevented the formation of political principles which
could have prompted Catholics to defend freedom and equal rights
resolutely. This dualism of patriotism and opposition robbed the
institutional churches and nationalist resistance movements in general of their ability to act decisively.[42]

The SD reports on religious affairs along with other documents
and theological publications suggest, however, that some members
of the Church acted more in accordance with Christian principles
than prominent critics have been willing to concede. Whether it
fully satisfies contemporary scholars or not, the Church did resist
Nazi totalitarianism. Conversely, the same documents and articles,

by elucidating the Church's spiritual power in defying the regime and undermining its ideology, could provide the grounds for a further question, which can probably never really be answered. If more vigorously applied, could the Church's considerable influence have significantly mitigated the horrors of National Socialism, or would the Nazi assault on Catholics have intensified, since those who resist in war can easily be labelled traitors? The SD reports, Catholic sermons and theological tracts indicate that the 'public silence' of the institution's hierarchy until late in the Third Reich was not assent or even support, but probably misplaced prudence. By opposing biological racism, some Catholics played a quiet, but outstanding, role in maintaining and nurturing moral responsibility. A perusal of the SD documents and theological materials indicates that the debate on values persisted throughout this period. It may not have been one publicised through the media, but such resistance constituted a significant grass-roots critique of the Nazi *Weltanschauung*.

By the time Catholic leaders realised that Nazi racism was not a gentle cleansing of the body politic, they were at war and could not directly attack Hitler without appearing unpatriotic. Theoretically, official Catholic doctrine on racial hygiene and the sanctity of the person diametrically opposed the National Socialist *Weltanschauung*, which Catholics for political reasons frequently dissociated from Hitler. But by compromises as they reacted to sterilisation, by delaying their wholesale condemnation of euthanasia, by adhering to historical anti-Semitism, and by defending Jewish converts to the faith rather than Jews as persons, Catholics publicly participated in softening up the conscience of the nation for radical racial policies. Even so, Catholics did not in general identify with racial eugenics, but rather with religious/cultural and socio-economic anti-Semitism, failing to understand the connection between 'normal' bigotry and the Final Solution in Hitler's Germany. But the 'Catholic conscience' did not develop in some rarefied atmosphere. Moral reasoning[43] is generally less a reflection of the developmental aspect of the individual than the psychology of the social group. Ideologically and theologically Catholic leaders condemned eugenic values, but did not seem to perceive that every member of a society must be equally supported for the entire political community to remain intact. Popular racism accepted by Catholics could and did support Hitler's Final Solution, even while Catholics on another front resisted, at least theologically, the biomedical politics practised by the Nazi state.

Evaluation of the Church's resistance can only be ascertained by knowing its goal, developed in relation to its capabilities. Physical resistance to Nazi totalitarianism would have resulted in self-destruction. Theological resistance sustained a viable option to Nazi values and maintained at least some institutional integrity for the Church until the end of Hitler's Reich. Only from hindsight can it be realised that anti-Semitism in any form supported Nazi racism and basically contradicted Catholic doctrine, ultimately threatening the Church itself. The refusal of Church leaders consistently and publicly to oppose Nazism by attacking racism and every form of anti-Semitism prevented them from being more effective. Practicality triumphed at the expense of morality. The Church had become too enmeshed in its support for the existing socio-political order, and, by perpetuating the ambiguity concerning Judaism, lost its very real potential as a significant source for dissent.

To encourage groups to resist, it seems necessary to change privately held and usually historically developed beliefs and values.[44] The Catholic critique of biological racism, although not of anti-Semitism *per se*, only posed a limited threat to Hitler's *Weltanschauung*. Catholics and Nazis, however, persistently struggled in this arena for the minds and hearts of men, and both the Catholic and Nazi records indicate that Catholic resistance to eugenic racism was taken seriously because of its potential results.

NOTES

1. U. Tal, 'On Structures of Political Theology and Myth in Germany Prior to the Holocaust', in Y. Bauer and N. Rotenstreich (eds), *The Holocaust as Historical Experience: Essays and A Discussion*, NY, 1981, pp. 43–50; H. Bach, 'Die neue Ordnung', *Der Morgen*, August 1933, pp. 161–6; D. Arieswelle, *Propaganda der Friedlosigkeit – Eine Studie zu Hitlers Rhetorik 1920–1933*, Stuttgart, 1972, p. 55.
2. D. J. K. Peukert, *Inside Nazi Germany: Conformity, Opposition, and Racism in Everyday Life*, trans. Richard Deveson, New Haven, 1987, pp. 208, 215; G. Bock, *Zwangssterilisation im Nationalsozialismus. Studien zur Frauen und Rassenpolitik*, Opladen, 1985; J. Noakes, 'Nazism and Eugenics: The Background of the Nazi Sterilization Law of 14 July 1933', in R. J. Buller *et al.* (eds), *Ideas into Politics: Aspects of European History 1880–1950*, London, 1984, pp. 75–94; K. Behnken (ed.), *Deutschland-Berichte der Sozialdemokratischen Partei Deutschlands (SOPADE) 1934–1940*, vol. 2, Frankfurt am Main, 1980, p. 1375.
3. Peukert, *Inside Nazi Germany*, pp. 217–18, 233; D. Blasius, *Der ver-*

waltete Wahnsinn. Eine Sozialgeschichte der Irrenhausen, Frankfurt am Main, 1980, pp. 155–72; G. Baader and U. Schultz (eds), *Medizin und Nationalsozialismus*, Berlin, 1980; Z. K. Brzezinski, *Ideology and Power in Soviet Politics*, London, 1962, p. 5; K.-J. Müller, 'The Structure and Nature of the National Conservative Opposition in Germany up to 1940', in H. W. Koch (ed.), *Aspects of the Third Reich*, NY, 1985; L. Volk, SJ, 'Der Widerstand der katholischen Kirche', in C. Klessmann and F. Pingel (eds), *Gegner des Nationalsozialismus*, Frankfurt am Main, 1980, pp. 126–39; K. Bindung and A. Hoche, *Die Freigabe der Vernichtung lebensunwerten Lebens*, Freiburg, 1920.

4. D. J. Dietrich, 'The Kulturkampf and the Psychodynamics of Catholic Anti-Semitism', in J. Fout (ed.), *Politics, Parties and the Authoritarian State: Imperial Germany, 1870–1919*, NY, 1989.

5. H. Rothfels, *Die deutsche Opposition gegen Hitler*, new and enlarged edn., ed. H. Graml, Frankfurt am Main, 1977; G. van Roon, *Widerstand im Dritten Reich*, 4th edn, Munich, 1987.

6. G. Lewy, *The Catholic Church and Nazi Germany*, NY, 1964; J. S. Conway, *The Nazi Persecution of the Churches, 1933–45*, Toronto–London–NY, 1968.

7. M. Marrus, *The Holocaust in History*, Hanover, NH, 1987, pp. 170–83; for a collection of reports on the resistance of Catholic and non-Catholic Germans, see K. Behnken (ed.), *Deutschland-Berichte der SOPADE*, 7 vols, Frankfurt am Main, 1980.

8. P. Matheson (ed.), *The Third Reich and the Christian Churches*, Grand Rapids, 1981, p. 1; E. Schlund, OFM, *Katholizismus und Vaterland*, Munich, 1923, pp. 32–3; P. T. Paffrath, OFM, 'Die alttestamentliche Religion und die semitischen Religionen', in E. Schlund, OFM (ed.), *Theologische Gegenwartsfragen*, Regensburg, 1940, pp. 107 ff.; G. Gundlach, SJ, 'Antisemitismus', *Lexikon für Theologie und Kirche*, 2nd rev. edn, Freiburg, 1930, 1:504; M. Buchberger, *Gibt es noch eine Rettung?*, Regensburg, 1931, pp. 97–8; Lewy, *Catholic Church and Nazi Germany* p. 275.

9. D. Dietrich, *Catholic Citizens in the Third Reich: Psycho-Social Principles and Moral Reasoning*, New Brunswick, NJ, 1988, esp. Ch. 6.

10. G. Mann (ed.), *Biologismus im 19. Jahrhundert. Vorträge eines Symposiums von 30. bis 31. Oktober in Frankfurt am Main*, Stuttgart, 1973; A. Ploetz, *Die Tuechtigkeit unsren Rasse und der Schutz der Schwachen*, Berlin, 1895, pp. 224–6; G. Lilienthal, 'Rassenhygiene im Dritten Reich!', *Medizinhistorisches Journal*, vol. 18, 1983, pp. 351–2, 366–71; R. Proctor, *Racial Hygiene: Medicine under the Nazis*, Cambridge, Mass., 1988, pp. 195–6.

11. K. Ackermann, *Der Widerstand der Monatsschrift Hochland gegen den Nationalsozialismus*, Munich, 1965, p. 121.

12. H. Muckermann, *Rassenforschung und Volk der Zukunft. Ein Beitrag zur Einführung in die Frage vom biologischen Werden der Menschheit*, Berlin, 1932; J. Mayer, *Gesetzliche Unfruchtbarmachung Geisteskranken*, Freiburg, 1927.

13. O. Schilling, 'Richtiges und Falsches bei der sog. Eugenik', *Schönere Zukunft*, vol. 7, 1932, pp. 570–2, 597–8.
14. K. Frank, 'Zur Eugenik', *Stimmen der Zeit*, vol. 128, 1935, pp. 316–24.
15. A Mitscherlich and F. Mielke, *Doctors of Infamy*, NY, 1949, p. 91.
16. K. Frank, 'Rassenkunde und Rassengeschichte der Menschheit', *Stimmen der Zeit*, vol. 127, 1934, p. 110; F. Walther, *Die Euthanasie und die Heiligkeit des Lebens. Die Lebensvernichtung im Dienste der Medizin und Eugenik nach christlichen und materialistischen Ethik*, Munich, 1935, p. 22; K. Nowak, *'Euthanasie' und Sterilisierung im 'Dritten Reich'. Die Konfrontation der evangelischen und katholischen Kirche mit dem 'Gesetz zur Verhütung erbkranken Nachwuchses' und der 'Euthanasie' Aktion*, Göttingen, 1978, p. 128.
17. Lewy, *Catholic Church and Nazi Germany*, p. 166; H. Müller, *Katholische Kirche und Nationalsozialismus. Dokumente 1930–1935*, Munich, 1963, p. 393.
18. W. Mariaux, *The Persecution of the Catholic Church in the Third Reich*, London, 1940, p. 457; M. Pribilla, 'Ehe und Familie', *Stimmen der Zeit*, vol. 134, 1938, pp. 53–6; M. Pribilla, 'Christliche Haltung', *Stimmen der Zeit*, vol. 135, 1939, pp. 169–75.
19. A. Artweiler, *Unser Glaube. Christliche Wirklichkeit in der heutigen Welt*, Munich, 1938, pp. 8–10, 36, 152–3, 157–60.
20. O. Schilling, 'Von der sozialen Gerechtigkeit', *Theologische Quartalschrift*, vol. 120, 1939, pp. 289–94.
21. W. Moock, 'Der Einzelne und die Gemeinschaft', *Hochland*, vol. 32, 1934–5, pp. 193–203.
22. P. Lippert, 'Der Gemeinschaftsmensch', *Stimmen der Zeit*, vol. 128, 1935, pp. 361–70.
23. I. Zeiger, 'Werde, der du Bist', *Stimmen der Zeit*, vol. 133, 1938, pp. 298–307.
24. R. Cecil, *The Myth of the Master Race: Alfred Rosenberg and Nazi Ideology*, NY, 1972, pp. 82, 85, 102–3, 111–20; M. A. Gallin, *German Resistance to Hitler: Ethical and Religious Factors*, Washington, DC, 1961, pp. 165, 171, 197; on Wilhelm Neuss and the attack on Rosenberg, see 'Ansprache von Bischofsvikar Teusch aus Anlaß der Promotion zum Dr. rer. pol. der Nanzen-Universität in Nagoya am 6. März 1975'.
25. In the *Frankfurter Zeitung*, 18 January 1937, cited in Mariaux, p. 457.
26. D. J. Dietrich, 'Catholic Resistance in the Third Reich', *Holocaust and Genocide Studies*, vol. 3, 1988, pp. 171–86.
27. S. Friedländer, *Kurt Gerstein: The Ambiguity of Good*, trans. Charles Fullman, NY, 1969, p. 147; M. G. Steinert, *Hitlers Krieg und die Deutschen. Stimmung und Haltung der deutschen Bevölkerung im zweiten Weltkrieg*, Düsseldorf, 1970, p. 259; R. Blaich, 'Rivalry for Ideological Leadership: The German Churches and National Socialism during the Second World War', Ph. D. dissertation, Washington State University, 1975, pp. 47, 245–50; US National Archives (hereafter NA), T-175/271, frame 2767004, 5 June 1942; T-175/266, frame 2760745, 2 October 1943.

28. Franz von Waldburg-Zeil, in NA, T-175/260, frame 2753630, 10 April 1941; NA, T-175/260, frames 2753097-2753099, 23 January 1941; H. G. Adler, *Der Kampf gegen die 'Endlösung der Judenfrage'*, Bonn, 1958, p. 56.
29. NA, T-175/262, frame 2756169, 12 March 1942.
30. NA, T-175/262, frame 2756536, 20 April 1942.
31. NA, T-175/265, frame 2760492, 20 September 1943.
32. *Hauptstaatsarchiv Düsseldorf*, G 21/5, 30655d-4, 5, 33, G/90 Rep. 27, No. 45-6JS 722/35, 1935; H. Boberach (ed.), *Berichte des SD und der Gestapo über Kirchen und Kirchenvolk in Deutschland, 1934–1944*, Mainz, 1971, pp. 77, 208.
33. B. Vollmer, *Volksopposition im Polizeistaat*, Stuttgart, 1957, pp. 259–60.
34. Ibid., p. 277.
35. NA, T-175/262, frame 2756538; T-175/258, frame 604; T-175/270, frame 2766400; Conway, *The Nazi Persecution of the Churches*, p. 273.
36. J. Neuhäusler, *Kreuz und Hakenkreuz. Der Kampf des Nationalsozialismus gegen die katholische Kirche und der kirchliche Widerstand*, vol. 2, Munich, 1946, pp. 357–9.
37. Ibid., pp. 359–63.
38. H. Portmann (ed.), *Bischof Graf von Galen Spricht! Ein apostolischer Kampf und sein Widerhall*, Freiburg, 1946, pp. 66–76; P. Blet *et al.* (eds), *Actes et Documents du Saint Siège relatifs à la Seconde Guerre Mondiale*, vol. 2, Vatican City, 1967, pp. 230–308.
39. R. A. Graham, '"The Right to Kill" in the Third Reich: Prelude to Genocide', *The Catholic Historical Review*, vol. 62, 1976, p. 57; W. Catel, *Grenzsituationen des Lebens. Beitrag zum Problem einer begrenzten Euthanasie*, Nuremberg, 1962; Nowak, *'Euthanasie' und Sterilisierung* pp. 158–77; G. Zillig, 'Über Euthanasie', *Hochland*, vol. 42, 1949/50, p. 351.
40. G. Zahn, *German Catholics and Hitler's Wars: A Study in Social Control*, NY, 1969; Müller, *Katholische Kirche*; Lewy, *Catholic Church and Nazi Germany*.
41. Müller, *Katholische Kirche*, p. xxii.
42. Ibid., p. xxiv; M. G. Steinert, *Hitler's War and the Germans: Public Mood and Attitude During the Second World War*, trans. T. E. J. de Witt, Athens, Ohio, 1977, p. 125.
43. L. Kohlberg, 'Stage and Sequence: The Cognitive-Developmental Approach to Socialization', in D. A. Goslin (ed.), *Handbook of Socialization Theory and Research*, Chicago, 1969; A. Damico, 'The Sociology of Justice: Kohlberg and Milgram', *Political Theory*, vol. 10, 1982, pp. 409–33.
44. R. Brown, *Social Psychology: The Second Edition*, NY, 1986, p. 40.

9

Social Unrest and
the Response of
the Nazi Regime,
1934–1936

Ian Kershaw

The effectiveness and brutality of the Nazi apparatus of repression, and the underlying general support from the great majority of the population for much of what the regime stood for, are two obvious broad reasons why there was never any likelihood that the Hitler state could be seriously threatened by popular opposition. On the other hand, there can be no doubt about the regime's sensitivity to adverse opinion, poor morale, signs of popular unrest, and the potential destabilisation which popular disaffection could stimulate. In particular, the '1918 syndrome' left a continuing mark on attitudes towards the working class – ambivalently regarded as the pillar of the new society and as the likeliest source of revolutionary ferment. A few years ago, Tim Mason argued that the Nazis' fear of the working class, arising from the legacy of 1918, was a key component of their inability to sustain control over the armaments economy, and that workers' industrial muscle in conditions of labour shortage provoked a general crisis of the Nazi system by 1938–9, amounting to a decisive factor in the timing and character of the war.[1] The second part at least of this argument has generally been critically received. One counter-argument was that the Nazi leadership showed little or no consciousness of a general crisis of the system or of the regime's stability's being endangered by worker unrest.[2] Labour problems and the condition of the economy have for the most part, therefore, been seen as less significant

157

in the timing of the war than strategic, military and diplomatic concerns – the international balance of power and the comparative armaments position of rival powers.[3]

In the mid-1930s, however, the situation was very different from what it became by 1938–9. Internally and externally, the Nazi regime was in nowhere near as strong a position in 1934–6 as it was on the eve of the war. Yet this period, it is generally accepted, was pivotal in the internal development of the regime, and contained immeasurable consequences for subsequent external relations. Beginning with the reconsolidation of the regime following the *Röhm-Putsch*, it ended with the placing of the economy on a new footing with the announcement of the Four Year Plan in September 1936. Between these dates, the regime faced arguably its worst crisis of disaffection before the very different conditions of the final phase of the war. The question which this essay poses, therefore, is whether in 1934–6, if not in 1938–9, the perceived threat posed by social unrest and opposition tendencies was taken so seriously by the Nazi leadership that it affected the character of political decisions, thus having a far-reaching effect on both the internal development of the regime and on the road to war. After briefly outlining the nature of the difficulties confronting the regime in those years, the essay offers some illustrations of the manifestations of unrest and of increased oppositional activity, before turning to concentrate on the regime's response.

Background to the Unrest

By late 1934 worrying signs of rising prices, especially for foodstuffs, were beginning to appear in Germany. By the summer of 1935, the situation had become significantly more serious, and with nominal wages pegged the price-rises amounted to a perceptible fall in real wages. A summary of the prices and wages situation prepared for Hitler on 4 September 1935 indicated that almost half the German work-force earned gross wages of 18 RM or less per week. Wages remained at the 1932 level (which were in any case substantially lower than in the last pre-Depression year of 1928). Meanwhile, the official rise of food prices since 1933 was put at 8 per cent, and the overall increase in living costs at 5.4 per cent. Average figures were, however, misleading, since price rises for some foodstuffs of 33 per cent, 50 per cent, and even 150 per cent had been reported.[4] By September 1935 the situation had so worsened that there was common reference to a 'food crisis'

(*Ernährungskrise*) or 'provisions crisis' (*Versorgungskrise*). The problem was certainly made more acute by conjunctural factors, including the bad harvest of 1934, and owed not a little to the inefficiency, mismanagement and harmful bureaucratisation of agricultural production and marketing which the reorganisation of farming under the Reich Food Estate had promoted. But the crisis was also an early indicator of the structural problems of the Nazi economy.

Already in 1934 dwindling currency reserves and a chronic shortage of foreign exchange had provoked a mini-crisis which led to Hjalmar Schacht being placed in charge of the economy, and to the introduction of the 'New Plan' aimed at the reorientation of Germany's foreign trade. With the 'terms of trade' running strongly against Germany – a trend enhanced by an understandable refusal to consider any devaluation of the currency – and with significantly rising armaments expenditures, the inbuilt tension between imports of raw materials for an industrial base already being tilted towards an arms economy and imports of foodstuffs now began to make itself felt. The tension was reflected in the growing contradiction between the demands of Schacht and of Walther Darré, Reich Minister for Food and Agriculture, for their respective spheres of interest. In the case of agriculture, the self-sufficiency effort which had set in by November 1934 in the proclaimed 'production battle' (*Erzeugungsschlacht*), though achieving a significant reduction in imports, in fact led, as a result of some early ill-judged measures by the Reich Food Estate, to a serious shortage of domestic fodder and a vicious circle of food shortages, with reserves of fats and eggs effectively used up by the autumn of 1935.[5] The supply of fatstuffs lagged way behind demand in 1935, reserves had already disappeared, and foreign exchange for imports could only be had at the expense of raw materials needed for industry. Future problems for agriculture seemed also preordained in the drop in livestock herds and the shortage of fodder. The difficulties were amplified by the inefficiency of the Food Estate.

Suddenly, it appeared, the shops were empty. Shortages of fats, butter, eggs and then meat became visible everywhere in the big cities. The situation was made more acute, as was commonly recognised, by farmers holding back their produce in the expectation of enhanced profits. The lowering of an already depressed standard of living in the big cities, and the blatant signs of economic difficulties revealed by the food shortages gave rise to the most worrying manifestations of popular unrest and of oppositional attitudes encountered since 1933 amongst the section of the

population which the regime had always held in greatest suspicion
– the working class.

Reports of Social Unrest and Popular Opposition

Reports emanating from the Nazi authorities and those reaching
the SOPADE, the exiled leadership of the former German Social
Democratic Party in Prague, concurred that the growth of unrest
was widespread, but was most noticeable among the working class
of major industrial areas, such as the Ruhr, Saxony and Berlin. The
situation reports of the Berlin police authorities will serve as an
example of the seriousness with which the unrest was viewed on
the local level. The Berlin reports are unusually frank and expressive, though it should be noted that from the autumn of 1935, the
city had been singled out for favourable treatment in the 'food
crisis', and special provisions were set aside for it.[6] Conditions
were said to be far worse in some other big cities, such as Leipzig.[7]

The report of the Berlin Gestapo for October 1935 stated that the
mood of the population had generally worsened in the month
under review – a deterioration caused mainly by the fats and meat
shortage, the rising cost of foodstuffs and the renewed growth of
unemployment. Shops selling butter had long queues outside
them, and sales had to be watched over by the police. There was
anger at the butter trade and those hoarding butter, and also at the
government. The need to curtail food provisioning in the interests
of rearmament was far from generally acknowledged; it was felt
that the government was not doing enough to pursue those responsible for causing the fats shortage, and confidence in press and radio
explanations was said to have disappeared. The price-rises while
wages remained constant had, it was noted, led to a disquieting
drop in the general standard of living of workers, and to further
bad feeling as people came to the conclusion that the government
was no longer capable of maintaining prices. And everywhere,
especially in bars and at weekly markets, the increase in unemployment formed a topic of conversation. There were rumours of 50
per cent dismissals in seasonal labour, and also of large-scale firings
in armaments factories because of raw-material shortages. The
report noted that confidential soundings had partly confirmed the
rumours, and that the number of unemployed had risen by 2.6 per
cent during October.[8]

In January 1936 the Berlin Gestapo carried out extensive and
thorough investigations into the mood of the people in all parts of

the city, and came up with pessimistic findings. A further deterioration had set in, attributable to a variety of causes, and growing discontent was evident from week to week. A 'directly negative attitude towards State and Movement' was said to prevail among a 'shockingly high percentage of the population', and otherwise there was widespread indifference and weariness. The need of the masses to express their growing criticism was 'now moving into uncontrollable territory, and thus manifesting itself in especially undesirable form'. The mood of the Berlin population, the report continued, was now as before influenced in the first instance by material want. There was no prospect of improvement in living standards, and the income of broad sections of the population stood in crass disproportion to living costs, especially since the prices of necessary foodstuffs had often risen sharply – one example being a 70 per cent increase in the price of frozen meat. These price-rises were causing significant unrest, not least since they stood in contradiction to official declarations and explanations. Rent-rises were also a matter of serious concern, and, though the provisioning situation had improved, people were worried by rumours of new butter shortages. 'The standard of living', it was noted, 'is still in reality extraordinarily miserable'. In addition, the seasonally conditioned rise in the unemployment level had led to sceptical and scornful expressions about the failure of the work-creation action. In various districts of the city, especially in Charlottenburg and Moabit, an active communist verbal propaganda in disguised form was recorded. The food stalls in the market-hall in Moabit and in the markets in Charlottenburg were favourite places for discussions which provoked 'bad feeling and discontent among shoppers'. Arrests for public avowals of communism had increased compared with the previous month.[9]

By March 1936, the mood was said to have deteriorated still further and 'to give rise to great worry with regard to internal political conditions'. A 'marked bitterness' could be registered in wide sections of the population. The 'Heil Hitler' greeting had as good as vanished, apart from uniformed civil servants and people from the provinces. The feeling was widespread that 'something must happen' soon, but views on what that might be gave rise to the most varied speculations. There was a lot of talk of a military dictatorship which would provide 'a fundamentally new and clean state leadership and administration under the dominant influence of the armed forces', and of a second '30 June' – the murder of the SA leadership in the so-called 'Night of the Long Knives' – to bring about 'a fundamental purge of all abuses'. In extraordinarily frank terms, the report regarded the discontent caused by the food shortages as merely a superficial manifestation of a more underlying and deep-seated lack of confidence in the leadership of the state and the Nazi movement which was grounded in the huge gulf between the poverty of the masses and the ostentatious wealth and blatant corruption among Party bosses, in the government and industry. For his toleration of such a deplorable situation, Hitler himself had become the target of criticism, and the report went so far as to claim that 'confidence of the population in the person of the *Führer* is also undergoing a crisis'.[10]

Reports from the SOPADE provide indications of left-wing oppositional assessments of the situation. Wishful thinking about the fragility of Nazi rule and a tendency to exaggerate the extent of anti-regime feeling are part of the built-in bias of the 'Germany Reports'. At the same time, the extracts from the internal reports just provided show that in this instance the SOPADE assessments were not out of line, even if their language is more expressive. From the Ruhr, in November 1935, it was reported that the food shortage had prompted 'an enormous tension' and 'feverish unrest in all sections of the population'. The report from Rhineland–Westphalia that same month spoke of ever-deepening unrest gripping all parts of the population, and amounting to the most serious crisis which the regime had faced. A report from Dresden claimed that in the whole of Saxony the anti-regime mood had deepened to such an extent in the light of the butter, meat and fats shortage 'that it only needed a light to the powder barrel to set off the explosion'. With equal exaggeration, in spite of reflecting a significant diminution of pro-Nazi sentiment, the Rhineland–Westphalia report for October 1935 had claimed that 'one can ask whom one wants to, all sections of the population are against the system. One can only wonder that this government can still exist.'[11]

The growth in social unrest manifested itself in a number of ways. As some of these extracts themselves indicate, there was a marked increase in verbal criticism of the regime. Comments revealing discontent abounded, the 'Hitler Greeting' was often refused, or – as in Berlin in the spring of 1936 – was not proffered except in official places, and jokes, scurrilous remarks and graffiti about leaders of the Party and state were commonplace. There were widespread reports of the revival of illegal opposition groups, especially attached to the KPD. Following the change in strategy for underground activity devised at the 7th Congress of the Comintern and the 'Brussels' Conference of the KPD in 1935, the illegal KPD in Germany made a deliberate attempt to turn its attention to stirring up unrest in factories and within Nazi organisations through its so-called 'Trojan Horse' tactic. The declining living standards, rising food prices, shortages and threats of an increase in unemployment offered favourable conditions for anti-regime verbal propaganda in the autumn and winter of 1935–6, though it is doubtful how much of the rise in social protest is attributable to organised communist agitation.[12]

In the prevailing climate, it was not hard to stir up feeling against the regime, not least in locations such as *Autobahn* construction sites, where living and working conditions were often atrocious, and which had long provided special trouble-spots in the eyes of the authorities. The decline in living standards also lay behind the upward trend in industrial protest at this time. Relative to the existential circumstances of the Third Reich, there was even something of a strike-wave in 1935–6 – though, of course, the strikes were invariably small-scale and short-lived affairs. One police file, labelled 'Strike Movement', contains reports of a great number of short strikes during 1935–6, usually directly prompted by wage issues and the living conditions of the workers.[13] All these signs of unrest were reflected in the growing numbers of workers who were sentenced by the 'Special Courts' in this period for 'political' offences, or were taken by the Gestapo into 'protective custody' or sent to concentration camps. In most cases, there was no indication that those sentenced by the 'Special Courts' had formerly belonged to left-wing organisations.

How did the regime respond to the reported unrest, and to the difficulties it was facing in 1935–6? Did the signs of real or potential opposition have any influence on the political decision-making process at that time? We turn now to consider these questions by looking chronologically at the mark left by the issues of prices, living standards, shortages, economic prognoses and reports of social unrest on the development and formulation of Nazi policy at this critical juncture.

The Regime's Response

Already in September 1934 Hitler himself had requested information on the course of fat and milk prices, following complaints, which Goering had forwarded to the Reich Chancellery, from numerous regions of Prussia about the price situation. According to a note from the head of the Chancellery, Hans-Heinrich Lammers, to Walther Darré, 'he [Hitler] has been repeatedly made aware on his journeys through the Reich that the population with low income is complaining about the price of fatstuffs. He would like to know whether these complaints are justified.'[14] Two months later, Hitler ordered the appointment of Carl Goerdeler, *Oberbürgermeister* of Leipzig, as Reich Commissar for Price Surveillance. He explained his reasons for the appointment and for the need to provide stricter controls over prices to a ministerial meeting on 5 November 1934: 'Since the present wage level was to be held to, there must not be price conditions which do not accord with the wage level. He [Hitler] has given the working class his word that he would allow no price increases. Wage-earners would accuse him of breaking his word if he did not act against the rising prices. Revolutionary conditions among the people would be the further consequence. He would not, therefore, allow the shocking driving up of prices.'[15]

In July 1935, Reich Minister of the Interior Wilhelm Frick sent to Lammers in the Chancellery extracts from political 'situation reports' from all parts of the Reich with the urgent request to bring to Hitler's attention the 'serious danger' of the wave of price-rises and the extremely unfavourable impact this was having upon the population, especially the working class.[16] Among the extracts he sent was a report of the Gestapo in Münster in Westphalia emphasising the 'depressed mood', especially among miners, as a result of price increases of between 20 and 150 per cent, while wages were insufficient to provide necessary food and clothing. The opposition was finding fertile ground for agitation. 'The mood prompts fears for the worst', the report added, referring also to rumours that the miners in and around Gelsenkirchen were planning a hunger-strike if nothing were done to help them. In another report, the *Regierungspräsident* of Minden in Westphalia pointed out bluntly that 'further food price rises would be politically intolerable'.[17] Similar reports were coming in thick and fast from the *Gauleiter* of the Nazi Party, from the Trustees of Labour and from other authorities.

On 27 August 1935 a meeting in Berlin of the Trustees of Labour from all regions of the Reich produced unanimous reports of successful communist agitation and a very poor mood among the workers. The Trustee for the *Nordmark* – the region centring on Hamburg – spoke of 'a devastating picture of the mood of the working class' which had emerged from investigations in his area. He saw 'extraordinarily great dangers' for the political situation if conditions did not improve. The Trustee for Bavaria somewhat apocalyptically prophesied that if things were not fundamentally altered 'we are not going to get through the next winter'.[18] All the Trustees demanded in the most forthright terms an immediate and significant reduction in prices.

Ten days before the meeting of the Trustees, presumably in the light of Frick's letter, Hitler had demanded a statistical report on the situation regarding working-class income and the price and provisions situation.[19] He was presented with the report, indicating generally poor standards of living with falling real wages and steep price increases in certain necessary commodities, in early September.[20] Later the same month, Hitler was informed about the serious consequences which the shortage boded for rearmament as well, in view of the critical depletion of foreign exchange. The amount of foreign currency needed for the import of fatstuffs (in particular, cheap margarine) to make up the deficiency was put at 300,000 RM per day, and even this was 110,000 RM per day less than Agriculture Minister Darré wanted. The implications for government policy were clearly stated: 'All foreign exchange [expended] for fats provisions has as a consequence a drop in raw material imports and therefore increased unemployment. But even this must be accepted, for the provisioning of the population with fatstuffs must take precedence over all other needs' – meaning, of course, temporarily even over rearmament.[21]

Towards the end of October 1935, Goerdeler, the Price Commissar, sent Hitler a memorandum containing a devastating analysis of Germany's economic position. Goerdeler pointed to structural problems in the economy which were causing the shortages, and stated that if things carried on as they were, only a hand-to-mouth existence would be possible from January 1936 onwards. Large supplies of foreign currency were urgently needed to import fatstuffs, which could only be done at the expense of other imports, meaning the withdrawal of foreign exchange for the import of raw materials. Goerdeler regarded 'the satisfactory provisioning of the population with fats, even in relation to armaments, as having political priority'. He advocated the return to a market economy, a re-emphasis upon exports and a corresponding reduction in the rearmament drive, which in his view was at the root of the economic problems. He saw only one alternative if his line were not followed: the reversion to a non-industrial economy, with drastic reductions in the standard of living for every German.[22]

Goerdeler had also reached the conclusion that the Reich Commissariat for Price Surveillance had become as good as redundant in the circumstances, and twice – in November 1935 and again in

February 1936 – suggested its immediate dissolution. On both occasions, however, Hitler typically decided – evidently out of considerations of image and propaganda – that a dissolution of the Price Commissariat could not be entertained 'until further notice'.[23] According to the later account of Alfred Sohn-Rethel, at that time closely aware of the thinking in business circles, Goerdeler's memorandum met with considerable support among leading representatives of industry – though not in the synthetic fuel-chemical lobby of IG Farben – and gave rise to lively debate about the future development of the economy, with some talk even of a possible *putsch*.[24]

In the same month of October 1935 Hitler, reacting to a request by Economics Minister Schacht, ordered a meeting between Schacht and Food Minister Darré, his rival in the struggle over foreign exchange, regarding the allocation of the scarce currency reserves. Typically, Hitler himself was not present, but Goering was mandated to decide on the allocations at the meeting which took place in the building of his Air Ministry in Berlin. To the surprise of Schacht and of many in business circles, Goering – certainly with Hitler's approval or at his behest – sided with Darré, and ordered Schacht to make available the necessary foreign exchange – amounting to an additional sum of 12.4 million Reichsmarks – for the import of oil-seed for margarine production.[25] The reason for the apparently surprising decision seems clear. Again, out of consideration for the likely psychological effect, the only alternative – food rationing – had to be avoided. According to the 'confidential information' of the press agency in November 1935, the *Führer* had 'decided that the card for fats should not be introduced and that instead sufficient currency for the import of foodstuffs should be made available by the Economics Minister'. It was reported that the War Ministry had been prepared to forgo a proportion of its allotted currency until the spring in order to make available foreign exchange for food.[26] For the short term at any rate, therefore, the armaments build-up had to take a back seat to imports of foodstuffs to quieten the unrest, which was adopting menacing proportions. To this extent, there seems a clear connection between popular opposition and significant policy decisions in autumn 1935, which soon came to have far-reaching consequences.

Hitler's concern about the domestic situation in 1935 is also reflected in a number of entries in Goebbels's diaries. According to the diary notes for 15 July 1935, 'domestic policy has him [Hitler] strongly in its grip'. On 11 August, Goebbels noted: 'Bad mood in the country. We must get a tighter grip on it.' A week later, on

19 August, Hitler was mentioned as pointing out a decline in the popular mood. Goebbels spoke three times in the following days – on 21, 25 and 27 August – with Hitler about the poor mood due to the food situation. According to Goebbels's notes of the lengthy discussion with Hitler on 27 August, Darré had failed to master the problem and Hitler had decided to deploy Goerdeler to bring prices back under control. As we have seen, little came of this goal. On 5 October 1935 a conference of leaders took place about the food situation, 'which is very serious', and immediate measures were adopted to provide special relief for Berlin.[27]

At the same time that the domestic unrest and food-supply difficulties were reaching their peak, Hitler was also becoming heavily preoccupied with foreign affairs in the wake of the Abyssinian crisis. In October 1935, according the Goebbels, he told ministers and army leaders that 'everything is coming for us three years too soon. . . . Rearm and get ready. Europe is on the move again. If we're clever, we'll be the winners.'[28] Sohn-Rethel's account suggests that it was around this time, in mid-October, and precisely at the juncture that the decision was made to provide currency for fats not armaments, that a sort of 'inner cabinet' was formed and met on a number of occasions in the Reich Chancellery to discuss the acceleration of rearmament. Present at the meetings were leading military figures (Admiral Raeder and General von Blomberg), the Foreign, Economics and Finance Ministers (Konstantin von Neurath, Schacht and Schwerin von Krosigk), the head of the Party (Rudolf Hess), Goering – the dominant figure in the discussions – and Hitler (who said little). According to Sohn-Rethel, there was some talk of necessary preparations for a coming war against the Soviet Union, and with this in mind a decision was taken at the end of November 1935 about the need for an acceleration in the rearmament drive.[29]

In contradiction to this, however, Hitler personally intervened, despite bitter objections from Schacht, in the spring of 1936 to provide Darré once more with the necessary scarce foreign currency – in this instance 60 million Reichsmarks – for the import of seed-oil.[30] Provision of consumer commodities still at this stage retained priority over the import of raw materials for rearmament. Yet the armament situation was becoming increasingly desperate, and Schacht had to explain to War Minister von Blomberg in December 1935 that an increase in raw-material imports was out of the question. By the spring of 1936, available supplies of raw materials for rearmament had sunk to a precariously low level.[31]

In the spring of 1936, then, the regime faced a very difficult situation. The tension on the socio-economic front, reflected in the popular unrest and growth in oppositional activity, posed a recognised danger, not of course in the sense of a revolutionary threat to the political hold of the regime, but indirectly, through the limits it was imposing on armaments policy and through the sustenance it was offering to alternative economic strategies which scarcely fitted the plans of the Nazi leadership. From the evidence assembled, it seems clear that Nazi leaders, including Hitler himself, were seriously concerned about the possible consequences of a lasting period of food shortages, rising prices, and social tension both in terms of domestic political stability and of the build-up of armaments. The regime showed itself prepared, at this critical point, to buy off possible further unrest with the cash it needed for rearmament. But at the same time, foreign-policy considerations were making the acceleration rather than retardation of rearmament vital. Nazi economic policy appeared to have run into a cul-de-sac, and the social unrest was a contributory factor in bringing the difficulties to a head. With both foreign exchange and the supplies of necessary raw materials in a critical state, influential figures in the economy – prominent among them Goerdeler and Schacht – were pressing for a slowing down of the rearmament drive, the revitalisation of exports, and for Germany's reintegration into the international market economy, while other economic lobbies – especially IG Farben and the armed forces leadership – placed their support behind accelerated rearmament and increased autarky.

As the reports cited earlier indicated, fears were also growing in the autumn of 1935 of a renewed rise in unemployment, which would certainly have followed the continued truncation of raw-materials supplies, a prolonged retardation of rearmament, and the reversion to conventional involvement in foreign trading which Goerdeler was advocating. In fact reports from the Reich Labour Ministry even as late as January 1936 were painting a gloomy picture of unemployment, still running at around two and a half million, and, it seemed, with little prospect of a further, lasting reduction.[32]

Finally, in the late winter of 1935–6, while police reports frequently pointed to increased opposition activity, especially on the part of a revived underground KPD, reports from Party agencies repeatedly alluded to the poor morale and sagging spirits of the membership.[33] All in all, the outlook for the regime did not appear to be especially rosy from the vantage point of February 1936. The 'break-out' from the seemingly intractable situation took the form of the risky 'forward moves' which were so typical of Nazi policy initiatives, and which contained such far-reaching consequences.

The 'Break-Out'

By late January 1936, Hitler was speaking of an early solution to the Rhineland question.[34] Certainly, diplomatic and strategic considerations in the light of the upheaval caused by the Abyssinian affair, most notably the position of Italy, were crucial to Hitler's thinking. But it seems likely that internal considerations also played a not inconsiderable role in influencing the timing. Certainly, this was the view of Foreign Minister von Neurath when speaking to the German Ambassador in Rome, Ulrich von Hassell. In fact, von Neurath went so far as to suggest that the question of reoccupying the Rhineland had 'only' domestic causes. In his view, Hitler was conscious of the general drop in enthusiasm for the regime which compelled him to search for a new national slogan to fire the masses again. The timing to coincide with the 'Heroes' Memorial Day' on 8 March was allegedly chosen deliberately in order to heighten the propaganda effect. Von Hassell agreed that domestic considerations were uppermost in Hitler's mind. The action, he suggested, offered a favourable opportunity to forget the provisions difficulties and also the clashes between the Party and the Catholic Church in the Rhineland.[35] Reports from the Rhineland itself before the reoccupation certainly painted a fairly dismal picture of the especially unfavourable economic conditions there, which, together with the 'Church struggle', were having a highly negative effect on the political attitude of the population.[36] Hitler himself, of course, was well aware of the domestic implications of plebiscites on foreign coups. The massive mobilisation for the 'election' of 29 March is, in fact, scarcely explicable without the recognition of the need to reinvigorate the masses after the problems of the preceding winter. Similarly, the cancellation at the last minute of the Works Councils elections scheduled for April 1936 is probably attributable to the presumption that the results would turn out to be far less favourable than those of the plebiscite.[37]

The Rhineland coup was certainly highly effective, as SOPADE reports make plain, in taking the wind out of the sails of the opposition.[38] There was a notable rallying round the regime, and in particular a massive boost to Hitler's personal popularity, as the prevailing poor mood dissipated at least temporarily, and morale within the Party revived. Moreover, against the gloomy prognoses of the Reich Labour Ministry, the unemployment figures showed a surprisingly sharp drop in the spring and summer of 1936, foodstuffs were returning to the shops, and, with prices of necessities falling again, the provisioning situation was returning to normal.

And a huge onslaught by the Gestapo which brought some 11,000 arrests of Communists on top of the 15,000 the previous year[39] meant that the short-lived revival of KPD activity had been effectively crushed by the summer of 1936.

The basic economic conflict between priorities for consumption and for armaments remained unresolved by the Rhineland spectacular. It reached its climax in the summer of 1936 after Goering, following his experiences of the previous winter, had been installed as a crisis-manager to find the necessary raw materials for rearmament, with supplies sufficient for only a further one to two months, and with Schacht demanding a reduction in the pace of rearmament.[40] The internal disputes in leading economic circles about future development ended during the culmination of the raw-materials crisis in summer 1936 by forcing Hitler to intervene with his memorandum on the Four Year Plan. The official launch of the Plan – marking the victory of the autarky lobby – followed at the Party Rally in September. In the event, neither of the alternatives which Goerdeler had suggested in his memorandum of October 1935 – an export-orientated or an agrarian economy – had been adopted, and his further memorandum of August 1936, conflicting with the autarky line, was rejected out of hand.[41]

Testimony to the continuing sensitivity to the dangers of price inflation was the appointment, within the framework of the Four Year Plan, of Josef Wagner, *Gauleiter* of Silesia, as Reich Commissar for Price Formation. His powers of intervention and control were theoretically wide; but much of his actual role fell within the realm of propaganda and political psychology, persuading the people that he represented the will of the Nazi leadership 'decisively to intervene in the interests of the broad public where lack of sense, profit lust and the irresponsibility of individuals or groups threatened to damage nation and state'.[42]

Conclusions

In a little-noticed passage in the Hossbach Memorandum of November 1937 Hitler himself apparently referred to the experiences of the 'provisions crisis', when he said: 'If I were not to act by 1943–45, any year could, owing to a lack of reserves, produce a food crisis, to cope with which the necessary foreign exchange was not available, and this must be regarded as a "waning point of the regime".'[43] This awareness of the dangers of popular unrest stemming from a crisis in food supplies matches Hitler's actions during the winter of 1935–6. During this period, he appears to have insisted on being kept informed of the situation, and responded by approving the temporary priority given to food supplies rather than armaments. This in itself drastically worsened the already precarious raw-materials situation to the extent that radical steps, presaged by Goering's appointment to deal with raw-material supply, were necessary to restore the priority to armaments. Indirectly, therefore, the social tensions unleashed by the food crisis of 1935–6 played a significant role in the process which culminated in the Four Year Plan. The crisis brought into the limelight the imminent tension in the economic policies of the regime, and showed that – at this juncture at any rate – the Nazi leadership's first priority was the safeguarding of social stability. The Four Year Plan provided a partial and provisional solution to the underlying economic problems by choosing forced rearmament on an autarkic basis (as far as this was possible), without attempting to depress living standards along the lines advocated by General Thomas and others in the *Wehrmacht's* economic bureau. The result was an off-balanced and overheated economy, and a work-force which in peacetime could not be kept indefinitely at the production levels demanded by the Plan.

As Tim Mason well demonstrated,[44] economic problems mounted alarmingly by 1938–9, even if it could be claimed that other factors were more significant in influencing the timing of hostilities. From 1936 onwards, however, there was no possibility of retreat from the course which Germany had adopted. This paper has attempted to show that the critical and complicated decision-making processes of the year 1936 had not a little to do with the causes, experiences and consequences of the social tension and opposition which were made visible to the Nazi leadership through the 'food crisis' of the winter of 1935–6.

NOTES

1. T. W. Mason, *Sozialpolitik im Dritten Reich*, Opladen, 1977, esp. Chs. 1 and 6; and 'Innere Krise und Angriffskrieg 1938/1939', in F. Forstmeier and H.-E. Volkmann (eds), *Wirtschaft und Rüstung am Vorabend des Zweiten Weltkrieges*, Düsseldorf, 1975, pp. 158–88.
2. This point was given special emphasis by L. Herbst, 'Die Krise des nationalsozialistischen Regimes am Vorabend des Zweiten Weltkrieges

und die forcierte Aufrüstung. Eine Kritik', *Vierteljahrshefte für Zeitgeschichte*, vol. 26, 1978, pp. 347–92.

3. See esp. J. Dülffer, 'Der Beginn des Krieges 1939: Hitler, die innere Krise und das Mächtesystem', *Geschichte und Gesellschaft*, vol. 2, 1976, pp. 443–70. The most hard-hitting attack on Mason's argument has recently come from R. Overy, 'Germany, "Domestic Crisis", and War in 1939', *Past and Present*, no. 116, 1987, pp. 138–68. For Mason's response, along with a comment from David Kaiser and a 'Reply' from Richard Overy, see 'Debate – Germany, "Domestic Crisis" and War in 1939', ibid., no. 122, pp. 200–40.

4. Bundesarchiv/Koblenz (hereafter BAK): R43II/318, Fos. 205–13, 28, 61–2 (and also Fos. 195–203, 214–15); R43II/318a, Fos. 45–53.

5. See J. E. Farquharson, *The Plough and the Swastika: The NSDAP and Agriculture in Germany 1928–45*, London–Beverly Hills, 1976, pp. 166–8.

6. BAK: NL118/62, entry for 5 October 1935; see also BAK: R43II/863. Fos. 69–83.

7. BAK: R43II/318a, Fo. 15, memorandum of Reich Price Commissar Carl Goerdeler, 26 October 1935.

8. BAK: R58/535, Bl. 91–6, report of Stapo Berlin for October 1935.

9. BAK: R58/567, Bl. 84–93, report of Stapo Berlin for January 1936.

10. Institut für Marxismus-Leninismus/Zentrales Parteiarchiv/East Berlin (hereafter IML/ZPA): St. 3/44/I, Fos. 103–7, report of Stapo Berlin, 6 March 1936.

11. *Deutschland-Berichte der Sozialdemokratischen Partei Deutschlands 1934–1940*, 7 vols, Frankfurt am Main, 1980, vol. 2, pp. 1013, 1251–5 (16 October, 12 November 1935).

12. See D. J. K. Peukert, *Die KPD im Widerstand. Verfolgung und Untergrundarbeit an Rhein und Ruhr 1933 bis 1945*, Wuppertal, 1980, pp. 204–50 for a good account of rising unrest among the Ruhr working class, but scepticism about the extent of the KPD's role in fostering it. For the changes in Communist strategy in 1935, see A. Merson, *Communist Resistance in Nazi Germany*, London, 1985, Ch. 8.

13. IML/ZPA: St. 3/463, 'Streikbewegung'.

14. BAK: R43II/193, Fol. 157, Lammers to Darré, 30 September 1934. The extracts from the reports sent by Goering are in the file. A number of top-level discussions, involving the *Gauleiter*, and, on one occasion, taking place in Hitler's own presence, followed the intervention. Ibid., Fos. 122–245.

15. BAK: R43II/315a, Fo. 31, extract from the minutes of a ministerial meeting, 5 November 1934.

16. BAK: R43II/318. Fo. 2, Frick to Lammers, 24 July 1935.

17. Ibid., Fos. 16, 19, 23, 28–9, Gestapo Münster, 15 July 1935; Regierungspräsident Minden, 5 July 1935. Further reports are contained in Fos. 1–29.

18. Ibid., Fos. 62, 64, minutes of a meeting of the Trustees of Labour, 27 August 1935.

19. Ibid., Fo. 31, Lammers to the President of the Statistisches Reichsamt, 17 August 1935.
20. Ibid., Fos. 205–13; BAK: R43II/318a, Fos. 45–53, 'Aufzeichnung über die Einkommensverhältnisse, über die Preislage und über die Versorgungslage in Deutschland', 4 September 1935.
21. BAK: R43II/318, Fos. 219–22, 'Vermerk' for Lammers, 20 September 1935; similarly in the prices and wages summary for Hitler of 4 September 1935, Fos. 205–13, and R43II/318a, Fos. 45–53.
22. BAK: R43II/318a, Fos. 11–31, Goerdeler Denkschrift, 26 October 1935.
23. Ibid., Fos. 35, 66, Goerdeler to Lammers, 1 November 1935; 'Vermerk über die Auflösung des Reichskommissariats für Preisüberwachung', 1 February 1936, with Lammers's note about Hitler's decision the following day.
24. A. Sohn-Rethel, Ökonomie und Klassenstruktur des deutschen Faschismus, Frankfurt am Main, 1975, p. 177. The date of the memorandum is given as November 1935 and it is said (p. 140) to have carried the title 'Über die wirkliche Lage in Deutschland'. Though Goerdeler was a prolific memorandum-writer, it seems almost certain that this is either the identical (untitled) report contained in BAK: R43II/318a, Fos. 11–31, or was closely based on this report.
25. D. Petzina. Autarkiepolitik im Dritten Reich, Stuttgart, 1968, pp. 32–3. See also Sohn-Rethel, Ökonomie und Klassenstruktur, pp. 105–6; Farquharson, Plough and Swastika, p. 168.
26. BAK: ZSg. 101/28, Fo. 331, 'Informationsbericht Nr. 44', 7 November 1935.
27. BAK: NL118/62, entries for 15 July, 11, 19, 21, 25, and 27 August, 5 October 1935.
28. Ibid., entry for 19 October 1935.
29. Sohn-Rethel, Ökonomie und Klassenstruktur, pp. 138–41.
30. Petzina, Autarkiepolitik, pp. 33–4.
31. Ibid., p. 35.
32. BAK: R43II/533 Fos. 91–6, reports of Minister Franz Seldte sent to Lammers.
33. The dullness of Party life in early 1936 is emphasised by D. Orlow, The History of the Nazi Party, 1933–45, Newton Abbot, 1973, pp. 170–5.
34. BAK: NL118/63, entry in Goebbels's diary for 21 January 1936; G. L. Weinberg, The Foreign Policy of Hitler's Germany: Diplomatic Revolution in Europe 1933–36, Chicago–London, 1970, p. 247.
35. E. Robertson, 'Zur Wiederbesetzung des Rheinlandes', Vierteljahrshefte für Zeitgeschichte, vol. 10, 1962, pp. 203–4; M. Funke, '7. März 1936. Fallstudie zum außenpolitischen Führungsstil Hitlers', in W. Michalka (ed.), Nationalsozialistische Außenpolitik, Darmstadt, 1978, pp. 278–9; J. Dülffer, 'Zum "decision-making process" in der deutschen Außenpolitik 1933–1939', in M. Funke (ed.), Hitler, Deutschland und die Mächte, Düsseldorf, 1978, pp. 196–7.

36. For example, BAK: R58/570, Fos. 104–8, report of Gestapo Cologne, 6 February 1936; BAK: NS22/vorl. 583, reports of Gauleiter Grohé of Cologne–Aachen from 8 June, 6 July and 10 December 1935, dealing with the economic disadvantages of the demilitarised zone and the strength of the Catholic Church's position.
37. Mason, *Sozialpolitik*, p. 206. Reich Labour Minister Seldte had no inkling of a postponement until he read the announcement of the *Deutsches Nachrichtenbüro* in the Berlin evening papers soon after the Rhineland invasion. Seldte was subsequently informed by telephone that Hitler wished a one-year postponement. It was later said that the reason was to prevent a large part of the population having to go to the polls again immediately after the Reichstag election. See BAK: R43II/547b. Fos. 2, 19.
38. See, e.g., DBS, vol. 3, pp. 304–8.
39. H. Weber, 'Kommunistischer Widerstand', in R. Löwenthal and P. von zur Mühlen (eds), *Widerstand und Verweigerung in Deutschland 1933 bis 1945*, Berlin–Bonn, 1984, p. 93.
40. Petzina, *Autarkiepolitik*, p. 35.
41. Ibid., p. 47.
42. BAK: R43II/315a, Fo. 7, Deutsches Nachrichtenbüro, 'Gauleiter Wagner über die Preisbildung', 2 December 1936.
43. J. Noakes and G. Pridham (eds), *Nazism 1919–1945: A Documentary Reader*, vol. 3, Exeter, 1988, p. 684.
44. Mason, *Sozialpolitik*, Ch. 6.

10

Peasants and Workers in their Environment: Nonconformity and Opposition to National Socialism in the Austrian Alps

Ernst Hanisch

I

The Bavaria-Project of Martin Broszat and his colleagues has elevated research on the National Socialist era to a new level.[1] It is my intention to analyse the diverse attitudes of the majority of the population in the Austrian *Alpengauen*, attitudes which did not show either enthusiastic endorsement or rejection of Nazi rule.

The social-scientific reflections of the term 'milieu' as a category of analysis have been applied to investigate the history of social identification in the Third Reich.[2] A socio-cultural milieu is defined as the concatenation of various structural aspects, such as a given economic situation, specific class characteristics, cultural orientation, and religious penetration.[3] In comparison to the concepts of class-consciousness or political party, the 'milieu' concept is restricted to a specific geographical area which is determined either by local or regional borders.[4] The milieu is thus distinguished through compact, highly integrated emotional relationships, for example, by the surrounding environment – a circle of daily contacts, relatives, friends, colleagues, acquaintances – and by intermediary associations – co-operatives, churches and political parties.[5] Émile Durkheim, the renowned sociologist, defined the 'social milieu' as resulting from two specific elements: people and things.[6] Included in the latter element 'thing' is the environment, which is especially characterised in the Alps by the economic importance and symbolic connotation of the mountains in relation to the forests, water, houses, churches, books, etc. In short, the milieu means the dialogue between ecology and culture, the interplay between local topography, flora, fauna and climate and the cultural repertoire determined by the inhabitants of a certain area.[7] The socio-cultural milieu can transcend certain class structures associated, for example, in the Catholic-agrarian milieu with the village social system including farmers, domestic servants and agricultural trade; it can, however, also remain a part of class-consciousness, as seen in the working-class milieu.

The establishment of the new totalitarian National Socialist regime was based, for the most part, on mass mobilisation, and thereby sought to weaken the influence of the socio-cultural milieu, if not to dissolve it completely. To cling to the milieu meant to stand in opposition to the demands of the government. The milieu was a potential shield that could retard the influence of State and Party in local society. As a result, a certain constellation developed out of this tense situation: conformist behaviour towards the NSDAP was interpreted as nonconformist behaviour toward the milieu of the village. A report by the SD (*Sicherheitsdienst* or Security Service of the SS) assessed the situation in Tyrol in 1940 as follows: 'The few National Socialist teachers in agrarian munici-palities are practically treated with hostility by the inhabitants, especially then when they have quit the Church.'[8] On the other hand, a conforming acceptance of the milieu – the continued celebration of the abolished traditional farmers' holidays, or the use of the customary greeting '*Grüß Gott*' – was seen by the Nazi authorities as a nonconformist stance toward the State and the Party. The extreme example of a conscientious objector and religious individualist, Franz Jägerstätter, revealed a double break with the existing situation. His behaviour showed a firm disinclination toward both National Socialism and the local milieu. He gave both Church and State reasons for feeling insecure.[9]

II

The predominant economic elements in rural society in the Austrian alpine provinces can be described as follows: animal husbandry, and hence a larger number of domestic servants, as well as

Table 10.1 Economic Sectors in the Austrian Provinces in 1934
(% employed)

	Primary Sector	Secondary Sector	Tertiary Sector
Salzburg	45.4	24.7	29.9
Styria	53.7	25.1	21.2
Carinthia	53.3	25.5	21.2
Tyrol	46.8	25.0	28.2

Source: G. Otruba, 'Wachstumsverschiebungen in den Wirtschaftssektoren Österreichs, 1869–1961' in *Vierteljahresschrift für Sozial- und Wirtschaftsgeschichte*, vol. 62, 1975, p. 61.

middle and large landowning farmers.[10] At the end of the nineteenth century this society had opened itself to tourism, which as a result brought relatively advanced development in this tertiary sector.[11]

In the typical tourist provinces, Tyrol and Salzburg, the tertiary sector had outdistanced the secondary sector by the eve of the First World War.

The Catholic-agrarian environment can be categorised by the following structural characteristics: the predominance of a possession-oriented ideology, a strong attachment to one's home and heritage, and dense social control through the local culture based on a traditional village sense of religiousness. The village social hierarchy was quite rigid, and infringements of the social scale in either direction were not tolerated. Stratification was based on property, age and sex.[12] The basic confrontation of agrarian society with National Socialism was a result of several factors: a long tradition of subjugation to outside powers and consequent rural insubordination,[13] and the attitude that National Socialism was comparable to a natural catastrophe, such as flooding or an avalanche. To survive, one had to grin and bear it – at least until the catastrophe was over.

In 1938 various traditions began to overlap. Between 1933 and 1938 Church and State played the old game of the Counter-Reformation in which the illegal National Socialists identified themselves with the revolutionary tradition of the Peasants' War. According to their interpretation, they were in alignment with the exploited masses – against Church and State – or, quite simply, against authority. In 1938, however, the poles changed rather radically. The National Socialists took over the powers of the State and began to oppress the Church with an ever-increasing intensity.

Table 10.2 Two Villages from the Salzburg District, Flachgau:
Großgmain and Dorfbeuern

Total population in 1939	Registered National Socialists (1945)			
	Absolute Numbers	Inhabitants %	Voters %	Share of VdU Votes %
Großgmain 909	106	12	15	24
Dorfbeuern 922	47	5	6	9

It became apparent that the Austrian people, in spite of disciplinary measures from above, were deeply Catholic. As the National Socialists began to remove crucifixes from the classrooms, to imprison priests in concentration camps, and to abolish certain religious holidays, they unknowingly reactivated the alliance between Austria and Catholicism. This constellation, which had been maintained by the powers that were since the Baroque period, found spontaneous support from the masses as a result of renewed persecution and suppression. That old rural insubordination came to the aid of the Church. This meant that the Catholic milieu could not be broken apart.

An additional factor to be considered is the form of settlement of the alpine farmers, which was characterised by small villages and numerous single-family farms. It is therefore clear why the totalitarian demands of the Nazi regime in many cases were not able to penetrate the rural structural hierarchy. The sources available to us describe the various types of villages. One village model shows a relatively unproblematic relationship between the Church and the NSDAP. Even those few individuals who belonged to the Party went to church on Sunday, sang in the church choir, and walked in church processions, much to the annoyance of the Gestapo. In this case, government demands for power were at least so refined that they did not create any marked conflicts in the local milieu. The other village type was characterised by a deep cleft between the Party and the Church in which a small, embittered war between the village party leader and the local priest broke out afresh on a daily basis. Thus, a particular structural reality can be summarised in the following thesis: the stronger the socialising influence of the Catholic Church, the weaker the National Socialist penetration. Such was the case at the beginning of the 1930s, and so it remained in the 1940s. More precise information on political structures is available to us for the Salzburg district of Flachgau. Based on my own investigation, two villages, with quite different political profiles, are used as examples (Table 10.2). Großgmain lies very close to the Bavarian border and is dependent upon tourism as a source of income. Dorfbeuern is situated in a remote area and was strongly influenced by a Benedictine monastery, Michaelbeuern. Comparable in size, these two villages show that in the case of Großgmain more than twice as many individuals were National Socialist Party members, indicating that these individuals gave their votes to the Association of Independents Party (VdU – *Verband der Unabhängigen*) in 1945.

III

The *Anschluß* gave alpine farmers access to the larger German market. A wave of mechanisation and a more tightly controlled market structure tore these farmers away from their moderate subsistence economy and subordinated them as never before to the decisions of the urban centres. At the same time, an absolute ban was enforced on compulsory auctions due to financial difficulties. This meant that the existence of these farmers, whose livelihood had been threatened by financial ruin, would be newly assessed and protected. Thus, the National Socialists were able to gain agrarian support in particular through an insolvency propaganda campaign. An exact study of this campaign has shown, however, that this was, in fact, a refinancing plan in which farm debts were concentrated and taken over by the state and the banks. The farmers were in reality not released from their debts, although they were given this impression. The new duties of the bloated agrarian bureaucracy now included keeping an exact record of each farm, thereby controlling and observing the internal affairs of farm life, both economic and familial. Those who profited the most from these measures were the middle-sized and large landowning farmers, especially those who were affected by the new farm inheritance law (*Erbhofgesetz*). In addition, the Third Reich guaranteed construction loans and subsidies. For example, each farmer in St Johann/Pongau received 1,632 *Reichsmarks* (RM) in loans and 6,443 RM in subsidies. These funds were a considerable amount for that period. Up to one-third of these monies were used for the purchase of new machines and tools. Economically speaking, the National Socialists were very supportive of the agrarian sector.[14]

In spite of these benefits, rural sentiment was less than cheerful.

In January 1939 the State Agrarian Counsellor commented that: 'The mood of the farmers is depressed and discouraged. A certain political radicalism among the lower-level party agencies and the tactless treatment by our comrades, who do not even belong to the party, have added to their depression.'[15] The farm inheritance laws, refinancing and the new market structure radically restricted the farmer's free property rights; a rural exodus created a shortage of farm-workers; the wages of the remaining workers increased rather significantly; and, in addition, the strife between Church and State intensified even more in the autumn of 1938.

Agrarian society had developed along two competitive lines since the middle of the nineteenth century. The older model, as characterised by Norbert Ortmayr, was a patron–client relationship based on a 'moral economy';[16] the other model, which had developed out of the class-formation process, penetrated agrarian society only minimally.[17] How did National Socialism affect the unstable balance between these two models? Although controlled by the state, the professionalisation of the farm-worker accelerated the development of free wage-work in the agrarian sector. In effect, the patron–client relationship was, thereby, virtually disbanded by the end of the 1930s. Whether the model resulting from the class-formation process – even indirectly or against one's will – was strengthened remains an open question. Nevertheless, male and female farm-workers belonged to that social class which clearly profited from National Socialism. Between 1938 and 1941 a wage-increase of 133 per cent for men and 176 per cent for women farm-labourers was put into effect in Upper Austria.[18] This explains why Hitler received such a positive reception from a certain sector of the rural milieu. Oral-history projects support this thesis; for example. 'Hitler came like a God for the little people . . .';[19] or, 'Hitler was good for the people because he gave us work';[20] or with respect to the year 1938: 'There was a feeling in the air as though paradise would come.'[21] This also explains why more people living in rural communities were apt to become Party members than, for example, in Vienna. In Vienna 8.9 per cent of the population, as opposed to 14.4 per cent in Tyrol and Vorarlberg, were members of the NSDAP in 1942.[22]

IV

With respect to the village, a clear social distinction must be made between the local dignitaries (the village bourgeoisie), on the one hand, and the indigenous rural élite, on the other. The local dignitaries – the doctor, the notary public, the judge, the teacher – formed part of a relatively mobile class, which could, only in part, establish itself in the village community. Since the nineteenth century, this group was either of Liberal or Pan-German political persuasion; as a rule, they quickly crossed over to National Socialism. Their organisational centre was usually the local sports association. The indigenous rural élites, on the other hand, were to a large degree mostly of a conservative Austrian Catholic persuasion and a patriotic disposition.

The National Socialist penetration of the village followed a certain social pattern: the village Party leader usually came from the dignitary class, whereas the mayor belonged to the indigenous rural élite.[23] The traditional rural élite remained, for the most part, resistant to Nazi penetration, and congregated around its village priests. An SD officer informed the regional *Gauleiter* that the Church had been able to establish a system of trusted followers which had increasingly developed into an instrument of political propaganda and a communication apparatus of the Church.[24] This was not resistance in the political sense, because it did not openly criticise the Nazi leadership; instead, it merely encouraged a firmer holding fast to traditional ways and means under the motto, 'as it always was, so it will always be'.

The penetration of the relatively closed village social system occurred in several ways:[25] one method involved the disintegration and instrumentation of the traditional sense of duty towards the state through military service. Evidence for this includes an undated wartime letter composed by nine mothers from a farming village in the vicinity of the city of Salzburg. They wrote the following:

> We, the undersigned mothers, who have already lost some of our sons in this crusade and some of whom still stand to support our flag, ask hereby from our heart, also for the other mothers in our village, almost all of whom have at least one son fighting at the front as well as children in school, that the crucifixes to which our children pray for the blessing of the Fatherland and the *Führer* be returned . . .[26]

These women protested against the removal of the crucifixes from the schools and also accentuated their traditional fidelity to the state, even the National Socialist state. Neither the right of the state to request the death of their sons for the Fatherland, nor the call for a supposed crusade against Bolshevism was challenged. But a crusade without a cross was meaningless; and this was where these women drew the line.

National Socialism continuously attempted to exploit the deeply rooted masculinity rituals in the village. A true man was always obliged to prove his masculinity, be it at work, while trading livestock, while fighting at the local pub, in bed or even at war. The ideal masculine model in the village was the avid hunter, the keen soldier. The militarisation of the village had already begun in the nineteenth century with the establishment of military conscription, fire brigades, veterans' organisations, war monuments and death cults. Even the old informal village youth clubs were newly integrated. A good example of one of these traditions was the custom of erecting the Maypole; this custom among rural youth was characterised by much local and sexual flavour, and was transformed by the NSDAP into a Party rally.[27] Furthermore, after the *Anschluß* the Hitler Youth (HJ) promoted the militarisation of young people. This, however, did not take place without a conflict. On the one hand, antagonisms emerged between the traditional authorities and the new state youth organisation. Farmers complained that the activities of the Hitler Youth kept boys from their work, and that the League of German Girls (BdM – *Bund deutscher Mädel*) and the 'Reich' Work Brigades raised girls to be 'whores'.[28] This generational conflict reached unheard-of dimensions. Under the protection of their HJ uniforms, youths became extremely self-confident, and more assured in opposing their elders. On the other hand, conflict among the young people themselves had also become unavoidable. This development was exemplified in the hostile relations between the State youth groups and the Church youth groups (which enjoyed support from the village priests).[29]

An additional element which helped to pry the rural village open was the fear of the East – the *Grande Peur* – in other words, the fear of Bolshevism. The longer the duration of the war and the more apparent the threat of a German defeat, the more intense Nazi anti-Communist propaganda became. A letter from a Catholic soldier fighting at the front addressed to his mother in 1944 gives us a valuable perspective about this fear as well as its influence as part of a stylised propaganda campaign:

> You have never seen a Russian, a Bolshevist of today, face to face. You have never seen such a distorted, grotesque face, like this primitive Asian race. . . . Do you want to punish me before God, whom I have never forgotten? If so, then I would no longer be among the living. You think of everything, but – don't you think about who will defend our homeland, who will defend our home, farm and land, and

Table 10.3 Prosecutions in Accordance with the Laws against
Insubordination

	% Farmers	% Workers
Lower Austria	8.5	27.3
Upper Austria	6.3	38.3
Salzburg (1942)	4.9	39.0

Sources: *Widerstand und Verfolgung in Niederösterreich 1934–1945. Eine Dokumentation*,
vol. 3, p. 599; Dokumentationsarchiv des Österreichischen Widerstandes
(ed.), *Widerstand und Verfolgung in Oberösterreich 1934–1945. Eine Dokumen-*
tation, vol. 1, Vienna, 1982, p. 359; *Justiz und Zeitgeschichte*, vol. 1, Vienna,
1977, p. 20.

you from those godless masses from the East or those Negroes from
the West! . . . What does our life on earth mean in comparison to
eternal life, which should still be our goal? You call me a Nazi! I have
accepted those parts of the party programme which I have found to be
correct for myself. I will never give up my positive Christian faith.
That is what distinguishes me from the Nazis. What has remained
mutual is our hatred toward our arch-enemy – the Jew![30]

The goals of the rural local milieu and the National Socialists were
to some degree similar. However, as far as the Church and the
practice of its traditional customs were concerned, rural society
developed an adamant stance. The Sunday sermon was a tremendous propaganda instrument for the Catholic Church, which knew
how to use it well. The Gestapo was completely perplexed about
the double meanings and subtle insinuations of the sermons, which
were metaphorically directed toward certain concrete developments in the Third Reich.

The resistance of the farmers was peculiarly silent. They expressed themselves in symbolic gestures: by attending church services, by participating in prohibited processions and pilgrimages,
by observing cancelled holidays, and by sharing meals with foreign
labourers. The above table on those charged with insidious behaviour shows a distinct under-representation of the rural population.

The 'speechlessness' of the rural milieu reflected in these statistics
corresponds to the high density of social control. The rural community wished to remain isolated, and, if possible, to keep the State
and Party at bay. In comparison to the city, a party informant was
seldom found in the village. Radomir Luza's study supports this
view. According to the results of his analysis, 49.1 per cent of the

workers, as opposed to 3 per cent of the farmers, were in some form direct resisters against the Nazi system.[31]

V

The working-class milieu can be characterised by the following structural characteristics: wage-dependent, relatively mobile and tendentially non-religious.[32] The old social awareness continued to exist in the housing settlements constructed for railwaymen and workers – even in 1938, when one could not be completely sure whether one of the others had not joined the opposing side. This communal living arrangement ensured worker solidarity, and was strong enough to outlive any newly imposed social modifications. A worker from a cigar factory in Hallein in Salzburg province expressed the worker's basic experience with National Socialism as follows: 'The main thing was that we had a job – at least that is what we thought. You could not even help yourself with the tremendous changes made by the state. You just had to face the facts. You could not do a thing *because one just cannot blow against a hurricane*'[33] [author's italics].

The mobilisation generated by the *Anschluß* also reached the working class. The provincial Social Democratic leaders had, for the most part, called year after year for a 'German' attitude, and also put the accent on anticlericalism. This resulted in a certain degree of co-operation between Social Democrats and Pan-Germans.[34] A new statistical election analysis has given us the following results for the years 1927–33: the Social Democratic milieu in Vienna held its ground during the NSDAP onslaught, whereas it lost ground in the provinces.[35] Of more consequence than all the propaganda espoused by 'German Socialism' were the repercussions of the continued high unemployment rate. New job opportunities and an improved standard of living, as a result of the *Anschluß*, appealed to many workers. A worker in Hallein authentically expressed the mood of this period: 'We all cheered as they came, all together . . .; we suddenly had a lot of new jobs.'[36] Class-conscious workers did not align themselves with the National Socialist party, but they also did not protest. They remained defensive within their milieu, withdrew into their private sphere, and offered some opposition by taking sick-leave and slowing down the work process. The same worker from Hallein seems to have characterised this situation quite accurately: 'Of course one had to adapt. You could not say a thing. As a matter of fact, you profited most if you did not say anything. If you protested, then they would fire you right away!'[37] The district governor of Zell am See made a similar observation, but from the perspective of the ruling class. On 31 January 1939, he reported: 'In spite of all our efforts, Marxist and Communist ideas have spread among the workers. . . . The greeting 'Heil Hitler' is a rarity between workers. If informants or overseers are present, on the other hand, they then fake National Socialist sentiments.'[38]

The village factory had always been an island of proletarian existence surrounded by an agrarian world. Because of a lack of other alternatives, the emotional identification and one's ties to the workplace were simultaneously strengthened. Social relationships were less anonymous and bureaucratic, and more personal than in those factories situated in metropolitan areas. A patriarchal system, which was either relaxed or tyrannical, existed in the village factory. The workers' housing complexes maintained their own small gardens and livestock breeding. These Nazi 'work communities' found a more welcome reception under these structural circumstances in the village than in large factories in industrial centres. The working man's dream of owning his own house was exploited by the German Labour Front (DAF – *Deutsche Arbeitsfront*). In contrast to the working milieu, the Catholic Church was a reliable institution that offered the rural milieu an organisation that outlived the Nazi period. A multitude of autonomous workers' organisations had already been eliminated by the 'Austro-Fascists' in 1934. This meant that the workers were in need of a strong organisation to shield them from the massive and clever National Socialist propaganda; but they lacked this. The only institution left offering any sort of protection was the Social Democratic milieu, which could only advocate worker solidarity.[39]

Solidarity was demonstrated in the following ways in the working-class milieu: monetary collections for imprisoned comrades, the distribution of illegal pamphlets, listening to Allied radio broadcasts, spreading rumours critical of the regime, and telling anti-Nazi jokes. In the light of these circumstances, the mountains offered a secret place and sense of refuge. This 'mountain' solidarity was quite effective, and even transcended the working-class milieu. A worker from the Salzkammergut, an alpine region near Salzburg, stated the following:

Even if many community members belonged to the party (NSDAP), they were certainly not 'keen' members. I am sure that they knew what was going on here in secret, but they did not say a thing. Had

they done so, then the Gestapo would have come and simply eliminated us. They were also mountain people; even if they were our
opponents, we still stuck together.[40]

Just as the illegal National Socialists had done before 1938, the now
illegal Social Democrats and Communists tried to remain active by
organising mountain hikes and holding meetings in secluded
mountain cabins; they exchanged information and pamphlets, sang
old revolutionary songs, and denounced the regime. A proud
saying could often be heard: 'Once a socialist, always a socialist!'[41]

The rituals practised to prove one's masculinity were less intense
in the working-class milieu. The pacifist stance promulgated by the
socialists certainly had left its mark on the workers; their willingness to let their sons die for the 'Fatherland' and Hitler was not as
strong as in the agrarian village. The following statement by a
female worker in Hallein stands in clear contrast to the letter quoted
above written by the farmers' wives: 'you don't count the work
and time involved in raising children . . . and then when they're
old enough you see them shot.'[42]

The railwaymen were a key group in the workers' milieu. They
were mobile, and this made the promotion of conspiracies among
them less problematic. In Salzburg alone approximately 250 railwaymen were imprisoned under National Socialist rule. Since 1939
a Communist group that existed among the railway workers had
been active in collecting money and distributing printed and non-
printed propaganda. During the war worker production declined.
In the spring of 1942 a member of the Gestapo uncovered the
Communist group and an inquisition was initiated. During the
investigation a larger group of 'Revolutionary Socialists' was also
discovered. The members of this group had been employed by the
Reich and by local railways. Under the leadership of Engelbert
Weiss and Alfred Reska, this organisation had contacts with a
Bavarian Social Democratic group called *Neu Beginnen* ('Beginning
Anew'). As a consequence of the Salzburg investigation, this resist-
ance group was also exposed.[43]

VI

Nothing would be more misleading than for the historian to
interpret such examples of internal solidarity in these socio-cultural
milieus as heroic gestures. An individual's decision actively to
partake in political resistance could indirectly be neutralised by the
acceptance or neutrality of the social milieu. The milieu, however,

would never compensate for such a decision. On the other hand, as the case of Franz Jägerstätter showed, one's decision could be made more difficult. A combination of partial collaboration and partial insubordination was, in many instances, characteristic of the reaction in the milieu.[44]

The most obvious difference between the working-class and the agrarian milieu was their respective degrees of political consciousness. The workers, thanks to the many years of commitment to the Social Democratic party, had developed a higher degree of political awareness, and, as a result, were exposed to greater pressure from the Nazi regime. For this reason, the workers practised measures of resistance more explicitly than did the farmers. The Gestapo files describe the typical example of worker insubordination: a frustrated worker enters a pub, drinks a few beers, and then loses his self-restraint without taking into consideration the fact that others are watching. One of the individuals present is an NSDAP member, who at first tries to calm the worker down. When this fails and the man becomes even more out of control, the Party member reports him to the Gestapo. The reaction in the agrarian milieu was a bit different. An example of their attitude in dealing with a difficult situation is described in the following incident. In spite of a Gestapo ban, a traditional pilgrimage was made to the village of Heiligenblut in Carinthia in 1940. Ninety-four individuals came together. Among others, one of the leaders of the procession was a 78-year-old man from Bruck, who had made this difficult pilgrimage sixty-four times in the past. The local police could not stop the group. In spite of tremendous hardships (there was a snowfall and fog), they crossed over the Tauern Alps and eventually reached their goal. In the end, this proved to be a successful triumph of old agrarian insubordination against the demands of the Nazi State and Party.[45]

The speed with which the political camps regrouped in 1945 shows that they did not cease to exist, but instead were in hibernation during the years of Nazi rule. Certain old party élites had been living in a type of internal emigration, and were waiting for the collapse of the regime. In 1945 these élites were once again fully present on the political landscape.

The political hierarchy in the resistance movement, as described by Martin Broszat with respect to Bavaria, can also be applied to Austria: the Communist resistance movement was devoted and often daring (with a large number of fatalities); Social Democratic resistance was a more passive opposition; and the Catholic-agrarian milieu offered indirect resistance.[46] One can clearly discern various

degrees of resistance: political resistance in the true sense was
evident above all among workers and the conservative intelligentsia; forms of social protest were to be found among workers and to
some extent the peasants; behaviour conforming to the 'milieu',
signifying a certain rejection of the Nazi code, was apparent above
all among the peasants.[47]

NOTES

1. M. Broszat *et al.* (eds), *Bayern in der NS-Zeit*, vol. 1, Munich–Vienna,
   1977.
2. U. Raulff (ed.), *Mentalitäten-Geschichte*, Berlin, 1987.
3. M. R. Lepsius, 'Parteisystem und Sozialstruktur. Zum Problem der
   Demokratisierung der deutschen Gesellschaft', in G. A. Ritter (ed.),
   Deutsche Parteien vor 1918, Cologne, 1973, pp. 56–80.
4. J. Falter, 'Die Wählerpotentiale politischer Teilkulturen 1920–1933', in
   D. Lehnert (ed.), *Politische Identität und nationale Gedenktage*, Opladen,
   1989, pp. 281–305.
5. R. Mann, *Protest und Kontrolle im Dritten Reich. Nationalsozialistische
   Herrschaft im Alltag einer rheinischen Großstadt*, Frankfurt am Main,
   1987, p. 1.
6. E. Durkheim, *Die Regeln der soziologischen Methode*, ed. R. König,
   Darmstadt, 1980, p. 195.
7. J. W. Cole and E. R. Wolf, *The Hidden Frontier: Ecology and Ethnicity in
   an Alpine Valley*, NY, 1974, p. 120.
8. J. Riedmann, 'Tirol als Bestandteil des national-sozialistischen Reiches
   (1938–1945)', in *Geschichte des Landes Tirol*, vol. 3, Innsbruck, 1988.
9. E. Putz, *Franz Jägerstätter*, Linz, 1987, and idem (ed.) *Gefängnisbriefe
   und Aufzeichnungen. Franz Jägerstätter verweigert 1943 den Wehrdienst*,
   Linz, 1987. See also G. Zahn, *In Solitary Witness: The Life and Death of
   Franz Jägerstätter*, NY, 1964.
10. M. Mitterauer, 'Formen ländlicher Familienwirtschaft. Historische
    Ökotypen und familiale Arbeitsorganisation im österreichischen
    Raum', in J. Ehmer (ed.), *Familienstruktur und Arbeitsorganisation in
    ländlichen Gesellschaften*, Vienna, 1986, pp. 185–323.
11. E. Hanisch, 'Wirtschaftswachstum ohne Industrialisierung. Fremden-
    verkehr und sozialer Wandel in Salzburg 1918–1938', in *Mitteilungen
    der Gesellschaft für Salzburger Landeskunde*, vol. 125, 1985, pp. 817–35.
12. J. Blum, *The End of the Old Order in Rural Europe*, Princeton, 1978; R.
    J. Evans (ed.), *The German Peasantry*, NY, 1986; G. Wilke, 'Village
    Life in Nazi Germany', in R. Bessel (ed.), *Life in the Third Reich*,
    Oxford, 1987, pp. 17–24.

13. W. Schulze, *Bäuerlicher Widerstand und feudale Herrschaft in der frühen Neuzeit*, Stuttgart, 1980; P. Bickle, *Deutscher Untertan. Ein Widerspruch*, Munich, 1981.
14. R. Stadler and M. Mooslechner, *St. Johann/Pongau 1938–1945*, St Johann, 1986; idem 'Landwirtschaft und Agrarpolitik', in E. Tàlos (ed.), *NS-Herrschaft in Österreich 1938–1945*, Vienna, 1988, pp. 69–94.
15. E. Hanisch, *NS-Herrschaft in der Provinz. Salzburg im 'Dritten Reich'*, Salzburg, 1983, p. 155.
16. N. Ortmayr, 'Ländliches Gesinde in Oberösterreich 1918–1938', in Ehmer (ed.), *Familienstruktur*, pp. 325–416.
17. E. Hanisch, 'Bäuerliche Kindheit in Österreich vor dem Ersten Weltkrieg', in R. G. Ardelt (ed.), *Unterdrückung und Emanzipation. Festschrift für Erika Weinzierl zum 60. Geburtstag*, Vienna, 1985, p. 132.
18. 'Landwirtschaft und Agrarpolitik', in Tàlos (ed.), *NS-Herrschaft*, p. 79.
19. N. Ortmayr, 'Beim Bauern im Dienst', in H. Ehalt (ed.), *Geschichte von unten*, Vienna, 1984, p. 125.
20. R. Girtler, *Aschenlauge. Bergbauernleben im Wandel*, Linz, 1987, p. 44.
21. M. Horner, *Aus dem Leben einer Hebamme*, Vienna, 1985, p. 54.
22. S. Karner, '. . . Des Reiches Südmark', in Tàlos (ed.), *NS-Herrschaft*, p. 484.
23. E. Hanisch, 'Nationalsozialismus im Dorf: Salzburger Beobachtungen', in H. Konrad and W. Neugebauer (eds), *Arbeiterbewegung–Faschismus–Nationalbewußtsein*, Vienna, 1983, pp. 69–82.
24. *Salzburger Konsistorialarchiv*: 12/21.
25. E. Hanisch, 'Austrian Catholicism between Accommodation and Resistance', in F. Parkinson (ed.), *Conquering the Past: Austrian Nazism Yesterday and Today*, Detroit, 1989.
26. *Salzburger Konsistorialarchiv*: 12/21. This letter was probably written in 1942 or 1943.
27. M. Mitterauer, *Sozialgeschichte der Jugend*, Frankfurt am Main, 1986, pp. 164–91.
28. Dokumentationsarchiv des Österreichisches Widerstandes (ed.), *Widerstand und Verfolgung in Niederösterreich 1934–1945. Eine Dokumentation*, vol. 3, Vienna, 1987, p. 559.
29. F. Klostermann, 'Katholische Jugend im Untergrund', in R. Zinnhobler (ed.), *Das Bistum Linz im Dritten Reich*, Linz, 1979.
30. A. Bader, '1670 Tage unterm Hakenkreuz', vol. 4, p. 186 (unpublished private manuscript).
31. R. Luza, *The Resistance in Austria 1938–1945*, Minneapolis, 1984, pp. 305–7.
32. K. Tenfelde, 'Proletarische Provinz. Radikalisierung und Widerstand in Penzberg/Oberbayern 1900–1945', in M. Broszat et al. (eds), *Bayern in der NS-Zeit*, vol. 4, Munich–Vienna, 1981, pp. 1–382.
33. I. Bauer, *Sozialisten und NS-Herrschaft in Salzburg, Mitteilungen des Karl-Steinocher-Fonds*, no. 7, 1986, p. 26.
34. E. Hanisch and U. Fleischer, *Im Schatten berühmter Zeiten. Salzburg in den Jahren Georg Trakls 1887–1914*, Salzburg, 1986.

35. J. W. Falter and D. Hänisch, 'Wählerfolg und Wählerschaft der NSDAP in Österreich von 1927 bis 1932', in *Zeitgeschichte*, vol. 15, 1988, pp. 223–44.

36. Oral-History-Project, Karl-Steinocher-Fonds, Salzburg.

37. Ibid.

38. Hanisch, *NS-Herrschaft*, p. 274.

39. P. Lösche and M. Scholing, 'Sozialdemokratie als Solidargemeinschaft. Eine Fallstudien', in R. Saage (ed.), *Solidargemeinschaft und Klassenkampf*, Frankfurt am Main, 1986, pp. 365–83.

40. H. Hummer, 'Region und Widerstand. Am Beispiel des Salzkammergutes', in *Die Pflicht zum Widerstand*, Vienna, 1986, p. 136.

41. *Widerstand und Verfolgung in Niederösterreich*, vol. 2, p. 20.

42. I. Bauer, 'Frauenleben und Frauenarbeit an der Peripherie. Die Halleiner Zigarren-Fabriksarbeiterinnen 1869–1940', Dissertation, Salzburg, 1988, p. 274.

43. Hanisch, *NS-Herrschaft*, pp. 273–9.

44. M. Broszat, 'Zur Sozialgeschichte des deutschen Widerstandes', in *Vierteljahreshefte für Zeitgeschichte*, vol. 34, 1986, pp. 293–309.

45. *Pfarrchronik*, Krimml.

46. *Bayern in der NS-Zeit*, vol. 6, Munich–Vienna, 1983, p. 9.

47. G. Botz, 'Methoden- und Theorieprobleme der historischen Widerstandsforschung', in H. Konrad and W. Neugebauer (eds), *Arbeiterbewegung–Faschismus–Nationalbewußtsein*, pp. 137–51.

11

Social Democratic Resistance Against Hitler and the European Tradition of Underground Movements

William Sheridan Allen

I

Throughout the twelve years of the Third Reich, the largest and most constant mass resistance to Nazism came from the members of the Social Democratic Party of Germany. No other anti-Nazi party continued as a coherent entity beyond 1933, excepting the German Communists (whose special problems will be discussed below). On certain limited issues the Evangelical and Catholic Churches opposed Hitler, but they did so within a context of overall compliance with the regime, and therefore never posed a fundamental threat to the Third Reich. The men of the 20 July movement certainly rejected Hitlerism completely and were determined to overthrow it; but they formed a conspiracy, not a mass movement. Their only potential mass support, apart from the hope that Germans would respond to their manifestos once Hitler had been removed from power, consisted of the German army. This forced the conspirators into tactics that ultimately proved ineffectual.[1]

But the SPD entered the Third Reich as a party with a million members, an organised mass backing of perhaps five million Germans, and the voting support of about one-fifth of the nation (in the last free election before Hitler became Chancellor). Because of long tradition and the intense cohesiveness of German Social

Democracy as a sub-community, very few of the party's followers deserted it when Hitler came to power. Moreover, the SPD rapidly developed an extensive clandestine organisation, with an executive committee-in-exile, an underground newspaper, and a nation-wide backing. Gestapo arrests broke the external structure of the socialist underground – its national organisation and underground newspaper distribution network – by 1936, but an informal and decentralised party remained intact throughout the rest of the Third Reich. More importantly, hundreds of thousands of Social Democrats retained their loyalty to the ideals and values of their party, and emerged at the end of the Third Reich ready to renew the struggle for a realisation of those ideals.[2]

This account raises a fundamental issue of interpretation. Given the determination, constancy and extent of the Social Democratic resistance, why was it ineffective?

The usual explanation is that Gestapo repression was simply too brutal for any anti-Nazi underground to survive. It is certainly correct to note that Hitler's regime achieved a level of repression exceeding that of virtually every prior government, though it should also be noted that this was a matter of degree, and that previous underground movements had flourished despite repression, the anti-tsarist Russian one being a prime example. Furthermore, Gestapo brutality was visited upon the occupied countries of Europe during the Second World War, and yet large and potent underground movements arose and grew in strength in France, the Netherlands, Denmark and even Poland – where Nazi brutality far exceeded anything perpetrated inside Germany. Historically, brutal repression has been a double-edged weapon that even authoritarian regimes must use with caution. It risks recruiting even more adherents to oppositional movements, rather than achieving its intended goal of discouraging them.

Another explanation for the failure of the socialist underground in Nazi Germany is that Joseph Goebbels' propaganda was too powerful. According to this hypothesis, Hitler won the hearts and minds of so many Germans that an underground party could not find backers and thus was foredoomed. One problem with this interpretation is that research has indicated the failure of this propaganda on key issues, such as support for Hitler's war or the use of overt violence against Germany's Jews.[3] Beyond that, Nazi propaganda was clearly never potent enough for the regime to rely upon it exclusively; the continued efflorescence of the SS, the Gestapo and the concentration camps attest to that. Yet propaganda did play a role in condemning the Social Democratic underground to futility, as will shortly be discussed.

This essay argues that the major reason the socialist underground failed to threaten the Third Reich was that it was acting within the established tradition of European underground movements. That tradition had developed for over a century prior to Hitler's dictatorship. Its rules of engagement had become clearly understood, and there was a record of success provided those rules were followed. However Hitler's government created new rules that changed the conditions of combat. It was this dichotomy between the traditional approach employed by the SPD and the new environment established by the Nazis that defeated the underground.

II

The fate of the German communist underground fits the above-described analysis. Nevertheless the KPD had its own special problems, which make the collapse of its mass-based resistance better understood as resulting from somewhat different factors. The size, structure and tactics used by Germany's communist underground rendered it particularly susceptible to the Third Reich's repressive measures.

In the first few years of the Hitler regime the German Communist Party was more active than the SPD, though not as widely established because of the communists' concentration in industrial centres. Yet this hyperactivity proved suicidal, and by 1936 communist cadres had been largely wiped out. The KPD's membership, even at the onset of the Third Reich, was substantially smaller than the SPD's: about 180,000 as opposed to around one million. Since the KPD traditionally had a very high turnover among its members (often over 100 per cent within a year), while the SPD's stability was legendary, this also limited the strength of the KPD in comparison with that of the SPD during the underground years. My estimate is that the real cadre of Germany's communists numbered about 60,000 in 1933; and by 1936 almost all of them were either in concentration camps, in exile or dead.

Consequently, the KPD maintained only a skeletal organisation in Nazi Germany after 1936; the centre of its effort was abroad. During the war years the KPD had a network of contacts in and between several major cities of the Reich, but what remained of its erstwhile membership – in so far as it was active at all – had merged with the SPD in the almost ubiquitous local 'Antifa' committees.[4]

At least part of the reason for the fate of Germany's Communist

Party was that the Gestapo saw it as much more of a threat to
Nazism than the SPD, and accordingly concentrated its efforts
against communists. The Gestapo was predisposed to do this
because its predecessor, the political police of Prussia and the other
states, had long since infiltrated the KPD with informers. This
practice dated back to the initial years of the Weimar Republic,
when attempted *coups d'état* by the KPD were frequent. The Prussian police never even opened a file on the SPD until the summer of
1932, less than a year before Hitler came into power. Secondly, the
early Nazi raids on Communist headquarters, starting in February
1933, yielded extensive written information about the personnel
and practices of the KPD. The Gestapo was thus extremely well
informed about the KPD, but generally ignorant about all except
the public figures of the SPD; and this helped the Social Democrats
in their struggle for survival. Finally, Communist organisation of
underground activity was rigid, predictable and widely known to
the police. The Gestapo had a clear grasp of its structure. The
Socialists, on the other hand, improvised their underground organisation, with considerable local variations, and so the police
were never sure about what the shape of an SPD formation really
looked like.

Communist practices in the early years of the Third Reich also
helped make its underground especially vulnerable to detection and
destruction. The KPD pressed for action regardless of risk, partly
because its doctrine assumed that Nazism could be quickly overthrown and partly because Leninist theory saw the rank and file as
expendable so long as the élite core of 'professional revolutionaries'
remained intact to provide continuity. Consequently German communists accepted losses that the more cautious and long-term
orientation of the SPD avoided.[5]

None of this is intended to belittle the courage and commitment
of Germany's communists during the Third Reich. However it
does help explain why the communist underground, large and
active as it was in the first years of the Third Reich, ceased to be a
mass organisation within a short while, and therefore never really
had the opportunity fully to test traditional assumptions against
Hitler's untraditional dictatorship.

III

We tend to think of European underground movements as excep-
tional and *ad hoc* responses to unusual situations, such as the

Metternichian 'Holy Alliance', the tsarist police state or the fascist dictatorships. In fact, illegal political movements have been fairly common phenomena in Europe since the end of the eighteenth century. Only a few nations have had no experience with them. In the twentieth century, for example, there are only three European countries whose governments have not included former underground figures (Britain, Sweden and Switzerland), though much of that was a legacy of the Nazi occupation of Europe during the Second World War. The historian of modern Europe should view underground movements as a regular and recurrent part of the political history of the continent, and as a generic response to all authoritarian regimes.

As with so much else in modern Europe, it was the French Revolution of 1789, with its creation of a new source of authority in 'the people', that originated underground political movements. Before then, covert organisations consisted of persecuted religious minorities trying to survive or élite anti-governmental conspiracies such as the *Fronde* or the Jacobites. Once the masses became a force and ideology a mobiliser, however, the potentiality of underground revolutionary movements arose. Governments either had to suppress this threat or else compete with the underground movements for the allegiance of the masses.

Political competition between authoritarian regimes and revolutionary underground movements for the ultimate allegiance of the masses became the essential theme of the European underground tradition in the nineteenth and twentieth centuries. Most governments have had little cause to fear a direct military challenge from underground movements. Modern states, so long as their armies have been adequately equipped and led, have easily handled armed confrontations with civilians. More importantly, underground movements aiming at armed insurrections have seldom even reached the point of mobilisation. Creating an army among a civilian population requires a pyramidal and conspiratorial organisation. On the one hand, such an organisation tends to be an élite rather than a mass structure, and consequently it is unlikely to win the allegiance of anything approaching a majority of the population. On the other hand, highly conspiratorial organisations have historically proved to be more easily penetrated by police informers than have broad and relatively open movements. Thus, no matter how counterintuitive it may seem, the record of insurrectionary underground movements in modern Europe indicates that they are relatively weak threats to all but the most moribund of regimes. So, also, are terrorist movements, and for much the same reason:

by definition they are small in size, are likely to win more sympathy for the government than for themselves, and are highly vulnerable to police action.

The real danger to an authoritarian regime has traditionally been a mass political movement. Such organisations threaten to delegitimise regimes, and against that strategy armies and police spies provide little protection. Once the bulk of a nation's people have turned against their government, force is the *ultima ratio* in the sense that there are no additional arguments available to a regime.

Excessive repression has also created unstable situations for modern states because neighbouring countries view any nation relying upon force rather than popular allegiance as vulnerable. Finally, unless a government has previously re-established sufficient popular backing, any partial relaxation of repression or any programme of pre-emptive reform can be the most destabilising moment of all. Consequently, mass political underground movements have historically confronted authoritarian regimes with a fatal dilemma; and that is one reason why such movements eventually established a tradition of success.

However, tradition is cumulative, and underground movements in Europe did not discover the above formulations until a lengthy period of trial and error made them manifest. In fact, the pioneer underground movements were élite conspiracies directed towards armed uprisings or *coups d'état*. The first, in the French Revolutionary period, was Theobald Wolfe Tone's United Irishmen, who rose in rebellion in 1798. This was a national independence movement that sought to end traditional sectarian divisions in Ireland by appeals to the ideology of radical democracy, and hoped to expel the British with the aid of a French army. That aspiration proved misplaced; but the fundamental flaw in this first true underground organisation was its élitist structure: there was no real mass base other than the potential mobilisation of peasant discontent. Despite a hierarchical cellular system the movement was easily penetrated by government spies; and the consequence was pre-emptive arrests, premature and ill-coordinated uprisings, and swift defeat in detail by British armed forces, who were aided by a substantial number of Catholic and Protestant militiamen.[6]

It is very questionable whether Wolfe Tone and his followers could ever have staged a more effective uprising; but certainly one of their major failures was inadequate political preparation and the lack of any reliable mass base. In the end a hurried and poorly thought-out, probably unrealistic, strategy did not produce a united uprising of all Irishmen against the British, but something closer to 'a civil war between Catholic and Protestant'.[7]

Less than two decades later there emerged what is generally considered the archetypal underground movement: the Carbonari, the universal bogymen of Metternichian Europe. These secret societies (they never fused either ideologically or organisationally) resembled Wolfe Tone's in being legacies of the French Revolution and the Enlightenment. Another similarity is that the Carbonari also failed to build a mass base. There seemed to be no need to, since Carbonari strategy was to infiltrate governments by recruiting key figures and then seizing power by a coup. They hoped their programme would win mass support; but mass involvement was never envisioned.

Nor did mass participation appear required by objective circumstances, since the targets of the Carbonari – at least in Italy, where the movement was most prevalent – were petty, reactionary principalities created after the downfall of Napoleon and themselves without popular support, being dependent ultimately upon Austrian military power. As many-centred élite conspiracies the Carbonari never even sought a defined ideology other than vague nationalism, unspecified liberalism and clear opposition to the individual governments they planned to replace, along with antipathy toward the Metternichian system which sheltered those governments.

That the Carbonari succeeded at all in overthrowing governments was less a result of their elaborate secret rituals than it was an index of the weakness of the governments they attacked. They managed to execute coups in Naples and Piedmont in 1820 and 1821 and revolts in Parma, Modena and the Papal States in 1831. A Spanish Revolution in 1820 successfully restored the constitution of 1812 there. All these efforts were defeated because of international interventions; but the ease with which Carbonari-inspired revolutions were crushed certainly derived from the lack of any widespread support for these élite-dominated conspiracies.

After the post-mortem analysis, Italian revolutionaries proceeded in two directions. Mazzini, the progenitor of 'Young Italy', believed the masses must be engaged, and set out to involve them through open propaganda. Filippo Buonarroti feared involving the masses, and instead stressed a clearer ideology: the unification of Italy under a republic. Both contributed to the origins of the 1848 revolutions, but neither formed effective instruments to assure success.[8]

Serial Polish uprisings in the first half of the nineteenth century reinforced the lessons of earlier failures in Ireland and Italy. In all three Polish instances (1830, 1846, 1863) the various Polish nationalist underground movements were élite-dominated, failed to include the masses in their organisation, and were defeated as much by social antipathies as by the superior military power of foreign overlords. It was not until the last quarter of the nineteenth century that the Polish nationalists began to build a movement based on mass involvement along with a political programme of land redistribution that eventuated in success (though an independent Poland ultimately required the defeat of Russia, Austria and Germany in the First World War).[9]

The first real triumph of an underground movement came in Germany. It was not the élitist, conspiratorial and partly terrorist *Burschenschaften* (which at best kept alive a nationalist consciousness in the period 1817–48) that showed how covert political action could prevail, but the outlawed Social Democratic movement of the 1880s. Driven underground by Bismarck in 1878, the infant socialist organisation forced the *Kaiserreich* to relegitimise it in 1890 by building a non-violent, political mass-based party which threatened to destabilise the nation.

Admittedly the SPD's victory was made possible by the relatively mild level of Bismarckian police repression, by a major legal loophole that permitted Social Democrats to participate in Reichstag elections and thus display their growing constituency, and by a valuable technicality in Bismarck's anti-socialist law: its 'sunset' provision, which put the burden of gaining a majority for renewal upon the government. Admittedly, the legalisation of the SPD did not overthrow Germany's semi-authoritarian government and put the socialists into power. All it accomplished was reinstating the right of democratic socialists to agitate openly, subject to ongoing sporadic harassment. It was the first instance, however, in which threatened political destabilisation compelled an otherwise entrenched government to eschew escalated repression in order to avoid a loss of mass allegiance. Moreover, the mere existence of the SPD was the major reason Bismarck created a welfare system for Germany, thus achieving one of the goals of democratic socialism. The lesson was clear: mass-based political action, even when covertly organised, worked.[10]

The Russian underground movements in the two decades before the Bolshevik Revolution provided even more instructive examples. Throughout the nineteenth century various élitist ventures, from the Decembrists to the terrorist 'Will of the People', had failed. Then mass-based organisations, from the Social Revolutionaries (SRs) to the Social Democrats (SDs, in Menshevik and Bolshevik forms) succeeded in organising discontent to the point at which the tsarist government collapsed. The tsarist regime was an outmoded and horrendously inefficient one. It vacillated between brutal repression and half-hearted reform. In the end it was nudged into oblivion not because of an armed uprising or an élite conspiracy, but because underground movements, through incessant political agitation, took away the regime's mass base at a time when a World War required combatant nations to enjoy mass support.[11]

This mechanism was obscured by the ultimate triumph of the Bolsheviks in Russia, which appeared to validate the explicit theories of Lenin. His concept of underground organisation, published fifteen years before he came to power, combined élitist theory with mass recruitment. A very small conspiratorial cadre was to provide continuity and coherence to endemic mass disaffection, partly because only 'professional revolutionaries' could presumably cope with the equally professional repressive forces.[12] Since Lenin eventually won, many believed that his theories had been proved by the ultimate test.

Germany's Social Democrats had been very closely associated with the Russian underground, and therefore knew that the Bolsheviks had little to do with the overthrow of the Tsar, but instead had 'won' through a post-revolutionary coup. Moreover, in the 1920s a variety of revelations demonstrated that the Bolshevik underground had been anything but 'professional', that its élitist structure had permitted an astonishing degree of police infiltration, and that its victory had not liberated the masses but had enslaved them.[13] If anything, Russia's experience reinforced the accumulated tradition that underground movements triumph only when they are mass-based political movements which threaten to delegitimise authoritarian regimes.

One other historical lesson immediately preceding the Third Reich also seemed initially to question the tradition of European underground movements as political and mass-based. That was the Irish independence movement, which began with an armed uprising (Easter 1916) and culminated in a successful guerrilla war leading to independence in 1922. This seemed all the more challenging to the traditional thesis because the apparent moving force behind success was an élitist conspiratorial revolutionary organisation: the longest continuous underground in European history, the Irish Republican Brotherhood (IRB, including its successor, the Irish Republican Army or IRA).

Closer inspection shows that the Irish Brotherhood's record is deceptive. In fact, the success of Ireland's independence movement reaffirms the tradition of European underground movements by showing the futility of conspiratorial insurrectionary organisations and the power of mass-based political ones.

The IRB (or 'Fenian' Brotherhood) was founded in 1858 with the goal of organising a secret army to expel the British from Ireland. Despite widespread recruitment it was so thoroughly penetrated by police informers that its uprising in 1867 was easily suppressed by the constabulary. For the next forty years the IRB atrophied, but then began to infiltrate legal nationalist organisations in ways that remind us of the Carbonari. The First World War drove the IRB to desperation, and it instigated the 'Easter Rising' of 1916: a small armed insurrection bereft of mass support which was swiftly suppressed. Subsequent British measures delegitimised their own rule in Ireland; but it was an open political movement that crystallised Irish nationalism into a successful confrontation with Britain. This organisation, 'Sinn Fein', was originally non-violent, and most definitely was not the creation of the underground IRB. Rather it represented the accumulated effort of a broad-based cultural-political movement that was given its chance by particularly inept British responses. In the end it became clear that the work of the Irish Republican Brotherhood was only symbolically causative. An open political movement with a mass-based structure led Ireland's revolution. The ensuing guerrilla war that expelled the British was not the work of any one underground organisation. Instead it resulted from a general political consciousness that delegitimised the government to the point at which even brutal repression was unavailing.[14] In Ireland, as in Russia, it was the ruling regime that recognised its helplessness and threw in the towel. A tradition had been established. No government can survive without the support of the people.

IV

Once Hitler had established his dictatorship, the SPD and KPD began to fight him using traditional underground tactics. Through illegal newspapers, pamphlets and leaflets they tried to win the masses to anti-Nazism. They expected that between Hitler's inevitable mistakes and their own persuasive efforts they could acquire a majority, and with it could destroy the Third Reich. It was not Gestapo repression that ended their reliance on this traditional strategy, though the communists gave it up when their organisation was shattered beyond repair. What caused the socialists to retreat from the attempt to expand their backing was neither fear nor any conviction that their ideals were wrong, but rather a growing sense that their efforts were futile.

From the outset it was obvious that Hitler's regime had many advantages never enjoyed by previous and more traditional authoritarian governments: an extensive mass base, a nation-wide party designed for constant propaganda, momentum from victory over a discredited system, the promise of novelty, a dynamic political agenda and revolutionary *élan*. Hitler's prime advantage, though, in combat with the underground was that he viewed them as only a nuisance factor. His true goal went far beyond their defeat. Hitler sought the allegiance of Germans not to solidify his own power, but because he needed a united nation to carry out his insatiable imperialistic ambitions. A Germany organised behind Nazism was merely a prerequisite to world domination.[15]

Because of this vast goal, Hitler's attitude toward the underground's challenge was never defensive, and his political measures were single-mindedly aggressive. He aspired to expand his mass base even after winning full power, and moved to do so even if that required measures which dismayed some of his own party fanatics. For example, Hitler recognised that overcoming the Depression was the single most important step toward winning himself full popular support. To defeat the Depression he ignored the economic radicals in his own party, and co-operated with Germany's business establishment. For the same reason he was initially even willing to prevent radical anti-Semitic actions until after he had achieved full employment.[16] However, ending the Depression was only part of an incessant and many-faceted Nazi programme to engender the fervent mass support which Hitler saw as vital to gearing up Germany for his intended wars of conquest.

National programmes were one part of this venture; Hitlerian foreign policy coups were another. Nazism, however, contained enough inefficiencies, internal contradictions and faulty conceptions, and Germans retained enough scepticism that a full engagement of the people could never come from such measures alone. Moreover, the Nazi party at the local level did not passively wait for Hitler's political ventures to win it public approval. Through organisational dominance and by using terrorist threats for outright compulsion, the Nazi party forced Germans into constant manifestations of enthusiastic allegiance. Whether they wanted to or not Germans had to display the swastika flag, march in parades, join in Nazi rallies and shout 'Heil Hitler!'[17] This compulsory external enthusiasm was often a charade; but it was also effective deception.

Both domestic and foreign observers came to believe that the vast majority of Germans really did endorse the Third Reich, since they so often behaved as if they did.

Evidently Nazi leaders themselves were also deceived by the charade their own organisations were staging. Most leading Nazis knew very well that the average German was not at all as enthusiastic as they wanted him to be. But these leaders also convinced themselves that there was some true emotion within the managed demonstrations of commitment. Propaganda may not have convinced Germans on individual issues, but in the aggregate it was self-validating.[18]

The result was that Hitler created a regime infused with a sense of purpose, and one that never showed a debilitating loss of self-confidence. Instead, it was the socialist underground that doubted its ability to gain enough mass support to destabilise the Third Reich. Survival rather than aggressive dynamism became the chief characteristic of the socialists. They continued to hate Nazism and to hope for a restored democracy; but they no longer believed they could influence events by their own efforts. Many expected Hitler to overextend himself and produce a catastrophe; at that moment the socialists would come forward again. In the face of the unending Nazi efforts to control and compel mass allegiance, traditional underground strategies had lost their power.

That the experience of Nazism did not mark a permanent end to the tradition of underground political competition for mass allegiance is clear from the recent success of the Solidarity movement in Poland. However, the Polish underground of the 1980s did not have to compete for mass support against a regime like Nazi Germany's in the 1930s. The German socialist underground in the Third Reich failed to overthrow Hitler because he refused to follow the traditional rules and instead created a regime that, in order to pursue its unique goals, rendered traditional underground tactics futile.

NOTES

1. The standard work on this is, of course, Peter Hoffmann's *History of the German Resistance*, rev. edn, Cambridge, Mass.–London, 1979. My own analysis of some of the problems confronting the Churches and the 20 July movement may be found in 'Objective and Subjective

Inhibitants in the German Resistance to Hitler', in F. H. Littel (ed.), *The German Church Struggle and the Holocaust*, Detroit, 1974, pp. 114–23.

2. W. S. Allen, 'Die sozialdemokratische Untergrundbewegung: Zur Kontinuität der subkulturellen Werte', in J. Schmädeke and P. Steinbach (eds), *Der Widerstand gegen den Nationalsozialismus. Die deutsche Gesellschaft und der Widerstand gegen Hitler*, Munich–Zürich, 1985, pp. 849–66.

3. W. S. Allen, 'Die deutsche Öffentlichkeit und die "Reichskristallnacht" – Konflikte zwischen Werthierarchie und Propaganda im Dritten Reich', in D. J. K. Peukert and J. Reulecke (eds), *Die Reihen fast geschlossen: Beiträge zur Geschichte des Alltags unterm Nationalsozialismus*, Wuppertal, 1981, pp. 397–412; M. G. Steinert, *Hitler's War and the Germans: Public Mood and Attitude During the Second World War*, trans. T. E. J. de Witt, Athens, Ohio, 1977.

4. R. N. Hunt, *German Social Democracy 1918–1933*, New Haven, 1964; W. H. Kraus and G. A. Almond, 'Resistance and Repression under the Nazis', in G. A. Almond (ed.), *The Struggle for Democracy in Germany*, Chapel Hill, 1949, pp. 3–68; L. J. Edinger, *German Exile Politics: The Social Democratic Executive Committee in the Nazi Era*, Berkeley, 1956; A. Merson, *Communist Resistance in Nazi Germany*, London, 1985.

5. Sources on this can be found in Allen, 'Sozialdemokratische Untergrundbewegung' (see n. 2, above).

6. M. Elliott, *Partners in Revolution: The United Irishmen and France*, New Haven, 1982; J. L. McCracken, 'The United Irishmen', in T. D. Williams (ed.), *Secret Societies in Ireland*, NY, 1973, pp. 58–67; T. Packenham, *The Year of Liberty: The Great Irish Rebellion of 1798*, London, 1966.

7. T. E. Hachey, J. M. Hernon, Jr., and L. J. McCaffrey, *The Irish Experience*, Englewood Cliffs, NJ, 1989, p. 49.

8. E. E. Y. Hales, *Mazzini and the Secret Societies*, NY, 1957; S. A. Woolf, *A History of Italy, 1700–1860*, London, 1979; D. Beales, *The Risorgimento and the Unification of Italy*, NY, 1971.

9. R. F. Leslie, *Polish Politics and the Revolution of November 1830*, London, 1956; R. F. Leslie, *Reform and Insurrection in Russian Poland, 1856–1865*, Westport, Conn., 1969; S. Kieniewicz, *The Emancipation of the Polish Peasantry*, Chicago, 1969; M. K. Dziewanowski, *Poland in the Twentieth Century*, NY, 1977; N. Davies, *God's Playground: A History of Poland*, vol. 2, Oxford–NY, 1984.

10. V. L. Lidtke, *The Outlawed Party: German Social Democracy under the Socialist Laws, 1878–90*, Princeton, 1963.

11. T. H. von Laue, *Why Lenin? Why Stalin? A Re-appraisal of the Russian Revolution, 1900–1930*, Philadelphia, 1964; A. B. Ulam, *Lenin and the Bolsheviks*, London, 1965; T. Dan, *The Origins of Bolshevism*, NY, 1964; R. C. Elwood, *Russian Social Democracy in the Underground*, The Hague, 1974; L. H. Haimson, *The Mensheviks*, Chicago, 1974.

12. V. I. Lenin, *What Is To Be Done? Burning Questions of Our Time*, Peking, 1969.

13. Before 1914 German Social Democrats provided the main technical support for both wings of Russian Social Democracy. For example, Lenin's newspaper *Iskra* was printed on Social Democratic presses. In the 1920s the Soviets published O. Piatnitsky's *Memoirs of a Bolshevist*, Moscow, 1925, which unabashedly described a hopelessly amateurish underground that survived only because the Russian police were even sloppier. The Soviets also exposed an extraordinarily extensive penetration by tsarist agents into the highest echelons of Lenin's organisation. See B. W. Wolfe, *Three Who Made a Revolution: A Biographical History*, NY, 1964, pp. 478–609.

14. R. Kee, *The Bold Fenian Men*, London, 1981, and *Ourselves Alone*, London, 1981; R. M. Henry, *The Evolution of Sinn Fein*, Port Washington, 1970; G. D. Boyce, *Nationalism in Ireland*, Baltimore, 1982; J. Lee, *The Modernisation of Irish Society, 1848–1918*, Dublin, 1983; T. D. Williams (ed.), *Secret Societies in Ireland*, Dublin, 1973, Chs. 9 and 13.

15. E. Jäckel, *Hitler's Weltanschauung: A Blueprint for Power*, trans. H. Arnold, Middletown, 1972; T. W. Mason, *Sozialpolitik im Dritten Reich: Arbeiterklasse und Volksgemeinschaft*, Opladen, 1977.

16. K. A. Schleunes, *The Twisted Road to Auschwitz: Nazi Policy toward German Jews, 1933–39*, London, 1972, especially pp. 62–91 and 93.

17. W. S. Allen, *The Nazi Seizure of Power: The Experience of a Single German Town 1922–1945*, rev. edn, NY, 1984, pp. 183–232, 249–92.

18. See Allen, 'Deutsche Öffentlichkeit' (n. 3, above).

12

Dutch Contacts with the Resistance in Germany

Ger van Roon

During the first year of the Third Reich Dutch clergymen, socialists and communists were among the first to react, in an otherwise reluctant and cautious Holland, to the events in Germany. The secretary of the Dutch branch of the 'World Alliance of Churches', an ecumenical organisation, the reformed Pastor J. C. Wissing, on the day that Hitler came to power was in Berlin for a meeting of the executive committee of the Alliance. Even though this was coincidental, it probably contributed to the more decisive attitude that this branch adopted towards events in Germany.[1] Furthermore, Wissing's agreement to be secretary of the 'Protestant Aid Committee for the so-called "non-Aryan" Christians' and his ensuing co-operation with Pastor Heinrich Grüber in Berlin, can also be seen as consequences of that same coincidence.

Shortly after the Berlin Reichstag went up in flames during the night of 27 February 1933 the Dutch communist Daan Goulooze met Georgi Dimitroff, already a prominent leader of the Comintern.[2] It was a very critical moment. Marinus van der Lubbe, an ex-member of the CPH, the Dutch Communist Party, was arrested on a charge of arson. The action of van der Lubbe, possibly meant as a signal for an uprising against National Socialism, was used by Hitler for political purposes. All Communists in Germany were declared outlaws. Dimitroff and Goulooze spoke at length about the political consequences of the action, and Goulooze could provide information about van der Lubbe, whom he knew well. Dimitroff, who was arrested shortly after this discussion on a charge of complicity to arson, was able to devise his defence strategy, aided by what Goulooze had told him. Later on, it was

Goulooze and his co-workers who collected material for the 'Brownbook', a publication edited by Willi Münzenberg about the Reichstag fire. At that time, Van der Lubbe's name emerged repeatedly in talks in the parental home of the Bonhoeffer family, which courageously resisted oppression and sacrificed four of its men: the theologian Dietrich Bonhoeffer, his brother Klaus, and two brothers-in-law, Hans von Dohnanyi and Rüdiger Schleicher. Dohnanyi was sent to witness the Reichstag fire trial on behalf of the German Ministry of Justice. Bonhoeffer's father, a medical doctor, was asked for psychiatric advice, and described van der Lubbe as 'a humanly not unsympathetic young man'.[3]

In March 1933 the Reformed pastor F. J. Krop, who was also secretary-general of the anti-Communist organisation 'Entente Fraternelle Internationale', wrote to the secretary of the Dutch Reformed Church: 'You will just like me feel anxious about the persecution of the Jewish people in Germany. Would it not be appropriate to write to the ecclesiastical authorities in Berlin or elsewhere to end these outrageous events? Can our synod do something? Or do they prefer to be informed first? If so, I shall turn to the *Kirchenbundesamt* in Berlin to inform you of my findings.'[4] Although the secretary-general did not encourage him, Krop nevertheless travelled to Berlin, and came back with information which he compiled in a brochure together with his colleague, J. R. Callenbach, and asked for adherence to it. It was now time, 'on the basis of the *Una Sancta* (the unity of Christians belonging to different churches, in different countries), to support the critical element in Germany'. Although most Dutch churches kept silent about the persecution of the Jews in Germany, the 'Remonstrants Brotherhood', a small liberal church founded in the seventeenth century, being the lone exception, it should have been the task of clergymen and laity to let the voice of Christian conscience be heard.

Already before 1933 the International Transport Federation, whose secretary-general, Edo Fimmen, had his office in Amsterdam, was aware of the danger that was arising in Germany. In the summer of 1933 Fimmen travelled to the Saar area, where he discussed with socialist leader Willi Eichler the possibilities of illegal work. Because Fimmen was too well known in Germany his secretary, J. H. Oldenbroek, made a trip to Berlin and Stettin in September, where he spoke with former union functionaries, encouraged them to carry on illegal work, and made arrangements to set up a communications network between the former German unions and Amsterdam. This marked the beginning of irregular

contact from Amsterdam with remnants of the German Trade
Unions.[5]

Soon after the Nazis came to power, the first refugees crossed the
border into the Netherlands, which was still possible at that time.
By August 1933 their number had grown to 6,000. Aid committees
were founded, such as the 'Committee for Jewish Interests', headed
by A. Asscher and D. Cohen, who at that time still had some
illusions about the position of the Jewish people in Germany. More
or less by chance, a small Dutch Protestant group became involved
in a German plan emanating from ecumenical circles to open an
office in Amsterdam for Jews who had to leave Germany. Parallel
with this, another contact developed as a consequence of the
attempts of the 'German Christians' to dominate the Protestant
Church. A Reich law of 14 July 1933 ordered ecclesiastical elections, in which the 'German Christians' won an overwhelming
victory on 23 July. Shortly before the elections, a German vicar
who had studied in Utrecht came to ask Dutch Protestants for help
on behalf of the ecclesiastical opposition group *Evangelium und
Kirche* in Bochum.[6] On 9 July, a group of fifteen people, among
them university theologians and clergymen, met with two German
visitors, H. Hausmann and G. Klose. Klose returned to Germany
with the message that Holland was willing to help financially and
otherwise, and that the Dutch would stay in touch with him and his
group. There were also consultations with the English ecumenical
movement about this contact with the church opposition in Germany. It was suggested that an international ecumenical secretariat
be opened in Utrecht to facilitate contacts between England, Germany and Geneva; but because the German ecumenical movement
was somewhat fearful of this tie, the plan to aid Jewish refugees
never materialised. This task was left to the Quakers, who opened
an aid centre in August 1933 in Amsterdam, and visited some
concentration camps near the German–Dutch border.

When the Dutch university professor, Ph. A. Kohnstamm visited Bochum in August 1933, he was asked whether some Dutch
people could come to Germany for consultations. Kohnstamm
accepted the request and wrote upon returning: 'It can, I think,
only add to the willingness to hold out our hands to each other,
when we see the incredible damage that has been done in Germany,
because the Church has neglected her hour.'[7] On 8 and 9 September 1933 the Dutch clergymen R. B. Evenhuis, E. Jansen Schoon-
hoven, G. W. Oberman, H. Faber and Professor G. W. Locher of
Leiden University, met with their German colleagues H. Ehren-
berg, H. Fischer and L. Steil of Bochum and K. Schmitz and

W. Thiemann of a group from Tecklenburg, at the vicarage of Kattenvenne near Osnabrück. After this meeting irregular contact developed, and in April 1934 the Germans met with a larger Dutch group in Woudschoten near Zeist. The information that was gathered was passed on from the Netherlands to ecumenical bodies in Geneva, without compromising the informants.

During 1933, particularly in its latter half, the *Kirchenkampf* ('Church struggle') started in Germany. Much attention was devoted to it in the Netherlands. When on 4 January 1934 the first Free Reformed Synod assembled in Barmen and published a declaration written by Karl Barth, a small Dutch Reformed church declared its adherence to this declaration at the suggestion of the parish of Rotterdam. Simultaneously, all the parishes were asked to show solidarity with the struggle of the German Church. In the letter to Barmen, gratitude was expressed for the fact that the 'Confessing Church' had not avoided this struggle. At the end of the letter the following amendment was added: 'in the firm conviction that your struggle is free of political aims, and in no sense constitutes opposition to your current government, but rather is a purely spiritual struggle'.[8] This adherence was an exception. A proposal by the Reformed pastor of Laren, J. Verkuyl, to start an aid programme for German clergymen and their families, was dismissed by the board of the clergymen's association of his Church.

Under the leadership of Daan Goulooze, an Amsterdam-based group of German communist refugees was selected to start up and co-ordinate illegal work in Germany. Dutch communists brought banned newspapers to Germany and established some contact between underground communist groups there and the KPD (Communist Party of Germany) group in Amsterdam. In addition, there was the 'International Red Aid' under the Dutchman Jan Postma. It received the refugees, collected money, and generally helped them as much as it could. Hans Tiemijer later described how one of these contacts developed at the border:

> I heard nothing else but that I had to pick up a person between 2 and 3 p.m. on a certain day, who would be reading *Zwischenfall in Rohwinkel* at the small station of Mariënberg, somewhere between Hardenberg and Almelo in Holland. In case the person was not there, I only had to make a phone call at a certain address in Almelo and say: 'He wasn't there'. If I did see him, I only needed to ask whether he came from Bielefeld.[9]

Security measures were needed, as spies tried to infiltrate the world of the emigrants. Sometimes warnings came from Germany about certain individuals. Goulooze augmented the money collected with Comintern funds and had it taken to Germany by couriers. In those years, he also delivered some money to Rosa Thälmann, so that she could do something extra for her husband, the well-known KPD leader, who was in gaol. The Social Democrats in the Netherlands also tried to set up aid and communication lines with illegal SPD groups in the neighbouring areas of Germany. For this purpose a border secretariat of the SPD was established in Antwerp under Ernst Schumacher. The activities of the leftists among and with German emigrants troubled the Dutch authorities, who feared German reprisals. Consequently, some German refugees were sent back across the border even when the Gestapo was waiting for them there.

On the Catholic side, it was especially Mgr. Poels from Heerlen (Limburg province) who, through his acquaintance with leaders of the German Catholic Workers' Movement such as Bernhard Letterhaus and Josef Joos, and contacts with ex-Chancellor Heinrich Brüning, was well informed about developments in Germany. On 2 February 1934 the Dutch Catholic bishops issued their first warning against fascism and National Socialism. It was owing to Poels's activities that the Jesuit priest Friedrich Muckermann could slip across the Dutch border at Gronau during the repression of the *Röhm-Putsch* in 1934. His life was in danger. That same year the first issue of *Der Deutsche Weg* was published in Oldenzaal, edited by Muckermann in an anti-Nazi fashion, strongly supported by Poels, and feared by the Gestapo. The paper had served as a warning for many German Catholics.

Some Dutch organisations still had contacts with their counterparts in Germany, who told them about the situation there. It was the attitude of Karl Barth that prompted more attention to be devoted in the Netherlands to the German church struggle. When he ran into difficulties, the Dutch Reformed Synod rejected a request to give him a theological chair at Utrecht University, but did not want to discourage any private initiative on his behalf.[10] A committee invited Barth to deliver some lectures at Utrecht in February and March 1935. Barth was still at Bonn University. From all parts of the Netherlands hundreds of clergymen and students streamed to Utrecht for his lectures. Barth came over every week. Once, as he was about to leave for the Netherlands, he was approached by someone from the Gestapo at the Bonn railway station, who informed him that a ban on speaking had been issued against him. Barth was clever enough to query whether this also applied to Utrecht; because the Gestapo official had no ready answer, he got on the train and went there.

German youth resistance also received support from outside the country. There were Germans abroad who themselves had been involved with the youth movement, and sometimes still had contacts with youth groups. One of these, who had fled to the Netherlands, was Theo Hespers. His origins were in the Catholic youth movement. From the Netherlands he contacted groups in different German cities. In the neighbourhood of Roermond there was a favourite campsite for youth groups from the Rhineland area, and during Whit Sunday of 1935 a conference of German youth leaders took place there. Hespers sometimes also went to Germany for a couple of days. At the end of 1935 the Gestapo became aware of these activities, and thirty people were arrested. It tried in vain to lure Hespers to the border.[11]

In 1935 there appeared in the Social Democratic newspaper *Het Volk* under a pseudonym articles by the vicar of the Confessing Church, Werner Koch. He was a student of Barth and an assistant to Bonhoeffer. He planned to provide the international press with informed articles about the church struggle. In early September 1935, during an ecumenical seminar in Geneva, he asked the Dutch student, B. J. Ader, to help him. In October Koch came to Amsterdam with a letter of introduction from Barth; there he visited the editorial staff of the Amsterdam newspapers, the *Algemeen Handelsblad* and *Het Volk*. Afterwards he wrote several articles for those papers. In the issues of 21 October and 23 December 1935 of *Het Volk* interviews with him were published.[12]

It took some years before a Protestant Aid Committee for Jewish Refugees was founded. Various Dutch politicians had discouraged this, and therefore its establishment had been made conditional on the founding of an international committee. When this happened a Dutch Protestant committee was also set up. The first meeting was held in the vestry of the cathedral church in Utrecht on 5 May 1936. On the committee the most important ecumenical organisations and most Protestant Churches were represented. It agreed to limit its concern to the Protestant so-called 'non-Aryan' Christians. Up to December 1937 the committee was able to facilitate the emigration of thirty people from Germany. The cost of immigration to their destination countries was sometimes very high.

In 1936 Barth again came to the Netherlands, this time to meet theologians of the Confessing Church. He had been expelled from Germany, but wanted to remain in touch with the Confessing Church. Barth thought a meeting in Germany too risky. Then thoughts turned to the Netherlands, and some Dutchmen, among them J. Eijkman and E. van Bruggen, were asked to prepare the meeting. The German B. Locher, who had studied in Utrecht, acted as contact-man with Germany. Under cover of a so-called 'Tulip Ride' to Katwijk fifteen theologians of the Confessing Church, including Asmussen, Immer, Vogel, Niesel, Obendiek, Hesse, Klugkist Hesse, Hellbardt, Harder, Albertz and Schlier, met from 13–16 April 1936 at the country house 'Landszegen' of the youth organisation *Algemene Maatschappij voor Jongeren* (General Society for Youth, AMVJ) near Doorn. There they discussed with Barth the situation in Germany.[13]

Initially, relations between the Hitler government and the Catholic Church had not been too bad, as a result of the complaisant attitude of some bishops and of the Vatican. The contradictions between them became more evident from 1934 onwards. That the suppression of Catholic organisations, the Catholic press and religious orders led to growing discontent among German Catholics was demonstrated by the mass attendance at a procession in Aachen in 1937. In the same year, the papal encyclical *Mit brennender Sorge* appeared. It is likely that Muckermann, who at that time was staying in Rome, was involved in its preparation. Possibly he corresponded with Poels about some formulations. Certainly, some information included in the document reached Rome through the Netherlands.

In 1937 Goulooze received instructions from Dimitroff to build a new Comintern apparatus. Owing to the increasing danger of war, the possibility existed that most lines of communication would be broken off, except via radio. Moreover, working with illegal foreigners living in Amsterdam was considered too dangerous in case of a German occupation. Hence, Goulooze was ordered to form a new group among Dutch communists. Couriers travelled to different places in Germany; meeting points and mailing addresses were agreed upon.

The inhabitants of the Dutch areas along the border with Germany had followed events there during and after 1933 in a more direct fashion than most of the Netherlands' population.[14] Because of the many reciprocal contacts and ties that existed, they felt more involved with events in Germany and were more affected by them. For instance, in the border area the church struggle was followed with much more attention. The Dutch regional newspaper *Tubantia*, for example, published an extensive article that was picked up by other papers about the commotion in the small town of Schüttorf (near Bentheim), where both local clergymen as well as a teacher were banned from their homes. They were given a send-off by thousands of people who had demonstrated earlier on the market square.

Because the 'Protestant Aid Committee for Jewish Refugees' received more and more requests for asistance, a reorganisation became desirable on a broader and increasingly businesslike basis. The direct cause of this change was a request from the Quakers for more aid. Therefore, in January 1938, the 'Protestant Aid Committee for Refugees because of Race and Religion' was founded, headed by a professor of the Free University, V. H. Rutgers, with J. C. Wissing as secretary and a businessman as treasurer. Furthermore, a Catholic aid committee was also founded, with Professor Schmutzer from Nijmegen University as chairman. They had to do a lot of work in the year of the *Anschluß* and the *Kristallnacht*.

In March 1938 anxious calls came from Vienna, where Mrs M. J. van Everdingen was working. She sent lists to the Dutch Committees of Jewish children who had to leave Austria immediately. Following a governmental directive of 7 May 1938, however, the admission of refugees to the Netherlands became much more restricted. Henceforth, every refugee could be treated as *persona non grata*. At the same time, the Netherlands was extending its trade ties with Germany.

The *Kristallnacht*, the pogrom of 9 November 1938, marked a turning point in the history of the Nazi persecution of the Jews. In telegrams, private individuals and organisations urged the Dutch government to pursue a broader admissions policy and to open the border. Some groups made relief homes and beds available. After the *Kristallnacht*, some Dutch clergymen, among them J. B. Th. Hugenholtz and H. Berkhof, cycled by different routes to Neuenhaus near Bentheim at the invitation of Reverend A. Rosenboom of the Confessing Church. They deliberated as to how clergymen belonging to the church should react to the *Kristallnacht*.[15] This meeting led to more contacts between them. Moreover, the chairman and secretary of the 'Protestant Aid Committee' went to Berlin for deliberations with Pastor Grüber, who was responsible for the care of Protestant Jewish-Christians in Germany. They discussed what the Dutch Protestant committee could do to help. Upon returning they reported on their findings. The minutes of the organisation's 1 December meeting were in this respect explicit:

> The secretary announces that consultations are going on with the Jewish and Catholic committees to found a Central Council. In Berlin the formation of a similar *Zentralstelle* will be considered. He [Grüber]

pointed out how much such a Council in Berlin is desired by the German Aid committees, and how the state of affairs in Germany forbids us to entertain any optimism regarding the future fate of non-Aryans in Germany, so that concerted action by various governments must indeed be pursued. Germany wants its more than one million non-Aryans to vanish, either by legitimate or illegitimate means. The legitimate means will be used if other governments will take the non-Aryans into their countries, the illegitimate if they don't.[16]

At that time much had been done by very few. As the representative of the Dutch Aid committees, M. C. Slotemaker de Bruïne, became the contact person in Berlin to Grüber. Until the summer of 1939 he worked there in the Dutch legation. Moreover, the Dutch Protestant and Catholic committees created a common emigration office in Utrecht.

The arrest of Pastor Martin Niemöller and the preparations for his trial revived in the Netherlands attention to the German church struggle. The Dutch Ecumenical Council devoted a special meeting to it, collected advice in England, but could not agree on steps to be taken. Attempts by some younger people to act and offer some help were smothered by their cautious elders. In July 1938, a second meeting between Barth and theologians of the Confessing Church, among them Gollwitzer, Schlink, Kreck, Graffmann, Steck, Dehn and Hellbardt, took place in Utrecht. This meeting, prepared by G. H. Slotemaker de Bruïne, H. Berkhof and B. Locher, was more secluded than before. None of the German participants were informed about the place of the gathering before entering Holland. They had all received invitations from unknown Dutch people to come for a visit. Their hosts brought them to the meeting-place. The main themes of these discussions were the religious and political situation in Germany and the relation between theology and politics.

A new series of lectures by Barth in March 1939 in neutral Holland led to a commotion because the police tried to prevent political utterances during the lectures. None the less, clergymen of the Confessing Church from border areas could attend and personally talk with Barth about their problems. Barth's visit also increased the activities of the 'Workgroup: German Church Struggle', headed by the clergymen J. Koopmans, D. Tromp, and J. Eijkman, who understood what could happen in the Netherlands. This led to the so-called 'Amersfoort theses' (1939),[17] an application of the 'Barmen theses' (1934) of the German Confessing Church to the situation in the Netherlands, which had a strong influence during

the early part of the occupation. The talks with Barth also led to the
publication of an information bulletin, *News from the German
Church Struggle*, that included contributions by clergymen of the
Confessing Church in Bentheim. The first issue contained the
following introduction by H. Berkhof:

> We start this publication in the firm conviction of rendering service to
> the Church of Jesus Christ in the Netherlands and in Germany. For
> many people, this publication can present a different, in any case a
> deeper and more vivid view of things. Thus, the goal envisaged will
> be deepened feelings of solidarity, more earnest prayers and a sharper
> alertness with regard to the signs of the times in our own country
> also.[18]

Until December 1939, when most communication lines with Germany were broken off, issues of the *News* continued to be published. Besides official declarations from the Confessing Church
and a prayer liturgy with regard to the threat of war, the issues
contained a sermon by a German clergyman (probably Bernds of
Uelzen) after the pogrom of 9 November, and a report about the
pastor of the Confessing Church, Paul Schneider, who had been
tortured to death by the Nazis in Buchenwald.

From the beginning Daan Goulooze had the task of maintaining
contacts between the group of German communists in Amsterdam, the illegal KPD in Germany, its *Auslandsleitung* in Paris, and
the Comintern in Moscow. In May 1939, Willy Gall travelled from
Amsterdam to Berlin as an instructor for some still existing illegal
groups. After returning to Amsterdam to report on his trip, he was
in Berlin again by August. There he stayed until he was arrested in
late 1939 or early 1940. In November 1939 an issue of the *Berliner
Volkszeitung* had been published under his inspiration. This issue
included a call for a fight against National Socialism: 'All of us have
one goal: Peace. Bring down the war criminal Hitler!'[19]

At the same time there was another line of communication
between Berlin and the Netherlands. Around 9 October 1939 a
mysterious figure appears in the records of the Dutch legation in
Berlin. This person was said to be an acquaintance of the military
attaché, Major Sas. Nobody besides Sas knew this man, and some
even doubted his existence. He was Colonel Hans Oster, deputy
chief of the German Military Intelligence Service. He belonged to
the military part of the German resistance, and was the son of a
clergyman. The church struggle and the forced resignation of the
Chief of Staff, General von Fritsch, whom Oster regarded highly,
had led him to become an opponent of the Nazis. Furthermore, it

was his opinion that in special and dangerous situations many traditional considerations should be of secondary importance. Therefore, he warned Major Sas and gave him detailed information in the hope that a quick reaction by the Western powers would render a German offensive impossible.

Major G. J. Sas had attended the war academy in Berlin in the early 1930s. He had been military attaché in Berlin in 1936 and 1937, and had been sent back to Berlin in 1939. There he had contacted his old acquaintances again, Oster being one of them. It would not be correct to say that Sas, or other Dutch and Belgian diplomats, relied solely on the information of Oster; rather, they combined it with their own observations and confirmed it from other quarters. Oster's information was an important and uncommon source. Unfortunately, however, the warnings that the Hague received from Sas were believed by hardly anyone, not even when Sas came to the Hague himself. Back in Berlin, he found an urgent message from Oster in his hotel room on 7 November, urging Sas to contact him. In an excited manner, Oster informed Sas of Hitler's decision to start the Western offensive on 12 November, and that he would not spare the Netherlands. He asked Sas to warn the Dutch government, so that precautionary measures could be taken. Returning to the Hague by night-train, Sas was received by a Cabinet committee. His warnings were only believed by the Minister of War, even though an English diplomat had provided similar information.[20]

During the first year of the occupation, 'neutralism' and 'adaptation' had a paralysing effect, although the *Geuzen*, one of the first resistance groups in the Netherlands, went into action as early as May 1940. But at that time the experience of contacts with the 'Other Germany' received a new immediacy. Inspired by the German church struggle, the 'Lunteren Circle', founded in the summer of 1940, became an early example of ecclesiastical resistance in the Netherlands. In late August 1940 some forty clergymen and laity, mostly of the Reformed Church, met in Lunteren. The initiators were Miss H. C. Kohlbrugge, who had worked in a Berlin parish of the Confessing Church, J. Koopmans, secretary of the *Nederlandse Christen Studenten Vereniging* (Dutch Christian Students Movement, NCSV), and G. H. Slotemaker de Bruïne, who had been involved in contacts with the Confessing Church since 1933. This meeting had three goals: to exchange information about the German church struggle relevant for the Dutch situation; to deliberate on current problems; and to found an illegal organisation to obtain better information and reach as many people as possible.

The group saw in German developments more or less a 'model' for what a country and Church under National Socialist domination could expect. Because of this example they were indeed better prepared. The first result of their activities was the publication of a leaflet written by Koopmans, entitled *Bijna te laat* ('Almost Too Late'), which the participants in the Lunteren meeting circulated throughout the Netherlands, 30,000 copies in all. The 'Lunteren Circle' was the focal point from which a series of ecclesiastical opposition activities within and outside the Reformed Church, both nationally and regionally, emerged.

Around that same time some other Dutch people came in contact with a representative of the German resistance, Wilhelm Staehle, who was from the border town of Neuenhaus, and had a Dutch mother.[21] Colonel Staehle had been pushed aside by the Nazis, who considered him an opponent. Staehle knew many of the senior officers of the German army, he met with Oster frequently, he belonged to the Confessing Church together with his wife and he hid Jews in his residence. Already in 1933 he had realised what dangers threatened Germany. Around 1937 he had established contact with Carl Goerdeler, the former mayor of Leipzig and one of the leaders of the political resistance, and was later asked to be a liaison person for Holland. Shortly after the outbreak of the Second World War, during the tense weeks at the end of 1939 and early in 1940, Staehle had also sent warnings to his relatives in the Netherlands. After the occupation of Holland Staehle visited his relatives and acquaintances to see if he could do something for them. Also, he offered his services to H. Colijn, the Dutch Prime Minister from 1933 to 1939, whom he met in Amsterdam. Staehle also remained in touch with Colijn during the latter's internment in Germany. In those years, Staehle assembled a large circle of Dutch contacts including resistance men, business people and government officials. Two bulbgrowers from Rijnsburg, J. van Egmond and Jac. Heemskerk, who had work near Berlin, acted as couriers. Several times Staehle provided them with train tickets and money to go to Holland with information and warnings.

As a result of the German attack against Western Europe in 1940 Goulooze had lost his carefully developed lines of communication. He had to start them up again and face the other problems that the occupation caused. This is why he was not able to establish new contacts with Germany until 1941. On 16 January 1941 Willy Seng left for Wuppertal. From there he was able to communicate with Holland. In July 1941, Alphons Kaps left for Düsseldorf disguised as a silver-polisher. Kaps contacted Seng. After this thin line of communication to the Rhineland had been established, attention turned to Berlin. In the late autumn of 1941 Alfred Kowalke went there, after first contacting Wuppertal and Düsseldorf. Werner Seelenbinder and Paul Hinze, who belonged to the Berlin Uhrig group, provided addresses where they could live and work. Couriers travelled between these cities in Germany and Amsterdam regularly.

One of the German resistance groups was the so-called *Kreisauer Kreis*.[22] It consisted of Catholics, Protestants and Socialists, and comprised mainly younger persons with some older members as advisers. Some of them had spent years in concentration camps, such as the ex-deputy to the Reichstag, Carlo Mierendorff, the political head of the group. It contacted former union and also Church leaders, such as Bishops Preysing, Faulhaber and Wurm, who were also encouraged to take a more critical attitude with regard to the Third Reich. The group's moving spirit was Count Helmuth James von Moltke. As an attorney he had aided persecuted Jews in the years since 1933. During the war, when he had found a place as an international-law expert in the Foreign Department of the German army, he tried to help prisoners of war and hostages. It was especially the Kreisau Circle, favouring European co-operation, that contacted resistance groups in occupied countries such as Norway, Poland, Belgium, Denmark and the Netherlands. These ties served three goals: (1) through them the German resistance had more possibilities for contact with the Allies; (2) from these resistance movements after the war national governments would have to be formed, and therefore co-operation with them was desirable; and (3) as much as possible the occupied areas should be warned of orders from Berlin for *razzias* and arrests.

When the diplomat Adam von Trott zu Solz, whose mother knew the Dutch secretary-general of the World Council of Churches then in process of formation at Geneva, Visser't Hooft, asked him in 1942 on behalf of the Kreisau Circle to be brought into contact with the Dutch resistance, Visser't Hooft passed on the request through one of the secretaries of the World Council, H. Schönfeld, to C. L. Patijn in The Hague. This was shortly after a memorandum of the Circle delivered by Visser't Hooft in London to the British government had remained unanswered. After some hesitation, Patijn sent a message that Trott was welcome. When Trott came to the Netherlands in early December, 1942, he was officially on a trip to discuss Far Eastern problems. At night, he went to Patijn's house. There he also met F. M. Baron van Asbeck, a professor of International Law at Leiden, the Dutch diplomat

J. H. van Roijen, and G. J. Scholten, who had met Trott before the war at a student conference in England. As a result of this meeting, co-operation between the Kreisau Circle and these Dutch people was agreed upon. A naturalised German banker, von Görschen, who sometimes had to go to Berlin on business and therefore had travel opportunities, acted as contact person.

In 1943 Moltke twice came to the Netherlands officially, in connection with action he was undertaking against the shooting of hostages. He met Görschen and van Roijen. About his talk with the latter, Moltke wrote to his wife:

> The Dutchman is a good man with an understanding of our problems; someone who hates the Germans but is reasonable enough to see that not all Germans can be treated alike and also that the Germans must have the possibility to live. His hate is not primarily against us, but mostly against A. A. Mussert [leader of the National Socialist movement of the Netherlands]. We talked for an hour and a half, and I expect that we can have good relations with this man.

In general, 1943 was a year of increased activity by the German resistance. Several times preparations were made for action against the Hitler regime. Since 1942, Staehle, being in contact with Trott, had acquired a communication line to the eastern Netherlands through friends in Neuenhaus. A Dutch Social Democrat named Duinkerken, released from gaol through mediation by Staehle, agreed to bring him into contact with resistance people. Duinkerken discussed this request with J. Cramer, who involved Van Heuven Goedhart, both members of the Social Democratic 'Parool' group of the Dutch resistance. The latter would negotiate with Staehle. It was first suggested they meet near Arnhem. Staehle did not turn up, probably because at the time the *Solf-Kreis*, with which he also had contact, had been discovered by the Gestapo. Sometime later, at the end of 1943, Duinkerken again received a message from Staehle via Neuenhaus. Staehle requested a meeting on short notice, not in Arnhem but in Coevorden. During this discussion in the back room of a shipping-café, Staehle asked for the Dutch conditions for co-operation with the German resistance. He disclosed some details, and announced that an overthrow of the regime could be expected. The Dutchmen trusted Staehle, and pointed out that only the Dutch government in London could decide on this. Therefore, after consultations with others in the resistance, a detailed report was sent to London by way of Geneva, with the request to be allowed to pursue this contact. To the dismay of those involved, the Dutch government forbade any official contact with the German resistance, as Prime Minister Churchill had advised, because he had no faith in it. It was not until 20 July 1944, when messages of an assassination attempt reached London, that the British were again interested.

In June 1944, more than a month before Colonel von Stauffenberg's act, Staehle was arrested after being interrogated twice. Through Neuenhaus he had warned his Dutch partners and mentioned names of people whom he had been asked about during the interrogations. Because Staehle, who was then sixty-six years old, knew a lot his arrest caused a commotion within the German resistance, and disquieted Stauffenberg.

Early in July 1944, just prior to the attempt on Hitler's life, Trott was in the Netherlands for the last time. Besides Görschen, Van Roijen and Patijn he also met H. J. Reinink, who worked at the Department of Education. Trott told them about the undertaking that was to take place in the coming weeks, inquired what reaction was to be expected from the Dutch side, and pleaded for a positive attitude by the Dutch government in London. He estimated the chances of success at 25 per cent.

After the failure of Stauffenberg's attempt, a manhunt was initiated that claimed many victims. Of those in the German resistance who had been in contact with the Dutch, Trott was executed in August 1944, Moltke and other Kreisauer members in January 1945, and Staehle during the night of 22 April 1945. He had been sentenced to two years' imprisonment, but was killed anyway as a former *Abwehr* man at about the same time as Canaris, Oster, Dohnanyi and Bonhoeffer, as the war drew to an end.

One of the German officers in the Netherlands who knew about the Stauffenberg plot was Major von Oldershausen, the town commander of Apeldoorn. In July 1944, shortly before the Stauffenberg attempt, he was telephoned by the Chief of Staff of the German Forces in the Netherlands, General von Wühlisch, and was asked what he would do if, on the next day, he was ordered to return to Germany with troops to fight against the SS. On 5 April 1945 von Oldershausen was arrested for his contacts with the Dutch resistance and his aid to British soldiers during and after the battle of Arnhem. He barely escaped execution.

During the period of the Third Reich the contacts and cooperation between the German and Dutch resistance reflected a common opposition to National Socialism as a dangerous element of the European, not merely the German, situation. Their common struggle was conditioned by the supra-national values of Christianity, Humanism and Socialism, which they considered to be the basis for future, post-war European co-operation. When the war ended in 1945 it was the survivors of the German and Dutch resistance who took the lead in promoting the renewal of relations between their two countries.

NOTES

1. G. van Roon, *Zwischen Neutralismus und Solidarität. Die evangelischen Niederlande und der deutsche Kirchenkampf 1933–1942*, Stuttgart, 1983, pp. 12 f.
2. G. Harmsen, *Daan Goulooze*, Utrecht, 1967, pp. 72 f.
3. E. Bethge, *Dietrich Bonhoeffer*, Munich, 1967, (trans. by Eric Mosbacher *et al.* as *Dietrich Bonhoeffer: Man of Vision, Man of Courage*, NY, 1970), p. 313.
4. Van Roon, *Zwischen Neutralismus und Solidarität*, p. 43.
5. H. Esters and H. Pelger, *Gewerkschaftler im Widerstand*, Hanover, 1967, rev. edn, Bonn, 1983, pp. 32 f.
6. Van Roon, *Zwischen Neutralismus und Solidarität*, pp. 79 f.
7. Ibid., p. 79.
8. Ibid., pp. 37 f.
9. Harmsen, *Daan Goulooze*, p. 70.
10. G. van Roon, *Protestants Nederland en Duidsland 1933–1941*, Utrecht, 1973, p. 16.
11. G. van Roon, *Het Duitse verzet tegen Hitler*, Utrecht, 1968.
12. Van Roon, *Zwischen Neutralismus und Solidarität*, pp. 93 f.
13. Ibid., p. 86.
14. Ibid., pp. 118 ff.
15. Ibid., p. 121.
16. Ibid., p. 108.
17. Ibid., pp. 179 f.
18. Ibid., p. 98.
19. Harmsen, *Daan Goulooze*, pp. 109 ff.
20. G. van Roon, *Kleine landen in Crisistijd*, Amsterdam, 1985, p. 335.
21. G. van Roon, *Wilhelm Staehle. Ein Leben auf der Grenze 1877–1945*, Munich, 1969 (reprint: Neuenhaus, 1986).
22. G. van Roon, *German Resistance to Hitler: Count von Moltke and the Kreisau Circle*, London, 1971.

13

The National-Conservatives and Opposition to the Third Reich before the Second World War

Leonidas E. Hill

In a stream of recent articles[1] and in his book on General Ludwig Beck,[2] Klaus-Jürgen Müller has provided a fresh analysis of the stages of development of the national-conservative opposition to the Third Reich before the Second World War. His arguments have apparently been widely accepted, and he defends them vigilantly against his critics.[3] A re-examination of the subject demands a summary of his views.

Müller expresses the prevailing view of German historians that the national-conservative opposition to Hitler and the Third Reich has been excessively idealised, that the moral dimension has been accentuated at the expense of recognition of their sympathy for Nazism and desire to preserve its achievements, and that their motives were self-interested, defined by the élites to which they belonged. He argues that the national-conservative opposition was composed of a small number of men in the military, the diplomatic service and the administration, the traditional power élite, which had concluded an *entente* with the Nazis in 1933, and collaborated with them for some years afterwards.[4] They did so in order to recover the power in the domestic sphere that they had lost since 1918, and to re-establish Germany's position as a great power in Europe and the world. They slowly and reluctantly turned against the Nazi regime, mainly because of their reaction to 30 June 1934, the removal of Generals von Blomberg and von Fritsch in 1938, and the crisis over the Sudetenland the same year. Their reaction to the first event was ambivalent: on the one hand they were pleased that Hitler acted in the spirit of the *entente* of 1933 when he disposed of Ernst Röhm and the SA, which especially threatened the army, the main pillar of strength of the national-conservatives. But their approval of the goal did not allay their unease about the method, murder, and especially the killing of conservatives and officers. After the Blomberg–Fritsch affair even the most radical of the national-conservative opposition urged no more than action against the Gestapo and SS. Thus they wanted reform of the regime and the dissolution or containment of the revolutionary Nazi organisations which had trapped the two officers, and which still threatened the national-conservative bastions of power. Not because they were idealistic and morally offended by the regime, but because their expectations were disappointed by it, did they show self-interested and narrow opposition early in 1938; yet they had no clear conception of an alternative to the Nazi system. Only because of the danger of a war over the Sudetenland, which they thought Germany would lose, did a few of them finally determine to depose or try to assassinate Hitler. By that time they had a fuzzy conception of a neo-conservative, authoritarian successor regime, one obedient to legal norms and purged of police terror and party arbitrariness.

This essay attempts a revision of Müller's analysis and a definition of national-conservative opposition to the Third Reich before the war by distinguishing clearly between generations in the ranks of its adherents, by surveying their shared characteristics and experiences as well as their differences before 1933, and by examining their reactions to the main features of Nazism rather than to a limited number of major events between 1933 and 1938. Müller's work does not acknowledge the depth and breadth of their opposition to National Socialism by 1938; instead, he writes as though the nature of their opposition was revealed in his detailed analysis of a few weeks at the end of the Sudeten crisis.

I

The national-conservatives can and should be grouped in two generations.[5] The older one was politically conscious during some of the pre-1914 Wilhelmine years; most of them wore a uniform and participated in the discussion of war aims during the First World War. Those of this generation mentioned for their opposition or resistance in 1938–9 include, in the order of their birthdates, Hjalmar Schacht (1877–1970), Ludwig Beck (1880–1944),

Erwin von Witzleben (1881–1944), Ulrich von Hassell (1881–1944), Ernst von Weizsäcker (1882–1951), Carl Goerdeler (1884–1945), Franz Halder (1884–1972), Wilhelm Canaris (1887–1945), Hans Oster (1888–1945), Ewald Heinrich von Kleist-Schmenzin (1890–1945) and Franz Liedig (1891–1967). Six of them were career officers, four in the army (Beck, Witzleben, Halder, Oster) and two in the navy (Weizsäcker, Canaris). Thus their education had been narrow, and they were taught very conservative values, such as adulation of the monarchy, acceptance of a hierarchical society and strict discipline. Three of them (Goerdeler, Hassell, Liedig) had a university legal education. Only Schacht had obtained a doctorate in political economy, had had experience in journalism, was a banker, and had not worn a uniform or seen combat in the war. All of them had lengthy experience as responsible administrators, whether in the military, municipal government (Goerdeler), the foreign service (Hassell; Weizsäcker after 1919) or banking (Schacht).

The younger generation, born closer to the turn of the century and mentioned as national-conservatives active in 1938–9, includes Helmut Groscurth (1898–1943), Friedrich Wilhelm Heinz (1898–), Henning von Tresckow (1901–44), Fritz Dietlof Count von der Schulenburg (1902–44), Albrecht von Kessel (1902–76), Hans von Dohnanyi (1902–45), Ulrich-Wilhelm Count Schwerin von Schwanenfeld (1902–44), Erich Kordt (1903–70), and Hans Bernd Gisevius (1905–74). Adam von Trott zu Solz (1909–44) returned to Germany from abroad in November 1938, and played a small part in the events in 1939; but his domestic political views were not conservative. Schulenburg, Kessel and Schwerin were cousins. It is striking that almost all the members of the younger generation, even Tresckow and Groscurth, who had fought in the Great War and eventually pursued military careers, obtained university degrees which included some legal studies after 1919. Groscurth administered an estate for a year before returning to the army in 1924; Tresckow pursued a somewhat similar curriculum, was subsequently a banker who travelled in Europe and North and South America, and only rejoined the army in 1926. Schulenburg, Schwerin, Kessel, Dohnanyi, Kordt and Gisevius completed their studies with law degrees in the 1920s, and Trott his during the 1930s, and they were then employed by the state at various levels except for Schwerin, who administered his family's hereditary estates.

II

The older national-conservatives were usually nostalgic for the Wilhelmine years; but their views about the House of Hohenzollern, monarchy, the republic and dictatorship varied. As a naval officer Weizsäcker had personal experience of the Kaiser, his family and the court, where a noble title was very important for an officer. When he obtained his title in 1916 he had long been critical of the Kaiser and his sons, as well as of the Prussian aristocracy. So was Kleist-Schmenzin, but on different grounds; whereas Hassell admired the monarchy and defended aristocratic privilege.[6] Weizsäcker's scathing assessment of Wilhelm II at the end of the war complemented his judgement that officers were not bound by their oath to the Kaiser at his abdication.[7] Beck thought that the army should have continued fighting to save the Kaiser, whom he apostrophised as an 'eminently noble, upright and elegant man'.[8] Although he was sentimentally a monarchist, Weizsäcker's experience of the royal family convinced him that the Hohenzollerns were finished; whereas Hassell and Kleist-Schmenzin thought a restoration was possible. However, Kleist-Schmenzin came to despise Wilhelm II for having supposedly embraced liberalism, capitalism and materialism; and he distrusted the Crown Prince.[9] In the early 1920s Beck wanted the latter to return and rule; but at the end of the decade opted for Hitler.[10] Similarly Canaris, Oster, Groscurth and Tresckow remained monarchists by sentiment until they fixed on Hitler.[11] Nothing in Weizsäcker's papers indicates any conceit about his title or special defensiveness against Nazi attacks on the aristocracy; whereas Hassell often expressed resentment of Nazi animosity towards his caste.[12] Schulenburg and probably the rest of the younger generation opposed or were sceptical of a restoration.[13] Even those like Oster, whose monarchism apparently legitimated his opposition to Nazism,[14] or Goerdeler, who is sometimes called a reactionary, did not think in the 1930s a restoration of the aristocracy to its pre-1914 position was feasible.

All of them rejected German guilt and even responsibility for the outbreak of the First World War. The available studies do not tell us much about their views on and knowledge of this issue, but the evidence is best for Weizsäcker, who knew more at close hand in 1914 than the rest, and read various collections of the relevant documents during and after the war. He was unusually critical of German blunders before 1914 and after Sarajevo.[15] Kleist-Schmenzin, like Weizsäcker, expressed severe strictures about Admiral von

Tirpitz's naval policy, which Hassell supported unreservedly, out of conviction and as the son-in-law of the Admiral.[16] Only Weizsäcker opposed unrestricted submarine warfare, a very unusual position for a naval officer; whereas Hassell was a passionate advocate of it, like Tirpitz, whose secretary he became.[17] Canaris eventually commanded a submarine, and probably opposed restraints on its use; but his stance on war aims is not recorded. Weizsäcker advocated a *status quo ante* peace during the First World War, and by the end of 1916 Beck concluded that a negotiated peace was essential. Kleist-Schmenzin would hear no disparagement of Ernst von Heydebrand[18] and Kuno, Count von Westarp,[19] so he presumably espoused their grandiose war aims; towards the end he set his hopes on Ludendorff to avoid defeat. Hassell, too, denounced a compromise peace, shared the extremist aims of Tirpitz and served on the Board of his *Vaterlandspartei*.[20] Weizsäcker deplored the plotting, lobbying and politicising of the military against the civilian leadership over war aims and the conduct of the war; Hassell, in contrast, participated in efforts to force the resignation of Bethmann Hollweg and install Hindenburg or Ludendorff as dictator.[21] These matters, however, hardly appear in the studies of the lives of the 'younger' generation.

Weizsäcker recognised that Germany had lost the war because the army was exhausted, could not find enough fresh troops, and faced increasingly strong Entente forces with the flood of American forces. He denied the claim of a 'stab-in-the-back' by 'November-criminals', and was critical of its authors, including Ludendorff, whose actions he had witnessed at close hand daily in the last months of the war. Beck knew why Germany had been defeated, but believed in the 'stab-in-the-back' myth nevertheless. So did Hassell, and he supported a party promoting it, the German National People's Party (DNVP), which included Admiral von Tirpitz and many members of his *Vaterlandspartei* and the Pan-German League.[22]

These people were anathema to Weizsäcker because of their megalomania during the war and because they subverted the Republic, which Weizsäcker accepted without enthusiasm. He observed the revolution of 1918–19 with equanimity, appreciated Friedrich Ebert's stabilising role (as did Tresckow), and was not driven by fear of Bolshevism. He consistently voted for Gustav Stresemann's German People's Party, referred to the conservatives as 'blockheads' in 1919, condemned the Kapp *Putsch* and feared the disintegration of Germany during the revolutionary events of 1923.[23] Hjalmar Schacht deeply feared Bolshevism in 1919 and

1923, and therefore did not condone revolution then or in 1920; but in 1919 he himself improbably belonged briefly to a Workers' and Soldiers' Council, was a founding member of and stayed in the Democratic Party until 1926, supported Ebert, respected Stresemann, and responsibly served the government from his currency reform in 1923 until his resignation in 1930.[24] Kleist-Schmenzin sided with Kapp, whom Canaris, Liedig and Heinz also joined, while Groscurth supported the *Putsch*, and resigned because of it.[25] Hassell might have been Kapp's foreign minister if the *Putsch* had succeeded in 1920, and although he thought an armed seizure of power might be expedient in the future, he recognised that such an attempt in 1923 would be a mistake.[26] Beck too wanted a dictatorship. Kleist-Schmenzin hoped that Seeckt would overthrow the Republic, yet was scathingly critical of Hitler's role in the Munich events. Schwerin and Eduard Brücklmeier[27] witnessed the débâcle on the Odeonsplatz, while Kessel and a number of his friends, Karl Ludwig, Freiherr von Guttenberg,[28] Gottfried von Nostitz[29] and Botho von Wussow,[30] minor figures in the resistance, were also in Munich at the time. They discerned incompetence and misjudgement by Hitler and his associates.[31]

When the murderer of Karl Liebknecht recounted his story to Weizsäcker in confidence, he advised him to flee. But he wrote later about Erzberger's assassination that he was far from being a friend of such acts.[32] Although the DNVP defended the assassins, and Kleist-Schmenzin was a member of it after 1923, he opposed political murder. Canaris supported the *Freikorps*, and worked closely with the 'Organisation Consul', which carried out such killings; indeed, he was implicated in the murders of Rosa Luxemburg and Liebknecht. Liedig and Heinz assisted Ehrhardt and his Brigade, for which Groscurth was a courier, while Kleist-Schmenzin and Tresckow hid weapons from Allied inspection teams.[33] Until the end of 1923 Heinz was in the SA, and from 1925 to 1928 was a leader in the *Stahlhelm*; but he was also sentenced to fourteen different prisons, and wrote a number of books.[34]

All the national-conservatives decried the terms of the Versailles Treaty, which was true of the entire political spectrum in Weimar Germany. In 1919 Goerdeler wanted a revolt in the east to resist the loss of territory in the Polish Corridor and East Prussia.[35] The futility of armed and passive resistance was exposed in 1923. The question thereafter was whether revision should be pursued through Stresemann's policy of fulfilment, the Dawes Plan, the Treaty of Locarno and the other negotiations and agreements that followed. As president of the Reichsbank, Schacht had an important role in the critical financial arrangements of fulfilment. Weizsäcker believed that at Locarno, as later, Stresemann gave away too much in exchange for too little. Yet Weizsäcker did not think anyone else could fill Stresemann's shoes, and he accepted the necessity of the Dawes and Young Plans rather than denouncing them as the DNVP did, especially in its campaign against the latter with the Nazis in 1929. Older national–conservatives, such as Hassell and Goerdeler, approved the DNVP's broad negativism towards Stresemann, fulfilment and all that went with it, although the party did participate in coalition governments with him as foreign minister.[36] Somewhat surprisingly Kleist-Schmenzin, a member and promoter of the DNVP, accepted the Treaties of Rapallo and Locarno as well as the Dawes Plan and Germany's entrance into the League of Nations. Weizsäcker was very critical of the League, but thought it useful for the promotion of German interests, and believed that if it died something like it would have to be created – not a view shared by other national–conservatives, especially in the military.

Most of the older and some of the younger national–conservatives obviously despised the parliamentary system, party politics, and coalition governments including the Left. They welcomed the fall of the 'Great Coalition' headed by the SPD's Hermann Müller in 1928–30, and probably agreed with Kleist-Schmenzin that signing the Young Plan was treasonous. In contrast, Weizsäcker did not like the Young Plan but thought it unavoidable, even wanted the Right to accept the Republic in 1930, and admired Müller as well as his successor Heinrich Brüning.[37] A number of the older national-conservatives welcomed the authoritarian elements in Brüning's government, but persisted with Hugenberg and the DNVP in opposition, and leaned toward dictatorship. Goerdeler broke with Hugenberg in order to be Brüning's Price Commissioner, then later urged Hugenberg to carry the DNVP into a coalition with the Centre and NSDAP under Brüning,[38] while Kleist-Schmenzin warned Hugenberg against the dangers of any coalition with Hitler. Early in 1931 Schacht urged Brüning to bring Hitler into his cabinet, and in October he attacked the government in a speech at the Bad Harzburg demonstration led by Hitler and Hugenberg.[39] Weizsäcker recognised the grave deficiencies of Chancellors Franz von Papen and Kurt von Schleicher, as did Goerdeler, who had expected to succeed Papen. Weizsäcker and Kordt judged that Hitler's losses in the last election of 1932 precluded his appointment, which they did not want, whereas Schacht believed Hitler as Chancellor was the only alternative to military dictatorship or civil

war, both of which he opposed.[40] He had given up hope for the
Republic.

Other national-conservatives had already gravitated to the
NSDAP: Beck in 1929, Tresckow in 1930, Schulenburg by sentiment in 1928 and as a party member in 1932. Hassell was in touch
with Hitler before 1933.[41] Beck, Tresckow and Schulenburg hoped
Nazism would restore the old Prussian ideal of the state, destroy
parliament and the political parties, and realise Oswald Spengler's
'Prussian Socialism', plus some of the ideas of Ernst Jünger and
August Winnig. They were also attracted by the vision of utopian
organic unity, the *Volksgemeinschaft*. More than the others Schulenburg shared Nazism's agrarian romanticism and its antagonism to
capitalism, industrialisation and urbanisation.[42] Heinz shifted from
the *Stahlhelm* to the SA and the NSDAP. Canaris was not alone in
being seduced by Nazi slogans. Despite reservations Oster and
Groscurth welcomed Hitler's appointment as Chancellor. Because
Beck liked Hitler's views on many matters, and also hoped for an
improvement in the position of the army, he wrote: 'It is the first
ray of hope since 1918.'[43] Only Kleist-Schmenzin had clearly stated
why National Socialism and Hitler were a danger, and tried to
prevent Hitler's appointment.

Some of the younger national-conservatives were much less
attracted by the Nazis. Kessel and Schwerin voted for the DVP or
the new Conservative People's Party so as to save the Weimar
Republic, supporting Stresemann and later Brüning. They disapproved of a coalition that included Hitler, which their cousin
Schulenburg opposed only because he wanted Hitler and the NSDAP
to retain their revolutionary *élan*. Kessel and Schwerin were alienated
by Hitler's support for the SA murderers of a communist in Potempa
in August 1932, but gave his regime the benefit of the doubt when he
assumed power.[44] Kordt voted for the Centre Party and followed a
similar course.[45] Dohnanyi belonged to a circle that included Dietrich
Bonhoeffer, and supported the Republic to the end.[46] Trott voted for
the Social Democrats, and foresaw Hitler's destruction of civil and
political liberties.[47]

This sketch reveals considerable differences in the experiences
and views before 1933 of both the older and the younger generation
of those called 'national-conservatives' for their roles between 1937
and 1939. In the older group Weizsäcker and Kleist-Schmenzin, in
the younger Kessel, Dohnanyi, Kordt and Trott zu Solz stand out
from the rest. With the exception of Kleist-Schmenzin they were
hardly extremists, and were loyal to the post-1930 authoritarian
Republic. Except for Trott they were both conservative and national-

istic. All belonged to various élites, yet none of this smaller group had advocated an *entente* with Hitler or his appointment. The great differences among these men reflect the splintering in conservative ranks in the last years of the Republic.[48] Obviously, however, the generalisations about an alliance of the élites with Hitler in order to increase or even restore their power are supported by the behaviour of others in both generations, especially army officers, at least one diplomat (Hassell), and some administrators (Goerdeler, Schulenburg). If this alliance partly defines the term national–conservative, yet a number of the men assigned this label and in those élites did not have such a relationship to Hitler, we must either reject the label or redefine the term. Redefinition would allow inclusion of those few, such as Weizsäcker, who considered but rejected resignation, who were encouraged by others to remain at their posts so as to provide experience and restraint to the raw and radical regime, and who expressed supportive sentiments at least partly because of their awareness of the very real dangers of police retaliation for criticism. The relationship of these men to the regime can be described as collaboration but hardly as an alliance; and their reasons for it cannot be reduced to personal advantage, dreams of Great Power status, or their own view of the state, although all of these factors certainly influenced their behaviour.

III

The emphasis by earlier historians such as Hans Rothfels, Gerhard Ritter and Eberhard Zeller[49] on the moral basis of the opposition to Hitler has been criticised, but this factor nevertheless played a major role. A number of the national-conservatives were offended by the cynicism and amorality, if not immorality, of the Nazis, and by their dismissal of the prescriptions of an 'eternal moral code'. During his conversations with the English industrialist A. P. Young in 1938–9, Carl Goerdeler referred many times to the 'eternal moral code which has guided civilised people for countless generations'.[50] Hassell observed how the Nazis violated 'all decent standards' and wilfully destroyed 'all ethical values and institutions'.[51] Oster and Hassell disliked the Nazi contempt for decency and propriety; the latter, Tresckow and Weizsäcker opposed Nazi intrusions into the realm of family morality.[52] Some historians dismiss recollections and testimony from after the war about the moral beliefs of these men. For example, at his trial Weizsäcker testified that the treatment of the Jews was a violation of the laws of Christianity.[53] Their morality was conventional and rooted in religion, as in the cases of Kleist and Schacht, or Oster and Groscurth, the pastors' sons. The lack of contemporary evidence for some national-conservatives does not prove their denial of such a code; then as now moral beliefs and religion were very private matters, seldom revealed. No doubt those in their ranks who would have described Goerdeler's old-fashioned views as naïve were the exception rather than the norm. Most of them were offended by the murder of their own. Officers such as Beck, Oster, Tresckow, Groscurth and Witzleben, and the civilians Weizsäcker, Goerdeler, Schacht, Gisevius, Kessel and Schulenburg, were shocked by the purge of 30 June 1934, particularly by the murders of Generals von Schleicher and von Bredow. Schulenburg had been a supporter of the murdered Gregor Strasser, and the SS apparently had looked for him, too.[54] Kleist might have been killed had he not fled. The Blomberg–Fritsch affair of January–February 1938,[55] when the two were ousted through the machinations of the Gestapo, had a comparable effect. The national-conservatives deplored murder in the first instance, deceit and dishonesty in the second; but an important element in some reactions was the code of honour of their profession and caste or class, predominantly the military and aristocracy. In both 1934 and 1938 some of them sought the satisfaction of legal investigations. Early in 1938 Canaris and General Friedrich Hossbach wanted to demand changes in the leadership of the Gestapo, while Gisevius, Oster and Goerdeler proposed the occupation of Gestapo headquarters,[56] although neither of these moves would have removed Hitler and Nazism from power. Only a few of the national-conservatives, such as Kessel in 1934, and Dohnanyi, Tresckow and Witzleben in 1937, concluded before 1938 that Hitler should be assassinated or overthrown.[57]

Goerdeler, Schacht, Hassell, Beck, Oster, Weizsäcker and Kordt frequently referred to the Nazis as 'gangsters' or 'criminals',[58] and these words capture nicely their antagonism toward the Nazis, whose manners, mores, language and delinquencies smacked of the underworld. Oster said that the methods used on 30 June 1934 were those of a band of robbers.[59] The brutality, greed and corruption of Nazis high and low were repellent to many national-conservatives. Hans von Dohnanyi kept a chronicle of the corruption of various *Gauleiter*; something similar is credited to Schulenburg.[60] Hitler's noisiness, volubility, vulgarity and brashness, his reliance on rhetoric and the use of the big lie, and his creation of a Ministry of Propaganda offended Hassell and Groscurth, and even Canaris, who despised Goebbels for his disreputable personal life as well as his radical political role, and Schacht, whose enmity for Goebbels was entirely reciprocated.[61] They also detested and feared Himmler and Heydrich and their Gestapo and SS,[62] for their brutal roles in the 1934 purge, the Blomberg–Fritsch affair and the 1938 pogrom. Kessell described Hitler as *petit-bourgeois* and a *Lausbub* to the Weizsäckers on 21 September 1937.[63]

Later in the Third Reich, and with increasing frequency, the national-conservatives objected to the arbitrary use of police power and the incarceration of its opponents in concentration camps, again apparently a subject of Dohnanyi's chronicle.[64] Few of them criticised this practice in the early years of the regime, when their special enemies, the Communists and Social Democrats, were persecuted. They also tended, like the Nazis, to object to intervention by the outside world on behalf of Hitler's victims, as in the campaign on behalf of Carl von Ossietzky and the award to him of the Nobel Peace Prize.[65] However, in a memorandum for Hitler dated 3 May 1935 Schacht wrote that 'the behaviour of the Gestapo earns us the contempt of the whole world . . . .'.[66] After talking with Paul Nikolaus Cossmann,[67] a conservative who in 1933 had experienced a camp, Hassell wrote that 'the mistreatment of prisoners beggared description'.[68] Goerdeler optimistically concluded that 'Conditions were so bad that . . . if the German people knew the whole truth [about the camps] a revolution against the present regime would be precipitated.'[69] In the summer of 1938 Beck referred to the 'nightmare of the Gestapo' and wanted 'an end to Tcheka methods'.[70] The national-conservatives became particularly aroused by Nazi misuse of police power against priests and pastors.

Probably all of these national-conservatives thought of themselves as Christians, even when they infrequently attended church (Beck went once a year for the music)[71] or otherwise demonstrated their adherence to their faith.[72] Early in the Third Reich the pulpits rang with words of support for the regime.[73] But the Nazis wanted to replace Christianity with their own church, ideology, forms of worship of the state, *Führer* and ritual.[74] This attack on a bastion of conservatism quickly angered Kleist-Schmenzin and Tresckow, somewhat later the two pastors' sons, Oster and Groscurth, Halder in December 1934, Schacht in his memorandum of 3 May 1935, and Schulenburg by May 1936.[75] The new *Kirchenkampf* was also abhorrent to Weizsäcker, whose wife was very concerned about the fate of the Evangelical Church. They concluded during a walk on 10 October 1937 that Christianity and National Socialism could not be reconciled if both remained unchanged.[76] Even Beck said in

January 1938 that one of the most evil aspects of the regime was 'its treatment of the religious question', and during the following summer he wanted a restoration of 'good relations with the Church'.[77] Hassell referred frequently to the persecution of the Churches, and wondered if they would be driven back into the catacombs.[78] Goerdeler said that 'Never, since the persecution of the Christians by the Roman Emperors, have Christians been so persecuted as is now happening in Germany.' He thought Hitler wanted to destroy Christianity.[79] He and most of the others were admirers of Pastor Martin Niemöller, whose services Schacht attended in his official car.[80] Protocol put Frau von Weizsäcker near Himmler at banquets, and she argued with him for the release of Niemöller from Sachsenhausen concentration camp.[81] The fundamental challenge to the Churches made the national-conservatives express their objections in more universal terms. The rights of other institutions and of individuals, at least of conservatives and the religious, had to be preserved against the state's harassment, and their ideas allowed expression.

Did many of these men view with alarm the burning of books on 10 May 1933? Only Oster is actually reported as having reacted strongly. On 1 September 1937 Ernst von Weizsäcker and his brother Viktor shared their anxiety about the plight of science and the decimation of humanistic *Bildung* in the schools and universities.[82] Schacht was so angered by Goebbels's publication of censored versions of his 18 August 1935 speech in Königsberg that he distributed 250,000 copies of the speech from counters of the Reichsbank.[83] Nazi control of the press, including conservative and church journals, aroused the national-conservatives to the point that in July 1938 Beck wanted the return of '*freie Meinungsäußerungen*', which Kleist had attempted to preserve in 1933 as an amendment to the Enabling Act.[84] When they stated their position on these matters after the outbreak of the war in order to lay a foundation for a new government, they wanted greater if not complete freedom of the press and ideas.[85]

In 1933 Kleist attempted to preserve the *Rechtsstaat*, and foresaw its destruction by the Nazis. Other national-conservatives later awakened to its loss and wanted to restore it. This is as evident in Schacht's memorandum of 3 May 1935 as in Erich Kordt's and Hasso von Etzdorf's paper about the nature of a successor regime at the end of October 1939.[86] Clearly the experience of the Nazi *Unrechts-Staat* had persuaded some national-conservatives who had been involved during the Weimar Republic in political murder and counter-revolutionary coups – a subversion of norms central to the *Rechtsstaat* – that a return to this ideal was essential. Many of them had legal training or experience in public administration, and army officers knew about military justice; they contrasted this ideal with what they experienced in Germany under the Nazis. Indeed, in July 1938 Beck called for the 'restoration of Justice in the Reich'.[87] Restoration of a *Rechtsstaat* is mentioned as an important impulse in the opposition to Nazism of Oster, Goerdeler, Kleist-Schmenzin, Schulenburg and Tresckow.[88] Central to such a *Rechtsstaat* was the rule of law. Hassell wrote that 'in the administration of justice [the Nazi regime], for instance, officially proclaims immoral principles'.[89] The conservatives had wanted an authoritarian regime to replace the Weimar Republic, and had favoured the abolition of political parties and trade unions.[90] Yet even while supporting these objectives the arch-conservative Kleist-Schmenzin had trenchantly criticised the Enabling Act, and suggested important amendments. After a period in which Weizsäcker, Tresckow, Schulenburg, and even Trott[91] expected and allowed for the initial excesses of the Nazi upheaval, they realised that there were few brakes against continuing revolution. In June 1933 Weizsäcker was pessimistic about the fate of Germany because of the revolutionary actions of the regime; and he, like Beck, believed that with Hindenburg's death some protection against the radicals was lost. Hence Canaris and Groscurth reportedly viewed the monarchy and parliamentary life in Britain more favourably,[92] while Goerdeler and Tresckow increasingly favoured constitutional monarchy. Yet they did not envisage a return to democracy.

Some national-conservatives feared that Hitler and the Nazis were determined to destroy capitalism and replace it with a system which smacked horrifyingly of socialism. Goerdeler opposed central planning, believed in the free play of economic forces and had confidence in a pre-established harmony. His 1936 memoranda contained arguments about the economy that unbeknownst to him contradicted objectives of the Four Year Plan.[93] Goerdeler told A. P. Young that German industrialists thought the Nazis would destroy capitalism, and repeatedly said this was the Nazis' aim.[94] Hjalmar Schacht shared Goerdeler's views, opposed the autarky in the Four Year Plan, and believed, as he told Walter Funk[95] in August 1939, that Nazi economic policies were headed down a blind alley.[96] Tresckow's study of economics and brief experience of the business world made him an admirer of Schacht and an early critic of the Nazi economic programme. Beck's scepticism about autarky is evident in his memorandum of 12 November 1937, and early in 1938 he emphasised the evil effects of these policies to the

British military attaché.[97] Hassell approvingly recorded the views
of Schacht and Robert Bosch that the Nazi regime interfered too
much in the economy.[98] These views were probably quite widely
shared by the former adherents of the DNVP and DVP, but there is
little evidence that objections to the perceived anti-capitalism of the
Nazis, which had attracted Schulenburg to them,[99] animated many
of the other national-conservatives. Still, they and Schacht opposed
autarky, the regulation of the economy, the state organisation of
producers and workers and its allocation of resources (particularly
for the armaments industry), the termination of the free market
economy, and the regime's financial policies.[100] They talked of
Nazi corruption and mismanagement of the economy. This was a
major indictment of the Nazi regime for some of them.

National-conservatives such as Kleist-Schmenzin, Tresckow,
Oster, Groscurth and Hassell perceived that this regime interfered
everywhere and wanted to control everything, that is, that it was
totalitarian.[101] This was not the authoritarian regime that they had
wanted, and was more than a dictatorship. The reassuring terms
and ideas of Nazi ideology revealed dangerous potential in its
racism, its economic ideas, and its aspirations in foreign policy, as
well as in its desire for war.

Usually the sources reveal little about the evolving views of the
national-conservatives on Nazi racism. Clearly, some degree of
anti-Semitism was widespread in their ranks in the Wilhelmine
years, and endured during the Weimar Republic, perhaps partly
accounting for the attraction of a few to the DNVP.[102] Some were
upset by the apparently increasing numbers of *Ostjuden*,[103] and by
what Weizsäcker and Schacht believed were too many Jews in the
professions and the cultural world. Schacht thought the Jews had to
be aware that they constituted a 'foreign element' in a state founded
on Christian civilisation.[104] Others with similar views, such as
Kleist and Schulenburg, had not entirely accepted Jewish emancipation, did not defend German Jews as equal citizens when they
were robbed of their rights, and thought of them as different from
themselves.[105] Canaris believed that there was a 'Jewish problem',
that Jews should be sent to a colony and should wear the Star of
David in Germany. It is not clear whether Beck introduced lectures
on racial hygiene and racial biology in the army out of conviction.
Apparently on grounds of honour rather than principle, Erich von
Manstein[106] and Witzleben complained about the application of the
'racial' laws in the army, while Tresckow, who rejected Nazi racial
doctrines and felt no hatred for Jews, was angered by the Nuremberg Laws of 1935. Kleist-Schmenzin condemned racism as incom-

patible with God's law. Groscurth commented in 1939 on the groundlessness of an SS man's racial theories.[107] None of them wrote as though they believed in Hitler's racial categories, in superior Aryans, inferior Slavs, or subhuman Jews who conspired to control the world. The anti-Semitism in their ranks was probably conventional and Christian.

However, they disapproved of violent action against Jews and their property. As Mayor of Leipzig Goerdeler prevented the SA from plundering Jewish shops early in 1933. On economic grounds Schacht intervened to protect individual Jews in business, and like Weizsäcker worried about the reaction of foreign powers.[108] Many probably joined him in believing that these excesses of the revolution would diminish in a future mature phase of the regime.[109] But pressures on the Jews increased. Goerdeler resigned as Mayor in April 1937 because the Nazis had removed a statue of Felix Mendelssohn from a public square. The pogrom of 9–10 November 1938 disabused them of their sanguine historical wisdom. Canaris viewed the pogrom as barbarous, and Tresckow was shaken by it. The day after the funeral for Ernst vom Rath in Paris Weizsäcker said the pogrom was inhumane and unworthy of a civilised people.[110] At a Christmas party for *Reichsbank* employees Schacht explicitly condemned it, and Hitler mentioned this when he fired him in January 1939. Hassell wrote of the vile and disgraceful treatment of the Jews, of his deep sense of shame, Groscurth of being ashamed to be a German.[111] On his own authority Schulenburg released some arrested Jews, and clashed with Goebbels over this. Goerdeler denounced as 'barbaric, sadistic and cruel [the] persecution of 10,000 Polish Jews in Germany'.[112] Most of these national-conservatives were already so opposed to Hitler that they had planned a *coup d'état* in September 1938. Their outrage was probably greater because of their objections to other aspects of the Nazi regime, and is of a piece with their reaction to the butchery of Poles and Jews during the conquest of Poland.

The chief menace obviously was war. The national-conservative opponents of Hitler did not object to the Nazi promotion of military values or to rearmament, which had so profoundly destabilised the balance of power after 1933. Indeed, many of them as officers were participants in the process, especially Beck. So was the Minister of Economics, Schacht, whose worries about damage to the economy from accelerated rearmament and the autarkical policies of the Four Year Plan were eventually shared at least partially by Beck.[113] Whereas Schacht struggled with Goering for control of the economy and lost, by 1938 Weizsäcker no longer mentioned disarmament agreements as a way to reduce tensions, although Goerdeler did in his 4 December 1938 memorandum. Beck and Oster were representative of the officers in their largely successful attempts to retain the army's monopoly on bearing arms, first against the SA and later the SS.[114]

Some of the national-conservatives, such as Goerdeler, were Social Darwinists, or were attracted by Social Darwinism's simple explanation of history.[115] But none of them sought war as desirable in itself, or believed, as Hitler did, that German youth would benefit from the experience of war.[116] In the early years Weizsäcker and Kessel, among others, feared defeat in a preventive war by Germany's opponents; and in 1937, like Beck and Witzleben, they were anxious about a war launched by Germany too early against an overwhelming coalition of opponents.[117] This was one of the reasons why all of them wanted a militarily stronger Germany, but also why the crisis over the Sudetenland occasioned the plot of 1938. A very few, like Weizsäcker and some of his associates in the Foreign Office, mentioned international law and the League of Nations[118] because they recognised that the world could not afford another World War. The National Socialists, Hitler foremost among them, in contrast subscribed to an atavistic Social Darwinism saturated with racism, and accepted no legal or organisational restraints on the raw struggle for life.

The national-conservatives' views about Germany's objectives were spread over a spectrum between Schulenburg at one extreme and Tresckow or Kleist-Schmenzin at the other. Schulenburg was always *Großdeutsch*: the incorporation of Austria, the Sudetenland, and the Corridor seemed to him completely justified. Very close to him was Beck, who wanted *Lebensraum*, but probably did not understand what Hitler meant by the term. Certainly for him the *Anschluß* was necessary, and in May 1938 he wrote that Czechoslovakia's boundaries were 'intolerable' to Germany. He would probably have said the same thing about Poland. Yet in neither case did Beck advocate annexation. Unlike Halder he did not think Danzig worth a war, and he wanted a Polish *Pufferstaat* after its conquest.[119] Other soldiers, such as Halder, Witzleben, Walter Count von Brockdorff-Ahlefeldt,[120] Paul von Hase,[121] Erich Hoepner[122] and Wilhelm Adam,[123] as well as Canaris, Oster and Groscurth in the *Abwehr*, all prospective participants in a coup during the Sudeten crisis, whose territorial aims in 1937–9 are ill-documented, would presumably have agreed with Beck. Goerdeler welcomed the *Anschluß* and the incorporation of the Sudetenland, and fully supported the demand for the Polish Corridor.[124] Hassell's views were probably very similar. Weizsäcker envisaged a federated *Großdeutsch-land*, and thought that the *Anschluß* was inevitable, without personally wanting it, because of his dislike for Austrians and for adding so many Catholics to Germany.[125] However, when it happened he was deeply moved.[126] Because he judged that if Germany obtained the Sudetenland the other Powers would reject German claims to the Polish Corridor, and because he did not assign the Sudetenland the same priority, he would have sought the Corridor first.[127] Among the younger members of the Foreign Office, Kordt and Kessel strongly supported the *Anschluß*, but shared Weizsäcker's views on the other territorial issues.[128] The published sources do not reveal the aims of Heinz and Liedig.[129] At the other extreme, Tresckow believed that a '*Großgermanisches Reich*' was a '*Hirngespenst*', and therefore did not want either the *Anschluß* or the annexation of the Sudetenland, although he considered the Corridor an '*Unfug*'.[130] Kleist-Schmenzin opposed the union of Berlin and Vienna; he thought Austrians and Germans had nothing in common with one another. Thus for him the *Anschluß* was the triumph of '*Unheil*'. He disputed all German historical claims to the Sudetenland, but was avid for Danzig and the Corridor. Like Weizsäcker, he worried about the reaction of the powers if Germany appeared to be achieving a hegemonial position. Furthermore, he grasped the extent of Hitler's ambitions, and warned the British against his *Weltherrschaftspläne*, as did Goerdeler, who told Young that Hitler 'had designs on Belgium, Holland, and Switzerland'.[131] Many of these men condemned the occupation of Prague as a grave mistake.[132] Only Weizsäcker among them had attempted to prevent this step, by his support for a Treaty of Friendship with rump-Czechoslovakia. But some of the military figures probably approved of the action on 15 March 1939, because of the strategic advantage it gave Germany over Poland.[133]

The national-conservatives were not megalomaniacs. They knew Germany's weakness in 1938–9. Although some of them implemented Hitler's combination of diplomacy and subversion (Weizsäcker, Canaris and Groscurth), they disapproved of his threats and willingness to wage war. They were more patient, at most wanted Austria, the Sudetenland and the Corridor, but repeatedly glimpsed disaster, *finis Germaniae*, as Beck, Canaris and Weizsäcker expressed it.[134] Their dreams were pinched in comparison with those of Hitler and the NSDAP.

Thus there were marked differences between Hitler and the Nazis and the national-conservatives over the military, Social Darwinism and imperialism. These differences were focused by

Hitler's desire for war, first against Czechoslovakia in September 1938 and then against Poland in September 1939. Thereafter he wanted ever more war. He thought it necessary and desirable, the fulfilment of a Social Darwinistic law. Many of the national-conservatives had experienced the First World War, and feared a repetition of it. They became convinced that Hitler's war against Czechoslovakia would expand into a larger European war, perhaps even a World War, in which Germany would once again be defeated. This conviction, combined with their other reasons for opposition to Hitler and the Third Reich, provoked this small group of ill-organised men to plan a *coup d'état* in August–September 1938.

IV

It remains to summarise this essay on the men who have been called national-conservatives for their role in 1938–9. There were two generations in their ranks, the older of which had experienced the Wilhelmine era and participated in the First World War, a number espousing extreme aims during it. Most opposed the Revolution of 1918 and the Weimar Republic, which many in both generations attacked or subverted in its early years. During and after the war Weizsäcker was an exception in his generation. Some of the younger ones, in contrast, did not experience the Revolution politically, and were not so adamantly opposed to the Republic, or even supported it. Most of the older generation turned to the Nazis between 1929 and 1932, whereas a higher percentage of the younger ones did not. But the lives of the older group do not confirm Klaus-Jürgen Müller's claims that 'they' envisaged a recovery of 'their' pre-1918 power through a Nazi regime, or that all allied themselves with the Nazis. Some did; others even became Nazis. 'Collaboration' better describes the relationship to the Nazis of a number of them. Continuity with the Wilhelmine era is evident in their nearly united effort to recover Germany's position as a *Großmacht*. They differed over the speed of rearmament, and some worried about causing a war by destroying the existing balance of power, although all wanted an end to the French alliance system. Among them were found a wide range of views about the *Anschluß* with Austria, and what should be sought in Czechoslovakia and Poland. Most of the older generation who recalled the Wilhelmine era with nostalgia either welcomed or fatalistically accepted a Nazi future, frequently influenced by Nazi slogans but also by various utopian visions of Prussian Socialism and organic national unity *à la* Spengler, Winnig, Moeller van den Bruck or Jünger.

Especially important events during the Third Reich, such as 30 June 1934 and the Blomberg–Fritsch affair, did turn these national-conservatives against Nazism, exactly as Müller has argued. But all of them were also alienated by other principal features of the regime, such as its condemnation of conventional morality, its attack on the Churches, its destruction of the *Rechtsstaat*, its autarkical and regulative economic policies, its totalitarian controls over public and private life, its anti-Semitism, its Social Darwinism and its aggressive foreign policy. The overriding objective of these national-conservatives, which brought them together and gave them a focus in 1938, was the prevention of a war that they thought Germany would lose. They shared these criticisms of the regime with many Germans, according to the work of Ian Kershaw.[135] Most of the members of the older generation had to move a long way from their counter-revolutionary attitudes after 1918 and their support of Nazism after 1929 to their position in 1938–9 of supporting a revolution against Nazism. However, the experience some had of supporting a *Putsch* in the early 1920s perhaps facilitated their shift in 1938. Weizsäcker and a number of the younger men had never assumed such radical positions earlier, and had been more sceptical about Nazism from the beginning, and thus did not have to shift so far to support opposition later. It also seems that in 1938–9 the younger generation still usually followed the older one, whereas after the oubreak of the war, in October–November 1939, some members of the former began to take the lead.

Many in both generations had reached a revolutionary stance by August 1938, when the slogans written by Beck would have expressed their domestic objectives better than any of their other pre-war documents. Yet in 1938 they did not have a clear conception of a new government, although it would not have been democratic or parliamentary.[136] Whether Beck thought his programme was reformist and was 'for the *Führer*', as Reynolds and Müller assert, or recognised and accepted the revolutionary implications of his programme, including the ouster of Hitler, and was already concerting with Witzleben for a *coup d'état*, as Krausnick and Hoffmann claim, is arguable.[137] Certainly Beck's proposal for a collective resignation of the generals, an idea he almost certainly took from the aftermath of the Fritsch–Blomberg crisis,[138] was unrealistic. Yet even though by mid-June the results of the wargame contradicted his arguments about certain disaster in an invasion of Czechoslovakia, many of the generals might have joined

him if Brauchitsch had not skilfully blocked him.[139] His humilia-
tion in the war-game and frustration by Brauchitsch surely provoked his own resignation, after which the plot against Hitler took
shape even without his close participation. Those involved constituted a small and apparently isolated group, but this appearance is
somewhat deceiving. If Hitler had commanded the invasion of
Czechoslovakia and a *coup d'état* had taken place, presumably many
of the generals who had supported Beck would have supported the
new government. So would large numbers of officials in other
Reich agencies, and probably a surprisingly high percentage of the
wider population, which was much more agitated at the prospect
of war in 1938 than it would be in the more favourable circumstances of 1939.[140]

Klaus-Jürgen Müller has properly warned us against the form of
historiography which consisted of citing all their criticisms of the
regime without referring to the collaborationist, professional work
which dominated their days. This also constituted a fundamental
part of their national-conservatism. But the elements of idealism
and decency attributed to them in the old historiography cannot be
made to disappear, and their views on the deficiencies of the Third
Reich help define their national-conservatism and explain their
opposition. Müller freshly analyses with new terminology their
already familiar plans and responses in August–September 1938,
and illuminates their differences about how to carry out a *coup
d'état*. The central beliefs of national conservatism did not determine the right moment, the means, the kind of action (such as the
arrest or assassination of Hitler), the make-up and constitution of
the interim regime or their judgement about support for Hitler and
Nazism in the army and the population. The label national-
conservative accommodates their differences about these issues.

Certainly these men were both nationalistic and conservative.
They promoted the appeasement of Hitler with territory before and
after they opposed or resisted him, and at every stage – that is,
during the war as well – the dominant group wanted to keep much
of what he had obtained. Their opposition to the facets of the Third
Reich examined here obviously did not imply a commitment to
restore something like the Weimar Republic. Their new state
would have been neither parliamentary nor democratic. Their
Rechtsstaat was an old model, for some of them virtually reactionary, because modelled on Prussia. But the conservative nature of their
views denies Adam von Trott zu Solz and Hans von Dohnanyi[141] the
label national-conservative. Weizsäcker, Kessel and Erich Kordt are
questionable because of elements in their biographies before 1938,

although in that year their views were in harmony with the national-conservatives. Such modifications in a liberal direction as were introduced after the war commenced were above all due to the widening of the coalition against Hitler beyond those who had collaborated before 1939.

From the outside, however, the national-conservatives seemed unchanged before the war. The British mistakenly believed that the national-conservatives scarcely differed from Hitler and the Nazis, especially in their foreign-policy objectives. They did not discriminate between the methods and the goals of the national-conservatives and Hitler. The national-conservatives accepted considerable subversion, but not limitless deceit or war risked with inferior forces, and their most ambitious territorial objectives were Austria, the Sudetenland, and the Corridor. Some would not have included the Sudetenland, had not Hitler made it a Nazi aim. When they spoke of *Lebensraum*, they did not grasp what it meant for Hitler, and the British did not credit the assertions by Kleist-Schmenzin and Goerdeler that Hitler's goals extended to the world. Above all, the British who heard these national-conservative emissaries were not interested in and paid virtually no attention to the implications of their important criticisms of the domestic policies of Hitler and Nazism.[142] Nor did they seriously consider using these conspirators for the destruction of Hitler without paying much of a price. Instead they dealt with him, and sacrificed Czechoslovakia so as to avoid war, despite the enormous immediate strategic gain for Germany, the predictable annexation of Bohemia–Moravia, and the grim prospect for Poland thereafter.

Had the British stood by Czechoslovakia, the conspirators' resolve would have been tested. Those who survived the war have claimed that up to the eve of the Munich Conference they were ready to act, obviously without any British promises. Appeasement deterred them, not the absence of promises. Without appeasement the conspirators might have lacked the nerve or opportunity to act, or might have failed. But even without speculating on might-have-beens it is clear that the Chamberlain Government and many of its advisers took the wrong measure of Hitler, the Nazi regime and its domestic and foreign goals, as well as of its German national-conservative opponents. The latter might have acted in 1938, whereas because of the enormous strategic shift accomplished by the Munich Agreement and the occupation of Prague, and perhaps also because of the change in German public opinion, and in views within their own ranks, only a few did anything to prevent war in the months before 1 September 1939.[143] There was no plot against Hitler. Not surprisingly, many of the historians who are most critical of the German national-conservative opposition insist that Chamberlain and his advisers could hardly have done other than what they did. Even a severe judgement about the national-conservative resistance does not, however, necessarily entail approval of appeasement. A more lenient verdict will return to them some of their patrimony, their claim to fundamental and often lofty motivation, and the recognition that 1938 was surely the time to have tested them.

NOTES

I thank The Social Sciences Humanities Research Council of Canada for grants which made this study possible and my wife Nancy for many revisions.

1. K.-J. Müller, 'Die deutsche Militäropposition gegen Hitler. Zum Problem ihrer Interpretation und Analyse', in his *Armee, Politik und Gesellschaft in Deutschland 1933–1945. Studien zum Verhältnis von Armee und NS-System*, Paderborn, 1979, pp. 101–23; idem, 'Die national-konservative Opposition vor dem Zweiten Weltkrieg: Zum Problem ihrer begrifflichen Erfassung', in Manfred Messerschmidt *et al.* (eds), *Militärgeschichte Probleme – Thesen – Wege*, Stuttgart, 1982, pp. 214–42; idem, 'The German Military Opposition before the Second World War', in W. J. Mommsen and L. Kettenacker (eds), *The Fascist Challenge and the Policy of Appeasement*, London, 1983, pp. 61–75; idem, 'Struktur und Entwicklung der nationalkonservativen Opposition', in Militärgeschichtliches Forschungsamt (ed.), *Aufstand des Gewissens. Der militärische Widerstand gegen Hitler und das NS-Regime 1933–1945*, Herford–Bonn, 1984, pp. 263–309; idem, 'Nationalkonservative Eliten zwischen Kooperation und Widerstand', in J. Schmädeke and P. Steinbach (eds), *Der Widerstand gegen den Nationalsozialismus. Die deutsche Gesellschaft und der Widerstand gegen Hitler*, Munich–Zürich, 1985, pp. 24–49; idem, 'Zu Struktur und Eigenart der nationalkonservativen Opposition bis 1938 – Innenpolitischer Machtkampf, Kriegsverhinderungspolitik und Eventual-Staatsstreichplanung', ibid., pp. 329–44; idem, 'The Structure and Nature of the National Conservative Opposition in Germany up to 1940', in H. W. Koch (ed.), *Aspects of the Third Reich*, London, 1985, pp. 133–78; idem, 'Der nationalkonservative Widerstand 1933–1940,' in K.-J. Müller (ed.), *Der deutsche Widerstand 1933–1945*, Paderborn–Munich–Vienna–Zürich, 1986, pp. 40–59.

2. K.-J. Müller, *General Ludwig Beck. Studien und Dokumente zur politisch–militärischen Vorstellungswelt und Tätigkeit des Generalstabschefs des deutschen Heeres 1933–1938*, Boppard am Rhein, 1980.
3. H. Krausnick, 'Zum militärischen Widerstand gegen Hitler 1933–1938. Möglichkeiten, Ansätze, Grenzen und Kontroversen', in Militärgeschichtliches Forschungsamt (ed.), *Aufstand des Gewissens*, pp. 311–64. For Müller's criticisms see his 'Nationalkonservative Eliten', pp. 46–7, n. 32.
4. J. Dülffer, 'Die Machtergreifung und die Rolle der alten Eliten im Dritten Reich', in W. Michalka (ed.), *Die nationalsozialistische Machtergreifung*, Munich–Vienna–Zürich, 1984, pp. 182–94.
5. Restricted to the military, and on other counts different from my analysis, is W. Schieder, 'Zwei Generationen im militärischen Widerstand gegen Hitler', in Schmädeke and Steinbach (eds), *Der Widerstand*, pp. 436–59.
6. L. E. Hill (ed.), *Die Weizsäcker Papiere 1900–1932*, Berlin, 1982, p. 15 (hereafter *WP 1900–1932*); B. Scheurig, *Ewald von Kleist-Schmenzin. Ein Konservativer gegen Hitler*, Oldenburg–Hamburg, 1968, p. 21. G. Schöllgen, 'Wurzeln konservativer Opposition. Ulrich von Hassell und der Übergang vom Kaiserreich zur Weimarer Republik', *Geschichte in Wissenschaft und Unterricht*, vol. 38, August 1987, p. 480, documents Hassell's opposition in 1918 to reform of the three-class voting system in Prussia.
7. *WP 1900–1932*, pp. 25–6, 318–19, 11.XI.18.
8. N. Reynolds, *Treason was no Crime: Ludwig Beck, Chief of the German General Staff*, London, 1976, pp. 28–9; Müller, *General Ludwig Beck*, pp. 43, 323, letter of 28 November 1918, and n. 2 about Beck's changing views of the 'stab-in-the-back' thesis.
9. *WP 1900–1932*, pp. 308–18; Scheurig, *Kleist-Schmenzin*, pp. 26, 28, 98, 102. There is evidence of Hassell's enduring monarchism in his diaries, of which there are now three versions: U. von Hassell, *Vom andern Deutschland, aus den nachgelassenen Tagebüchern 1938–1944*, Zürich, 1947, the translation of this as *The von Hassell Diaries 1938–1944*, introduction by A. W. Dulles, Garden City, NY, 1947, and the greatly expanded *Die Hassell-Tagebücher 1938–1944. Ulrich von Hassell. Aufzeichnungen vom Andern Deutschland*, ed. F. Freiherr H. von Gaertringen in collaboration with K. P. Reiß, Berlin, 1988. Consequently citations of Hassell's diary here will provide only the date of the entry and no pagination.
10. Reynolds, *Beck*, p. 34; Müller, *General Ludwig Beck*, pp. 41, 43, 51. During the war Goerdeler and Beck considered the temporary installation of the Crown Prince despite their objections to him. H.-A. Jacobsen (ed.), *'Spiegelbild einer Verschwörung.' Die Opposition gegen Hitler und der Staatsstreich vom 20. Juli 1944 in der SD-Berichterstattung. Geheime Dokumente aus dem ehemaligen Reichssicherheitshauptamt*, 2 vols, Stuttgart, 1984, vol. 1, p. 352.
11. H. Höhne, *Canaris*, Garden City – London, 1979, pp. 130, 259; R. G.

Count von Thun-Hohenstein, *Der Verschwörer. General Oster und die Militäropposition*, Munich, 1984, p. 28; H. Groscurth, *Tagebücher eines Abwehroffiziers 1938–1940*, ed. H. Krausnick and H. C. Deutsch, Stuttgart, 1970, p. 24; B. Scheurig, *Henning von Tresckow. Eine Biographie*, Oldenburg–Hamburg, 1973, pp. 20, 38.

12. *WP 1900–1932*, p. 30; Hassell, 17, 29 September 1938, 26 January 1939.
13. H. Mommsen, 'Fritz-Dietlof Graf von der Schulenburg und die preußiche Tradition', *Vierteljahrshefte für Zeitgeschichte*, vol. 32, April 1984, p. 234.
14. H. Graml, 'Hans Oster', in idem (ed.), *Widerstand im Dritten Reich. Probleme, Ereignisse, Gestalten*, Frankfurt am Main, 1984, p. 226.
15. *WP 1900–1932*, p. 28.
16. Scheurig, *Kleist-Schmenzin*, p. 21; Schöllgen, 'Wurzeln konservativer Opposition', p. 479.
17. Schöllgen, 'Wurzeln konservativer Opposition', p. 479; Count Westarp, *Konservative Politik im letzten Jahrzehnt des Kaiserreiches. 2. Teil 1914–1918*, Berlin, 1935, pp. 107, 117, 118. Hassell's advocacy of unrestricted submarine warfare is vividly evident in his correspondence during the war with Admiral Adolf von Trotha.
18. Ernst von Heydebrand (1851–1924), from 1880 to 1918 deputy in the Prussian Legislative Assembly, from 1903 to 1918 also deputy in the Reichstag; in both a Conservative; during the war a supporter of extreme war aims.
19. Kuno, Count von Westarp (1864–1945), Reichstag deputy and since 1913 Chairman of the Conservative Caucus; after 1920 sat in the Reichstag for the DNVP, 1926–28 as Chairman of the Caucus. During the war an opponent of a compromise peace and of domestic reform.
20. Hassell–Trotha correspondence. The belief that during the First World War the national-conservatives 'probably remained untouched by Pan-German fantasies and crude dreams of hegemony' is incorrect. H. Graml, 'Resistance Thinking on Foreign Policy', in idem *et al.*, *The German Resistance to Hitler*, Berkeley–London, 1970, p. 4.
21. Hassell–Trotha correspondence. These efforts have been described as a kind of 'proto-fascism' by Dirk Stegmann, 'Vom Neokonservatismus zum Proto-Fascismus: Konservative Parteien, Vereine und Verbände 1893–1920', in idem, B.-J. Wendt, P.-C. Witt (eds), *Deutscher Konservatismus im 19. und 20. Jahrhunderte*, Bonn, 1983, pp. 217–23.
22. Schöllgen, 'Wurzeln konservativer Opposition', pp. 481–2.
23. *WP 1900–1932*, pp. 25–31.
24. H. Schacht, *Confessions of 'The Old Wizard'. The Autobiography of Hjalmar Horace Greeley Schacht*, Cambridge, Mass., 1956, pp. 136 ff.
25. Scheurig, *Kleist-Schmenzin*, p. 38; Höhne, *Canaris*, pp. 73, 77; Groscurth, *Tagebücher*, p. 18.
26. Schöllgen, 'Wurzeln konservativer Opposition,' p. 481 is sceptical of

the claim in J. Erger, *Der Kapp-Lüttwitz-Putsch. Ein Beitrag zur deutschen Innenpolitik 1919–1920*, Düsseldorf, 1967, p. 86, about Hassell's contemplated role; but Stegmann, 'Vom Neokonservatismus', p. 228, confirms it. Hassell's views in 1923 are in a document entitled 'Gedanken über die Taktik der rechtsgerichteten Elemente in Deutschland' in Tirpitz's *Nachlaß*, BA/MA, N253, D13.

27. Eduard Brücklmeier (1903–44), in the Foreign Office, particularly close to Erich Kordt.

28. Karl Ludwig, Freiherr von Guttenberg (1902–45), estate-owner, editor of the 'Weißen Blätter', after 1939 in the Abwehr.

29. Gottfried von Nostitz (1902–76): 1930–2 German embassy, Belgrade; 1934–8 Vienna; 1938–40 Foreign Office, Berlin; 1940–5 Geneva. Quite closely connected with Hassell and Weizsäcker.

30. Botho von Wussow (1901–1971), estate-owner, in Chile for eleven years, after 1935 in Ribbentrop's *Büro*, eventually transferred to Spain.

31. U. W. Schwerin, 'Der Weg der "Jungen Generation" in den Widerstand', in Schmädeke and Steinbach (eds), *Der Widerstand*, p. 468.

32. *WP 1900–1932*, p. 325, 16.I.19(T); 2 Sept. 1921, E. v. W. to his wife.

33. Liedig and Heinz in Höhne, *Canaris*, pp. 73, 77.

34. Thun-Hohenstein, *Oster*, p. 52. His books were *Sprengstoff* (1930); *Kameraden der Arbeit. Deutsche Arbeitslager: Stand, Aufgabe und Zukunft* (1933); *Die Nation greift an. Geschichte und Kritik des soldatischen Nationalismus* (1933); *Mensch unbekannt. Begegnung und Erinnerung* (1935), written with others.

35. G. Ritter, *Carl Goerdeler und die deutsche Widerstandsbewegung*, Munich, 1965, pp. 24 ff.; E. Kosthorst, 'Carl Friedrich Goerdeler', in R. Lill and H. Oberreuter (eds), *20. Juli. Portraits des Widerstands*, Düsseldorf–Vienna, 1984, p. 114.

36. From 1919 to 1930 Hassell was in Rome, Barcelona and Copenhagen, and Goerdeler in Königsberg. Neither of them seems to have played an important part in the internal or parliamentary politics of the DNVP after 1919.

37. *WP 1900–1932*, pp. 41–3, 45–7, 393, 20.x.29, 401, 16.III.30.

38. Ritter, *Goerdeler*, p. 63; Kosthorst, 'Goerdeler', p. 115; M. Krüger-Charlé, 'Carl Goerdelers Versuche der Durchsetzung einer alternativen Politik 1933 bis 1937', in Schmädeke and Steinbach (eds), *Der Widerstand*, pp. 385–6.

39. Schacht, *Confessions*, pp. 258, 268–70; idem, *Account Settled*, London, 1949, pp. 32–3, 40. See E. Eyck, *A History of the Weimar Republic*, vol. 2, Cambridge, Mass., 1963, pp. 332–5.

40. *WP 1900–1932*, p. 49; E. Kordt, *Nicht aus den Akten*, Stuttgart, 1950, p. 50; Schacht, *Confessions*, pp. 271, 273.

41. A. Krebs, *Fritz-Dietlof Graf von der Schulenburg. Zwischen Staatsraison und Hochverrat*, Hamburg, 1964, p. 75; see the criticism of Krebs's biography as representative of the old apologetic resistance literature which emphasised only the moral–ethical component, by U. Heinemann,

'Fritz Dietlof Graf von der Schulenburg', in Schmädeke and Steinbach (eds), *Der Widerstand*, p. 419; Mommsen, 'Schulenburg', p. 215; E. von Weizsäcker, *Erinnerungen*, Munich–Leipzig–Freiburg im Breisgau, 1950, p. 143.

42. Mommsen, 'Schulenburg', in Graml (ed.), *Widerstand im Dritten Reich*, p. 215. See also K. Sontheimer, *Antidemokratisches Denken in der Weimarer Republik. Die politischen Ideen des deutschen Nationalismus zwischen 1918 und 1933*, Munich, 1962.

43. Reynolds, *Beck*, p. 44; especially, Müller, *General Ludwig Beck*, pp. 54, 63 ff., 339, Doc. no. 8, 17 March 1933.

44. Schwerin, 'Der Weg der "Jungen Generation"', pp. 467–9.

45. Kordt was a Catholic, originally from Düsseldorf.

46. C. Strohm, 'Der Widerstandskreis um Dietrich Bonhoeffer und Hans von Dohnanyi', in Schmädeke and Steinbach (eds), *Der Widerstand*, pp. 296–7.

47. C. Sykes, *Tormented Loyalty: The Story of a German Aristocrat Who Defied Hitler*, NY–Evanston, 1969, pp. 48, 79; H. O. Malone, *Adam von Trott zu Solz. Der Werdegang eines Verschwörers 1909–1938*, Berlin, 1986, pp. 47–8, 86–7.

48. See A. Schildt, 'Die Illusion der konservativen Alternative', in Schmädeke and Steinbach (eds), *Der Widerstand*, p. 160.

49. H. Rothfels, *Die deutsche Opposition gegen Hitler*, new and enlarged edn, Frankfurt am Main, 1977; Ritter, *Goerdeler*; Eberhard Zeller, *Geist der Freiheit*, 5th edn, Munich, 1965.

50. A. P. Young, *The 'X' Documents*, ed. S. Aster, London, 1974, p. 135; see also pp. 10, 106, 114.

51. Hassell, 22 March, 3 April, 30 May 1939.

52. Höhne, *Canaris*, p. 260 (on Oster); Hassell, 22 March, 3 April, 30 May 1939; Weizsäcker, *Erinnerungen*, p. 208.

53. Weizsäcker testimony, transcript Case 11 (English), pp. 8556, 9228.

54. R. Pommerin, 'Erwin von Witzleben', in Lill and Oberreuter (eds), *20. Juli*, p. 353; L. E. Hill (ed.), *Die Weizsäcker Papiere 1933–1950*, Berlin, 1974–82, p. 84, 4.VII.34(B) (hereafter *WP 1933–1950*); H. C. Deutsch, *Hitler and his Generals: The Hidden Crisis of January–June 1938*, Minneapolis, 1974, p. 50.

55. Deutsch, *Hitler and his Generals*, pp. 232 ff., 238–9, 255–6, 291 ff., 372–6, 399 ff., 416–17; A. von Kessel, *Verborgene Saat. Das 'Andere' Deutschland*, unpublished MSS, 1944–5, p. 26.

56. Deutsch, *Hitler and his Generals*, pp. 313–15, 377–82.

57. Höhne, *Canaris*, p. 266 (Dohnanyi).

58. Young, *The 'X' Documents*, pp. 54, 76, 152, 179; Hassell, 20 December 1938, 3 April 1938. In affidavits for Kordt's denazification trial Hans von Herwarth and Freiherr von Brandt zu Neidstein recollected that during visits to Moscow and Paris in 1934 Kordt had spoken of the regime as criminal because of 30 July 1934. *Akten der Spruchkammer München*, VIII, Akt. Zeichen VIII/1494/46.

59. Jacobsen (ed.), *Spiegelbild einer Verschwörung*, vol. 1, p. 451.

60. Höhne, *Canaris*, p. 266 (Dohnanyi); Jacobsen (ed.), *Spiegelbild einer Verschwörung*, vol. 1, pp. 325–8, 454–5, 518.
61. Hassell, 17 January 1939, 18 February 1939, 4 July 1939.
62. Hassell, 27 November 1938.
63. Unpublished private and contemporary source that cannot be cited.
64. Höhne, *Canaris*, p. 266; Jacobsen (ed.), *Spiegelbild einer Verschwörung*, vol. I, p. 519.
65. *WP 1933–1950*, p. 94, 19.I.36.
66. Schacht, *Confessions*, p. 316.
67. Paul Nikolaus Cossmann (1869–1942): 1904–1933 founder and manager of 'Süddeutschen Monatshefte'; after 1921 political adviser to 'Münchner Neuesten Nachrichten'; 1933 arrested for a year; 1938 put in a camp near Munich; 1942 transferred to Theresienstadt, where he died. In the First World War a proponent of extreme war aims; a nationalistic opponent of the Treaty of Versailles and the Weimar Republic.
68. Hassell, 1 December 1938.
69. Young, *The 'X' Documents*, p. 77.
70. Müller, *General Ludwig Beck*, p. 556, Doc. no. 51, 19 July 1938.
71. Reynolds, *Beck*, p. 76.
72. In 1934 General Werner von Fritsch, *Chef der Heeresleitung*, ordered the officer corps to participate in church services. H. Krausnick, 'Vorgeschichte und Beginn des militärischen Widerstandes gegen Hitler', in Europäische Publikation e.V. (ed.), *Vollmacht des Gewissens*, vol. 1, Frankfurt am Main–Berlin, 1960, p. 247.
73. K. Scholder, *Die Kirchen und das Dritte Reich*, vol. 1, Frankfurt am Main–Berlin–Vienna, 1977.
74. Weizsäcker, *Erinnerungen*, p. 208; J. S. Conway, *The Nazi Persecution of the Churches 1933–45*, Toronto, 1968, pp. 140–57.
75. Heinemann, 'Schulenburg', p. 422.
76. Weizsäcker, *Erinnerungen*, p. 108; unpublished private and contemporary source that cannot be cited.
77. Müller, *General Ludwig Beck*, p. 556, Doc. no. 51, 19 July 1938.
78. Hassell, 2 June 1939.
79. Young, *The 'X' Documents*, pp. 139, 153, 161.
80. Groscurth, *Tagebücher*, 30 December 1938; Hassell, 3 April 1938; Scheurig, *Kleist-Schmenzin*, p. 142; Reynolds, *Beck*, p. 140; Thun-Hohenstein, *Oster*, p. 125; Young, *The 'X' Documents*, p. 47; Schacht, *Confessions*, p. 327. Niemöller (1892–1984) was arrested in July 1937, tried in February 1938, found innocent of the charges, but nevertheless imprisoned again.
81. On one of these occasions Himmler told her 'we shall not rest until we have rooted out Christianity'. In his published *Erinnerungen*, p. 207, Weizsäcker does not name the Nazis to whom she talked, but names Himmler, Goering, *Statthalter* Murr of Württemberg and the Police President of Berlin in the (March 1945) early version of his memoirs. For the reasons that he deleted names from the

published version see L. E. Hill, 'The Genesis and Interpretation of the Memoirs of Ernst von Weizsäcker', *German Studies Review*, vol. 10, 1987, pp. 453–4. Niemöller was in Sachsenhausen 1938–41, in Dachau 1941–5.

82. Unpublished private and contemporary source that cannot be cited. See Weizsäcker, *Erinnerungen*, p. 145. Viktor von Weizsäcker was a professor of neurology at Heidelberg University.

83. Schacht, *Confessions*, pp. 318–21. For Goebbels's reaction see E. Fröhlich (ed.), *Die Tagebücher von Joseph Goebbels. Sämtliche Fragmente*, Munich–NY–London–Paris, 1987, part 1, vol. 2, pp. 505–6, 511–16.

84. Müller, *General Ludwig Beck*, p. 556, Doc. no. 51, 19 July 1938.

85. Groscurth, *Tagebücher*, pp. 498–503. See also Jacobsen (ed.), *Spiegelbild einer Verschwörung*, vol. 1, p. 150.

86. Schacht, *Confessions*, p. 316; Kordt, *Nicht aus den Akten*, pp. 359–66; Groscurth, *Tagebücher*, pp. 498–503.

87. Müller, *General Ludwig Beck*, p. 556, Doc. no. 51, 19 July 1938.

88. Jacobsen (ed.), *Spiegelbild einer Verschwörung*, p. 452. See the suggestive article by P. Steinbach, 'Wiederherstellung des Rechsstaats als zentrale Zielsetzung des Widerstands', in Schmädeke and Steinbach (eds), *Der Widerstand*, pp. 617–36.

89. Hassell, 4 September 1938.

90. Scheurig, *Tresckow*, p. 46; Graml, 'Hans Oster', p. 224; M. Krüger-Charlé, 'Carl Goerdelers Versuche', pp. 386–7.

91. Scheurig, *Kleist-Schmenzin*, p. 128; *WP 1933–1950*, p. 70, 23.III.33(B), 30.III.33(B), 22.IV.33(B), p. 75, *Ende August* 1933(T); Scheurig, Tresckow, p. 45; Mommsen, 'Schulenburg', p. 218; Sykes, *Tormented Loyalty*, p. 84.

92. Unpublished private and contemporary source about Weizsäcker that cannot be cited, from 28 June 1938; *WP 1933–1950*, p. 85, 5.VIII.34(B); Müller, *General Ludwig Beck*, pp. 58–9; Groscurth, *Tagebücher*, p. 26; Scheurig, *Tresckow*, pp. 20, 38.

93. Kosthorst, 'Goerdeler', p. 118.

94. Young, *The 'X' Documents*, pp. 78, 153, 161.

95. Walter Funk (1890–1960): 1933–8 Government Press Chief; 1937–45 Reich Economics Minister; 1939–45 President of Reichsbank.

96. A. E. Simpson, *Hjalmar Schacht in Perspective*, The Hague–Paris, 1969, pp. 110, 125, 130; Hassell, 15 August 1939.

97. Müller, *General Ludwig Beck*, p. 499; Reynolds, *Beck*, p. 122.

98. Hassell, 10, 11 August 1939. Bosch (1861–1942) founded factories in Stuttgart to produce ignition and electrical parts for automobiles. He became renowned for his liberal employment policies and philanthropic endeavours. For some indications of his role during the Nazi period see W. Treue, 'Widerstand von Unternehmern und Nationalökonomen', in Schmädeke and Steinbach (eds), *Der Widerstand*, pp. 928–34.

99. Mommsen, 'Schulenburg', pp. 221, 234.

100. Simpson, *Schacht*, pp. 142, 146, 150; G. Schulz, 'Nationalpatriotismus im Widerstand', *Vierteljahrshefte für Zeitgeschichte*, vol. 32, 1984, pp. 338–43.
101. Hassell, 28 November 1938.
102. For an indication of the limitations of DNVP in comparison with Nazi anti-Semitism see H. Graml, *Reichskristallnacht. Antisemitismus und Judenverfolgung im Dritten Reich*, Munich, 1988, p. 113; A. Thimme, *Flucht in den Mythos. Die Deutschnationale Volkspartei und die Niederlage von 1918*, Göttingen, 1969, pp. 116–17.
103. On the antipathy of the Right to the *Ostjuden* see G. L. Mosse, 'Die Deutsche Rechte und die Juden', in W. E. Mosse (ed.), *Entscheidungsjahr 1932. Zur Judenfrage in der Endphase der Weimarer Republik*, Tübingen, 1965, pp. 227, 230. For further background see S. E. Aschheim, *Brothers and Strangers: The East European Jew in German and German Jewish Consciousness, 1800–1923*, Madison, 1982.
104. *WP 1900–1932*, p. 44; Schacht, *Confessions*, p. 325.
105. On Schacht see the comments of R. Rürup, 'Das Ende der Emanzipation: Die antijüdische Politik in Deutschland von der "Machtergreifung" bis zum Zweiten Weltkrieg', in A. Paucker (ed.), *Die Juden in Nationalsozialistischen Deutschland/The Jews in Nazi Germany 1933–1943*, Tübingen, 1986, p. 102.
106. Erich von Manstein (1887–1973), General Field Marshal.
107. Groscurth, *Tagebücher*, pp. 25, 169, 3 March 1939.
108. Schacht, *Confessions*, pp. 315, 322; but see the sceptical remarks about Schacht's claims in Rürup, 'Das Ende der Emanzipation', p. 110, n. 54. *WP 1933–1950*, p. 62, 13.III.33.
109. *WP 1933–1950*, p. 62, 13.III.33(B), p. 70, 17.III.33(B), 23.III.33(B), 30.III.33(B), p. 75, Ende August 1933(T).
110. Affidavit of Luisa Countess Welczeck for Weizsäcker's trial, but apparently not introduced as evidence. Weizsäcker *Nachlaß*. See also *WP 1933–1950*, p. 509, n. 149.
111. Hassell, 25, 27 November, 20, 25 December 1938; Groscurth, *Tagebücher*, p. 157.
112. Young, *The 'X' Documents*, p. 139.
113. Schacht, *Confessions*, pp. 331, 337–8.
114. Simpson, *Schacht*, Ch. 6; Young, *The 'X' Documents*, p. 155; Reynolds, *Beck*, pp. 48, 50, 61–6; Müller, *General Ludwig Beck*, pp. 48, 53, 66–73, 91, 134, 169, 344, Doc. no. 9, 14 December 1933; Jacobsen (ed.), *Spiegelbild einer Verschwörung*, vol. 1, pp. 526, 528–9; Graml, 'Oster', p. 226.
115. On Goerdeler see H. Mommsen, 'Social Views and Constitutional Plans of the Resistance', in H. Graml et al., (eds), *The German Resistance to Hitler*, p. 72. Müller, *General Ludwig Beck*, p. 157, explicitly denies that Beck was a Social Darwinist.
116. *WP 1933–1950*, p. 168, *Mitte Oktober* 1939.
117. Weizsäcker wrote of the necessity to bring Germany through a 'Gefahrenzone', ibid., p. 82, June 1934.

118. *WP 1900–1932*, pp. 35–7, 408; *WP 1933–1950*, pp. 96–7, July 1936, p. 111, ?.ɪ.37. Kordt, *Nicht aus den Akten*, pp. 18, 22, 40–1 speaks of his interest and studies in international law. After the Second World War he became a professor in that field.

119. Reynolds, *Beck*, pp. 142, 151–2, 183 (Halder); G. R. Ueberschär, 'Ansätze und Hindernisse der Militäropposition gegen Hitler in den ersten beiden Kriegsjahren (1939–1941)', in Militärgeschichtliches Forschungsamt (ed.), *Aufstand des Gewissens*, p. 348; Müller, *General Ludwig Beck*, pp. 147–50, 154–5, 157–8, 255.

120. Walter, Count von Brockdorff-Ahlefeldt (1887–1943), General of the Infantry; 1938–1939 Commander of the 23rd Infantry Division, stationed near Berlin.

121. Paul von Hase (1885–1944), Lieutenant-General; 1934–1938 Commander of Infantry Regiment 50, during the war District Commandant of Berlin; executed after 20 July 1944.

122. Erich Hoepner (1886–1944) Colonel-General; 1938 Commander First Division, 1942 retired; executed after 20 July 1944.

123. Wilhelm Adam (1877–1949), General of the Infantry; March–November 1938 commander of Army-Group 2, 31 December 1938 retirement.

124. Young, *The 'X' Documents*, pp. 154, 232–4; Jacobsen (ed.), *Spiegelbild einer Verschwörung*, vol. 1, p. 353.

125. *WP 1933–1950*, p. 111, ?.ɪ.37.

126. Ibid., p. 123, 15.ɪɪɪ.38(B); Weizsäcker, *Erinnerungen*, p. 150.

127. *WP 1933–1950*, p. 152, 16.ɪɪɪ.39(T), p. 173, *Mitte Oktober 1939*. It is important to note that he did not even mention the Sudetenland as an objective in his list of July 1936. Ibid., pp. 97–8.

128. Kordt, *Nicht aus den Akten*, pp. 38–42, 221–4; Kessel, *Verborgene Saat*, p. 68.

129. Heinz wrote memoirs, *Von Wilhelm Canaris zum NKWD*, which are available on microfilm at the Institut für Zeitgeschichte in Munich.

130. Scheurig, *Tresckow*, pp. 60–2.

131. Scheurig, *Kleist-Schmenzin*, pp. 150–2, 166; Young, *The 'X' Documents*, pp. 153, 161.

132. Scheurig, *Kleist-Schmenzin*, p. 169; Hassell, 22 March 1939; Young, *The 'X' Documents*, pp. 178–9; Jacobsen (ed.), *Spiegelbild einer Verschwörung*, vol. 1, p. 353 (Goerdeler), p. 354 (Schacht); *WP 1933–1950*, pp. 152–3, 16.ɪɪɪ.39(T), 27.ɪɪɪ.39(T), pp. 173–4, *Mitte Oktober 1939*; Kordt, *Nicht aus den Akten*, p. 298.

133. *WP 1933–1950*, pp. 152–3, 16.ɪɪɪ.39(T), 27.ɪɪɪ.39(T), pp. 173–4, *Mitte Oktober 1939*.

134. Reynolds, *Beck*, pp. 158, 164, 172, 182; Höhne, *Canaris*, p. 295; *WP 1933–1950*, p. 122, 5.ɪɪɪ.38(T).

135. See I. Kershaw, 'The Führer Image and Political Integration: The Popular Conception of Hitler in Bavaria during the Third Reich', in G. Hirschfeld and L. Kettenacker (eds), *Der 'Führerstaat': Mythos und Realität. Studien zur Struktur und Politik des Dritten Reiches*, Stuttgart,

1981; see also the elaboration of this argument in Kershaw's *Der Hitler-Mythos. Volksmeinung und Propaganda im Dritten Reich*, Stuttgart, 1980, and the expanded English version, *The 'Hitler Myth': Image and Reality in the Third Reich*, Oxford, 1987; also his *Popular Opinion and Political Dissent in the Third Reich: Bavaria 1933–1945*, Oxford, 1983.

136. See Mommsen, 'Social Views', pp. 55–147.
137. Reynolds, *Beck*, p. 161; Müller, *General Ludwig Beck*, p. 309; P. Hoffmann, 'Ludwig Beck: Loyalty and Resistance', *Central European History*, vol. 14, 1981, pp. 346–7; idem, *German Resistance to Hitler*, Cambridge, Mass.–London, 1988, p. 83.
138. Deutsch, *Hitler and his Generals*, pp. 399–402; Müller, *General Ludwig Beck*, p. 307. Halder thought the plan utopian; see H. Countess Schall-Riaucour, *Aufstand und Gehorsam. Offizierstum und Generalstab im Umbruch – Leben und Wirken von Generaloberst Franz Halder, Generalstabschef 1938–1942*, Wiesbaden, 1972, p. 222. Krausnick, '*Vorgeschichte*', p. 321 judges it unrealistic.
139. Müller, *General Ludwig Beck*, pp. 298–306.
140. Kershaw, 'The Führer Image', pp. 151–4; idem, *The 'Hitler Myth'*, pp. 133–42; idem, *Popular Opinion*, pp. 107, 152.
141. Strohm, 'Der Widerstandskreis', in Schmädeke and Steinbach (eds), *Der Widerstand*, pp. 296–7.
142. Their remarks on Hitler's goals in the world and his objectionable domestic politics are ignored by B.-J. Wendt, 'Konservative Honoratioren – Eine Alternative zu Hitler? Englandkontakte des deutschen Widerstands im Jahre 1938', in D. Stegmann, B.-J. Wendt, and P.-C. Witt (eds), *Deutscher Konservatismus im 19. und 20. Jahrhundert*, Bonn, 1983, pp. 347–67.
143. Kershaw, *The 'Hitler Myth'*, pp. 139, 141.

14

Between England and Germany: Adam von Trott's Contacts with the British

Henry O. Malone

In 1734 Elector George Augustus of Hanover founded a university at Göttingen which rapidly became one of the great institutions of higher learning in Europe. Since the Elector was also King George II of England the Georg-August Universität had, from its inception, a special relationship with England. That relationship remained firm even after the separation in 1837 of the Hanoverian and English Crowns, and also continued following the Prussian annexation of Hanover in 1866.

In view of this background, it is interesting to note that at the beginning of the winter semester of 1927/8, Adam von Trott zu Solz, whose own life would be closely bound up with England and English people, matriculated as a student in the Faculty of Law and Public Administration at the University of Göttingen. Although he had already studied one semester in Munich, and would study two more in Berlin, Göttingen became his academic home, the university to which he would always return, and at which he took his first examination and his doctorate. During Trott's five semesters in Göttingen, he worked under Professor Herbert Kraus, Director of the Institute for International Law and Diplomacy, an academic who was himself at home in the world of Anglo-American scholarship and who was a staunch believer in liberal democratic government.[1] Certainly, this academic atmosphere had its influence on Trott's interest in England.

But even before Trott's university years he had had relations with English people. His earliest British contact took place on

9 August 1909, when Louisa Barrett, the Trott children's English nanny, saw him for the first time in Potsdam, a few hours after his birth.[2] Through Miss Barrett he was exposed to the English language for five years, until the outbreak of war in 1914. Even after her departure, there was his mother Eleonore, a granddaughter of the American Minister to Vienna John Jay, who sometimes spoke and corresponded with him in 'her mother's' tongue. And there was her brother, Eberhard von Schweinitz, who had been one of the first German Rhodes scholars at Oxford from 1903 to 1905.

Despite these Anglo-Saxon influences, English was not one of Trott's school subjects, since he was a pupil in a classical *Gymnasium* where French was the one modern language prescribed. Consequently, when he first matriculated as a student at Munich in the summer semester of 1927, his English composition still left much to be desired. For example, writing to his mother with regard to two American student acquaintances he reported: '. . . through the Americans I became very good conexions to America! . . . I sea as longer I write as bader becomes my English!'[3] However, his ability to write and speak the language improved markedly in the next years, probably due in part to some extra-curricular English lessons and the further chance to associate with English-speaking people.

Contacts as a Student

After two semesters in Göttingen, Trott used his mother's connections with ecumenical church leaders to facilitate an invitation for him to Geneva in September 1928. That trip brought him into contact not only with the Scotsman Charles Freer Andrews, a friend of Tagore and Gandhi, but also with Bernard Shaw and an Oxford student, Geoffrey Wilson of Oriel College. Moreover, the American Conrad Hoffman, one of the leaders in Geneva of the World's Student Christian Federation, knowing of Trott's interest in visiting England, made arrangements with the London staff of the Student Christian Movement of Great Britain and Ireland (SCM) for Trott to go to England to participate in the quadrennial conference of SCM, held in Liverpool during the first week of January 1929. That conference afforded Trott the opportunity to renew his friendship with Geoffrey Wilson and to lay the groundwork for a period of study at Oxford as a special student. Through the SCM staff Trott was able during the conference to meet Professor W. G. Adams of All Souls College and the Reverend Dr William B. Selbie, Principal of Mansfield College, who took a liking to him and agreed that he could spend Hilary term at his College. During that two-month period, Trott made a wide range of new friendships, running all the way from the Chichele Professor of Military History, Major-General Sir Ernest Swinton, and All Souls Fellow A. L. Rowse, to an Indian student called Humayum Kabir, later Minister of Scientific Research and Cultural Affairs in New Delhi. He learned much about England, and began to understand some of the fundamental differences between English and German perspectives on life, politics and society. He characterised the English student as a 'man of action', as manifested by the socialist activism of Oxford students, and contrasted him with the German student as a 'man of thought'. He aspired to combine the English 'man of action' motif with the German 'man of thought' ideal, and thus at the age of nineteen he began the task of trying to find a basis for Anglo-German solidarity born out of a common need of each for the other.[4] His effort to integrate the Anglo-Saxon and Germanic viewpoints was a task which would engage him for the rest of his life. But of all the insights he gained from his first trip to England, the most important, he concluded, was that it enabled him to experience what 'democracy' can mean.[5]

After the term at Mansfield College, Trott matriculated at the University of Berlin, where he became a close friend of a young British diplomat, Hugh Montgomery, the third secretary in the British Embassy. Montgomery introduced him to the 'fascinating' world of Embassy political circles and to social acquaintance with interesting and influential people, both English and German.[6] Ironically, it was Montgomery who brought Trott together with two young attachés in the German Foreign Office, Albrecht von Kessel and Josias von Rantzau, who would later be instrumental in recruiting him for the Wilhelmstraße.[7] The year in Berlin also gave Trott the opportunity for more frequent visits to his uncle, Eberhard von Schweinitz, a Prussian civil servant, with whom he could exchange ideas about experiences in England. Indeed, it was von Schweinitz who gave Trott the particulars on how one applied for a Rhodes Scholarship, a step Trott took after returning to Göttingen for his law examination. In his application, Trott emphasised not only his general interest in international problems, but also his hope that his experiences at Oxford might yield something useful for the problems of his own country. Once he was selected as a Rhodes Scholar, early in 1931, he chose Balliol as his college, following in the footsteps of his uncle.[8]

Trott's return to Oxford as a regular student enabled him to renew old friendships as well as to have the chance to meet a large number of new acquaintances in the Anglo-American world. Among his contemporaries were David Astor, Christopher Hill, Peter Calvocoressi, Con O'Neill, John Stafford Cripps, the Americans Dean Rusk and Carl Albert and the Canadian David Lewis. But he also had contact with both the younger faculty and those of more mature years, within and outside the university, such as Richard Crossman, Isaiah Berlin, A. D. Lindsay, Humphrey Sumner, John Fulton, R. G. Collingwood, H. A. L. Fisher, Christopher Cox, John Buchan, Sir Stafford Cripps and the Marquess of Lothian. The two years of the Rhodes Scholarship were of decisive importance in Trott's life, forming as it were a watershed. By going up to Oxford in 1931 he had not only postponed the beginning of his prescribed postgraduate legal *practicum*, but had also thereby taken himself out of Germany just when the final struggle to preserve the country as a constitutional state was beginning. Although he kept in touch with his socialist friends in Germany, and visited them whenever possible, the fact was that he found himself outside Germany during these crucial years, unable to participate in the effort to prevent the collapse of the Weimar Republic. But, because he was abroad, he saw developments from a different perspective. Thrust automatically by his position as a German Rhodes Scholar into the role of a representative of his country, whether of Weimar or of the National Socialist state, he had to consider carefully what he said, and be certain of where he should take his stand. With the coming of the National Socialists to power, his own career plans were overturned, and it became necessary to answer the question: *Was sollen wir tun?* (What must be done?). The basis for his ultimate answer came quickly, as he recognised at once the fundamental evil represented by the 'dangerous crowd' which had taken over the state. He understood what his task would be, and he knew he had to return to Germany to accomplish it. As his Balliol college friend, Charles Collins, recalled: 'At a very early age he had done what few people do – he had recognised the nature of the task to which he proposed, in one form or another, to address his life – to help in resolving the problem of Germany's place in Europe and the world.'[9] Trott believed that task could not be carried out as an *émigré*. But the years in Oxford had given him the background which later made possible his specific contribution within the German resistance to Hitler.

Maintaining Contact in the Early National Socialist Era

Many of Trott's British acquaintances could not understand why he should return to a Germany ruled by Hitler unless he was sympathetic to National Socialism. This simplistic view was fuelled by a letter Trott wrote in early 1934 to the *Manchester Guardian*, in which he questioned the view that the German judiciary had allowed itself to become an instrument of anti-Semitic persecution. On the basis of his own experience of several months in the Hessian judiciary, he argued that there was another side of the story, and offered his views as a corrective to what he considered a biased and sensationalised article in the newspaper. Although Trott's letter did not cause his close friends at Oxford to believe he had opted for National Socialism, it did create problems for them in trying to defend his action or explain his real intent. But among those who did not know Trott well, there was a tendency to think the worst: that he had become an apologist for National Socialism. The damage to his reputation in Oxford had been done and persisted, with one rumour going so far as to say that he had joined the NSDAP. Almost from the moment he mailed the letter Trott recognised that it was ill-advised. But what was his real motive? Quite simply, he felt that if the foreign press were to take note of the dissenting body of opinion in Germany, the more rational elements in the country would be encouraged to form factions within the Nazi Party organisation, or else to break away altogether, thus driving a wedge between the regime and the majority. Trott felt an obligation to aid this process; and that desire was the fundamental motive behind his communication to the *Manchester Guardian*. Unfortunately, the letter was remembered in official British circles, and later helped to damage his credibility.[10]

During the years of his judicial *practicum*, Trott received periodic visits from English friends, and brought some of his German socialist friends into contact with similar circles in England. For example, J. P. Mayer, a representative of the younger and more militant wing of the former German Social Democratic Party led by Carlo Mierendorff and Theodor Haubach, wanted to foster a connection with the British Labour Party leadership in order to gain moral support from socialist groups outside Germany in case of an early displacement of Hitler. Trott sent Mayer to see Sir Stafford Cripps in June 1934, and asked this English friend to put Mayer into contact with other Labour Party notables, such as Clement Attlee and George Lansbury.[11]

Late in 1934 Trott was transferred back to Berlin for a period of practical experience in international law with the law firm of Dr Paul Leverkühn, work that Trott found more compatible with his real interests. He was also elected secretary of the German Rhodes Scholarship Selection Committee, which brought him into even closer contact with Lord Lothian, secretary of the Rhodes Trust. Although Hugh Montgomery was no longer in Berlin, Trott met a number of the younger persons in the diplomatic corps, in particular George P. (Jerry) Young, who like Montgomery earlier was Third Secretary at the British Embassy. This contact led to an introduction to the British Ambassador, Sir Eric Phipps.[12]

When Trott completed his prescribed training period in Berlin early in May 1935, he had a two-week interlude before the beginning of duty at the court in Kassel. That provided him with a chance to visit England for the first time since 1933. Most of his fellow undergraduates had gone down from Oxford by the time he returned, so his reunion was primarily with the dons and other faculty. He was a guest of Professor W. G. Adams, Warden of All Souls, and spent a weekend with Sir Stafford Cripps at his country home, at Lechlade, Gloucestershire. During the last week of May 1935 he attended a Rhodes Trust dinner in London as a member of the German selection committee, and had a chance to see his contemporaries at college, David Astor and Charles Collins. He made a particular point of talking with R. H. Tawney, whom he held in high regard, and saw R. G. Collingwood, who assured him of his steadfast and sustaining friendship. Nevertheless, most of Trott's acquaintances knew little if anything of the actual circumstances under which he lived in Germany, or of his ties to dissident circles. Some felt that he had compromised himself by remaining in Germany and working within the National Socialist legal system, despite their recognition of his lack of sympathy for National Socialist ideology. Thus in May 1935, when they found him unwilling indiscriminately to repudiate everything that had happened in Germany over the past two years, and even expressing hope of a change for the better, they doubted the authenticity of his opposition to the National Socialist regime. If he were really an opponent, now that its actual character had become apparent, why did he not leave and come to England as an *émigré*, as so many of his like-minded fellow-countrymen had done? The trip to England had a polarising effect on his English acquaintances. Either they were strengthened in their doubts about him, being unable to accept his view that decent people had a duty to remain in Germany rather than abandon the country to the National Socialists, or else they admired him for following a difficult and courageous course.[13]

In the autumn of 1935 Trott was transferred to a post in Hamburg, and there he first met John Wheeler-Bennett, during a visit with his friend, Shiela Grant Duff, to the estate of Albrecht Count von Bernstorff in nearby Holstein. This meeting put Trott in touch with the Englishman generally regarded as the best informed on German affairs, one with whom Trott was destined to collaborate closely in the future.[14] Another English contact during his Hamburg tenure came through the mediation of a young German-Jewish woman, Ingrid Warburg, who had also been a student at Oxford while Trott was there. Miss Warburg introduced him to a Hamburg lawyer, Dr Peter Bielenberg, who was married to an English woman, and, like Trott, was in the midst of his legal *practicum*. Bielenberg and his wife, Christabel, née Burton, a niece of newspaper baron Lord Northcliffe, became fast friends of Trott. Later, he would say that Chris Bielenberg was his 'English conscience'.[15]

Early in 1936, following the training period in Hamburg, Trott found it necessary to interrupt his *practicum* in order to fulfil a National Socialist requirement that all potential *Assessoren* spend a period in a camp, a *Referendarlager*, in which they would undergo physical conditioning, military-type training and political indoctrination. The authorities in Kassel scheduled him to attend the eight-week course at Jüterborg. Not long after his arrival there, his presence in the camp became known in England, and gave rise to a new set of rumours that he had either joined the Party or was sympathetic to its aims.[16] How Trott could stay in Germany, seemingly indifferent to his own personal safety, at a time when other Germans who opposed Hitler were flocking to England as refugees, was beyond the comprehension of many of his English acquaintances. They were neither able to understand the sense of duty that compelled him to stay in Germany, preparing for a better day, nor could they fathom his conviction that things could be changed. The rumours persisted, and Trott was virtually helpless to check them. In a mood of desperation, he wrote: 'Sometimes I feel I never want to go to England again, whatever kind of home-sickness I feel toward it.'[17]

During the final year of his legal *practicum*, Trott continued to serve as secretary of the German Rhodes Scholarship Selection Committee as he prepared for the *Assessor* examination, and began to think seriously of leaving Germany temporarily to make a study trip to the Far East. During October 1936 Trott and his fellow Rhodes Scholar, Fritz Schumacher, met together in Berlin to discuss whether they should stay in Germany or become *émigrés*.

Trott emphasised their duty to remain and work for the downfall of the National Socialist regime, but Schumacher disagreed. Each stuck to his position and could not persuade the other.[18] Upon completion of his examination in October 1936, Trott's status as a civil servant ended, and he was no longer under the control or discipline of the Ministry of Justice. 'I am as much a free man as one is likely to be under the circumstances', he wrote.[19] In November Trott spent three weeks in England to gain the sanction of the Rhodes Trust for his plan to use a postponed third year of his Rhodes Scholarship for a study tour of China. The joy at the prospect of leaving National Socialist rule for a while was tempered by the realisation that, ultimately, he would not be able to escape his destiny: 'The idea of leaving Europe next year is hard, but still the only way I can deal with the future before me.'[20]

Trott's principal contacts in these weeks were with Lord Lothian, who supported his proposal for study abroad, R. H. Tawney, John Wheeler-Bennett, H. A. L. Fisher, himself a Rhodes trustee, and Dr C. K. Allen, Warden of Rhodes House, who was not in favour of Trott's plan. Lothian's will prevailed over Allen's, and the trustees approved the project, with the intent of allowing Trott to gain the necessary expertise to qualify for an appointment as a Far Eastern specialist in a German University.[21] Lothian sought the assistance of Edward C. Carter, Secretary-General of the Institute of Pacific Relations in New York, in arranging university connections for Trott, putting him into direct contact with the organisation and its head.[22]

Toward Anglo-German Co-operation in the Far East

Late in February 1937, Trott journeyed once more to England, *en route* to China via North America. In Oxford he saw Isaiah Berlin, Maurice Bowra and A. L. Rowse, who introduced him to Helmuth Count von Moltke. In London he stayed with the Astors in St James's Square, and for the first time met David Astor's celebrated mother Nancy Astor, MP for Plymouth,[23] as well as the Chinese Ambassador and Lord Halifax, who would be Foreign Secretary by the time Trott returned.

About six weeks after arriving in North America in mid-March 1937, Trott travelled to Montreal and then to Ottawa, where he was the guest of Lord Tweedsmuir, whom he had known in Oxford as John Buchan. He also got to meet and have long talks with his Oxford student friend, David Lewis, Secretary of the Co-operative Commonwealth Federation, the Canadian Socialist

Party.[24] An extended stay in California to study China and its language gave Trott an opportunity to reflect on the political situation in Europe. In concert with arguments he had made earlier in a monograph on Hegel's concept of international law, Trott maintained that an international order based on recognition of national sovereignty was the only 'tool' available to Europe for solving the existing crisis. Yet that sovereignty had to be informed and directed by a rational element dedicated to justice and peace within each national state. In Britain he saw that element in the Labour Party; but Germany had a corresponding 'peace element' capable of changing the state 'from inside'. Those moderating forces in Germany, to which Trott felt incapable of contributing at that time, along with the rearmament under way in Great Britain, together created a 'more stable balance' of power in Europe, and thus diminished the chances for war.[25] The problem he faced personally was to determine how to make a constructive contribution to the 'peace element' in his own country. His sojourn in China was intended in part to help him resolve that fundamental issue.

The trip to China was financed by Sir Stafford Cripps. Additional funds to supplement the £350 allocated to Trott by the Rhodes Trust were provided by another English friend, H. N. Spalding. Ten days before Trott sailed in July 1937, the Japanese attack on the Marco Polo bridge in Lukouchiao rekindled the Sino-Japanese conflict. As a result Peking was cut off by Japan by the time the ship reached Hong Kong, and Trott, together with his travelling companion, sinologist Dr Wolfram Eberhard, made a diversionary trip into Canton. Meanwhile, Warden Allen of Rhodes House tried to scuttle Trott's entire trip because of the changed circumstances, but Lothian would not allow this to happen. Trott proceeded to Peking later in the autumn of 1937, and became affiliated with Yenching University. Despite the Japanese military occupation, the foreign diplomatic missions remained in place, even though the government to which they were accredited had withdrawn. Therefore Trott soon made contact with his Berlin friend, Jerry Young, who had risen to a position of some prominence in the British Legation.[26] He also became acquainted with John Brett Robey, an Oxford graduate and British consular official. Robey liked Trott on a personal level, and felt certain that he was opposed to totalitarianism. But on the official level, Robey was uncertain just how far Trott was prepared to accept the existing situation in Germany. British officials in Peking and elsewhere hesitated to believe that Trott was in Peking simply to pursue academic studies. Since he seemed intent on returning to Germany, and maintained contact with the German Legation in Peking, they tended to assume that he was there under official German Government sponsorship. At the least they assumed he had some official task to carry out in exchange for the freedom of travel he enjoyed. Consequently, suspicion began to grow, and it appears likely that he was under British security surveillance. Although no reports to this effect have been uncovered, direct and indirect evidence suggests that such reports were compiled and forwarded to London.[27]

On the occasion of the anniversary of the foundation of the Bismarckian Reich, Trott was asked to deliver a lecture on Anglo-German relations to the Peking German community. The lecture, published in April 1938 as an article entitled 'Deutscher und Englischer Wille zur Macht',[28] called for intensive efforts by both Great Britain and Germany to work together. Apart from his close personal ties to both countries, and a natural desire to see them maintain friendly and co-operative relations, he was convinced that Anglo-German co-operation was the key to maintaining peace in Europe. That conviction was given more concrete form in a paper he prepared in the summer of 1938. Its basis was the shift in German policy, predicted by the Anti–Comintern Pact of 1936, and fulfilled in the ascendancy of Ribbentropp over von Neurath early in 1938 and the subsequent withdrawal of the German advisory group to Chiang Kai-shek. With English and German interests in East Asia suddenly brought into greater conflict, Trott sought a solution. His essay summed up his observations and proposals for a peaceful settlement in the Far East, resting on a joint initiative by Germany and Great Britain. Arguing that British and German interests were threatened equally by the expansion of Japan's power, Trott believed that further advances into Central and South China would make her military and political position on the Asiatic continent increasingly precarious and, at the same time, intensify her differences with the major world powers. Since diplomatic and financial sanctions had proved ineffective in halting the Japanese advance, the danger of an overwhelming anti–Japanese combination, including even Soviet Russia, should be obvious. Such a combination would prove fatal to Japan, and Trott believed responsible statesmen and soldiers in Japan realised this danger and had a genuine desire to stop the fighting. However, only a major international gesture would offer these constructive elements in Japan the pretext to assert themselves. Moreover, Japan needed Germany's military and even moral support, and also required British economic assistance. Japanese military men would listen to

German counsel, whereas Japanese politicians and businessmen would be sensitive to British representations. Thus, a joint move by both would prove almost irresistible. What was the alternative? A continuation of war which would lead to an indefinite deterioration of Western influence in the Far East and on the international balance overall. Specific provisions of Trott's proposal included: recognition of the government of Chiang Kai-shek as the legal government of China; assistance to the Chungking government to diminish the power of the Chinese Communists; inclusion of Japan in economic development plans for China; and the continued Japanese presence in all strategic locations then held by their forces in China. Mediation on this basis would be in the best interest of Japan and would offer the maximum political support at that juncture for China. Joint assertion of Western interests in a settlement of the conflict would prevent expanding Japanese interests from attaining a monopolistic position, while China would be given the chance to blunt the impact of one foreign competitor with the aid of other powers, and thereby to build up her newly reinforced national unity.

The German version of the paper was called 'Ostasiatische Möglichkeiten' and was sent in July to some fifty friends, industrialists, government officials and professors in Germany, including *Reichsbank* President Hjalmar Schacht and German Ambassadors Dirksen in England, Trautmann in China and Ott in Japan.[29] An early English version for Lord Lothian, called 'First Draft of a Memorandum on the Present Situation in the Far East', was carried back by Peter Fleming, who returned to England by air early in July. A more polished version was widely distributed in September by Rhodes House, called 'Far Eastern Possibilities'.[30] When Lothian received Trott's memorandum, he transmitted it at once to Lord Halifax, who since Eden's resignation in February had been Foreign Secretary. Lothian's view was that the course of action set forth in the paper had the potential for bringing a fair peace to the Far East, and that Anglo-German co-operation along the lines suggested by Trott just might pave the way to better relations in Europe.[31] Although Halifax's personal reaction is unknown, it was probably favourable, since the response of his subordinates was positive. One of them wrote on 10 August 1938: 'This is an interesting paper. It is written in a thoroughly German idiom, but the underlying argument and the common sense behind it are clear enough.'[32] The commentator realised that the principal obstacle standing in the way of Trott's proposal was the difficulty in persuading the National Socialist regime that economic considerations sometimes have to override ideological ones. Nevertheless, he felt the possibilities were well worth examining, and that 'Herr von Dirksen' should be sounded out upon his return to London.

The paramount difficulty with such a proposal for Anglo-German co-operation in August 1938 was the build-up of tension between the two countries over the German moves to bring the Sudetenland into the Reich. Although a second official found the Trott proposal worth bearing in mind and perhaps cautiously pursuing, on balance he thought consideration of it ought to be postponed until September,[33] evidently expecting a relaxation of tensions. However, these had intensified by then, as the Sudeten crisis moved Europe close to war. When the paper was considered again on 19 September, another official thought that the existing critical situation in Central Europe precluded any hope of raising the question with the Germans at that time, and suggested it be taken up the following month, presumably after there had been some accommodation.[34]

In the wake of the Munich Accord, and the damage it inflicted on Anglo-German relations, there is no evidence that the Foreign Office gave any further consideration to Trott's plan. Some commentators have called his proposals naïve or unrealistic, and with hindsight one can more easily say that they were, given the ideological gulf between the National Socialist regime and His Majesty's Government. However, Harold Nicolson reported having offered a proposal closely resembling Trott's to Hugh Dalton and Albrecht von Bernstorff in June 1937.[35] Quite apart from that, it was a remarkable feat for a young man, completely lacking official standing or any credentials, to put forward a plan proposing a fundamental reorientation of British foreign policy that was taken seriously at the highest level in Whitehall. Had there been a different outcome of the Sudeten crisis, occasioned by a British determination to stand firm against Hitler and grant no concessions, the prospect of the Foreign Office's pursuing Trott's proposal in October 1938 might have been greater.

During Trott's homeward journey from the Far East, his ship docked at the port of Colombo in Ceylon on 10 November. It was there that he first heard details of the infamous *Kristallnacht* pogroms in Germany. His thoughts turned at once to his Jewish friend in Berlin, Wilfrid Israel, as he wrote to a friend in England: 'You know that it is we who are humiliated by what has passed and it is for us to wonder whether our former friends wish to have anything more to do with one who, after all (in my case through my very absence), has to accept his full share of the guilt and the responsibility.'[36] His sense of responsibility demanded his presence in Germany. He knew that many of his English friends, representatives of British public opinion, had resigned themselves to the belief that only the military defeat of Germany in war would return Europe to peace and stability. Trott rejected and abhorred such a fatalistic outlook, urging an English friend not to 'let your mind get trapped in the hopeless view that only war can make things right again'. He firmly believed that 'peace, even painful peace, is ultimately better, and may still give us a chance to disentangle the destinies of our two countries'.[37]

Efforts to Preserve Peace

Before Trott went to the Far East he had opposed the National Socialist regime, but had not conspired against it with the aim of a forcible overthrow. At some point, no later than the time he was on the way home, his attitude toward such action had changed. But he felt that a crucial factor in any political conspiracy aimed at removing Hitler's government from power was the maintenance of peace. During the months following his return, the refrain that frequently fell from his lips was: 'War does not solve any problems.'[38] He was persuaded that it would be far more difficult, if not impossible, to mobilise key elements in Germany against the dictator if the country were engulfed in a war and caught up in the accompanying surge of patriotism. In 1930, as a student in Göttingen, he had entered in a notebook his attitude toward war in the twentieth century: 'We should strive today for self-assertion of the state on the lines of a development of law, not on those of war. As a just verdict of the world tribunal concerning a people's historical right to exist, war is today an absurdity.'[39] In accordance with this view, Trott embarked in 1939 on an effort to preserve peace, not only to prevent the ultimate disaster for Europe and Germany, but also to maintain a situation more likely to favour effective internal resistance to the regime. His contacts with England were the fundamental basis for that effort.

During a trip to England in February 1939 Trott renewed personal ties with Lord Lothian, David Astor, John Wheeler-Bennett, Sir Stafford Cripps, and Geoffrey Wilson, who was by then acting as an occasional assistant to Cripps. Although these and other English contacts meant a great deal to Trott, some of his Balliol contemporaries, such as Con O'Neill, who had resigned from the Foreign Service after Munich, were troubled by his decision to remain in Germany.[40] 'People of my own generation', Trott wrote to his mother, 'have become a little estranged.'[41] In separate conversations with *émigré* Göttingen Professor Gerhard Leibholz and New College Fellow Isaiah Berlin, he found full agreement with his own view that Great Britain should take a very firm stand towards Hitler.[42]

After Trott's return to Germany, Geoffrey Wilson came over for a visit, giving Trott an opportunity to let his English friend gain a first-hand impression concerning the extent of opposition sentiment in Germany. Trott's intent, of course, was that Wilson would report the results back to Sir Stafford Cripps. In a trip of several days to Kassel, Heidelberg, Freiburg im Breisgau and Berlin, Trott brought Wilson into contact with numerous people who were opposed to the Hitler regime and prepared to co-operate in an effort to remove it from power. Trott explained to Wilson that he was attempting to find a way to mobilise the wide-ranging internal disapproval of the Nazi government into a channel for effective action against it. The first message he wanted Wilson to take back was that opposition to Hitler did exist in Germany throughout a broad spectrum of society: among the military, in Socialist circles, in the Civil Service, and in both the Roman Catholic and Protestant religious communities. Many of the people in the various groups were, he explained, moving into positions from which they might be able to contribute to the downfall of the Hitler regime. The second point he wanted Wilson to make in England was the absolute necessity, in case war had broken out by the time Hitler was removed, of an Allied willingness to extend reasonable, nonpunitive terms to a successor German government. Geoffrey Wilson passed on his impressions to Sir Stafford Cripps, but the latter, although intensely interested, was in no position to influence official policy.[43]

In the spring and summer of 1939 Trott established closer relations with Helmuth Count von Moltke. But, before the Moltke group emerged as a cohesive part of the German resistance, Trott undertook an initiative aimed at influencing international politics in such a way that peace could be preserved long enough to enable the resistance to gain sufficient strength to eliminate Hitler. Fundamental to Hitler's success, Trott believed, was the dictator's identification of National Socialist foreign-policy objectives with German grievances against territorial adjustments and armament limitations imposed by the Treaty of Versailles. In Trott's view, if the Anglo-French coalition could be persuaded to make a good-faith gesture toward resolving some of these grievances, then Hitler would lose the basis for much of the popular support of his bellicose and intransigent attitude. Since it was unlikely that further concessions would indeed restrain Hitler, it would become quickly apparent to the Army leadership and the German people that Hitler's continued irresponsible and illegal conduct demanded and justified his forcible removal.[44]

Somewhat earlier in the year a distant cousin of Trott introduced him to a fervent National Socialist member of Hitler's inner circle, Walter Hewel, a liaison officer between the Foreign Office and the Reich Chancellery. Using this connection, Trott got Hewel's backing for an 'information-gathering' trip to England, using that as a cover for his actual mission. After discussing the strategy at length with his friend, Peter Bielenberg, Trott went to England in early June 1939. Ernst von Weizsäcker, State Secretary at the German Foreign Office, was apprised by Kessel of Trott's trip and allowed it to go forward. However, it would be incorrect to say that Trott was 'sent' by either Hewel or von Weizsäcker.

Once in England, Trott contacted his Balliol College friend, David Astor, to whom he confided the broad outlines of his plan, and received crucial assistance in gaining access to the decision-making level of the Government. David Astor took Trott to his parents' country estate, Cliveden, where both the Foreign Secretary, Lord Halifax, and Lord Lothian, the Ambassador Designate to Washington, were guests. Another visitor at Cliveden that June weekend has left an account of Trott's discussion over the dinner-table with the Foreign Secretary:

> I heard a discussion about international politics between a British cabinet minister and a young German called von Trott. Von Trott, as passionate an anti-Nazi as he was a patriot, spoke with a perfect mastery of English, of the aspirations of the German nation as a whole. While allowing for the mistrust engendered in the British mind by the activities of the Nazi leaders – a mistrust which he fully shared – he seemed to be trying to impress upon the Minister the necessity of an immediate adjustment of the *status quo*. He argued that some gesture of good will, not verbal, but actual, should be made toward Germany, not only to satisfy her just desire for a revision of the Versailles Treaty, but also – and this might be decisive – to remove some of the planks from Hitler's political platform and thus pave the way to power for those who had the interests of the world, as well as Germany, at heart.[45]

In the conversation at Cliveden, Trott attempted to create a climate in which the British would be prepared to act favourably on a possible proposal from the German government for restoration of the independence of Czechoslovakia, excluding the Sudetenland, in exchange for the cession of Danzig to the Reich and the establishment of a motor corridor linking isolated East Prussia to Pomerania.[46] Following the Cliveden weekend, Lord Astor set up a meeting for Trott in London with the Prime Minister. Neville Chamberlain was favourably disposed toward Trott, and was said to have remarked later that he was precisely the type of person one would like to see as a mediator, because he had the capacity to perceive both sides of the issue.[47]

After the meetings with Halifax, Lothian and Chamberlain Trott returned to Berlin, and, in collaboration with Peter Bielenberg, composed a report on the trip designed to stimulate a German initiative on an adjustment of the status quo in the East.[48] The report, which passed through the hands of Hewel and Ribbentropp, was placed before Hitler; but Trott was never summoned for a meeting on the subject with either Hitler of Ribbentropp, and the report alone did not prompt high-level consideration in Berlin of such an adjustment.[49] The one tangible result of the early June 1939 trip to England was a speech by Halifax at Chatham House on 29 June, in which he expressed sympathetic understanding for the situation of patriotic Germans who deplored the excesses of the National Socialist regime, yet felt that Germany's legitimate aspirations should be fulfilled.[50] In reality, Hitler was in no mood to entertain any compromise put forward by Great Britain as far as Eastern Europe was concerned. All he wanted from the British was a free hand in the East. And the prospect of an agreement with Stalin, a change well-known among informed circles in Berlin,[51] gave him the confidence to take a hard line at that moment.

Later in June 1939 Trott returned once more to England, and met a number of Oxford acquaintances. Among the dons he found 'infinite suspicion' about just what he was trying to do.[52] Most of them felt that anyone who was not persecuted by the Nazis must have something wrong with him, and since Trott would not take the only public stand that was in their view valid – emigration – they judged him to be 'morally ambiguous'.[53] Feeling desperate in the face of this rejection by many of those he had counted as friends, Trott threw caution to the winds and confided to Maurice Bowra, Warden of Wadham College, that he was there as a representative of the opposition in Germany and that he was able to make the trip because of a connection to the German Foreign Office. Bowra was incensed, and, deciding Trott was 'playing a double game', ordered him out of the house.[54]

Early in July David Astor visited Berlin at Trott's behest, and, upon returning to London, sent a report to Halifax advocating maintenance of the dialogue between Britain and Germany at all costs while Hitler's opponents inside Germany worked to bring about his downfall.[55] In mid-July Trott returned once more, his last visit to England, to put forward the same view, but with no discernible result. As the European continent edged its way ever closer to war that summer Trott believed he could not leave Berlin again; but he arranged for Peter Bielenberg and another friend called Curt Bley to travel to England in mid-August in a last desperate effort to stimulate the British government to give Hitler a clear signal that he was mistaken about the lack of British resolve to fight if he moved on Poland.[56] But with the signing of the Nazi-Soviet Non-aggression Pact a few days later, the attempt to preserve peace failed, and the German opponents of Hitler were faced with an even more difficult task after 1 September 1939.

Trott's efforts to prevent war in the summer of 1939 have been judged far-fetched and out of touch with reality, because his proposal in early June was based on further 'appeasement' of Hitler. It is argued that had Trott not been so far removed from the change in international politics in Europe after Munich, he would not have advocated an appeasement policy during his discussions in England. The problem with that argument, however, is that it is badly flawed, avoiding the clear distinction between Chamberlain's appeasement policy as practised before October 1938 and the policy Trott advocated in the summer of 1939. The Chamberlain government's appeasement policy proposed concessions to Hitler for the purpose of reaching a settlement and thus avoiding war. Trott also proposed concessions with the aim of avoiding war; however, he and his fellow conspirators were not trying to reach a settlement with Hitler, but instead to overthrow him.

Wartime Contacts

One of the American recipients of Trott's paper proposing Anglo-German co-operation in the Far East had been Edward C. Carter of the Institute of Pacific Relations. Carter had been sufficiently impressed by the paper's argument that he suggested to Lord Lothian shortly after Trott's return from East Asia that the Rhodes Trust consider providing financial support to allow the Institute to bring Trott to New York for six months to serve as a member of the organisation's International Secretariat.[57] During the spring Carter had confirmed the invitation, and also invited Trott to participate in an international conference sponsored by the Institute to deal with problems of the Pacific Ocean area.[58] Trott had proposed to Hewel that he be allowed to leave Germany for this purpose, and the latter had agreed, even arranging that the Foreign Office would provided a stipend to Trott for the passage and support during the time abroad.[59]

With the outbreak of war, it seemed as though the trip would have to be cancelled, but Carter urged both British and German authorities nevertheless to allow Trott to make the trip.[60] Trott's principal objective was to gain the support of the American government for the German opponents of the Hitler regime; but that part of his mission was doomed to failure before he ever left Germany. When Trott had confided in June to Maurice Bowra his true role as a representative of the German opponents of Hitler, he had also told him of his plans to go to America in the autumn. Bowra decided to do whatever he could to block Trott's attempts to influence the American government, and this took the form of a letter to Felix Frankfurter of the United States Supreme Court, warning against favourable consideration of Trott's proposals by the President.[61] Despite Trott's initial success in dealing with American officials, notably Assistant Secretary of State George S. Messersmith, with whom former Reich Chancellor Heinrich Brüning interceded directly on Trott's behalf, Frankfurter was able to cast enough doubt on Trott's intentions to prevent him from seeing Roosevelt or retaining the full confidence of Messersmith and others.[62] However, another aspect of Trott's visit to America that was eminently successful was his contact with British officials.

By the time Trott came to America in the autumn of 1939 Lothian was Ambassador and Wheeler-Bennett one of his advisers. Lothian had a secret meeting with Trott in Washington, and Wheeler-Bennett kept in close touch with him throughout his visit to the United States. The result of Wheeler-Bennett's collaboration with Trott was a strong appeal to the Foreign Office by this influential British official, calling on Whitehall to recognise the opponents of Hitler within Germany as allies and to co-operate in their struggle to rid Germany of National Socialism.[63] Both Halifax and Chamberlain saw Wheeler-Bennett's appeal, but nothing came of it.

Upon Trott's return to Germany in the spring of 1940 via Tokyo, Peking and Moscow, he entered the Foreign Office as chief of a section in the Political Intelligence Department (*Informationsabteilung*) dealing with both American and East Asian affairs. This official position gave him the opportunity to work against the

Hitler regime from within the government. It also allowed him to travel outside Germany, and during 1940 and 1941 he journeyed five times to Switzerland on behalf of the resistance. Staying with his friend Gottfried von Nostitz, German Consul in Geneva, he used the good offices of another old friend, Dr W. A. Visser't Hooft of the World Council of Churches, to facilitate the contacts he wanted to make abroad, particularly with people in Great Britain. In due course he was able to get into direct contact with the historian, Dr Elizabeth Wiskemann, who was an attaché with the British Legation in Berne.[64]

Trott had already formed a close tie to Helmuth von Moltke before his trip to America in 1939, and this was strengthened after his return in 1940. By the end of that year he was identified with the secret socio-constitutional planning group known posthumously as the Kreisau Circle. In the spring of 1942 Trott prepared a memorandum, in English, representing the views of the Moltke group, and sent it via Visser't Hooft to Sir Stafford Cripps, by then a member of Churchill's War Cabinet. The memorandum outlined the structure and aims of Hitler's German opponents, and called on the British to offer some measure of encouragement to their efforts so that they could widen and strengthen the base of support for resistance to Hitler within Germany. Despite Cripps's positive reaction, Whitehall was not only unprepared to give any encouragement, but did not even answer Trott or the group he represented. Instead, when Cripps suggested that Miss Wiskemann be told to 'cool off' Adam von Trott on the grounds that he was too valuable, one Foreign Office official disagreed energetically, since Trott's 'value to us as a "martyr" is likely to exceed his value to us in post-war Germany'.[65] Yet another official, one who had been a friend of his at Oxford and had visited him in Germany, was willing to recognise the significance of Trott's group only in terms of how it might be 'misdirected' by the British Foreign Office 'in ways useful to H. M. G.'.[66] When Trott made a return trip to Geneva in June 1942 Visser't Hooft told him of the negative character of the British reaction to the appeal from the German resistance, and that news became a major discouragement to the conspirators.[67]

During the remainder of 1942 and into 1943 Trott turned a major focus of his activity towards opening contacts with ecumenical church and governmental circles in Sweden and with the Dutch resistance in Amsterdam. In each case the aim was similar: to stimulate the respective contact groups into helping to convince Britain of the need to give some indication of recognition to a movement in Germany that wanted to bring an end to the Hitler regime.

In the autumn of 1943 Lieutenant-Colonel Claus Schenk Count von Stauffenberg, having recovered adequately from severe wounds received in North Africa, was assigned as Chief of Staff to General of the Infantry Friedrich Olbricht, Head of the General Army Office of the Army High Command (OKH). As soon as Stauffenberg was appointed to that post, Trott began to visit him periodically in the Bendlerstraße, and their relationship became close in the months that followed.[68] Late October and early November 1943 found Trott once again in Stockholm, but this time he had direct contact with British officials at the Legation there. His discussions were aimed at getting behind the unconditional surrender formula to find out something about what the Allies planned for a defeated Germany, particularly in the area of collaboration between Britain and the Soviets.[69] Despite a basic sympathy that the Special Operations Executive (SOE) representatives had for Trott and the cause he represented, the officials involved were not able to make any real decisions or to function as a political, as opposed to an intelligence, contact.

In March 1944 Trott went once again to Stockholm, and communicated with the same British officials through a Swedish intermediary. He suggested that if Allied peace terms, known to be then under discussion, should be published soon, it would aid in an attempt to get rid of Hitler by giving the German people a concrete alternative, as opposed to the vagueness of the unconditional surrender formula. He offered to return to Stockholm at any point when one of the Allied Legations was prepared to establish political contact.[70]

At the beginning of June 1944 Stauffenberg's promotion to full colonel and assignment as Chief of Staff to *Generaloberst* Erich Fromm, Commander of the Home Army, gave the conspirators a new opportunity, since Stauffenberg would have periodic access to Hitler. With renewed optimism, plans for an attempt to bring a quick end to the National Socialist regime were readied for action. At the end of the month Trott made his final visit to Sweden, disregarding the danger he faced as the result of an indiscretion by the BBC German Service in referring to a 'German Rhodes Scholar' putting out 'peace-feelers' in Stockholm.[71] This time he met with a different British official, purportedly a 'political contact', but in effect a member of SOE's rival organisation, the Secret Intelligence Service (MI6). The MI6 agent asked Trott to prepare a memorandum giving his assessment of the situation, including the names of the individuals involved in the resistance. Trott was reluctant to name individuals in view of the lack of good faith shown by the British side, but he did prepare a paper which gave a picture of the opposition in general terms that ended with a plea for a political contact as the only way to achieve co-operation toward ending the National Socialist regime and establishing a new government in Germany.[72] No response ever came from the British side.

At the beginning of July Trott made one last attempt to open a line of communication to London, by travelling to the Netherlands and informing the Dutch resistance of plans for a forthcoming coup in Germany. His objectives was to have the Dutch inform London by radio as soon as the action was under way, thereby giving an outside view of the honourable intentions of the German resistance. When the Dutch asked Trott about the prospect of success for the projected coup, he answered that it was no more than 25 per cent.[73] That trip ended five years of 'resistance diplomacy' centred on the relationship the resisters hoped to establish with Britain.

Following the unsuccessful coup on 20 July, Trott was arrested on the 25th, largely owing to the suspicion thrown on him as a result of his close association with Stauffenberg.[74] The SS informed the German Foreign Office on 11 August of his forthcoming death sentence,[75] Trott's trial took place on 15 August, and, after eleven further days of interrogations, he was executed on 26 August 1944. In September his death sentence was announced in *The Times*, which is how many of Trott's English friends learned of his fate. Charles Collins, an official in the Foreign Office who had known Trott well at Oxford, was among those who got the news and experienced a great sense of personal loss: 'It was', he said, 'as though a light had gone out in our hopes for the future.'[76] Yet, on another level, the opposite was true. By taking action against the Hitler regime, despite the lack of any reasonable hope of political success, Trott and his fellow conspirators demonstrated that there were Germans prepared to challenge evil even at the cost of their own lives. This clear signal that the moral decision of conscience was not dead, in a state that had lost moral direction, was itself a beacon of hope for the future.

NOTES

1. Cf. H. Kraus, *The Crisis of German Democracy: A Study of the Spirit of the Constitution of Weimar*, Princeton, 1932.
2. Louisa Barrett to Diana Hopkinson, 15 February 1946, in the Trott Collection (hereafter TC), Berlin, binder 2.
3. Adam von Trott to his mother, 28 July 1927, TC.
4. Adam von Trott, 'Impressions of a German Student in England', (typed MS, p. 1), TC. Cf. his much shorter article of the same title in *The World's Youth: A Magazine for Leaders of Youth*, vol. 5, no. 9, November 1929.
5. Trott to his father, Oxford, 5 March 1929, TC.
6. Trott to his mother (postcard), Berlin, postmarked 11 November 1929, TC; letters to his mother, Berlin, undated [Wednesday, mid-October 1929] and Berlin [20 February 1930], TC.
7. Interviews by the author with Albrecht von Kessel, Bonn–Bad Godesberg, 10 June 1970, and Dr Gottfried von Nostitz, Gauting, Bavaria, 3 April 1971.
8. Application by Trott for the Rhodes Scholarship, 23 November 1930, Rhodes House.
9. Trott to Shiela Grant Duff, [Berlin], 2 April 1933. The Trott–Grant Duff correspondence is now in published form thanks to Klemens von Klemperer (ed.), *A Noble Combat: The Letters of Shiela Grant Duff and Adam von Trott zu Solz, 1932–1938*, Oxford, 1988. Quotation from a letter by Charles E. Collins to David Astor, Cheltenham, 30 December 1968, Papers of Hon. David Astor, London.
10. Trott to the Editor, *Manchester Guardian*, 21 February 1934; Paul Gore-Booth, Memorandum to the Foreign Office, 25 September 1944, C13339, FO 371/39066, Public Record Office, London (hereafter PRO).
11. Interview by the author with J. P. Mayer, Stoke Poges, Buckinghamshire, 1 May 1971. Also, Trott to his father, Hanau, 3 May 1934, and to his mother, Hanau, 10 May 1934, TC.
12. D. Hopkinson, *The Incense Tree*, London, 1968, pp. 137 f.; Trott to his father, Berlin, 2 March 1935, TC.
13. Diana Hopkinson, typewritten memoir of Trott's life, 1931–40, pp. 60 f. Copy in Julie Braun-Vogelstein Collection, Leo Baeck Institute, New York City; Trott to his father, Berlin, 9 May 1935, TC; to his mother, Oxford, 17 May 1935 and undated [Kassel, 28 August 1935], TC; Isobel Henderson to Trott, Oxford, 27 April 1935, TC; R. G. Collingwood to Trott, Oxford, 23 May 1935, TC; interviews by the author with David Astor and Charles E. Collins.
14. S. Grant Duff, *The Parting of Ways: A Personal Account of the Thirties*, London, 1982, p. 96. Despite Wheeler-Bennett's claim not to have been in Germany in 1935 (cf. his autobiography, *Knaves, Fools and Heroes*, NY, 1974, p. 92), his own memorandum to the Foreign Office in 1943 confirms Miss Grant Duff's account, despite placing the date in

1933: 'Adam von Trott and Peace Feelers', 21 April 1943, C5218, FO 371/3449, PRO. Contemporary confirmation is provided in Trott's own letter to his father, Hamburg, 18 October 1935, TC.

15. Interview by the author with Christabel Bielenberg, Hangelar bei Bonn, 14 October 1969. Also see her memoir, *The Past is Myself*, London, 1969 [1968], pp. 40 f.

16. Hopkinson MS, p. 73; Countess Russell (Patricia Spence) to Clarita von Trott zu Solz, Cambridge, 28 November 1945, TC; Isobel Henderson to Trott, Oxford, 6 February 1936, TC; Shiela Grant Duff to Trott, Chelsea, 29 February 1936, originals in the possession of Shiela Sokolov Grant. The relevant portion of this letter is omitted from the published letters edited by Klemperer.

17. Hopkinson MS, p. 73

18. Ibid., p. 79

19. Trott to his father, Berlin, 23 October 1936, TC.

20. Hopkinson MS, p. 80.

21. Lord Lothian to [Dr C. K.] Allen, London, 16 November 1936, Rhodes House; Trott to Lothian, 25 November 1936, TC; Dr C. K. Allen to the Secretary of the Rhodes Trust [Lothian], Oxford, 27 November 1936, Rhodes House; Trott to his mother, London, 27 November [1936], and to his father, Berlin, 1 December 1936, TC.

22. Edward C. Carter to Allen Dulles, [New York], 11 October 1946, copy in author's files; Trott to Carter, Imshausen, 27 December 1936, TC.

23. Trott to his mother, London, 5 March 1937, TC; Trott to Shiela Grant Duff [at sea, early March 1937], in Klemperer, *A Noble Combat*, pp. 215–18; A. L. Rowse, *All Souls and Appeasement*, London, 1961, p. 95.

24. Trott, 'Amerikanische Eindrücke' (typewritten essay), pp. 13 f., TC; Trott to Shiela Grant Duff, *en route* to California [about 10] May 1937, in Klemperer, *A Noble Combat*, pp. 229 ff. Cf. also D. Lewis, *The Good Fight: Political Memoirs 1909–1958*, Toronto, 1981, pp. 64 f. Lewis says they never met again after Trott went down from Oxford, but Trott's contemporary letter to Miss Grant Duff contradicts Lewis's recollection of over thirty years later.

25. Hopkinson MS, pp. 91 f.

26. Trott to Shiela Grant Duff, [Peking], 21 October 1937, in Klemperer, *A Noble Combat*, pp. 285 ff.

27. John Brett Robey to the author, Rotherfield, Sussex, 30 May 1977; Robey to the British Embassy in Washington, Cincinnati, 12 September 1944, C13339. FO 371/19066, PRO; P. H. Gore-Booth to the British Foreign Office, Washington, 25 September 1944 (same PRO reference); Lord Gore-Booth to the author, 4 January and 21 March 1977; interview notes of Christabel Bielenberg with W. G. Adams, Oxford [1962].

28. Trott to his father, Peking, 15 January 1938. A copy of the printed article is in TC, but the name of the journal is unknown. It appeared in issue 58, April 1938, vol. 6, pp. 34–6.

29. Trott to his mother, Peking, 7 July 1938, TC. Other recipients included Finance Minister Schwerin von Krosigk, Hans von Dohnanyi, Wilfrid Israel, Peter Bielenberg, Professor Herbert Kraus, Gottfried von Nostitz, Hans Muhle, and Herbert Goering.
30. Both versions are found in TC.
31. Lord Lothian to Lord Halifax, London, 2 August 1938, F8608, FO 371/22109, PRO.
32. File F8608, as above, FO 371/22109, PRO.
33. Ibid., note dated 17 August 1938.
34. Ibid., note dated 19 September 1938.
35. See H. Nicolson, *Diaries and Letters 1930–1939*, London, 1966, p. 302.
36. Hopkinson MS, pp. 106 ff., quoting a letter from the end of November 1938.
37. Trott to Shiela Grant Duff, Hong Kong, 28 October 1938, in Klemperer, *A Noble Combat*, p. 335.
38. Interview with Christabel Bielenberg, 14 October 1969.
39. Trott wrote in his notebook as follows: 'Die Selbstbehauptung des Staates auf den Wege der Rechtsentwicklung nicht dem des Krieges ist heute zu erstreben. Krieg als gerechte Entscheidung des Weltgerichts über die historische Daseinsberechtigung eines Volkes ist heute eine Absurdität.'
40. Con O'Neill to Christabel Bielenberg, Helsinki, 10 April 1962 (Christabel Bielenberg Materials).
41. Trott to his mother, London, 15 February 1939, TC.
42. Interview by the author with Constitutional Court Justice Gerhard Leibholz, Karlsruhe, 5 October 1970; interview by the author with Sir Isaiah Berlin, Oxford, 15 May 1971.
43. Geoffrey Wilson to Curt Bley, Washington, DC, 19 December 1960, TC; interview by the author with Sir Geoffrey Wilson, London, 28 April 1971. Cf. also M. Dodd, *Through Embassy Eyes*, NY, 1939, p. 278: 'As a matter of fact there is still a good deal of organised opposition among the people of Germany.'
44. Interview by the author with Peter Bielenberg, County Carlow, 22 May 1971.
45. W. Douglas-Home, *Half-Term Report*, London, 1954, p. 113; interview by the author with the Hon. William Douglas-Home, London, 17 May 1971.
46. *Documents on German Foreign Policy 1918–1945* (hereafter DGFP), Series D (1937–1945), vol. 6, *The Last Months of Peace, March–August 1939*, London, 1956, pp. 674 ff. A shorter account of the report, stamped 'hat dem Führer vorgelegen', is in Handakten Hewel 6, Deutschland, T-Z, 1938–42, Politisches Archiv des Auswärtigen Amtes, Bonn (hereafter PA).
47. Interview with Sir Isaiah Berlin.
48. Interview with Peter Bielenberg.
49. See DGFP, n. 46, above.
50. Lord Halifax, speech at Chatman House, 29 June 1939, extract in

Documents on International Affairs, 1939–1946, issued under the auspices of the Royal Institute of International Affairs, vol. 1: March to September 1939, London, 1951, pp. 297–304.

51. Interview by the author with Margret Boveri, Berlin, 31 October 1969.
52. Hopkinson MS, p. 115, quoting from a letter in mid-June 1939.
53. Interview by the author with Stuart Hampshire, Oxford, 7 May 1971.
54. Interview by the author with Sir Maurice Bowra, Oxford, 6 May 1971; M. Bowra, *Memories 1898–1939*, London, 1966.
55. David Astor to Lord Halifax, London, 9 July 1939, with attached memorandum, in file 4538, FO 800/316, PRO. Cf. also FO 371/22974, file 4453.
56. Interview by the author with Peter Bielenberg; David Astor and Peter Bielenberg, memorandum, 24 August 1939 and letter (c.c.), David Astor to [Lord Halifax], 19 August 1939, in the Astor Papers, London; Curt Bley to David Astor, Varel, 19 October 1945, Astor Papers.
57. Edward C. Carter to Trott, New York, 22 March 1939, TC.
58. Ibid.
59. Walter Hewel to Trott, Salzburg, 18 August 1939, Handakten Hewel 6, Deutschland, T-Z, 1938–42, PA.
60. See Carter's letter to Philip C. Jessup, Lee, Mass., 15 September 1939, Exhibit 1118 of Senate Internal Security Subcommittee Hearings on the Institute of Pacific Relations, Part 14, Washington, DC, 1952, p. 5195.
61. Bowra interview, (see n. 54, above).
62. Memorandum, George S. Messersmith, Assistant Secretary of State, to the Secretary and the Undersecretary, 20 November 1939, printed in H. Rothfels, 'Dokumentation: Adam von Trott und das State Department', *Vierteljahrshefte für Zeitgeschichte*, vol. 8, 1959, p. 329.
63. John W. Wheeler-Bennett to Sir Robert Vansittart, New York, 27 December 1939, with attached memorandum dated 28 December 1939, file 4426, FO 371/24363, PRO. Both Halifax and Chamberlain saw this communication. H. Rothfels published the memorandum (based on a carbon copy Trott had left in New York with Julie Braun-Vogelstein) in the *Vierteljahrshefte für Zeitgeschichte*, vol. 12, 1964, pp. 316–17.
64. Interview by the author with Elizabeth Wiskemann, London, 14 May 1971; see also her *The Europe I Saw*, London, 1968, p. 168.
65. This remarkable comment was penned on 12 June 1942 by Foreign Office German expert G. W. Harrison, file C5428/48/18, FO 371/30912, PRO.
66. The author of this 'appreciation' is not identified, but both internal and external evidence make it certain that Trott's one-time friend R. H. S. Crossman wielded the poison pen.
67. W. A. Visser't Hooft, *Memoirs*, London-Philadelphia, 1973, pp. 155–8. See also H. Rothfels, 'Memorandum von Schönfeld und Trott', *Vierteljahrshefte für Zeitgeschichte*, vol. 5, 1957, pp. 388–97.

68. Information from Delia Ziegler, Secretary to *General der Infanterie* Friedrich Olbricht, Chief of the General Army Office in the *Oberkommando des Heeres* (OKH), contained in notes of an interview by Sophie-Mathilde von Buch, Bonn, July 1963. Author's collection.
69. Political Memorandum, No. 143 by R. P. H. [Roger P. Hinks], British Legation, Stockholm, 5 November 1943, C13371, FO 371/34462, PRO.
70. Political Memorandum, No. 41, Stockholm Legation, 23 March 1944, FO 371/39059, PRO.
71. Freiburg historian Gerhard Ritter heard the broadcast, as recounted in his address before the Royal Institute of International Affairs: 'The German Opposition to Hitler', *The Contemporary Review*, vol. 177, January–June 1950, p. 341. Interviews with Alste Horn and Alexander Werth confirm the episode, based on accounts they saw independently of each other in Swedish newspapers.
72. The memorandum was published by H. Lindgren, 'Adam von Trotts Reisen nach Schweden 1942–1944', *Vierteljahrshefte für Zeitgeschichte*, vol. 18, 1970, pp. 274–91.
73. Interviews by the author with J. H. van Roijen, Wassenaar, Netherlands, 4 March 1971; and with G. J. Scholten, Amersterdam, 5 March 1971.
74. Alexander Werth, memorandum concerning Adam von Trott, November 1957, TC.
75. [Gustav Adolf] Sonnenhol, memorandum to 'Herrn Gruppenleiter Inland II', Berlin, 11 August 1944, Inland IIg, 59, PA.
76. Charles E. Collins, Notes on Adam von Trott, 19 November 1946, TC. Also published by H. Rothfels in *Vierteljahrshefte für Zeitgeschichte*, vol. 12, 1964, pp. 310–13.

15

Waiting for Action:
The Debate on the
'Other Germany' in Great Britain
and the Reaction of
the Foreign Office to German
'Peace-Feelers', 1942

Rainer A. Blasius

The attempts of German opposition circles to establish contact with Whitehall reached a climax in May–June 1942. This very period, with hindsight, appears to have been unsuitable for commencing a fruitful dialogue. At the beginning of May, the War Cabinet confirmed Prime Minister Churchill's 'policy of absolute silence', which he had introduced on 20 January 1941.[1] Also, later in May, the Government agreed to Article II of the British-Soviet Treaty, which stated: 'The High Contracting Parties undertake not to enter into any negotiations with the Hitlerite Government or any other Government in Germany that does not clearly renounce all aggressive intentions, and not to negotiate or conclude except by mutual consent any armistice or peace treaty with Germany or any other State associated with her in acts of aggression in Europe.'[2]

Article II did not say exactly how the 'contracting parties' were to respond to some kind of approach by German anti-Hitlerites. Neither did the treaty prohibit all contact with opposition circles within Germany, as they did not yet constitute a government in their own right nor could they be regarded as such. However, the British-Soviet Treaty deprived the opposition to Hitler of any chance to divide the Grand Alliance once Hitler's regime had been overthrown. Since the 'peace-feelers' were most probably aiming either to reach some arrangement with London and Washington or to conclude a separate peace with Moscow, but not a combination of both, opposition circles could not hope for a more favourable climate in future negotiations. This paper will show how the Foreign Office reacted to the 'peace-feelers' in the spring of 1942, and the public attitudes which were adopted towards them. Consideration will be paid especially to the deliberations on political warfare at that time, because it is possible that British propaganda towards Germany could have had either an encouraging or a retarding effect on the actions of the German opposition to Hitler.

First, however, it is useful to look at the public debate on the image of Germany in Britain. This debate was triggered by Stalin, who had pointed out in his Order of the Day of 23 February 1942: ' . . . it would be ludicrous to identify Hitler's clique with the German people, with the German state. The experience of history indicates that Hitlers come and go, but the German people and the German state remain.'[3] This line of propaganda, which drew a distinct line between the German people and the National Socialists, was championed in London by politicians who believed in the existence of the 'Other Germany', hoped for the fall of Hitler, and pleaded for eventual reconciliation with Germany.

In the House of Commons on 24 February 1942, just after a Cabinet reshuffle, John Rhys Davies (Labour) harshly criticised Churchill's Cabinet's policy, which he considered 'exactly the same as that of the previous one, that is, death or victory, fight on to the last man, the last shilling and the last drop of blood'. Davies advocated some appeal to 'moderate' Germans and Italians, with whom he hoped to go beyond the principles enunciated in the Atlantic Charter.[4] He was supported by Richard Stokes (Labour), who spoke in favour of a 'more constructive' declaration towards the Germans when he asked '. . .what German would attempt to overthrow the existing regime in Germany in order to be downtrodden and disarmed by the invading Powers?' Of Stalin's Order of the Day he said: 'He has treated the situation in a realistic way and has completely disproved the advice put about by what I call the Vansittart gang.'[5] In the *Evening Standard*, journalist Frank Owen referred to Stalin's order while discussing the arguments of Lord Vansittart: 'Vansittart indicts the whole German race. . . . He belongs to those who see not men, good or evil or merely ignorant, confused or frightened, but races good and evil. Yellow races.

Black races. German races. In this matter Vansittart is a kind of
Nazi, inside out.' With reference to Vansittart's comparison between Germans and beasts, Owen wrote:

> Is the wolf to be kept alive forever in Europe, chained – with always
> the chance that he will slip the chain? That is the Vansittart policy – for
> not even Vansittart proposes to kill the wolf. There is no public man
> in Britain who will get up and propose either to kill all the Germans
> alive or to sterilize the race. What is the alternative? Teach the wolf.
> Train him. Make him into a house-dog. The house-dog was once a
> wolf.[6]

Attacks of this sort in public were a reaction to the six lectures
Vansittart had given on the BBC Overseas Programme which were
broadcast between 24 November and 5–6 December 1940. In these,
he had mused about 'the character of the German people'. He
argued that this aggressive nature had essentially remained unchanged, thus furthering the notion of collective guilt. The British
press quoted extensively from these talks. In January 1941, the
same month that Churchill rid himself of the Chief Diplomatic
Adviser to His Majesty's Government by elevating Vansittart to
the House of the Lords, the lectures appeared as a brochure entitled
Black Record. Germans Past and Present, which instantly became a
best-seller. In February 1942, by the time Victor Gollancz, the
prominent publisher of Jewish descent and member of the Labour
Party, published his notable reply, *Black Record* had sold half a
million copies.

In the preface to his book, *Shall our Children Live or Die? A Reply
to Lord Vansittart on the German Problem*, Gollancz characterised the
ideas of the former diplomat as 'Vansittartism' – that is, a kind of
thought which would play into the hands of Nazi Propaganda
Minister, Joseph Goebbels, and therefore weaken 'the growing
movement of German revolt'. With disquietude he recorded that
Vansittart had received applause from both the 'Right' and the
'Left', and noted that even 'one very high official of the Labour
Party is a perfervid adherent of the Vansittart school'. Towards the
notion of collective guilt he felt outspoken distaste:

> It is vulgar to blame the German people – the toy maker of Nurem-
> berg or the steel worker of the Ruhr – for something the roots of
> which lie deep in history. It is doubly vulgar, when the blame comes
> from those whose national history has been far more fortunate; and
> trebly so, when it comes from people who would sell their souls to the
> devil precisely to prevent a revolution of any kind whatsoever.

Gollancz also referred to Stalin as a witness against Vansittart, and wrote:

> Here is, explicitly, the antithesis to Vansittart's analysis, and, by implication, the antithesis to his cure. The revolution must and will start with the revolt of the German army, which is led by the officer corps, but is now simply the part of the German people that is bearing arms. When Hitler is beaten or can no longer conceal the certainty of defeat, the German people will turn its arms against the officers, the Gestapo and the regime, and the revolution will be on. Here – in the people in arms – will be the beginning of a revolutionary government.

Evaluating the result of a possible Russian breakthrough in the East, followed by a sweep of the Red Army across Poland and Germany into France, ending with the Soviet occupation of the continent of Europe, Gollancz wrote: 'If it happens, the problem we have been discussing disappears and another one takes its place. This issue would be, not Vansittartism, but "Stalinisation".' The most promising propaganda approach, he thought, lay in telling the Germans that 'they have everything to gain, and nothing to fear, from the overthrow of Hitler's tyranny, and that it is only by their own act that they can win freedom for themselves and the world'. An attitude of menace directed especially towards the war criminals, he felt, would be unlikely to destabilise Germany. Perhaps it would achieve the opposite effect, particularly since Goebbels's recent line of propaganda about his own military front had switched to saying: 'You have made yourself so permanently detested by your crimes that, if you lose this war, you will be annihilated – so do everything, however foul, to prevent defeat.'[7]

Vansittart began to snap back at his critics in early March 1942, when he argued in favour of a drastic policy towards post-war Germany. On 2 March he told Oxford students that he would be the last to deny the existence of some 'good' Germans: 'The percentage [however] is not worth arguing about. The point is that when you want them, they are not there. The whole of their past leads you to distrust them. . . . There will be no revolution in Germany.'[8] In his maiden speech in the House of Lords on 18 March, during a debate on the employment of emigrants in the BBC and other institutions dealing with political warfare, he took a negative stand. He rejected the 'anti-Nazi' attitude of emigrants as an unreliable criterion. Moreover, the theory of the 'two Germanys' – the 'good' and the 'bad' – was considered false. Vansittart called the book by Gollancz 'an example of the poison at work. It is easy to see where that bookmaker gets his stuff. That kind of anti-Nazism is not only worthless but flat-catching.'[9] Referring to his personal pre-war experience with anti-Hitlerites,[10] he told his audience:

> Perhaps I am peculiarly entitled to be sceptical in regard to anti-Nazism because, during all the years I was at the Foreign Office before the war, perfectly good Germans and perfectly genuine anti-Nazis continually came to me and said 'why cannot you get your Government to stand up to Hitler? Make them push him to the verge of war, or even into war. Then of course he will have to arm us, and we will finish him off in no time.' And some of them went so far – and very often went so far – as to suggest that the good Germans would do the job. I think any comment on these fictions is superfluous, except to say that the tune of the good Germans is still played over for practice, and I am not at all sure that we have yet heard the last of it.[11]

In Blackpool on 5 May 1942, Home Secretary Herbert Morrison spoke in favour of equal economic opportunities for all nations after the war. Since he had explicitly included the Germans, Vansittart asked for a debate in the House of Lords on the policy to be adopted *vis-à-vis* Germany after the war. On 19 May, when British–Soviet negotiations were in their final stage, he rose to present his interpretation of German history since 1871. Vansittart emphasised the 'martial character' of the Germans, and turned vehemently against 'new appeasers', like Morrison, who asked for justice for Germany. 'We are not fighting this war to give Germany yet another chance.' In particular, he rejected Morrison's suggestion to disarm 'the Fascists' only. In this case, Vansittart warned, Britain would be left 'with a nice portion of the German Army' on its hands.[12]

It is interesting to note that in his public statements, Vansittart made no really practical suggestions on how to deal with Germany. However, in general terms he talked of complete disarmament, and the need to re-educate the Germans over a period of a hundred years. He rather tried to promote an image of Germany which made no distinction between the people and its leadership; it fostered distrust against the regime and its opposition alike. Among his fellow peers, he was supported by the Marquess of Donegall, who on 10 May 1942 had written in a newspaper article on Morrison's speech: 'The implication is that he imagines that Germany's 90,000,000 population consists of about 10,000 nasty Nazis and 89,990,000 nice, kind German people only waiting for Colonel Briton to say the word "Go" over the BBC, to rise up, tear asunder their shackles and overthrow the Nazi oppressor.'

Donegall emphatically agreed with Vansittart's arguments in *Black Record*, and attacked the Home Secretary: 'Where the Home Secretary and I differ is this: He stands for Justice for the German People. I don't. I stand for German Justice for 90,000,000 German vermin.'[13] In the House of Lords, at least, the Marquess did not clarify his ideas on possible ways of destroying the 'German vermin', but reaffirmed: '. . . it was Germany that made Hitler'. About Morrison's arguments he said: 'Fortunately, also, the vast majority of people in this country do not agree with the Home Secretary.'[14]

Among those in the House of Lords who stood up against Vansittart and his followers were Lord Perth, Lord Rankeillour and Lord Wedgewood. Of these, the last-mentioned argued: 'We are fighting the Fascists, the Nazis; we are fighting a school of thought. This is an international war. You have got both sides in this country, and you have got both sides in Germany. . . . This is the reproduction of the Thirty Years War – a war between two different religions, the religion of freedom and the religion of authority.'[15] In the Commons on 19 May 1942 John McGovern (Independent Labour) rose to attack not only Vansittart but also Churchill. He reproached the latter for not having distanced himself in public from the one-time diplomat. He arrived at the conclusion that for Hitler, 'every speech made by Lord Vansittart is equivalent, in my estimation, to two or three divisions of infantry. . . .'[16]

On 3 January 1942 R. H. S. Crossman (whom Vansittart held responsible for the allegation that the *Wehrmacht* belonged to the 'good' part of Germany) submitted a memorandum on Political Warfare to the Foreign Office. Crossman headed the 'German Section' within the Political Warfare Executive (PWE) for which the Foreign Office and the Ministry of Information shared responsibility. The PWE essentially had two tasks. It analysed enemy propaganda, and also prepared British psychological warfare for both the 'black' and the 'white' service. The latter promoted official British views broadcast by the BBC. Crossman, in retrospect, once acknowledged that in these BBC broadcasts 'exaggeration, excitement, threats and extravagances in all forms were avoided'.[17] They painstakingly stuck to the 'strategy of the truth' right from the start of the war, and did so even in 1942, when the situation for Britain was bad. These broadcasts proposed to keep the German people informed about news and editorial opinion unavailable from their own media. Thus, the 'German Service' of the BBC aimed at counterbalancing the propaganda of Goebbels.[18]

The efficiency of psychological warfare depended above all on the military situation. Since Great Britain was on the defensive for the greater part of 1942, preconditions for the successful work of the PWE were bleak early in that year. In a 'Central Directive' of 8 October 1942 it was recognised that until that time the propaganda initiative had rested with Hitler and Goebbels, and that London accordingly was limited to reactive action.[19] Improvement eventually came in January 1943, when the end of the battle of Stalingrad brought about the turn of the tide for PWE. The aforementioned 'black' service of PWE, which operated through radio and leaflets, was inaccessible to the British public. In fact, it was kept highly secret, particularly the existence of Sefton Delmer's German-language transmitting stations.[20] Sometimes, indeed, the content of the leaflets was not in line with the official British view.

In February 1942 a career diplomat and expert on eastern European questions, R. H. Bruce Lockhart, was appointed Director General of the PWE. He was to succeed in achieving a firmer control by the Foreign Office over psychological warfare. He resisted attempts from politicians and high officials 'to make foreign policy by means of propaganda instead of being content to support policy by propaganda'.[21] Since propaganda was to support policy, its line towards Germany generally had to take into account the plans and intentions of the British government. As far as the 'white' service was concerned, which was accessible to Britons, too, propaganda had to fit in perfectly with official policy. Thus propaganda could not ignore obligations Great Britain had accepted or was to accept when concluding alliances against Hitler. This became clear in the reaction of the Foreign Office to Crossman's memorandum of 3 January. In this paper he recommended that they emphasise the responsibility of Hitler, the Gestapo and the Nazi party for the fate of the German people. Moreover, he wished to promote domestic tensions, following the damaging effect of the battle of Moscow in December 1941 on Hitler's reputation, by highlighting the existence of opposition to Hitler in Germany:

We should do everything possible to publicise Christian opposition in Germany and thereby to promote a violent attempt by the Gestapo to crush it. Note: It will not be necessary in open propaganda to draw any conclusions about relations between the Church opposition and the generals. Such conclusions will readily be drawn in Germany since the wish will be father to the thought. We must not compromise ourselves by actually suggesting that H.M.G. is ready for peace with the 'Christian generals', but we might be able to deceive them into drawing false conclusions on this point.

If Great Britain should decide to publish a 'Black List' of war

criminals, which the governments in exile had asked for and which
the USSR would possibly endorse, then care should be taken that
'any such statement narrowing down the number of the guilty
would provide that "escape clause" for the ordinary German without which our Political Warfare must be relatively ineffective.'[22]

G. W. Harrison of the Central Department in the Foreign Office
did not share Crossman's optimism about the domestic situation in
Germany. He pointed out some of the dilemmas for British propaganda in the coming months:

> . . . as I see it we have the choice either of intensifying the 'Hope'
> theme, i.e. emphasising the 'relatively pleasant existence which the
> Germans may expect once their present leaders have been over-
> thrown' (as Mr. Roberts put it last October) or of going all out on an
> 'Intimidation' theme and making it clear that the longer the Germans
> hold out the less chance there is of a reasonable future for the German
> people.

The Secretary of State for Foreign Affairs, Anthony Eden, agreed
with Harrison's second alternative as warmly as he approved of a
comment from R. M. Makins, Head of the Central Department,
suggesting that public statements should be restricted to the economic aspects of Germany's future; in view of the proposals which
Stalin had put to Eden in December 1941 on the dismemberment of
Germany, it would not be easy 'to provide a convincing picture of
any future for the Germans'. When Assistant Under-Secretary of
State William Strang urged caution concerning statements on peace
directed to the 'Christian generals', Eden noted: 'I agree. I don't
like this for Russian reasons.'[23]

Permanent Under-Secretary of State Sir Alexander Cadogan,
himself sceptical about encouraging German opposition circles,
wrote on 8 January 1942 on British propaganda policy:

> As between the 'Hope' and 'Intimidation' themes, I have always
> found that the former is more likely to be effective in producing
> discussion in Germany. A vast number of people in Germany (and
> very many at the top) remember 1918 and what followed, and I
> should imagine that the one thing that would keep them united would
> be determination to resist exposure to another and a worse Versailles.
> But there might be, as suggested by Mr. Harrison, a combination of
> the two. 'We are going to draw your claws, but we don't intend then
> to starve and beat you, so long as you rid yourselves of the bandits.
> But you'd better to be quick about it, or our intentions may change.'[24]

In spite of all the public debates and demands for a clarification of

Allied war aims and of attempts by German opposition circles to establish contact with the Foreign Office, this view was to remain the guideline for British declarations directed to Germany. As time passed, the temporary nature of the offer to the Germans, promising economic prosperity, gradually moved to the fore. London saw precisely this as the advantage of British propaganda policy *vis-à-vis* the Soviet approach, which made a distinction between the German people and the Nazis. Harrison was now completely in agreement with Eden's speech made at Coventry on 30 August 1941. On 2 March 1942 he called 'the military threat with the economic carrot' the basis of political warfare. 'On the other hand it is essential to avoid putting the German people in the position of being able "to have it both ways", i.e. in trying to induce them to overthrow their leaders we must place on them responsibility for doing so sooner rather than later. It seems to be the weakness of M. Stalin's order of the day that he does not do so.'[25]

Towards the end of April 1942 Crossman recommended a statement by the Secretary of State for Foreign Affairs saying that 'we wanted the decent elements in Germany to form a strong Germany after the war'. But Eden rejected it, remarking to E. Williams of the BBC: 'Not so long as I am Secretary of State for Foreign Affairs.' In a conversation with Bruce Lockhart later, Williams commented on Eden's attitude: 'This justifies everything Vansittart says.'[26] In a speech given at Edinburgh on 8 May, Eden publicly clarified his opinion, both about the responsibility of the German people and the tasks and trustworthiness of German opposition circles. He said:

> The longer the German people continues to support and to tolerate the régime which is leading them to destruction, the heavier grows their own direct responsibility for the damage that they are doing to the world. Therefore, if any section of the German people really wants to see a return to a German state which is based on respect for law and for the rights of the individual, they must understand that no-one will believe them until they have taken active steps to rid themselves of their present régime.[27]

In the weeks following Eden's speech, the German Anti-Hitlerites were to learn that Britain was unwilling to grant any concessions prior to Hitler's overthrow. Instead, British officials asked for visible activities indicating that the opposition circles meant business. Perhaps the most significant encounter between members of German opposition circles and representatives of the Western Allies during the war took place in the Swedish town of Sigtuna on

31 May 1942. At that time George K. A. Bell, the Bishop of Chichester, was touring the neutral Scandinavian kingdom in order to renew British–Swedish relations. His mission had been both initiated and organised by the British Ministry of Information. It had been publicly announced, and the British Press had made Bell's trip widely known. Independently of each other the German pastors Hans Schönfeld and Dietrich Bonhoeffer had decided to pay a visit to Stockholm in order to meet him.

For Whitehall and a part of the British public, Bell was a somewhat controversial figure. Immediately after the Nazi take-over, he had publicly condemned anti–Christian features of National Socialism, and had consequently been severely criticised in many quarters in Britain. The same criticism was provoked ten years later by his disapproval of Allied bombing raids on civilian targets in Germany. The 1930s had seen him support the *Bekennende Kirche*. On 13 December 1939 he had endorsed Lord Darnley's *démarche* to the British Government in favour of accepting the offer made by the Dutch Queen Wilhelmina and the Belgian King Leopold III to mediate peace.[28] In a letter to *The Times* on 17 April 1941 he had proposed a mutual cessation of the bombing of non–military targets.[29] In a broadcast to Germany at Christmas 1941 he had paid homage to Pastor Martin Niemöller, the Protestant Bishop of Württemberg, Theophile Wurm, and the Catholic Bishop of Münster, Count von Galen: 'Help to save your country's soul by resisting the evil spirit by which it is now possessed. Your fellow Christians everywhere are by your side. Your struggle is our struggle. The days are dark, but Christmas brings salvation. Light will break through. Hold fast, never yield. Trust in the power of God, and the Love of Christ.'[30] Whitehall looked with distrust at Bell, who was always guided by Christian principles, who pleaded against a 'propaganda of lies and hatred',[31] who from the middle of 1942 had become the most important champion of the 'other Germany' in England, and who after 1943 turned most ardently against Vansittart's ideas. When Eden learned of Bell's visit to Sweden, he refused to meet him before his departure. Also, he was irritated by the official approval of his tour by the Ministry of Information: 'This seems a strange choice. I thought he was a pacifist.'[32] Vansittart was later to call Bell 'a political priest', who moved outside his province.[33] Schönfeld was Director of the Research Department of the Ecumenical Council of Churches at Geneva. He had known Bell since 1929. Behind Schönfeld stood the so-called *Kreisauer Kreis*, an opposition group around Helmuth James Count von Moltke and Peter York Count von Wartenburg, which was in contact with the Christian community abroad. The ideas of this group on foreign policy, mainly formulated by the diplomats Hans-Bernd von Haeften and Adam von Trott zu Solz, a former Rhodes Scholar, together with Eugen Gerstenmaier, found their way into the memorandum which Schönfeld wrote for Bell at Stockholm.[34] Bonhoeffer and Bell had enjoyed cordial relations with each other since 1933, when Bonhoeffer had acted as adviser to Bell during his session as President of the Ecumenical Council for Practical Christendom. Officially, Bonhoeffer worked for the *Amt Ausland/Abwehr* of Admiral Wilhelm Canaris, under cover of which a group around General Hans Oster and Hans von Dohnanyi worked against Hitler. He continued contact, however, with his old friend Haeften; prior to his departure he had a long conversation on the external situation with him, and briefed him after his return as well.[35]

The meeting with Schönfeld and Bonhoeffer made a deep impression on Bell. Immediately after returning to Britain in mid-June he reported first to the Foreign Office and later to the American Ambassador, John Winant.[36] On 18 June he briefed the Head of the Northern Department, Christopher Warner, on the importance of the Sigtuna talks. Warner put on record that in Bell's opinion 'this was something more than one of the usual peace feelers'. The British minister to Sweden, Victor Mallet, could have confirmed his view.[37] Bell intended to submit a paper to the Foreign Office on the meeting along with a memorandum by Schönfeld. He therefore asked for an appointment with Eden himself.

In his paper Bell outlined the different elements within German opposition circles, such as army officers, civil servants, functionaries of the former trade unions and members of both Christian Churches. The political blueprint for 'the opposition' in the time after Hitler he summarised as follows: Germany would abjure aggression. It would repeal the Nuremberg Laws and actively co-operate in finding an international solution to the 'Jewish Question'. The German Army would be gradually withdrawn from states either under occupation or being invaded. German support for Japan would cease. Moreover, the new government would assist the Allies both in ending the war in the Far East and in rebuilding those areas which had been destroyed by the war or had suffered damage. On behalf of 'the opposition' both clergymen had enquired whether, on the basis of the preconditions listed above, the Allies would be prepared to enter into peace negotiations with a new German Government. The subsequent peace should safeguard the following principles: (1) the establishment of the reign of law in

Germany alongside far-reaching self-determination in the 'main different provinces'; (2) close economic ties among the European nations in order not only to obtain a balance of prosperity in Europe, but also to act as a guarantee of the strongest possible kind against militarism; (3) the creation of a representative federation of free nations or states, including free Polish and Czech nations; and (4) the creation of a European army under a central command, into which the German army would be integrated. However, 'the opposition' had complete faith in the *Wehrmacht*, and could carry on with the war until 'its bitter end' if the Allies refused talks with a new German government. Also, the anti-Hitlerites would explicitly warn against a continuation of the war 'on the present or a greater scale', as this would condemn further millions of people to death.

With regard to the USSR Bell noted: 'The opposition, while having some hesitations with regard to Soviet Russia, has the hope (as a result of impressions made by some of the high Russian officers on some of the German officers) of the possibility of reaching an understanding.' The anti-Hitlerites would be waiting for some encouragement in the form of a reaction to the proposals mentioned: 'The answer to this might be privately given to a representative of the opposition through a neutral country.' Furthermore, the question had been raised whether the Allies could 'announce publicly to the world' in the 'clearest terms' that they were prepared to negotiate for peace with a post-Hitler government, along the lines put forward by 'the opposition', provided of course the said preconditions were met.

Although the Schönfeld memorandum emphasised the hope for economic and social co-operation, it played the anti-Bolshevist card more strongly than Bell presented it in his paper. In fact, Schönfeld had written on the attitude of 'the opposition' towards the USSR: '. . . they are not convinced that the totalitarian methods of revolutionary brutal warfare would be changed without very effective guarantees, even when the totalitarian regime in Central Europe had been abolished.' Furthermore, 'they would regard the building up of an Orthodox Russian Church by the renewal of Christian faith in Russia as a real common basis which could further more than anything else the co-operation between Russia and the European Federation.'[38] Such statements were directed against Stalin's political system because, as Bell explained after the war, Schönfeld thought of a peace between Germany and the western Allies once Hitler had been disposed of. The only alternative, which Schönfeld and his 'friends' saw and conveyed to Bell, was 'further chaos' followed by the rise of Bolshevism in Germany.[39]

Bonhoeffer, in contrast (and Bell's paper failed to mention this), favoured the idea of considering the forthcoming action of the opposition as an 'act of repentance'.[40] Both pastors argued that the Allies should encourage German opposition circles. However, Bonhoeffer was aware of the incompatibility of the demands with Christian principles and Schönfeld's peace conditions.[41] Although he did not say so in public during the war, Bell felt more inclined towards Bonhoeffer's line. The bishop was no advocate of a peace settlement with Germany based on concessions, especially territorial ones. His attempts in the second half of 1942 to induce Whitehall into making a direct and positive 'address' to the *Wehrmacht* was therefore meant as a purely functional measure. He thought that only the armed forces could be expected to launch an action against the Nazi regime which had any scope for success. But his own political attitude was quite similar to the official British point of view, and not identical with the ideas of the 'nationalist' section of the German anti-Hitlerites.[42]

Before Bell eventually met Eden on 30 June, the Foreign Office received more information on the German resistance that was seeking contact with Britain and their ideas for peace. In May the Foreign Secretary of the Dutch Government in exile, van Kleffens, handed to the Foreign Office a paper on a conversation with Willem Visser't Hooft. Visser't Hooft, then the Secretary General of the World Council of Churches (Preparatory Committee), had relayed the foreign-policy goals of opposition circles with whom he was in touch. After the *coup d'état*, German troops would be withdrawn from Western and Northern Europe behind the 'old German frontiers'. But this would not apply to the forces both in the Balkans and on the Eastern front unless the Western democracies were to guarantee Germany's safety against Russian revenge. The future of Austria should be subject to a plebiscite. Post-Hitler Germany, however, would be willing to join a European Federation, and, in that case, would be prepared 'to renounce some considerable part of her sovereign rights to the federation'.[43] Visser't Hooft's memorandum did not change the attitude of British officials. Kleffens had already told Visser't Hooft that he considered the opposition group 'very unrealistic in its outlook'. P. F. Hancock of the Foreign Office found the ideas 'quite ridiculous', and Harrison urged 'the decent German elements' to act, as this was necessary before Britain would be 'prepared to believe even in their existence'.[44]

In May 1942 Visser't Hooft had also approached Ivone Kirkpatrick.

Before the war he had been First Secretary of the British Embassy in Berlin under Sir Neville Henderson. After the meeting Kirkpatrick, who since late autumn 1941 had been the 'European controller' of the BBC's European Division, reported to Eden that 'well-informed Germans' were 'fully aware of German atrocities in occupied areas'. This knowledge was 'filtering through to the masses', who had begun to worry about what would happen to them after the war. He also cited a German industrialist who said during a visit to Switzerland that there was developing a 'general fear of the Russians and the possibility of a Russian invasion' in Germany.[45] In reaction to these kinds of reports on the mood of the German population and atrocities in the occupied areas, Cadogan drafted a new propaganda formula:

> You Germans, you have been stunned and are being crushed by the machine to which you have delivered yourselves. Look at the bestialities that it commits in your name: think of the feeling that this must arouse against you, and of the retribution from which perhaps no power will be able to protect you. Unless you give some sign you will be forever identified with it. Etc.

Eden agreed to Cadogan's proposal on 22 May. Thinking perhaps of his speech of 8 May he noted in the file: 'We are, I think, already on this line.'[46] However, on 8 May Eden had only talked of the growing responsibility of the Germans 'for the damage' that they were doing to the world. He did not explicitly speak, like Cadogan, of responsibility for war crimes, since this would lead easily (at least from the perspective of the Allies) to the identification of all Germans with their leadership. This finally could end up in the notion of the 'collective guilt' of all Germans. Cadogan deliberately wished to arouse the fear that all Germans would be treated just the same as the important Nazi criminals if Hitler was not overthrown.

Nevertheless, the British Government continued to emphasise the guilt of individuals. On 21 May, the Secretary of State for the Colonies, Viscount Cranborne, spoke in the House of Lords of 'justice stern and unflinching for those Germans who have been guilty of the abominable crimes we have witnessed'. His colleague, the Minister of Economic Warfare, the Earl of Selborne, said on 4 June: 'Great Britain will never propose a peace of revenge. Individuals . . . who have been guilty of atrocities will and must be punished, but that is not revenge; that is justice.'[47] A memorandum of the PWE of 20 June 1942 accordingly ruled that the German programme of the BBC was to consider the statements of both Cranborne and Selborne, together with the principles laid down in the Atlantic Charter. In fact, it was considered 'vital' that the Germans 'should be given every opportunity of hearing them'.[48]

Also in May the Foreign Office received a memorandum addressed to Sir Stafford Cripps, which Adam von Trott had given to Visser't Hooft in Geneva the month before. Copies were also received by Arnold J. Toynbee and Sir Alfred Zimmern of the Foreign Research and Press Service.[49] The authors of the memorandum, Trott and members of the 'Kreisau Circle' such as Schönfeld and Gerstenmaier,[50] argued that 'the earliest possible overthrow of the Regime in Germany' would be 'the most urgent and immediate task to stave off catastrophe in Europe'. This could be achieved either 'by way of anarchical dissolution' following the success of Soviet arms, which would lead to a 'world revolution by military means', or by the establishment of a German government firmly based on the standards of civilised Europe. A group inspired by the European Christian tradition did exist; but, as Trott's memorandum pointed out, the seizure of power by this group would be hindered by obstacles such as the threat the USSR posed to Germany, and 'control of the entire national life by the police [Gestapo]'. Also, the group felt 'complete uncertainty of the British and American attitude towards a change of government in Germany'. Eventually they feared 'movements of indiscriminate hatred in the event of a sudden relaxation of German control in the occupied parts of Europe.' The political concept Trott presented embraced a decentralised Germany together with a European Federation, which would include Great Britain. Co-operation with other continents should be close. In exchange for free access to raw materials overseas, the memorandum suggested 'the renunciation of economic autarky'. Also, the new Germany must be willing 'to co-operate in any international solution of the Jewish problem' which would help to overcome the 'misery' existing in countries 'under Nazi rule'. However, Trott, who more than some others of the 'Kreisau Circle' favoured the principle of the national state, emphasised the necessity of 'ethnographic frontiers', in view of the reconstitution of a 'free Polish and a free Czech state'.[51] Thus Trott demanded quite clearly that the Sudeten area, the city of Danzig, the Corridor and Austria should be integrated into the new Germany, although he did not say so explicitly.

Ideas on foreign policy of this kind understandably aroused suspicion rather than excitement in Whitehall. The Foreign Office at first made enquiries about the political reliability of Visser't Hooft, and since no incriminating evidence turned up against the messenger, suspicion was focused on the author of the memorandum.[52] T. H. Marshall of the Foreign Research and Press Service approached Crossman, who had been at Oxford with Trott in the 1930s. On 27 May 1942 Crossman let Marshall know that he and Trott had never been confidants. Nevertheless, he believed that the group which Trott claimed to represent did really exist. Trott's friends, so he thought, could be of some importance for British political warfare as they could be 'misdirected . . . in ways useful to H.M.G.'. About Trott's political acumen Crossman conveyed a poor opinion: 'Adam von Trott is not fully aware of his ingenuousness in politics, can claim a really extensive knowledge of England, and may therefore be able to persuade harder headed men than himself to share his illusions.'[53]

Eden himself, though he did not take up the idea of instrumentalising Hitler's opponents in such a way, accepted Crossman's assessment of Trott as a *homo politicus* to at least some extent. In a letter to Cripps, who knew Trott and whose son John was a friend of the former Rhodes Scholar, Eden described him as: 'a curious mixture of high-minded idealism and political dishonesty'. He found the memorandum 'interesting'. Also, he thought it likely that there would be quite a number of Germans 'who would endorse it'. Fundamentally, however, he saw 'no evidence' that Hitler's enemies in Germany would form an 'organised group'. Moreover, they could perhaps be used themselves by 'more hard headed individuals, e.g. as a cover for peace overtures'. Therefore, Eden decided: 'We do not ourselves attach much importance as yet to these people, nor do we propose to respond to any overtures from them. Our view is that until they come out into the open and give some visible sign of their intention to assist in the overthrow of the Nazi regime, they can be of little use to us or to Germany.'[54] Cripps did not wish to leave Eden's denigrating remarks about Trott unanswered, and reminded the Foreign Secretary that Trott had chosen to stay in Germany even though he could have taken the 'very simple solution' of 'resigning from the service of the Nazi regime'. He had instead assumed the far higher risk in 'refusing to join the Nazi regime', and going back to Germany 'to fight for the things which he believed to be right'.[55]

In June Cadogan summarised the British attitude towards the German anti-Hitlerites, what Britain could promise them and what German opposition circles would have to do in order to gain British acceptance:

> What would be interesting would be to see what any group of this kind can *do*. We are not going to negotiate with any Government in

Germany that has not thoroughly purged its soul and we must have some convincing of *that* and we have got to be convinced first. Total defeat and disarmament is probably the only possible answer.[56]

Apparently there was no scope for negotiations prior to a radical change of government in Germany. If Bishop Bell had been optimistic in this respect, the final communication with Eden on the subject of the German 'opposition' informed him of the futility of his effort. On 30 June Eden let Bell know that Great Britain wished to avoid arousing even the slightest suspicion of entering into 'negotiations with the enemy', for reasons concerning the USA and the USSR.[57] A couple of weeks later, on 17 July, Eden wrote to Bell that both the Schönfeld memorandum and Bell's report had been thoroughly analysed. However, the Government had arrived at the conclusion that 'it would not be in the national interest for any reply whatever to be sent to them'.[58] When Bell insisted and asked for a public statement explaining that Whitehall neither considered Vansittart's ideas to be its own nor wished to enslave a post-war Germany, Eden reminded the bishop of his speech of 8 May 1942, and of the growing responsibility of all Germans for the Nazi crimes.[59] On 17 August Bell terminated his correspondence with Eden, at least for the time being. He emphasised that the Allies had promised to liberate the nations under Nazi rule, but had failed to promise the same to the German people. However, he accepted that German opposition circles had to contribute their share to the overthrow of Hitler, especially in view of the atrocities:

Certainly the pastors and their friends in Germany are fully alive to the grave character of responsibility borne by the German people for the crimes committed by the Nazis in their name. The hopes of a return to a German state based on the respect for law and the rights of the individual, after the overthrow of the Nazis, and of a place for a reformed Germany in the future of Europe, ought to be powerful factors in making the opposition declare itself more and more plainly.[60]

Towards the end of June at Geneva, Visser't Hooft conveyed to Adam von Trott the 'essentially negative' reply of the British government to his memorandum of April 1942. Trott, according to Visser't Hooft, was 'near despair'.[61] Cripps had told Visser't Hooft before his departure for Geneva that he had been impressed by Trott's paper. Churchill had called it 'most encouraging',[62] but had not committed himself to any answer. At first Germany, Cripps had said, had to be defeated, since there had to be 'a clear demonstration that National Socialism could not be tolerated'. After the defeat, however, the Germans would receive 'fair treatment'.[63]

Conclusion

There are four main reasons for the negative response of the British leadership to the overtures of the German anti-Hitlerites. All of them reflect the fundamental attitude of London towards both Germany and British concepts on post-war planning.

First, Great Britain did not want to arouse suspicion in Moscow that London and Washington secretly wished to conclude a separate peace with Germany. The anti-Soviet remarks and allusions the German opposition circles put into their memoranda confirmed British fears that Hitler's enemies in Germany intended to split the Grand Alliance against Nazi Germany. This alliance, however, which Great Britain had strengthened with its treaty with the USSR of May 1942, had become a key element of British policy. Thus, the anti-Soviet attitude of the German opposition turned out to be counter-productive.

London confirmed its policy of 'absolute silence'. The overtures of Schönfeld and Trott were treated accordingly. Since contacts with German opposition circles could become a source of suspicion and misunderstanding, a conference of senior officials of the Foreign Office on 4 November 1942 suggested a tripartite agreement on 'peace-feelers'. A memorandum on this meeting stated that Great Britain already kept both Washington and Moscow informed about approaches made by German opposition circles.[64] At the Moscow Conference of Foreign Ministers, Eden submitted a 'British Draft of Resolution on Peace Feelers from Enemy Countries'. This was included in the secret protocol of the conference of the Foreign Ministers of Great Britain, the USSR and the USA on 1 November 1943.[65]

Secondly, Great Britain gradually reached the conclusion that Germany could only be brought to its senses by a complete military defeat.[66] Information on atrocities committed by the National Socialists, which were increasingly coming to light, strengthened this attitude. This was the case especially from spring 1942 onwards. The declaration of the United Nations of 1 January 1942 already obliged its signatories to pursue 'complete victory over their enemies'. The leading article of *The Times* of the same day called such a victory 'absolute and without compromise'. On 11 November 1942 King George VI emphasised the determination of the Allies 'to fight on to complete victory, with no thought of parley'. The Labour politician Arthur Greenwood on 18 December 1942 called 'complete military victory' the goal of the Allied war effort: 'Any feeble discussions based on appeasement would defeat the high objects for which we fight.'[67] Thus the attitude and the ideas which were to lead to the demand for unconditional surrender were already circulating, though a crystal-clear formula was only to come at Casablanca on 24 January 1943. Such a war aim, which laid down the essential preconditions for a cease-fire, created ideal conditions for planning the future of Germany. It allowed ample scope for the formulation of idealistic goals about the post-war social, political and economic order. If the formulation of post-war goals depended on the mutual consent of the Allies, the demand for unconditional surrender meant that the interests of the enemy countries need not be taken into account.

This basic assumption underpinning post-war planning was rarely emphasised because it was taken for granted. A case in point was the statement of Brigadier van Cutsem of the Military Sub-Committee, who on 18 February 1942 had already written to the Foreign Office on the subject of an armistice with Germany and Italy: 'The terms should include a preamble whereby the defeated states admit their unconditional surrender. They should provide for the immediate occupation of all enemy territory not already occupied during the course of hostilities.'[68] Cadogan evidently thought along very similar lines when he wrote in November 1942:

> But after the war, if we are to be just to surviving Germans, we must be stern as well. Germany must be completely disarmed and to a great extent controlled. We must stop our ears against all whinings about a *Diktat*. It's got to be a *Diktat*, if only for the good of the poor dear Germans who remain, and who will only learn slowly and painfully through generations, how to govern and behave themselves.[69]

Therefore, only those anti-Hitlerites stood a chance of acceptance abroad who, like Bonhoeffer or Count von Moltke, saw the absolute need of Germany's total defeat and disarmament. Moltke had considered total defeat a necessity as early as April 1941.[70]

Thirdly, distrust and scepticism towards German opposition circles were widespread in the Foreign Office. The 'Venlo Incident' of 1939 was still remembered. On that occasion the German Security Service (*Sicherheitsdienst*, SD) had kidnapped two British intelligence officers who were deluded into thinking they were meeting opponents of Hitler. When the Foreign Office made inquiries about Trott, the Special Operations Executive described him on 27 September 1942 as an 'extraordinarily suspicious character.'[71] He was considered an 'appeaser'. Before the war he had been in contact with well known appeasers like the Astors and Viscount Halifax. In the summer of 1939 he had submitted a plan to the British Government suggesting the restoration of Czech independence in exchange for Polish concessions to Germany in Danzig and the Corridor.[72]

A summary of German peace-feelers from April 1941 to June 1942, which the Foreign Office sent to Churchill, concluded: 'There is a good reason to believe that many of these overtures, perhaps the majority, have been inspired by the German Secret Service, which seems to have made special study of the strategy and tactic of the peace feelers. The purpose is obvious – to try to sow dissension between the Allies and to slow up the tempo of their war effort.'[73] Eventually, the Foreign Office was sceptical as to the wisdom of accepting Trott and Schönfeld as foreign-policy planners. Their demand for concessions prior to Hitler's overthrow was not well received. References to the strength of the German army and the German intention to fight on in case the Western Allies failed to meet the demands of the German 'opposition' were also not well received. In October 1942, J. W. Wheeler-Bennett in particular pointed out the 'impossibility of negotiating a war-time Munich with Germany'.[74] Unfortunately, German opposition circles were compelled to ask that concessions be granted prior to the overthrow of Hitler.[75] Many *Wehrmacht* officers in key positions of command could not be won over unless the Allies pledged to respect the territorial and national integrity of a post-Hitler Germany.

Finally, the position of the British government was not such that it could commit itself to any binding concept concerning the future of Germany. There were too many factors which had to be considered. Therefore, the War Cabinet had decided on 9 October 1939 to avoid any explicit declaration of British war aims.[76] This guideline remained in force until 1945. One advantage of leaving Germany's future open was that the Dominions had entered the war mainly on moral grounds, and wished to consider the feelings of their German minorities. Also, it was felt that the British government could not ignore the opinion of the USA and the USSR in 1942. Any decision on the future of Germany had to be taken in agreement with these Allies, which were militarily stronger than Britain. Furthermore, the Allies had to consider the feelings of the governments in exile, especially those of Poland and Czechoslovakia. There was a certain concern to keep up the will to resist the Nazis in Poland, Czechoslovakia and elsewhere. A soft attitude on Germany's future could do much damage. Frank Roberts, Head of the Central Department in the British Foreign Office from the summer of 1942, conceded this on 16 August 1942, and said that British policy towards Germany was in fact one 'of disarmament and military weakness, coupled with a bright economic future for Germany'.

Moreover, Britain had to expect that the Russians and 'our minor Allies' would have 'very different views', and would 'favour a much more drastic policy of keeping Germany down in every way.'[77] And in October 1942, when London was concerned that the USA might recognise German politicians in exile, Geoffrey Harrison of the Central Department wrote in a minute: 'In short, in our view, whatever government emerges in Germany after the war will consist of Germans who have been through the war in Germany. It should further be noted that active encouragement even of anti-Nazi organisations would be sure to arouse suspicion in the countries now suffering under German oppression and in particular among our European Allies.'[78] The fact that Britain refused to give some official status to German politicians in exile was favourable to some extent for those opponents of the Nazis who considered Hitler's overthrow to be a domestic affair and were worried about another 'stab in the back' myth. British silence on Germany's future was also helpful, since the knowledge of British plans such as 'the transfer of population' would have strengthened the position of Hitler.

The Foreign Office was not even prepared to oppose publicly Vansittart's notion of a German collective guilt. It did not follow the line taken by Stalin, who in his speeches made clear distinctions, on the one hand, between the National Socialists and the German people, and, on the other hand, between Hitler's army and some other organised military force which could come into being in post-war Germany.[79] In contrast, the directives of the Foreign Office for the PWE aimed at keeping the Germans in a state of uncertainty. British propaganda therefore left the Germans guessing about who would be treated as National Socialists and/or war criminals, and who would be forgiven.[80]

In the second half of 1942 such a middle-of-the-road approach served a twofold purpose. First, it took into consideration British public opinion, which began to favour punitive measures for those who were held responsible for atrocities against both Jews and the populations of the occupied countries. Public concern was so strong, indeed, that it compelled the Government to make its position clear. On 7 October 1942[81] and again on 17 December

1942[82] statements were made on this subject in the House of Commons. Secondly, it justified British strategic 'carpet bombing', which caused suffering among the 'good' and the 'bad' Germans alike. This kind of air warfare could not be justified if public opinion considered the overwhelming majority of the potential victims as innocent people who had had the bad luck of being governed by a gang of criminals.

On 2 December 1942, after German opposition circles had failed to meet the demand for positive action in May, Eden told the House of Commons that he had lost hope of a change of government in Berlin. Like Vansittart, he supported his view with remarks about the aggressive character of the German people:

> During the last 70 years – these are unpleasant facts which we have to face – successive German Governments have consciously and consistently pursued a policy of world domination. This policy and the philosophy that is behind it is the first threat to enduring peace, and it will be the first and imperative duty of the United Nations on the morrow of their victory to elaborate such a settlement as will make it impossible for Germany again to dominate her neighbours by force of arms. That lies at the root of the business, and it would be sheer folly to allow some non-Nazi German Government to be set up, and then, so to speak, to trust to luck. The rooting out of the old false gods will be a long and strenuous business, but it must be accomplished.[83]

Thus Eden gave expression to the view that henceforth the overthrow of Hitler would not be enough. At the same time he demanded far-reaching intervention in the internal affairs of Germany, subsequently asking for a change in the German attitude towards armed conflicts in general (e.g. mental disarmament in combination with material disarmament), something which entailed the re-education of the whole nation. Therefore, if Germany was to be recreated and launched with the ultimate goal of becoming a 'civilised member of the family of nations', then, according to the perspective of the Allies, unconditional surrender was the indispensable precondition. Unconditional surrender, however, narrowed the scope of manoeuvre for German opposition circles, which depended on the support of essential parts of the officer corps for success. Thus, the demand of Hitler's opponents in Germany for concessions and the war aims of Great Britain cancelled each other out.

NOTES

I wish to thank Herbert Behrendt for his help in translating this article.

1. See R. A. Blasius (ed.), *Dokumente zur Deutschlandpolitik*, First Series, vol. 1, 3 September 1939 – 31 December 1941: Documents on British Foreign Policy Toward Germany (hereafter DzD I/1), Frankfurt am Main, 1984, p. 269.
2. R. A. Blasius (ed.), *Dokumente zur Deutschlandpolitik*, First Series, vol. 3, 1 January – 31 December 1942: Documents on British Foreign Policy Toward Germany (hereafter DzD I/3), Frankfurt am Main, 1989, p. 385.
3. J. Stalin, *On the Great Patriotic War of the Soviet Union. Speeches, Orders of the Day, and Answers to Foreign Press Correspondents*, London–NY–Melbourne, 1944, p. 27.
4. DzD I/3, 1942, p. 152.
5. Ibid., pp. 156 f.
6. Ibid., p. 157, n. 6.
7. V. Gollancz, *Shall our Children Live or Die? A Reply to Lord Vansittart on the German Problem*, London, 1942, pp. 3, 5, 32, 36, 95, 113 f. and 116 f.
8. See 'Lord Vansittart and Germany: "No Revolution"', *The Times*, 3 March 1942.
9. DzD I/3. 1942, p. 215. Some German emigrants like Curt Geyer and Walter Loeb supported Vansittart's view *vis-à-vis* Gollancz. See T. D. Burridge, *British Labour and Hitler's War*, London, 1976, p. 61; A. Glees, *Exile Politics during the Second World War: The German Social Democrats in Britain*, Oxford, 1982; A. Goldman, 'Germans and Nazis: The Controversy over "Vansittartism" in Britain during the Second World War', *Journal of Contemporary History*, vol. 14, 1979, p. 171. The majority of Social Democrats in exile, however, strongly opposed these '*deutsche Vansittartisten*'. See W. Röder, *Die deutschen sozialistischen Exilgruppen in Großbritannien 1940–1945. Ein Beitrag zur Geschichte des Widerstandes gegen den Nationalsozialismus*, 2nd edn, Bonn, 1973, pp. 168 ff.
10. See R. A. Blasius, *Für Großdeutschland – gegen den großen Krieg. Staatssekretär Ernst Freiherr von Weizsäcker in den Krisen um die Tschechoslowakei und Polen 1938–39*, Cologne–Vienna, 1981, pp. 102, 150 ff.
11. DzD I/3, 1942, p. 213.
12. Ibid., p. 359.
13. Ibid., pp. 372 ff., n. 10.
14. Ibid., pp. 367 f. (on 21 May 1942).
15. Ibid., p. 370.
16. Ibid., pp. 359 f., n. 9.
17. Quoted in A. Briggs, *The War of Words*, London–NY–Toronto, 1970, p. 429, n. 5.
18. See C. Pütter, *Rundfunk gegen das Dritte Reich. Deutschsprachige*

302   *Rainer A. Blasius*

Rundfunkaktivitäten im Exil 1933–1945. Ein Handbuch, Munich–London–NY–Paris, 1986, p. 94.

19. See M. Balfour, *Propaganda in War 1939–1945: Organisation, Politics and Publics in Britain and Germany*, London–Boston, 1979, pp. 267 ff.
20. Ibid., p. 95; U. Reusch, 'Die Londoner Institutionen der britischen Deutschlandpolitik 1943–1948. Eine behördengeschichtliche Untersuchung', *Historisches Jahrbuch*, vol. 100, 1980, p. 348.
21. R. H. Bruce Lockhart, *Comes the Reckoning*, London, 1947, p. 155.
22. DzD I/3, 1942, p. 20, n. 1.
23. Ibid., pp. 21 f. and p. 23, n. 15.
24. Ibid., p. 23.
25. Ibid., pp. 191 f., n. 2.
26. Ibid., p. 312. See also Briggs, *War*, p. 427.
27. DzD I/3, 1942, p. 336. Eden again took up Chamberlain's view holding the whole of the German people responsible for the prolongation of the war, which he had made public on 9 January 1940. See DzD I/1, 1939–1941, p. 108.
28. In view of the Third Reich's brutal conduct of war, Bell saw only two alternatives for Great Britain: either to fight until the bitter end, or to seek peace by negotiation soon. See Hansard, *House of Lords*, vol. 115, pp. 254 f.
29. See *The Times*, 17 April 1941.
30. See G. K. A. Bell, 'Christmas Broadcast to Germany, 24 December 1941', in Bell, *The Church and Humanity, 1939–1946*, London–NY–Toronto, 1946, p. 69.
31. So Bell, in an essay of November 1939. See Bell, *Church*, pp. 26 f.
32. Quoted in R. Lamb, 'The Foreign Office Response to the Overtures from the Trott-Goerdeler Conspirators', MS, Leeds, May, 1986, p. 8.
33. Quoted in R. C. D. Jasper, *George Bell: Bishop of Chichester*, London–NY–Toronto, 1967, p. 279.
34. G. van Roon, *Neuordnung im Widerstand. Der Kreisauer Kreis innerhalb der deutschen Widerstandsbewegung*, Munich, 1967, p. 314; P. Hoffmann, *Widerstand – Staatsstreich – Attentat. Der Kampf der Opposition gegen Hitler*, 4th rev. edn, Munich, 1985, p. 265.
35. See Roon, *Neuordnung*, p. 313; Hoffmann, *Widerstand*, p. 269.
36. DzD I/3, 1942, p. 646.
37. Ibid., p. 504.
38. Ibid., pp. 498 ff., 503.
39. G. K. A. Bell, 'Die Kirche und die Widerstandsbewegung', in *Dietrich Bonhoeffer. Gesammelte Schriften*, ed. E. Bethge, vol. 1, Munich, 1958, pp. 517 f.
40. Ibid., p. 519.
41. See P. Hoffmann, 'Peace through Coup d'État. The Foreign Contacts of the German Resistance 1933–1944', *Central European History*, vol. 19, 1986, p. 32.
42. See H. Ben-Israel, 'Im Widerstreit der Ziele. Die britische Reaktion auf den deutschen Widerstand', in J. Schmädecke and P. Steinbach

(eds), *Der deutsche Widerstand gegen den Nationalsozialismus. Die deutsche Gesellschaft und der Widerstand gegen Hitler*, Munich–Zürich, 1985, p. 742.
43. DzD I/3, 1942, p. 347.
44. Ibid., p. 348.
45. Ibid., p. 349, n. 8.
46. Ibid., p. 349.
47. Ibid., pp. 33, 372, 451.
48. Ibid., p. 508.
49. Lamb, 'The Foreign Office Response', p. 10.
50. Hoffmann, *Staatsstreich*, p. 266.
51. For the text of the memorandum, see H. Rothfels, 'Zwei außenpolitische Memoranden der deutschen Opposition [Frühjahr 1942]. Dokumentation', *Vierteljahrshefte für Zeitgeschichte*, vol. 5, 1957, pp. 392 ff.
52. A. Boyens, *Kirchenkampf und Ökumene 1939–1945. Darstellung und Dokumentation unter besonderer Berücksichtigung der Quellen des Ökumenischen Rates der Kirchen*, Munich, 1973, p. 211.
53. Quoted in R. Lamb, *The Ghosts of Peace, 1939–1945*, Wilton, Salisbury, 1987, p. 256.
54. Quoted in ibid., pp. 259 f.
55. Quoted in ibid., p. 260.
56. DzD I/3, 1942, p. 497, n. 4.
57. Ibid., p. 498, n. 1.
58. Ibid., p. 615.
59. Ibid., pp. 633, 648.
60. Ibid., p. 668.
61. W. A. Visser't Hooft, 'The View from Geneva', *Encounter*, vol. 52, September, 1969, p. 92. See also Lamb, *Ghosts*, p. 264.
62. See Visser't Hooft, 'View', p. 92: 'very encouraging'; Lamb, *Ghosts*, p. 264: 'most encouraging' (with reference to Visser't Hooft and Rothfels as sources). Churchill's minute is obviously known only on the basis of oral sources. Moreover, it referred to the existence of some German opposition group rather than to their political ideas.
63. Visser't Hooft, 'View', p. 92. Visser't Hooft referred in this context to Crossman, who was supposed to have said that in the case of a successful overthrow of Hitler: 'a new situation would be created and new possibilities might arise'. Visser't Hooft called this the 'unofficial view'. Crossman, apparently, saw such an arrangement only from the propaganda point of view. He wished to use the German 'opposition' for British interests. When Cripps suggested that Elisabeth Wiskeman, who worked at the British Legation at Berne, should 'calm down' Trott, G. W. Harrison commented on 12 June 1942 that the value of Trott as a 'martyr' would be higher than his possible value in post-war Germany. See N. Shepard, *Wilfried Israel*, Berlin, 1985, pp. 291 f; Lamb, *Ghosts*, p. 257.
64. DzD I/3, 1942, p. 949. See also *Foreign Relations of the United States* (hereafter FRUS), 1943, vol. 1, p. 484, n. 1.

65. See *FRUS*, 1943, vol. 1, p. 737.
66. See Visser't Hooft, 'View' p. 93: 'This point came up in practically every conversation in Britain about the Trott memorandum.'
67. DzD I/3, 1942, pp. 3, 6, 981 and 1167.
68. Ibid., pp. 114 f.
69. Ibid., p. 950.
70. For the text of the Moltke memorandum, see Roon, *Neuordnung*, pp. 507 ff.
71. Quoted in Lamb, *Ghosts*, p. 261.
72. See R. A. Blasius, 'Über London den "großen Krieg" verhindern. Ernst von Weizsäckers Aktivitäten im Sommer 1939', in Schmädecke and Steinbach (eds), *Widerstand*, p. 699. See also about Trott: R. A. Blasius, 'Adam von Trott zu Solz', in R. Lill and H. Oberreuther (eds), *20 Juli. Portraits des Widerstands*, Düsseldorf–Vienna, 1984, pp. 324 ff.; K. von Klemperer, 'Adam von Trott zu Solz and Resistance Foreign Policy', *Central European History*, vol. 14, 1981, pp. 351 ff. Trott's friend and contemporary at Oxford, David Astor, assessed Trott's activities in July 1939 as the last attempt of some group in the Foreign Ministry at Berlin to give Hitler Danzig and the Corridor without war. This group, however, would have launched this scheme in order to gain time for the preparation of a military *coup d'état* against Hitler. For this argument, which is most improbable and cannot be verified, see D. Astor, 'Adam von Trott: A Personal View', in H. Bull (ed.), *The Challenge of the Third Reich*, Oxford, 1986, p. 27.
73. See 'Summary of Principal Peace Feelers, April 1941 to June 1942', in L. Kettenacker (ed.), *Das 'Andere Deutschland' im Zweiten Weltkrieg. Emigration und Widerstand in internationaler Perspektive*, Stuttgart, 1977, pp. 188 ff. The policy of 'absolute silence' to German peace-feelers was exploited in this summary as well as in the telegram of the Ministry of Information of 28 June 1942, which went to all British Legations and Embassies; see DzD I/3, 1942, p. 620, n. 1.
74. DzD I/3, 1942, p. 881.
75. See K. von Klemperer, 'Nationale oder internationale Außenpolitik des Widerstands', in Schmädecke and Steinbach (eds), *Widerstand*, pp. 639 ff.
76. See Kettenacker, *Das 'Andere Deutschland'*, pp. 146 f.
77. DzD I/3, 1942, p. 654.
78. Ibid., p. 931, n. 1.
79. Stalin, *Great Patriotic War*, p. 44 (on 6 November 1942). See also R. A. Blasius, 'Zweifel an Uncle Joe's Treue? Chancen eines sowjetisch-deutschen Sonderfriedens vor Casablanca im Urteil des Foreign Office', in W. Michalka (ed.), *Der Zweite Weltkrieg. Forschungsbilanz und Perspektiven*, Munich–Zürich, 1989.
80. See DzD I/3, 1942, pp. 952 f.
81. Ibid., pp. 846 ff.
82. Ibid., pp. 1162 f.
83. Ibid., p. 1095.

16

German Soldiers in the 1938 Munich Crisis

Harold C. Deutsch

Few aspects of the National Socialist period of German history have so engaged contemporaries and posterity as the role of the Army. No matter what aspect of the Third Reich is under scrutiny, the question of how the military fitted into the course of events is likely to arise. On some issues one must anticipate perennial controversy.

In the formidable domestic and international ferment known as the Munich crisis the centrality of the topic scarcely requires delineation. The question of what the Army would or would not do was never a decisive factor, as the crisis was cut short by the western powers through the concessions made to and reluctantly accepted by Hitler. Our problem must of necessity thus fall among the might-have-beens of history.

So much has been written about the relations of the Army with the Hitler regime that its more general aspects need be dealt with only to highlight essential points. The German officer corps under the Weimar Republic was among the most élite in history. Limited by the Versailles Treaty to 4,000, it could be selected from among battle-tested veterans of the Great War. Its small size allowed it to be the most aristocratic army of any for a century. The contrast is especially striking when drawn against the last peacetime army of the Empire, whose comparatively swollen ranks (nearly 900,000 men) forced it to reach farther down the social structure than it found comfortable. This was one factor that kept the German army from exceeding the size of the French. In view of its composition, the officer corps of the Republican *Reichswehr* was solidly conservative. The national spirit inherent in armed forces was also accentuated by the festering wounds of the 1918 defeat and the humiliations and restrictions of the Treaty.

Comparatively few elements of the *Reichswehr* fell prey to National Socialist agitation before Hitler took power. On the other hand, many officers and men adopted a positive attitude toward such Nazi programmes as reviving the national spirit, rearming, and more intensively pursuing the revision of the Treaty of Versailles. Such attitudes largely prevailed even among officers who later were most alienated from Nazi rule.

Significant, too, was a dichotomy between the command structure and the junior and middle grades. Many of the latter were inclined to recognise fresh, forward-looking viewpoints that held promise of a new era. The senior levels, however, hoped for a return to what they thought best in pre-war society, and their disappointments turned uneasiness into alarm. The extent of this reaction has frequently escaped students of the period because of two factors that are often overlooked. The first of these is the degree to which the regime, though exacting obedience, failed to win the hearts of most of the *Generalität* (general officers). The evidence lies in their reaction to 'treasonable' overtures. Except for an infinitesimal group of Nazi sympathisers, almost all active commanders in the period 1938–44 were approached. Men like Rundstedt, List, Manstein, Guderian, Beck and uncounted others were sounded out by 'recruiters', many of them on repeated occasions. (We leave aside such as did make some kind of commitment, such as Witzleben, Hoepner, Halder, Leeb, Heinrich von Stülpnagel, Falkenhausen and Speidel.) Yet there seems to have been only a single case, Fritz Fromm, in which the unwilling recruit obeyed regulations by reporting the situation to a superior. When one considers that failure to do so was an act of high treason punishable by death, it is remarkable that cases such as Fromm's occurred so rarely. It assuredly denotes a basic distaste if not detestation for the regime against which the plots were directed. A second aspect frequently overlooked in judging attitudes in the *Generalität* is the degree to which it had to be purged to assure Hitler a grip on those who remained. Of the military leaders he had inherited from the Republic, those who were still active in 1945 were mostly outright Nazis, crass opportunists, or *nur-Soldaten* (just soldiers) of limited horizons and purely professional outlook.

In the five years before 1938 a considerable number of prominent military figures were dismissed from their posts or even from the service entirely. The great purge of January–February 1938 claimed first and foremost the Minister of War, Werner von Blomberg, and the Army commander, Werner von Fritsch, who was relieved on trumped-up charges of homosexuality. Hitler took advantage of this moment of confusion for a wholesale clean-up. Fourteen top generals were summarily retired, and forty others switched to unfamiliar command environments. The new commander-in-chief, Walther von Brauchitsch, was both ill-equipped and ill-placed to stand up to the dictator. He felt totally at a loss in dealing with a man with so little regard for the amenities. As one in whom social graces had been implanted while serving as a page to Germany's last empress, Hitler's rude outbursts when roused to fury left him literally speechless. Brauchitsch's tortured responses to confrontations were doubtless augmented by the circumstances of his appointment. To enable him to take up a post of such dignity, Hitler had financed a divorce which his wife otherwise would not have granted. Even worse than this straightjacket of obligation was the probability of Hitler's knowing about the questionable background of his second spouse. Brauchitsch could scarcely doubt the danger of becoming troublesome. Indeed, Hitler may have appointed him because of this vulnerability.[1]

Taken together, these psychological handicaps were formidable obstacles to confronting Hitler on any issue or presenting an unwelcome opinion with the power of conviction. It scarcely eased matters that Brauchitsch also carried on his conscience the burden of the price exacted for his appointment. He had to promise to bring the Army closer to the National Socialist state and to sacrifice Chief of Staff Ludwig Beck if, as the very raising of the question made all but certain, Hitler should wish it. Thus, although Brauchitsch himself was troubled by Nazism, any inclination to do something about it was quickly stifled.

The most significant aspect of the Fritsch affair was its role as the prelude to the plot of September 1938. As Hitler repeatedly stated to his *Wehrmacht* adjutant, Captain Engel, he bitterly resented Fritsch and Beck building an Army with a largely defensive posture, something he considered a hindrance to his increasingly aggressive policies. He knew that few general officers shared his visions of Germany's future. As long as he publicly based his claims to Austria and the Sudetenland on self-determination, the generals, like most Germans and many persons abroad, were sympathetic. But his obsession with unlimited expansion and extreme racist fantasies generated little support. In any event, virtually the entire *Generalität* felt that another European war must be avoided at almost any cost. Beck largely shared his colleagues' attitudes, but thought far more deeply than they, and also recognised the wider implications. No doubt he hoped again to see Germany a European power, but he viewed the German situation much as Bismarck had done after the war with France, when he said that the new Empire was now just big enough to be tolerable for Europe. Further expansion would compel the other powers to combine against Germany. Thus an unbridgeable gap opened between Beck and Hitler. When one adds to Hitler's sense of grievance Beck's insistence that the General Staff was the 'conscience of the Army', and must be consulted before any call to arms, it is clear that a break was imminent. Hitler called Beck the 'saboteur' of his policies, said that he lived in the mentality of the 100,000-man Army, and claimed that he opposed war as such. Beck must therefore be made to disappear (*verschwinden*).[2]

The beginning of the end was signalled by Hitler's declaration to party, state and military leaders on 28 May 1938 that he was determined to smash Czechoslovakia. Two days later a directive to the service chiefs demanded readiness for action by the end of September. Brauchitsch, though deeply disturbed, could not summon the courage to confront Hitler on so fundamental an issue. Beck now sought to induce him to call on the *Generalität* for a general strike if Hitler persisted in his plan. Failing that, Brauchitsch should order Witzleben of Military District III (Berlin) to co-ordinate action with Chief of Police Count Helldorff for seizing control of the capital. This was to be done 'for the *Führer*', to free him from the nefarious influences surrounding him.

Politically unsophisticated as Brauchitsch undoubtedly was, he could hardly have been impressed by so naïve a formulation; and the problem with the dictator was almost daily growing worse. The most important of Beck's memoranda passed on to Hitler by Brauchitsch were left unread for a week. When Hitler did read them, he exploded to his military adjutants about Beck trying 'to discourage warlike intentions on my part'. Beck, he said, was 'lying' to him about the relative strength of the French and German forces by including the Mobile Guards and traffic police on the French side, and not even mentioning the SS and SA on the German.[3]

On 4 August Brauchitsch convened the Army group and corps commanders to hear Beck's appeal for solidarity to avert the catastrophe of a European war. This, the Chief of Staff insisted, would be the inevitable consequence of an attack on Czechoslovakia. He was warmly seconded by General Adam, who as group commander in the West had primary responsibility for fending off the French.[4] All but two commanders voiced basic agreement.

General von Reichenau insisted that the decision for peace or war was the *Führer*'s prerogative, and that he undoubtedly would do what was best. General Busch chimed in with fatuous remarks about the duty of soldiers to obey. Unanimity thus was not achieved, and the support of Brauchitsch had been lukewarm at best. Any impact on Hitler was further reduced when the weak-kneed Brauchitsch transmitted Beck's memorandum through the dismayed Captain Engel rather than presenting it himself. Hitler's first impulse was to dismiss Beck out of hand, but he was persuaded by Brauchitsch that so brusque a move would offend the *Generalität*. So Hitler determined to force Beck's resignation; and he set about doing so with adroit brutality. Addressing the chiefs of staff of the commanding generals on 10 August, and the latter themselves at an artillery exercise at Jüterborg on 15 August, he skilfully defended his decision on Czechoslovakia in terms insulting to the unnamed Beck. There was now no alternative to resignation, and Beck communicated his to Brauchitsch on 18 August. He was too much the creature of his profession to defy Hitler's order not to publicise his departure – a fateful feature in the following crisis, which he was to regret bitterly.

On 31 August Beck turned over his emptied desk to General Halder, who assumed his functions on the following day, together with the burden of directing the conspiracy which was now well along. Halder had hated the regime almost from its inception, and his denunciations of it had never lacked vehemence. During the Fritsch affair he had pressed so vigorously for action that it had led to some coolness between him and Beck. The latter's conversion had not much improved matters. Halder resented Beck's interminable meetings with Lieutenant-Colonel Oster of the *Abwehr*, and felt left out. The tone and manner of his post-war statements reveal this.[5] 'I believe your conception was the right one', Beck said in parting, 'Now it is up to you [to lead the take-over].'

Yet Halder believed that Beck had withheld much from him, and, his pride offended, may have decided to play something of a game of his own. He never felt completely in control in the following critical weeks. Awareness of the infinitely greater prestige of his predecessor was no doubt a psychological burden. It may have played some part in his decision not to engage in a systematic sounding of the corps commanders in the hope of committing them to support his plans. In July he had sounded out Hitler-hating Wilhelm Adam, and begged him to approach his friend Rundstedt. The wholly negative response of the latter to the completely committed Adam may have discouraged Halder from going any farther. In Berlin he already had ties with Witzleben, who had been enlisted originally by Hjalmer Schacht, the Reichsbank President and Minister of Economics. Unquestionably, Schacht was one of the two or three major instigators of the September plot. Though the Reich Cabinet was to meet no more after the previous February, his formal ministerial status carried weight with the hierarchically-minded *Generalität*. Halder wished to know him better, and paid Schacht a call that has been variously reported.[6]

Halder knew Witzleben's great prestige with his fellow corps commanders, and had told Adam in July that once Witzleben struck, he hoped the others would join in. The dichotomy of functions now agreed upon left Witzleben in charge of the seizure of the capital. Halder himself would signal the start of the *Putsch* and would see to it that Brauchitsch would step forward once Hitler was eliminated. He would further arrange the military deployment against Czechoslovakia in such a manner that troops would be available wherever they were needed for the coup.[7]

Considering its centrality in the scheme of things, Halder had little contact with the beehive of activity in *Abwehr* headquarters on Tirpitz Ufer. Until the arrest of Hans Oster and Hans von Dohnanyi in the spring of 1943, all conspiratorial threads were gathered in there. Being charged with collecting information at home and abroad (the former supposedly only in counter-intelligence work), the *Abwehr* was the eyes and ears of the conspiracy. Almost alone among government agencies, it seems never to have been penetrated by the SS. Most vital for the opposition were the key placements of Wilhelm Canaris and Hans Oster.

In both historical and fictional writing, as well as in films, the figure of Canaris rivals in the attention he has received such Nazi leaders as Goering, Goebbels and Himmler. Controversy about his personality and motivations will no doubt persist. For the purpose of this essay it must suffice to bear in mind that, after welcoming the Third Reich, Canaris became so utterly disillusioned that he set about assembling in the *Abwehr* directorate a core group of anti-Nazis, down to the secretaries. He was a moving spirit for action during the Fritsch crisis, and, through the spring of 1940, he played a vital part in all resistance projects. Thereafter, frustrated and the victim of a pronounced fatalistic streak, he confined himself to a supportive role.[8] Canaris was apprised of all plans and preparations for September 1938, but left an essentially free hand to those in his entourage who were the prime movers of revolt. Of these, Chief of Staff and Central Division head Oster was by far the most noteworthy. He was direct where Canaris was deliberate and at times devious, impulsive where the admiral was wary, and of an heroic mould that no one would ascribe to his chief. The final crossing of what he called his personal Rubicon came only during the war, when overthrowing the regime became inexorably linked to German victory or defeat. We know so much about how Oster pursued his cause that it is at times easy to overlook the gaps in our knowledge. Here and there one catches a glimpse of activities about which history has thus far been silent.[9] What we know about his part in the September plot is far from complete.

A study of the military in September 1938 must confine itself to the points at which the civilian sector interlocks with it. Civilian opponents, of course, knew that to overthrow the regime they needed the help of soldiers and policemen. The *Abwehr* was the most convenient meeting ground for their interconnected activities. Oster, in fact, would have been hard put to pursue his designs without the aid of civilian helpers whose fierce dedication matched his own. Three civilians and the spouse of one of them were the core of this support group. Their chief was Hans Bernd Gisevius. Though not yet associated with the *Abwehr*, he veritably haunted its offices, and jumped at any service Oster might assign him. One of the more controversial figures of opposition history, his extensive writings have been accused of embellishing his own role and disparaging those whom he disliked. Yet they are the only detailed source on many aspects of civilian resistance, and when used with caution, are indispensable.[10] Though Hans von Dohnanyi also did not yet belong to the *Abwehr*, he had forged links with its opposition leaders during the Fritsch crisis, when he had done yeoman work on behalf of the defence. The son of a famous musician, and linked through his wife to the distinguished Bonhoeffer family, he could reach into circles otherwise difficult to penetrate. For years in the Ministry of Justice he had assembled evidence of Nazi crimes. Theodor and Elisabeth Struenck had met Oster and Gisevius in their Düsseldorf home, and had moved to Berlin largely to be helpful and to be near the action. As persons of some means, who possessed a motor car and initially lived in the Hotel Continental, their services to the opposition were many and varied. Their quarters were always available for a conspiratorial rendezvous, and Frau Struenck was ever ready to help as a messenger, go-between and chauffeur. One can indeed think of her as a sort of secondary clearing-house.

From the *Abwehr* offices lines of communication ran into many other departments and agencies of government. They did not stop short of the Reich Chancellery and the SS. Fritz Wiedemann, Hitler's personal adjutant, reported to Oster and Dohnanyi on what went on around the *Führer*.[11] Gisevius had close ties with Arthur Nebe, one of Himmler's principal department heads (Criminal Police), who provided invaluable information about developments in the SS leadership. He had also cultivated a relationship with Count Helldorff, whose deputy, Fritz Dietlof von der Schulenburg, was a key member of the conspiracy. Most important in many ways were the links with the Foreign Office, where State Secretary (deputy minister) Baron von Weizsäcker protected a group that reached especially into the London and Rome embassies. Since service communications between the Foreign Office and the General Staff were prohibited, the *Abwehr* again was the channel. Canaris, who had regular dealings with the General Staff, was the principal go-between. Halder found him a difficult conversationalist, who dealt largely in allusions and kept pressing for action. He considered the *Abwehr* chief more of a fervent 'whipper-upper' (*Aufpeitscher*) than a doer. Oster replaced Canaris when he was away on business. Halder complained that Oster conveyed more of a 'burning hatred' of Hitler than the solid political orientation that was needed.

As conviction hardened that only the certainty of a European war resulting from an attack on Czechoslovakia could induce the generals to help overthrow the regime, the touchstone became the position of the western powers. To encourage the appropriate posture, a string of opposition missions beat a path to London and Paris during the summer of 1938. All but the first and the last of these are amply recorded in history; so discussion here will bear mainly on the missing links. Hitherto unknown is the mission of Carl Goerdeler a few weeks after his well-reported visits of March and April 1938. It was the immediate result of Hitler's having put the generals on notice of his intention to invade Czechoslovakia by 1 October. The major contact of the Goerdeler group in France was former Chancellor Joseph Wirth.[12] For some time he had been the chief informant of a French intelligence venture financed by Jewish bankers and assisted by the government.[13] In late May or early June Wirth brought three Germans to Manfred Simon, the executive arm of the committee which managed the operation. One of the three was a military man, but it was Goerdeler who did the talking. He described the villainous manoeuvre by which Hitler had rid himself of Fritsch. Now Hitler was planning to attack Czechoslovakia in the early autumn. If other means failed, the military leadership was prepared to forestall this by a *coup d'état*. He referred specifically to Beck, Halder, Heinrich von Stülpnagel and others. He also stressed the role of the *Abwehr*, and mentioned Oster and Canaris. None of these names could be confided to paper.[14] Goerdeler said it was vital that the western powers make clear that an attack on Czechoslovakia was equivalent to one upon themselves. Then the generals could count on the backing of a nation that was far from bellicose. He hoped to secure such assurances from Prime Minister Daladier and Foreign Minister Bonnet. Simon strongly advised against approaching the later arch-appeaser Bonnet. He personally drove Goerdeler, however, to Daladier's residence at about six o'clock the next morning for a meeting arranged by Alexis Léger, secretary general at the Quai d'Orsay.

That afternoon a dejected Goerdeler reported that Daladier, though cordial, had stated categorically that France could only do what Britain would do. Thus, all depended on London, to which Goerdeler then departed. There he would see Sir Robert Vansittart, Chief Adviser in the Foreign Office, and Frank Ashton-Gwatkin, head of its Department of Economics. He had already spoken with both during his March–April visit. When Simon next made his monthly report to Vansittart, who, together with Ashton-Gwatkin, was the official British contact for his intelligence operation, he encountered only cynicism: 'I don't see how these Germans can ask us to make their revolution for them.' Ashton-Gwatkin, who thought highly of Goerdeler, and in 1970 still expressed pride in having been his friend, deeply regretted Vansittart's rigid response.[15]

Goerdeler, who had gone to the very top in France, probably had hoped to see Chamberlain and Halifax in Britain, but either was discouraged by Vansittart's reception or by his refusal to mediate a meeting with them. The significance of Goerdeler's misfired *tour de force* for opposition history depends, of course, on who initiated the enterprise. It cannot be entirely ruled out that he acted on his own. That he travelled with two companions, one of them military, speaks against this. Most probably he dealt at least with Beck, whom he had known since 1935, and who was to use the same channel of communication with France three months later. That Halder was involved is hinted at by his enigmatic remark to Adam in late July that, 'without the foreknowledge of his superiors [i.e. Brauchitsch and Beck]', he had 'established relations with the English Cabinet'.[16] Did Halder really take so much on himself while only Deputy Chief of Staff? Or might he, Canaris and Oster, dismayed by Beck's hesitations, have cooked up the mission among themselves? These are questions that may never be answered. That the circle was a restricted one is suggested by the fact that, aside from Ashton-Gwatkin and the leaders of the French intelligence venture, none remained after 1945 to testify regarding Goerdeler's mission. The absence of evidence in declassified British documents says little. At least one reference there, concerning a conversation with Goerdeler in 1939 that is actually listed in the printed index, consists of only one page, blank but for a laconic 'to be released in 2015'.

As the fateful month of September drew near, a mood of desperate urgency about Western support took over in resistance ranks. In mid-August it spawned two missions which, though independent of one another, originated largely in *Abwehr* headquarters. The London trips of Ewald von Kleist and Colonel Boehm-Tettelbach appear to have been inspired by Oster, though authorised by Beck, and, in the second instance, also by Halder. The poor colonel never managed to penetrate government quarters. Kleist was more fortunate, and conducted himself well; but also could show no positive results. Equally well-known are two attempts by Weizsäcker to make an impression in London. He used his close friendship with the Swiss League of Nations High Commissioner in Danzig, Carl Jacob Burckhardt, to approach the British legation in Berne. The second endeavour presents the dramatic scene of Germany's official representative in London, *chargé d'affaires* Theo Kordt, tiptoeing through the garden gate of No. 10 Downing Street to orient no less a personage than Foreign Minister Halifax!

The latter mission must have played some role in Beck's acting in parallel to alert the French. It has hitherto been assumed that no such revelations as flooded London were extended to Paris, which was notorious for leaks of confidential information. Moreover, France, as Daladier had said, could be counted upon to do whatever Britain did. London, therefore, was a much more significant target than Paris. But, as the crisis deepened in the second week of September, Beck apparently determined not to leave even this final stone unturned. His posture in the critical days of September is certainly more nebulous than in any other phase of opposition history. Whatever cards he held were kept so close to his chest that scholars are uncertain of the game he was then conducting.[17] Halder insists that Beck kept all threads in his hands, and even played off various opposition centres against one another.[18] The truth may well lie in between: Beck was probably exercising a broad directive influence, but was taking no part in the action.

Sometime in mid-September Manfred Simon was alerted by ex-Chancellor Wirth that a major figure opposing Hitler would meet them in a hotel room in Basle. When Wirth and Simon entered the room in question, the man they encountered was the Chief of the German General Staff! Beck pleaded for France to remain firm in the prevailing crisis. The Hitler regime would be overthrown if it were made clear to the German army and people that an attack on Czechoslovakia meant a world war. The amazed Simon exclaimed: 'But how can generals accomplish this in a totalitarian state?' Beck solemnly responded that the situation was too precarious to reveal details. 'You know who I am and that I must know whereof I speak.'[19]

If Beck's excursion to the Swiss border town of Basle was something of an afterthought, the decision also to alert the United States must have been even more of an improvisation. It is the similarly hitherto untold story of what later befell Jacob Beam, then on the staff of the Berlin embassy.[20] Like other American diplomats such as Douglas Miller and Sam Woods, Beam was the occasional beneficiary of confidences from Erwin Respondik, former Reichstag whip of the Catholic Centre Party.[21] On an undetermined date in early or mid-September, Beam was invited to a *Herrenabend* (gentlemen's evening party) at Respondik's home. Other guests were a colonel of the *Luftwaffe*, introduced as a former deputy commander of the Richthofen squadron, and an academic named Muckermann. After the hostess withdrew, her husband pronounced: 'Now we can get to the business of the evening', and launched into a tirade against Hitler in which the airman happily joined. There followed the revelation of the existence of a conspiratorial group under Halder determined to assassinate Hitler and overthrow the regime if he moved to the brink of war.

Next morning Beam composed a memorandum for Ambassador Hugh Wilson, but showed it first to military attaché Truman Smith. Smith ridiculed such a story concerning German generals. Nevertheless, Beam forwarded the memorandum to the State Department, where it probably reached J. Pierrepont Moffat of the Western European Division. Beam never heard what happened to the matter thereafter. The purpose of this initial 'opening to Washington' can only have been to encourage the United States to recommend firmness to London and Paris. Respondik was something of a loner, and may have acted entirely on his own. On the other hand, he may have had something like a standing brief on opposition contacts with the American embassy. His pin-pointing of Halder reflects inside knowledge of what was afoot. Once again we see the tip of an informational iceberg, that may indicate the dimensions, but not the configuration, of what lay beneath.

The contours and much detail about plans and preparations for the September coup are well known; but there are disappointing gaps and formidable contradictions. Here and there, as evidenced in this study, unimagined angles may appear. Controversy is sure to continue on such central issues as Beck's place in the scheme of things. There are equal uncertainties on the role of Brauchitsch. At Nuremberg he was a sadly confused man, and made highly questionable statements.[22] He claimed to have known little or nothing about the September plot, and had certainly made no commitment. Halder testified that he was informed, and had agreed with the decision to press the button on 28 September. On that day Brauchitsch invited Fritsch to confer with him in his suite in the Hotel Continental, which can only mean that he sought to bring Fritsch into the picture at that point.[23] Fritsch's own role in September is close to a total riddle. During the summer he had received inklings of a planned *Putsch*, but understood so little about it that he feared others were taking chances for his sake, and sought to discourage it. To him Himmler was still the great villain, rather than Hitler.[24] We can only guess his response to Brauchitsch's overture.

Up to the last minute there were thus attempts to bring in further recruits. Witzleben and others kept worrying about the uninformed and uncommitted corps commanders. Several had been sounded out in some way during the Fritsch affair, and were regarded as safe once Hitler was eliminated. The key personage among the senior generals was, of course, von Rundstedt. Witzleben, who knew nothing of Halder's prior sounding via Adam, recognised Rundstedt's importance if he could be alerted and committed to action. To explore this possibility, Witzleben used a family gathering on 11 September (the birth of his first grandchild) to invite the wife of his cousin Hermann for a walk in his garden to tell her of the coup now lying just ahead. He wanted her advice, he said, on two soldiers she knew well; Rundstedt, in whose house she had 'virtually grown up', and Fritz Fromm, head of the *Allgemeines Heeresamt*, whom she and her husband met regularly at horse-shows. She disposed of Fromm in few words. Rundstedt's heart, politically speaking, she thought to be in the right place; but she could see no prospect of his taking any initiative.[25]

Oster and Canaris never ceased to enlarge the circle of conspirators or sympathisers. Canaris at this stage can indeed be labelled the 'circuit rider' of the opposition. When he regularly conferred with his representatives at corps headquarters he used such occasions to explore their political orientation, and, wherever possible, to enlist them in the opposition.[26]

As the month wore on, Halder's sorely tried nerves approached the breaking-point. When Captain Engel called on him (apparently on 26 September), he seemed 'a completely nervous and over-irritated person' who complained about being 'pursued and shadowed'. He laid a pistol on his desk, and proclaimed that he would not allow himself to be shot down.[27] There are uncertainties about Halder's post-war claim of having been about to press the button on 14 September when interrupted by the report of Chamberlain's coming to Berchtesgaden. At that moment the September plot seemed to be going into eclipse, only to be saved by Hitler's intransigence. About the Godesberg meeting of Hitler and Chamberlain the plotters had running reports from interpreter Paul Schmidt. Appeasement seemed on the way out.

The critical days were 27 and 28 September. On 27 September Hitler staged the military parade through Berlin that was meant to give the impression of units proceeding to the Bohemian frontier. He was, of course, hoping to whip up war sentiment in the Berlin population. But the immediate stimulus came from decoded intercepts of the British and French embassies, which pictured the mobilisation against Czechoslovakia as incomplete. The parade was thus a tactic in the prevailing war of nerves. Hitler's fury about the frigid response of the Berliners was somewhat allayed by new reports that the bluff was working with the Western embassies.[28] But the popular mood was apparently decisive with the dictator, and he allowed appeasement to take its course. On the 28 September he accepted Mussolini's London-inspired proposal for the meeting at Munich. Therewith, all prospect of Hitler's overthrow in September 1938 vanished.

To most of the German people, as well as to much of the *Generalität*, Munich could only appear a brilliant triumph of Hitler's policies. Many who had been sceptical of his capacities were shaken to the point of doubting their own judgement. Only in the autumn of 1939, when he became obsessed with a daft determination to launch a lightning war at the least suitable season of the year, did the generals again feel that he was heading for disaster. The result was a second round of the military conspiracy. As for Hitler, Munich left him more convinced than ever that the Army was the most unsure element in the state, worse, he told Reichenau, than the Church or the Ministry of Justice.[29] He had taken the sharpest issue with the plans and dispositions for the campaign against Czechoslovakia, and his insistence on changes was a harbinger of the dictatorial controls he was to impose upon the military during the war.

Those conspirators who lasted the course from 1938 to 1944 and survived the grisly climax of 20 July agreed that no later period could match in organisation or design the September 1938 rehearsal. The comings and goings thereafter of key military figures as the demands of their war service dictated, the unceasing purges of the best general officers, and finally the exigencies of life in the ruins of Berlin all inhibited continuity and compelled improvisation. In 1938 all Nazi power centres had been pinpointed and troops allotted to seize them. The faithful Frau Struenck had driven Witzleben and Brockdorff (the Potsdam divisional commander) over 2,000 kilometres about the city to accomplish this. The two commando-type troop formations designated for the Reich Chancellery had decided among themselves to kill Hitler while 'resisting arrest'. The wisdom of hindsight confirms that a *Führer* left alive for a show trial or psychiatric tests would have increased the odds against the plotters astronomically.

The might-have-beens of September 1938 crowd the pages of history, with the central questions clustering about the course of events if there had been no appeasement or if its high points had been slightly delayed. A key problem that has thus far escaped study in depth concerns the probable response to a coup of the field-grade officers and the Army rank-and-file. The vital feature again would have been the irrevocable elimination of Hitler. The same applies to the Navy and Air Force, where the known conspirators may be counted on the fingers of the hand. This was the phase of opposition history least sullied by anything like personal pique or ambition, and most noteworthy for moral dedication. In the early war period, when even pro-Nazis like Reichenau might have joined in to stop the insanity of an autumn offensive, the material factors were more evident. The same may be said of July 1944, when the hope of saving something from the wreck of the Reich might, after a successful start, have brought in such *nur-Soldaten* as Guderian.

As was the case throughout the history of the German resistance, the designs and groundwork of 1938 revealed the short-comings of amateur revolutionaries innocent of conspiratorial experience or aptitudes. Even so, as in the previous fumblings of the Fritsch crisis, the dress rehearsal of September had some value. It provided models of organisation and planning for a take-over that could be dusted off, refurbished and expanded.

NOTES

1. Hitler's actual knowledge is now established. Captain Engel tells of an outburst when Brauchitsch was about to dismiss from the Army a lieutenant who had made a girl of 'respectable' family pregnant, but wanted to marry her. Hitler shouted that he knew well with whom Brauchitsch had slept, and indeed lived, before his divorce. This was the general's own business; but the same was true of the lieutenant. The dismissal was immediately cancelled. Engel interview, 11 May 1970.
2. Engel interviews, 11 May and 24 June 1970.
3. Ibid.
4. W. Adam, *Memoirs* (MS), p. 455; interview with Walter Warlimont, 7 February 1970.
5. In a conversation with the author, 19 June 1958.
6. Schacht claimed that he was asked to take charge of foreign contacts in a new government. Schacht interview, 2 October 1969. Halder denied raising the topic. Halder letter to Helmut Krausnick, 14 July 1955, a copy of which was given by Helmut Krausnick to the author.
7. Ibid.; Halder interview, 19 June 1958.
8. For more full-length portraits by the author of Canaris and most of the personages appearing in this study, see H. Deutsch, *The Conspiracy against Hitler in the Twilight War*, Minneapolis, 1968, and *Hitler and his Generals: The Hidden Crisis of January–June 1938*, Minneapolis, 1974.
9. A prime example is Oster's systematic cultivation of the foreign military attachés. We know much about his wartime relations with the Dutchman, Guijsbertus Sas. Untold as yet are his close ties with Yugoslav attaché Vladimir Vauhnik, whom, with the consent of Canaris, he warned of the 6 April 1941 attack on Yugoslavia and the scheduled bombardment of Belgrade. Vauhnik does not mention Oster by name in his post-war memoirs, but told his brother Milos about the contact. Interviews with Milos Vauhnik, 30 September and 15 December 1969 and 9 April 1970. A copy of Vauhnik's statement on Oster is in the possession of the author.
10. The author first met Gisevius under OSS (Office of Strategic Services) auspices in June 1945, and got to know him well during later visits and encounters. When the personal factor is not too intrusive, he regards him as an insightful and basically reliable witness.
11. Wiedemann interview, 11 July 1970.
12. G. Ritter, *Carl Goerdeler und die deutsche Widerstandsbewegung*, Stuttgart, 1954, p. 257.
13. An analysis of this venture in *Intelligence and National Security*, known familiarly as the *Comité du Cirque*, has been completed by the author and awaits publication.
14. Simon recalled the names from memory, and may well have included some that became engraved in his recollections after the war. He insists that names were mentioned, and that the *Abwehr* chiefs were included.

320 *Harold C. Deutsch*

Simon interviews, 18 November 1969 and 13 April 1970.
15. Interview with Ashton-Gwatkin, 21 June 1970.
16. Adam MS, p. 252.
17. For example, N. Reynolds in his perceptive *Treason Was No Crime: Ludwig Beck, Chief of the German General Staff*, London, 1976.
18. Halder interview with Helmut Krausnick, 11 October 1952.
19. André Meyer and Georges Wormser of the *Comité du Cirque* confirm (interviews on 27 October 1972 and 8 May 1973) that Simon reported to their Committee on his return from Basle, and that the information was transmitted to Alexis Léger, who in a general way confirmed this (interview, 12 April 1970). Hans Speidel, who commanded a battalion at Mannheim in south-west Germany, had a surprise visit from Beck (they were sons of cousins) in mid-September. Beck gave him details of the Fritsch affair, and stressed how much he regretted not having acted then. He added, 'I know that I can depend on you.' Beck's niece and nephew, children of his brother, tell of his surprise visit to Biebrich about the time of their parents' wedding anniversary (16 September), and the girl's amazement that he should have come from Basle. Interviews with Walter Beck and Gertrud Newbauer, née Beck, 29 May and 10 June 1970.
20. Beam interview, 16 December 1974.
21. Only many years after the war did it become known that Respondik was Sam Woods's informant on Hitler's plans to attack the Soviets.
22. Such as that he had never talked with Gisevius; but Elisabeth Struenck engineered the meeting and watched some of its progress. Interview, 18 April 1970.
23. Interview with Colonel Otto Heinz Grosskreuz, 15 January 1970. Grosskreuz stood watch in the hallway while the meeting was in progress.
24. Letter of General Hans von Salmuth, to whom Fritsch addressed these sentiments, to Helmut Krausnick, 7 August 1955.
25. Conversations with Hermann and Ursula von Witzleben, 9 and 11 February 1970. Apparently unaware that Witzleben was playing with the same idea, Halder sounded out Fromm about this time, and found him non-committal. A later attempt by Halder to enlist him (31 October 1939) led to Fromm's covering himself by a formal report to Brauchitsch. Letter of Halder to Hermann von Witzleben, 4 June 1953. Fromm appears to have been the sole officer of the Hitler period who reported an attempt to enlist him in a conspiracy.
26. The story of the later General von Pfuhlstein illustrates dramatically how Canaris worked on such occasions. He approached only the wives of those of whose attitude he could also feel sure. Interview with Alexander von Pfuhlstein, 14 February 1970. Especially fascinating is the case of Renate Piekenbrock. Her husband, probably the ablest of Canaris's lieutenants in the *Abwehr*, was not a conspiratorial activist, but nevertheless knew well what was in progress. When telling Canaris of his coming marriage he confided that the bride-to-be was a

fanatical Nazi; Canaris smiled: 'Let that be my business.' He wrought so well that in time she would not blink when the best ways of assassinating Hitler were debated in her presence. Interview with Renate Piekenbrock, 21 February 1970.

27. G. Engel, *Heeresadjutant bei Hitler, 1938–1943*, Stuttgart, 1974, p. 35.
28. Ibid., pp. 39–40.
29. Ibid., p. 41.

17

Individual Loyalty and Resistance in the German Military: The Case of Sub-Lieutenant Oskar Kusch

Heinrich Walle

In a dark prison cell, two chess-players sit at a table. The candle-light makes the haggard features of one of the players stand out in a menacing fashion. He has obviously just checkmated his opponent, who sits with his back facing the beholder. The loser of the game slumps dejectedly in front of the table, propping his head against his right arm full of resignation. This gloomy picture is a charcoal drawing made by Sub-Lieutenant Oskar Heinz Kusch in a cell of the Kiel–Wik Naval Prison shortly before his execution by firing-squad on 12 May 1944. It expresses, in a deeply moving way, all the despair and hopelessness of the 26-year-old officer who has portrayed himself in the figure of the loser, thus expressing with this drawing that he was hopelessly in the hands of a diabolical power embodied in the figure of his death-like opponent.

The drawing was apparently first published in the collection of documents entitled *Gegen den Strom*,[1] which appeared in 1958. It was published again, along with three other drawings by Kusch, in the novel *Wer das Schwert nimmt*,[2] which appeared in 1987. The novel describes the wartime experiences of two naval officers of the Class of 37A (that is, call-up year 1937), 'Count Torra' and 'Oskar Burk'. Thanks to the painstakingly described episodes, it was not difficult to establish that the author had based his novel on his own experiences and on those of his friend and class-mate, Oskar Kusch.

Klenck/Luttitz, quite obviously aware of what actually happened, has related, above all, the tragic fate of Oskar Kusch, even if the character of 'Oskar Burk' in the novel differs in certain respects from the figure on which it is modelled.

The Kusch case is very well documented. The files covering his trial are almost completely extant, from his three and a half months of imprisonment until his execution.[3] The legal proceedings conducted against Kusch's judges in 1949 and 1950 have been documented by Jörg Friedrich in his compilation published in 1983.[4] In the same year, former Commander Gerd Nehls, writing in Letter II/83 of the Class of 37A, recalled Oskar Kusch, and published some statements by class-mates who had known him more closely.[5] In 1986, Rear-Admiral Karl Peter compiled an as yet unpublished account of Kusch entitled: 'Der Fall des Oberleutnants zur See Kusch: "Wider besseres Wissen zum Tode verurteilt". Stimmt das?' ('The Case of Sub-Lieutenant Kusch: "Sentenced to Death Against Better Judgement" – Is this Statement True?').[6] In this account, retired Admiral Peter has reproduced, among other things, some of the court files and the sentence and the grounds for the sentence, but above all statements and comments by naval officers who knew Kusch and were acquainted with his case. He has also described the efforts made by Kusch's father after the war to get his son rehabilitated, and has published remarks made by his defence counsel, who pleaded the case in court in 1949 and 1950, together with a statement by Kusch's former navigator aboard submarine U 154 on its first war patrol under Kusch's command. The most recent author to recall Kusch's fate was Lothar Günther Buchheim, in his third illustrated volume about the U-boat war, published in 1988.[7] Probably the most comprehensive appreciation of Oskar Kusch is in Karl Peter's collection of documents. However, he – like the other authors – did not have all the existing files at his disposal.[8] Thus the publications hitherto dealing with the Kusch case have only used the sentence, the grounds for the sentence and the record of the execution, while not considering the other files, which are, however, the crucial sources for providing an answer to the question of whether Oskar Kusch is to be considered part of the military resistance against Hitler and the Nazi regime.

Who Was Oskar Kusch?

Oskar Heinz Kusch was born in Berlin on 6 April 1918.[9] At the age of ten, he joined the *Bündische Jugend* youth organisation,[10] in which he was a member of the *Deutsche Freischar* and later of the *Deutscher Pfadfinderbund* (German Boy Scouts). In 1933 his *Bund* was transferred to the *Jungvolk* of the Hitler Youth (HJ) and, until 1935, he belonged to the corps of honour of the HJ unit in Berlin-Charlottenburg. In the same year, the process of *Gleichschaltung* was finally completed, and for that reason Kusch left the Hitler Youth. He had been a *Scharführer* (troop leader) in his youth group,[11] and had for a time led a 'Group Oskar'.[12] This 'transfer' of groups from the *Bündische Jugend* to the Hitler Youth was part of the destruction of all independent, political and religious youth organisations by the new rulers. After 30 January 1933 the Hitler Youth alone, as the official state youth organisation, was to have a monopoly on extra-curricular youth education.

Kusch must have experienced personally the terror associated with the crushing of the youth organisations and their *Gleichschaltung* during his time at secondary school. In 1944 he was accused of having made remarks to the effect that he 'had never belonged to the Hitler Youth, but to the *Bündische Jugend*, which had resisted the pretensions of the Hitler Youth. In fact, he said, there had also been a charge against him, and he had almost been arrested, as some of his friends were; but the fact that he had been accepted into the Navy led to the affair's being forgotten.'[13] In the autumn of 1936 Kusch took his school-leaving examination at the Hohenzollerngymnasium in Berlin, and subsequently served his compulsory period in the Reich Labour Service (RAD) until April 1937.[14] However, he was still evidently in touch with his friends in the former *Bündische Jugend*: according to information supplied by the Berlin Gestapo, dated 26 January 1944, he had written letters while in the RAD to his ex-group leader expressing himself in 'blunt terms'[15] about the Labour Service. The RAD had obviously censored letters without the knowledge of the sender.

On 3 April 1937 Kusch joined the German Navy as an officer cadet. He thus belonged to the class of 37A, the naval officer cadet groups still being officially named after the year in which they entered. Kusch decided to take up the profession of a naval officer for several reasons. Two of these were undoubtedly patriotism and the desire to participate in the defence of Germany. Fascination with the Navy, seafaring, *wanderlust*, the romantic appeal of distant countries, the attraction of the technological perfection of modern warships and on-ship camaraderie, as well as the international traditions of the Navy, probably also influenced the young Kusch – along with many of his class-mates – in his choice of profession.[16]

However, the accusations made by Sub-Lieutenant Abel[17] also indicate a further motive: by applying to become an officer cadet, Kusch had tried to escape persecution by Nazi Party officials. At that time, *Wehrmacht* servicemen were still not allowed to be members of a political party, including the NSDAP. The *Wehrmacht* – and above all the Navy – was considered by many people to be a kind of island on which it was possible to elude the direct influence of the Party. It is apparent from many individual accounts by former *Wehrmacht* officers and from the biographies of those who were later involved in the military resistance that it is quite legitimate to consider Kusch's 'escape' to the Navy as a serious motive for his choice of profession.

After successfully completing the customary naval officers' training with his class, Kusch was promoted to midshipman on 25 August 1939.[18] From May 1939, until he was transferred to U-boats on 1 April 1940, he served on the cruiser Emden. On 29 July 1940, after a few intermediate assignments, he commenced his training in the U-boat Instructional Division. On 25 June 1941 Kusch received his first active assignment as officer of the watch on U 103, which operated in the northern, western and central Atlantic. From June to August 1941 he served as second officer of the watch under the command of Lieutenant-Commander Victor Schütze, and from August 1941 to July 1942 under Lieutenant Werner Winter. On 1 September 1942 he was promoted to Sub-Lieutenant, and on 10 November 1941 awarded the Iron Cross (Second Class) and the U-boat badge for his achievements as officer of the watch. From July 1942 to 7 February 1943, Kusch served as first officer of the watch under Lieutenant Gustav-Adolf Janssen. On 24 June 1942, he was awarded the Iron Cross (First Class). On 8 February 1943 Kusch assumed command of U 154.[19] His days as a U-boat commander came to an end after two sea patrols, when he was arrested for sedition on 20 January 1944.[20]

His penultimate commander, Lieutenant Werner Winter,[21] described Kusch's service on U 103 in his evaluation report in the following manner:

> Kusch has developed into an excellent young officer. He has matured in the war; his impeccable disposition, his fine aptitude and quickness of mind make him a valuable aid to the commander. As a superior he is warm-hearted and cheerful, but also firm towards his subordinates. He is artistically inclined and very well educated. In the face of the enemy he has always shown great tenacity, bold daring tempered by careful consideration, a high degree of reliability and a sense of responsibility. His knowledge is very good and he masters his tasks in all situations. As weapons control officer he has always been accurate,

prudent and very reliable. . . . After his next patrol as first officer of the watch, he will be very well qualified to be a U-boat commander.[22]

After his first war patrol as Commander of U 154, the Commander of the Second U-boat Flotilla, Commander Ernst Kals, who had also been awarded the Knight's Cross,[23] wrote that Kusch was well-qualified to be a U-boat commander.[24]

Remarks by his class-mates, made from memory thirty-nine years after his death and with no knowledge of the files, round off the picture of Kusch's character. Commander Victor Nonn, a successful and highly decorated U-boat commander (German Cross in Gold), described him as: '. . . actually a very quiet fellow-sailor who liked to be spoken to, but who also came out of his shell in the course of discussions and was quite able to put his views into words. His opinion counted for something. He was hard-working . . . quick-witted and very prompt to react.'[25] Lieutenant Heinz Wolff noted that: 'He was an intelligent, very sensitive person, who was very withdrawn but never unlikeable. I had the feeling that he enjoyed being a naval officer and was thus very ambitious. He always behaved in a comradely manner.' Commander Eberhard Wallrodt stated:

> The 'crime' he was accused of was committed by more or less all of us: listening to enemy radio stations and talking disparagingly about the bigwigs. I can, for instance, remember very well a heated discussion around the fireplace of the officers' mess in Mürwik, where we – company commanders and training unit chiefs – were not willing to agree with the new commander, Captain Wolfgang Lüth, that Heinrich Himmler was a competent man of integrity.

Former navigator Chief Petty Officer Heinrich Lüdmann, who acted as third officer of the watch on the first patrol of U 154 under Kusch's command, told Admiral Peter on 24 April 1985: 'Kusch was an upstanding man and a brave officer and, what is more, a devout Christian [Catholic]. In his cabin there was not only a crucifix, but also – above his bunk – a small metal altar.' Lüdmann also remembers with gratitude the many discussions which Kusch had with him. He stresses that Kusch did occasionally – even in the presence of others – 'make teasing remarks', but never negative ones, about the system and Hitler (as he was later to be accused of doing).[26] In a personal souvenir album Lüdmann had written, under the picture of the commander, a brief account of Kusch's tragic fate, in which he gave expression to the esteem in which he held him: 'If the party member and Hitler supporter, Dr Abel, had not been on board U 154 with us, our fine commander would never have been court-martialled. The "submariner spirit" was different.'[27]

In the evaluation reports written by his direct military superiors – both of whom were outstanding, successful and experienced U-boat commanders – Kusch was said to possess all the qualifications that an officer required to command a U-boat successfully under wartime conditions. His last two commanders, Werner Winter and Gustav-Adolf Janssen, must have thought very highly of him, as is apparent from the glowing report written by Winter, who was later also named by Kusch as a character witness, and unequivocally spoke up for him in his statement to the court-martial. In his evaluation report, Winter remarked that Kusch was 'warm-hearted and cheerful, but also firm towards his subordinates'. Winter also mentioned Kusch's artistic inclinations in his evaluation report. The pictures published by Arno Klönne and Klenck/Luttitz which Kusch had drawn in his death cell clearly demonstrate his artistic talent, which is also referred to in a letter from his friend, First-Lieutenant Dieter Berger, dated Berlin, 1 March 1944.[28]

Because of his intellectual and artistic inclinations, to which his class-mates also attested, Kusch did not fully correspond to the prototype of a U-boat officer, despite his excellent military knowledge. A sensitive and reflective man, Kusch obviously sensed this, and consequently behaved in such a withdrawn manner. Given the cramped living conditions on board a U-boat, this was bound to lead to disagreements with subordinate officers, who could neither share nor empathise with this attitude. Thus when Kusch encountered a fanatical adherent of National Socialism and an ambitious older reserve officer of the same rank, who obviously also fancied himself to be professionally superior to him, the fatal conflict was inevitable.

Oskar Kusch as Commander of U 154

U 154, of which Kusch assumed command on 8 February 1943, was a large Type IX C ocean-going submarine.[29] It had been commissioned in 1941, and belonged to the Second U-boat Flotilla, stationed at that time at Lorient. Its commander was Ernst Kals. The Flotilla was under the control of the 'Commander of U-boats in the West', Captain Hans Rudolf Rösing.

The U-boat campaign reached its peak in the spring of 1943. After great initial successes, the enemy's defences had improved to such a degree that, from March onwards, German losses started to assume increasingly threatening proportions. In May 1943 they were so heavy – 43 sinkings – that Admiral of the Fleet Karl Dönitz was forced to discontinue the 'Battle of the Atlantic', and ordered his U-boats to withdraw to more remote parts of the ocean, where the threat posed by the enemy was considered to be less serious. The U-boat war had thus been lost for good.[30]

Kusch took over his vessel at a time when it was no longer possible for single U-boats to achieve major successes, and when simply surviving a patrol and returning home safely was an achievement which required great skill and luck. Kusch was fully aware of the technological inferiority of his U-boat type, and, according to witnesses, made no secret of what he thought.[31] Similarly, he regarded the radio messages received under the code-word 'Rose', designed to enhance the Navy's fighting spirit, as 'whip-cracking' and 'slave-driving'.[32] Just how seriously Admiral Dönitz took his order to 'stick it out' is shown by his 'Decree to Counter the Mania for Criticism and Grumbling', dated 9 September 1943, in which he demanded: 'Grumblers who openly transmit their pathetic attitude to their fellow sailors or other German citizens, thereby crippling their will to assert themselves forcefully, are to be mercilessly called to account before a court-martial for sedition.'[33]

On 20 March 1943, U 154 left Lorient and operated initially off the Brazilian coast. On 8 May, it torpedoed a tanker off Recife, but the vessel did not sink because of torpedo failure.[34] On 15 May, U 154 was refuelled by U-boat tanker U 460. Kusch noted in its visitor's book: 'After 9 weeks at sea we have still not sunk anything – a bitter fate. The new fuel and rations make it easier for us to bear this.'[35] U 154 now transferred its area of operations to the Caribbean, where, on 27 May, it encountered a convoy of twelve steamers and five screening vessels. It succeeded in sinking one ship, and two others were hit by torpedoes but did not sink. The submarine was often attacked from the air, and did not succeed in sinking any more ships. At the end of June, it started its return journey to Lorient. It passed through the Bay of Biscay – a particularly dangerous region – together ·with U 126, so that the two U-boats could give each other covering fire in the event of air raids. During the night of 2–3 July 1943 there was a surprise air raid, which claimed U 126 and its entire crew within eyesight of U 154. U 154 reached its base on 6 July. On 25 September 1943 Kusch set sail on his final patrol. The area of operations was once again the Caribbean. U 154 did not succeed in approaching a convoy, and was once again the target of numerous air raids. U 154 returned to Lorient on 20 December 1943 without having succeeded in sinking any ships.

Following Kusch's arrest for sedition, Lieutenant Gemeiner took over command of his submarine.[36] In the spring of 1944 he undertook a patrol to the Caribbean, and was likewise unable to sink any ships using torpedoes. On 3 July 1944, while setting sail on a new mission, U 154 and its entire crew were the victims of an American anti-submarine force east of the Azores.[37] The sea area around the West Indies had still been a worthwhile theatre of operations for the U-boats in 1942. However, from 1943 onwards the Americans had considerably reinforced and perfected their anti-submarine defences in this region, with the result that almost complete surveillance by superior air and naval forces had been achieved. The American historian G. T. M. Kelshall has established that, in 1943, 40 individual submarines carried out 45 missions in the Caribbean, and were only able to sink 31 ships and damage one other. In 1942, such a result was the monthly average in the area.[38]

Denunciation, Arrest, Sentence and Execution

The former first officer of the watch of U 154, Reserve Sub-Lieutenant Dr Ulrich Abel, denounced Kusch in a report dated 12 January 1944, with the following words: 'On 2 missions, with a total of 189 days on patrol in the course of 1943, I repeatedly experienced unmistakable signs of an attitude on the part of Kusch which was strongly opposed to the political and military leadership of Germany. I therefore consider him incapable of being a U-boat commander.'[39] Abel then proceeded to enumerate in eleven points the following accusations against Kusch:

1. In March 1943, shortly before setting sail on his first patrol as commander, Kusch had had the only picture of Hitler on board the U-boat removed from the officers' mess and replaced by a 'strange picture of a ship which he had painted himself, saying: "Take that picture away, we don't worship idols here!"'

2. In numerous discussions, Kusch's strongly 'anti-National Socialist', 'totally unpatriotic and unmilitary' attitude had been apparent. His exact words are said to have been: 'Only the overthrow of Hitler and his party can bring peace and a cultural rebirth for the German people. If the German people summon up

the energy for this overthrow, the others will be prepared to conclude peace with us. Indeed, the people are suffering terribly under the burden of this regime, and not until it is removed will the true energies of the people be able to flourish.'

3. Abel retold one of the so-called 'whispered jokes' that were circulating among the population at that time, and which Kusch had circulated among the crew: 'What do the German people and a tapeworm have in common? Answer: They are both surrounded by a brown mass and in permanent danger of being killed.'

4. Critical remarks by Kusch about the Hitler Youth, which have been mentioned earlier.

5. A description of how Kusch had warned the two *Fähnriche* (midshipmen) attached to his U-boat on the first voyage against Nazi propaganda, and had told them to submit such statements to critical analysis. Abel hastened to add that he had exhorted the cadets to show 'unconditional loyalty to the present-day leaders' and to the *Führer*.

6. Kusch described the *Führer* as an 'insane utopian, megalomaniacal and pathologically ambitious'. He has it from a reliable source that 'the *Führer* often has fits, rants and raves, pulls the curtains down and rolls around on the floor'.

7. A mention of Kusch's remarks on the 'Code-word Rose' radio messages, which have already been quoted.

8. 'Kusch scarcely doubts that the Reich will be defeated in this war. . . . He is convinced that the war will be terminated by Germany's defeat before the end of this year. In his opinion, this will in no way be a disaster, since the Western Powers do not want to destroy us and will protect us against Russian incursions.'

9. References to the reasons for such a defeat – the shortage of equipment and total obsolescence of the current type of U-boat.

10. Kusch's contention that the alleged objective of world Jewry to destroy Germany is nothing but a propaganda lie, and the suggestion that Kusch obtained his political information by listening to enemy radio stations.

11. The statement that Kusch was of the opinion that enemy air raids on German cities were directed primarily against military targets.

332   *Heinrich Walle*

In a further paragraph, Abel stated:

> What seems particularly dangerous to me is the fact that Kusch simply thrust his views upon us officers and always pronounced them in such a way that at least some ratings and NCOs were bound to hear them, i.e. at least the radio operator at the sound locator, the cook and the officers' messman. However, Kusch also did not shrink from revealing his views on the conduct of the war, etc., in the control room.

Abel concluded by referring to a lack of fighting spirit which Kusch, in view of his inner attitude, had demonstrated on three occasions, which he (Abel) would deal with in more detail in a separate report. Abel apologised for not having submitted his report to the flotilla commander immediately after entering port on 20 December 1943; but he had still been undecided. 'I did not make my decision until the commander, at a meeting of officers on 23 December, had commented particularly forcefully on the war situation. Moreover, I had one more talk with Kusch which did not lead to any result.'

After entering port at Lorient, Kusch had to write an evaluation report on his First Officer of the Watch, because Abel had been transferred to the Third U-boat Instructional Division, where he was to attend the preparatory course for assuming command of a submarine. In the report, dated 25 December 1943, Kusch, although critical of Abel's 'inflexibility, rigidity and one-sidedness', nevertheless confirmed Abel's suitability to be a front-line U-boat commander, and concluded by saying that he was a good officer of average talent.[40] This evaluation report was acknowledged by Flotilla Commander Kals and the Commander of U-boats in the West, Captain Rösing. It was not usual at that time for evaluation reports to be disclosed to those evaluated. However, it must be assumed that Abel knew exactly how he had been assessed by his commander. The fact that the commander, who was six years younger and not university-educated, had written of the doctor of laws holding the same rank that his thinking and behaviour were marked by inflexibility, rigidity and one-sidedness must have hurt Abel badly. Kusch stated that there was no harmony between himself and Abel, which, given the cramped conditions on board a U-boat, must have led to quarrels during the long periods at sea, as may be inferred from some of the accusations the latter brought against him. Kusch himself explained the origins of the report by the total difference in character between himself and his accuser.

When criticised for having reported his commander for personal reasons, Abel replied, when questioned on 24 January 1944, that he had not written his report 'out of spite'.[41] Under the 1939 'Ordinance on Reporting by the People'[42] every German aged eighteen and over was obliged immediately to report any derogatory remarks about the Nazi regime, or face the most severe penalties as an accessory. In Abel's report of 12 January 1944, accusations were made relating to incidents that had happened on Kusch's first patrol in the spring of 1943, and which consequently should have been reported in July after sailing into Lorient. The unpleasant impression that Abel waited until a further mission was over to commit his accusations to paper remains, despite its being cloaked by the reference to his conflict of conscience, the fruitless discussion with Kusch, and the speech by the flotilla commander on 23 December 1943. In his collection of documents, Karl Peter reports that apparently several of Kusch's superiors attempted to get Abel to withdraw his report or at least to tone it down, but that Abel rejected such requests. Captain Claus Korth, himself a successful U-boat commander and holder of the Knight's Cross, claims to remember that even Admiral von Friedeburg, then Commanding Admiral of U-boats, attempted personally to get Abel to change his mind.[43] However, this conflicts with the statement made by Kusch's classmate, Georg Bohlken, who thinks he can remember that Friedeburg later refused to reprieve Kusch because of the 'fundamental significance of the case.'[44]

On 20 January 1944 Sub-Lieutenants Funke and Druschel, Kusch's fellow crew-members on U 154, were questioned as the first witnesses by Naval Judge Advocate Dr Hans Egon Breinig. The 38-year-old reserve officer Funke stated:

> The report by Sub-Lieutenant Dr Abel dated 12 January 1944, page 1 of the file, has been disclosed to me. It reflects the general opinion of the officers of our submarine based on our observations of our commander, Sub-Lieutenant Kusch. It corresponds to the general agreement by the officers to submit, through the senior officer, a report on our experience with the commander.[45]

Funke then spoke about the accusations relating to Kusch's remarks on the last mission, which he confirmed in full. In addition, he stated that Kusch had repeatedly made these remarks, and that they thus reflected his inner conviction:

> . . . which he also tried to thrust upon us. [This sentence was underlined in pencil by Breinig.] These statements appeared especially dangerous to me, if I think what effect they might have on younger, impressionable and immature officers. Luckily, we were older reserve

officers and were not impressed in the slightest by these remarks. Nor was the younger chief engineer, Sub-Lieutenant Druschel, who was in fact a regular officer, impressed. He was in full agreement with us as far as our rejection of the person of the commander was concerned.

Funke claimed that Kusch had 'tried to impose his opinion on the medical captain' [the words 'tried to impose' were also underlined by Breinig]. Funke went on to describe how Kusch had listened to foreign news broadcasts with the loudspeaker volume turned down, and then passed on this information to his officers. [This whole passage was heavily underlined by Breinig.]

In his statement, 23-year-old Sub-Lieutenant Kurt Druschel confirmed all the accusations made by Abel, with the exception of item 4; he claimed he could not remember Kusch making disparaging remarks about the Hitler Youth. As evidence additional to Abel's report, he stated that Kusch had said: '. . . that in the event of an overthrow he would be one of those marching to Berlin, if this took place following defeat in the war. He would then help to shoot the members of the present regime, whom he called war criminals'. [The words 'help to shoot' were underlined in pencil by Breinig.] He [Kusch] said that the *Führer* had been working towards a war for years, and had started it. On another occasion, Kusch said: 'Germany can only achieve an acceptable peace if the current regime is removed and a military dictatorship installed in its place.' Both Funke and Druschel swore to their evidence. The other witnesses from Kusch's crew made their statements during the trial in Kiel on 26 January 1944.

It seems clear from the words of Abel, Funke and Druschel that Dr Abel was the initiator of this tragedy, that he found an obviously like-minded person in Funke, and that both of them had dragged the considerably younger Druschel into their denunciation. The unpleasant fact that this may almost have amounted to a plot by the officers of a warship against their commander is apparent from Funke's introductory remarks. Judge Advocate Breinig must also have felt this when, in his questioning of Abel on 24 January, he grilled him at length about the motives behind his report. Abel not only denied having acted against his commander out of personal motives, but also stated emphatically that 'he had not spoken again to Druschel at all, nor had they written to each other about this case, especially after he [Druschel] had gone on leave [probably after 23 December 1943]'.[46] What is also striking is the obvious endeavour by Funke in his report to exonerate Druschel. For his part, Druschel had also had a strained relationship with his commander, as is apparent from the remarks made by Kusch during his hearing on 21 January 1944.[47]

Nevertheless, in view of the fact that the statements made by the three officers amounted to a serious charge of sedition, the suspicion that the true reason for this denunciation may have lain in a personal aversion to a military superior was dropped. Already, submariners were aware of the outrageous nature of this incident, namely that a commander who could not be accused of any misdemeanours whatsoever, was being denounced by his officers and thus sent to his death. Captain Jeppener, at the time responsible for personnel administration for U-boat officers, has stated: 'There was a lot of talk about this affair among submariners. . . . We were shocked that a submariner could be charged with something like this. And we could not understand the officer who had submitted the report. He was doing nobody a good turn.'[48]

On January 1944, the Commander of the Second U-boat Flotilla Kals instituted preliminary proceedings against Sub-Lieutenant Kusch for 'sedition, insulting the Reich and so-called atrocity propaganda'.[49] On the same day, an arrest warrant was issued. On 20 January 1944 Kusch was committed to Angers Military Prison, and shortly afterwards transferred to Kiel, where he was committed to Kiel-Wik Naval Prison on 25 January 1944.[50] Because most witnesses had to be summoned, the date of the trial was fixed for 26 January 1944 at Kiel, since it was easiest to gather the witnesses there.

On 25 January 1944 Dr Abel submitted a supplement to his report of 12 January in which he accused his former commander of having failed on three occasions to show 'the necessary fighting spirit' because of personal fear. He stated that, at the end of March, Kusch had not been resolute enough in pursuing a convoy reported by reconnaissance aircraft in the Atlantic; that in the case of the convoy attacked on 27 May 1943, Kusch could have sunk far more ships if he had shown more courage; and that in November 1943, out of cowardice, he had deliberately not approached a sighted convoy in such a way as to permit firing.[51] Since this additional report dealt with purely tactical questions, the court lacked the technical knowledge to evaluate the charges made therein, and therefore appointed as an expert witness Lieutenant Wilhelm Franken who, as a U-boat commander, had been awarded the Knight's Cross of the Iron Cross on 30 April 1943.[52] On January 1944 this experienced U-boat commander refuted Abel's accusations of 'cowardice in the face of the enemy'. Franken stated that Kusch had probably made false estimations, as sometimes happened among young, inexperienced commanders, and that his indecision in those situations should not necessarily be taken as a sign of cowardice.[53] In the subsequent trial, the court did not go into these accusations any further.

The trial commenced in Kiel at 9 a.m. on Wednesday, 26 January 1944, as a 'public session of the Court-Martial of the Commander of U-boats in the West'.[54] The judge was Naval Chief Judge Advocate Karl Heinrich Hagemann; the counsel for the prosecution Naval Judge Advocate Dr Hans Egon Breinig; and the military assessors Lieutenant-Commander Wolfgang Dittmers and Sub-Lieutenant Otto Westphalen, who was a U-boat commander himself, and who had been appointed to this office by pure chance, because he happened to be in Kiel on official business at the time.[55] Kusch was defended by the Kiel lawyer and notary Gerhard Meyer-Grieben. Seven witnesses had been summoned to the trial: Sub-Lieutenants Dr Abel, Druschel, and Meyer, Medical Captain Dr Nothdurft, and the former *Fähnriche* (in the meantime *Oberfähnriche*), Kirchhammer and Fröhlich. At Kusch's suggestion, his former commanders, Lieutenant-Commander Winter and Lieutenant Janssen, had also been called. Sub-Lieutenant Funke was unable to attend the trial.

In accordance with the bill of indictment dated 25 January 1944, Kusch was accused of crimes against Section 5, Paragraph 1, Sub-Paragraphs 1 and 2 of the 'Special Wartime Penal Code' (KSSVO) dated 17 August 1938, and under Section 1 of the 'Ordinance Concerning Extraordinary Radio Measures' dated 1 September 1939.[56] The most serious charges were the accusations falling under Section 5 of KSSVO, which governed the penalties for crimes of 'sedition'.[57]

The trial, which was attended by several officers from the staff of the Commanding Admiral of U-boats, went off quietly and without dramatic scenes; Kusch is said to have made a calm, self-assured and totally normal impression.[58] He did not make any inflammatory speeches against the Nazi regime in court.[59] After all the evidence had been heard, the counsel for the prosecution demanded a total sentence of ten years and six months imprisonment, along with forfeiture of the right to serve in the armed forces and loss of civil rights. The court did not go along with this demand, but instead sentenced Oskar Kusch 'to death and one year's imprisonment for continued sedition and listening to foreign radio stations'. The defendant was also to forfeit his right to serve in the armed forces, and his civil rights for the rest of his natural life.[60]

The charges brought against Kusch in the reports of Abel, Funke and Druschel were obviously true. In his first interrogation on 21 January 1944,[61] and later in the trial on 26 January, Kusch had not denied his conduct and the statements of which he was accused, but tried to modify their contents in such a way that they no longer incriminated him. His attempts to make light, above all, of the remarks about Hitler were vehemently opposed by Abel and Druschel in their statements to the court. The statements of the witnesses Sub-Lieutenant Meyer, Medical Captain Dr Nothdurft and the two midshipmen were merely confined to repeating the major accusations, and it is thus fair to conclude that they had been dragged into the affair by the two spokesmen of the denunciation, Abel and Funke. A denial would undoubtedly have made them accessories, and rendered them liable to prosecution as well. Midshipman Horst Fröhlich was the only one who claimed to have heard nothing of Kusch's remarks against the Nazi regime, but he still had to admit: 'I have the impression that the accused rejects the Third Reich and its institutions.'[62] The court made the officers who had testified against Kusch swear to their evidence, but did not do so in the case of the two cadets, which may be a reflection of the unpleasant fact that here two officer cadets were forced to testify against their commander. In his questioning on 21 January 1944 Kusch had named his two previous commanders, Winter and Janssen, as witnesses for the defence. They were the only ones who unreservedly stood by him, and fully confirmed the good impression they had of him. They could not, however, comment on the matter in question.[63]

In the grounds for the sentence, dated 29 January 1944 and comprising eight pages,[64] Naval Chief Judge Advocate Hagemann considered all the charges brought against Oskar Kusch by Dr Abel in his report dated 12 January 1944 as proved, since there was no doubt as to the credibility of all the witnesses, both those who had made sworn statements and the two cadets. Kusch's defence counsel, the lawyer Meyer-Grieben, had completely denied that his client had committed a criminal offence, since the accused had not acted in public on his submarine, and had made his remarks mostly in the officers' mess or, in some cases, on the bridge (i.e. the conning-tower). However, Hagemann stated that, according to Druschel's testimony, in addition to the officers, the cook, the officers' messman and the sound locator operator had been able to overhear these conversations; and Abel testified that the sailors on the bridge had made derisive remarks about the commander's attitude. These facts were sufficient for him 'to claim a public action by the accused, without requiring an interpretation of the term "public" as it was defined in peacetime criminal law. . . . At all events, the accused acted in public in the broad interpretation given to this term by the Reich Military Court of Justice . . .' The court conceded that the accused 'did not set out to disparage the *Führer* or to incite people against the system of government and the political and military leadership with the aim of breaking down the German people's will to resist'.

Kusch's above-average education, the positive features of his character and his military competence were, indeed, acknowledged in the grounds for the sentence; they were not considered in the slightest degree as mitigating, but rather as aggravating factors, since such a highly-qualified officer should have been fully aware of the dangerous effects of his remarks on his interlocutors. Although there was no immediate intent to commit sedition, 'as the Reich Military Court . . . so aptly states, not only actions which are aimed directly at committing sedition and are performed for this purpose, are dangerous, but also, to no less a degree, such actions by perpetrators who, while not intending a seditious effect by their conduct, are fully aware of this and are not thereby deterred from committing the offence'. The actual grounds for the death sentence were that Oskar Kusch 'no longer believed in final victory'; 'his liberal tendencies, which had led him to leave the Hitler Youth in 1935', had caused him to 'reject National Socialism'; and 'the frequent occurrence of seditious remarks made by the accused, which did not even stop at the person of the *Führer*, and some of which bore the character of high treason'.

It is evident from the court records that no attempts were made to find grounds which could have exonerated the accused, and that the political remarks, regardless of their actual effects, were the sole reason for the death sentence. The assumption of limited intent which under Section 5, Paragraph 1, Sub-Paragraph 3 of the KSSVO, should have led to the case being a 'less serious offence' for which the penalty would have been imprisonment, was – as Hagemann stated in 1950 in the Kiel Regional Court – due solely to the fact that the court wished to give the accused a chance for a reprieve, which, if he had been found guilty of full intent, would have been impossible from the outset.[65] Defence counsel Meyer-Grieben must evidently have tried to appeal against the sentence – a memorandum dated 30 January 1944 stated that the condemned man would express his dissent through him. However, the same memorandum also stated that prosecution 'for breach of official duty out of fear' had initially been dropped 'because the hearing of evidence on this will take longer'.[66] Thus there was no questioning of further crew-members, who, according to Kusch's former navigator, Heinrich Lüdmann, had heard nothing of his negative remarks against the Nazi regime.[67]

The conduct of the naval court which sentenced Oskar Kusch to death for sedition reflects in a fatal manner the statements made by the head of the *Wehrmacht* Legal Section, Rudolf Lehmann, to the generals in 1939, in which he said that:

> . . . it was not the task of the court to seek a truth *per se* which did not exist; it was, rather, its responsibility 'to preserve, within the framework of the community in which it is placed, this very community with the instruments of the law'. Misdemeanours committed by the individual against the spirit of the community were to be regarded as aggravating factors.[68]

The notorious Sections 5 (Sedition) and 5a (Increase of Penalty) of the KSSVO, drafted in 1938 by *Wehrmacht* jurists, thus allowed for the most severe punishments, including death, for offences which, under the military code of criminal justice, were only punishable by more or less lengthy prison sentences. A brutal judiciary made intensive and extensive use of these instruments. Manfred Messerschmidt's opinion that 'A closer examination of the sentencing practice leads to ascertaining a participatory ideological "purification work by the military judiciary"; put more plainly, this means that not only did the inevitable happen, but that there was also thoroughly deliberate ideological co-operation [between military courts and regime]', applies without qualification in the case of Oskar Kusch. This conclusion is also confirmed by a description of the function of courts-martial announced in February 1942 by Vice-Admiral Warzecha:

> The courts-martial have a command function, in fact a dual one: they are an organ of the general state leadership, in that they ensure, through the severity of criminal law, that national policy directives are implemented in all spheres of life. In addition, however, they are – and this distinguishes them fundamentally from all other courts – an organ of the military command.[69]

This definition imposed severe constraints on the independence of judges, and considerably strengthened the influence of the convening authority by means of a 'voluntary link' to the military claim to leadership.

The interpretation of the term 'public' in the grounds for the sentence, which was based on the sentencing practice of the Reich

Court of Military Justice,[70] points to a characteristic of National
Socialist law. At that time, laws were mostly kept very short, and
had numerous general clauses which gave judges, public prosecutors and civil servants great scope for interpretation. The jurisdiction of this period gives the impression that, in the vast
majority of cases, decisions were taken to the detriment of those
accused, although a different decision would have been possible
according to the text of the standards for those applying the law.[71]

The death sentence imposed on Kusch was passed unanimously;
that is, in addition to Naval Chief Judge Advocate Hagemann as a
professional judge, the two military assessors, Lieutenant-
Commander Dittmers and Sub-Lieutenant Westphalen, as lay
judges also voted for the execution of their fellow sailor. In 1950, as
witnesses at the Kiel Regional Court, they both stated that for
purely military reasons they had considered Kusch to be so guilty
that his crime could only be atoned by death. Their sentence had
not been in the slightest respect politically motivated; in their
opinion, with his remarks Kusch had greatly endangered the operational capability of his vessel, and thus put the lives of its crew at
risk.[72] The death sentence was confirmed by Reichsmarschall Hermann Goering and by the Chief of the *Wehrmacht* High Command, Field Marshal Wilhelm Keitel, on 10 April 1944.[73] The
regulations governing the conduct of trials by court-martial obviously made provision for an independent opinion by the judges on
the question of clemency, which was to be addressed directly to the
High Command of the Navy. It occasionally happened that they
recommended that the death sentence be commuted to probationary service in a front-line unit or to imprisonment.

The extant files still include an empty envelope marked:
'Opinion of the judges on the question of clemency in the criminal
case of Sub-Lieutenant Kusch. May only be opened by the High
Command of the Navy!'[74] Sub-Lieutenant Westphalen stated to
Admiral Peter that he personally suggested that a petition for
clemency with probation to a fighting unit be supported.[75] He may
have done this in a memorandum which was forwarded in the
still-extant envelope. However, as far as Westphalen can remember
it was not possible to get Kusch to submit a petition for clemency.
His class-mate, Victor Nonn, assumes: 'In so far as I knew Kusch, I
do not believe that he would have submitted a petition for clemency.' Lieutenant-Commander Winter then tried to use his influence with Admiral of the Fleet Dönitz and Admiral von Friedeburg
on Kusch's behalf, but in vain.[76] Lieutenant Janssen also acted
similarly when, during the entire course of a car journey from

Lorient to Berlin, he tried to dissuade Dönitz from going ahead with the execution. Dönitz, however, categorically refused to accede, stating that an example had to be made in this case.[77] In a message dated 6 February, the convening authority, the Commander of U-boats in the West, Captain Rösing, declined 'support for an act of clemency'.[78]

However, after receiving the reasons for the sentence, Kusch's lawyer, with the consent of his client, had submitted a petition for clemency, which, to be on the safe side, his wife had personally delivered to the High Command of the Navy in Berlin.[79] In view of the circumstances described above, it had no chance of success. Nevertheless, Kusch still hoped that he would not be shot. This hope was also expressed in three of his four letters which are to be found in the files. Moreover, he was profoundly convinced of his innocence. In the two letters which he addressed on 27 February 1944 to his former navigator, Lüdmann,[80] and to his radio operator, Janker, Kusch described the circumstances of his denunciation and arrest. In view of the fact that he was not able to produce any evidence to the contrary, he wrote, the court had believed the sworn testimonies of the denouncers and sentenced him to death. In the letter to Janker, he then wrote: 'What is more, you yourself, who knew what the mood was like on the vessel and were station supervisor, must know whether and how I committed sedition and undermined discipline.' He expressed himself in similar terms in his letter to Lüdmann: 'You, who were with me on my very first patrol, must know whether and to what extent I committed sedition on board our vessel and undermined discipline. If only they would ask the crew, then I think they would get a different picture from that of the testimonies of Abel and Druschel.' These two letters never reached their addressees. They are still extant in the original, and were filed away by Naval Judge Advocate Ernst Meinert, who was responsible for supervising the execution of the sentence, because he considered their contents 'seditious', as was apparent from a memorandum dated 29 March 1944 in which Kusch complained about this treatment.[81]

Kusch's feelings and his soldierly attitude are revealed most clearly in his letter to the brothers Peter and Karl Flindt, both no doubt friends from the youth movement, dated 8 March 1944:

But the irrevocably final decision is getting nearer and nearer. Its deadly seriousness and significance cast their shadows over every day, every hour. I am trying to come to terms with it inwardly, to accept the thought that it will soon be all over for good. But it's extremely difficult. Especially the idea of such a desolate, ignominious end. That's the most bitter thing. How often did we expect to die out there, from air raids, depth-charges and all the ways of submarine warfare – but it's a different matter to have to suffer it here in this fashion. How I would love to be out there again now, at sea! In the confinement and loneliness of my cell, this yearning is particularly agonizing and painful. You know how fond I was of my profession – it was my true vocation. That's also gone forever. It's so bitter that I dare not even think about it. Never again will I be able to set sail with a crew or be a commander. If only they would give me a boat now! Just think of what I could do with my experience and ability, how I would endeavour to correct their false picture. I believe and know that this would be of more use to everyone than an execution, especially to the U-boat force and the state.[82]

Just how much Kusch was considered to be a political delinquent is shown by the reaction of Naval Judge Advocate Meinert to letters written to Kusch by his friends. In the already quoted letter dated 1 March 1944[83] Dieter Berger tried to encourage Kusch, and showed sympathy for his sad fate. The brother of Kusch's fiancée, Lieutenant Henning von Foris, expressed similar sentiments in a letter no longer extant. Meinert had Berger's letter forwarded via the High Command of the Navy to the Commander-in-Chief of the *Luftwaffe* (Berger was obviously a *Luftwaffe* officer) with the intention of securing a reprimand.[84] In an order regarding the forwarding of Lieutenant von Foris's letter to the High Command of the Navy, Meinert wrote:

> It must strike one as strange that a German officer, if he still cares for his honour, should write such a letter to a man sentenced to death and to forfeiture of his right to serve in the armed forces. I suggest that the letter be forwarded to the appropriate commander-in-chief [probably of the Army, since Lieutenant von Foris was an army officer] to give him an opportunity to take further measures.[85]

On 1 April 1944, Meinert returned to Lieutenant von Foris his letter to Kusch which had been deemed objectionable, and called upon him as a German officer, in view of the circumstances which had led to Kusch's being sentenced to death, to disassociate himself from him immediately and to cease all correspondence with him. In addition, Meinert warned him that he would report him immediately if he attempted to write to Kusch again.

Following confirmation of the sentence on 10 April 1944, the Legal Section of the High Command of the Navy on 8 May 1944 issued to the court of the Commander of U-boats in the West the order to execute the death sentence.[86] On 11 May 1944 the date for this was fixed as 12 May 1944; and on the same day Kusch was informed that he would be shot the next morning at 6.30 a.m.[87] In the night preceding his execution, Kusch wrote a final letter to his friend Gustav-Adolf Janssen, the original of which is still in the files: 'Dear Gustav – Fate has decided against me after all. I give you my thanks, best wishes for the future and my final regards. Keep me in kind remembrance. You know that I die innocent. But that still doesn't help me. I give you my hand one last time. Your faithful friend, Oskar.'[88] It is doubtful whether Lieutenant Janssen ever received this final message from his friend. On the day of the execution, Meinert wrote on the envelope: 'contents dubious!'

During his final night, Kusch made another drawing, which was found in his cell and submitted to the court of the Senior Commander of U-boat Training.[89] It shows, facing the observer, a firing-squad immediately after releasing the fatal volley, and, with his back to the observer, the victim with his arms spread out wide at the moment of collapse. His class-mate, Horst Freiherr von Luttitz, published this haunting picture in his novel as Kusch's final drawing.[90] According to the record dated 12 May 1944, the execution took place on that day as scheduled, at the Kiel–Holtenau shooting-range.[91] On the same day Kusch's parents received a letter from the court of the Senior Commander of U-boat Training, informing them that the death sentence against their son had been executed, and forbidding them to publish notices of his death or obituaries.[92] Kusch's father had a facsimile of this letter published in the Berlin *Neue Zeitung* of 8 July 1946.[93]

On 9 May 1946, one year after Germany's surrender, Oskar Kusch's father filed a demand for prosecution with the Kiel Higher Regional Court. He brought charges against the judge, Naval Chief Judge Advocate Hagemann, the two assessors Dittmers and Westphalen, the counsel for the prosecution, Naval Chief Judge Advocate Meinert, Sub-Lieutenants Dr Abel and Druschel, and Medical Captain Dr Nothdurft for the murder of his son. The legal basis for these charges was Law No. 10, enacted by the Allied Control Council, which provided for the punishment of persons found guilty of war crimes, crimes against peace or crimes against humanity. In the 8 July 1946 issue of the Berlin *Neue Zeitung*, a report was published, obviously at the instigation of his father, under the heading: 'The Case of Sub-Lieutenant Kusch; a Father Accuses a Naval Court of Murder – "Sentenced to Death Against Better Judgement".' An account of the three post-war trials dealing with the Kusch case and its legal background would exceed the scope of this paper. Jörg Friedrich has described it in detail, along with numerous other cases, in his collection of documents.[94] All were acquitted in three trials in 1949 and 1950. Kusch's name was later included in the roll of crew-members of U 154 on one of the bronze plaques of the U-boat memorial in Kiel–Möltenort.

Oskar Kusch and the Military Resistance

It can be said that Sub-Lieutenant Oskar Kusch was an irreproachable and conscientious officer. The accusations made against him, in the trials of those who had tried and condemned him, in 1949 and 1950, namely that he had reduced the operational readiness of his vessel to zero, are inconsistent with the extant sources. If he had failed as a commander on his last mission, as he was accused of doing five years after the end of the war, his military superiors would have been bound to notice it in the thirty days which elapsed between the day he sailed into port and the day he was arrested, when evaluating the war diary and during the customary exchange of information in the course of which those members of the crew holding important functions were debriefed. Kusch would then undoubtedly have been relieved of his command. However, in the records of the trial of 26 January 1944 only potential military effects of his remarks against the Nazi regime are mentioned.

Oskar Kusch conducted himself in a thoroughly dignified manner before his judges. The fact that he tried to save his life by modifying his remarks – which he did not deny making – is totally understandable, and these modifications cannot be called 'lame excuses',[95] as his defence counsel had apparently asserted in court in September 1950. Most of those involved in the attempted *coup d'état* of 20 July 1944, when on trial before the People's Court, had only admitted to those offences of which they could unequivocally be proved guilty. Moreover, in his own defence Kusch never allowed himself to be carried away and make opportunistic declarations of support for National Socialism in order to prove his 'right' way of thinking; nor did he show remorse or ask for clemency himself. In his letters to friends and acquaintances, he was convinced of his innocence, and showed himself to be a patriot who wished to place his military abilities and experiences at the disposal of 'the state', and not of a National Socialist regime. Nor was he the victim of occasional expressions of displeasure about the Nazi regime or its functionaries in the officers' mess, which, according to his classmate Wallrodt, he made fairly often. Oskar Kusch had already had personal experience, in his youth, of the pressures exerted by the National Socialist dictatorship; and he refused to accept them. He must have been profoundly disgusted by the mendacity of this system, and its *Führer* who had thrust Germany into a hopeless war, with the result that time and again he unequivocally opposed this injustice and these lies. Of course, he had not expected to be denounced by his own officers.

Since 1984, when military resistance was the subject of an exhibition by the Federal Armed Forces Historical Research Office entitled 'Rebellion of Conscience: Military Resistance Against Hitler and the Nazi Regime',[96] the resistance by *Wehrmacht* servicemen has been considered to have been more than just the act of the men of 20 July 1944. 'Thus, military resistance should be seen as a spectrum of widely varying activities, in which servicemen of all ranks opposed injustice in different ways, thereby risking and sometimes sacrificing their lives.'[97]

Sub-Lieutenant Oskar Kusch is thus clearly to be ranked among the host of men who offered military resistance to Hitler and the Nazi regime, and whose number it will never be possible to determine exactly. There were undoubtedly many servicemen who, like Kusch, expressed their inner disgust at the criminal system of National Socialism in words and deeds, even if only the tragic cases are known in which such men had to lay down their lives following a denunciation. Kusch was undoubtedly aware of the danger to which he was exposing himself through his pointed remarks, even if he did trust in the camaraderie of all submariners, and did not expect such brutal consequences. He is proof of the fact that there were servicemen in the *Wehrmacht* who performed their difficult duty for their fatherland but not for its National Socialist rulers. This makes him a model for future generations of German officers.

Rear Admiral Erich Topp, one of the most successful U-boat commanders in the German Navy (he was awarded the Knight's Cross of the Iron Cross with Oak Leaves and Swords), recently wrote the following about the Kusch case:

> Whatever the political environment may have been, it would still have been in place here for Dönitz to speak to his commander at least once and to stand by him. Or was he so naïve that he did not know what people were saying in the U-boat messes about the Party and the *Gröfaz* [a scornful abbreviation of the way Hitler was apostrophised in Nazi propaganda as the *Größter Feldherr aller Zeiten*, the 'Greatest Commander of All Times']. . . . If we comprehend tradition as being in touch with and continuing lofty intellectual currents, then

Sub-Lieutenant Kusch undoubtedly fits into this pattern, whereas Admiral of the Fleet Dönitz does not.[98]

Lieutenant Robert Hering, the senior member of the Class of 37A, has expressed the legacy of his class-mate Oskar Kusch at the most basic level: 'He was not willing to swap the truth for lies.'

NOTES

1. A. Klönne, *Gegen den Strom. Ein Bericht über Jugendwiderstand im Dritten Reich*, Hanover–Frankfurt am Main, 1958, p. 142.
2. W. Klenck (i.e., H. Freiherr von Luttitz), *Wer das Schwert nimn ι . . . Erleben im Luft- und Seekrieg 1940–1945. Bericht und Mahnung*, Munich, 1987, following p. 468, further drawings following p. 528.
3. Bundesarchiv Zentralnachweisstelle/Aachen–Cornelimunster (hereafter ZNS): File No. 3140: 1. Investigation Files of the Court of the Commander of U-boats in the West (F.d.U.-West) St.L.J.I. 9/44 (75 pp.); 2. Replacement File (30 pp.); 3. Reference Files (46 pp. and 12 pp.).
4. J. Friedrich, *Freispruch für die Nazi-Justiz. Die Urteile gegen NS-Richter seit 1948. Eine Dokumentation*, Reinbek, 1983, pp. 175–82. These proceedings still exist in the *Gerichtsaktensammlung* in Schleswig.
5. G. Nehls, 'Erinnerung an Oskar Heinz Kusch', in *Crewbrief der Crew 37A*, II/83, pp. 5–12. This letter was published privately and edited by the senior class-member, former Lieutenant Robert Hering.
6. This account, in manuscript form, was made available to the author by the Chairman of the Association of German Submariners, former Captain Kurt Diggins.
7. L. G. Buchheim, *Zu Tode gesiegt. Der Untergang der U-Boote*, Gütersloh, 1988, pp. 172–3.
8. ZNS K 3140, Reference Files, p. 11: Letter from Rear-Admiral Peter to the ZNS dated 12 May 1985 requesting a copy of the record of execution, which, according to a note in the margin, he received on 8 July 1985. Cf. also ibid., pp. 9, 11: Letter from former Commander Nehls dated 28 June 1983 requesting access to the files on behalf of the class of 37A. On 10 August 1983, Nehls received from the ZNS a copy of the grounds for the sentence with the names obliterated. Karl Peter presumably obtained it from Gerd Nehls.
9. ZNS K 3140, Investigation Files, p. 39: Teletype message from Gestapo Central Headquarters in Berlin to Gestapo Headquarters in Kiel, dated 26 January 1944.
10. ZNS K 3140, Investigation Files, p. 41: Court of the F.d.U.-West St.

L.J.I. 9/44, Grounds for the Sentence, dated 29 January 1944.

11. NS K 3140, Replacement File, p. 9: Court of the F.d.U.-West St. J.I. 9/44, Record of Interrogation of Sub-Lieutenant Kusch dated 21 January 1944.

12. ZNS K 3140, Investigation Files, p. 39.

13. ZNS K 3140, Replacement File, pp. 1–2: Copy of the report submitted by Sub-Lieutenant Dr Ulrich Abel to the 3rd U-boat Instructional Division, dated 12 January 1944.

14. ZNS K 3140, Replacement File, p. I: Abbreviated extract from the identity card of Sub-Lieutenant Oskar Kusch.

15. ZNS K 3140, Investigation Files, p. 39.

16. R. Hering (ed.), *Chronik der Crew 37A 1937–1987*, Selbstverlag, Gärtringen, 1987, p. 7, where the senior class-member enumerates these motives. Cf. also the novel by Klenck/Luttitz (n. 2, above) who points, above all, to the fascination with the Navy as a kind of ideal and honourable society.

17. ZNS K 3140, Replacement File, pp. 1–2 (see n. 13, above).

18. ZNS K 3140, Replacement File, p. 1; and K. Peter, 'Der Fall des Oberleutnants zur See Kusch: "Wider besseres Wissen zum Tode verurteilt". Stimmt das?', manuscript, 1986, p. 3.

19. ZNS K 3140, Replacement File, p. 1; and Peter, p. 5. See also Bundesarchiv–Militärarchiv (hereafter BA–MA), Freiburg, RM 98/358, Kriegstagebuch U 154, p. 86.

20. ZNS K 3140, Reference Files, p. 6: Angers Wehrmacht Prison, Notice of committal of Sub-Lieutenant Kusch on 20 January 1944; ZNS K 3140, Replacement File, p. 15: Court of the F.d.U.-West St.L.J.I. 9/44 gives the date as 16 January 1944.

21. W. Lohmann and H. Hildebrand, *Die deutsche Kriegsmarine 1939–1945*, vol. 3, 'Personalien', Bad Nauheim, n.d., p. 436. Winter was promoted to Lieutenant-Commander on 1 June 1943. After being replaced as Commander of U 103, he was Commander of the 7th U-boat Flotilla until September 1944.

22. ZNS K 3140, Investigation Files, p. II: Copy of the evaluation report written upon the change of commander, dated 26 June 1942.

23. Lohmann and Hildebrand, *Die deutsche Kriegsmarine*, p. 159.

24. ZNS K 3140, Investigation Files, p. III: Copy of the evaluation report on Sub-Lieutenant Oskar Kusch, Commander of U 154, dated 25 September 1943.

25. *Crewbrief Crew 37 A*, II/83, p. 9 f. For the following see ibid., pp. 11, 12 and 10 f.

26. Peter, 'Der Fall', Appendix A: Note on a discussion between the author and Heinrich Lüdmann, first mate of U 154, on 24 April 1985 in Kiel–Schilksee. However, according to his personnel file (see n. 16, above), Kusch was a Protestant.

27. Peter, 'Der Fall', Appendix C: photocopy from the album of Heinrich Lüdmann, Kiel–Schilksee.

28. ZNS K 3140, Reference Files, p. 26.

29. For technical data see E. Rössler, *Geschichte des deutschen U-Bootbaus*, vol. 1, Koblenz, 1986, p. 72.
30. M. Salewski, *Die Deutsche Seekriegsleitung 1935–1945, vol. 2, 1942–1945*, Munich, 1975, pp. 305 f.
31. ZNS K 3140, Replacement File, p. 1 and p. 10: Court of the F.d.U.-West J.I. 9/44, Record of Interrogation of Sub-Lieutenant Kusch, dated 21 January 1944.
32. ZNS K 3140, Replacement File, p. 1 and Investigation Files, p. 32: Public Session of the Court-Martial of the F.d.U-West St. L.J.I. 9/44 on 26 January 1944, at which Abel repeated this remark.
33. 'Erlaß gegen die Kritiksucht und Meckerei', 9 September 1943, KTB B V, BA–MA II M 1005/8, quoted in Salewski, *Die deutsche Seekriegsleitung*, vol. 2, p. 639.
34. ZNS K 3140, Replacement File, p. 1, for sailing time. J. Rohwer and G. Hümmelchen, *Chronik des Seekrieges 1939–1945*, Oldenburg–Hamburg, 1968, p. 354. Cf. also G. T. M. Kelshall, *The U-Boat War in the Caribbean*, manuscript in the author's possession, p. 305. See also BA–MA, RM 98/358, Kriegstagebuch U 154, pp. 96–7.
35. Peter, 'Der Fall', Appendix D: Photocopy of the entry made in the guest-book of U 460 on 15 May 1943.
36. Kelshall, *The U-Boat War*, p. 431.
37. Rohwer and Hümmelchen, *Chronik des Seekrieges*, pp. 421, 450.
38. Kelshall, *The U-Boat War*, pp. 427, 429.
39. For this and the following, see ZNS K 3140, Replacement File, pp. 1–2.
40. ZNS K 3140, Investigation Files, p. 2a.: Copy of the evaluation report on Sub-Lieutenant Abel (Ulrich) for the period from 5 January 1943 to 3 January 1944, dated 25 December 1943.
41. Ibid., p. 12: Court of the F.d.U.-West J.I. 9/44, Record of interrogation of Sub-Lieutenant Kusch, dated 21 January 1944 (also in Replacement File, p. 9); ibid., p. 25: Note on the interrogation of Sub-Lieutenant Dr Abel on 24 January 1944.
42. BA–MA: N 104/3: pp. 52–3: Draft 'Ordinance on Reporting by the People', dated September 1939.
43. Peter, 'Der Fall', p. 11.
44. *Crewbrief, Crew 37A*, p. 7.
45. ZNS K 3140, Investigation Files, p. 7: Court of the F.d.U.-West L.J.I. 9/44; for the following, see ibid. and pp. 8–9.
46. Ibid., p. 25.
47. Ibid., p. 13: Court of the F.d.U.-West J.I. 9/44, hearing on 21 January 1944.
48. *Crewbrief, Crew 37A*, p. 7.
49. ZNS K 3140, Investigation Files, pp. 3–4: Court of the F.d.U.-West St.L.J.I. 9/44, dated 16 January 1944.
50. ZNS K 3140, Reference Files, pp. 6, 8; ZNS K 3140, Replacement File, p. 15: Court of the F.d.U.-West St.L.J.I. 9/44 gives the date for commitment to Angers as 16 January 1944.

51. ZNS K 3140, Reference Files, pp. 11–12.
52. Lohmann and Hildebrand, *Die deutsche Kriegsmarine*, p. 81.
53. ZNS K 3140, Reference Files, p. 13: J.I. 9/44.
54. ZNS K 3140, Investigation Files, p. 31.
55. Peter, 'Der Fall', p. 9.
56. ZNS K 3140, Investigation Files, p. 30: Court of the F.d.U.-West J.I. 9/44, Bill of Indictment against Sub-Lieutenant Oskar Kusch, HQ 2nd U-boat Flotilla, dated 25 January 1944.
57. The text of this section is reproduced in M. Messerschmidt and F. Wüllner, *Die Wehrmachtjustiz im Dienste des Nationalsozialismus. Zerstörung einer Legende*, Baden-Baden, 1987, p. 133.
58. Remark made by Captain Jeppener, who attended part of the trial, in the audience, in *Crewbrief, Crew 37A*, p. 8; and personal communication from Lieutenant Rüdiger Burchhards, who also was present at the trial, to the author, dated 21 July 1987.
59. Klenck, *Wer das Schwert nimmt*, pp. 480 ff.
60. ZNS K 3140, Investigation Files, p. 36: Public session of the Court of the F.d.U.-West St.L.J.I. 9/44 on 26 January 1944.
61. Ibid., pp. 12–13: Court of the F.d.U.-West St.L.J.I. 9/44.
62. Ibid., p. 33: Public session of the Court-Martial of the F.d.U.-West St.L.J.I. 9/44 on 26 January 1944.
63. Ibid., p. 34: Public session of the Court-Martial of the F.d.U.-West St.L.J.I. 9/44 on 26 January 1944.
64. For these and the following, ibid., pp. 40–9: Court of the F.d.U.-West St.L.J.I. 9/44, sentence dated 29 January 1944. Some passages were heavily underlined.
65. Friedrich, *Freispruch*, p. 178 (see n. 4, above).
66. ZNS K 3140, Investigation Files, p. 51: Memorandum by Naval Chief Judge Advocate, dated 30 January 1944.
67. Peter, 'Der Fall', Appendix A.
68. R. Lehmann, 'Die Aufgaben der Wehrmacht', in *Deutsches Recht*, 1939, pp. 1265–9, quoted in Messerschmidt and Wüllner, *Wehrmachtjustiz*, pp. 27, 32.
69. ZNS, unnumbered regulations, speech by the Chief of the General Navy Office (to which the Legal Section was subordinate), Vice-Admiral Warzecha, to leading naval chief judge advocates and ordinary naval judge advocates in February 1942, ibid., pp. 35, 183.
70. M. Messerschmidt, 'Deutsche Militärgerichtsbarkeit im Zweiten Weltkrieg', in *Die Freiheit des Anderen. Festschrift für Martin Hirsch*, Baden-Baden, 1981, pp. 122 ff.
71. D. Majer, 'Justiz zwischen Anpaßung und Konflikt', in *Justiz und Nationalsozialismus*, J. H. Schoeps and H. Hillermann (eds), *Studien zur Geistesgeschichte*, vol. 8, Stuttgart–Bonn, 1987.
72. Friedrich, *Freispruch*, pp. 179 f.
73. ZNS K 3140, Reference Files, p. 35.
74. ZNS K 3140, Investigation Files, p. 50.
75. For this and the following, see Peter, 'Der Fall', pp. 13, 21.

76. *Crewbrief, Crew 37A*, II/83, p. 7.
77. Peter, 'Der Fall', p. 11.
78. ZNS K 3140, Reference Files, pp. 13–14: Order and teletype message from the Court of the F.d.U.-West to the High Command of the Navy, dated 6 February 1944.
79. Peter, 'Der Fall', Appendix B, Paragraph 6.
80. ZNS K 3140, Reference Files, p. 27.
81. Ibid., p. 22: Report to the Court of the Senior Commander of U-boat Training (HKU), Attention: Naval Judge Advocate Meinert, by Sub-Lieutenant Kusch, dated 29 March 1944.
82. Ibid., p. 18: Copy of a letter to Frau Flindt (presumably the mother of the two addressees).
83. Ibid., p. 26.
84. Ibid., p. 17: Court of the HKU, dated 11 March 1944.
85. Ibid., pp. 20, 21, and 29: Court of the HKU to the High Command of the Navy, dated 23 March 1944 (see the same source also for the following).
86. ZNS K 3140, Investigation Files, p. 53: High Command of the Navy Mar/Wehr/R III No. 796 g II Ang (Secret) to the Court of the F.d.U.-West.
87. Ibid., p. 55: RHJ 90/44, notification of execution on 11 May 1944.
88. ZNS K 3140, Reference Files, p. 28.
89. Ibid., pp. 41–2: Wehrmacht HQ Kiel to the Court of the HKU, dated 15 May 1944.
90. Klenck, *Wer das Schwert nimmt*, following p. 528.
91. ZNS K 3140, Investigation Files, p. 56: RHJ 90/44, Record of the execution of the death sentence on Sub-Lieutenant Oskar Kusch, HQ 2nd U-boat Flotilla, dated 12 May 1944.
92. Klönne, *Gegen den Strom*, p. 142.
93. *Die Neue Zeitung*, 8 July 1946, in Peter, 'Der Fall', p. 23.
94. Friedrich, *Freispruch*, p. 175.
95. Ibid., p. 182.
96. Militärgeschichtliches Forschungsamt (Federal Armed Forces Historical Research Office) (ed.), *Aufstand des Gewissens. Militärischer Widerstand gegen Hitler und das NS-Regime 1933–1945*, Herford–Bonn, 1984.
97. H. Walle, 'Loyalität im Konflikt', in *Offizierbrief 17*, ed. Evangelisches Kirchenamt der Bundeswehr, n.d., p. 31.
98. Buchheim, *Zu Tode gesiegt*, pp. 172 f. The author of this text is said to be 'a surviving U-boat commander'. The author was personally informed on 8 September 1988 that this was former Rear-Admiral Erich Topp.

18

'Resistance' to 'No Surrender': Popular Disobedience in Württemberg in 1945

Jill Stephenson

The kind of German 'resistance' which has been the subject of Peter Hoffmann's writings was mostly high-profile, politically-motivated and often idealistic opposition to the rule of evil in Nazi Germany. A liberal interpretation of the term 'resistance' in the Third Reich would, however, also encompass more mundane and less spectacular activities or single deeds by individuals, small groups or tight-knit communities, to frustrate the will of officers of the Nazi dictatorship. Much of what falls into this category would be regarded merely as 'dissent' or, at most, 'disobedience' in a pluralistic polity. In the Third Reich, however, it can legitimately be designated 'resistance', because that was how despotic Nazi leaders perceived it. As Detlev Peukert has observed, 'National Socialism politicised society by importing political claims into domains that had previously been private.'[1] Where disagreement or dissent cannot be openly expressed without fear of severe retribution, and where the rulers regard these sentiments as dangerous to their own position – and therefore as axiomatically 'political' – each act of dissidence can become a statement of opposition to the existing order. This is particularly the case in time of national emergency, where defiance, or mere criticism, of that order can be branded as unpatriotic. For example, the threat of the death penalty for anyone caught listening to enemy 'black' radio in the Nazi empire in wartime could turn defiance into an act of heroism. Furthermore, where a regime has a monopoly on expressions of public opinion, it can portray its own interests as being congruent with those of the nation at large, and any undermining of these as treason. The leaders of the Third Reich propagated this connection relentlessly. This is why even small acts of disobedience were truly resistance, because they threatened the totalitarian claims of the Nazi leadership.

Yet under the veneer of propaganda and the enforcement through terror of orders from Hitler and other senior Nazis, there was significant scope for non-compliance in everyday life, even in wartime – perhaps *especially* in wartime. With increasing numbers of able-bodied men away from home on military service, it became more and more difficult to police the population at large. Inside Germany, the chief preoccupations were the preservation of public order and the maintenance of control over both suspected political opponents and the growing number of workers conscripted from outside the Reich, whose self-confidence and assertiveness developed as the war turned against the Germans.[2] There was also the growing problem of disorder among sections of the nation's youth.[3] But where dissent did not threaten public order, it could be tolerated: indeed, it was the staple diet of the surveillance officials of the *Sicherheitsdienst* (SD), among other agencies. By the end of the war, there were few civilian policemen to enforce observance of the law on a disaffected population, although the Gestapo could still be deadly if brought in to investigate allegations of 'defeatism'. Similarly, 'defeatism' on the part of serving soldiers, mostly manifested through desertion, was growing in 1945, although retribution was swift and harsh.[4] This, too, can be seen as a kind of resistance, superficially against military discipline but in reality because soldiers knew when they were beaten, and wanted to escape from the pointless, life-threatening conflict.

It is generally easier to identify acts of 'resistance' in occupied countries than in Germany itself. Abroad, any act of dissent or subversion could be portrayed – if only clandestinely – as patriotic. Sabotage of the German war effort in France, for example, or hit-and-run partisan raids on Axis forces in Yugoslavia, were intended not merely to hinder the occupying power but also to strengthen national morale. The tiny pin-pricks of defiance which M. R. D. Foot has described[5] were resistance to domination of mind and body by an alien tyrant. In Germany too, instances of defiance, however small, can be seen as acts of resistance. Sabotage in war-related industry was undoubtedly resistance, and was often carried out by politically-committed former socialist or communist factory workers. But while go-slows or absenteeism were not necessarily political in motivation, their effect was nevertheless to

Map 1 The new districts of the province of Württemberg, issued by the Württemberg Innenminister-Landesvermessung, Topographisch-Kartographische Abteilung, Stuttgart, 1938 (courtesy of the Hauptstaatsarchiv, Stuttgart).

frustrate the will of the NSDAP's leadership, even if in many cases such behaviour was due to fatigue rather than subversion. Similarly, German hoarders, barterers and black marketeers were accused of weakening the war effort by refusing to put 'the common good before self-interest'.[6] If detected, they and others guilty of offences against the War Economy Regulations might be sentenced to a term in gaol, as punishment and also *pour encourager les autres*. Certainly, perpetrators of major acts of resistance, such as industrial sabotage, were severely punished, often by execution. But, especially after 1943, small fry like hoarders and petty black-marketeers might have their prison term 'deferred' until after the war, in order to maintain their contribution to the war effort, since they were generally workers or producers of some kind.[7] This undoubtedly did 'encourage the others' to believe that they, too, could get away with black-marketeering and other petty crimes, at least for the duration of the war. In this way, a culture of popular defiance and disobedience developed in the face of Nazi orders and requirements, in circumstances where it seemed that retribution would be difficult or impractical to administer.

In this spirit of opportunism, German civilians increasingly sought to deal with their manifold practical problems during the Second World War, and particularly at its end. By early 1945, they were looking not for a heroic death but merely an end to the slaughter, and, especially, to the bombing. Any remaining faith in the Nazi leadership, which had inflicted this disaster on them and which made few and feeble attempts to mitigate its effects, plummeted. As Ian Kershaw has shown, Bavarians' perception of Hitler himself grew increasingly unfavourable as early as 1942, while the NSDAP's stock was low long before that.[8] Nazi promises of a better deal for small farmers, for example, had remained unfulfilled; on the contrary, the misconceived aims and incompetence of the *Reichsnährstand* (Reich Food Authority) only exacerbated their precarious condition. The small Württemberg farmer was described, no doubt extravagantly, as being almost an endangered species even before the war, and his position only deteriorated during it.[9] For urban civilians the position was in some respects even worse, with acute food shortages by the end of the war, and time and energy being spent standing in endless queues for scarce commodities. The worst aspect of urban life was, of course, the frequent bombing, which killed people and destroyed homes, schools, shops and offices, and drove survivors to spend uncomfortable nights in bunkers or cellars. Essential services – transport, gas, electricity, water – were disrupted by air attacks. All in all, by the early months of 1945 most German civilians confronted a daily battle for survival, both in the face of an imminent takeover by enemy forces and in negotiating the complex obstacle-race which they experienced in getting to work, obtaining basic supplies and seeking a refuge from the bombers.[10]

It is against this background that the piecemeal surrender of German territory to the invading Allies in 1945 should be assessed. In the east, fear of what retribution the Red Army might inflict on the homeland which had bred the murderers and torturers of countless Russians concentrated the attention of most Germans on trying to halt the Soviet invasion.[11] But in western and southern Germany there was little commitment to a long-drawn-out defeat which seemed, in early 1945, the only alternative to speedy surrender. Some Bavarians even claimed in February 1945 that 'as long as the Russians don't come here, we can put up with anything'.[12] But Hitler's 'Nero decree' of 19 March 1945 demanded that German soldiers and civilians resist to the end, and that a 'scorched earth' policy be followed.[13] Especially in the final weeks of March and April 1945, conflict developed in many towns and villages between the zealots, who were determined to implement Hitler's orders to the letter, and others who became increasingly bold in refusing – often at great personal risk – to participate in obviously hopeless attempts to block the advancing enemy's inexorable progress. Sometimes the inhabitants of a town or village simply decided to surrender before further damage or loss of life were sustained, while in other places a lead was given by people who had clearly been 'politically reliable' enough to prosper in the Third Reich. 'Resistance' in this sense was obviously not the prerogative of committed anti-Nazis, but often a matter of simple common sense. Even a Nazi mayor, like Karl Strölin of Stuttgart, could see that inflicting additional misery on ordinary citizens who had already suffered much was indefensible. Trying to defend every last town and village would also ensure that places which had escaped the bombing raids would now feel the full force of military operations in a fight to the finish. Nevertheless, some NSDAP functionaries, notably *Gauleiter* (regional leaders), *Kreisleiter* (district leaders) and SS officers, were convinced that this was·a price worth paying to try to avoid the ignominy of surrender.[14]

In Württemberg, Peter Hoffmann's home state, civilians took the opposite view: since the result of the war was not in doubt, hostilities should cease forthwith. In any case, they were confident that 'it isn't the Russians who are coming, but, on the contrary, civilised people, and it's clear from areas already under Allied control that the inhabitants are finding the occupation tolerable'. The eagerness with which the arrival of American forces was anticipated in some places was deplored by Propaganda Minister Goebbels, but was nevertheless palpable; in particular, there was exhilaration at the prospect of an end to the fighting.[15] There was even resigned acceptance when it was clear that in some areas the invading forces were French (including North African colonial troops); Württembergers braced themselves for possible French retaliation, after what the French had suffered at the hands of German occupiers during 1940–4. By March 1945, the over-whelming mass of ordinary people wanted peace, at almost any price. They certainly did not believe that Germany could salvage its position, and few expected a miracle in the shape of 'new weapons' which would dramatically transform Germany's fortunes.[16] The 'V-weapons', promised for so long,[17] had only limited value, and could not alone rescue Nazi Germany. In any case, there were totally inadequate supplies of even conventional weapons for the *Volkssturm* (Home Guard) and anyone else who might be expected to resist the invader on the ground.[18]

Yet Hitler's 'Nero decree' was underscored by repeated similar instructions from Martin Bormann,[19] and there were still plenty of fanatical Nazis who were determined to enforce these. *Gauleiter* Wilhelm Murr of Württemberg–Hohenzollern was one who insisted that there should be no surrender in his territory. On 10 April, with the invader on course to take Stuttgart and calling upon Germans to surrender peacefully, Murr proclaimed: 'Whoever submits to the enemy will face proscription and contempt. Whoever pays heed to the enemy's words forfeits his life.' Two days later, he issued a more explicit threat: ' . . . any attempt either to obstruct the closing of an anti-tank barrier, or to open an anti-tank barrier that is closed, will be punished by summary execution. Similarly, anyone who shows a white flag will be executed.'[20] As late as 18, 19 and 20 April 1945 the NSDAP's newspaper in Stuttgart, the *NS-Kurier*, insisted that all was not lost, that faith in the *Führer* remained unstinting and that defiance, not cowardice, characterised the popular mood. But these were its last editions, and Murr himself fled the city before it was taken by the French on 22 April.[21] Even so, there remained in Württemberg ardent Nazis, including SS commanders, who insisted on a last-ditch defence, as well as army officers who were reluctant to flout similar orders from above, however much they realised the hopelessness of the cause.

It was clear for all to see that by March 1945 the western Allies' advance into Germany was irresistible. They could perhaps be delayed by determined defenders, but the ultimate outcome was not in doubt for anyone prepared to be realistic. But as surely as Hitler continued to wait for a miracle and ordered all others to hold out until it occurred, so the 'little Hitlers' showed an equal lack of concern for life, limb and property in their areas. In some places, conflict developed between the diehards, with their *Götter-dämmerung* mentality and, on the other side, local notables who had supported Hitler's regime and, up to a point, his war, but who were now prepared formally to accept defeat rather than risk total destruction. In other places, however, the hapless civilian population was at the mercy of a diehard leadership, apparently condemned either to live out the nightmare to its end or to risk summary execution for defeatism.

The contrasting experiences of two of Württemberg's cities, Stuttgart, the capital, with a population of over 400,000, and, further north, Heilbronn, with over 60,000 inhabitants, provide a good illustration of the two choices before Germans in April 1945. Both had suffered dreadfully from bombing, especially in 1943–5: Stuttgart sustained altogether fifty-three attacks, while in Heilbronn over 7,000 people were killed and 80 per cent of the city destroyed in one air raid on 4 December 1944.[22] But Stuttgart was protected from additional damage by the determination of its mayor, Dr Karl Strölin, to surrender the city without a fight. On 4 April, he told Murr that Stuttgart could not be successfully defended against the French and American troops who surrounded it, and he asked that it be declared an open city. Murr refused to countenance this, and so Strölin, having consulted some local notables who shared his view, opened negotiations with the Allies on 10 April with a view to handing the city over to them peacefully, which he did on 22 April.[23] Given Murr's fanatical determination to punish 'defeatists' and the propensity of Nazi officials in the mayhem of April 1945 to mete out arbitrary penalties indiscriminately, Strölin's stand was a courageous one. Furthermore, he was no closet anti-Nazi emboldened by the prospect of an end to the Third Reich: he was a district leader of the NSDAP, and the proud mayor of 'the city of ethnic Germans abroad', who could see how criminal it was to sacrifice others for a patently lost cause. Strölin had also recently been president of the International Association for Housing and Town Planning,[24] and it may be that this interest partly motivated him to surrender his already battered city. Thus, Stuttgart was spared the kind of final agony that was inflicted on the city of Heilbronn. The reign of terror presided over by the NSDAP's Heilbronn district leader, Richard Drauz, saw numerous people summarily shot or hanged for displaying a white flag, and culminated in a week's bitter hand-to-hand fighting before the invader claimed his inevitable victory.[25]

These two instances help to show that by April 1945 there was no effective central authority in the parts of Germany not yet under Allied control. But there were still instances where local preferences were overridden by an external authority. In Tübingen, for example, the presence of 6,000 wounded soldiers in 1944 had led to requests that it be recognised as a 'hospital town' under the terms of the Geneva Convention, to exempt it from bombing raids. The proposal was made by a group of local notables, including the senior army doctor in Tübingen, the *Rektor* of the University, the deputy mayor and the NSDAP district leader of the area. But it came to nothing because the Ministry of Armaments refused to undertake not to divert war industry there. While Tübingen was not an industrial centre, it was now being considered as a possible site for a branch of the Daimler works as part of the decentralising of industry away from the major cities which were prime bombing targets.[26] Again, the presence in a town of an army unit with orders simply to defend German territory against the invader could mean that civilians had no influence on whether their town was to be defended or surrendered. This was the case in Wolpertswende (Ravensburg district), where in April 1945 there remained a German garrison with plentiful equipment. On the arrival of French troops, a battle ensued in which the casualties included a local woman, after which the French took control of the town, burning down three buildings as retribution for the military resistance which they had encountered.[27] Thus, townsfolk were punished for conduct over which they had had no control.

It is true that Hitler's, or Bormann's, instructions still reached some provincial Party officials, but since the orders remained the same – to defend German territory unconditionally – the fate of individual towns and villages depended largely on the attitude of the local population and its leaders. Where they were at one in seeking an early end to the bloodshed, the *Führer*'s directives were disregarded and surrender to an Allied· army was speedy and generally bloodless, although there were individual cases of indiscriminate shootings, or of rape, committed by the invading troops. Many reports, however, tell of the 'correct' behaviour of the occupying forces – particularly the Americans – and news of this undoubtedly encouraged people in areas not yet under enemy control to surrender without a fight. Where punitive action was taken against Germans, it generally meant requisitioning certain goods or letting foreign labourers and prisoners-of-war loose to plunder at will from their former masters. These rather unpleasant experiences were, however, felt to be much preferable to the prospect of trying to hold a town or village against an invader who was infinitely better-equipped and, almost as important, better fed and clothed.[28]

Although the diehards were often fanatics determined to exit dramatically, since victory was to be denied them, in many places the decision to defend a town or village was taken soberly, in the full knowledge of what it would mean for the community. Sometimes the local inhabitants were ordered to leave, so that they might avoid attacks which would possibly destroy their homes. Alternatively, they might be told to take cover in bunkers or other shelters for the duration of the action. These tactics were most likely where there was an army or SS unit with adequate arms. Local people did not welcome this, since it implied an anticipation of severe damage to the town or village; but there was little that they could do about it. Where there were only token army or SS troops, they might force civilians to construct anti-tank barriers and destroy any bridges which would be of use to the invader. In these places, units of the *Volkssturm*, founded in the autumn of 1944, or of the Hitler Youth might be the only forces available for defence, and they were likely to be poorly armed, inadequately trained and low in morale.[29] If there was no Party, SS or army commander to compel them to make a stand, they probably would not do so, regardless of orders issued in Berlin. But if there was a leader determined to follow his *Führer* to the end, then a battle of wills was likely to ensue, with the leader using dire threats to frighten local people into compliance. Sometimes this succeeded, but in other cases it did not. In view of the readiness with which SS officers, in particular, were given to uttering threats of execution, which they did not shrink from carrying out, it is hardly surprising that in many places preparations to resist the enemy were made, albeit with the utmost reluctance.

Where there was a stalemate between German civilians and Party, SS or army officers about what action to take, the invader could lose patience. In Bächlingen (Crailsheim district) on 11 April, where the American commander of an advance party feared the arrival of German reinforcements, he announced that, unless the town raised the white flag by the following morning, it would be burned down. Sure enough, the flag appeared, but shortly afterwards was removed by a German army unit which had just arrived.

Its leader threatened the civilians and refused to meet their request that, to preserve the town, the soldiers should withdraw from it. The American commander declared a cease-fire for two hours to enable the civilians to flee. He was so taken with the beauty of the place that he ordered his men to avoid damaging buildings which were not in the hands of the defending German soldiers. But two days of bitter close-range fighting were enough to leave the town centre devastated; altogether, one-third of all houses were destroyed, as well as business premises. This disaster befell Bächlingen for two reasons. First, Hitler's insistence that every inch of territory be defended for as long as possible was implemented by the local Party leaders, who supervised the construction of anti-tank barriers and mobilised the *Volkssturm*. Then, the arrival of a German army detachment, small in number and poorly-equipped but with orders to defend the town, ensured that the civilians' desire to surrender was disregarded. Thus, a place which had been relatively unscathed by bombing found itself unwillingly in the front line because of 'the arbitrary destruction order of a madman'.[30]

By contrast, in Friedrichshafen to the south, a town which had suffered bombing raids because of its important industrial sector, the mayor's view that any attempt at defence would be 'senseless and irresponsible' in the end prevailed. The local NSDAP *Kreisleiter*, however, brushed aside all such talk as 'defeatism and cowardice' and threatened to shoot anyone who favoured surrender. On 28 March, with French forces advancing, he summoned the civic authorities to announce Hitler's order that 'every house and every place must be defended, all essential supplies must be destroyed' and the town evacuated. There could be no doubt about the mood of the inhabitants: they urged their leaders to surrender. But the military commander of the region, who had been told to defend Friedrichshafen with the 1,400 or so German soldiers and the similar number of Hungarians under his authority, declared that he had never disobeyed an order and was not about to do so now. Finally, however, on 29 April he agreed not to order his men to proceed with defence measures, such as blowing up the town's bridges, and thereby left the way open for civilian negotiators to approach the advancing French forces and to order the dismantling of the various anti-tank barriers which had been constructed for the defence of the town. But this became possible only once the Friedrichshafen NSDAP district leader and local police chief, who was an SS officer, had departed, seeking refuge further east. The seriousness of their original position was revealed when the leader of the French tank company told the mayor that, if a defence had been mounted, he would have called up airborne reinforcements which would have 'given the town a bad time'.[31]

It is not clear whether the fanatics really believed that a last-ditch attempt at defence could save the Third Reich. They seem mostly to have been the kind of Nazi or SS criminal whose only options in the spring of 1945 were suicide, arrest followed by either imprisonment or execution, or going down fighting – and taking with them not only their own immediate followers but also civilians who wanted no part in the armed conflict. In some places, an SS or army unit did score temporary successes, recapturing a town or village from the invader, only to lose it for good a few days later. Crailsheim endured this sort of struggle, which caused massive destruction.[32] In Nufringen (Böblingen district), an SS-led force counter-attacked within twenty-four hours of the town's being occupied; there were some casualties on both sides and, as a punishment for the SS assault, French troops burned down a large building in Nufringen. The SS attackers – who were perhaps reminiscent of the *Freikorps* of the post-1918 years – departed in the direction of Tübingen, and were cut to pieces by enemy artillery on the way.[33] In Oberdorf (Aalen district), an incident after the Americans had occupied the town cost the lives of twelve people, 'in order to prolong the life of a criminal regime by a few days'.[34]

But in Waldsee (Ravensburg district), where anti-tank barriers indicated a readiness to defend the town, even the local NSDAP leader, who was also mayor, gave up the idea of making a stand, because there was strong popular opposition to it. This was confirmed by the large group of citizens who besieged the town hall, demanding immediate surrender and cheering as some of their number raised the white flag. But the local army commander insisted that it be removed: even at this late date, on 23 April, he remained determined to defend Waldsee because he feared that, if he did not, 'he would lose his head'. He was, however, eventually persuaded that saving the town was what mattered, and he therefore agreed to withdraw his forces into the nearby woods so that it could be surrendered to the French without bloodshed or destruction.[35] Mostly, however, army discipline among garrison troops held, and they generally carried out orders to defend an area whatever their chances of success, often, no doubt, because of the threat of summary execution by SS squads.[36] But even in the face of this, the hopelessness of the German position increasingly led to desertions. In Waldburg (Ravensburg district), two German soldiers who had deserted were condemned to death by an *ad hoc* court-martial: they were hanged from a nearby tree, and their bodies buried in a gravel-pit.[37] In what was probably a rare instance, in Adelmannsfelden (Aalen district) the army general who arrived on 15 April managed to restrain the SS from enforcing the pointless defence of the town.[38] But although there was by now some disarray among German forces, with convoys of retreating troops from the western front passing through these southern towns and villages, soldiers seem on the whole to have continued fighting, even when surrounded, heavily outnumbered and outgunned, if ordered to do so by their superiors, whether or not an SS execution squad was in the vicinity.

Where defence depended almost entirely on the civilian population, however, it was easier to refuse to mount it, because it was even more hopeless and less likely to succeed without military support of some kind. Yet this was not considered a sufficient cause for surrender, and terror was frequently employed to try to enforce defence. *Kreisleiter* Drauz in Heilbronn was a particularly grim exponent of it, but there were plenty of others, too. To act as a deterrent, however, the threat of reprisals had to be immediate, in a way that threats emanating from Hitler's bunker in Berlin were not: the potential defeatist had to be accessible to an authority such as an SS officer, for example, who could threaten summary retribution for showing a white flag or dismantling an anti-tank barrier. In Aalen the young SS leader whose contingent arrived to defend the town in April 1945 declared that 'if the Americans attack, they will find themselves biting on granite', adding 'if anyone leaves his post, I'll have him hanged'. He, together with the newly-appointed NSDAP *Kreisleiter*, further warned that anyone opening an anti-tank barrier or ignoring the call to join the *Volkssturm* would be shot or hanged.[39] But, as Drauz of Heilbronn found in outlying parts of his district, orders carried much less force at a distance: in Brettach, three wooden anti-tank barriers had indeed been erected on 3 and 4 April, on his orders, but with the approach of the enemy they were dismantled. Reinforcing this response, the local *Volkssturm* unit and Hitler Youth group failed to obey Drauz's strict instructions to stand and defend Brettach.[40] Given the logistics of the situation, there was little that he could do about it, as the Brettach villagers were no doubt well aware.

By contrast with the army, which remained relatively well-disciplined, in the *Volkssturm* and the Hitler Youth (HJ) there were many cases of disobedience. It is perhaps too much to call it 'mutiny', since these were hastily-mustered troops who had received only the most rudimentary military training with regard to both technique and discipline. Nevertheless, they were treated like army conscripts and expected to submit to military discipline. But the chief effect of SS attempts in Bavaria to brutalise HJ boys of fifteen or sixteen into 'volunteering' for service in the *Waffen-SS* late in March 1945 was to shock the youths and their families, friends and neighbours, and thus to promote widespread defeatism.[41] Attempts in Württemberg, in Honhardt (Crailsheim district) to recruit boys born in 1928, 1929 and 1930 into HJ military formations were actually prevented by the refusal of the parents to countenance it.[42] Clearly, ordinary people felt that they could disobey the orders and disrupt the processes of the military and political authorities, but only where there was no threat of direct retribution. There was an apparent confidence of safety in numbers. But that could be a risky assumption, as was demonstrated in the case of an unfortunate woman in Bad Windesheim who was shot by SS men after being singled out as token ringleader of a group of women demonstrating against the use of their town as a defensive bastion.[43]

There were, however, places where the call-up of the *Volkssturm* met with little response, even when punitive action was threatened. The *Volkssturm*'s value was at best limited, even where it was well-organised. Its equipment was inadequate, and many of its members and leaders regarded it realistically as barely a serious military force.[44] In Friedrichshafen the *Volkssturm* was some 4,000 men strong; but they were 'entirely unarmed', and convinced that there was nothing they could do to stem the French advance. They gladly dismantled the anti-tank barriers when the mayor gave the order.[45] In Aalen there were, 'on paper only', five *Volkssturm* companies of 120 men each. When they were called to action, they mustered a mere 100 men altogether; in spite of threats of 'rope and bullet', the rest of them simply stayed at home. Their unhappy commander was threatened with a court-martial, yet he was powerless: he could not produce anything like the full complement 'by magic'. In neighbouring Wasseralfingen, the picture was much the same. All in all, the capability, motivation and morale of the *Volkssturm* were severely overrated by leaders at both the local and national levels.[46]

The one event which did most to prevent further destruction of towns and villages in the last days of the war was the sudden flight of a Party leader or SS commander who had been trying to enforce Hitler's orders on an unwilling population. With Allied troops within reach of their goal, many erstwhile fanatics realised that, while they might be prepared to bludgeon other Germans into fighting to the death, they were reluctant to mount a last stand themselves. The hurried flight of a Party district leader, probably taking the only available transport with him, opened the way for civilians to treat with the invader. Even SS units were not above abandoning their posts and fleeing after a realistic appraisal of the situation, although many stood and fought. In Dalkingen (Aalen district) it was a matter of great relief to the civilian population when, with American forces only a day's march away, the SS unit which had been forcing women, girls and old men to construct defences around the village suddenly left, removing the worst threat to their safety.[47] In Adelmannsfelden (Aalen district) the sight of the head of the Americans' tank column was enough to persuade the remaining SS men in the town to withdraw, thus enabling the Americans to take over 'without incident'.[48]

There can be little doubt that most Germans wanted the Reich to win Hitler's war, and to do so quickly. The reversal of the Versailles Treaty, the humbling of both Poland and France, and the victory over 'Bolshevism' that came tantalisingly close in 1941, were all widely welcomed. But when it became apparent, from mid–1944 especially, that Germany was going to lose, people generally wanted defeat to come sooner rather than later. The devastation from repeated bombing raids on towns and cities, with the promised *Vergeltung* (retaliation) failing to materialise, convinced ordinary civilians and, increasingly, also some Nazi officials that unless Germany called a halt – even if it meant 'unconditional surrender' – the entire country would be destroyed. Once Germany was being invaded from both east and west, there was a widespread desire for an immediate end to the destruction and therefore to the war. It is perhaps not surprising that Hitler should have been sufficiently removed from reality, inside his bunker during the last weeks of the war, to believe that a change of fortune was possible. But local Party leaders and SS officers were often living in communities which had been mercilessly bombarded from the air, with only the prospect of a further battering from ground forces to look forward to. It is hard to fathom the mentality of those, like the NSDAP *Kreisleiter* of Heilbronn and Friedrichshafen, who were determined that their citizens should fight to the last man. In Württemberg this threat seems to have hung over many communities right up to the final minute, when the popular will, expressed by a mayor, a group of local notables or a determined crowd, in the end prevailed.[49] Some places, such as Heilbronn or Crailsheim, were less fortunate in being made into an involuntary battleground by fanatics who were prepared to abandon the town once the game was up, leaving its remains to a grieving citizenry. How far the very local, small-scale and *ad hoc* opposition detailed here can genuinely be called 'resistance' is perhaps questionable. Yet, it often took considerable courage to resist orders to work for the probable devastation of one's home town or village. The breakdown of central control, at both the national and *Land* levels, made the complexion of authority in the localities very much a lottery in those confused last days of the war, with the normal civil and criminal law suspended in favour of arbitrary Party, SS or Gestapo 'justice'. Württembergers did enjoy one advantage, in that they had news of the positive experience of the Allied take-over of other parts of western Germany to go on. This persuaded many of them that surrender and occupation would be orderly and, on the whole, less punitive and vindictive than the Nazi regime in its brutal death-throes. This undoubtedly strengthened the resolve of many to stand up to the remaining adherents of the Third Reich at the very end, and to resist their demands. Perhaps Peter Hoffmann, who experienced these events at first hand as a boy in Württemberg, can provide a clearer appraisal of their significance than can this author.

NOTES

I am grateful to the British Academy for the generous grant which made possible the research on which this essay is based.

1. D. J. K. Peukert, *Inside Nazi Germany: Conformity, Opposition and Racism in Everyday Life*, New Haven – London, 1987, p. 84; see also the discussion on pp. 118–20.
2. J. Stephenson, '"Emancipation" and its Problems: War and Society in Württemberg, 1939–1945', *European History Quarterly*, vol. 17, 1987, pp. 355–8.
3. Peukert, *Inside*, pp. 152–74, 246.
4. E. R. Beck, *Under the Bombs: The German Home Front 1942–1945*, Kentucky, 1986, pp. 182–3, 190 ff; M. G. Steinert, *Hitler's War and the Germans*, Ohio, 1977, pp. 296, 299–301; Staatsarchiv Ludwigsburg (hereafter StAL), K110, Büschel (hereafter Bü) 58, *Sicherheitsdienst* report, 'Betrifft: Stimmung und Meinungsbildung', 27 March 1945.
5. M. R. D. Foot, *Resistance*, London, 1976, pp. 42–8.
6. Nazi Party Programme of 1920, point 24, found in J. Noakes and G. Pridham (eds), *Nazism 1919–1945: A Documentary Reader*, vol. 1, Exeter, 1983, pp. 14–16.
7. J. Stephenson, 'War and Society in Württemberg, 1939–1945: Beating

the System', *German Studies Review*, vol. 8, 1985, pp. 94–100.

8. I. Kershaw, *The Hitler Myth: Image and Reality in the 'Third Reich'*, Oxford, 1987, pp. 84–7, 91–104, 180–9; Steinert, *Hitler's War*, pp. 154–5, 194, 220, 284.

9. Stephenson, 'Beating the System', pp. 93, 104.

10. Beck, *Bombs, passim*, and especially pp. 177–86.

11. Ibid., pp. 137, 159, 171.

12. M. Broszat *et al.* (eds), *Bayern in der NS-Zeit*, vol. 1, Munich–Vienna, 1977, p. 682 (24 February 1945); Steinert, *Hitler's War*, pp. 299, 304, 306, 308.

13. Beck, *Bombs*, pp. 187–8.

14. Ibid., pp. 189–95; Broszat *et al.* (eds), *Bayern*, pp. 682–3 (7 March 1945); pp. 685–6 (7 April 1945); pp. 686–8 (17 April 1945).

15. Beck, *Bombs*, pp. 188–9; Steinert, *Hitler's War*, p. 308; StAL, K110, Bü58, 27 March 1945.

16. Ibid., Broszat *et al.* (eds), *Bayern*, p. 684 (25 March 1945).

17. G. Kirwin, 'Waiting for Retaliation – A Study in Nazi Propaganda Behaviour and German Civilian Morale', *Journal of Contemporary History*, vol. 16, 1981, pp. 565–83.

18. Steinert, *Hitler's War*, pp. 281, 301–2; Hauptstaatsarchiv/Stuttgart (hereafter HStAS), section J170, Bü1 (Aalen): 'Die letzten Wochen vor un[d] die ersten Wochen nach der Besetzung in Neresheim', undated; and 'Bopfingen im zweiten Weltkrieg', undated. The J170 files comprise a collection of reports from the *Gemeinden* (communes), organised by *Kreis* (district), in response to a questionnaire dated 14 July 1948 and circulated to the *Kreise* by the Württemberg *Statistisches Landesamt* after the capitulation about 'the last days of the war' at the local level. In some cases the answers were very brief, but in others a leading figure – e.g. a mayor, teacher or cleric – wrote a personal account of his own and his area's experience, often in great detail. These reports form the main primary source material for this essay. The *Büschel* numbers refer to the districts, normally in alphabetical order: e.g., Bü1 = Aalen, Bü4 = Crailsheim, Bü65 = Ravensburg.

19. Beck, *Bombs*, pp. 187–8.

20. HStAS, Bü78 (Tübingen); P. Sting, 'Der große Szenenwechsel. Tübingen in Niemandsland', *Schwäbisches Tageblatt*, 19 April 1955.

21. P. Sauer, *Württemberg in der Zeit des Nationalsozialismus*, Ulm, 1975, pp. 495–6.

22. K. Weller and A. Weller, *Württembergische Geschichte im südwestdeutschen Raum*, Stuttgart–Aalen, 1975, p. 308.

23. K. Leipner (ed.), *Chronik der Stadt Stuttgart 1933–1945*, Stuttgart, 1982, pp. 1021–4.

24. Berlin Document Center, file on Karl Strölin, letter from Strölin to Martin Bormann, 10 November 1941.

25. Sauer, *Württemberg*, pp. 492–4.

26. HStAS, Bü78 (Tübingen); Paul Sting, 'Der große Szenenwechsel', 19 April 1955.

27. Ibid., Bü65 (Ravensburg), 18 November 1960.
28. Ibid., Bü1 (Aalen), Aalen (town), 'Das letzte Aufgebot', 9 October 1948; Adelmannsfelden, undated; Kerkingen, 15 January 1950; Dankoltsweiler, 6 February 1949; Bü3 (Böblingen): Kuppingen, 4 October 1948; 'Geschichtliche Darstellung der letzten Kriegstage', Leinfelden, 20 December 1948.
29. Ibid., Bü1 (Aalen), Aalen (town), 9 October 1948; Bü4 (Crailsheim), 'Die Kämpfe um Bächlingen im April 1945', undated; Bü77 (Tettnang), Walter Bärlin, 'Die Übergabe der Stadt Friedrichshafen und Ihre Vorgeschichte', 9 April 1946; Bü78, (Tübingen), Paul Sting, 'Der große Szenenwechsel', 19 April 1955.
30. Ibid., Bü4 (Crailsheim), 'Kämpfe um Bächlingen'.
31. Ibid., Bü77 (Tettnang), Walter Bärlin, 9 April 1946.
32. Sauer, *Württemberg*, pp. 489–90, 493.
33. HStAS, Bü3 (Böblingen), 'Geschichtliche Darstellung der letzten Kriegstage', Nufringen, 20 October 1948.
34. Ibid., Bü1 (Aalen), Karl Laib, Oberdorf, 25 October 1948.
35. Ibid., Bü65 (Ravensburg), Josef Ehrhart, 'Waldsee vor der unmittelbaren Besetzung durch den Feind!', 18 July 1945.
36. Ibid., Bü4 (Crailsheim), 'Kämpfe um Bächlingen'.
37. Ibid., Bü65 (Ravensburg), 'Ausmaß der Zerstörungen im zweiten Weltkrieg in den einzelnen Gemeinden', Waldburg, 5 December 1960.
38. Ibid., Bü1 (Aalen), Baron Dr Gottfried von Franz, 'Geschichtliches zu den letzten Kriegstagen', Adelmannsfelden, undated.
39. Ibid., Bü1 (Aalen), Aalen (town), 9 October 1948.
40. Ibid., Bü8 (Heilbronn), Brettach, undated.
41. Broszat *et al.* (eds), *Bayern*, p. 683 (24 March 1945). See also J. H. Grill, *The Nazi Movement in Baden, 1920–1945*, Chapel Hill, 1983, p. 457.
42. HStAS, Bü3 (Crailsheim), Honhardt, 29 October 1948. See also ibid., Bü1 (Aalen), von Franz, Adelmannsfelden.
43. Broszat *et al.* (eds), *Bayern*, pp. 685–6 (7 April 1945).
44. HStAS, Bü4 (Crailsheim), 'Kämpfe um Bächlingen'; Bü1 (Aalen), 'Besetzung in Neresheim'.
45. Ibid., Bü77 (Tettnang), Walter Bärlin, 9 April 1946.
46. Ibid., Bü1 (Aalen), Aalen (town), 9 October 1948; Hugo Theurer, 'Die letzten Kriegstage von Aalen', undated; Bü4 (Crailsheim), 'Kämpfe um Bächlingen'; Grill, *Baden*, p. 457.
47. HStAS, Bü1 (Aalen), 'Geschichtliche Darstellung der letzten Kriegstage', Dalkingen, 5 November 1948; 'Geschichtliche Darstellung der letzten Kriegstagen in Oberkochen', 5 November 1948; Bü77 (Tettnang), Dr Gmelin, 'Wie es zur Übergabe der Stadt Friedrichshafen kam', undated.
48. Ibid., Bü1 (Aalen), von Franz, Adelmannsfelden.
49. Ibid., 'Kriegsereignisse in der Gemeinde Zipplingen Kreis Aalen' undated.

19

The Uses of Remembrance:
The Legacy of
the Communist Resistance in
the German Democratic Republic*

Eve Rosenhaft

The German Communist Party (KPD) was the only major political party in Germany that attempted to maintain a coherent organisational structure during the Third Reich and to mobilise popular resistance through illegal activity. In the attempt, the party's cadres were bled almost to the point of extinction, and active opposition on the part of the working population remained a distant dream in the face of massive indifference, police terror and the sheer struggle for survival. From the ruins of war, the German communists rescued their honour and a powerful impulse towards social and political reconstruction. This legacy suffered very different fates in divided Germany. In the West, the communist resistance became an object of cultivated oblivion; in the East, of pious celebration.

In the Federal Republic, the incompatibility of communism and the national tradition is a matter of judicial record. The banning of the KPD in 1956 represents not only a defensive gesture of the budding security state but also a more than symbolic purging of the anti-fascist tradition, a closing-off of one channel of organised memory. A similar function was served by the official harassment of the *Vereinigung der Verfolgten des Nazi-Regimes* (Association of Persecutees of the Nazi Regime, VVN), a pressure group of former prisoners and resistance fighters which had been founded in 1946 on an interzonal basis, and continued to have links with East Germany after 1949. As early as 1950 its members were barred from public employment. The 1956 law on compensation to the victims of Nazism stipulated that people who had opposed the constitutional order after May 1949 could not claim compensation, and this provision was invoked against members of the VVN as well as against active communists. In 1959 the West German government attempted to outlaw the VVN on the grounds that it was a communist front organisation.[1] It was left to a younger generation to raise the claims of the communist and labour-movement resistance again in the 1970s.

At the same time, it is a striking feature of the West German attitude to the recent past that even the sections of the German resistance that the Federal Republic claims as its own – those of liberal intellectuals, churchmen and women, and army officers determined at the last to save the honour of the 'other Germany' – have been treated with nearly as much embarrassment as National Socialism itself. This attests to some uncertainty about the value of historical remembrance. This uncertainty has been confronted in recent West German debates about the proper form and purposes of memorials to the Nazi period. But it remains the case – and a telling index of the official mentality of the Federal Republic – that West Germans celebrate only one secular national holiday apart from 1 May. That is not 20 July, but 17 June, the day of the workers' uprising in East Germany – a celebration of somebody else's political activity.

Even at the level of visible memorials, the contrast with East Germany is striking. Since 1945 the second Sunday in September has been celebrated in the Soviet Zone and the German Democratic Republic (GDR) as a national 'Memorial Day for the Victims of Fascism', and 11 September was a school holiday well into the 1960s. What is more apparent to the visitor, particularly in Berlin, is that the events and individuals of the Third Reich are everywhere memorialised – in the names of streets, squares, schools and factories, in monumental sculpture and 'tradition cabinets', in which school pupils and factory workers display the results of pious research about their respective local heroes, and in innumerable plaques. These mark not only the sites, for example, of destroyed synagogues, Gestapo offices and 'unofficial' concentration camps, but also the homes and workplaces of individual resisters and deportees. This practice of tying the terror and heroism of the Third Reich to very specific and very ordinary places and individuals, with its unmistakable hortatory function, is only now beginning to be echoed in the Federal Republic;[2] it is highly reminiscent of the long-standing practice of French municipalities in memorialising local resistance movements.

This is not entirely accidental, since the national identity of the GDR rests on the depiction of National Socialism as a kind of occupying power from which the German people had to be liberated. If the liberation in the end came from without, through the agency of the Red Army, then the activity of the German resistance bore witness to the moral claim of the people as a whole, which until 1988 allowed the government of the Democratic Republic to renounce any responsibility for compensation to the victims of Nazism. *Per contra*, an articulate construct of this kind clearly makes it easier to identify publicly, through both symbolic representations and institutions, with both the victims and the opponents of Nazism. The activities of the resistance are acknowledged as having laid the foundations for the new order. For their service to society, resistance fighters and other victims of Nazi persecution resident in the GDR (and their children) were rewarded with privileged access to housing, health and education, as well as special pensions, in one of the first legislative acts of the new republic.[3] All resisters and victims are thus honoured. In the formal celebration of the resistance, the communist opposition to Hitler has a special place because it embodies the link between native anti-fascism, the Soviet Union as liberator and protector, and the first generation of political leaders in the GDR; its activities confirm the historical claim to leadership of the Socialist Unity Party (SED), the KPD's successor and state party, and thereby testify to the legitimacy of the political system in which it has a key position.

But the idea of a clean break with the Nazi past has never been unproblematic. In contrast to those countries for which resistance to Nazism was unequivocally part of a national liberation struggle, neither East nor West Germany has been able simply to draw a line between 'us' and 'them'; emerging from an immediate post-war situation in which the policies of the occupying powers discouraged such line-drawing, both German states have had in the end to find ways of representing (in all senses of the word) both 'us' and 'them', and where possible mobilising both in the construction of post-war society. In the GDR the plausible construction of a continuous tradition of revolutionary socialist and communist opposition which informs the celebration of the resistance as national heroes disguises a process by which some aspects of the resistance have been selected and instrumentalised at the expense of others. In practice, this meant that from a very early stage in the history of the Republic the experiences of certain members of the communist movement were accorded a greater weight than others, in spite of their common suffering and indeed their common heroism.

This theme seems to me to be worth pursuing not only for its intrinsic interest, but also for its relevance to wider questions about the character of the East German polity. The celebration of the resistance has several functions in the GDR. It has first of all the legitimating function outlined above. It also serves to provide examples and role models of the kind that are essential tools in the government's efforts to mobilise the population in fulfilment of the phrase 'work, plan, govern yourself' which appears in the GDR's constitution. The question of how effective the myth of resistance and its propagation have been in generating a culture of socialist reconstruction cannot be answered within the scope of this essay, or even within the confines of a more detailed study of the treatment of the resistance theme in East German society. What such a study can do is to throw some light on the plausibility of the moral and political message for the population at large, in terms of its formal structure and relationship to other aspects of state policy. This essay aims to sketch out in preliminary form some of the relevant aspects of the communist resistance and its aftermath.

Although the KPD was the first victim of Hitler's 'legal revolution', following the Reichstag Fire in 1933, the party continued in the first years after the Nazi take-over to pursue a policy by which it deliberately exposed itself to the full force of political terror.[4] The 'ultra-left' analysis of the world situation, in force in the Comintern since 1928, anticipated the relatively rapid bankruptcy of National Socialism, and insisted that the national Communist Parties must exercise leadership independent of all other parties in order to win the working class and the lower middle class to the revolutionary cause. For the KPD, this meant maintaining its posture of hostility to Social Democracy, while continuing as far as possible to demonstrate its own presence and commitment through public actions such as the distribution of leaflets. Although the KPD's achievements in moving printed material produced illegally in Germany or smuggled into the country were prodigious, this kind of activity was calculated to attract the attention of the authorities. But wherever the communists continued to carry on 'business as usual', even in the most constructive forms, they and their allies were exposed. In Wuppertal, for example, communists and social democrats came together in the autumn of 1934 to rebuild the trade unions, and managed to organise some 400 workers in individual factory sections; but the very size of the undertaking guaranteed that it would be uncovered by the Gestapo, as it was in 1935. It was already clear by the summer of 1934 that the KPD was critically weakened; it had reportedly lost some two-thirds of its pre-1933 membership of over 300,000, and the regional leadership cadres had had to be reconstructed seven and eight times following arrests. The capture by the Gestapo of the KPD's 'operational leadership' in Berlin in March 1935, followed by a second wave of mass arrests throughout the country, climaxed the development which led to a change in policy at the end of 1935.

The party's 'Brussels Conference', which actually met in Moscow in October, took the decision to reorganise the party underground. In place of the old centralised structure, the initiative would now be left largely to small, independent groups, who would maintain contact with the party in exile through instructors. The instructors were sent into Germany from KPD bases in neighbouring states – Czechoslovakia, Switzerland, France, Belgium, the Netherlands and Denmark – and these 'section leaderships', in turn, received instructions from an 'External Secretariat' in Paris. Instead of carrying out independent actions, communists were now urged to infiltrate fascist organisations, and, in concert with social democrats, to use them as the basis for propagating democratic demands. On the whole, neither communists nor social democrats were inclined to adopt this tactic. Rather, in the mid-1930s, when oppositional work was generally made more difficult by the economic recovery, local communist groups devoted themselves to exploiting the opportunities for workplace agitation offered by circumstances of near-full employment. As the leadership candidly complained, however, communist activity had no apparent impact on 'the masses'; even in the autumn of 1938, when circumstances appeared to confirm the warnings of Hitler's opponents that Nazism meant war, it was not possible to mobilise popular anxiety into an oppositional movement. At the same time, all efforts to form an alliance with the Social Democrats, whether at the level of local or national leaderships or in negotiations between the Second and Third Internationals, proved fruitless. The result was a further shift in policy, from early 1939, towards the renewal of centrally directed independent action by KPD sections. In the wake of the Hitler–Stalin pact the KPD was urged to rebuild its regional organisations and set up a new headquarters in Germany – a return to the dangerous tactics of the early thirties.

The strategy of reconstructing a co-ordinated resistance movement from outside the country was critically undermined by the outbreak of war in 1939. The successive occupation of the countries in which the KPD had its external bases severely restricted the activities of the communists in Western Europe (even where they managed to escape internment and deportation to Germany). At the same time, the war meant heightened police watchfulness and sharpened political terror in Germany. The attempts by KPD instructors to set up illegal organisations in Germany during this period are remarkable for their tenacity and for their maintenance, against the odds, of a drum-roll of oppositional propaganda. But their history is on the whole one of false starts, inexcusable gambles and premature imprisonments. Communist resistance activity within Germany intensified during the war, and this was at least in part a response to the urgings of the party leadership; ironically, though, resistance groups had if anything a better chance of survival the longer they remained cut off from foreign contacts. The group of young Berlin Jews around Herbert Baum, for example, came together as early as 1936, and managed to avoid discovery until their attempt to fire-bomb an anti-Soviet exhibition in May 1942 – an entirely symbolic act inspired by the KPD call to action, which led to the arrest and execution of the members of the group and to reprisals against the Berlin Jewish population. By contrast, the underground networks built up by Anton Saefkow in Berlin and by Georg Schumann, Theodor Neubauer and Martin Schwantes in Central Germany maintained a more or less continuous activity from late 1940 until they were swept up in the wave of arrests that followed the 20 July 1944 assassination attempt; although the official East German history accords them collectively the status of a second 'operational leadership' of the KPD, they operated largely in isolation from the communists in exile and did not undertake open propaganda actions.

For most of the life of the Third Reich the mass of politically active communists was in prison or in concentration camps; at the outbreak of war, between 60 and 70 per cent of the party's pre-1933 membership was under lock and key. It was hardly possible to organise an uprising from this position. Hitler's camps and prisons did, however, provide the communists with an institutional framework within which they were able to prosecute their party's claim to leadership and sustain and cultivate its political traditions in anticipation of liberation. In concentration camps like Dachau, Buchenwald and Sachsenhausen, in which prisoners played a part in camp administration, communists sought out positions in the induction centres and the infirmaries or, very commonly, acted as *Blockälteste*; in this role they had to answer to the camp commandants for order in their respective blocks, but they were also in a position to negotiate with the SS, to procure food, medicine and other necessities for their fellow-prisoners, and to maintain net-

works of information and communication on a camp-wide level
and even between camps. In some cases, contacts were established
between prisoners and members of the communist underground
still at large. In spite of their brutal regime, the concentration
camps, like the prisons which housed large numbers of political
prisoners, became centres of political education and debate, in
which communists argued, recruited and self-consciously developed their plans for a future after the defeat of Nazism.[5]

A further consequence of the outbreak of war in 1939 was the
definitive transfer of leadership within the KPD to the Politburo in
Moscow. The KPD Chairman, Wilhelm Pieck, had been there
since 1935, and had been joined by Politburo Secretary Walter
Ulbricht and others in 1938. For the most part, this group had no
direct contact with the underground party, but had heretofore
drawn its information from instructors by way of the West European sections. As a result of the difficulties of carrying out a
continuous exchange of information across the German border, its
members remained only imperfectly informed about the actual
situation of the resistance in Germany. The practical contribution
of the Moscow leadership to the development of a resistance
movement in Germany therefore consisted mainly in the formulation of policy and its transmission to communists and sympathisers
through radio broadcasts. In addition, after the German attack on
the Soviet Union in June 1941 agents of the KPD began to build up
a separate arm of the opposition to Hitler through propaganda and
re-education efforts among German prisoners of war, the *Nationalkomitee Freies Deutschland* (NKFD). In both of these areas of activity, the exile leadership had to orient itself according to
considerations other than the immediate concerns of the communist underground, whether these were the military-strategic im-
peratives as perceived from the vantage point of the Soviet Union
or the need to appeal to the particular interests of captured members of the German officer corps.[6]

It is hardly surprising, then, that differences emerged between
the communists inside and outside Germany.[7] 'Are those people in
Moscow living on the moon?' was the response of one underground organiser to the instruction from Moscow to build
workers' and soldiers' councils.[8] On the whole, activists in the
underground retained their optimism about the possibility of organising popular opposition once the time was right, while they
confined themselves in the interval to building networks, and,
through their illegal publications, encouraging such actions as
could be taken at a local or individual level. By contrast, the exile

leadership staked everything on the call for organised resistance, and when this failed engaged in extensive debates about how far the working-class had succumbed to fascism; by 1945, KPD members in Moscow were broadly of the opinion that the working class as a whole had capitulated. These differing perceptions of the possibility for popular action against Hitler in wartime correlate with divergent expectations about the appropriate balance between the organisational activity of party cadres and popular mobilisation that emerged in the period of liberation and reconstruction.

In their articulate programmes for post-war Germany, too, the respective views of the exile and underground communists echo their varying experiences. The general trend in the political views of the leading underground communists is exemplified in the May 1944 declaration 'We Communists and the *Nationalkomitee Freies Deutschland*', which was drafted by Saefkow, Neubauer and the Hamburg communist Franz Jacob, and circulated among communist prisoners in Sachsenhausen. It envisaged the collapse of the Nazi regime as a moment of popular revolution. Local commissions would form the basis of a popular democracy of a 'new kind', which would in turn create the conditions for the rapid establishment of a 'purely proletarian democracy', or socialism. A range of views was represented among communists in the prisons and concentration camps, particularly on the question of co-operation with the social democrats. But they shared an expectation that the new order would be a socialist one, in which the party of the working class would take the lead. In 1945, after twelve years of struggle and suffering, they felt their turn had come.

This attitude inspired a wide range of independent actions by communists in the days leading up to the arrival of the Allied forces and in the weeks that followed. They played a central part in the take-over of concentration camps by their prisoners, and participated in the formation of local popular reconstruction committees, or Anti-fascist Commissions – sometimes in co–operation with members of other political groups, sometimes to their exclusion.[9] In Buchenwald, where prisoners had made extensive preparations for an armed uprising in the last months of the war, the communists carried out a review of their members and began to organise as a KPD section within days of the liberation of the camp by American troops. In Berlin, in the same areas where communists were already working in Anti-fascist Commissions, numerous 'KPD party offices' sprang up, in spite of the continuing ban on party-political activity. From these offices came posters and leaflets calling for the dictatorship of the proletariat. On the island of

Usedom communists declared that the dictatorship of the proletariat had already arrived; and in many other parts of Mecklenburg, red militias and commissariats were established, their members identifiable by armbands with the hammer and sickle emblem. In Pirna the population was instructed to address members of the new local administration as *Du* and 'Comrade', and to use the greeting 'Red Front'. Meanwhile, parts of Saxony, Thuringia and Brandenburg witnessed the spontaneous formation of Communist–Social Democratic Unity parties with democratic socialist programmes.[10]

The leadership in Moscow took a different view of the prospects for social revolution. Between 1935 and 1945 its policy oscillated between characterising the fight against fascism as a phase in the revolutionary struggle of the working class and propagating an alliance between all anti-fascist groups in the spirit of popular democracy. By 1944 the certainty of a military victory over Hitler, the continued ineffectuality of the communist resistance, and the preoccupation with the symbolic successes of the NKFD among non-socialist soldiers and officers all contributed to the decision that the KPD needed a programme for action, and that that programme should be a democratic rather than a revolutionary socialist one. In October 1944 leading members of the Central Committee drafted an 'Action Programme for the Fighting Democratic Block'. Further discussions in early 1945 led to drawing up detailed plans for action to be undertaken by the new administrations in Soviet-occupied territories. These provided the guidelines for the three groups that took up their work in Germany behind the Russian lines in the last days of the war – groups led by Ulbricht in Berlin, Anton Ackermann in Saxony and Gustav Sobottka in Mecklenburg. And their message was repeated in the declaration issued by the KPD on 11 June 1945, after the Soviets had lifted the provisional ban on political parties for their zone of occupation. The essential points of the programme expressed in all these documents were as follows: the triumph of National Socialism, its penetration into all sections of the population and the failure of the German people as a whole to overthrow it were the result of long-term weaknesses within German society, and in particular of the infirmity of the democratic tradition. Post-war Germany must therefore complete the task that the revolutionaries of 1848 had begun, namely the firm establishment of bourgeois democracy. The economic correlates of this were a democratic land-reform and maintenance of private ownership in the economy, except for energy-related and transport industries or the property of Nazi leaders and war criminals, which should be taken over by local or regional government. In order to create the institutional foundation for these measures, proven anti-fascists from the churches, the intelligentsia and the urban and rural lower middle classes, as well as from the working class, should from the start be encouraged to participate in local administration. In all of this, the Communist Party had a leading role to play; but it must act as a party among parties, and it could only carry out that role effectively if it was systematically rebuilt on the basis of democratic centralism.[11]

This programme implied a whole series of rebuffs to the old communists. The idea that the transformation should be a democratic rather than a socialist one, which stood in marked contrast to the emphatic calls for socialisation on the part of the new SPD, met with blank incomprehension on the part of many, as indeed did the idea that they should abandon the political high ground in favour of co-operation with their old enemies. In meetings and speeches during the weeks following the issuing of the 11 June declaration, Central Committee members had repeatedly to emphasise that the democratic programme was not a tactical manoeuvre, but represented the only possible basis for social and political reconstruction; even in the medium term, socialism was not a realistic prospect. They complained among themselves that the majority of the old comrades still maintained 'sectarian attitudes', that they were 'stuck in the politics of 1933', that they carried out the new line only half-seriously – 'and then their slogan is still "Red Front"'.

The leadership position also implied a discounting of the experience and achievements of the communist underground. Not only did it acknowledge that the communists had no monopoly on anti–fascist sentiment; it also served to emphasise the embarrassing ineffectuality of the communist opposition, as did the repeated admission by the leadership that the KPD had made mistakes, which in the circumstances had the character not of necessary self-criticism but of an attempt to curry favour with potential allies. Moreover, the new programme was based on a vision of popular acquiescence to National Socialism from which those communists who had exercised only passive resistance or who had retreated into the private cultivation of tradition and local networks were not excluded.

In the longer term, the fact that the communists were at the same time assigned a leading role in reconstruction put the old resistance fighters in the painful position of having to defend to their fellow-Germans the Soviet policies of dismantling and reparations that were premised on their common complicity in the crimes of National Socialism. And this paradox was typical for the communist movement in the second half of 1945. For while the Central Committee criticised the old 'sectarians' for isolating themselves from other anti-fascist elements, it could not envisage the leading role of the party except as one exercised under its own direction independent of the effective influence of other popular movements. The forming of alliances had to await the consolidation of the respective parties. The beginning of the process of formally re-building the party thus brought an end to the phase of popular mobilisation and spontaneous alliances in which communists had played an active part. Instead of 'messing around [*Rummurkserei*] with Anti-fa[scist Commissions]' (thus Ulbricht to Dimitroff), the Communists should bring reliable anti-fascists into the party. By July 1945 the Anti-fascist Commissions had either been dissolved or their members had been absorbed into formal local administrations. At the same time, the party called a halt to all local initiatives towards organisational unity between Communists and Social Democrats. These measures, although generally successful in their execution, met variously with passive resistance and open protest from the old activists.

In the first phases of the liberation, the Communist leadership operated on the basis of a clear hierarchy of political authority in which the old resistance fighters had no independent role to play. The first groups to take up their work behind the Russian lines in 1945 consisted exclusively of members of the KPD who had been in Moscow and re-educated prisoners of war. Subject to the needs and decisions of the Soviet military authorities, these exile communists were responsible for appointing people to posts in local administration; in filling these posts they were advised by the Central Committee to draw first on members of pre-1933 'anti-fascist organisations' who had been active in the resistance, and then on 'responsible and adaptable' members of the intelligentsia who had not belonged to the Nazi Party or the Hitler Youth. Similarly, in the reconstruction of the KPD itself, the old communists found they had no automatic claim to a place of honour; rather, they had to submit to a review of their actions during the past twelve years, giving oral and written assurances and naming witnesses who could vouch for their good behaviour. Communist activists returning to party work from concentration camps were summoned before a commission of the Central Committee to answer for their own and other KPD members' activities while in confinement. For the party press it was self-evident 'that we must set particularly high standards for the Communist Party members of 1932/33'; by virtue of their very seniority, they were most open to the suspicion of passivity or complicity after 1933. By contrast, Ulbricht urged that Catholics who were proven anti–fascists should be encouraged to join the party without any discussion as to their religious beliefs or practices.

How serious was the breach between the exile leadership and the rank and file? On this question, interpretations turn to a considerable extent on political sympathy, which finds Western Marxists generally convinced of the authenticity of grass-roots sentiment, and Marxist-Leninist writers subscribing to the authority of the party.[12] The sources themselves are ambiguous. In this context, the best work of Marxist-Leninist scholars is valuable for its reminder that party discipline and respect for the authority of the leadership in the last resort are active values within the communist tradition which serve an important integrative function, perhaps doubly so in times of trial and crisis. In general, the case for the tactical correctness of the anti-fascist–democratic programme is a strong one; even authors critical of the Ulbricht leadership comment on the illusory character of the expectations of the underground communists, and the most recent West German work has made it clear that the range of deviant attitudes among the rank-and-file was too broad to permit us to speak of a coherent opposition to Ulbricht.[13] It is even possible to present the practice of the Moscow leadership in the spring and summer of 1945 as privileging the old communists,[14] and in particular as honouring the active resistance fighters by definitively marking them out from the mass.

At the same time, there is independent evidence for a generalised distrust of the old rank-and-file on the part of the Moscow leadership, and especially Ulbricht – a distrust which formed the complement to the strategic aim of broadening the basis of support for the party's programme both within and outside its own ranks.[15] The readiness of the new leadership to shake off the old communists was thus in keeping with the policy of centralisation of power within the party that goes under the name of Stalinisation. The Stalinisation of the KPD has often been depicted as a continuous process beginning in the mid-1920s.[16] It is arguable, however, that the leadership posture of 1945 had a prior history, not so much in the Stalinisation of the pre-1933 party as in the failure to transform the KPD into the perfectly articulated machine of the Stalinist dream. Although the KPD's leaders had indeed pursued their (and the Comintern's) tactical vision in increasing isolation from the daily life of the party, they had never succeeded either in making themselves independent of the rank-and-file or in purging the movement of the utopian impulses and rootedness in particular proletarian milieus that made it at once volatile and immobile. The wartime sojourn in Moscow brought the Politburo closer to the ideal of independence, and from 1945 on the Ulbricht leadership successfully neutralised the rank-and-file by large-scale recruiting of 'new blood'. The old activists were reduced to a minority, and kept in their place with exhortations against complacency and the enforcement of a scale of values that expressly placed performance before political qualification.[17]

Within four years after the liberation, much of the policy of 1945 had been reversed or abandoned as having fulfilled its purpose. In April 1946 the KPD and SPD combined to form the SED. As early as the autumn of 1945 the range of private firms subject to expropriation was expanded, and the SED went into the local elections of 1946 with the slogan 'Peace, Democracy, Socialism'. During 1948 the SED began a programme of transforming itself from a mass party back into a cadre party, a process which involved extensive purges over the next three years. The emerging Republic regularly paid formal homage to the victims and opponents of Nazism, and activists who had spent the Hitler years in Germany took up prominent positions in party and government. It was not the old communists who benefited from the restructuring of the party, however, but rather new cadres whose political reliability was matched by technical and managerial skills. The move towards socialism was accompanied, on the one hand, by the imposition of management structures and practices which had no pedigree in the German socialist tradition,[18] and, on the other, by the continuing constitutional arrangement of an alliance between democratic parties, in which even the old Nazis were allowed a party of their own (the NDPD, founded in May 1948).

At the same time articulated perceptions of the resistance ever more clearly reflected the current policy preoccupations of the SED. A central concern of the late 1940s and early 1950s was to raise productivity by encouraging individual and collective initiative in the form of the *Aktivistenbewegung*, with its hero in the miner Adolf Hennecke, who overfulfilled his norm by 280 per cent. Early popular accounts of the communist resistance were dedicated to the Hennecke Activists; people who had been politically active in the first period after the liberation, many of them resistance fighters emerging from prison or underground, were later celebrated under the title *Aktivisten der ersten Stunde*.[19] In this phase, the resistance fighters were honoured for their embodiment of past activism, but they were equally summoned to continued activity as the qualification for recognition.

In the late 1950s the resistance again became a theme in party debates and official policy, but now in the context of concerns about the stability of the socialist system as a whole, and the resistance tradition was appealed to as a means of legitimating the leadership and communicating socialist values. The 1950s had a dual character in East Germany. On the one hand, they were years of consolidation after the hardships and uncertainties of the post-war period. By the same token, however, the 1950s were charac-terised by more or less continuous crisis, since what the leaders of the new Republic were seeking to consolidate was a new kind of social and political order. Popular opposition to the policies of forcing productivity under the first Five Year Plan culminated in the uprising of 17 June 1953. After 1956 continuing discontent combined with the promise of liberalisation throughout Eastern Europe to fuel an apparent challenge to Ulbricht's leadership within the SED. At the thirty-fifth plenary session of the SED Central Committee, at the beginning of February 1958, the argu-ments of the opposition for a decentralisation of economic decision-making and for a 'gentle' path to socialism were put forward for the last time, and formally rejected.

Among the apparently less important topics before the Central Committee on that occasion was the proposal of the Politburo, 'in response to suggestions from the population', to institute a medal for resistance fighters.[20] It may have been the presence of this item on the agenda that prompted a remark which accounts of the Central Committee meeting rarely fail to mention. Fritz Selbmann, one of the group critical of the current policy, characterised the difference between them and the Ulbricht group with the words: 'Some sat in prison, or in concentration camps, the others talked on the radio.' The discussion in which this remark was made was essentially a debate about economic policy, in which Selbmann spoke from the point of view of practical experience as Deputy Chairman of the State Planning Commission (he was shortly to be censured by Ulbricht for 'managerism'). Moreover, the remark itself overstates the clarity of the divide in the Central Committee; not all of the prominent liberalisers and critics of Ulbricht disci-plined during 1957 and 1958 had spent the years of illegality in Germany. The reference to older differences, with its implicit invocation of an alternative communist tradition, nevertheless struck a nerve. In the ensuing discussion, Selbmann's comments were interpreted as a personal attack on Ulbricht, and answered with highly personal observations on his own failings, in which he was accused among other things of complacency and arrogance –

the conventional sins of old communists.

On 22 February, less than three weeks after the beginning of the Plenum, the Council of Ministers announced the institution of the Medal for Fighters against Fascism 1933–45, to be awarded 'for services to the German people in the anti-fascist resistance struggle'; those persecuted by the Nazi regime were eligible for the award 'in so far as they retained their anti-fascist attitudes after 1945 and actively support the development of the rule of the workers and peasants in the GDR'.[21] One of the functions of the new award was thus to delimit the category of 'official' resistance by setting ideological as well as practical preconditions. The new definition of resistance was further elaborated at the March 1958 meeting of the Committee of Anti-fascist Resistance Fighters in the GDR. (This body replaced the VVN in the GDR, which was dissolved in 1953 on the grounds that its aims were now official government policy.)[22] The meeting voted its approval for the decisions of the Central Committee, and declared the resistance fighters 'most closely allied with the Central Committee of the SED, whose whole policy is informed by the lessons and experiences of the anti–fascist resistance against barbaric Hitler-Fascism'. It expressed its 'outrage' at 'Fritz Selbmann's attempt to set the comrades who sat in fascist concentration camps against those who actively fought fascism from exile, especially from the Soviet Union', an attempt which 'serves only the enemies of socialism and peace. . . . The title "Resistance Fighter" belongs only to those who acknowledge the leadership of the party of the working class, defend the unity of the party and do everything to build socialism in the GDR.' In the same declaration, the Committee emphasised the more general function of commemoration: 'Every anti-fascist resistance fighter must be a socialist educator of our working people and youth. . . . Part of the socialist education of our people is the transmission of the lessons and experiences of the anti–fascist struggle.' The role of the resistance was thus firmly linked to the task that the SED had set itself in early 1958, namely to combine new methods in the *Aktivistenbewegung* with new forms of 'socialist propaganda'. In recognition of the principle that 'questions of socio-economic transformation and of the transformation of consciousness are closely linked', Ulbricht would turn his attention in the following months towards the codification of 'socialist morality' and the development of cultural policy.

The principles on which the medal was awarded appear to have been designed to confirm a particular set of lessons. The West German index of prominent figures in the GDR compiled in 1963 names 163 recipients of the medal.[23] The list comprises the most prominent of the first batch of recipients (including both Ulbricht and Selbmann). The vast majority of those named (141) had been communists or the children of communists before 1933. The next largest group (14) comprised men and women who had been Social Democrats before 1945 and gone on to be active in the SED. A further 3 had begun their political careers as prisoners of war in the NKFD. There were also a Catholic priest, Karl Fischer, who had been involved in non-communist resistance activities before 1945, and was a leading figure in the East German CDU (and a member of the executive of the Committee of Anti-fascist Resistance Fighters), and a leading academic and former editor of the liberal *Vossische Zeitung*. The message was as clear as it was familiar. The old communists had won special honours in the resistance, but the contributions of exiles and illegals had been of equal value; and they had not been the only ones. When Otto Grotewohl told his audience at the formal opening of the Buchenwald Memorial in September 1958, 'The resistance struggle against Hitler-Fascism was organised and led by the working class and its parties', the emphasis was on the plural. And in 1960 the Committee called on the population of Berlin to celebrate 11 September in the names equally of the KPD leader Thälmann, the SPD leader Breitscheid and the Protestant Pastor Schneider, all murdered in Buchenwald.[24]

The mention of Buchenwald recalls us to a nodal point in the commemoration of the resistance. It is certainly a coincidence that the Buchenwald Memorial was opened in the year of the Central Committee debate and the institution of the anti-fascist medal (to be followed by the opening of the Ravensbrück Memorial a year later, and the Sachsenhausen Memorial in 1961). That event had a long and complicated prehistory. Within ten days of their liberation, former prisoners had erected a wooden obelisk in the camp grounds, and this was the first of several provisional monuments to be constructed at various sites in the environs of Buchenwald and the city of Weimar. By 1948 discussions were also under way about developing what was left of the camp as a museum. In this phase, the initiative lay with former prisoners organised in the VVN; yet in spite of the support and encouragement of the regional authorities, plans for a memorial repeatedly foundered on the shortage of money and materials. The turning-point came in the 1950s; in 1951, the SED Central Committee voted funds for a museum on the camp grounds, and in 1954 the Council of Ministers of the GDR gave its approval to a government proposal for the construction of a separate memorial some distance away. These decisions brought the development of the site firmly within the purview of the party and the state at the central level, the more so as the new Committee of Anti-fascist Resistance Fighters, unlike the VVN, existed only as a central body without local organisations.

This did not exclude discussion, contradiction or ambivalence. For example, it is characteristic of the problems of consolidation of the early 1950s that the symbolic statement of Buchenwald had to compete for funds with the demands of housing construction. Moreover, the designs for the memorial were widely circulated among the public, and popular interest was mobilised through appeals to contribute money or volunteer to work towards its construction. Buchenwald's message as a quintessential 'anti-fascist monument' was worked out in the course of its planning, where there was a shift in emphasis from illustrating the horrors of Nazi terror and memorialising the victims to celebrating the element of active resistance in the camp and the inevitability of victory over fascism;[25] but this was the outcome of extensive discussions, in which former camp inmates took part along with the participating artists and representatives of state and party. The result was a complex whose ambivalence none the less clearly reflects its origins in a period when the past as well as the future was being definitively reconstructed. On the north-west slope of the hill lie the remains of the camp itself, from the beginning a place of education as well as of pilgrimage, with exhibitions repeatedly updated to reflect new research and new perceptions of the character of Nazi persecution. On the south slope, a kilometre away, lies the monument of 1958. It is constructed around a series of mass graves, but it is more than a cemetery; nor is it simply a memorial (*Denkmal*): it is also a reminder and warning (*Mahnmal*). It, too, aims to educate a wider public, though its message is communicated through a series of monumental bas-reliefs and sculptures, and not least through their ingenious arrangement in the landscape.

As an object in itself, this new Buchenwald seems to exemplify a process by which the image of the resistance was detached from its lived reality and recreated in symbolic and discursive terms. This process echoes, and indeed has its beginnings in, the early demobilisation of the old communists. In the medium- and long-term perceptions of many former prisoners and resistance fighters, the Democratic Republic clearly established its right to invoke their struggle by realising the aims to which the survivors of Buchenwald committed themselves in April 1945: the punishment of the guilty and the extirpation of Nazism. In 1945, though, anti-fascist transformation from above was still a promise, which served to justify the retreat from grass-roots revolutionary action. That demobilisation constitutes a break in the continuity between the immediate past and hope for the future that made action possible and meaningful in the wake of liberation. Permanent loss of momentum and withdrawal from political activity would be normal consequences of such a breach, and this may help to account for the situation of the 1950s, in which the will to action had to be recreated in the form of activism.

NOTES

*This paper was completed too early to take into account the drastic changes which occurred in the German Democratic Republic at the end of 1989.

1. M. Oppenheimer (ed.), *Vom Häftlingskomitee zum Bund der Antifaschisten. Der Weg der Vereinigung der Verfolgten des Naziregimes*, Frankfurt am Main, 1972, pp. 5–84.
2. Cf. U. Puvogel (ed.), *Gedenkstätten für die Opfer des Nationalsozialismus. Eine Dokumentation*, Bonn, 1987, p. 151.
3. See the article 'Wiedergutmachung', in *DDR-Handbuch*, Cologne, 1985, p. 1484; *Die Rechtliche Stellung der anerkannten Verfolgten des Naziregimes in der DDR*, Hrsg. vom Zentralvorstand der VVN in der DDR, Berlin, 1950.
4. The following account is based primarily on D. J. K. Peukert, *Die KPD im Widerstand*, Wuppertal, 1980; A. Merson, *Communist Resistance in Nazi Germany*, London, 1985; B. Herlemann, *Auf verlorenem Posten. Kommunistischer Widerstand im Zweiten Weltkrieg. Die Knöchel-Organisation*, Bonn, 1986; A. Sywottek, *Deutsche Volksdemokratie. Studien zur politischen Konzeption der KPD 1935–1946*, Düsseldorf, 1971; Institut für Marxismus-Leninismus beim ZK der SED, *Geschichte der deutschen Arbeiterbewegung*, vol. 5, Berlin, 1966.
5. See F. Pingel, *Häftlinge unter SS-Herrschaft*, Hamburg, 1978, pp. 59 ff., 106 ff.
6. Sywottek, *Deutsche Volksdemokratie*, pp. 123 ff.; B. Scheurig, *Freies Deutschland. Das Nationalkomitee und der Bund deutscher Offiziere in der Sowjetunion 1943–1945*, Cologne, 1984.
7. On the various conceptions within the KPD for post-war reconstruction, see Sywottek, *Deutsche Volksdemokratie*; *Geschichte der deutschen Arbeiterbewegung*; G. Benser, *Die KPD im Jahre der Befreiung. Vorbereitung und Aufbau der legalen kommunistischen Massenpartei*, Berlin, 1985; F. Stössel, *Positionen und Strömungen in der KPD/SED 1945–1954*, Cologne, 1985; D. Staritz, *Sozialismus in einem halben Lande. Zur*

Programmatik und Politik der KPD/SED in der Phase der antifaschistisch-demokratischen Umwälzung in der DDR, Berlin, 1976.
8. Herlemann, *Auf verlorenem Posten*, p. 101.
9. Pingel, *Häftlinge*, pp. 219 ff.; L. Niethammer, U. Borsdorf and P. Brandt (eds), *Arbeiterinitiative 1945*, Wuppertal, 1976, pp. 179 ff.; S. Thomas, *Entscheidung in Berlin*, Berlin, 1967, pp. 31 ff.
10. See the works of Benser, Stössel and Staritz for extensive accounts of communist activity in early 1945 (from which these examples are drawn). These authors also provide evidence for the divergence between leadership and rank-and-file attitudes outlined below, as do Sywottek and Thomas. Another important source is the letters and speeches of Walter Ulbricht, in *Zur Geschichte der deutschen Arbeiterbewegung*, vol. 2 and supplement, Berlin, 1963 and 1966.
11. The documents are reprinted in H. Laschitza, *Kämpferische Demokratie gegen Faschismus*, Berlin, 1969, pp. 193–228; *Dokumente der Kommunistischen Partei Deutschlands 1945–1956*, Berlin, 1965, reprint, n.p., 1973, pp. 1–8.
12. The former tendency is best represented by Dietrich Staritz, the latter by Günter Benser.
13. For example, Staritz, *Sozialismus*, p. 32; and Stössel, *Positionen und Strömungen, passim*.
14. G. Sandford, *From Hitler to Ulbricht: The Communist Reconstruction of East Germany 1945–46*, Princeton, 1983.
15. The *locus classicus* for Ulbricht's cynical attitude to rank-and-file action is W. Leonhard, *Die Revolution entlässt ihre Kinder*, Cologne–Berlin, 1955.
16. See, for example, W. Müller, *Die KPD und die 'Einheit' der Arbeiterklasse*, Frankfurt am Main–NY, 1979, elaborating a general interpretation best represented by the work of Hermann Weber.
17. Staritz, *Sozialismus*, p. 89. Cf. R. Schwarzenbach, *Die Kaderpolitik der SED in der Staatsverwaltung*, Cologne, 1976, pp. 66 ff.
18. Staritz, *Sozialismus*, pp. 111 ff; Stössel, *Positionen und Strömungen*, p. 634 and *passim*.
19. K. Kühn, *Die letzte Runde. Widerstandsgruppe NKFD*, Berlin, 1949; *Neues Deutschland* (hereafter ND), 17 April 1965.
20. For the following account, see ND, 2, 25, and 26 February and 9 March 1958. Cf. M. McCauley, *Marxism-Leninism in the German Democratic Republic*, London, 1979, p. 101; M. Jänicke, *Der dritte Weg. Die antistalinistische Opposition gegen Ulbricht seit 1953*, Cologne, 1964, pp. 91 f.; H. Weber, *Geschichte der DDR*, Munich, 1985, pp. 287 ff., 309 ff.
21. *Gesetzblatt der Deutschen Demokratischen Republik*, 1959, I, pp. 212 f; F. Bartel, *Auszeichnungen der DDR von den Anfängen bis zur Gegenwart*, Berlin, 1979, pp. 157 f.
22. A. Heldring, *The International Federation of Resistance Movements: History and Background*, The Hague, 1969, p. 60; *SBZ von A bis Z*, Bonn, 1966.
23. *SBZ-Biographie*, Bonn, 1965.

24. *SBZ von 1957–1958*, Bonn, 1960; *SBZ von 1959–60*, Bonn, 1964. The medal for resistance fighters, which was still in the official list of GDR awards in 1989, bears the portraits of Thälmann and Breitscheid.
25. H. Koch, *Nationale Mahn- und Gedenkstätte Buchenwald. Geschichte ihrer Entstehung*, Buchenwaldheft 31, Weimar–Buchenwald, 1988. Cf. V. Frank, *Antifaschistische Mahnmale in der DDR. Ihre künstlerische und architektonische Gestaltung*, Leipzig, 1970.

20

Conclusion:
How Far Could
the German Resistance Have
Changed the Course of History?*

Michael Balfour

A. J. P. Taylor has said that establishing what actually did happen, and why, is in itself so difficult that no time should be wasted on speculating what might have happened differently. Yet, how can we appreciate the importance of what did happen without occasionally speculating as to what the alternatives may have been? How can one learn from mistakes if one does not weigh up what would have been needed to avoid making them? The following exercise in counterfactual history is offered with a view to establishing what might have happened *if* the anti-Nazi Germans had been more skilful or more fortunate. The question calls for two separate answers, one relating to the period before the Nazi accession to power, the other to the period after it.

I. Prior to 30 January 1933

Fascism is something which is so hard to eject once it has gained power that every effort should be made to prevent it from doing so. Was this practicable in Germany? Obviously, if one takes the discussion far enough back, all sorts of alternative scenarios are conceivable. But even if one keeps to the three years after 1930, it looks in retrospect as though on at least five occasions relatively small changes in the behaviour of relatively few individuals would have kept Hitler out of power, viz. at the times of (1) Brüning's resort to government by decree under Article 48 in 1930; (2) his enforced resignation at the end of May 1932; (3) Papen's take-over as Reich Commissioner for Prussia in July 1932; (4) Schleicher's attempt to split the Nazis by forming a coalition with Gregor Strasser in December 1932; and (5) Hitler's appointment as Chancellor.

Yet when one looks at them more closely, one sees that it was not altogether by chance that the occasions developed as they did. The weakness of the anti-Nazis lay not so much in their lack of skill or bad luck as in lack of numbers. This deficiency was above all due to the refusal of the overwhelming majority of Germans, in defiance of Schiller's maxim that *Die Weltgeschichte ist das Weltgericht*, to accept the verdict of the First World War, both as regards to the establishment of a democratic regime domestically and in terms of the rejection of Germany's claim to a larger share in international affairs. This verdict was felt to be incompatible with the picture of the world which had been inculcated into Germans during the preceding century. In 1919 they had had little choice but to accept the terms imposed upon them (although the situation would have been clarified if they had refused all co-operation). But by 1930 the forces which had made such a *Diktat* possible were no longer available for maintaining the result. Externally, the victors had been weakened by the withdrawal of America into isolation and the growing concern in Britain about her economic and political strength. Internally, the settlement embodied in the Weimar Republic was something which the majority of Germans would probably never have chosen for themselves, and which finally lost its authority with the onset of economic depression. The people who should have defended Weimar inside Germany were demoralised by its political failure and afraid that an appeal to force would result in their total defeat. It is easy to say that death on the barricades between 1930 and 1933 would have been preferable to death in the concentration camps afterwards. But how many reinforcements would have appeared from either inside or outside Germany through the spectacle of workers dying on the barricades? The subsequent example of Spain is not encouraging.

But even if one accepts that Germany was bound to relapse into authoritarian government and renew its claim to world power, did it necessarily follow that the leader of this attempt had to be Hitler? Surely, a nationalist government is conceivable which would have contented itself with Germany's 1914 frontiers and with the moderate amount of anti-Semitic prejudice which was endemic in

German society. The British and French, aware that theirs was a position which they were not strong enough to hold against a determined assault, would have gone far to meet the demands of such a government. The German Restoration could have been achieved without provoking war.

How long, though, would a nationalist Germany have remained content with a mere return to its 1914 status, when it had been precisely a desire to improve on that status which had been the ultimate cause of war in that year? Moreover, the nationalists' attempt to take over the government failed dismally in 1932. They needed popular support if they were to reverse the verdict of 1918, and such public approval could only be forthcoming if nationalism could be made to look socialist. Could that have been achieved by someone like Goebbels or Gregor Strasser, or was the personality of Hitler indispensable? It is tempting to say that, if events had taken an unfavourable turn for him at one of the crucial moments between 1930 and 1933, his support would have dwindled even more than it did in the late summer of 1932, and he ultimately would have gone down in history as a rabble-rouser from the lunatic fringe. Nevertheless, the forces making for his access to power were a good deal stronger than such a judgement would imply. We must believe, if we are to attach any value to morality and human creativity, that individuals are able to change the course of history. But deflecting a historical movement is like stopping an express train or a supertanker. The process has to start far back if it is to be effective at the critical moment.

Suppose, however, that an isolated individual, alive to Hitler's menace, had assassinated him before 1933. Such a deed would have been easier to achieve then than later. How much difference would have been made? The victim would have become a martyr for his followers to avenge. The demand for vengeance would have raised the temperature of German politics. Posterity would never have imagined the misdeeds of which Hitler proved capable. All in all, there is little likelihood that such an assassination would have improved the prospects for democracy's survival in Germany. Even if it is a mistake for that form of government to turn the other cheek too often, things are coming to a pretty pass if its chances of enduring have to depend on its enemies being murdered quickly!

Behind these speculations lies a more profound question. Was Hitler primarily the cause of Germany's (temporary) success or the engineer of its downfall? Germany might not have got as far as it did in 1941–2 if it had not had an infinitely ambitious leader prepared to take risks based on his intuitions. Yet that leader had misjudged Britain's readiness to fight in 1939, Russia's ability to resist in 1941 and the strength of hostility which his effort to exterminate the Jews would arouse throughout the world. The result was the complete collapse of 1945. Germany's chances of achieving a lasting improvement in its position might have been greater if it had had leaders more inclined to weigh chances against capacities. As the British diplomat William Strang wrote in 1939, 'Without Hitler, Germany might be less evil but not necessarily less dangerous.' Or would the generals, left to themselves, have been so cautious that they would never at any point have risked attacking anyone?

II. The Third Reich 1933–45

When we turn to the period after the Nazis had gained power, the question to be asked automatically changes. What were then the chances of ousting them by action inside Germany, and what consequences might have been expected if that had been done?

For a number of reasons successful action against the National Socialists had become more difficult:

1. Their firm grip on the coercive machine and the radical way in which they exploited it disillusioned those who had imagined that it would still be possible to continue offering the kind of opposition with which men and women had faced earlier tyrannies. Not only was the Gestapo even less humane than the Inquisition had been, massacre had also become mechanised; while bureaucracy made it easier to identify subversion, and the media and education to control thought.

2. Although the increase in the number of acts which were forbidden under Nazism led to an increase in the number of ways in which nonconformity could be shown, the shortage of democrats in Germany meant that those who did want to make a demonstration were deprived of the very thing which Mao later described as vital to an underground movement, namely a sympathetic population. As soon as dissidence became significant, either in character or scale, it was almost certain to be noticed and repressed.

3. Until about 1938, the belief that Hitler was benefiting Germany was nourished by his achievements at home and abroad. He so often proved the prophets of doom wrong that many doubters became convinced of his genius. This was exploited by the Nazi propaganda apparatus.

4. Apprehension about Hitler's methods (rather than his objectives) developed between 1938 and 1940 in the General Staff and the higher ranks of the German administration, but never quite came to the point of action to remove power from his hands. Whether such a step would have been successful (e.g. in September 1938) is questionable. The possibility was checked, in any case, by his successes between 1938 and 1941.

5. Although a good deal of optimism must have been needed to go on believing in victory after the winter of 1942–3, the prospects of a stalemate and compromise peace must have seemed quite reasonable to many Germans until July 1944. But, since the enemy had meanwhile become confident of victory, attempts to negotiate such a settlement failed; and anti-Nazi Germans therefore had to reckon with the possibility that they might not significantly improve Germany's prospects by a change of leadership.

All these factors made the prospects of unarmed action hopeless. Those Germans who had the authority to give orders to armed organisations were unwilling to take the responsibility of using them to switch leaders. Those who lacked such power, yet were convinced of the need for a change, were driven to plan an assassination (which could only be done within the military structure). Yet assassination was not easy to carry out. Those with access to the target were not prepared to strike; those prepared to do so did not have access, or only under conditions which made it a hit-or-miss affair. Hitler's removal had, in the end, to be the work of foreign bayonets.

Nevertheless, three attempts to kill him came close to success. What was likely to have followed if any one had accomplished its goal?

a. Elser's bomb in the Munich beer-cellar on 8 November 1939

This was the work of an individual with no collaborators or plans for what was to follow. No blame would have attached to the *Wehrmacht*, and the likelihood is that a coalition of moderate Nazis and generals under Hitler's designated successor, Hermann Goering, would have taken over. They would have renewed the *Führer's* October peace offer, and the chances of its being taken up would have been better. The future disposition of the Sudetenland and of the Polish Corridor would have been stumbling-blocks, but the indications were that the British and French would have wished to compromise. Yet any settlement would have been precarious. Germany, having rearmed, would have looked for improvements in its 1937 position, and its demands would sooner or later have been more than the other powers were willing to concede.

b. The Tresckow–Schlabrendorff bomb in Hitler's aircraft on 13 March 1943

This misfire not only provides the most interesting opportunity for speculation, but is also a classic instance of the way in which small material accidents can affect the course of human affairs. Goering would presumably have claimed the succession, and it is hard to see who could have challenged him immediately – neither Himmler nor Goebbels possessed the necessary popularity. To judge by the evidence from 1944, the public would have reacted violently against the perpetrators. If the part played by General von Tresckow and Lieutenant von Schlabrendorff had come to light, the generals would have faced a choice between letting them be put on trial or, by protecting them, precipitating a clash with the SS, which could not be ruled out in any event. But a safer assumption is that an uneasy truce would have been established between Army and Party, and a provisional government representing both set up. The generals would presumably have made clear how slim the chances of victory had become; and before long authoritative peace-feelers would have been extended.

Although it was only seven weeks since the demand by the Allies for unconditional surrender had been announced, it is hard to believe that Roosevelt and Churchill would have stuck to the formula for long or been allowed to do so by their respective publics. Territorially, a return to the 1937 frontiers (rather than those of 1914) might have provided a starting-point for negotiation; but difficulties would have arisen over such areas as Austria, the Corridor, the Sudetenland and possibly Alsace. If Stalin had demanded the slice of Poland which he had gained in 1939 (and lost again in 1941), Roosevelt and Churchill could hardly have agreed, yet could not have prevented him from taking it; nor could they have compensated Poland by persuading the Germans to give the Poles German-inhabited land on their eastern frontier. There would have been ample support in Germany for re-establishing the rule of law, rescinding specifically Nazi laws, and releasing political prisoners. The anti-Semitic programme could have stopped at once. A thorough purge of Party members from key positions, and their punishment for acts of inhumanity, would have been harder

to agree upon, as would steps towards disarmament. The first
negotiations would almost certainly have ended in deadlock, and
the Germans would have had to accept harsher terms than they had
reckoned with. Yet it is hard to believe that, if Hitler had been
killed in March 1943, the war would have gone on for another
twenty-six months, or that German power would have been reduced to the level fixed at Potsdam. A great number of lives would
have been saved and a good deal of physical destruction avoided.
Many Germans would again have refused to accept that they had
been beaten. Germany would have changed substantially less than
it has done since 1945, and would have stayed united. The Reich
would have remained more and the Soviet Union less of a potential
menace to the post-war security of the rest of Europe.

c. The Stauffenberg bomb on 20 July 1944

If this had killed Hitler, there would probably have been an immediate clash between the *Wehrmacht* and the SS, with the pre-
ponderance of public opinion on the side of the latter. Even if
fighting had not broken out at once, animosities would have
seriously interfered with the handling of the military situation
between 1 August and 15 September. Sooner or later the German
forces would have had no alternative but to surrender unconditionally, thus permitting the occupation arrangements of 1945 to be put
into effect. However, a large number of Germans would have
remained unconvinced that they had been beaten in a fair fight, and
they would have put the blame once again on internal weakness. A
number of lives would have been saved, although the SS might
have executed without trial such conspirators as came into their
hands. Much destruction would have been avoided. Conceivably,
the Anglo-Americans and the Russians would have been drawn
into opposite sides of a German civil war.

There is one other possibility which deserves to be considered. The
military position on 20 August 1944 was much worse for Germany
than it had been a month earlier. If the generals had not been
inhibited by the knowledge of how the conspirators were being
treated, they might have decided that the moment had finally come
when power had to be removed from Hitler's hands. But if Count
von Stauffenberg had not become General Fromm's Chief of Staff
in July 1944, he could never have obtained access to Hitler, and
there would have been neither a bomb nor vengeance taken on
those involved in exploding it. There was something to be said for

General von Hammerstein's advice: 'Don't kill him too early.' Yet a *Putsch* in August would have come too late to avoid the need for accepting unconditional surrender, and would have created the impression that internal treachery and not inferiority in battle had been the cause of Germany's defeat.

The upshot of these speculations would seem to be that: the elimination of Hitler in November 1939 would not have obviated the need to fight the war; his elimination in July or August 1944 would not have made any significant difference in the result of the war for Germany, except by providing a spurious explanation for the defeat; and his elimination in March 1943 would have led to the war's ending with a compromise peace rather than unconditional surrender.

Which of these outcomes would have led to the most desirable form of peace and contributed most to the subsequent happiness of mankind? Most anti-Nazi Germans among the upper classes believed firmly that a lasting peace was most likely to have been achieved by terms which left their country in roughly the same position as it was in 1914 or 1937. They believed it to be in the general interest that Germany should dominate Central and South-Eastern Europe, if not the Continent as a whole, thereby bringing order and with it prosperity. A number of British and Americans shared this view. They wanted to end as soon as possible the cruelties and damage which, as they saw it, the need to defeat Hitler was forcing them to inflict upon the Reich. They trusted in the good faith of the conspirators, and thought that the experience of the Third Reich would make Germans generally more appreciative of democratic ideas and institutions, and keener to hold on to liberty now that they knew what life was like without it. They thought that Europe needed not only a prosperous Germany, but also one powerful enough to hold back the Soviet Union.

The core resisters in Germany believed that complete defeat was what Germany deserved, and that such a defeat was a necessary prelude to thoroughgoing internal reform. Other non-Germans were reluctant to take the chance that what had failed before (namely, leaving Germany to carry out her own reconstruction) would succeed at the second attempt. They knew that many Germans, even within the conspiracy, still felt that democracy was ill-suited to the country's position in the world and to the mentality of its inhabitants. They saw a need to change German society which they did not trust the Germans, if left to themselves, to carry far enough. They feared that if Germany were allowed a dominant position in Europe, it would in due course use it to extend its power outside Europe. They asked what assurances there could be that the 'good' Germans, if helped to achieve power, would be able to hold it against the 'bad' Germans, when this had not proved possible hitherto. Was it not desirable to fight the war to the conclusion of unconditional surrender not merely to have a say in the political and social shape of post-war Germany but also to demonstrate as clearly as possible the limits to German strength? Even if the extra months of a longer war involved a cost in lives, this would be less than was likely to result from a Third World War (even before it was realised that such a war would be nuclear). This view was widely shared in countries which the Germans had occupied. The most numerous of all the German anti-Nazi groups was meanwhile hoping that a Soviet victory would lead to the establishment of a Communist Germany.

In practice, it was the second policy which was at first put into effect, to be discarded gradually for a combination of the first and third. It is too early to pass judgement on this solution, which was not wholly premeditated. Whether a peace endures largely depends on whether it establishes an order (boundaries, constitutions, possessions) giving to each signatory a position roughly corresponding (and recognised as corresponding) to the terms which that state might hope to achieve as the result of further fighting. As has been said above, the main defect of Versailles was that it did not accomplish this. For forty-five years the arrangements made at Yalta and Potsdam have (although not altogether in the way intended) done so. West Germany has known that any attempt to regain the eastern territories would be met by Russia with overwhelming conventional forces, thereby unleashing on the part of America the totally unprecedented weapon of a nuclear strike. The USSR has known that a similar response would meet any attempt to extend Communism by force into Western Europe. The Federal Republic has become and remained a democratic state largely as an implicit condition of receiving military and economic aid from the US. The result has disproved the view that democratic government did not suit Germany. There are signs that this condition of affairs may be breaking up; but it is altogether too early to try to evaluate their likely significance.

If, however, the Americans continue to maintain their position in Western Europe, and civil war can simultaneously be avoided in Eastern Europe, it might seem that the conspirators against Hitler risked and lost their lives unnecessarily. For it cannot be said that they played much part in bringing about the present state of world affairs. It can be argued that they would have done better to have kept themselves in existence so as to be available for public service in post-war Germany. Once Hitler had gained access to power he should, on this view, have been left to exercise it, in the confident hope that such evil was bound sooner or later, somehow or other, to bring about its own downfall. *Alle Schuld rächt sich auf Erde.* But not merely does this view imply that no attempt should be made to decide politics on moral grounds. It also leaves out of account the inability of some human beings to 'endure an hour and see injustice done'. What chance does virtue have of prevailing in the long run if nobody is prepared to listen to its promptings at particular moments? The example thus matters more than the result.

NOTE

*This paper was completed too early to take into account the drastic changes which occurred in Eastern Europe at the end of 1989.

Contributors

WILLIAM SHERIDAN ALLEN was emeritus professor of history at the State University of New York at Buffalo when he passed away in 2013. His books include *The Nazi Seizure of Power: The Experience of a Single German Town 1922–1945* (1965, 1984) and *The Infancy of Nazism: The Memoirs of Ex-Gauleiter Albert Krebs 1923–1933* (1976), which he edited and translated. He also wrote scholarly articles on aspects of the Third Reich.

MICHAEL BALFOUR, CBE, taught politics at Oxford until the Second World War, and history at the University of East Anglia from 1966 to 1974, where he became emeritus professor. He was director of the branch of the Control Commission supervising the German information media in the British occupation zone in Germany from 1946 to 1947, and chief information officer of the HM Board of Trade from 1947 to 1964. His many books include *The Kaiser and His Times* (1964); *Propaganda in War 1939–1945: Organisations, Policies and Publics in Britain and Germany* (1978); (with Julian Frisby) *Helmuth von Moltke: A Leader Against Hitler* (1972); and *Withstanding Hitler in Germany 1933–1945* (1988). He passed away in 1995.

RAINER A. BLASIUS has been an editor at the *Frankfurter Allgemeine Zeitung* since 2000; and honorary professor of modern history at the Rheinische Friedrich-Wilhelms-Universität in Bonn since 2003. From 1980 to 1990 he was a historian at the Gesamtdeutsches Institut in Bonn. He is the author of *Für Großdeutschland – gegen den großen Krieg. Ernst von Weizsäcker in den Krisen um die Tschechoslowakei und Polen 1938/39* (1981), and of scholarly articles on Adam von Trott zu Solz and the foreign policies of England and Germany during World War II. He is the editor of several volumes in *Dokumente zur Deutschlandpolitik*, and was director of the Außenstelle des (Münchener) Instituts für Zeitgeschichte im Auswärtigen Amt until April 2000. He was also scholarly director of the series *Akten zur Auswärtigen Politik der Bundesrepublik Deutschland*.

JOHN S. CONWAY is emeritus professor of history at the University of British Columbia. He is author of *The Nazi Persecution of the Churches, 1933–1945* (1968), and of scholarly articles on German church history, the churches and the Holocaust, the Vatican and peace studies.

HAROLD C. DEUTSCH was emeritus professor of history at the University of Minnesota when he passed away in 1995. He was also professor for thirteen years at the National and US Army War Colleges. His many publications include the books *The Conspiracy Against Hitler in the Twilight War* (1968) and *Hitler and his Generals: The Hidden Crisis, January–June 1938* (1974), as well as many scholarly articles on German military history and the German resistance to Hitler.

DONALD DIETRICH was emeritus professor of theology at Boston College when he passed away in 2013. His books include *The Goethezeit: Metamorphosis in Catholic Theology in the Age of Idealism* (1979); *Catholic Citizens in the Third Reich: Psycho-Social Principles and Moral Reasoning* (1988); *God and Humanity in Auschwitz: Jewish-Christian Relations and Sanctioned Murder* (2008); and *Human Rights and the Catholic Tradition* (2007). He also edited *Christian Responses to the Holocaust: Moral and Ethical Issues* (2003), and authored many articles on church history in Germany during the nineteenth and twentieth centuries. He served on the Committee on Church Relations and the Holocaust at the US Holocaust Memorial Museum and as chairperson of the Theology Department at Boston College, and was the recipient of many awards and grants.

ROBERT P. ERICKSEN is Kurt Mayer Chair in Holocaust Studies and professor of history at Pacific Lutheran University. He is the author of *Theologians under Hitler: Gerhard Kittel, Paul Althaus and Emanuel Hirsch* (1985) and *Complicity in the Holocaust: Churches and Universities in Nazi Germany* (2012); and is co-editor with Susannah Heschel of *Betrayal: German Churches and the Holocaust* (1999). He is presently completing *Christians in Nazi Germany* for the Cambridge University Press Short History Series. He is a founding member on the board of editors of *Kirchliche Zeitgeschichte* and the online journal *Contemporary Church History Quarterly*, and is chair of the Committee on Ethics, Religion and the Holocaust at the US Holocaust Memorial Museum.

ROBERT GELLATELY is the Earl Ray Beck Professor of History at Florida State University. He has edited *The Nuremberg Interviews: An American Psychiatrist's Conversations with the Defendants and Witnesses at the Nuremberg Trials* (2004) and co-edited *The Specter of Genocide: Mass Murder and other Mass Crimes in Historical Perspective* (2003); *Social Outsiders in Nazi Germany* (2001);

and *Accusatory Practices: Denunciation in Modern European History, 1789–1989* (1997). He is the author of *The Politics of Economic Despair: Shopkeepers and German Politics, 1890–1914* (1974); *The Gestapo and German Society: Enforcing Racial Policy, 1933–1945* (1990); *Backing Hitler: Consent and Coercion in Nazi Germany, 1933–1945* (2001); *Lenin, Stalin and Hitler: The Age of Social Catastrophe* (2007); and *Stalin's Curse: Battling for Communism in War and Cold War* (2013).

ERNST HANISCH is emeritus professor of history at the University of Salzburg. He is the author of *Die Ideologie des politischen Katholizismus in Österreich 1918–1938* (1977); *Nationalsozialistische Herrschaft in der Provinz. Salzburg im Dritten Reich* (1983); *Der Lange Schatten des Staates. Österreichische Geschichte 1890–1990* (1994); and *Der Obersalzberg. Das Kehlsteinhaus und Adolf Hitler* (2008). He also co-edited *NS-Herrschaft in Österreich* (1988), and authored scholarly articles on modern Austrian history.

LEONIDAS E. HILL was emeritus professor of history at the University of British Columbia when he passed away in 2012. He edited *Die Weizsäcker-Papiere 1933–1950* (1974) and *Die Weizsäcker-Papiere 1900–1932* (1982); co-edited *Mein Leben in Deutschland vor und nach 1933; und Der Anti-Nazi, Handbuch im Kampf gegen die NSDAP* (2003); and authored numerous scholarly articles on Ernst von Weizsäcker and Nazi foreign policy, and on the German resistance to Hitler.

KAROL JONCA was professor of law and history at the University of Wrocław before he passed away in 2008. His books include *German Social Policy in Silesian Heavy Industry* (in Polish, 1966); *The Nationality Policy of the Third Reich in Silesia* (in Polish, 1970); *Nuit et Brouillard. L'action terroriste Nazie* (1981); and *The Economic History of Poland* (in Polish, 1983). He was editor of the journal *Studia nad Faszyzmem i Zbrodniami Hitlerowskimi* (Studies of Fascism and the Crimes of Hitlerism).

IAN KERSHAW held the chair in modern history at the University of Sheffield until his retirement in 2008. He is the author of *The Hitler Myth: Image and Reality in the Third Reich* (1987); *Hitler: Hubris, 1889–1936* (1998); *Hitler: Nemesis, 1936–1945* (2000); *The Nazi Dictatorship: Problems and Perspectives of Interpretation* (4th ed., 2000); *The End: Germany 1944–45* (2011); and other works on Germany in the Nazi era. He is currently writing a two-volume history of Europe in the twentieth century.

HENRY O. MALONE, chief historian of the US Army Training and Doctrine Command, headquartered at Fort Monroe, Virginia, passed away in 2008. He authored *Adam von Trott zu Solz. Werdegang eines Verschwörers 1909–1938*

(1986), and scholarly articles on Adam von Trott zu Solz and the German resistance to Hitler and National Socialism.

FRANCIS R. NICOSIA is professor of history and the Raul Hilberg Distinguished Professor of Holocaust Studies at the University of Vermont. He earned his Ph.D at McGill University under Peter Hoffmann. He is the author of *Nazi Germany and the Arab World* (2014); *Zionism and Anti-Semitism in Nazi Germany* (2008, 2010); *Zionismus und Antisemitismus im Dritten Reich* (2012); and *The Third Reich and the Palestine Question* (1985, 2000); and is co-author of *The Columbia Guide to the Holocaust* (2000). He has edited several documents volumes, co-edited six volumes of scholarly essays, including *Wer bleibt, opfert seine Jahre, vielleicht sein Leben. Deutsche Juden 1938–1941* (2010), and authored articles on aspects of Nazi Jewish policy and Nazi foreign policy, and on German Jewish history in the Weimar and Nazi periods.

ARNOLD PAUCKER, OBE, was director of the Leo Baeck Institute in London from 1959 to 2001, and editor of the *Yearbook of the Leo Baeck Institute* from 1970 to 1992. He is the author of *Der jüdische Abwehrkampf gegen Antisemitismus und Nationalsozialismus in den letzten Jahren der Weimarer Republik* (1969); *Deutsche Juden im Widerstand 1933–1945. Tatsachen und Probleme* (1999); *Deutsche Juden im Kampf um Recht und Freiheit. Studien zu Abwehr, Selbstbehauptung und Widerstand der deutschen Juden seit dem Ende des 19. Jahrhunderts* (2004); and *German Jews in the Resistance 1933–1945: The Facts and the Problems* (2005). He is also editor or co-editor of ten symposium volumes, including *Die Juden im Nationalsozialistischen Deutschland / The Jews in Nazi Germany 1933–1943* (1986) and *Juden und deutsche Arbeiterbewegung bis 1933* (1992), and author of scholarly essays on German Jewish history in the nineteenth and twentieth centuries.

GER VAN ROON, emeritus professor of contemporary history at the Free University of Amsterdam, is the author of *Neuordnung im Widerstand. Der Kreisauer Kreis innerhalb der deutschen Widerstandsbewegung* (1967); *Wilhelm Staehle. Ein Leben auf der Grenze 1877–1945* (1969); *German Resistance to Hitler: Count von Moltke and the Kreisau Circle* (1971); *Widerstand im Dritten Reich. Ein Überblick* (1979); *Zwischen Neutralismus und Solidarität. Die evangelischen Niederlande und der deutsche Kirchenkampf 1933–1942* (1983); and of scholarly articles on the resistance to National Socialism in Germany and Holland.

EVE ROSENHAFT is professor of German historical studies at the University of Liverpool. She studied at McGill University and the University of Cambridge, and has held fellowships in Britain, Germany and the United States. She has published widely on aspects of German social history since the eighteenth century, including labor, gender, urban culture and issues of race and ethnicity. She is the author of *Beating the Fascists? The German Communists and Political Violence, 1929–1933* (1983); and most recently of *Black Germany: The Making and Unmaking of a Diaspora Community 1884–1960* (2013). She also co-edited *The State and Social Change in Germany, 1880–1960* (1989).

JILL STEPHENSON is emerita professor of history at the University of Edinburgh. She is the author of *Women in Nazi Society* (1975); *The Nazi Organisation of Women* (1981); *Women in Nazi Germany* (2001); *The Third Reich in Colour* (2002); *Hitler's Home Front: Württemberg under the Nazis* (2006); and of scholarly essays and articles on aspects of German social history during the Third Reich. She is also co-editor of *Hitler's Scandinavian Legacy: The Consequences of the German Invasion of the Scandinavian Countries, Then and Now* (2013).

LAWRENCE D. STOKES was emeritus professor of history at Dalhousie University in Halifax, Nova Scotia, when he passed away in 2007. He edited *Kleinstadt und Nationalsozialismus. Ausgewählte Dokumente zur Geschichte von Eutin 1918–1945* (1984); and *Der Eutiner Dichterkreis und der Nationalsozialismus 1936–1945. Eine Dokumentation* (2001). He also authored scholarly articles on Germany and especially Schleswig-Holstein during the Third Reich.

HEINRICH WALLE was Fregattenkapitän (commander senior grade), and from 1979 to 1994 staff officer and historian at the Militärgeschichtliches Forschungsamt in Freiburg im Breisgau. He is the author of *Deutsche Jüdische Soldaten 1914–1945, Katalog zur Wanderausstellung im Auftrage des Bundesministeriums der Verteidigung* (1987); *Die Tragödie des Oberleutnants zur See Oskar Kusch* (1995); *Aus Feldpostbriefen junger Christen 1939–1945* (2005); and *100 Jahre Marineflieger 1913–2013* (2013); and the editor of *Aufstand des Gewissens. Der militärische Widerstand gegen Hitler und das NS-Regime 1933–1945. Katalog zur Wanderausstellung im Auftrage des Militärgeschichtlichen Forschungsamtes* (2000). In 1987 he received the Ben Gurion Medaille of the State of Israel and the Bundesverdienstkreuz (am Bande), in 1995 he received the Ehrenkreuz der Bundeswehr (in Gold) and in 2013 he was awarded the Bundesverdienstkreuz (1.Klasse).

Bibliography

This bibliography is divided into two parts. The first lists printed sources dealing primarily with the German resistance cited by the contributors to this volume. In the second part are found a selected number of additional titles which treat the same subject. Peter Hoffmann's publications on the German resistance appear separately at the end of the Introduction.

I

Ackermann, K., *Der Widerstand der Monatsschrift Hochland gegen den Nationalsozialismus*, Munich, 1965

Adler, H. G., *Der Kampf gegen die 'Endlösung der Judenfrage'*, Bonn, 1958

Allen, W. S., 'Objective and Subjective Inhibitants in the German Resistance to Hitler', in F. H. Littel (ed.), *The German Church Struggle and the Holocaust*, Detroit, 1974

——, *The Nazi Seizure of Power: The Experience of a Single German Town 1922–1945*, rev. edn, NY, 1984

Aster, S., 'Carl Goerdeler and the Foreign Office', in A. P. Young, *The 'X' Documents*, S. Aster (ed.), London, 1974

Astor, D., 'Adam von Trott: A Personal View', in H. Bull (ed.), *The Challenge of the Third Reich: The Adam von Trott Memorial Lectures*, Oxford, 1986

Behnken, K. (ed.), *Deutschland-Berichte der Sozialdemokratischen Partei Deutschlands (SOPADE) 1934–1940*, 7 vols, Frankfurt am Main, 1980

Bell, G., 'The Background of the Hitler Plot', *The Contemporary Review*, vol. 168, 1945

Bergmann, K. H., *Die Bewegung Freies Deutschland in der Schweiz 1943–1945*, Munich, 1974

Bethge, E., *Dietrich Bonhoeffer: Man of Vision, Man of Courage*, trans. Eric Mosbacher *et al.*, NY, 1970

Blasius, R. A., *Für Großdeutschland – gegen den großen Krieg. Staatssekretär Ernst Freiherr von Weizsäcker in den Krisen um die Tschechoslowakei und Polen 1938–39*, Cologne–Vienna, 1981

——, 'Adam von Trott zu Solz', in R. Lill and H. Oberreuther (eds), *20. Juli. Portraits des Widerstands*, Düsseldorf–Vienna, 1984

Botz, G., 'Methoden- und Theorieprobleme der historischen Widerstandsforschung', in H. Konrad and W. Neugebauer (eds), *Arbeiterbewegung, Faschismus, Nationalbewußtsein*. *Festschrift zum 20jährigen Bestand des
Dokumentationsarchivs des Österreichischen Widerstandes und zum 60. Geburtstag von Herbert Steiner*, Vienna, 1983

Boyens, A., *Kirchenkampf und Ökumene 1933–1945*. *Darstellung und Dokumentation unter besonderer Berücksichtigung der Quellen des Ökumenischen
Rates der Kirchen*, Munich, 1973 (Vol. 1, 1933–1939, pub. 1969; Vol. 2,
1939–1945, pub. 1973)

Bramke, W., 'Der unbekannte Widerstand in Westsachsen 1933–1945.
Zum Problem des Widerstandsbegriffs', *Jahrbuch für Regionalgeschichte*,
vol. 13, 1986

——, 'Der antifaschistische Widerstand in der Geschichtsschreibung der
DDR in den achtziger Jahren. Forschungsstand und Probleme', *Aus
Politik und Zeitgeschichte. Beilage zur Wochenzeitung Das Parlament*, 8 July
1988

Broszat, M., 'Zur Sozialgeschichte des deutschen Widerstands', *Vierteljahrshefte für Zeitgeschichte*, vol. 34, 1986

——, 'Vom Widerstand. Bedeutungswandel in der Zeitgeschichte', in
H. Graml and K. D. Henke (eds), *Nach Hitler. Der schwierige Umgang mit
unserer Geschichte – Beiträge von Martin Broszat*, Munich, 1987

Brothers, E., 'On the Anti-Fascist Resistance of German Jews', *Year Book
of the Leo Baeck Institute*, vol. 32, 1987

Buchstab, G., Kaff, B., and Kleinmann, H.-O. (eds), *Verfolgung und
Widerstand 1933–1945. Christliche Demokraten gegen Hitler*, Düsseldorf,
1986

Conway, J. S., *The Nazi Persecution of the Churches 1933–45*, Toronto–
London–NY, 1968

Deutsch, H., *The Conspiracy against Hitler in the Twilight War*, Minneapolis, 1968

——, *Hitler and his Generals: The Hidden Crisis of January–June 1938*,
Minneapolis, 1974

Dietrich, D. J., 'Catholic Resistance in the Third Reich', *Holocaust and
Genocide Studies*, vol. 3, 1988

Dokumentationsarchiv des Österreichischen Widerstandes (ed.), *Widerstand und Verfolgung in Oberösterreich 1934–1945. Eine Dokumentation*, 2
vols, Vienna, 1982

—— (ed.), *Widerstand und Verfolgung in Niederösterreich 1934–1945. Eine
Dokumentation*, 3 vols, Vienna, 1987

Dröge, F., *Der zerredete Widerstand. Zur Soziologie und Publizistik des
Gerüchts im 2. Weltkrieg*, Düsseldorf, 1970

Dülffer, J., 'Die Machtergreifung und die Rolle der alten Eliten im Dritten
Reich', in W. Michalka (ed.), *Die nationalsozialistische Machtergreifung*,
Munich–Vienna–Zürich, 1984

Edinger, L. J., *German Exile Politics: The Social Democratic Executive Committee in the Nazi Era*, Berkeley, 1956

Ericksen, R. P., 'Widerstand als ambivalenter Gegenstand historischer

Forschung: Am Beispiel der evangelisch-theologischen Fakultät der Universität Göttingen', *Kirchliche Zeitgeschichte*, vol. 1, 1988

Eschwege, H., 'Resistance of German Jews against the Nazi Regime', *Year Book of the Leo Baeck Institute*, vol. 15, 1970

Esters, H. and Pelger, H., *Gewerkschaftler im Widerstand*, rev. edn, Bonn, 1983

Europäische Publikation e. V. (ed.), *Vollmacht des Gewissens*, 2 vols, Berlin–Frankfurt am Main, 1960–5

Foot, M. R. D., *Resistance: An Analysis of European Resistance to Nazism 1940–1945*, London, 1976

Friedländer, S., *Kurt Gerstein: The Ambiguity of Good*, trans. Charles Fullman, NY, 1969

Gallin, M. A., *German Resistance to Hitler: Ethical and Religious Factors*, Washington, 1961

Glees, A., *Exile Politics during the Second World War: The German Social Democrats in Britain*, Oxford, 1982

Graml, H. (ed.), *Widerstand im Dritten Reich. Probleme, Ereignisse, Gestalten*, Frankfurt am Main, 1984

——, Mommsen, H., Reichhardt, H.-J. and Wolf, E., *The German Resistance to Hitler*, Berkeley–London, 1970

Groscurth, H., *Tagebücher eines Abwehroffiziers 1938–1940, mit weiteren Dokumenten zur Militäropposition gegen Hitler*, ed. H. Krausnick and H. C. Deutsch, Stuttgart, 1970

Hanisch, E., 'Austrian Catholicism between Accommodation and Resistance', in F. Parkinson (ed.), *Conquering the Past: Austrian Nazism Yesterday and Today*, Detroit, 1989

Hassell, U. von, *Die Hassell-Tagebücher 1938–1944. Aufzeichnungen vom anderen Deutschland*, ed. F. Freiherr H. von Gaertringen in collaboration with K. P. Reiß, Berlin, 1988

Heldring, A., *The International Federation of Resistance Movements: History and Background*, The Hague, 1969

Herlemann, B., *Auf verlorenem Posten. Kommunistischer Widerstand im Zweiten Weltkreig – Die Knöchel-Organisation*, Bonn, 1986

Hill, L. E. (ed.), *Die Weizsäcker Papiere*, 2 vols, 1900–1932, 1933–1950, Berlin, 1974–82

——, 'Towards a New History of German Resistance to Hitler', *Central European History*, vol. 14, 1981

Höhne, H., *Canaris*, trans. J. M. Brownjohn, Garden City–London, 1979

Hummer, H., 'Region und Widerstand. Am Beispiel des Salzkammergutes', in H. Hummer, R. Kannonier and B. Kepplinger (eds), *Die Pflicht zum Widerstand. Festschrift für Peter Kammerstätter zum 75. Geburtstag*, Vienna, 1986

Institut für Demoskopie Allensbach, *Der Widerstand im Dritten Reich. Wissen und Urteil der Bevölkerung vor und nach dem 40. Jahrestag des 20. Juli 1944*, Allensbach, 1984

Jacobsen, H. A. (ed.), *July 20, 1944: The German Opposition to Hitler as Viewed by Foreign Historians – An Anthology*, Bonn, 1969

—— (ed.), *'Spiegelbild einer Verschwörung'. Die Opposition gegen Hitler und der Staatsstreich vom 20. Juli 1944 in der SD-Berichterstattung – Geheime Dokumente aus dem ehemaligen Reichsicherheitshauptamt*, 2 vols, Stuttgart, 1984

Kershaw, I., *Popular Opinion and Political Dissent in the Third Reich: Bavaria 1933–1945*, Oxford, 1983

Kettenacker, L. (ed.), *Das 'andere Deutschland' im Zweiten Weltkrieg. Emigration und Widerstand in internationaler Perspektive*, Stuttgart, 1977

Klemperer, K. von, 'Adam von Trott zu Solz and Resistance Foreign Policy', *Central European History*, vol. 14, 1981

—— (ed.), *A Noble Combat: The Letters of Shiela Grant Duff and Adam von Trott zu Solz 1932–1939*, Oxford, 1988

Klessmann, C., and Pingel, F. (eds), *Gegner des Nationalsozialismus. Wissenschaftler und Widerstandskämpfer auf der Suche nach der historischen Wirklichkeit*, Frankfurt am Main, 1980

Klönne, A., *Gegen den Strom. Ein Bericht über den Jugendwiderstand im Dritten Reich*, Hanover–Frankfurt am Main, 1958

Kordt, E., *Nicht aus den Akten . . . Die Wilhelmstraße in Frieden und Krieg – Erlebnisse, Begegnungen und Eindrücke 1928–1945*, Stuttgart, 1950

Kraus, W. H. and Almond, G. A., 'Resistance and Repression under the Nazis', in G. A. Almond (ed.), *The Struggle for Democracy in Germany*, Chapel Hill, 1949

Krebs, A., *Fritz-Dietlof Graf von der Schulenburg. Zwischen Staatsraison und Hochverrat*, Hamburg, 1964

Kühn, K., *Die letzte Runde. Widerstandsgruppe NKFD*, Berlin, 1949

Kwiet, K. and Eschwege, H., *Selbstbehauptung und Widerstand. Deutsche Juden im Kampf um Existenz und Menschenwürde 1933–1945*, Hamburg, 1984

Lill, R. and Oberreuter, H. (eds) *20. Juli. Portraits des Widerstands*, Düsseldorf–Vienna, 1984

Lindgren, H., 'Adam von Trotts Reisen nach Schweden 1942–1944. Ein Beitrag zur Frage der Auslandsverbindungen des deutschen Widerstandes', *Vierteljahrshefte für Zeitgeschichte*, vol. 18, 1970

Locke, H. G. (ed.), *The Church Confronts the Nazis: Barmen Then and Now*, NY, 1984

Löwenthal, R. and von zur Mühlen, P. (eds), *Widerstand und Verweigerung in Deutschland 1933 bis 1945*, Berlin–Bonn, 1984

Luza, R., *The Resistance in Austria 1938–1945*, Minneapolis, 1984

Malone, H. O., *Adam von Trott zu Solz. Der Werdegang eines Verschwörers 1909–1938*, Berlin, 1986

Mann, R., *Protest und Kontrolle im Dritten Reich. Nationalsozialistische Herrschaft im Alltag einer rheinischen Großstadt*, Frankfurt am Main, 1987

Marßoleck, I. and Ott, R., *Bremen im Dritten Reich. Anpaßung–Widerstand–Verfolgung*, Bremen, 1986

Mason, T. W., 'Injustice and Resistance: Barrington Moore and the Reaction of German Workers to Fascism', in R. J. Bullen *et al.* (eds), *Ideas into Politics: Aspects of European History 1880–1950*, London–Totowa, 1984

——, 'The Third Reich and the German Left: Persecution and Resistance', in H. Bull (ed.), *The Challenge of the Third Reich*, Oxford, 1986

Merson, A., *Communist Resistance in Nazi Germany*, London, 1985

Militärgeschichtliches Forschungsamt (ed.), *Aufstand des Gewissens. Der militärische Widerstand gegen Hitler und das NS-Regime 1933–1945*, Herford–Bonn, 1984

Mommsen, H., 'Fritz-Dietlof Graf von der Schulenburg und die preußische Tradition', *Vierteljahrshefte für Zeitgeschichte*, vol. 32, April 1984

——, 'Die Geschichte des deutschen Widerstands im Lichte der neueren Forschung', *Aus Politik und Zeitgeschichte*, vol. 50, 1986

Müller, K.-J., 'Die deutsche Militäropposition gegen Hitler. Zum Problem ihrer Interpretation und Analyse', in Müller, *Armee, Politik und Gesellschaft in Deutschland 1933–1945. Studien zum Verhältnis von Armee und NS-System*, Paderborn, 1979

——, *General Ludwig Beck. Studien und Dokumente zur politisch–militärischen Vorstellungswelt und Tätigkeit des Generalstabschefs des deutschen Heeres 1933–1938*, Boppard am Rhein, 1980

——, 'Die national-konservative Opposition vor dem Zweiten Weltkrieg: Zum Problem ihrer begrifflichen Erfassung', in Manfred Messerschmidt *et al.* (eds), *Militärgeschichte Probleme – Thesen – Wege*, Stuttgart, 1982

——, 'The German Military Opposition before the Second World War', in W. J. Mommsen and L. Kettenacker (eds), *The Fascist Challenge and the Policy of Appeasement*, London, 1983

——, 'The Structure and Nature of the National Conservative Opposition in Germany up to 1940', in H. W. Koch (ed.), *Aspects of the Third Reich*, NY, 1985

—— (ed.), *Der deutsche Widerstand 1933–1945*, Paderborn, 1986

Neuhäusler, J. B., *Kreuz und Hakenkreuz. Der Kampf des Nationalsozialismus gegen die katholische Kirche und der kirchliche Widerstand*, 2 vols, Munich, 1946

Nowak, K., *'Euthanasie' und Sterilisierung im 'Dritten Reich'. Die Konfrontation der evangelischen und katholischen Kirche mit dem 'Gesetz zur Verhütung erbkranken Nachwuchses' und der 'Euthanasie'-Aktion*, Göttingen, 1977 (limited edn), 1978

Paucker, A., *Der jüdische Abwehrkampf gegen Antisemitismus und Nationalsozialismus in den letzten Jahren der Weimarer Republik*, 2nd edn, Hamburg, 1969

——, 'Jewish Self-Defence', in Paucker (ed.), *Die Juden im nationalsozialistischen Deutschland/The Jews in Nazi Germany 1933–1943*, Tübingen, 1986

Peukert, D. J. K., *Die KPD im Widerstand. Verfolgung und Untergrundarbeit an Rhein und Ruhr 1933 bis 1945*, Wuppertal, 1980

——, *Inside Nazi Germany: Conformity, Opposition, and Racism in Everyday Life*, trans. Richard Deveson, New Haven–London, 1987

—— and Bajohr, F., *Spuren des Widerstands. Die Bergarbeiterbewegung im Dritten Reich und im Exil*, Munich, 1987

Pommerin, R., 'Demokraten und Pazifisten oder Rowdies und Rebellen?

Die Einschätzung der "Edelweißpiraten" im britischen Außenministerium 1944/45', *Geschichte im Westen*, vol. 2, 1987

Portmann, H. (ed.), *Bischof Graf von Galen spricht! Ein apostolischer Kampf und sein Widerhall*, Freiburg, 1946

Pütter, C., *Rundfunk gegen das 'Dritte Reich'. Deutschsprachige Rundfunkaktivitäten im Exil 1933–1945 – Ein Handbuch*, Munich–London–NY–Paris, 1986

Putz, E., *Franz Jägerstätter. . . . besser die Hände als der Wille gefesselt*, 2nd edn, Linz, 1987

—— (ed.), *Gefängnisbriefe und Aufzeichnungen. Franz Jägerstätter verweigert 1943 den Wehrdienst*, Linz, 1987

Reynolds, N., *Treason Was No Crime: Ludwig Beck, Chief of the German General Staff*, London, 1976

Ritter, G., 'The German Opposition to Hitler', *The Contemporary Review*, vol. 177, January–June 1950

——, *Carl Goerdeler und die deutsche Widerstandsbewegung*, Stuttgart, 1954

Röder, W., *Die deutschen sozialistischen Exilgruppen in Großbritannien 1940–1945. Ein Beitrag zur Geschichte des Widerstandes gegen den Nationalsozialismus*, 2nd edn, Bonn, 1973

Roon, G. van, *Wilhelm Staehle. Ein Leben auf der Grenze 1877–1945*, Munich, 1969 (reprint, Neuenhaus, 1986)

——, *German Resistance to Hitler: Count von Moltke and the Kreisau Circle*, trans. Peter Ludlow, London, 1971

——, *Widerstand im Dritten Reich. Ein Überblick*, 4th edn, Munich, 1987

Rothfels, H., 'Zwei außenpolitische Memoranden der deutschen Opposition [Frühjahr 1942]. Dokumentation', *Vierteljahrshefte für Zeitgeschichte*, vol. 5, 1957

——, *Die deutsche Opposition gegen Hitler. Eine Würdigung*, new and enlarged edn, ed. H. Graml, Frankfurt am Main, 1977 (English version of 1st edn, *The German Opposition to Hitler*, London, 1970)

Schall-Riaucour, H., *Aufstand und Gehorsam. Offizierstum und Generalstab im Umbruch – Leben und Wirken von Generaloberst Franz Halder, Generalstabschef 1938–1942*, Wiesbaden, 1972

Schacht, H., *Account Settled*, London, 1949

——, *Confessions of 'The Old Wizard'. The Autobiography of Hjalmar Horace Greeley Schacht*, Cambridge, Mass., 1956

Scheurig, B., *Ewald von Kleist-Schmenzin. Ein Konservativer gegen Hitler*, Oldenburg–Hamburg, 1968

——, *Henning von Tresckow. Eine Biographie*, Oldenburg–Hamburg, 1973

——, *Freies Deutschland. Das Nationalkomitee und der Bund Deutscher Offiziere in der Sowjetunion 1943–1945*, Cologne, 1984

Schlabrendorff, F. von, *Revolt against Hitler*, ed. G. von S. Gaevernitz, London, 1948

Schmädeke, J. and Steinbach, P. (eds), *Der Widerstand gegen den Nationalsozialismus. Die deutsche Gesellschaft und der Widerstand gegen Hitler*, Munich–Zürich, 1985

Schöllgen, G., 'Wurzeln konservativer Opposition. Ulrich von Hassell und der Übergang vom Kaiserreich zur Weimarer Republik', *Geschichte in Wissenschaft und Unterricht*, vol. 38, August 1987

Schulz, G., 'Nationalpatriotismus im Widerstand', *Vierteljahrshefte für Zeitgeschichte*, vol. 32, 1984

Stephenson, J., 'War and Society in Württemberg, 1939–1945: Beating the System', *German Studies Review*, vol. 8, 1985

Stokes, L. D., 'Sozialdemokratie contra Nationalsozialismus in Eutin 1925–1933', *Demokratische Geschichte. Jahrbuch zur Arbeiterbewegung und Demokratie in Schleswig-Holstein*, vol. 2, 1987

Sykes, C., *Tormented Loyalty: The Story of a German Aristocrat Who Defied Hitler*, NY–Evanston, 1969

Tenfelde, K., 'Proletarische Provinz. Radikalisierung und Widerstand in Penzberg/Oberbayern 1900–1945', in M. Broszat *et al.* (eds), *Bayern in der NS-Zeit*, vol. 4, Munich–Vienna, 1981

Thun-Hohenstein, R. G. von, *Der Verschwörer. General Oster und die Militäropposition*, 2nd edn, Munich, 1984

Vollmer, B., *Volksopposition im Polizeistaat. Gestapo- und Regierungsberichte 1934–1936*, Stuttgart, 1957

Weizsäcker, E. von, *Memoirs*, trans. J. Andrews, Chicago–London, 1951

Wendt, B.-J., 'Konservative Honoratioren – eine Alternative zu Hitler? Englandkontakte des deutschen Widerstandes im Jahre 1938', in D. Stegmann, B.-J. Wendt and P.-C. Witt (eds), *Deutscher Konservativismus im 19. und 20. Jahrhundert. Festschrift für Fritz Fischer*, Bonn, 1983

Wenke, B., *Interviews mit Überlebenden. Verfolgung und Widerstand in Südwestdeutschland*, Stuttgart, 1980

Zahn, G. C., *In Solitary Witness: The Life and Death of Franz Jägerstätter*, NY, 1964

Zeller, E., *The Flame of Freedom: The German Struggle against Hitler*, trans. R. P. Heller and D. R. Masters, London, 1967

——, *Geist der Freiheit. Der Zwanzigste Juli*, 5th edn, Munich, 1969

II

Abendroth, W., 'Historische Funktion und Umfang des Widerstandes der Arbeiterbewegung gegen das Dritte Reich', in P. von Oertzen (ed.), *Festschrift für Otto Brenner zum 60. Geburtstag*, Frankfurt am Main, 1967

Abshagen, K. H., *Canaris*, trans. A. H. Brodrick, London, 1956

Adolph, H. J. L., *Otto Wels und die Politik der deutschen Sozialdemokratie 1894–1939. Eine politische Biographie*, Berlin, 1971

Akademie der Künste (ed.), *Zwischen Widerstand und Anpassung. Kunst in Deutschland 1933–1945*, Berlin, 1978

Andreas-Friedrich, R., *Schattenmann: Berlin Underground 1938–1945*, trans. B. Mussey, NY, 1989

Badische Kunstverein (ed.), *Widerstand statt Anpassung. Deutsche Kunst im Widerstand gegen den Faschismus 1933–1945*, Berlin, 1980

Balfour, M., *Withstanding Hitler in Germany: 1933–45*, London, 1988

—— and Frisby, J., *Helmuth von Moltke: A Leader against Hitler*, London, 1972

Baum, W., 'Marine, Nationalsozialismus und Widerstand', *Vierteljahrs-hefte für Zeitgeschichte*, vol. 11, 1963

Beck, D., *Julius Leber. Sozialdemokrat zwischen Reform und Widerstand*, Berlin, 1983

Beck, L., *Studien*, H. Speidel (ed.), Stuttgart, 1955

Beer, H., *Widerstand gegen den Nationalsozialismus in Nürnberg 1933–1945*, Nuremberg, 1976

Beier, G., *Die illegale Reichsleitung der Gewerkschaften 1933–1945*, Cologne, 1981

Bell, G. K. A., 'Die Ökumene und die innerdeutsche Opposition', *Viertel-jahrshefte für Zeitgeschichte*, vol. 5, 1957

Berglund, G., *Deutsche Opposition gegen Hitler in Presse und Roman des Exils. Eine Darstellung und ein Vergleich mit der historischen Wirklichkeit*, Stockholm, 1972

Besier, G., *et al.* (eds), 'Der Widerstand von Kirchen und Christen gegen den Nationalsozialismus', *Kirchliche Zeitgeschichte*, vol. 1, 1988

Bethge, E., 'Adam von Trott und der deutsche Widerstand', *Vierteljahrs-hefte für Zeitgeschichte*, vol. 11, 1963

Bielenberg, C., *The Past is Myself*, London, 1969 [1968]

Biernat, K. H. and Kraushaar, L., *Die Schulze-Boysen/Harnack Organisation im antifaschistischen Kampf*, Berlin, 1970

Billstein, A., *Der eine fällt, die anderen rücken nach . . . Dokumente des Wider-standes und der Verfolgung in Krefeld 1933–1945*, Frankfurt am Main, 1973

Bleistein, R., 'Alfred Delp SJ (1907–1945)', in J. Aretz, R. Morsey and A. Rauscher (eds), *Zeitgeschichte in Lebensbildern. Aus dem deutschen Katholi-zismus des 19. und 20. Jahrhunderts*, Mainz, 1984, vol. 6

Bludau, K., *Gestapo – geheim! Widerstand und Verfolgung in Duisburg 1933–1945*, Bonn–Bad Godesberg, 1973

Boberach, H. (ed.), *Berichte des SD und der Gestapo über Kirchen und Kirchenvolk in Deutschland 1934–1944*, Mainz, 1971

—— (ed.), *Meldungen aus dem Reich 1938–1945. Die geheimen Lageberichte des Sicherheitsdienstes der SS*, Herrsching, 1984

Bosch, M. and Niess, W. (eds), *Der Widerstand im deutschen Südwesten 1933–1945*, Stuttgart, 1984

Bösch, H., *Heeresrichter Dr. Karl Sack im Widerstand. Eine historische–politi-sche Studie*, Munich, 1967

Boehm, E. H. (ed.), *We Survived: The Stories of Fourteen of the Hidden and the Hunted of Nazi Germany*, New Haven, 1949

Bonhoeffer, D., *Letters and Papers from Prison*, enlarged edn, ed. E. Bethge, London, 1971

Boveri, M., *Treason in the 20th Century*, trans. Jonathan Steinberg, London, 1961

Bracher, K. D., 'Anfänge der deutschen Widerstandsbewegung', in W. Berges and C. Hinrichs (eds), *Zur Geschichte und Problematik der Demo-kratie. Festgabe für Hans Herzfeld*, Berlin, 1958

Braubach, M., *Der Weg zum 20. Juli 1944. Ein Forschungsbericht*, Cologne–Opladen, 1953

Bremer, J., *Die sozialistische Arbeiterpartei Deutschlands (SAP). Untergrund und Exil 1933–1945*, Frankfurt am Main, 1978

Bretschneider, H., *Der Widerstand gegen den Nationalsozialismus in München 1933 bis 1945*, Munich, 1968

Brill, H. L., *Gegen den Strom*, Offenbach, 1946

Broszat, M. *et al.* (eds), *Bayern in der NZ-Zeit*, 6 vols, Munich–Vienna, 1977–83

Bryans, J. L., 'Zur britischen amtlichen Haltung gegenüber der deutschen Widerstandsbewegung', *Vierteljahrshefte für Zeitgeschichte*, vol. 1, 1953

Büchel, R., *Der deutsche Widerstand im Spiegel von Fachliteratur und Publizistik seit 1945*, Munich, 1975

Bücheler, H., *Hoepner. Ein deutsches Soldatenschicksal des 20. Jahrhunderts*, Herford, 1980

Buchheim, H., 'Ernst Niekischs Ideologie des Widerstandes', *Vierteljahrshefte für Zeitgeschichte*, vol. 5, 1957

Cartarius, U., *Bibliographie 'Widerstand'*, Munich–NY, 1984

Colvin, I., *Master Spy: The Incredible Story of Admiral Wilhelm Canaris*, NY, 1951

Delp, A., *Im Angesicht des Todes, geschrieben zwischen Verhaftung und Hinrichtung*, 9th edn, Frankfurt am Main, 1965

Dipper, C., 'Der deutsche Widerstand und die Juden', *Geschichte und Gesellschaft*, vol. 9, 1983

Dohms, P., 'Literaturbericht und Quellenübersicht zu Widerstand und Verfolgung im Rhein–Ruhrgebiet 1933–1945', in Dohms (ed.), *Flugschriften in Gestapo-Akten. Nachweis und Analyse der Flugschriften in den Gestapo-Akten des Hauptstaatsarchivs Düsseldorf*, Siegburg, 1977

Donohoe, J., *Hitler's Conservative Opponents in Bavaria 1930–1945: A Study of Catholic, Monarchist and Separatist Anti-Nazi Activities*, Leiden, 1961

Drozdzynski, A. (ed.), *Das verspottete tausendjährige Reich. Witze*, Düsseldorf, 1978

Duhnke, H., *Die KPD von 1933 bis 1945*, Cologne, 1972

Dulles, A. W., *Germany's Underground*, NY, 1947

Durzak, M. (ed.), *Die deutsche Exilliteratur 1933–1945*, Stuttgart, 1974

Ehlers, D., *Technik und Moral einer Verschwörung. Der Aufstand am 20. Juli 1944*, Bonn, 1964

Elser, J. G., *Autobiographie eines Attentäters. Aussage zum Sprengstoffanschlag im Bürgerbräukeller, München am 8. November 1939*, L. Gruchmann (ed.), Stuttgart, 1970

Finker, K., *Stauffenberg und der 20. Juli 1944*, Berlin, 1967

———, *Graf Moltke und der Kreisauer Kreis*, Berlin, 1978

Foitzik, J., *Zwischen den Fronten. Zur Politik, Organisation und Funktion linker politischer Kleinorganisationen im Widerstand 1933 bis 1939/40 unter besonderer Berücksichtigung des Exils*, Bonn, 1986

Ford, F. L., 'The Twentieth of July in the History of the German Resistance', *American Historical Review*, vol. 51, 1946

Freyberg, J. von, *Sozialdemokraten und Kommunisten. Die Revolutionären Sozialisten Deutschlands vor dem Problem der Aktionseinheit 1934–1937*, Cologne, 1973

Friedrich-Ebert-Stiftung (ed.), *Widerstand und Exil der deutschen Arbeiterbewegung 1933–1945. Grundlagen und Materialien*, Bonn, 1981

Gersdorff, R.-C. von, *Soldat im Untergang*, Frankfurt am Main–Berlin, 1977

Gerstenmaier, E., 'Der Kreisauer Kreis', *Vierteljahrshefte für Zeitgeschichte*, vol. 15, 1967

Gisevius, H. B., *To the Bitter End*, trans. R. and C. Winston, London, 1948

Gitting, H., *Illegale antifaschistische Tarnschriften 1933 bis 1945*, Frankfurt am Main, 1972

Goeb, A., *Er war sechzehn als man ihn hängte. Das kurze Leben des Widerstandskämpfers Bartholomäus Schink*, Reinbek, 1981

Goguel, R. *et al.*, *Antifaschistischer Widerstand und Klassenkampf. Die faschistische Diktatur 1933 bis 1945 und ihre Gegner – Bibliographie deutschsprachiger Literatur aus den Jahren 1945 bis 1973*, Berlin, 1976

Gollwitzer, H., Kuhn, K. and Schneider, R. (eds), *Du hast mich heimgesucht bei Nacht. Abschiedsbriefe und Aufzeichnungen des Widerstandes 1933–1945*, Munich, 1954

Graml, H., 'Der Fall Oster', *Vierteljahrshefte für Zeitgeschichte*, vol. 14, 1966

Grant Duff, S., *The Parting of Ways: A Personal Account of the Thirties*, London, 1982

Grasmann, P., *Sozialdemokraten gegen Hitler 1933–1945*, Munich, 1976

Gross, B., *Willi Münzenberg: A Political Biography*, trans. M. Jackson, East Lansing, 1974

Grossmann, K. R., *Die unbesungenen Helden. Menschen in Deutschlands dunklen Tagen*, Berlin, 1957

——, *Ossietzky. Ein deutscher Patriot*, Munich, 1963

——, *Emigration. Geschichte der Hitler-Flüchtlinge 1933–1945*, Frankfurt am Main, 1969

Gruber, H., 'Willi Münzenberg: Propagandist for and against the Comintern', *International Review of Social History*, vol. 10, 1965

Gruchmann, L., 'Jugendopposition und Justiz im Dritten Reich', in W. Benz *et al.* (eds), *Miscellanea. Festschrift für Helmut Krausnick zum 75. Geburtstag*, Stuttgart, 1980

Hammerstein-Equord, K. von, *Flucht. Aufzeichnungen nach dem 20. Juli*, Olten, 1966

Hebel-Kunze, B., *SPD und Faschismus. Zur politischen und organisatorischen Entwicklung der SPD 1932–1935*, Frankfurt am Main, 1977

Helmreich, E. C., *The German Churches under Hitler: Background, Struggle and Epilogue*, Detroit, 1979

Henderson, J. L., and Caldwell, M., *The Chainless Mind: A Study of Resistance and Liberation*, London, 1968

Herlemann, B., *Die Emigration als Kampfposten. Die Anleitung des kommunistischen Widerstandes in Deutschland aus Frankreich, Belgien und den Niederlanden*, Königstein, 1982

Herwarth von Bittenfeld, H.-H., *Zwischen Hitler und Stalin. Erlebte Zeitge-schichte 1931 bis 1945*, Frankfurt am Main, 1982

Herzfeld, H., 'Johannes Popitz. Ein Beitrag zur Geschichte des deutschen Beamtentums', in R. Dietrich and G. Oestreich (eds), *Forschungen zu Staat und Verfassung. Festgabe für Fritz Hartung*, Berlin, 1958

Hildebrand, K., 'Die ostpolitischen Vorstellungen im deutschen Wider-stand', *Geschichte in Wissenschaft und Unterricht*, vol. 29, 1978

Hoch, A., 'Das Attentat auf Hitler im Münchner Bürgerbräukeller 1939', *Vierteljahrshefte für Zeitgeschichte*, vol. 17, 1969

Hochhuth, R., *Tell 38 [Maurice Bavaud]*, trans M. W. Rolloff, Boston, 1984

Hochmuth, U., *Faschismus und Widerstand 1933–1945. Ein Verzeichnis deutschsprachiger Literatur*, Frankfurt am Main, 1973

—— and Meyer, G., *Streiflichter aus dem Hamburger Widerstand 1933–1945. Berichte und Dokumente*. Frankfurt am Main, 1969

Höhne, H., *Codeword: Direktor – The Story of the Red Orchestra*, trans. R. H. Barry, London, 1971

Horn, D., 'Youth Resistance in the Third Reich: A Social Portrait', *Journal of Social History*, vol. 7, 1973

Hüttenberger, P., 'Vorüberlegungen zum "Widerstandsbegriff"', in J. Kocka (ed.), *Theorien in der Praxis des Historikers*, Göttingen, 1977

Irving, D., *The Trail of the Fox: The Life of Field-Marshal Erwin Rommel*, London, 1977

Jahnke, K.-H., *Weiße Rose contra Hakenkreuz. Der Widerstand der Geschwis-ter Scholl und ihre Freunde*, Frankfurt am Main, 1969

——, *Entscheidungen. Jugend im Widerstand 1933–1945*, Frankfurt am Main, 1970

Jedlicka, L., *Der 20. Juli 1944 in Österreich*, Vienna, 1965

Jens, I. (ed.), *At the Heart of the White Rose: Letters and Diaries of Hans and Sophie Scholl*, trans. J. M. Brownjohn, NY, 1987

Joffroy, P., *A Spy for God: The Ordeal of Kurt Gerstein*, trans. N. Denny, NY, 1971

Kater, M. H., 'Anti-Fascist Intellectuals in the Third Reich', *Canadian Journal of History*, vol. 16, 1981

Kennan, G. and Weber, H. (eds), 'Aus dem Kadermaterial der illegalen KPD 1943', *Vierteljahrshefte für Zeitgeschichte*, vol. 20, 1972

Kerschbaumer, M.-T., *Der weibliche Name des Widerstands. Sieben Berichte*, Olten, 1980

Klemperer, K. von, 'Glaube, Religion, Kirche und der deutsche Wider-stand gegen den Nationalsozialismus', *Vierteljahrshefte für Zeitgeschichte*, vol. 28, 1980

Klönne, A. (ed.), *Jugendkriminalität und Jugendopposition im NS-Staat. Ein sozialgeschichtliches Dokument*, Münster, 1981

——, *Jugend im Dritten Reich. Die Hitler-Jugend und ihre Gegner*, Cologne, 1984

Klotzbach, K., *Gegen den Nationalsozialismus. Widerstand und Verfolgung in Dortmund 1930–1945 – Eine historisch-politische Studie*, Hanover, 1969

Kluke, P., 'Der deutsche Widerstand. Eine kritische Literaturübersicht', *Historische Zeitschrift*, vol. 169, 1949

Kopp, O. (ed.), *Widerstand und Erneuerung. Neue Berichte und Dokumente vom inneren Kampf gegen das Hitler-Regime*, Stuttgart, 1966

Kosthorst, E., *Die deutsche Opposition gegen Hitler zwischen Polen- und Frankreichfeldzug*, 3rd edn, Bonn, 1957

Kramarz, J., *Stauffenberg: The Architect of the Famous July 20th Conspiracy to Assassinate Hitler*, trans. R. H. Barry, NY, 1967

Krammer, A., 'Germans against Hitler: The Thaelmann Brigade', *Journal of Contemporary History*, vol. 4, 1969

Krausnick, H., 'Erwin Rommel und der deutsche Widerstand gegen Hitler', *Vierteljahrshefte für Zeitgeschichte*, vol. 1, 1953

Krispyn, E., *Anti-Nazi Writers in Exile*, Athens/Georgia, 1978

Kühnrich, H., *Die KPD im Kampf gegen die faschistische Diktatur 1933 bis 1945*, Berlin, 1983

Kwiet, K., 'Problems of Jewish Resistance Historiography', *Year Book of the Leo Baeck Institute*, vol. 24, 1979

Laack-Michel, U., *Albrecht Haushofer und der Nationalsozialismus*, Stuttgart, 1974

Langbein, H., *. . .nicht wie die Schafe zur Schlachtbank. Widerstand in den nationalsozialistischen Konzentrationslagern 1938–1945*, Frankfurt am Main, 1980

Laska, V., *Nazism, Resistance, and Holocaust in World War II: A Bibliography*, Metuchen, 1985

Leber, A. (ed.), *Conscience in Revolt: Sixty-Four Stories of Resistance in Germany 1933–45*, trans. R. O'Neill, London, 1957

——— (ed.), *Das gewissen entscheidet. Bereiche des deutschen Widerstandes von 1933–1945 in Lebensbildern*, 4th edn, Berlin, 1960

Leber, J., *Schriften, Reden, Briefe 1920–1945*, D. Beck and W. F. Schoeller (eds), Munich, 1976

Lehmann, H. G., *In Acht und Bann. Politische Emigration, NS-Ausbürgerung und Wiedergutmachung am Beispiel Willy Brandts*, Munich, 1976

Leithäuser, J. G., *Wilhelm Leuschner. Ein Leben für die Republik*, Cologne, 1962

Lipgens, W., *Europa-Föderationspläne der Widerstandsbewegungen 1940–1945. Eine Dokumentation*, Munich, 1968

Ludlow, P., 'Papst Pius XII, die britische Regierung und die deutsche Opposition im Winter 1939/40', *Vierteljahrshefte für Zeitgeschichte*, vol. 22, 1974

Lühe, I. von der, *Elisabeth von Thadden. Ein Schicksal unserer Zeit*, Düsseldorf–Cologne, 1966

Maier, H., 'Die SS und der 20. Juli 1944', *Vierteljahrshefte für Zeitgeschichte*, vol, 14, 1966

Mammach, K., *Die deutsche antifaschistische Widerstandsbewegung 1933–1939*, Berlin, 1974

———, *Widerstand 1933–1939. Geschichte der deutschen antifaschistischen Widerstandsbewegung im Inland und in der Emigration*, Berlin, 1984

Mann, G., 'Helmuth James von Moltke', *Journal of European Studies*, vol. 4, 1974

Mann, R., 'Widerstand gegen den Nationalsozialismus', *Neue Politische Literatur*, vol. 22, 1977

Mason, T. W., *Arbeiterklasse und Volksgemeinschaft. Dokumente und Materialien zur deutschen Arbeiterpolitik 1936–1939*, Opladen, 1975
——, 'Arbeiteropposition im nationalsozialistischen Deutschland', in D. J. K. Peukert and J. Reulecke (eds), *Die Reihen fast geschlossen. Beiträge zur Geschichte des Alltags unterm Nationalsozialismus*, Wuppertal, 1981
——, 'Arbeiter ohne Gewerkschaften. Massenwiderstand im NS-Deutschland und im faschistischen Italien', *Journal für Geschichte*, vol. 5, 1983

Matthias, E., *Sozialdemokratie und Nation. Ein Beitrag zur Ideengeschichte der sozialdemokratischen Emigration in der Prager Zeit des Parteivorstandes 1933–1938*, Stuttgart, 1952
——, 'Resistance to National Socialism: The Example of Mannheim', *Past and Present*, No. 45, 1969
—— and Link, W. (eds), *Mit dem Gesicht nach Deutschland. Eine Dokumentation über die sozialdemokratische Emigration – Aus dem Nachlaß von Friedrich Stampfer*, Düsseldorf, 1968
—— and Morsey, R. (eds), *Das Ende der Parteien 1933. Darstellungen und Dokumente*, new edn, Düsseldorf, 1984

Mausbach-Bromberger, B., *Arbeiterwiderstand im Frankfurt am Main gegen den Faschismus 1933–1945*, Frankfurt am Main, 1976

Meier, K., *Der evangelische Kirchenkampf*, 3 vols, Göttingen, 1976–84

Melnikow, D. E., *20. Juli 1944. Legende und Wirklichkeit*, 2nd rev. edn, Hamburg, 1968

Mendel, K. H., *'Blick in die Zeit' 1933–1935*, Berlin, 1983

Meyer, G., *Nacht über Hamburg. Berichte und Dokumente*, Frankfurt am Main, 1971

Miller, M., *Eugen Bolz. Staatsmann und Bekenner*, Stuttgart, 1951

Moltke, H. J. von, *A German of the Resistance: The Last Letters*, 2nd and enlarged edn, London, 1948
——, *Briefe an Freya 1939–1945*, B. Ruhm von Oppen (ed.), Munich, 1988

Mommsen, H., 'Die deutschen Gewerkschaften zwischen Anpassung und Widerstand 1930–1944', in H. O. Vetter (ed.), *Vom Sozialistengesetz zur Mitbestimmung. Zum 100. Geburtstag von Hans Böckler*, Cologne, 1975

Moraw, F., *Die Parole der 'Einheit' und die Sozialdemokratie. Zur parteiorganisatorischen und gesellschaftspolitischen Orientierung der SPD in der Periode der Illegalität und in der ersten Phase der Nachkriegszeit 1933–1948*, Bonn–Bad Godesberg, 1973

Müller, C., *Oberst i.G. Stauffenberg. Eine Biographie*, Düsseldorf, 1970

Müller, J., *Bis zur letzten Konsequenz. Ein Leben für Frieden und Freiheit*, Munich, 1975

Müller, K.-J., 'Militärpolitik, nicht Militäropposition! Eine Erwiderung', *Historische Zeitschrift*, vol. 235, 1982

Müller, W., 'Opposition und Widerstand gegen die nationalsozialistische

Herrschaft im Alltag', *Internationale wissenschaftliche Korrespondenz zur Geschichte der deutschen Arbeiterbewegung*, vol. 20, 1984

Münchheimer, W., 'Die Verfassungs- und Verwaltungsreformpläne der deutschen Opposition gegen Hitler zum 20. Juli 1944', *Europa-Archiv*, vol. 5, 1950

Muth, H., 'Jugendopposition im Dritten Reich', *Vierteljahrshefte für Zeitgeschichte*, vol. 30, 1982

Namier, L., 'Ernst von Weizsäcker', in Namier, *In the Nazi Era*, London, 1952

Nebgen, E., *Jakob Kaiser. Der Widerstandskämpfer*, Stuttgart–Berlin, 1967

Nitzsche, G., *Die Saefkow-Jakob-Bästlein-Gruppe. Dokumente und Materialien des illegalen antifaschistischen Kampfes (1942 bis 1945)*, Berlin, 1957

Noakes, J., 'The Oldenburg Crucifix Struggle of November 1936: A Case Study of Opposition in the Third Reich', in P. D. Stachura (ed.), *The Shaping of the Nazi State*, London–NY, 1978

'L'opposition allemande à Hitler', *Revue d'histoire de la deuxième guerre mondiale*, No. 36, 1959

Paetel, K. O. (ed.), *Deutsche Innere Emigration. Anti-nationalsozialistische Zeugnisse aus Deutschland*, NY, 1946

——, 'Revolutionäre und restaurative Tendenzen in der deutschen Widerstandsbewegung', *Die Neue Gesellschaft*, vol. 2, 1955

Pechel, R., *Deutscher Widerstand*, Erlenbach–Zurich 1947

Peters, H., *Verfassungs- und Verwaltungsreformbestrebungen innerhalb der Widerstandsbewegung gegen Hitler*, Münster, 1961

Peterson, E. N., *Hjalmar Schacht: For and Against Hitler – A Political-Economic Study of Germany 1923–1945*, Boston, 1954

Peukert, D. J. K., *Ruhrarbeiter gegen den Faschismus. Dokumentation über den Widerstand im Ruhrgebiet 1933–1945*, Frankfurt am Main, 1976

——, 'Edelweißpiraten, Meuten, Swing, Jugendsubkulturen im Dritten Reich', in G. Huck (ed.), *Sozialgeschichte der Freizeit. Untersuchungen zum Wandel der Alltagskultur in Deutschland*, Wuppertal, 1980

——, *Die Edelweißpiraten. Protestbewegungen jugendlicher Arbeiter im 'Dritten Reich'. Eine Dokumentation*, 3rd enlarged edn, Cologne, 1988

Pikarski, M. and Uebel, G., *Die KPD lebt. Flugblätter aus dem antifaschistischen Widerstandskampf der KPD 1933–1945*, Berlin, 1980

Pingel, F., *Häftlinge unter SS-Herrschaft. Widerstand, Selbstbehauptung und Vernichtung im Konzentrationslager*, Hamburg, 1978

Plum, G., 'Die KPD in der Illegalität. Rechenschaftsbericht einer Bezirksleitung aus dem Jahre 1934', *Vierteljahrshefte für Zeitgeschichte*, vol. 23, 1975

Poppinga, O., Barth, H. M. and Roth, H., *Ostfriesland. Biographien aus dem Widerstand*, Frankfurt am Main, 1977

Portmann, H., *Cardinal von Galen*, trans. R. L. Sedgwick, London, 1957

Prittie, T., *Germans against Hitler*, Boston–London, 1964

Radkau, J., *Die deutsche Emigration in den USA. Ihr Einfluß auf die amerikanische Europapolitik 1933–1945*, Düsseldorf, 1971

Regler, G., *The Owl of Minerva: The Autobiography of Gustav Regler*, trans. N. Denny, London, 1959

Reichhardt, H.-J., 'Neu beginnen. Ein Beitrag zur Geschichte des Widerstandes der Arbeiterbewegung gegen den Nationalsozialismus', *Jahrbuch für die Geschichte Mittel- und Ostdeutschlands*, vol. 12, 1963

Reichhold, L., *Arbeiterbewegung jenseits des totalen Staates. Die Gewerkschaften und der 20. Juli 1944*, Vienna, 1965

Röder, W., 'Deutschlandpläne der sozialdemokratischen Emigration in Großbritannien 1942–1945', *Vierteljahrshefte für Zeitgeschichte*, vol. 17, 1969

—— and Strauss, H. A. (eds), *Biographisches Handbuch der deutschsprachigen Emigration nach 1933/International Biographical Dictionary of Central European Emigres 1933–1945*, 4 vols, Munich–NY, 1980–3

Rohe, K., *Das Reichsbanner Schwarz Rot Gold. Ein Beitrag zur Geschichte und Struktur der politischen Kampfverbände zur Zeit der Weimarer Republik*, Düsseldorf, 1966

Romoser, G. K., 'The Politics of Uncertainty: The German Resistance Movement', *Social Research*, vol. 31, 1964

Roon, G. van, 'Hermann Kaiser und der deutsche Widerstand', *Vierteljahrshefte für Zeitgeschichte*, vol. 24, 1976

—— (ed.), *Völkerrecht im Dienste der Menschen. Dokumente – Helmuth James Graf von Moltke und die völkerrechtliche Gruppe bei Ausland-Abwehr*, Berlin, 1985

Rosenhaft, E., *Beating the Fascists? The German Communists and Political Violence 1929–1933*, Cambridge–NY, 1983

Rothfels, H. (ed.), 'Ausgewählte Briefe von Generalmajor Helmuth Stieff', *Vierteljahrshefte für Zeitgeschichte*, vol. 2, 1954

——, 'The German Resistance in its International Aspects', *International Affairs*, vol. 34, 1958

——, 'Die Roten Kämpfer. Zur Geschichte einer linken Widerstandsgruppe', *Vierteljahrshefte für Zeitgeschichte*, vol. 7, 1959

—— (ed.), 'Dokumentation: Adam von Trott und das State Department', *Vierteljahrshefte für Zeitgeschichte*, vol. 7, 1959

——, 'Trott und die Außenpolitik des Widerstandes', *Vierteljahrshefte für Zeitgeschichte*, vol. 12, 1964

Salm, F., *Im Schatten des Henkers. Vom Arbeiterwiderstand in Mannheim gegen faschistische Diktatur und Krieg*, 2nd rev. edn, Frankfurt am Main, 1979

Sandvoß, H.-R., *Widerstand in einem Arbeiterbezirk. Wedding 1933–1945*, Berlin, 1983

Schabrod, K., *Widerstand an Rhein und Ruhr 1933–1945*, Düsseldorf, 1969

——, *Widerstand gegen Flick und Florian. Düsseldorfer Antifaschisten über ihren Widerstand 1933–1945*, Frankfurt am Main, 1978

Schadt, J. (ed.), *Verfolgung und Widerstand unter dem Nationalsozialismus in Baden. Die Lageberichte der Gestapo und des Generalstaatsanwalts Karlsruhe 1933–1940*, Stuttgart, 1976

Schellenberger, B., *Katholische Jugend und Drittes Reich. Eine Geschichte des katholischen Jungmännerverbandes 1933–1939 unter besonderer Berücksichtigung der Rheinprovinz*, Mainz, 1975

Scheurig, B. (ed.), *Verrat hinter Stacheldraht? Das Nationalkomitee 'Freies*

Deutschland' und der Bund Deutscher Offiziere in der Sowjetunion 1943–1945, Munich, 1965

—— (ed.), *Deutscher Widerstand 1938–1944. Fortschritt oder Reaktion?*, 2nd edn, Munich, 1984

Schlabrendorff, F. von, *The Secret War against Hitler*, trans. H. Simon, NY, 1965

Schmölders, G., *Personalistischer Sozialismus. Die Wirtschaftsordnungskonzeption des Kreisauer Kreises der deutschen Widerstandsbewegung*, Cologne–Opladen, 1969

Schnell, R., *Literarische innere Emigration 1933–1945*, Stuttgart, 1976

Scholder, K. (ed.), *Die Mittwochs-Gesellschaft. Protokolle aus dem geistigen Deutschland 1932 bis 1944*, Berlin, 1982

——, *The Churches and the Third Reich*, trans. J. Bowden, 2 vols, London–Philadelphia, 1987–8

Scholl, I., *The White Rose: Munich 1942–1943*, trans. A. R. Schultz, Middletown, 1983

Schorr, H. J., *Adam Stegerwald. Gewerkschaftler und Politiker der ersten deutschen Republik*, Recklinghausen, 1966

Schramm, T.-D., *Der deutsche Widerstand gegen den Nationalsozialismus. Seine Bedeutung für die Bundesrepublik Deutschland in der Wirkung auf Institutionen und Schulbücher*, Berlin, 1980

Schramm, W. von, *Conspiracy among Generals*, trans. R. T. Clark, London, 1956

—— (ed.), *Beck und Goerdeler. Gemeinschaftsdokumente für den Frieden 1941–1944*, Munich, 1965

Schüddekopf, O.-E., *Der deutsche Widerstand gegen den Nationalsozialismus. Darstellung in Lehrplänen und Schulbüchern der Fächer Geschichte und Politik in der Bundesrepublik Deutschland*, Frankfurt am Main, 1977

Schultz, H. J. (ed.), *Der zwanzigste Juli. Alternative zu Hitler?*, Stuttgart, 1974

Schulze, H. (ed.), *Anpassung oder Widerstand? Aus den Akten des Parteivorstands der deutschen Sozialdemokratie 1932/33*, Bonn–Bad Godesberg, 1975

——, *Otto Braun oder Preußens demokratische Sendung. Eine Biographie*, Frankfurt am Main–Berlin, 1977

Schumann, W., *Ihr seid den dunklen Weg für uns gegangen . . . Skizzen aus dem Widerstand in Hann. Münden 1933–1939*, Frankfurt am Main, 1973

Schuster, K. G. P., *Der Rote Frontkämpferbund 1924–1929. Beitrag zur Geschichte und Organisationsstruktur eines politischen Kampfbundes*, Düsseldorf, 1975

Shamir, H., '"Anklage gegen den Volksverderber Hitler". Ein Beitrag zur Geschichte der Opposition im Dritten Reich', *Jahrbuch des Instituts für Deutsche Geschichte*, vol. 5, 1976

Steinberg, H.-J., *Widerstand und Verfolgung in Essen 1933–1945*, Hanover, 1969

Stern, C., *Ulbricht: A Political Biography*, trans. A. Farbstein, NY, 1965

Sywottek, A., *Deutsche Volksdemokratie. Studien zur politischen Konzeption der KPD 1935–1946*, Düsseldorf, 1971

Techniczek, M., 'Die deutsche antifaschistische Opposition und der spanische Bürgerkrieg', *Jahrbuch des Instituts für Deutsche Geschichte*, vol. 3, 1974

Thielenhaus, M., *Zwischen Anpassung und Widerstand. Deutsche Diplomaten 1938–1941 – Die politischen Aktivitäten der Beamtengruppe um Ernst von Weizsäcker im Auswärtigen Amt*, Paderborn, 1984

Trepper, L., *The Great Game: The Story of the Red Orchestra*, London, 1977

Ueberschär, G. R., 'Generaloberst Halder im militärischen Widerstand 1938–1940', *Wehrforschung*, vol. 3, 1973

——, 'Gegner des Nationalsozialismus 1933–1945', *Militärgeschichtliche Mitteilungen*, vol. 35, 1984

Vassiltchikov, M., *The Berlin Diaries 1940–1945*, London, 1985

Vielhaber, K., *Gewalt und Gewissen. Willi Graf und die 'Weiße Rose' – Eine Dokumentation*, Freiburg, 1964

Vyvyan, M., 'The German "Opposition" and Nazi Morale', *The Cambridge Journal*, vol. 2, 1948/9

Wagner, E. (ed.), *Der Generalquartiermeister. Briefe und Tagebuchaufzeichnungen des Generalquartiermeisters des Heeres General der Artillerie Eduard Wagner*, Munich, 1963

Ward, J. J., '"Smash the Fascists . . .": German Communist Efforts to Counter the Nazis 1930–31', *Central European History*, vol. 14, 1981

Weber, H., *Kommunismus in Deutschland 1918 bis 1945*, Darmstadt, 1983

Wehner, H., *Zeugnis*, ed. G. Jahn, Cologne, 1982

Weisenborn, G., *Der lautlose Aufstand. Bericht über die Widerstandsbewegung des deutschen Volkes 1933–1945*, 4th edn, Frankfurt am Main, 1974

Weiss, P., *Die Ästhetik des Widerstands. Roman*, 3 vols in one, Frankfurt am Main, 1983

Weissbecker, M., *Gegen Faschismus und Kriegsgefahr. Ein Beitrag zur Geschichte der KPD in Thüringen 1933–1935*, Erfurt, 1967

Weizsäcker, R. von, 'Der 20. Juli 1944 – Attentat aus Gewissen', in Weizsäcker, *Die deutsche Geschichte geht weiter*, Berlin, 1983

Werner, G., *Aufmachen! Gestapo! Über den Widerstand in Wuppertal 1933–1945*, Wuppertal, 1974

Wette, W., 'Mit dem Stimmzettel gegen den Faschismus? Das Dilemma des sozialdemokratischen Antifaschismus in der Endphase der Weimarer Republik', in W. Huber and J. Schwerdtfeger (eds), *Frieden, Gewalt, Sozialismus. Studien zur Geschichte der sozialistischen Arbeiterbewegung*, Stuttgart, 1976

Zeller, E., 'Claus und Berthold Stauffenberg', *Vierteljahrshefte für Zeitgeschichte*, vol. 12, 1964

Zentner, K., *Illustrierte Geschichte des Widerstandes in Deutschland und Europa 1933–1945*, Munich, 1966

Zerna, H. (ed.), *Darauf kam die Gestapo nicht. Beiträge zum Widerstand im Rundfunk*, Berlin, 1966

Zimmermann, E. and Jacobsen, H.-A. (eds), *Germans against Hitler: July 20, 1944*, trans. A. and L. Yahraes, 4th edn, Bonn, 1964

Zipfel, F., *Kirchenkampf in Deutschland 1933–1945. Religionsverfolgung und*

Selbstbehauptung der Kirchen in der nationalsozialistischen Zeit, Berlin, 1965

Zorn, G., *Widerstand in Hannover. Gegen Reaktion und Faschismus 1920–1946*, Frankfurt am Main, 1977

zur Mühlen, P. von, *'Schlägt Hitler an der Saar!' Abstimmungskampf, Emigration und Widerstand im Saargebiet 1933–1935*, Bonn, 1979

——, *Spanien war ihre Hoffnung. Die deutsche Linke im spanischen Bürgerkrieg 1936 bis 1939*, Bonn, 1983

Selected Works since 1990

Arnold, Klaus Jochen. 'Verbrecher aus eigener Initiative? Der 20. Juli 1944 und die Thesen Christian Gerlachs.' *Geschichte in Wissenschaft und Unterricht*, vol. 53, 2002.

Barkai, Avraham. *"Wehr Dich!" Der Centralverein deutscher Staatsbürger jüdischen Glaubens, 1893–1938.* Munich, 2002.

Benz, Wolfgang. *Der deutsche Widerstand gegen Hitler.* Munich, 2014.

Benz, Wolfgang, and Walter H. Pehle (eds.). *Encyclopedia of German Resistance to the Nazi Movement.* New York, 1997.

———. *Lexikon des deutschen Widerstandes.* Frankfurt, 2008.

Berg, Nicolas. *Der Holocaust und die westdeutschen Historiker.* Göttingen, 2003.

Beuys, Barbara. *Sophie Scholl. Biografie.* Munich, 2010.

Blasius, Rainer. 'Appeasement und Widerstand 1938.' In Peter Steinbach and Johannes Tuchel (eds.), *Widerstand gegen die nationalsozialistische Diktatur 1933–1945.* Bonn, 2004.

Brakelmann, Günter. *Helmuth James von Moltke 1907–1945. Eine Biographie.* Munich, 2007.

Brown-Fleming, Suzanne. *The Holocaust and the Catholic Conscience: Cardinal Aloisius Muench and the Guilt Question in Germany.* Notre Dame, IN, 2006.

Brysac, Shareen Blair. *Resisting Hitler: Mildred Harnack and the Red Orchestra.* New York, 2000.

Carsten, Francis. *Widerstand gegen Hitler. Die deutsche Arbeiter und die Nazis.* Berlin, 1996.

Clements, K. W. *Bonhoeffer and Britain.* London, 2006.

Conze, Eckart. 'Aufstand des preußischen Adels. Marion Gräfin Dönhoff und das Bild des Widerstands gegen den Nationalsozialismus in der Bundesrepublik Deutschland.' *Vierteljahrshefte für Zeitgeschichte*, vol. 51, 2003.

Conze, Eckart, et al. *Das Amt und die Vergangenheit. Deutsche Diplomaten im Dritten Reich und in der Bundesrepublik.* Munich, 2010.

Coppi, Hans, Jürgen Danyel and Johannes Tuchel (eds.). *Die Rote Kapelle im Widerstand gegen den Nationalsozialismus.* Berlin, 1994.

Daniel, Silvia. "'Troubled Loyalty'"? Britisch-Deutsche Debatten um Adam von Trott zu Solz 1933–1969.' *Vierteljahrshefte für Zeitgeschichte*, vol. 52, 2004.

Danyel, Jürgen (ed.). *Die geteilte Vergangenheit. Zum Umgang mit Nationalsozialismus und Widerstand in beiden deutschen Staaten.* Berlin, 1995.

Dramm, Sabine. *Dietrich Bonhoeffer and the Resistance.* Minneapolis, MN, 2009.

Ericksen, Robert P., *Complicity in the Holocaust: Churches and Universities in Nazi Germany.* New York, 2012.

Erler, Hans, Arnold Paucker and Ernst Ludwig Ehrlich (eds.). *"Gegen alle Vergeblichkeit."* Jüdischer Widerstand gegen den Nationalsozialismus. Frankfurt, 2003.

Fest, Joachim. *Staatsstreich. Der lange Weg zum 20. Juli.* Munich, 1994.

———. *Plotting Hitler's Death: The Story of the German Resistance.* New York, 1996.

Fleischhauer, Ingeborg. *Diplomatischer Widerstand gegen 'Unternehmen Barbarossa'. Die Friedensbemühungen der deutschen Botschaft Moskau 1939– 1941.* Frankfurt, 1991.

Garbe, Detlef. *Zwischen Widerstand und Martyrium. Die Zeugen Jehovas im "Dritten Reich."* Munich, 1998.

Gerlach, Christian. 'Männer des 20. Juli und der Krieg gegen die Sowjetunion.' In Hannes Heer and Klaus Naumann (eds.), *Vernichtungskrieg. Verbrechen der Wehrmacht 1941 bis 1944.* Hamburg, 1995.

Geyer, Michael, and John W. Boyer (eds.). *Resistance Against the Third Reich, 1933–1990.* Studies in European History from the Journal of Modern History. Chicago, IL, 1995.

Geyken, Frauke. *Wir Standen nicht abseits. Frauen im Widerstand gegen Hitler.* Munich, 2014.

Gillmann, Sabine, and Hans Mommsen (eds.). *Politische Schriften und Briefe Carl Friedrich Goerdelers.* 2 vols. Munich, 2003.

Graml, Hermann (ed.). *Widerstand im Dritten Reich. Probleme, Ereignisse, Gestalten.* Frankfurt, 1994.

Griech-Polelle, Beth. *Bishop von Galen: German Catholicism and National Socialism.* New Haven, CT, 2002.

Gyßling, Walter. *Mein Leben in Deutschland vor und nach 1933 und Der Anti-Nazi Handbuch im Kampf gegen die NSDAP.* Bremen, 2003.

Haeften, Barbara von. *"Nichts Schriftliches von Politik". Hans Bernd von Haeften. Ein Lebensbericht.* Munich, 1997.

Hamerow, Theodore. *Die Attentäter. Der 20. Juli - von der Kollaboration zum Widerstand.* Munich, 1999.

———. *On the Road to the Wolf's Lair: German Resistance to Hitler.* Cambridge, MA, 1997.

Heinemann, Ulrich. *Ein konservativer Rebell. Fritz-Dietlof Graf von der Schulenburg und der 20. Juli.* Berlin, 1990.

————. 'Arbeit am Mythos. Neuere Literatur zum bürgerlich-aris-
tokratischen Widerstand gegen Hitler und zum 20. Juli (Teil 1).'
Geschichte und Gesellschaft, vol. 21, 1995.

————. 'Arbeit am Mythos. Der 20. Juli 1944 in Publizistik und wissen-
schaftlicher Literatur des Jubiläumsjahres 1994 (Teil 2).' *Geschichte und
Gesellschaft*, vol. 23, 1997.

Herder, Raimund. *Wege in den Widerstand gegen Hitler*. Vienna, 2009.

Hormayr, Gisela. *"Ich sterbe stolz und aufrecht."* *Tiroler SozialistInnen und
KommunistInnen im Widerstand gegen Hitler*. Vienna, 2012.

Jens, Inge (ed.). *Hans Scholl und Sophie Scholl. Briefe und Aufzeichnungen*.
Frankfurt, 2005.

Jessen, Olaf. *Die Moltkes. Biographie einer Familie*. Munich, 2010.

Kelly, Geoffrey, and F. Burton Nelson (eds.). *A Testament to Freedom: The
Essential Writings of Dietrich Bonhoeffer*. New York, 1995.

Keval, Susanna. *Die schwierige Erinnerung. Deutsche Widerstandskämpfer über die
Verfolgung und Vernichtung der Juden*. Frankfurt, 1999.

Kieffer, Fritz. 'Carl Friedrich Goerdelers Vorschlag zur Gründung eines
jüdischen Staates.' *Zeitschrift der Savigny-Stiftung für Rechtsgeschichte*, vol.
125, 2008.

Kißener, Michael (ed.). *Widerstand gegen Judenverfolgung*. Konstanz, 1996.

Klemperer, Klemens von. *German Resistance against Hitler: The Search for
Allies Abroad, 1938–1945*. New York, 1992.

————. *Die verlassene Verschwörer. Der deutsche Widerstand auf der Suche nach
Verbündeten 1938–1945*. Berlin, 1994.

Koehn, Barbara. *Der deutsche Widerstand gegen Hitler. Eine Würdigung*. Berlin, 2007.

Kroeger, Matthias. Über die Kostbarkeit von Mut und Klarheit. Stuttgart,
2010.

Kroh, Ferdinand. *David kämpft. Vom jüdischen Widerstand gegen Hitler*. Berlin,
2000.

Krusenstjern, Benigna von. *"daß es Sinn hat zu sterben - gelebt zu haben." Adam
von Trott zu Solz 1909–1944*. Göttingen, 2009

Lamberti, Marjorie. 'The Search for the "Other Germany": Refugee
Historians from Nazi Germany and the Contested Historical Legacy
of the Resistance to Hitler.' *Central European History*, vol. 47, 2014.

Large, David Clay. '"A Beacon in the German Darkness": The Anti-Nazi
Resistance legacy in West German Politics.' In David Clay Large (ed.),
Contending with Hitler: Varieties of German Resistance in the Third Reich.
Cambridge, 1991.

Madelung, Eva, and Joachim Scholtyseck. *Heldenkinder Verräterkinder. Wenn
die Eltern im Widerstand waren*. Munich, 2007.

Malinowski, Stephan. *Vom König zum Führer. Deutscher Adel und
Nationalsozialismus*. Frankfurt, 2004.

Meding, Dorothee von. *Courageous Hearts: Women and the Anti-Hitler Plot of 1944.* New York, 1997.

Meehan, Patricia. *The Unnecessary War: Whitehall and the German Resistance to Hitler.* London, 1992.

Metaxas, Eric. *Bonhoeffer: Pastor, Martyr, Prophet, Spy.* Nashville, TN, 2010.

Möller, Lenelotte. *Widerstand im Dritten Reich.* Wiesbaden, 2013.

Mommsen, Hans. 'Außenpolitische Illusionen des nationalkonservativen Widerstands in den Monaten vor dem Attentat.' In Jürgen Schmädeke and Peter Steinbach (eds.), *Der Widerstand gegen den Nationalsozialismus. Die deutsche Gesellschaft und der Widerstand gegen Hitler.* Munich, 1994.

———. 'Der Kreisauer Kreis und die künftige Neuordnung Deutschlands und Europas.' *Vierteljahrshefte für Zeitgeschichte,* vol. 42, 1994.

———. 'Der deutsche Widerstand gegen Hitler und die Überwindung der nationalstaatlichen Gliederung Europas.' In Manfred Hettling and Paul Nolte (eds.), *Nation und Gesellschaft in Deutschland. Historische Essays.* Munich, 1996.

———. *Alternative zu Hitler. Studien zur Geschichte des deutschen Widerstandes.* Munich, 2000.

———. *Alternatives to Hitler: German Resistance under the Third Reich.* London, 2003.

———. *Germans Against Hitler: The Stauffenberg Plot and Resistance Under the Third Reich.* London, 2009.

———. *Die rote Kapelle und der deutsche Widerstand gegen Hitler.* Essen, 2012.

Mosse, George. *Confronting History: A Memoir.* Madison, WI, 2000.

Nelles, Dieter, and Armin Nolzen. 'Adam von Trott zu Solz' Treffen mit Willy Brandt in Stockholm im Juni 1944. Kontakte zwischen dem Kreisauer Kreis und dem linkssozialistischen Exil.' In Christoph Dieckmann, Babette Quinkert and Thomas Sandkühler (eds.), *Kooperation und Verbrechen. Formen der "Kollaboration" im östlichen Europa 1939–1945.* Göttingen, 2003.

Nelson, Anne. *Red Orchestra: The Story of the Berlin Underground and the Circle of Friends Who Resisted Hitler.* New York, 2009.

Neugebauer, Wolfgang. *Der österreichische Widerstand 1938 bis 1945.* Vienna, 2008.

Nicosia, Francis R. 'Resistance and Self-Defence. Zionism and Antisemitism in Inter-War Germany.' *Leo Baeck Institute Yearbook,* vol. XLII, 1997.

Parssinen, Terry. *Die vergessene Verschörung. Hans Oster und der militärische Widerstand gegen Hitler.* Munich, 2008.

Paucker, Arnold. *Deutsche Juden im Widerstand 1933–1945. Tatsachen und Probleme.* Berlin, 1999.

———. *Deutsche Juden im Kampf um Recht und Freiheit. Studien zu Abwehr, Selbstbehauptung und Widerstand der deutschen Juden seit dem Ende des 19. Jahrhunderts.* Berlin, 2004.

Phayer, Michael. *The Catholic Church and the Holocaust, 1930–1965.* Bloomington, IN, 2001.

———. 'Questions about Catholic Resistance.' *Church History,* vol. 70, 2001.

Pope, Michael. *Alfred Delp S.J. im Kreisauer Kreis. Die rechts- und sozialphilosophischen Grundlagen in seinen Konzeptionen für eine Neuordnung Deutschlands.* Mainz, 1994.

Reich, Ines. *Carl Friedrich Goerdeler. Ein Oberbürgermeister gegen den NS-Staat.* Cologne, 1997.

Ringshausen, Gerhard. *Hans-Alexander von Voß. Generalstabsoffizier im Widerstand.* Berlin, 2008.

———. *Widerstand und christlicher Glaube angesichts des Nationalsozialismus.* Berlin, 2008.

Sabrow, Martin and Christian Mentel (eds.). *Das Auswärtige Amt und seine umstrittene Vergangenheit. Eine deutsche Debatte.* Frankfurt, 2013.

Sandvoß, Hans-Rainer. *Die "andere" Reichshauptstadt. Widerstand aus der Arbeiterbewegung in Berlin von 1933.* Berlin, 2007.

Schad, Martha. *Frauen gegen Hitler. Schicksale im Nationalsozialismus.* Munich, 2001.

Scheurig, Bodo. *Henning von Tresckow. Ein Preusse gegen Hitler.* Berlin, 2004.

Schilde, Kurt. *Jugendopposition 1933–1945.* Berlin, 2007.

——— (ed.). *Eva-Maria Buch und die "Rote Kapelle". Erinnerungen an den Widerstand gegen den Nationalsozialismus.* Berlin, 1992.

Schlabrendorff, Fabian von. *The Secret War Against Hitler.* New York, 1994.

Schmädeke, Jürgen, and Peter Steinbach (eds.). *Der Widerstand gegen den Nationalsozialismus. Die deutsche Gesellschaft und der Widerstand gegen Hitler.* Munich, 1994.

Schöllgen, Gregor. *Ulrich von Hassell 1881–1944. Ein Konservativer in der Opposition.* Munich, 1990.

———. *A Conservative Against Hitler. Ulrich von Hassell: Diplomat in Imperial Germany, the Weimar Republic and the Third Reich 1881–1944.* New York, 1991.

Scholtyseck, Joachim. *Robert Bosch und der liberale Widerstand gegen Hitler 1933 bis 1945.* Munich, 1999.

———. '"Bürgerlicher Widerstand" gegen Hitler nach sechzig Jahren Forschung.' *Jahrbuch zur Liberalismus-Forschung,* vol. 17, 2005.

Schulte, Jan Erik, and Michael Wala (eds.). *Widerstand und Auswärtiges Amt. Diplomaten gegen Hitler.* Munich, 2013.

Schwerin, Detlef Graf von. *Die Jungen des 20. Juli 1944.* Berlin, 1991.

Sifton, Elizabeth, and Fritz Stern. *No Ordinary Men: Dietrich Bonhoeffer and Hans von Dohnanyi. Resistance Against Hitler in Church and State.* New York, 2013.

Sigler, Sebastian (ed.). *Corpsstudenten im Widerstand gegen Hitler.* Berlin, 2014.

Smid, Marikje. *Hans von Dohnanyi – Christine Bonhoeffer. Eine Ehe im Widerstand gegen Hitler.* Güterslohe, 2002.

Steffahn, Harald. *Die Weiße Rose.* Berlin, 2007.

Steinbach, Peter. *Widerstand im Widerstreit. Der Widerstand gegen den Nationalsozialismus in der Erinnerung der Deutschen.* Paderborn, 2001.

———. *Der 20. Juli 1944. Gesichter des Widerstands.* Berlin, 2004.

Steinbach, Peter, and Johannes Tuchel (eds.). *Widerstand gegen die nationalsozialistische Diktatur 1933–1945.* Bonn, 2004.

Stoltzfus, Nathan. *Resistance of the Heart: Intermarriage and the Rosenstrasse Protest in Nazi Germany.* New York, 1996.

Strauch, Dietmar. *Ihr Mut war grenzlos. Widerstand im Dritten Reich.* Weinheim, 2008.

Thies, Jochen. *Die Moltkes. Biografie einer Familie.* Munich, 2010.

Tuchel, Johannes. 'Die Gestapo-Sonderkommission "Rote Kapelle".' In Hans Coppi, Jürgen Danyel and Johannes Tuchel (eds.), *Die Rote Kapelle im Widerstand gegen den Nationalsozialismus.* Berlin, 1994.

——— (ed.). *Der vergessene Widerstand. Zur Realgeschichte und Wahrnehmung des Kampfes gegen die NS-Diktatur.* Göttingen, 2005.

Ueberschär, Gerd (ed.). *NS-Verbrechen und der militärische Widerstand gegen Hitler.* Darmstadt, 2000.

———. *Für ein anderes Deutschland. Der Widerstand gegen den NS-Staat 1933–1945.* Frankfurt, 2006.

———. *Stauffenberg und das Attentat vom 20. Juli 1944.* Frankfurt, 2009.

Ullrich, Volker. *Der Kreisauer Kreis.* Berlin, 2008.

Vogel, Thomas. *Aufstand des Gewissens. Militärischer Widerstand gegen Hitler und das NS-Regime 1933–1945.* Begleitband zur Wanderausstellung des Militärgeschichtlichen Forschungsamtes. Hamburg, 2000.

Wollenberg, Jörg (ed.). *The German Public and the Persecution of the Jews, 1933–1945.* Atlantic Highlands, NJ, 1996.

Wuermeling, Henric L. *Doppelspiel. Adam von Trott zu Solz im Widerstand gegen Hitler.* Munich, 2004.

Index

www.ingramcontent.com/pod-product-compliance
Lightning Source LLC
Chambersburg PA
CBHW060018030426
42334CB00019B/2086

9 781782 388159